Instant SQL Server 2000 Applications

Greg Buczek

Osborne/McGraw-Hill

New York Chicago San Francisco
Lisbon London Madrid Mexico City Milan
New Delhi San Juan Seoul Singapore Sydney Toronto

Osborne/**McGraw-Hill**
2600 Tenth Street
Berkeley, California 94710
U.S.A.

To arrange bulk purchase discounts for sales promotions, premiums, or fund-raisers, please contact Osborne/**McGraw-Hill** at the above address. For information on translations or book distributors outside the U.S.A., please see the International Contact Information page immediately following the index of this book.

Instant SQL Server 2000 Applications

1234567890 CUS CUS 01987654321

Book p/n 0-07-213321-X and CD p/n 0-07-213322-8
parts of
ISBN 0-07-213320-1

Publisher	Brandon A. Nordin
Vice President & Associate Publisher	Scott Rogers
Acquisitions Editor	Rebekah Young
Project Editor	Jennifer Malnick
Acquisitions Coordinator	Paulina Pobocha
Technical Editor	Lee Jensen
Copy Editor	Robert Campbell
Proofreader	Linda and Paul Medoff
Indexer	Jack Lewis
Computer Designers	Michelle Galicia, Elizabeth Jang, Roberta Steele
Illustrators	Michael Mueller, Beth E. Young
Series Design	Roberta Steele

This book was composed with Corel VENTURA™ Publisher.

This book is dedicated to my readers. Thank you for your kind words, enthusiasm, and interest.

About the Author

Greg Buczek is a Microsoft Certified Solutions Developer and a Microsoft Certified Trainer working as an Independent Consultant in Albuquerque, N.M., in addition to being the author of five previous titles, *Instant ASP Scripts Edition 1*, *Instant ASP Scripts Edition 2*, *Instant Access Databases*, *Instant ASP Components*, and *ASP Developer's Guide*. He has created and managed numerous Web sites in which he strives to bring dynamic data-driven content to the Internet. In his role as Webmaster, Greg has extensive experience with SQL Server as well as with ASP, Visual Basic, and Access; and he has developed numerous Visual Basic applications, ActiveX Components, and ActiveX Controls. As an MCT, Greg has taught and developed curriculum for the MCSD courses. You can e-mail Greg at **books@netstats2000.com**. When e-mailing, please include the title and edition of the book. Do not send attachments. Also, to avoid the spreading of viruses, please do not add him to your e-mail address list.

Contents

Acknowledgments

I wish to acknowledge and thank Joyce Buczek for her tremendous support and assistance during this project. I would also like to thank Lee Jensen, my technical editor.

In addition, I must thank all the folks at McGraw-Hill who have given me the opportunity to write this book—and others—over the past few years.

Introduction

Book Structure

This book is divided into four sections: SQL Server Basics, Visual Basic/SQL Server Applications, Access/SQL Server Applications, and ASP/SQL Server Applications. The first section will introduce you to some of the SQL Server concepts used in the rest of the book. The other sections have chapters made up of solutions that have SQL Server back-end database with either a VB, VB.NET, Access, or ASP front end used to access the database.

The complete solutions for those chapters in the last three sections can be found on the accompanying CD. (See Appendix C for instructions on using the CD.) Each solution is presented in a chapter in the same format. First, an overview of the application is discussed. Here, through figures, you will see the functionality of the tool. Then the back-end SQL Server database is reviewed. In that section, you will read about the tables, fields, stored procedures, views, and other objects that make up the database. After that, the code of the front end is presented.

Final Note

As you are reading, reviewing, and playing with the solutions presented in this book, always think about how you could modify the code to satisfy a different need. Don't pass by one solution because you think you will never use it. Open your mind and think about how you could mold it for your own needs or how you could use a procedure or technique within your specific situation.

PART I

SQL Server Basics

CHAPTER 1

Database Tables and Fields

In this chapter, we will review some of the basics of working with a SQL Server database through the SQL Server Enterprise Manager.

Working with Databases, Tables, Fields, Relationships, and Users

First, you will look at creating a database and adding tables. You will review adding fields to tables, data types, primary keys, and indexes. After that, you will look at relationships between tables and data diagrams. Finally, you will review adding users to SQL Server and the permissions given to those individuals.

Creating a SQL Server Database

All of the tasks discussed in this chapter require that you are in the SQL Server Enterprise Manager. To launch the Enterprise Manager, select it from the Microsoft SQL Server folder under your Start menu.

Creating a new database is easy. Within the Enterprise Manager, browse down to the Database folder. Right-click it and select New. You should see the dialog box displayed in Figure 1-1.

The General tab of the New Database dialog box supplies a place for you to give your database a name. That is sometimes all you need to do to create a database. Just click the OK button and your database is created.

You do have additional options on this tab. First, you can set the Collation Name property. The collation refers to how data is sorted when it is returned from the query. If you leave this property as is, the collation that is set at the server level will be used. But you could choose to collate the data according to another language.

If you change to the second tab in the dialog box, you should see something like what is displayed in Figure 1-2. A database is actually made up of at least two physical files. The data is stored in a data file, and the transactions are stored in a transaction log file. From the second tab of the dialog box, the Data Files tab, you can change the name and the location of the data file. You can also choose more than

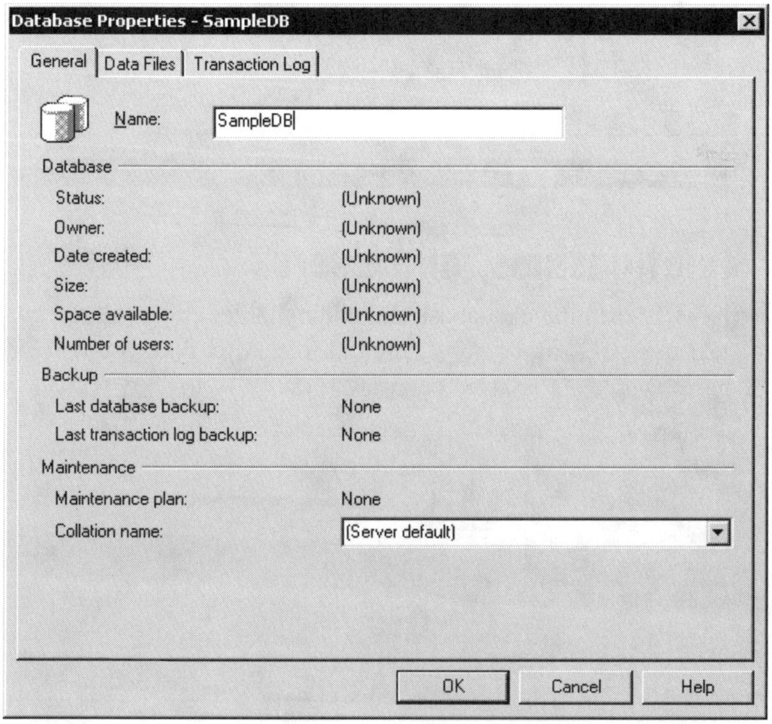

Figure 1-1 *General tab of the New Database dialog box*

one file for your database to store its data in a way that enables you to have a database that exists across drives.

At the bottom of the tab you can set properties that determine how the database grows and shrinks. Most of the time, the defaults work fine. By selecting the check box to allow the data file to automatically grow in size and selecting the Unrestricted File Growth property, you allow SQL Server to manage the size of the database as it sees fit. In the File Growth box, you set whether you want SQL Server to increase the size of the database by a percentage of the overall size of the file or by a specific number of megabytes.

There is, of course, a danger in letting SQL Server increase the size of your data file. It could potentially use up all the space on the hard drive, causing your system

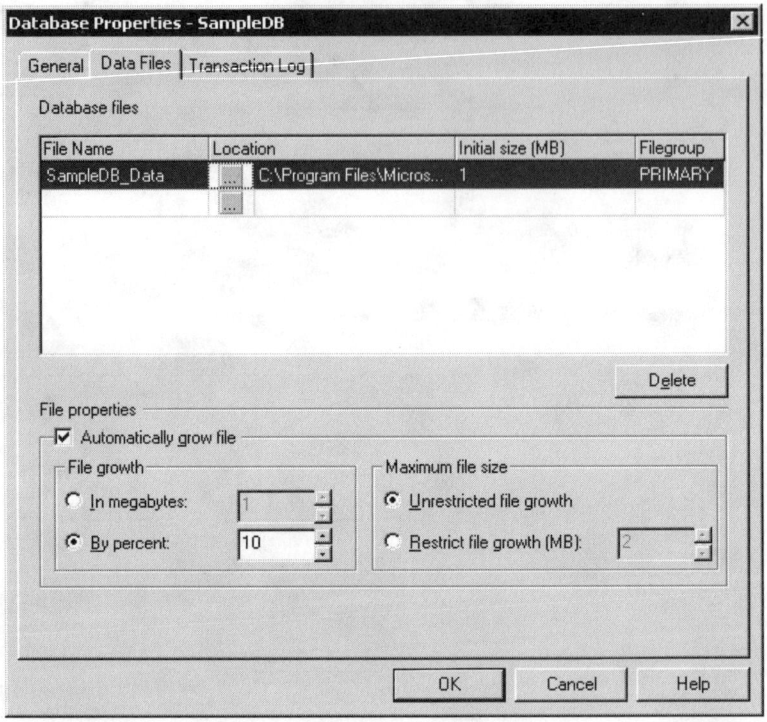

Figure 1-2 *Data Files tab of the New Database dialog box*

problems. But if you ever worked with earlier versions of SQL Server where this wasn't an option, you probably experienced having your data file running out of space in the middle of the night, bringing down any activity to the data file. So, I have found that the risk of running out of hard drive space is lower than the risk of forgetting to increase the size of the database.

Figure 1-3 shows the third tab of this dialog box. A Transaction Log file stores changes that are being made to the database. This provides the server with a way of rolling back data in case a transaction fails. The Transaction Log tab of the New Database dialog box provides a way for you to specify the location of the physical file that contains the transactions. You can also set the file growth properties from this dialog box.

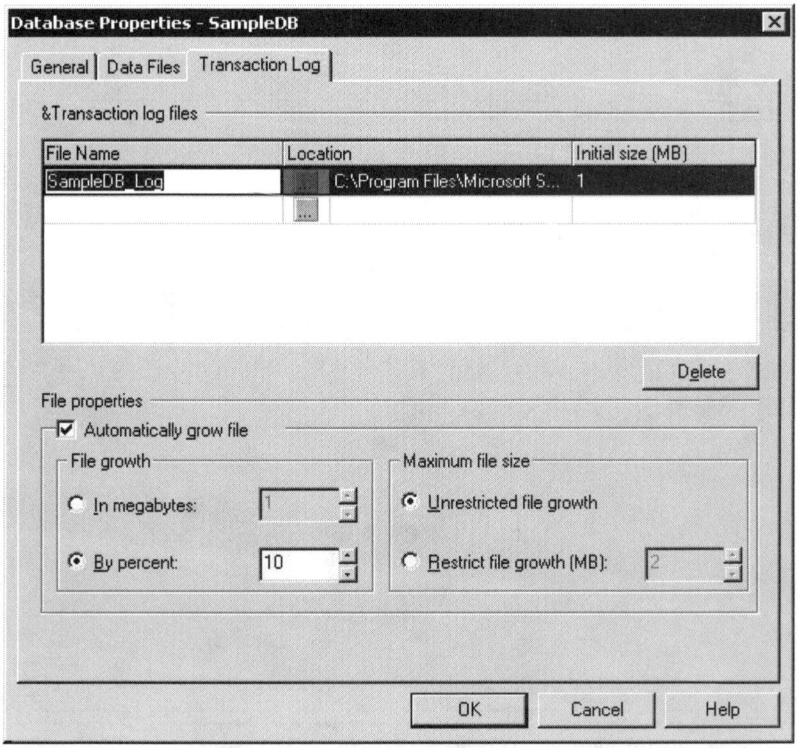

Figure 1-3 *Transaction Log tab of the New Database dialog box*

Creating a Table with the Enterprise Manager

If you have ever created a table using Microsoft Access, you should be pretty comfortable creating a table in SQL Server 2000. The design view of a table has a layout and grid format similar to Access.

To create a new table, browse to the database that you want to add the table to. Right-click the Tables folder and select New Table. You should see a design view like the one displayed in Figure 1-4.

Alternatively, you can enter the design view of an existing table by right-clicking the table and selecting Design Table. The dSesign view is divided into two sections. The top

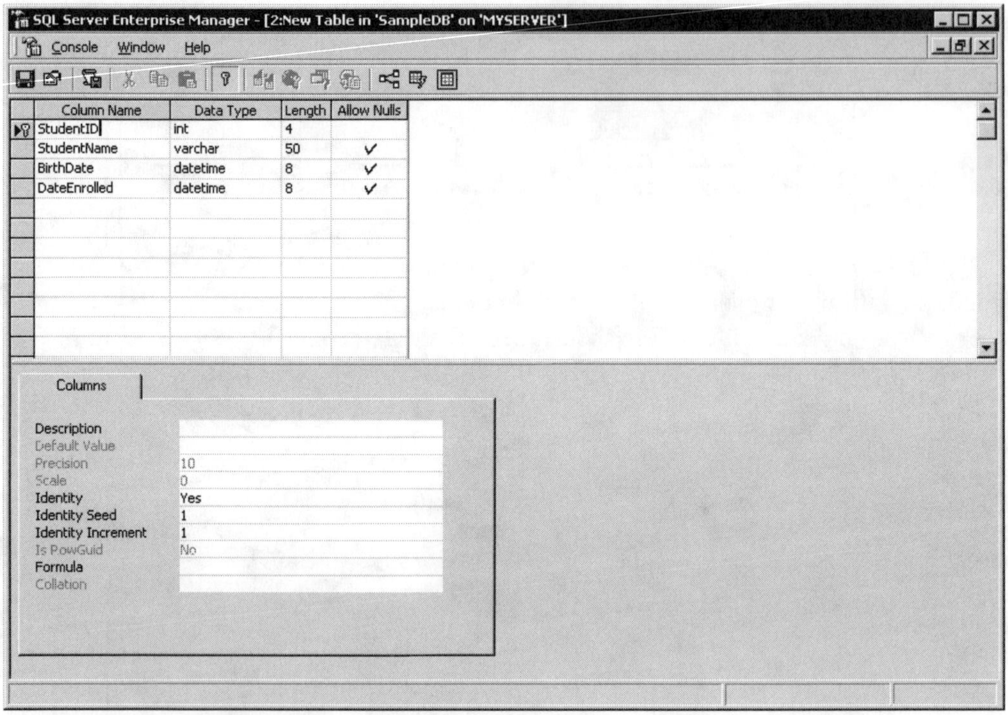

Figure 1-4 *Table design view for a number field*

section is where you specify general information about the fields, allowing you to easily see all that information across the table. At the bottom of the form you see specific properties for the field that are enabled or disabled according to the field type.

The first column in the top section of the form is where you specify the name of the field. Then, in the second column, you select the data type. (We will review these types in the next section.) The third column shows the length of the field. For some data types, like int, you can't change the size. The type determines the size. But for other types, such as varchar, you can set the length within certain limits.

The fourth column is a check box that indicates whether the field can contain null values. If you deselect this property, data must be placed in the field.

The first field, displayed in Figure 1-4, is a numeric field. Note the yellow key icon to the left of the field. That means this field is a primary-1 key field. A *primary key* uniquely identifies each record in the table. To make a field the primary-1 key, select it and then click the Key button on the toolbar. You can also create a composite primary key, which is a primary key made up of more than one field. You can do this by selecting more than one field and then clicking the Key button on the toolbar.

In this table, the StudentID field is also an identity column. Note that the Identity property is set to Yes. When you create an Identity column, you are creating a field that SQL Server automatically populates with a unique number.

Note that the Identity Seed property is set to 1. This means that the first record added to the table will get a value of 1 in the StudentID field.

The Identity Seed property is also set to 1, which means that as more records are added, the number of each is one more than the last record added. So the second record would have a value of 2 in the StudentID field.

Another property for this field type is the Description property. Here you can place information about the field that is just for you to remember something about the field. Maybe the name of the field is not intuitive as to its value. So, in the Description property, you could put in better information about the field.

Other Number fields can have the Precision and Scale properties enabled. The Precision property stores the maximum number of digits allowed for data in the field. The Scale field stores the maximum number of decimal places allowed for the data type.

Figure 1-5 shows the properties enabled for a date data type. Note that the date field has different properties available. One of the properties that can be used with this type, and many of the data types, is the default value property. This allows you to enter a value that should be used for this field when a new record is added but a value for the field is not specified. For a field like City, maybe you would default to a city name that is used in most of your record insertions. But you can also use a dynamic value for the default value, as is the case with this date field. Here you specify that each time a record is added to this table, and the DateEnrolled field is not specified, you insert the current system date:

```
GetDate()
```

The next figure, Figure 1-6, shows the properties that can be set for a field that will store text data. One of the properties that is available with this type of field is the Collation. Here you can specify how the records are collated at the field level.

To manage Indexes on the table, you can select the Manage Indexes button from the toolbar. You should then see the dialog box displayed in Figure 1-7.

An *index* is an internal mechanism that SQL Server uses to more efficiently return records that are sorted or limited according to a specific field. For example, say that

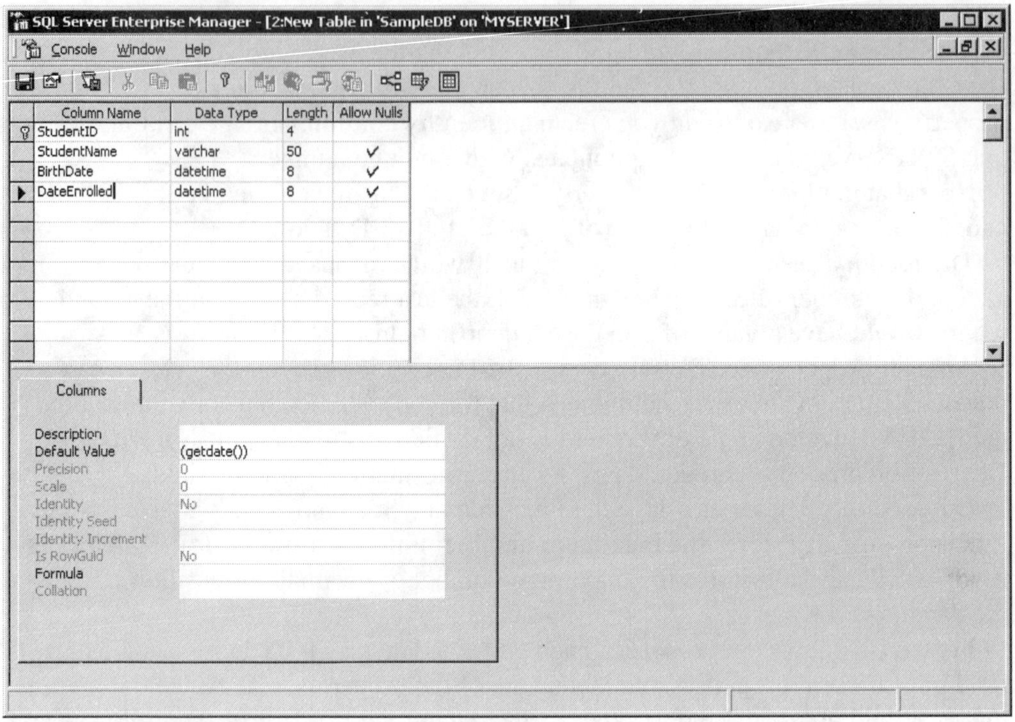

Figure 1-5 *Table design view for a date field*

you had a query that returned all the students that were born on today's date. Without an index, the SQL Server would have to look at each record to see whether the birth date field matched today's date. But if you index the field, SQL Server stores a list of all the birth dates sorted, as well as pointers to the full record. So the server could use the index to quickly find the matching records and return them.

So why not just index every field? There is a performance penalty paid for each index, because each time a record is added, edited, or deleted in a table, the server must also update the data in the index table. So an extra modification has to be made beyond the table itself. Therefore, you should use indexes where the fields are searched or sorted frequently, and avoid indexes on those fields that are not.

Creating an index is simple. Just click the New button in the Indexes dialog box. Select the field or fields that the index is to use and supply a name for the index in the Index Name property.

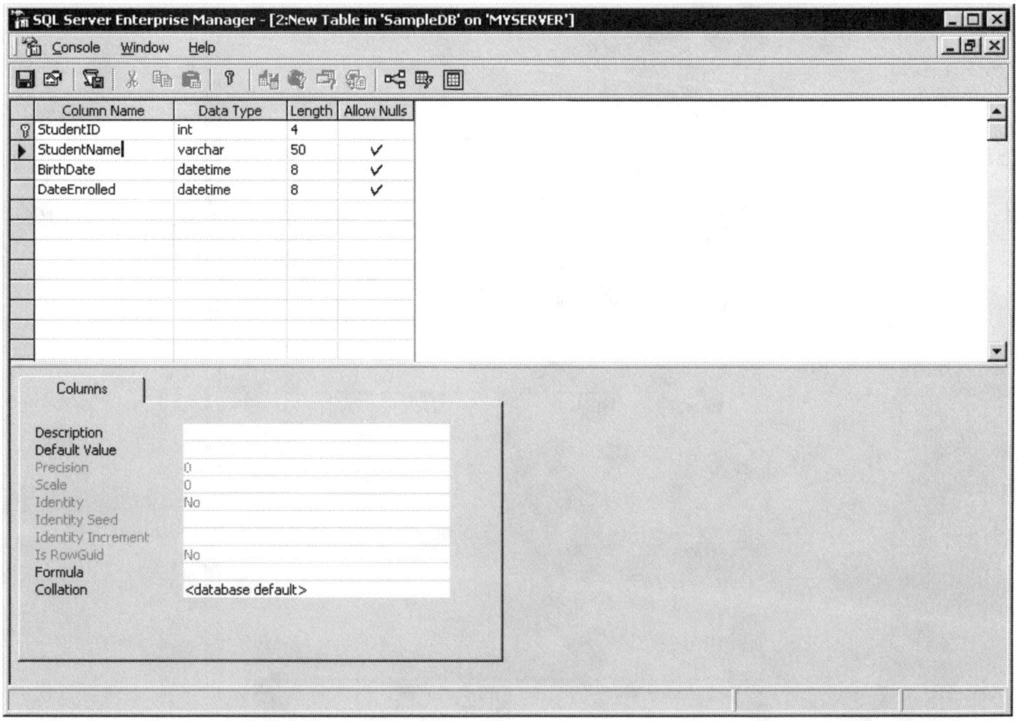

Figure 1-6 *Table design view for a text field*

Data Types

SQL Server provides a variety of data types that you can use when creating fields in tables. Using the correct data type can help make your database more efficient and provide you with the needed functionality. In this section you will review the different data types.

Strings

Strings are used to store nonnumeric information of variable length. This could be anything from a person's name, their sex or address, to the content of a book. The different string data types can be chosen according to their length and character sets.

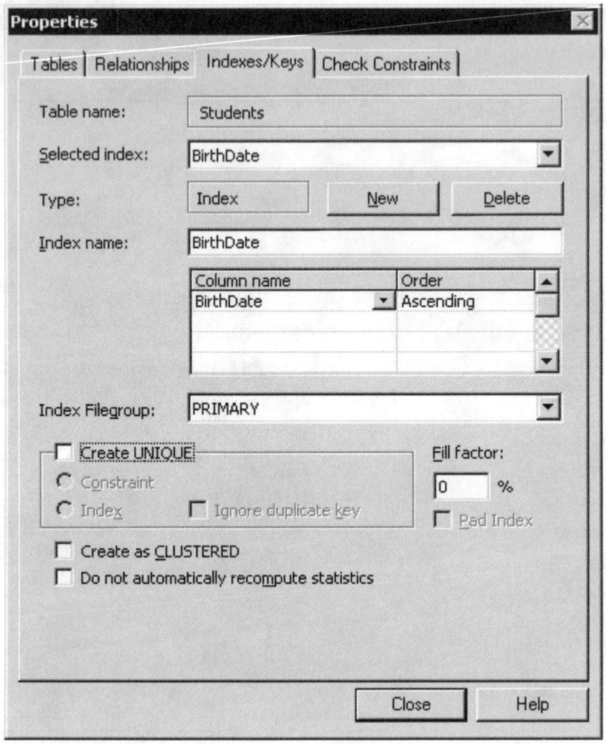

Figure 1-7 *Indexes dialog box*

Each of the different field types in this section occurs as the simple type and then the type with an "n" before it, for example, text and ntext. The difference lies in the characters that are to be stored in the field. The non-"n" data types store a single character per byte, but the "n" types store each character as two bytes in the Unicode format. Therefore, the maximum length of the "n"- types is half as long as the corresponding non-"n" types.

The char and nchar data types allow you to store string data that is of a fixed width. The char can be up to 8,000 characters in length, and the nchar can hold up to 4,000 characters. Since the field is of a fixed width, the field takes up the defined size no matter how long the data is.

Contrasting with that are the varchar and nvarchar data types. They, too, have maximum lengths of 8,000 and 4,000 characters, respectively. But they are of variable length. So, if you define a varchar field as having a length of 50 and the data in the field takes up only 10 characters, then only 10 bytes would be used.

Another pair of string data types are the text and ntext data types. These fields are used for extended text. They can have a length of over two billion characters for the text data type and one billion for the ntext data type. These fields are helpful for extended notes or comments. However, the data is not stored in the same location as the rest of the record. Instead, a pointer is used to locate where the text is within the data file.

Binary Data

Binary data, such as pictures, sound, or presentations, can be stored in any of three different types. These are the binary, varbinary, and image data types. Both the binary and the varbinary data types can store up to 8,000 bytes. The binary data type stores the information as fixed width, and the varbinary data type stores the information as variable length. The image data type allows you to extend beyond the length of the other data types to over two billion characters, but, as with the text and ntext data types, the data is not stored within the record.

Whole Numbers

Whole number fields are exact numbers that do not have a fractional portion. The smallest is the bit data type. It can have a value of 0 or 1. If you have more than one of these flags in a table, SQL Server will attempt to store them together in a single byte.

The next size up is the tinyint. This data type can be a whole number in the range of 0 to 255. The next size is the smallint. It has a range of just above +/– 32,000. Larger than that is the int data type. This data type can have whole numbers that are just above +/– 2 billion. The largest exact whole number is the bigint. It has a range that exceeds the quadrillions.

Exact Decimal Numbers

SQL Server also provides a few data types that have a fractional amount, but that are stored in their exact value. Such a type is needed to store money—where you need to know the exact dollar and cent amounts—but you need a fraction of a dollar.

For such a purpose, SQL Server provides the money and smallmoney fields. Both provide accuracy out to four decimal places. They differ in their range. Smallmoney has a range just above +/– 214,000. The money data type has a range that exceeds +/– 900 trillion.

SQL Server also provides another exact decimal field that is called decimal or numeric. This field gives you the flexibility of setting the decimal precision. So, if you need the number to be up to six decimal places and you need the number to be exact, this is the right data type to choose.

Floating-Point Numbers

Floating-point numbers differ from the types described in the two previous sections in that they are not precise numbers, but they allow you to store data ranging from extremely small values to extremely large ones. There are two data types, Float and Real, that fall into this category. They differ only in range. The Float data type has a range of –1.79E + 308 to 1.79E + 308. The Real data type has a range of –3.40E + 38 to 3.40E + 38.

Dates and Times

SQL Server provides two date and time data types. They are the datetime and the smalldatetime data types. The difference is in their range. The smalldatetime data type stores dates and times to the minute for the twentieth and most of the twenty-first centuries. The datetime data type stores dates, times, and fractions of a second. The dates also allow a range that goes up to the year 9999, the next Y2K-type marker.

Special Types

SQL Server also provides a couple of special data types. These are the unique identifier and the timestamp data types. The uniqueidentifier is a global unique identifier, GUID. These values are supposed to be unique in time and space. In other words, they should never be repeated at any time in any place. These are values that you could find in your system Registry. If you create a field of this type and set the Is RowGUID property to "yes," then the field is automatically populated with a GUID. Here is an example of such a number:

```
{621EA25F-6C4A-494C-9589-033ED2EBAD95}
```

The timestamp data type provides a number that is unique across the database. It is automatically populated when a new record is added and changes its value when the record is updated.

Database Diagrams and Relationships

If two tables relate, they can relate in one of three ways. They can relate one-to-one, one-to-many, or many-to-many. For example, if you had a Students table and you had a Significant-Others table, you could say that the tables relate in a one-to-one relationship. That is to say that each Student record can have one record in the Significant-Others table.

An example of a one-to-many relationship would be a Students table and a Phone-Numbers table. Each student could have many phone numbers, but each phone number record goes with a particular student.

An example of a many-to-many relationship would be if you had a Students table and a Courses table. Each student could take many courses, and each course could have many students enrolled in it. Since you can't link two tables logically in such a relationship, you actually end up with a third table. In this case, you would have something like a StudentCourses table. That table would relate to both of the other tables in a one-to-many relationship.

SQL Server provides an excellent visual tool for linking tables together in relationships and for enforcing these relationships. To create a *database diagram,* right-click the Diagrams folder for the database that you want to add a database diagram to and select New Database Diagram. SQL Server will then bring up a wizard that allows you to add tables to your diagram. Alternatively, you can click the Add Table on Diagram button on the toolbar. Once you add the table, you can create relationships like the ones displayed in Figure 1-8.

In the Database Diagram tool, you can link your tables together by dragging from one field in the relationship to the other field. When you do that, SQL Server brings up the dialog box displayed in Figure 1-9.

You can also right-click the relationship in the diagram and select Properties to see this dialog box. From within this dialog box, you can supply a name for the relationship. Then, within the grid portion, you select the fields that relate the tables together.

At the bottom of the dialog are a variety of checks. If the Check Existing Data on Creation check box is selected, SQL Server will verify that the relationship is correct when you create it.

If the second box, Enforce Relationship for Replication, is selected, the relationship will be enforced in replaced copies of this database. If you choose to

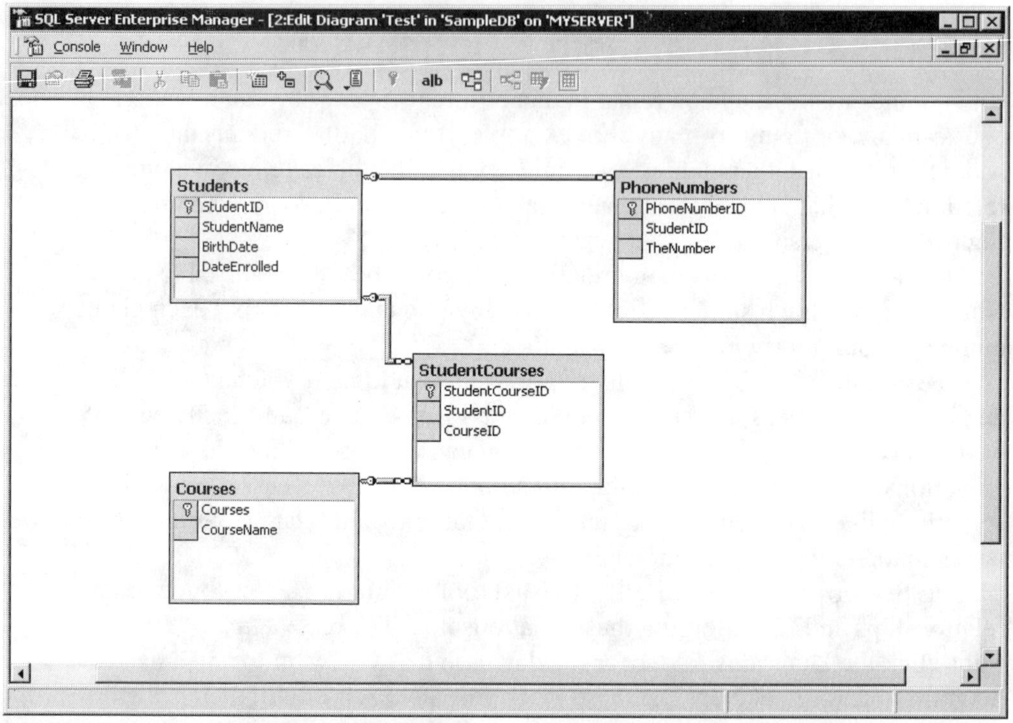

Figure 1-8 *Database diagram*

enforce the relationship with inserts and updates, that means that a new record in one table cannot be added or edited without a matching record in the other table. For example, if you selected this, you could not enter the ID of a student in the PhoneNumbers table for a student that did not exist.

The two cascade properties have to do with what action to take when the parent record is updated or deleted. For example, say that you changed the ID of a student record. If the Cascade Update option was selected, the related phone number records would be updated as well. Similarly, if you delete a student and the Cascade Delete option is set, the child records in the PhoneNumbers table would also be deleted.

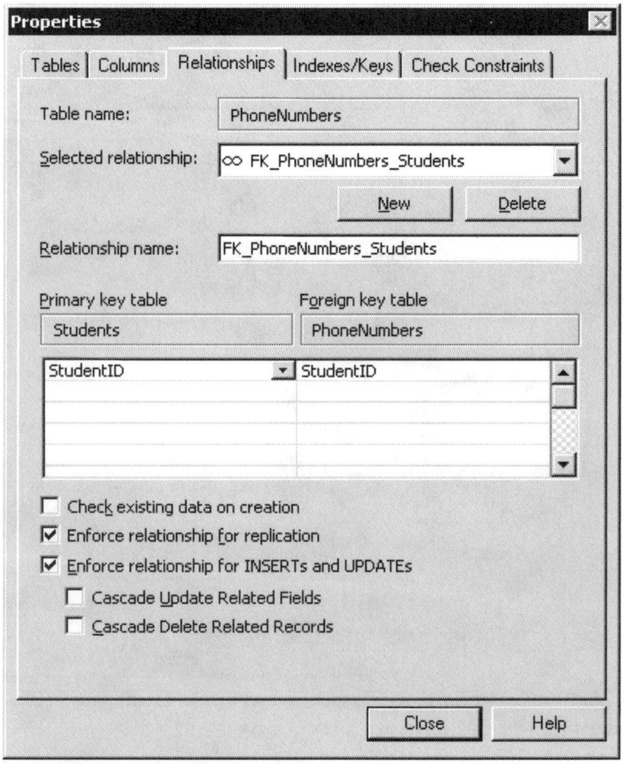

Figure 1-9 *Relationship properties*

Allowing Users to Access Your Database

Frequently, you will want to create users to access just portions of your database, or, as you will see in Part IV of this book, sometimes you only want to allow a user to access your database through stored procedures.

The first step in providing such a capability is to add a new user to SQL Server. To do that, right-click the Login item in the Security folder and select New Login. You should see the dialog box displayed in Figure 1-10.

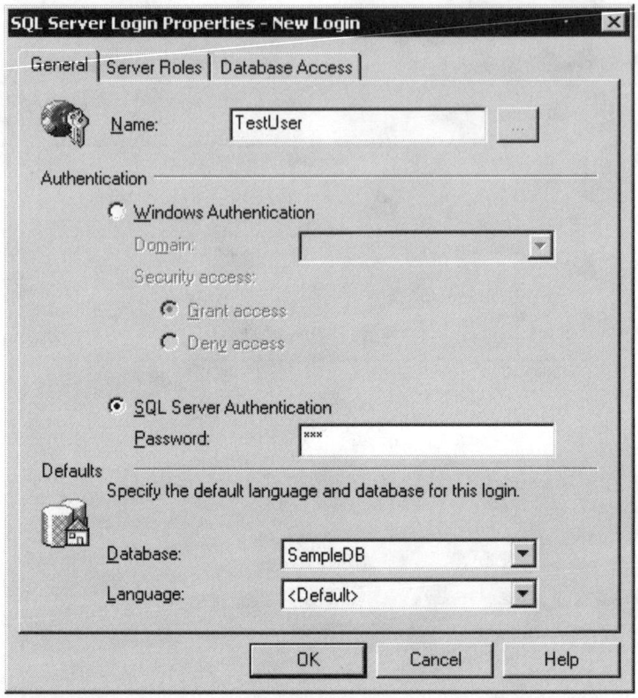

Figure 1-10 *General tab of New Login dialog box*

First, you need to determine if this user is a Windows user or if you are creating a SQL Server user. If the former is true, then the user will access the database through Windows security. If the latter is true, the user will be asked to provide their login information when entering the database or you will provide that information as part of a connection string in your code.

In this case, we are creating a SQL Server user, so we enter a name and the password for the user. We can also enter the default database that they will be connected to if none is selected.

Now change over to the Database Access tab of the dialog box. You should see the tab displayed in Figure 1-11. From here, you select the database or databases that you want this user to have access to. Here, we have selected the sample database that contains the student tables discussed in the preceding section.

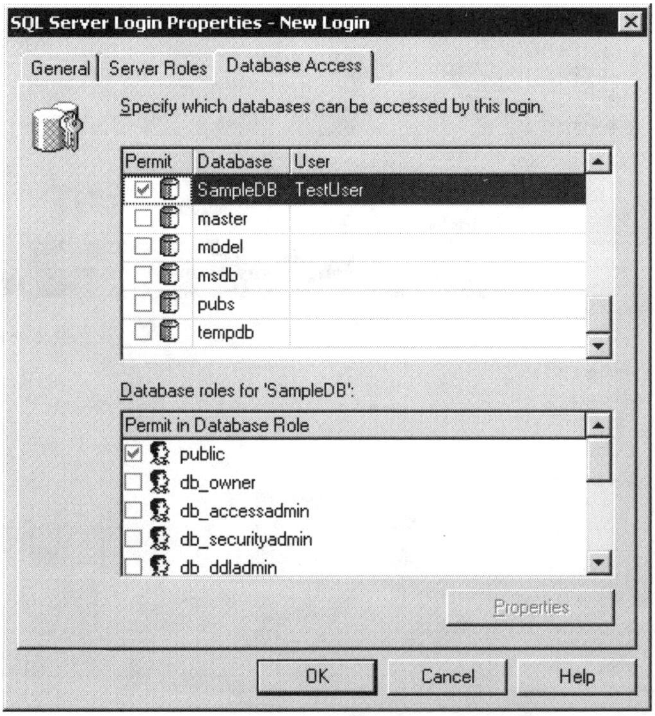

Figure 1-11 *Database Access tab of the New Login dialog box*

Next, you need to give the permissions within your database. Browse to the Users item in the database that you want to give permissions for. Right-click the user you just added and select Properties. Then click the Permissions button to see the dialog box displayed in Figure 1-12.

From here you can grant the user very specific privileges within a database. By selecting the SELECT column for a table, you could allow them to be able to see that table but not change anything. You could allow the user to add data but do nothing else by choosing the INSERT column. If you click the Columns button, you can even grant access to specific columns within a table; or you can really tighten up security and only allow the user to access your database through a view or through a stored procedure, as is done in this example.

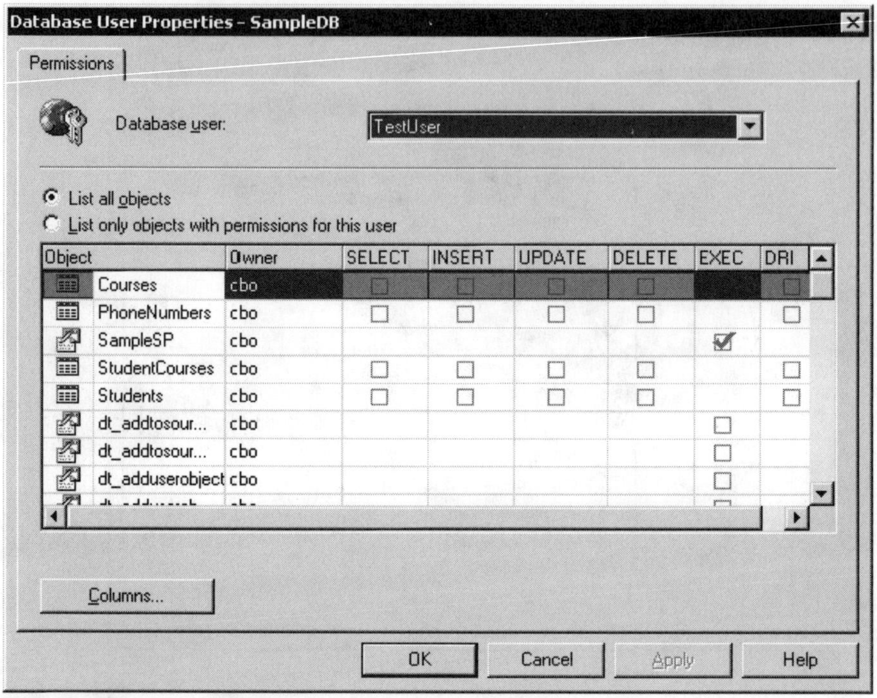

Figure 1-12 *Permissions dialog box*

CHAPTER

2

Views, Stored Procedures, and Triggers

You can allow users of your databases access directly through tables. But there are two main reasons you don't want to do that. First, it is inefficient to do so. When all you want to do is display two fields from 10 records, allowing access to the entire table is overkill.

You could define a query in your code that retrieved just those specific fields and records. But when you do that, the query isn't compiled. That would mean that every time you made the call to grab those records, SQL Server would create a temporary query and have to figure out the best strategy for retrieving those records. If, instead, you created the query as a view or a stored procedure, SQL Server would compile that query and you would have a much more efficient use of resources when you needed to retrieve the specific records and fields.

The other main reason that you don't want to allow users to access your tables directly is security. As you saw in the previous chapter, you can secure tables so that users can only read them or write records to the table. You can even limit their access to certain columns in the table. But, if you use views, triggers, and stored procedures, you can refine the user's access to a much more specific level. For example, you could allow users to see only records that they entered themselves, or you could allow them to see only records that were created or edited after a certain date. Then you could use triggers to activate other code that you wanted to run, regardless of who changed the data and in what way.

In this chapter, you will look at how to create views, triggers, and stored procedures. You will also look at the structure of these objects.

Views

Simply put, *views* provide a way for you to look at the data in a table or in tables that are joined together. A view is the result of running a SQL Select statement. For example, you could create a view that showed you all the students whose last name started with "B." You could create a view that showed you the total amount of sales in the current month grouped by department. Or you could create a view that showed you the name of the person who sold the most of a specific product at your company.

SQL Server 2000 comes with a design tool that makes creating views pretty simple. To create a view, browse to the database that you want the view contained in, select the Views folder, right-click it, and select New View. You should then see the View tool displayed in Figure 2-1.

The View window is divided into four panes. The top pane shows the tables that you have included in your view. The second pane shows the fields within the table or tables that are part of your view. The third pane shows the SQL syntax needed to derive the view that you have created. And when you run your query, the bottom pane shows the results of your view.

Now take a look at the buttons on the toolbar at the top of the View window. The first button is a typical icon used to save the view. When a view is saved, it is compiled and becomes part of your database. The second button allows you to view some properties of the view, like the comment property. The four buttons after that are used to toggle whether you want to see the four different panes in the View window. The red exclamation point icon is used to execute your view. The next button allows you to stop the execution of a query. The one after that can be used to verify that your SQL syntax is correct. The third icon from the right can be used

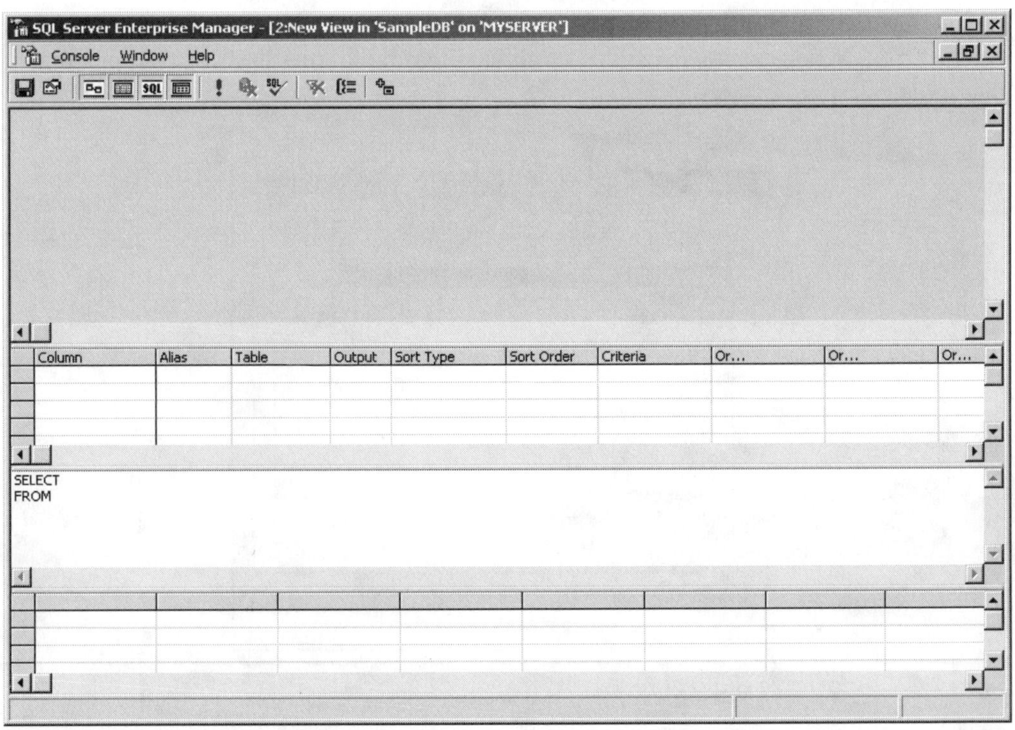

Figure 2-1 *New View window*

to remove a filter on the view. The second-to-last icon toggles the Group By option; we will look at that option later in this section. And the last button is used to add tables or other views to your view. When you click it, you should see the dialog box displayed in Figure 2-2.

The Add Table dialog box is used to specify the items that you want to be part of this view. Just select the item and click the Add button. Now take a look at Figure 2-3 where a table has been added to the view.

The table you just added is in the top pane of the View window. You add fields to your view by double-clicking them or by selecting them from the Column column in the Fields pane.

The Fields pane is made up of several columns. The first is the name of the field that is to be included in the view. In this example, we have included the StudentName and DateEnrolled fields.

The second column is called Alias. This is where you can give the field a different name when it is output. For example, we could alias the StudentName field as Student Name so that it would be output with a more readable column name.

The third column in the Fields pane shows the name of the table that the field comes from. When the view includes only a single table, this list just contains that one table.

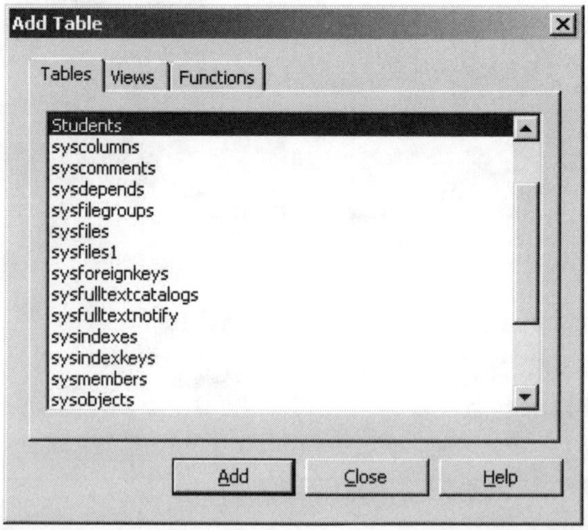

Figure 2-2 *Add Table dialog box*

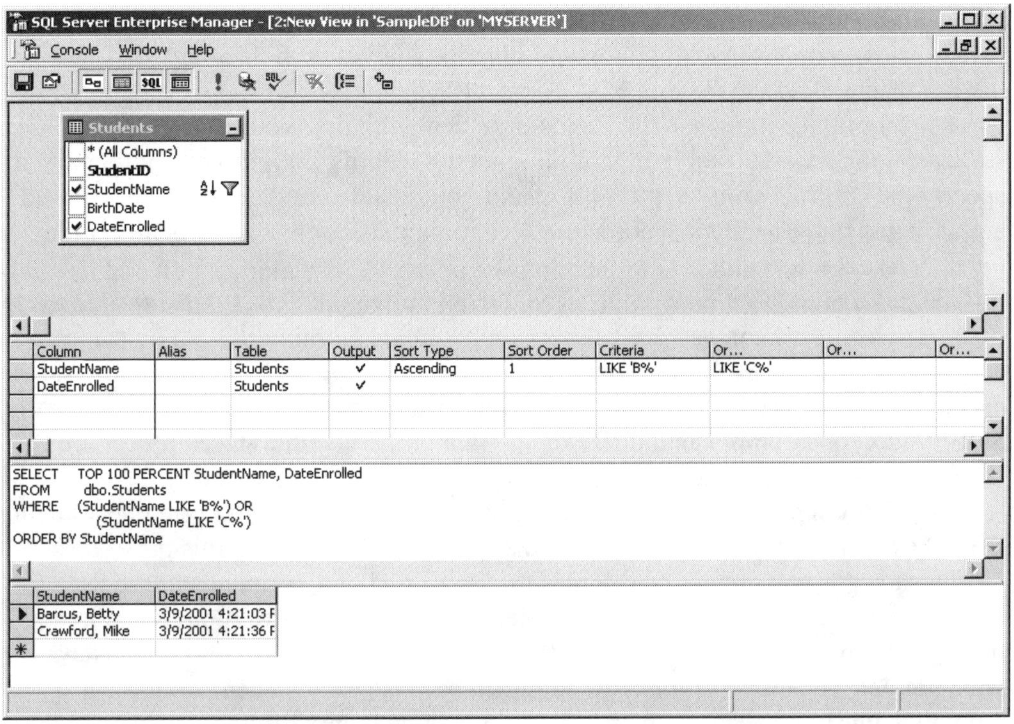

Figure 2-3 *Simple Select view*

The next column is a check column called Output. If it is checked, the field is included in the results of the query. Otherwise, it is not. You may use this as a way of filtering the records by a specific field but not outputting that field. For example, say that you wanted to return all the students who were born on today's date. You would need to include the BirthDate field in the Field pane so that you could specify limiting criteria. But what would be the point in including the field in the output? All the records that were returned should have the same date as the current date in that field.

The next two columns are used to specify the sorting of the records. In the Sort Type column, you indicate whether the field is used for sorting. If so, you specify the sorting order. Then, in the next column, you specify the ranking of that field within the sort. This is only relevant if you include more than one field to sort by. A ranking of one indicates that the field is used as the top-level sort order. A ranking of two would indicate a second level of sorting priority. For example, if you wanted to sort by an employee's name, you would give the LastName field a rank of 1 and the FirstName field the rank of 2.

The rest of the columns in the Fields pane deal with the Where clause of the SQL statement, the criteria used in determining which records are returned. Here you specify the criteria that a record must meet to be included in the query. The criteria are arranged horizontally if records can meet either criterion, and vertically if they must included both criteria.

Under the Field pane is the SQL pane. Here you see the SQL syntax needed to run your view. This can be very helpful when you are learning SQL. You can use the drag-and-drop feature to quickly create a view and then learn from it the expression needed to run the view. I find that I sometimes still come into this view to create the SQL syntax for a complicated query that I want to include in a stored procedure. Even if you know the syntax, it is sometimes quicker to go this route.

At the bottom of the view is the Result pane. When you run your view by clicking the red exclamation icon, the results of the query are displayed in this pane.

In Chapter 1, you created four tables that were part of a sample database used to produce a data diagram. Three of the tables that were created were involved in a many-to-many relationship. You had a Students table and a Courses table. They were defined as a many-to-many relationship because each student could be in more than one course and each course could include many different students.

You also required a third table that was used to connect the two main tables together. Since you established these relationships within the database, you can add these tables to your query and easily link them together.

Take a look at Figure 2-4. The additional tables were added just as the first was, through the Add Table dialog box. But since the relationships were in place, you didn't need to link them together here. Now you can view data from any of the three tables joined together. In this example, you see the name of each course that all the students whose name starts with a "B" or a "C" are enrolled in.

Figure 2-5 shows an example of a Group By view. Notice that the Field pane includes a new column, the Group By column. This is because the Group By button on the toolbar has been clicked. With this column, you can group or aggregate your data. In this example, you can see that the StudentName field is being grouped. So you are telling the compiler to combine all the records in the Students table

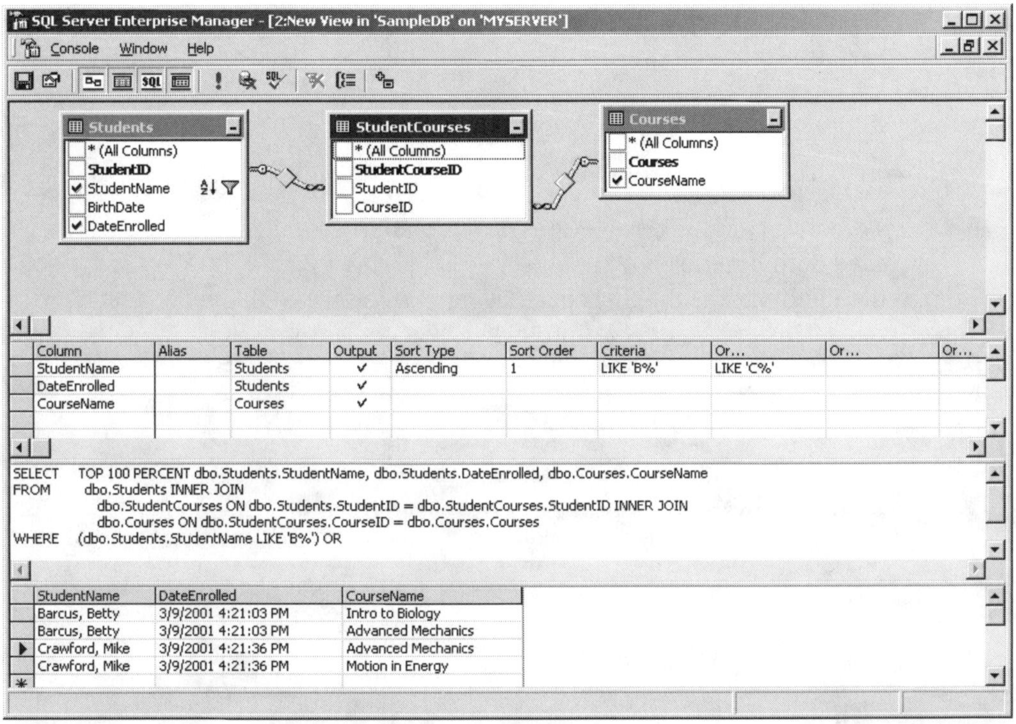

Figure 2-4 *View with three tables joined together*

connected with the StudentCourses table according to the name of the student. Then, in the second field included in the view, you are telling the compiler to count the number of courses that the student is enrolled in.

Notice the different icon used to demonstrate the link between the tables in this view and in the last. Here, you see that the diamond shape is boxed off on one end. This was done by right-clicking the link and selecting all the records from the Students table. When you take an action like this, you are performing a left join, which means that you want all the records from the Students table to be included in the results, even if they are not enrolled in any courses. Note that you can now see the student "Smith, Jon" included in the output of the view, even though the student is not enrolled in any classes.

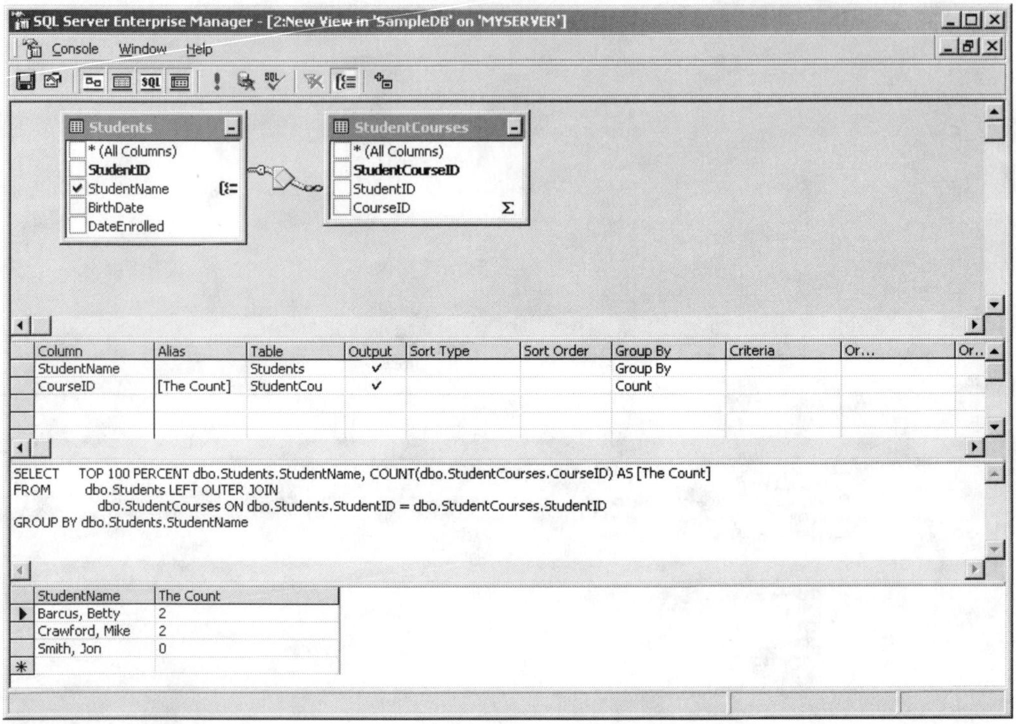

Figure 2-5 *Group By view*

Stored Procedures

Throughout this book—in fact, in every solution—stored procedures are used to provide access to the data and are used to control modifications done on the data. Stored procedures provide a way for you to add an efficient and secure mechanism for users to connect to your database.

To create a stored procedure, right-click the Stored Procedures item in the database that you want to add a stored procedure to and select New Stored Procedure. You should see a dialog box like the one displayed in Figure 2-6.

The bulk of the New Stored Procedure window consists of the area where you type in the code for the stored procedure. Note the buttons in the window. The Permissions button provides an easy way for you to allow other users to execute the stored procedure.

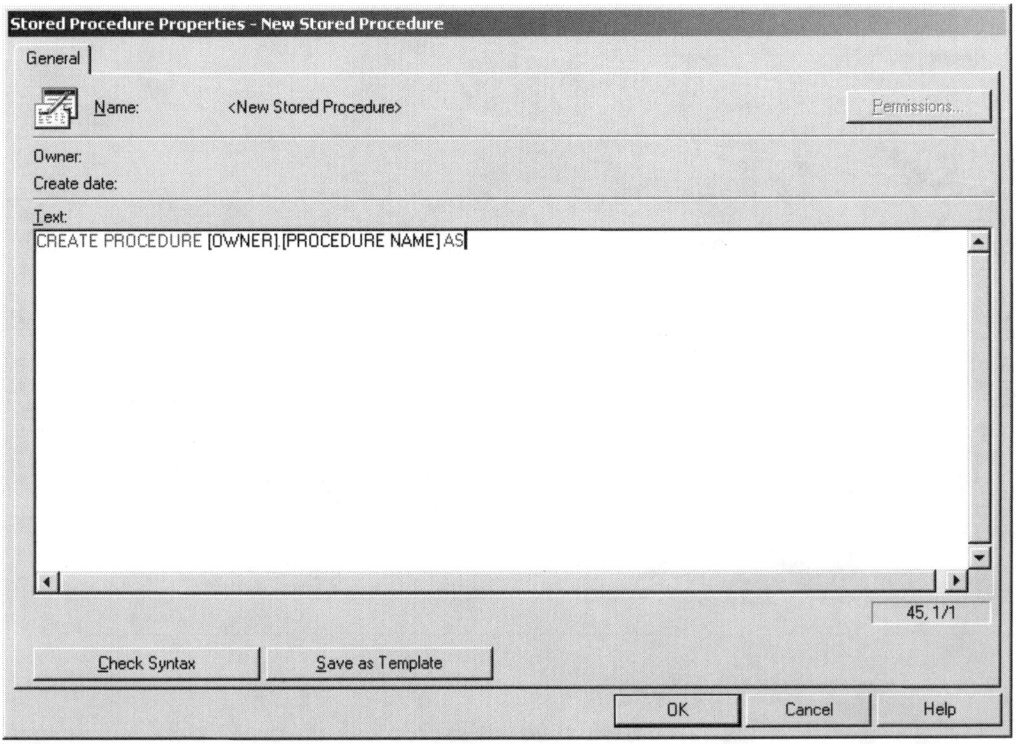

Figure 2-6 *New Stored Procedure window*

The Check Syntax button, when clicked, verifies that the code in your stored procedure is valid. The error messages that it produces rarely give you much of a clue about what the problem is, but they do generally indicate a point close to the line that the actual error is on. Many of the times simply a comma is missing, an extra one is inserted, or you left off the word "Select" at the beginning of an assignment statement.

When you create a new stored procedure, the initial text that it displays comes from the template for a stored procedure. In this case, it is the default text that you see in Figure 2-6. But maybe you always want to start your stored procedures with a comment block or some other text. You could type that information in once and then click the Save As Template button. Then, the next time you created a new stored procedure, the text you typed in would appear.

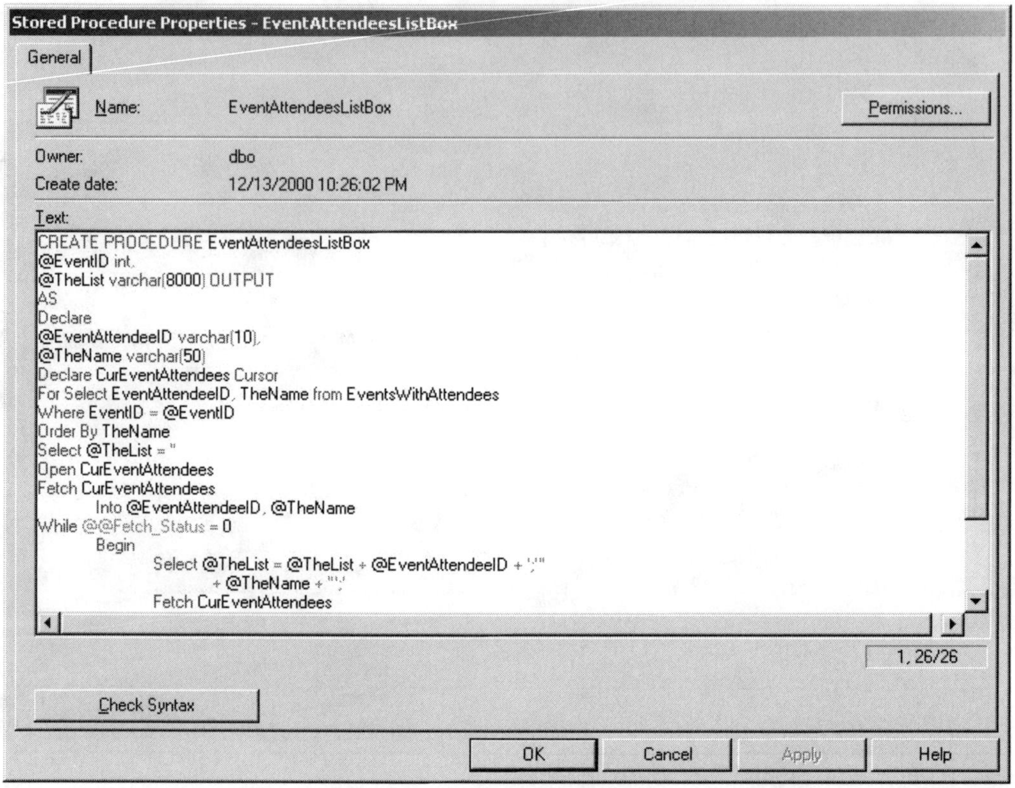

Figure 2-7 *Completed stored procedure*

Figure 2-7 shows a completed stored procedure that comes from one of the tools used later in this book.

Note that the header information for the stored procedure is filled in and that the Permissions button is now enabled. SQL Server also does a nice job of coloring your code to make it easier for you to pick out a string, a statement, or a global variable.

Let's take a closer look at the code in this stored procedure to review its structure.

```
CREATE PROCEDURE EventAttendeesListBox
@EventID int,
@TheList varchar(8000) OUTPUT
AS
Declare
```

```
@EventAttendeeID varchar(10),
@TheName varchar(50)
Declare CurEventAttendees Cursor
For Select EventAttendeeID, TheName from EventsWithAttendees
Where EventID = @EventID
Order By TheName
Select @TheList = ''
Open CurEventAttendees
Fetch CurEventAttendees
      Into @EventAttendeeID, @TheName
While @@Fetch_Status = 0
      BEGIN
            Select @TheList = @TheList + @EventAttendeeID + ';"'
                  + @TheName + '";'
            Fetch CurEventAttendees
                  Into @EventAttendeeID, @TheName
      END
Close CurEventAttendees
Deallocate CurEventAttendees
GO
```

A stored procedure begins with the CREATE PROCEDURE directive followed by the name you supply for the procedure:

```
CREATE PROCEDURE EventAttendeesListBox
```

That is followed by a list of *parameters* for the procedure. Parameters are variables that must be passed into the procedure from the calling application when it is called. They are the way you pass information into and out of a procedure.

The first parameter in this procedure is an input parameter. It is used to pass a value into the procedure. Note that the names of parameters, as well as any variables declared within a procedure, start with the @ symbol followed by the name. If you see a variable that starts with two @ characters, that means it is a global variable.

Note that after the name of the variable is the data type for the variable. Except for a couple of extra ones, these are the same as the field types in a table that you reviewed in the previous chapter.

Now notice that the data type is followed by a comma:

```
@EventID int,
```

That means that you have another parameter to follow it with. Here you have an output parameter. That means it is used to return data to the calling application. Notice it does not end in a comma. That means it is the last parameter:

```
@TheList varchar(8000) OUTPUT
```

The parameter list is followed by the keyword AS:

```
AS
```

Now you are in the code body of your stored procedure. You can now declare variables that you will use to complete your task. You do that by using the Declare keyword:

```
Declare
```

As with the parameters, local variables start with the @ character. Note that local variables come into scope when the procedure is called and go out of scope when the procedure ends. You end the line of code with a comma:

```
@EventAttendeeID varchar(10),
```

because you have another variable to declare:

```
@TheName varchar(50)
```

Next, you declare a variable that was not one of the types that a field in a table can be. It is a *cursor.* In Visual Basic terms, a cursor is like a Recordset object. It provides a way for you to retrieve a group of records from a table or tables joined together. You do this when you want to manipulate or iterate through a group of records:

```
Declare CurEventAttendees Cursor
```

Once you declare a Cursor object, you follow that with the specific Select statement that should be used to populate the Cursor object with records:

```
For Select EventAttendeeID, TheName from EventsWithAttendees
     Where EventID = @EventID
     Order By TheName
```

Now you are done with your declarations and can proceed with the code in the procedure. This first line of code is assigning a value to a variable. Note that the line starts with the Select statement. Select or Set must be present when assigning a value to a variable. Typically, you don't have to initialize a variable as you are doing here. In this case, you need to do it because you will be using the variable itself in a concatenation statement:

```
Select @TheList = ''
```

At some point, you need to open a Cursor object. Until you do that, the cursor is not connected to the record source:

```
Open CurEventAttendees
```

Once you do that, the cursor is connected to the record source but has not retrieved any records. You retrieve a record from a Cursor object using the Fetch statement. The first parameter in the Fetch statement is the cursor that you are fetching records from. That needs to be followed by a variable list for each of the fields that the cursor is retrieving data for. In the Select statement a couple of lines before this line, you have selected two fields. So, here you must provide two variables to select those fields into:

```
Fetch CurEventAttendees
      Into @EventAttendeeID, @TheName
```

Typically, when you retrieve data through a cursor, you want to process each of the records that are retrieved, taking some action based on the values of the field. So, here you enter an iterative loop. The line begins with the keyword While. The code in the loop will process until the condition specified in the While statement evaluates to False. In this case, you are looking at a global flag that SQL Server will set once your cursor is out of records. Therefore, what you are saying here is, keep looping until there are no more records to process:

```
While @@Fetch_Status = 0
```

A BEGIN keyword and an END keyword are used in stored procedures to mark the beginning and end of a logical code block. This typically tells the compiler what code should be run within a condition or an iterative loop. In this case, the code from BEGIN to END goes with the While statement. This code block runs with every iteration of the While statement:

```
BEGIN
```

Within that logical block of code, you have another assignment statement. Note the use of the + character, which is the concatenation character. Also note the use of the single quotes to denote the beginning and the end of a literal string:

```
Select @TheList = @TheList + @EventAttendeeID + ';"'
      + @TheName + '";'
```

This next line of code retrieves another record through the Cursor object:

```
Fetch CurEventAttendees
      Into @EventAttendeeID, @TheName
```

And now you reach the END statement, which marks the point that you loop back up to check the condition in your While statement:

```
END
```

Whenever you use a cursor, you must eventually close it:

```
Close CurEventAttendees
```

and remove it from memory:

```
Deallocate CurEventAttendees
```

BEGIN and END code blocks are also very important with If statements in stored procedures. Take a look at this code block.

```
If (dbo.ProjectIDCheck(@ProjectID)) = 0 and @ProjectID <> 0
      BEGIN
            set @ReturnStatus = 0
            set @ReturnMessage = 'The EventID entered ' +
                  'was not found.'
      END
Else
      If @ProjectID = 0
            BEGIN
                  /* some code */
            END
      Else
            BEGIN
                  /* some code */
            END
/* code for all */
```

This stored procedure fragment uses an If statement with a further embedded If statement to demonstrate the use of the BEGIN and END tags. You start with the first If statement. The line starts with the If keyword followed by a statement that is to be evaluated. Note the absence of the keyword Then found in Visual Basic languages:

```
If (dbo.ProjectIDCheck(@ProjectID)) = 0 and @ProjectID <> 0
```

If that entire expression evaluates to True, the code between the following BEGIN and END statements will run:

```
      BEGIN
```

In this case, you are using the Set keyword to assign a value to a couple of variables:

```
set @ReturnStatus = 0
set @ReturnMessage = 'The EventID entered ' +
      'was not found.'
```

The END here marks the end of the code block that is paired with the first If statement:

```
END
```

If that first If statement evaluated to False, the code would flow here:

```
Else
```

You then have an embedded If statement. This T-SQL line is equivalent to an ElseIf statement in Visual Basic:

```
If @ProjectID = 0
```

If that If statement evaluated to True, the code between the next BEGIN and END statements would run:

```
BEGIN
      /* some code */
END
```

If both If statements evaluated to False, the code would flow here:

```
Else
```

and the next code block would run:

```
BEGIN
	/* some code */
END
```

Then, regardless of the conditional code just described, all calls to the procedure would run this code:

```
/* code for all */
```

In that first stored procedure you reviewed, you returned information to the calling application through an output parameter. But take a look at this example.

```
CREATE PROCEDURE GetGlossaryTerm
@GlossaryID integer
AS
BEGIN
	Select GlossaryTerm, TermDefinition
		From GlossaryTerms
		Where GlossaryID = @GlossaryID
END
GO
```

Here, you return information to the calling application through a Select statement. In this case, two fields are returned:

```
Select GlossaryTerm, TermDefinition
	From GlossaryTerms
	Where GlossaryID = @GlossaryID
```

But, as you can see in this example, you don't have to return anything from a stored procedure:

```
CREATE PROCEDURE SupportPersonDelete
@SupportPersonID integer
AS
	BEGIN
		Delete from  SupportPeople
			Where SupportPersonID = @SupportPersonID
	END
GO
```

Triggers

Triggers provide a way for you to have code that runs according to an event in a table regardless of why that event fires. The events that you can write a trigger on a table for are those when a record is added, edited, or deleted in the table. Since the code runs regardless of why the record change has occurred, the code runs whether the change is due to a stored procedure or to a direct modification of the table.

Triggers are used to modify other records, often in other tables in response to some change in one table. For example, maybe you want to have a field that stores the total amount of a customer's order. You would have one record that contained this field for the customer's order, and then many records that stored the items ordered by the customer. The trigger would be on this order items table. Every time a record was added, edited, or deleted from the order items table, you would want to update the customer's order record.

To add a new trigger, right-click the table that the trigger goes with, select All Tasks, and then select Manage Triggers. You should then see the dialog box displayed in Figure 2-8.

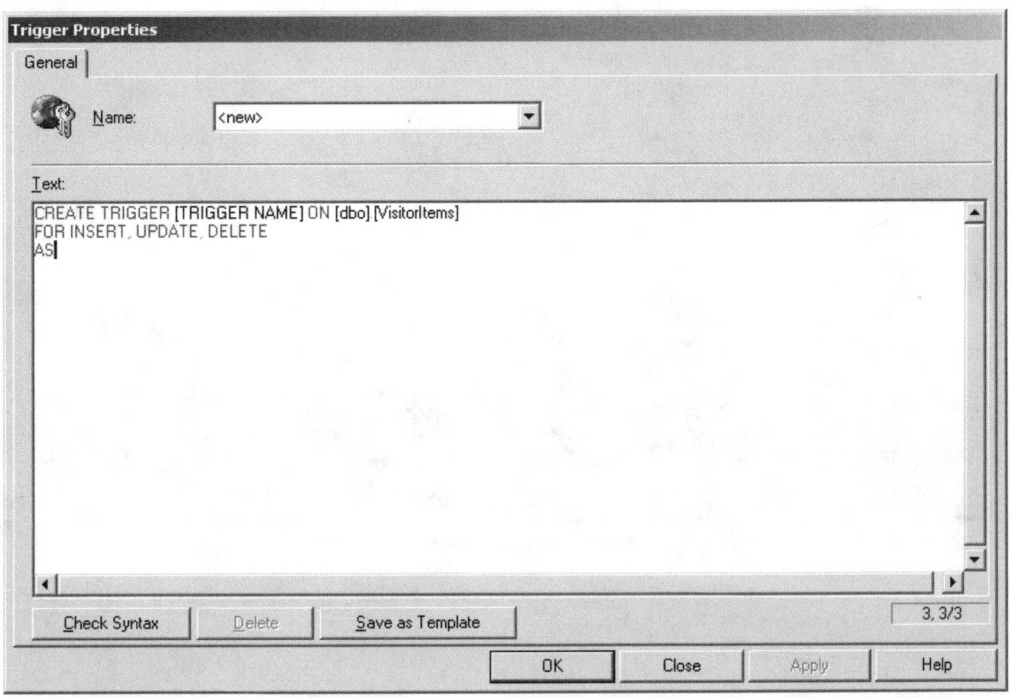

Figure 2-8 *New Trigger window*

The Trigger window has features similar to the Stored Procedure window. The bulk of the window is made up of the text box you use to type in the trigger. Notice the drop-down Name list at the top of the window. If you pull this window down, you will see a list of all the triggers associated with the current table. Figure 2-9 shows the window as it appears with a full trigger in place. Now the list shows the name of the trigger that we are currently viewing.

The Check Syntax button allows you to test the syntax of your code with the compiler. As with stored procedures, the error messages received aren't very helpful, but they do point you close to the erring line of code. The Delete button is used to remove the current trigger. The Save as Template button allows you to save the current text in the Trigger window as the default code you see when a new trigger is created.

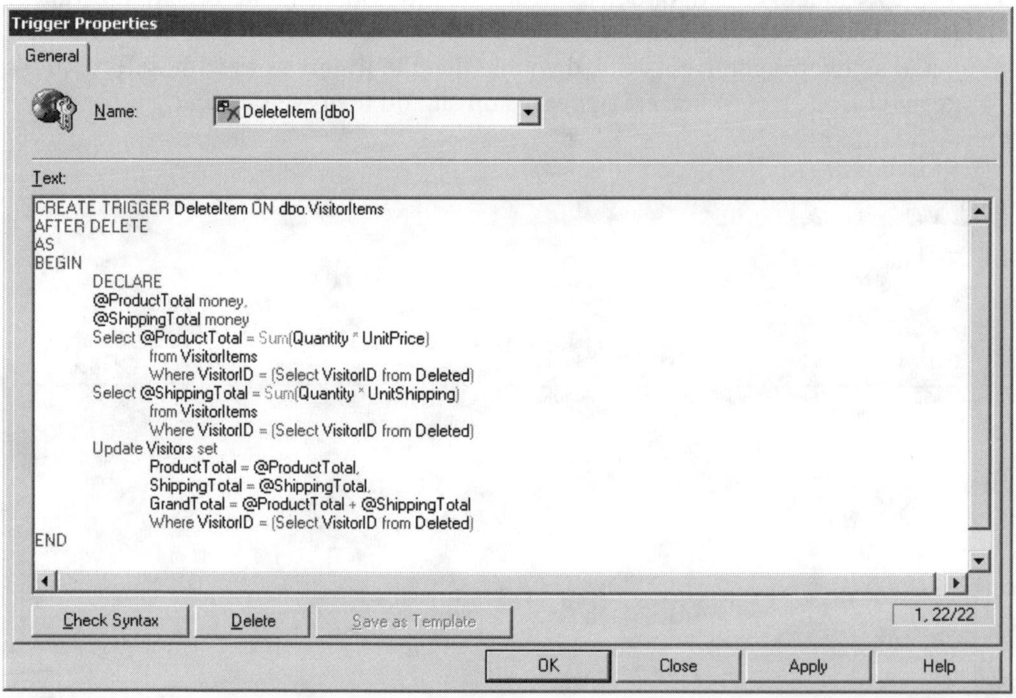

Figure 2-9 *Trigger window with an existing trigger*

Let's take a closer look at the syntax of a trigger.

```
CREATE TRIGGER DeleteItem ON dbo.VisitorItems
AFTER DELETE
AS
BEGIN
      DECLARE
      @ProductTotal money,
      @ShippingTotal money
      Select @ProductTotal = Sum(Quantity * UnitPrice)
            from VisitorItems
            Where VisitorID = (Select VisitorID from Deleted)
      Select @ShippingTotal = Sum(Quantity * UnitShipping)
            from VisitorItems
            Where VisitorID = (Select VisitorID from Deleted)
      Update Visitors set
            ProductTotal = @ProductTotal,
            ShippingTotal = @ShippingTotal,
            GrandTotal = @ProductTotal + @ShippingTotal
            Where VisitorID = (Select VisitorID from Deleted)
END
```

The syntax of a trigger starts with the CREATE TRIGGER keyword. That is followed by the name of the trigger and the table that it fires on. In this case, the trigger is called DeleteItem and it fires on the VisitorItems table:

```
CREATE TRIGGER DeleteItem ON dbo.VisitorItems
```

A trigger can fire after a record is deleted, added, or edited. In this case, the trigger needs to fire for any record that is deleted from the VisitorItems table. The next line of code states that:

```
AFTER DELETE
```

That is followed with the AS keyword, which indicates the beginning of the trigger code:

```
AS
```

You start it by indicating the beginning of a logical code block with the BEGIN keyword. Note that you can use the BEGIN and END blocks to mark your own logical code blocks just to make your code easier to read:

```
BEGIN
```

As with a stored procedure, you start your code with a variable declaration block. Note that you can declare variables in other places. It makes your code more readable to declare all the variables at the top of a procedure:

```
DECLARE
```

This procedure declares two variables. Note that variables start with the @ character. Also note that the line of code ends with a comma:

```
@ProductTotal money,
```

since it is followed with another variable declaration:

```
@ShippingTotal money
```

This next line of code is assigning a value to a variable. Therefore, it starts with the Select statement. But, more important, note the use of a table called Deleted. That table contains the values of the fields for the record that was deleted when this trigger fired. Each time this trigger is called, since it is a Delete trigger, the Deleted table will be populated with the record that was deleted:

```
Select @ProductTotal = Sum(Quantity * UnitPrice)
      from VisitorItems
      Where VisitorID = (Select VisitorID from Deleted)
```

Another variable is assigned to a value based on the value of a field in the record that was deleted:

```
Select @ShippingTotal = Sum(Quantity * UnitShipping)
      from VisitorItems
      Where VisitorID = (Select VisitorID from Deleted)
```

Now you are taking an action on a record in a table that is different from the table where the record was deleted. In this case, you are updating some product order totals with the items ordered from a visitor after the record was deleted. Again the Deleted table is used to indicate the specific record that is to be updated in the top-level table:

```
Update Visitors set
      ProductTotal = @ProductTotal,
      ShippingTotal = @ShippingTotal,
      GrandTotal = @ProductTotal + @ShippingTotal
      Where VisitorID = (Select VisitorID from Deleted)
```

Next, you close your logical code block with an END statement:

```
END
```

The special SQL Server table used in a trigger where a record was deleted is now deleted. But what about a trigger based on a record being added to a table? Take a look at this code block.

```
CREATE TRIGGER InsertItem ON dbo.VisitorItems
AFTER INSERT
AS
BEGIN
      DECLARE
      @ProductTotal money,
      @ShippingTotal money
      Select @ProductTotal = Sum(Quantity * UnitPrice)
            from VisitorItems
            Where VisitorID = (Select VisitorID from Inserted)
      Select @ShippingTotal = Sum(Quantity * UnitShipping)
            from VisitorItems
            Where VisitorID = (Select VisitorID from Inserted)
      Update Visitors set
            ProductTotal = @ProductTotal,
            ShippingTotal = @ShippingTotal,
            GrandTotal = @ProductTotal + @ShippingTotal
            Where VisitorID = (Select VisitorID from Inserted)
END
```

Note that the trigger fires after a record is deleted from the VisitorItems table:

```
CREATE TRIGGER InsertItem ON dbo.VisitorItems
AFTER INSERT
```

Also note the special table used in the Select and Update statements:

```
Select @ProductTotal = Sum(Quantity * UnitPrice)
      from VisitorItems
      Where VisitorID = (Select VisitorID from Inserted)
```

Instead of using the special Deleted table, you use the Inserted table. This table contains the values of a new record or the new values for the fields in an edited record.

PART II

Visual Basic/SQL Server Applications

CHAPTER

3

Visual Basic as a Front End to SQL Server

In this section of the book, we will look at solutions that use Visual Basic as the front-end application accessing the data in SQL Server databases. The first two solution chapters in this section will present front ends that were developed using Visual Basic 6.0. The other three solution chapters present front ends that were developed using Visual Basic.Net.

Using Visual Basic with SQL Server

In this chapter, we will look at the reasons to use or not use Visual Basic as the tool to develop a front end with. Then we will look at using tools within Visual Basic 6.0 and Visual Basic.Net to manipulate the objects and content in a database. After that, we will review referencing ADO with these tools, since the ADO library will be used for all the solutions in the section.

Advantages and Disadvantages of Using Visual Basic

I have been asked by many students of mine about when they should use Visual Basic to create a database solution. The argument goes, if the database solution is desktop based, why not use Access? If the database solution is browser based, then ASP should be used.

There are two main reasons to use Visual Basic as the front end. One is that Visual Basic allows you to do things in code and design that you cannot do with Access and SQL Server. The other reason has to do with marketing the product that you are developing.

Programming in Access really gives you just a subset of the functionality that Visual Basic offers. With Access, you can reference libraries to manipulate databases just as you can in Visual Basic. You can perform similar tests on data and the basic language is the same. However, if your project grows large in size, you can't break your Access database apart into the controls, components, and environments as you can with Visual Basic. Access works fine for developing a basic solution; but if you have a team of developers and you need to encapsulate your code, making it more object oriented and reusable, you need Visual Basic.

As mentioned, the other main reason to use Visual Basic over ASP or Access is the marketing appeal if you are trying to sell the product you are developing. If your company creates a solution that helps a specific type of business manage its data, it may not be as well received if it was developed using Access. Many people have the perception that if a tool was developed using Access, they could easily re-create it with their own internal staff. However, if your tool was created with Visual Basic, it is shipped as an executable. The perception then is that you have created something from the ground up that would take too much time for another company to try to re-create.

With the power of Visual Basic come some of the largest disadvantages. Say that you have spent six months getting your database solution to work just right. You are now ready to install the front end on the client machines. If you are using Access and your clients have Access on their own machines, you just need to stick the front-end database on their computer and maybe create a DSN.

If you use ASP, you just need to send an e-mail message out to your users and supply them with a link to your new site; but if you developed your tool in Visual Basic, you need to provide an installation disk that has been tested on many different environments with many different setups and hope that you haven't left out a support library that was needed by one of the components that you reference.

An additional disadvantage of using Visual Basic is releasing new versions of your tool. If you use ASP, you simply put the new version on your server and anyone who accesses your site now has the new tool. With Access, you could just supply your users with a new front-end database, if you weren't storing any data locally; but with Visual Basic, you may need to send out an entirely new installation. Add to that the complications of dealing with users who may have missed one of the interim updates.

So Visual Basic has its place. It is a great tool when you are trying to create a complete system that has the level of complexity beyond a basic database or one that you wish to better market to your customers.

Visual Basic 6.0 Data View Window

Within Visual Basic 6.0, you can manage the contents and the structure of some of your databases, SQL Server and otherwise. These database links are managed

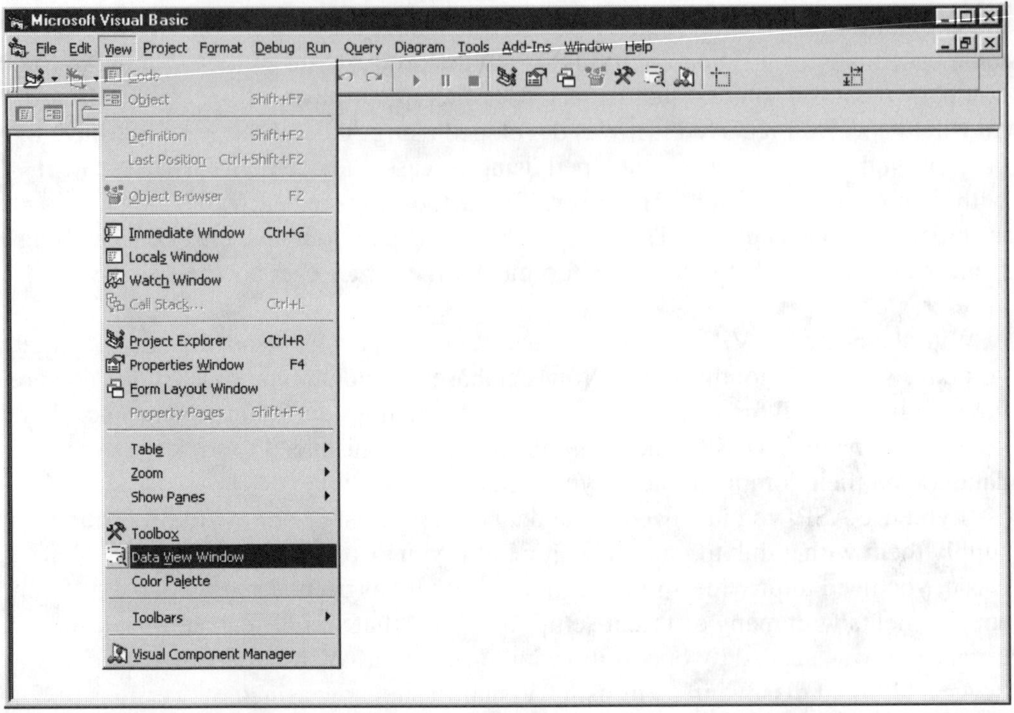

Figure 3-1 *View menu*

externally from a Visual Basic project, so you can see the links from project to project or just by opening Visual Basic 6.0 without a project.

From within Visual Basic 6.0, select Data View Window from the View menu, as shown in Figure 3-1. When you select that item, you should see the Data View window, as displayed in Figure 3-2. In this list, you will see all the databases that you have linked to. Listed here I have databases that are Access and SQL Server databases. These databases are located on four different computers, some of which are on my local network while others are linked to through the Internet.

To add a link to a database in the list, right-click the Data Links folder and select Add a Data Link. When you do that, you should see the dialog box displayed in Figure 3-3.

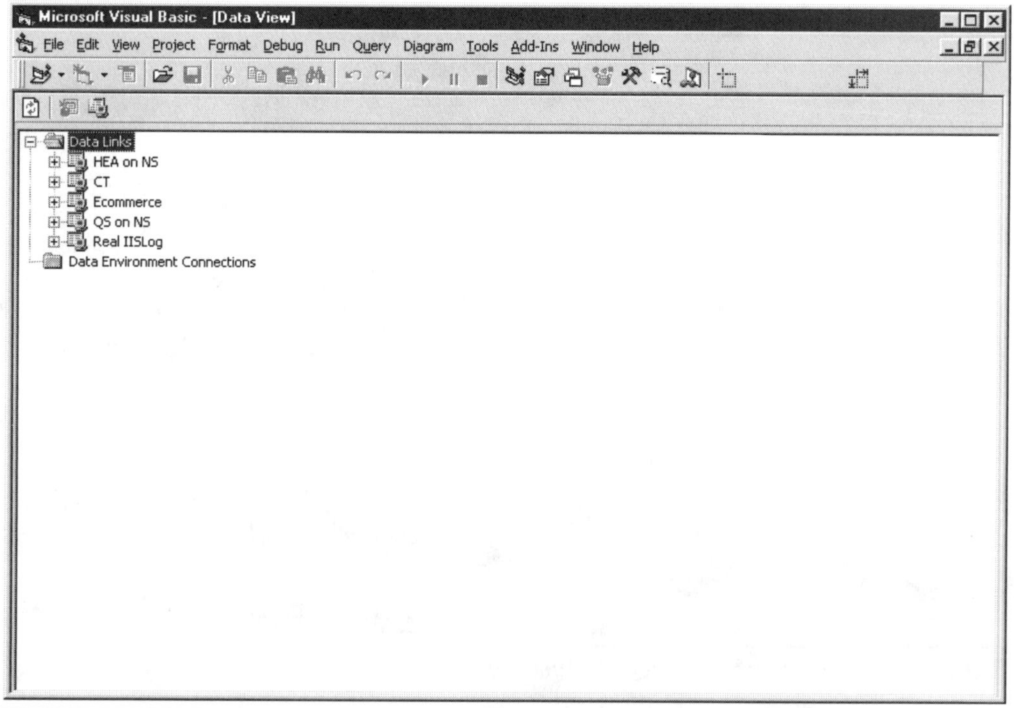

Figure 3-2 *Data View window*

The first step is to select the provider or library for the database that you are trying to connect to. In this example, we will connect to a database used in a later chapter of this section, so we need to select the SQL Server item highlighted. Then click Next to see the property page displayed in Figure 3-4.

In step 1, you would enter the name of your database server. If this connection was through the Internet, you enter the server's IP address. Then enter your user name and password for that database server. You can also choose to save the password with the connection. This allows you, in the development environment, to open the connection to the database without supplying your password again.

In step 3, you need to select the database that you want to link to. Here, we have selected the database that will be used in the next chapter. You could then click the Test Connection button to make sure everything that you have entered was set up correctly.

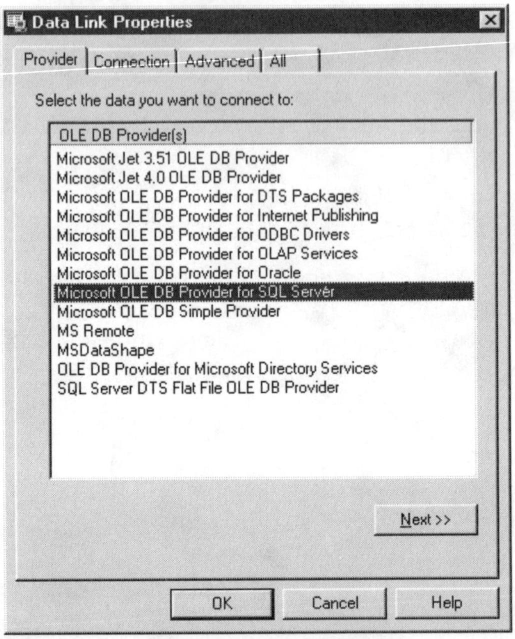

Figure 3-3 *Provider page of the Data Link Properties*

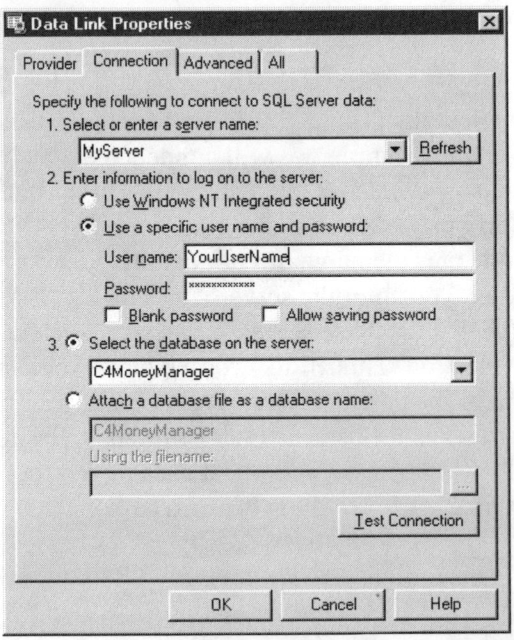

Figure 3-4 *Connection page of the Data Link Properties dialog box*

Click OK to close the dialog box and save the link. You can then give your link a name. If you expand the link in the Data View window, you should now see the Tables, Views, and Stored Procedures items like those shown in Figure 3-5.

Visual Basic.Net Server Explorer

Visual Basic.Net has a similar tool that you can use to manipulate databases. You access the tool through the Server Explorer. To view the Server Explorer, select it from the View menu, as shown in Figure 3-6.

When you select that item, you will see the Server Explorer window like the one shown in Figure 3-7.

One of the top-level items in the Server Explorer is the Data Connections item. This is where you can add connections to databases that you wish to manipulate. To

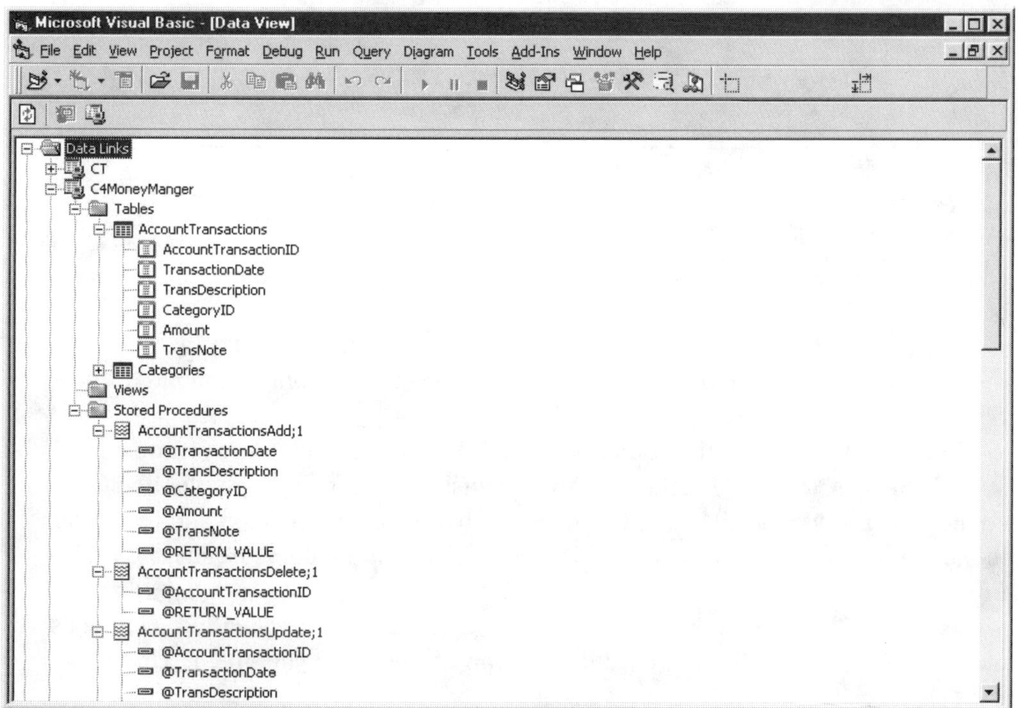

Figure 3-5 *Data View window showing linked database*

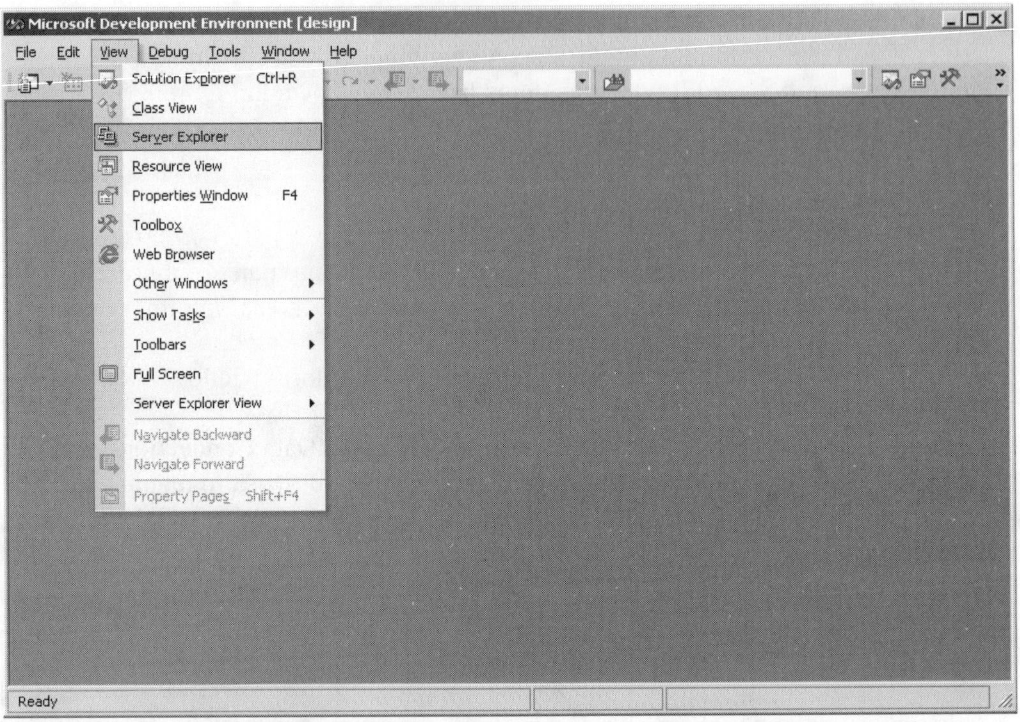

Figure 3-6 *Selecting the Server Explorer from the View menu*

add a data connection, select the Add Connection item; you should see the dialog box displayed in Figure 3-8.

As we did in the previous section, we need to select the provider that we will use to gain access to the database. Then click Next to see the Connection page shown in Figure 3-9.

Here we have entered the database server, user name, and password information. We have also selected the database that we wish to link to. When you click OK, the connection is added to the Data Connections list. You can then expand the database in the list to see and work with the different objects in the database, as shown in Figure 3-10.

Listed here is a stored procedure that adds a record to a table called Attendees. Note the blue box around the field list portion of the Insert statement. This new

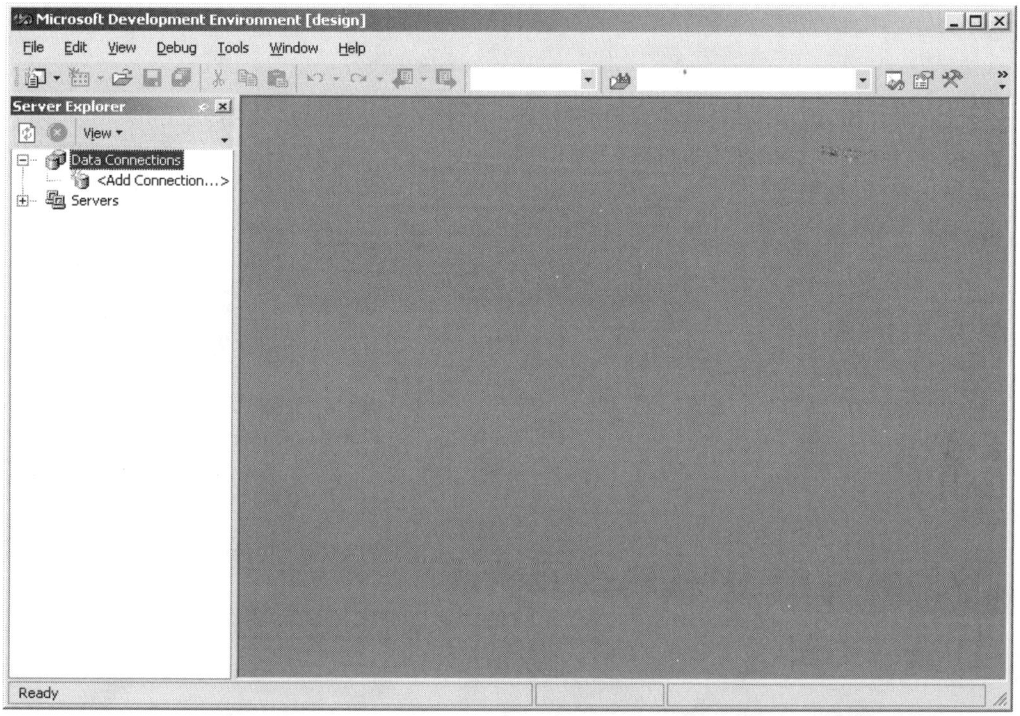

Figure 3-7 *Server Explorer*

feature of Visual Basic.Net allows you to edit portions of your stored procedures through a designer. Right-click the text within the blue box and select Design SQL Block. You should then see the window displayed in Figure 3-11.

You could then use this window to drag and drop fields into your Insert statement, simplifying the writing of Stored Procedures.

Referencing ADO from Visual Basic 6.0

Throughout the solutions in this section of the book, ADO is used to gain access to your SQL Server databases from Visual Basic. For you to use the objects in the ADO library, the library needs to be referenced in your project.

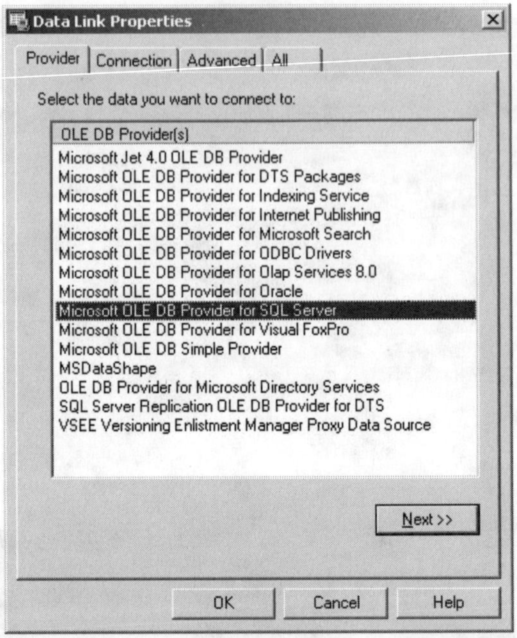

Figure 3-8 *Provider page of Data Link Properties*

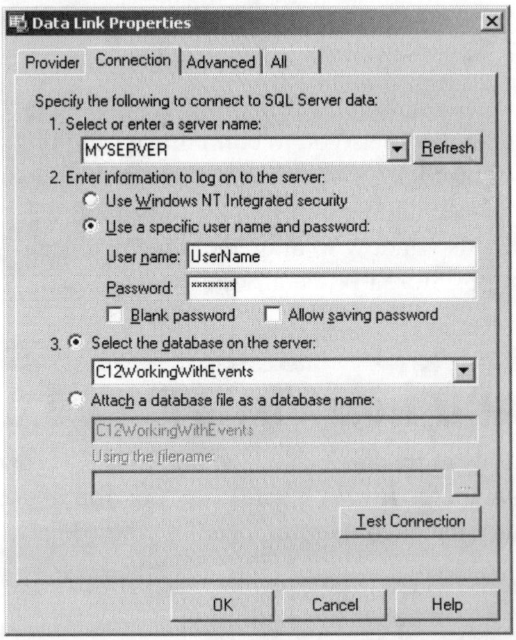

Figure 3-9 *Connection page of the Data Link Properties dialog box*

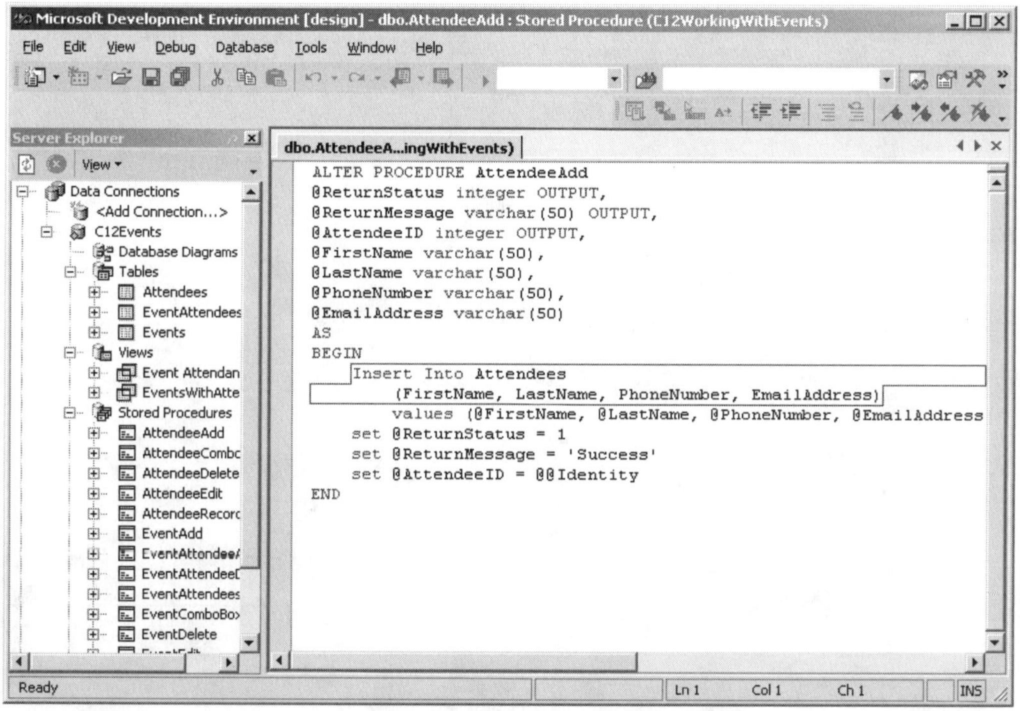

Figure 3-10 *Working with a database through a Data Connection*

To reference the ADO library from Visual Basic 6.0, start VB and open the project that you want to add the reference to. From the Project menu, select References to see the Reference dialog box displayed in Figure 3-12. Once you have the dialog box opened, you simply need to find ADO in the list, select it, and click OK. You can now create instances of the ADO objects within your project.

Referencing ADO from Visual Basic.Net

To reference ADO from a Visual Basic.Net project, you need to open your project and then select Solution Explorer from the View menu. One of the folders in the Solution Explorer should be References. Right-click that folder and select Add Reference to see the dialog box displayed in Figure 3-13.

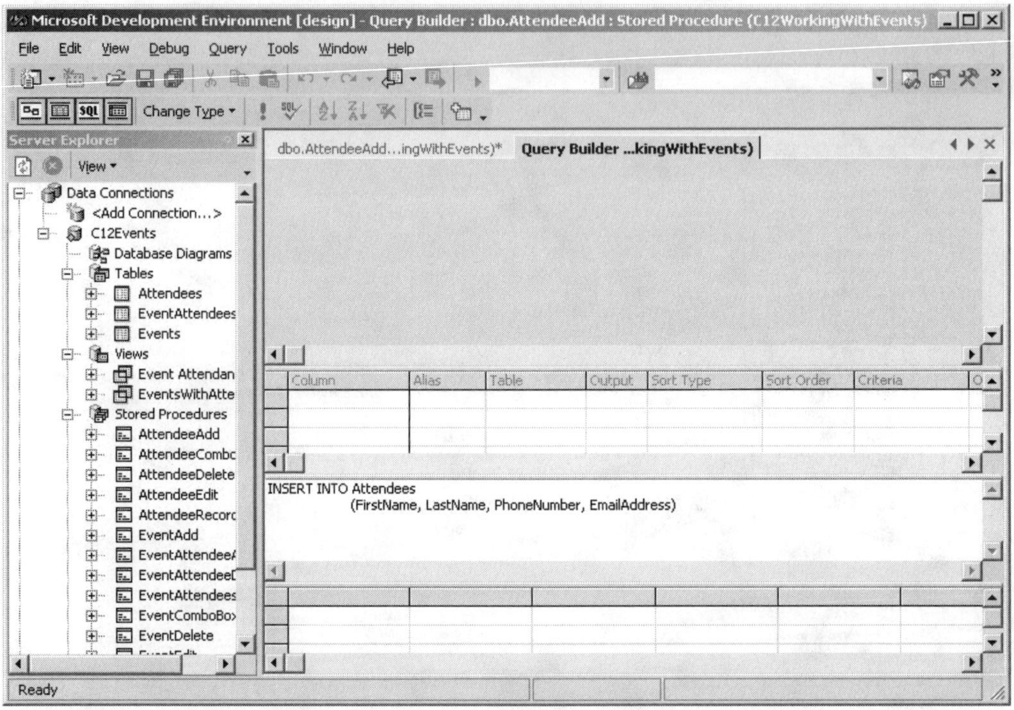

Figure 3-11 *Query Builder*

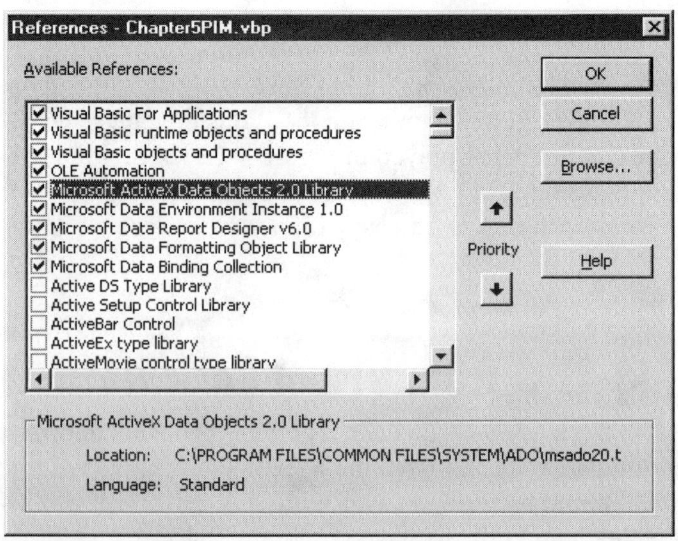

Figure 3-12 *Referencing ADO from Visual Basic 6.0*

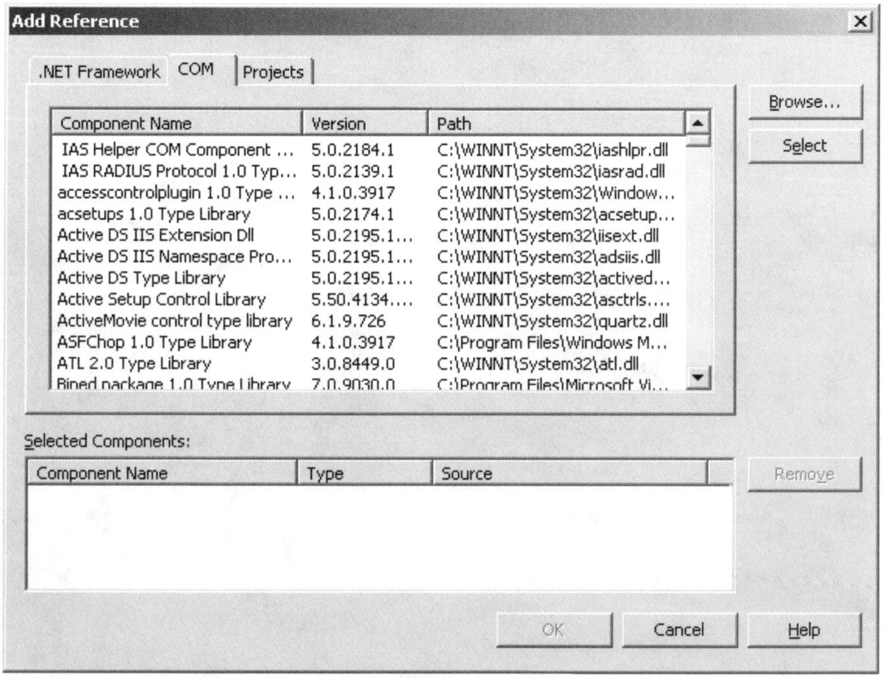

Figure 3-13 *Add Reference dialog box*

From within that dialog box, select the COM tab, and then find the ADO item in the list and click Select. After that, click OK. ADO is now referenced in your Visual Basic.Net project, so you should be able to create instances of the objects in that library.

CHAPTER

4

Money Manager

IN THIS CHAPTER:

C4SQLObjects.sql

AccountTransactions.txt

Categories.txt

Chapter4MoneyManager.vbp

The solution in this chapter allows the user to manage debits and credits in a bank account. Each of the ledger entries entered belongs to a particular category.

Working with Debits and Credits

Reports allow the user to see all the items in a category and to view items that are in a range. The SQL Server back-end database is accessed by the user through a Visual Basic 6 project. As you review this solution, pay close attention to how the grid is populated without using data controls. Also note the simple use of the Printer object for reporting purposes.

Application Walk-Through

When the Visual Basic project is launched, the user is asked to enter their user name and password. Once they have entered that information, they see the Menu form displayed in Figure 4-1.

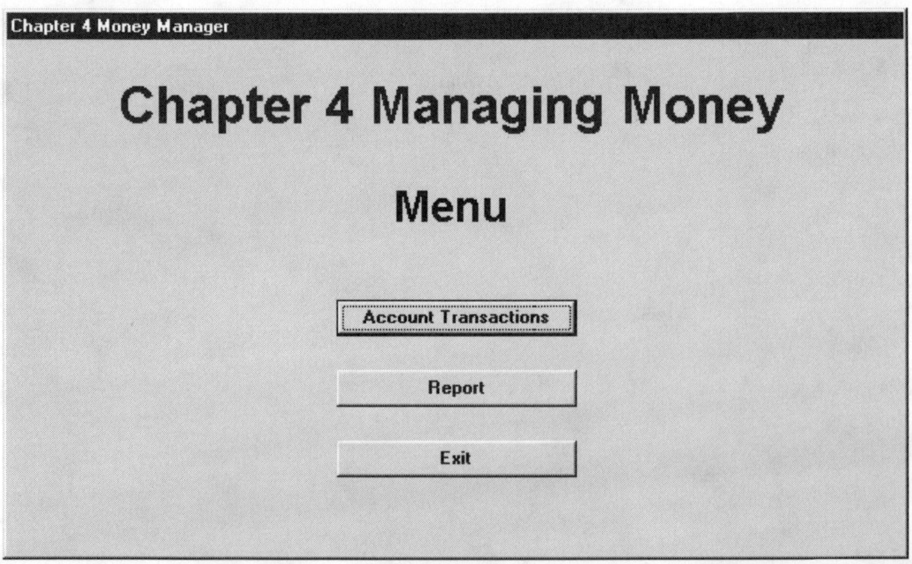

Figure 4-1 *Menu form*

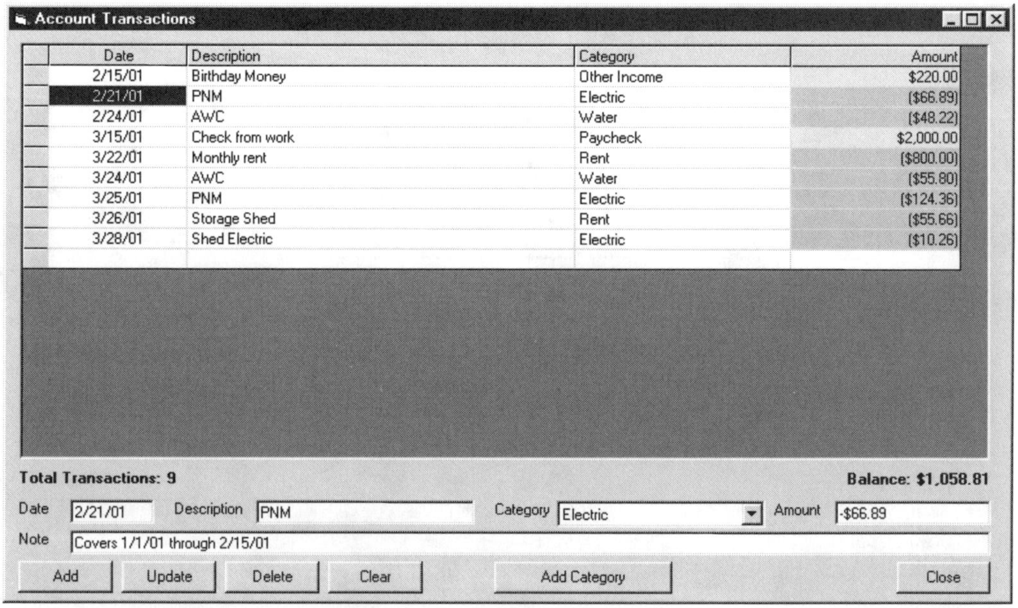

Figure 4-2 *Account Transactions form*

From the Menu form, the user can access the two other forms in this project. If the user presses the Account Transactions button, they see the Account Transactions form displayed in Figure 4-2. This form is where the user would enter and modify all of their account activity. The bulk of the form is made up with a grid that shows all their account transactions. The amount column is color coded so that a debit is a different color than a credit.

When the user clicks any of the rows, that row becomes the active row and the information for that row is displayed in the bottom part of the form. From there they can see the note that goes along with the record. They can also choose to edit or delete the record.

When the user wants to Add a new record, they can click the empty row in the grid or they can click the Clear button. They then enter the information for the transactions and press the Add button. When they do that, the record is added to the grid, the balance is updated, and the total number of transactions is updated.

Each of the entries made belongs to a particular category. The combo box on the form allows the user to select from this fixed list. If the user wanted to add a new category, they press the Add Category button. When they do that, they see the dialog box displayed in Figure 4-3.

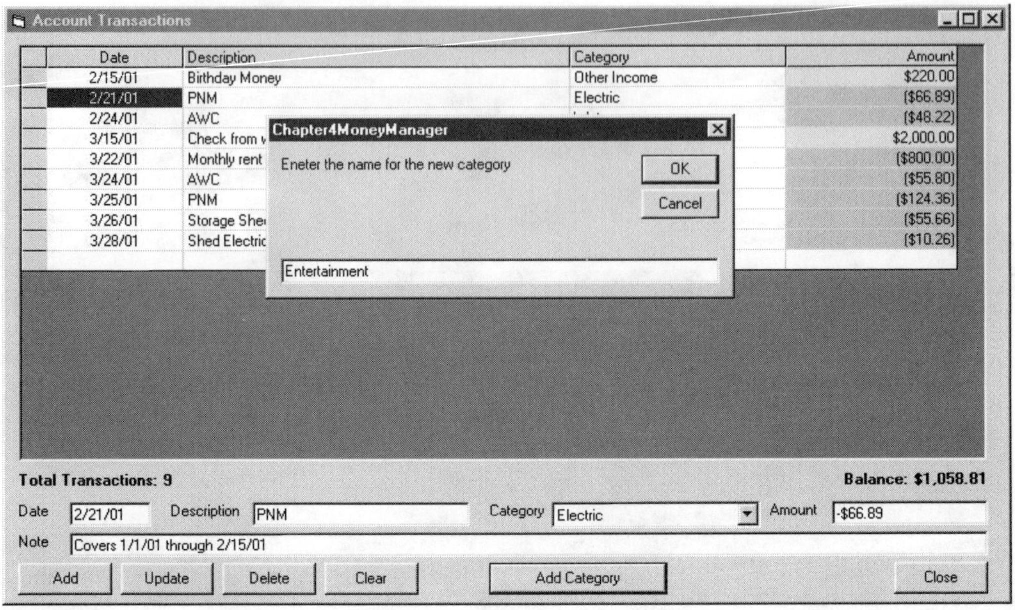

Figure 4-3 *Add Category dialog box*

If the user enters a category that does not yet exist, the category is added to the Categories table and the new category becomes part of the combo box so that the user can select it.

The other form in this application is the Reports form, displayed in Figure 4-4. The bulk of the Reports form is made up of a Label object that is used to preview the report. The report can be used in two ways. The first way is displayed in Figure 4-4. Here, the user has selected the Category object and has selected a particular category. When they click the Preview button, they see all the items in that category displayed in the label. The user could then click the Print button to have their report printed through the Visual Basic Printer object.

The other report that can be generated using this form is displayed in Figure 4-5. Here, the user has chosen to see all transaction items in a specific data range. They enter the date range and click the Preview button to see the transaction items in the date range that they entered. Again, the user can click the Print button to get a hard copy of their report.

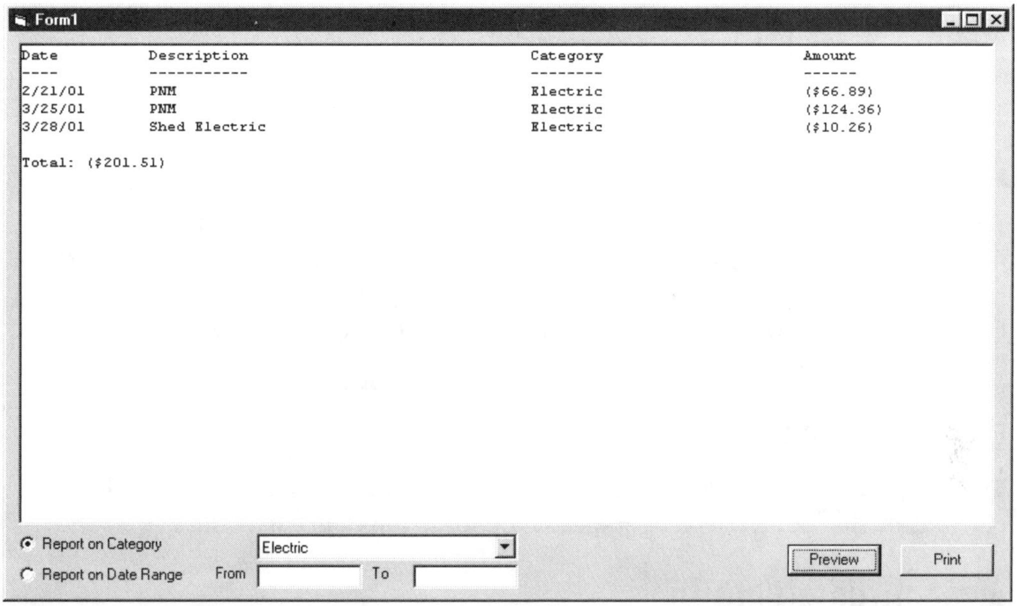

Figure 4-4 *Reports form*

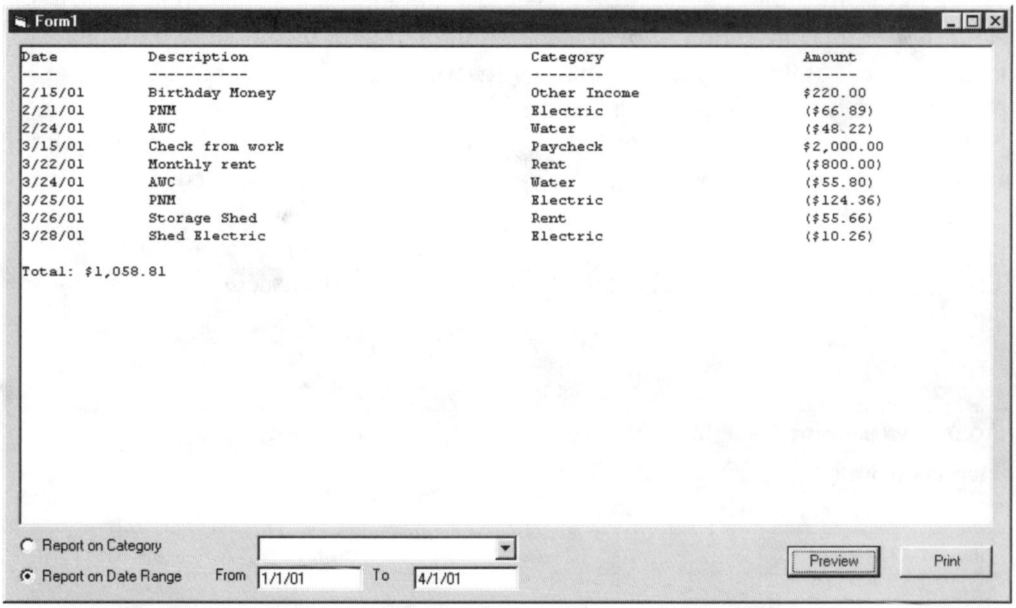

Figure 4-5 *Data Range report*

Tables and Relationships

C4SQLObjects.sql

AccountTransactions Table

The SQL Server database contains two tables for this solution. The first is the AccountTransactions table. This table contains all the debit and credit entries for the user's account. The table is in a one-to-many relationship with the Categories table. Each of the transactions goes in a particular category, but each category can be used by many transactions.

Categories Table

The other table in the SQL Server database is the Categories table. This table contains the list of all the categories that a transaction item can be in.

AccountTransactions Table

AccountTransactions.txt

The field specifications for the AccountTransactions table are displayed in Table 4-1.

The AccountTransactionID field is the primary key for this table. It uniquely identifies each of the records. It is an identity column, so it is automatically populated when a new record is added.

The TransactionDate field stores the date of the transaction. The TransDescription field stores a brief name or title for the transaction, which is displayed in the ledger.

The CategoryID field is a foreign key that links this table with the Categories table. The Amount field stores the dollar amount for the debit or credit. And the TransNote field allows for a lengthier note regarding the transaction.

Field Name	Field Type	Notes
AccountTransactionID	int	Primary Key, Identity Column
TransactionDate	datetime	
TransDescription	varchar	Length = 50
CategoryID	int	Foreign Key
Amount	money	
TransNote	varchar	Length = 200

Table 4-1 *AccountTransactions Table Field Specifications*

Field Name	Field Type	Notes
CategoryID	int	Primary Key, Identity Column
CategoryName	varchar	Length = 50

Table 4-2 *Categories Table Field Specifications*

Categories Table

Categories.txt

The field specifications for the Categories table are displayed in Table 4-2.

The CategoryID field is the primary key in this table. The other field, CategoryName, stores the name of the category.

Stored Procedures

AccountTransactionsAdd Stored Procedure

The AccountTransactionsAdd stored procedure provides the mechanism for adding a new record to the AccountTransactions table.

```
CREATE PROCEDURE AccountTransactionsAdd
@TransactionDate datetime,
@TransDescription varchar(50),
@CategoryID integer,
@Amount money,
@TransNote varchar(2000)
AS
BEGIN
        Insert Into AccountTransactions
            (TransactionDate, TransDescription, CategoryID,
            Amount, TransNote) values
            (@TransactionDate, @TransDescription, @CategoryID,
            @Amount, @TransNote)
        Select @@Identity as TheNewID
    END
GO
```

The procedure requires five input parameters. Each of these parameters contains the data for that field to be inserted into the new record:

```
@TransactionDate datetime,
@TransDescription varchar(50),
@CategoryID integer,
@Amount money,
@TransNote varchar(2000)
```

You then use a SQL Insert statement to add a new record to the AccountTransactions table:

```
Insert Into AccountTransactions
        (TransactionDate, TransDescription, CategoryID,
        Amount, TransNote) values
        (@TransactionDate, @TransDescription, @CategoryID,
        @Amount, @TransNote)
```

The procedure returns the AccountTransactionID of the record that was just added:

```
Select @@Identity as TheNewID
```

AccountTransactionUpdate Stored Procedure

The calling application uses the AccountTransactionUpdate stored procedure to edit an existing record.

```
CREATE PROCEDURE AccountTransactionsUpdate
@AccountTransactionID integer,
@TransactionDate datetime,
@TransDescription varchar(50),
@CategoryID integer,
@Amount money,
@TransNote varchar(2000)
AS
    BEGIN
        Update AccountTransactions set
            TransactionDate = @TransactionDate,
            TransDescription = @TransDescription,
            CategoryID = @CategoryID,
            Amount = @Amount,
            TransNote = @TransNote
            Where AccountTransactionID = @AccountTransactionID
    END
GO
```

The first parameter passed into the stored procedure contains the ID of the record to be edited:

```
@AccountTransactionID integer,
```

The other parameters passed in are the new values for the existing record:

```
@TransactionDate datetime,
@TransDescription varchar(50),
@CategoryID integer,
@Amount money,
@TransNote varchar(2000)
```

You then use a SQL Update statement to update the desired record:

```
Update AccountTransactions set
        TransactionDate = @TransactionDate,
        TransDescription = @TransDescription,
        CategoryID = @CategoryID,
        Amount = @Amount,
        TransNote = @TransNote
        Where AccountTransactionID = @AccountTransactionID
```

AccountTransactionsDelete Stored Procedure

The AccountTransactionsDelete stored procedure provides the mechanism for removing a transaction record from the AccountTransactions table.

```
CREATE PROCEDURE AccountTransactionsDelete
@AccountTransactionID integer
AS
    BEGIN
        Delete from  AccountTransactions
            Where AccountTransactionID = @AccountTransactionID
    END
GO
```

The procedure requires a single parameter, the ID of the record that is to be deleted:

```
@AccountTransactionID integer
```

That record is then removed from the AccountTransactions table:

```
Delete from  AccountTransactions
        Where AccountTransactionID = @AccountTransactionID
```

GetAllActivity Stored Procedure

When the Visual Basic Account Transactions form is first opened, it displays all the AccountTransactions records. The GetAllActivity stored procedure returns the data needed to display that information on the form.

```
CREATE PROCEDURE GetAllActivity AS
Select AccountTransactionID, TransactionDate,
    TransDescription, Categories.CategoryName, Amount
    from AccountTransactions Left Join Categories on
    AccountTransactions.CategoryID = Categories.CategoryID
    order by TransactionDate
GO
```

The procedure does not require any parameters. It simply returns the basic transaction information along with the name of the category instead of the ID through a Select statement. Note that a join is used to connect the Account-Transactions table with the Categories table.

```
Select AccountTransactionID, TransactionDate,
        TransDescription, Categories.CategoryName, Amount
        from AccountTransactions Left Join Categories on
        AccountTransactions.CategoryID = Categories.CategoryID
        order by TransactionDate
```

GetBalance Stored Procedure

The Visual Basic Account Transactions form must also display the current balance of all the account transactions. The GetBalance stored procedure returns this data.

```
CREATE PROCEDURE GetBalance AS
    Select Sum(Amount) as TheBalance
        from AccountTransactions
GO
```

A Select statement is used to return the sum total of the Amount field into an output field called TheBalance:

```
Select Sum(Amount) as TheBalance
    from AccountTransactions
```

GetTransactionRecord Stored Procedure

When the user clicks any of the records in the ledger on the Account Transactions form, the full information for that record is displayed in the bottom portion of the form. The GetTransactionRecord stored procedure returns that information.

```
CREATE PROCEDURE GetTransactionRecord
@AccountTransactionID integer
AS
BEGIN
    Select * from AccountTransactions Where
        AccountTransactionID = @AccountTransactionID
END
GO
```

The procedure requires a single input parameter, the ID of the record that the calling application wants returned:

```
@AccountTransactionID integer
```

That record is then returned through a Select statement:

```
Select * from AccountTransactions Where
        AccountTransactionID = @AccountTransactionID
```

CategoryAdd Stored Procedure

When the user clicks the Add Category button on the Account Transactions form, the category they enter needs to be added to the Categories table. This is done through the CategoryAdd stored procedure.

```
CREATE PROCEDURE CategoryAdd
@CategoryName varchar(50)
AS
    Declare @IsInUse integer
    Select @IsInUse = Count(CategoryID) from Categories
        Where CategoryName = @CategoryName
    If @IsInUse = 0
        BEGIN
```

```
                Insert Into Categories
                    (CategoryName) values
                    (@CategoryName)
                Select @@Identity as TheNewID
            END
        Else
            BEGIN
                Select 0 as TheNewID
            END
GO
```

The procedure requires a single parameter. The name for the new category:

```
@CategoryName varchar(50)
```

You will also need a local variable:

```
Declare @IsInUse integer
```

which is set to the number of occurrences that the category name supplied is found in the Categories table:

```
Select @IsInUse = Count(CategoryID) from Categories
        Where CategoryName = @CategoryName
```

If the category is not in use, the variable will be set to 0:

```
If @IsInUse = 0
```

You can then add the new category:

```
Insert Into Categories
       (CategoryName) values
       (@CategoryName)
```

and return the ID of the category added:

```
Select @@Identity as TheNewID
```

Otherwise, the category exists and is not added; you then return 0 from this procedure:

```
Select 0 as TheNewID
```

GetAllCategories Stored Procedure

On the Account Transactions form and the Reports form, the user selects a category from a combo box. Those combo boxes are populated through the return from the GetAllCategories stored procedure.

```
CREATE PROCEDURE GetAllCategories AS
    Select * from Categories
        Order By CategoryName
GO
```

The procedure uses a Select statement to return the information sorted by the name of the category:

```
Select * from Categories
        Order By CategoryName
```

GetAllActivityInCategory Stored Procedure

One of the reports accessed on the Reports form displays all the transactions in a category. That data is returned through the GetAllActivityInCategory stored procedure.

```
CREATE PROCEDURE GetAllActivityInCategory
@CategoryID integer
AS
Select TransactionDate,
    TransDescription, Categories.CategoryName, Amount
    from AccountTransactions Left Join Categories on
    AccountTransactions.CategoryID = Categories.CategoryID
    Where Categories.CategoryID = @CategoryID
    order by TransactionDate
GO
```

The procedure requires a single parameter, the ID of the category for which you want transactions returned:

```
@CategoryID integer
```

The basic transaction information is returned for the records in that category along with the name of the category. The name of the category is returned through the join of the two tables:

```
Select TransactionDate,
        TransDescription, Categories.CategoryName, Amount
        from AccountTransactions Left Join Categories on
        AccountTransactions.CategoryID = Categories.CategoryID
        Where Categories.CategoryID = @CategoryID
        order by TransactionDate
```

GetAllActivityInDateRange Stored Procedure

The other report on the Reports form displays all the transactions in a date range. That data is returned from the GetAllActivityInDateRange stored procedure.

```
CREATE PROCEDURE GetAllActivityInDateRange
@FromDate datetime,
@ToDate datetime
AS
Select TransactionDate,
    TransDescription, Categories.CategoryName, Amount
    from AccountTransactions Left Join Categories on
    AccountTransactions.CategoryID = Categories.CategoryID
    Where TransactionDate >= @FromDate and
    TransactionDate <= @ToDate
    order by TransactionDate
GO
```

The procedure requires two parameters. The first is the starting date for the records that are to be included:

```
@FromDate datetime,
```

The other is the ending date:

```
@ToDate datetime
```

A Select statement is used to return the records in that date range:

```
Select TransactionDate,
        TransDescription, Categories.CategoryName, Amount
        from AccountTransactions Left Join Categories on
```

```
AccountTransactions.CategoryID = Categories.CategoryID
Where TransactionDate >= @FromDate and
TransactionDate <= @ToDate
order by TransactionDate
```

Application Notes

Chapter4MoneyManager.vbp

No DSN is required for this application, since it uses a full connect string. If you call your database something different than what is in the code, you will need to modify the connect strings.

Since the application uses ADO, it must be referenced through the References dialog box. The project also uses the MSFlexGrid control for the ledger on the Account Transactions form. Therefore, it is included in the Components dialog box.

Take a look at the properties for the project displayed in Figure 4-6. The Startup Object property is set to Sub Main. That means that a form is not loaded automatically when the project starts. Instead, a subroutine called main is called and must be included with the project in a module.

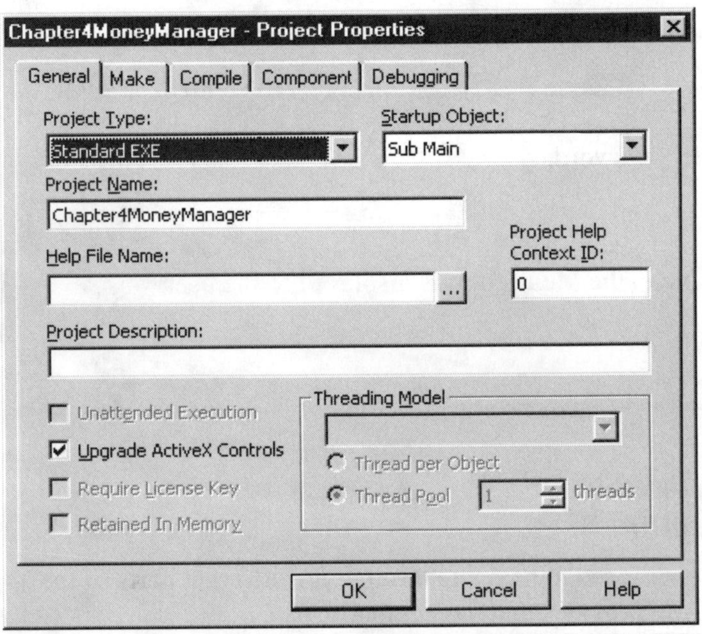

Figure 4-6 *Project Properties dialog box*

Modules

modPublicProcs Module

The front-end Visual Basic project contains a single module called modPublicProcs. The module has the following variables declared in the General Declarations:

```
Public SQLUserName As String
Public SQLPassword As String
```

These variables are available and are used throughout the application, since they have public scope. The first variable is used to store the name of the user, and the second is used to store the password of the user.

When the user first enters the application, the Main procedure fires:

```
Public Sub Main()
    SQLUserName = InputBox("Please enter your user name.")
    SQLPassword = InputBox("Please enter your password.")
    frmMenu.Show
End Sub
```

The procedure prompts the user for their SQL Server user name:

```
SQLUserName = InputBox("Please enter your user name.")
```

as well as their password:

```
SQLPassword = InputBox("Please enter your password.")
```

Once complete, the Menu form is displayed to the user:

```
frmMenu.Show
```

Forms

frmMenu Form

The Menu form is used to navigate through the different parts of the application. The code on the form provides that navigation.

The first code block fires when the Account Transactions button is clicked.

```
Private Sub cmdAT_Click()
    frmAccountTransactions.Show
    Unload Me
End Sub
```

The code opens the Account Transactions form:

```
frmAccountTransactions.Show
```

and closes the Menu form, which is what the Me keyword refers to in this case:

```
Unload Me
```

The next code block fires when the Report button is pressed.

```
Private Sub cmdReport_Click()
    frmReport.Show
    Unload Me
End Sub
```

The code opens the Report form:

```
frmReport.Show
```

and then closes the Menu form:

```
Unload Me
```

When the user clicks the Exit button, the program ends:

```
Private Sub cmdExit_Click()
    End
End Sub
```

frmAccountTransactions Form

The Account Transactions form provides the functionality for managing all the account transaction activity. This first code block appears in the General Declarations section.

```
Option Explicit
Private MyConnection As New ADODB.Connection
```

You start with option Explicit, which means that a variable declaration is required:

```
Option Explicit
```

You then declare an ADO Connection object that you will use in many locations on this form:

```
Private MyConnection As New ADODB.Connection
```

The form contains two of its own procedures. The first is used to update the balance and transactions totals.

```
Public Sub CalcBalance()
    Dim RSTheBal As ADODB.Recordset
    Set RSTheBal = MyConnection.Execute("Exec GetBalance")
    lblBalance.Caption = "Balance: " & FormatCurrency(RSTheBal(0))
    lblTotTrans.Caption = "Total Transactions: " _
        & (grdTrans.Rows - 2)
End Sub
```

The procedure will need a Recordset object:

```
Dim RSTheBal As ADODB.Recordset
```

That Recordset object is set to the return of a call to your GetBalance stored procedure:

```
Set RSTheBal = MyConnection.Execute("Exec GetBalance")
```

The balance returned from the stored procedure is set to be displayed as currency and is placed in a label:

```
lblBalance.Caption = "Balance: " & FormatCurrency(RSTheBal(0))
```

Next, you set the number of transactions to the total number of rows in the grid control minus two. One is subtracted for the black row at the bottom of the grid, and the other is subtracted for the column headers:

```
lblTotTrans.Caption = "Total Transactions: " _
    & (grdTrans.Rows - 2)
```

The other user-defined procedure on this form is used to populate the combo box.

```
Public Sub UpdateCombo()
    Dim RSAllCategories As ADODB.Recordset
    Set RSAllCategories = MyConnection.Execute("Exec GetAllCategories")
    Do Until RSAllCategories.EOF
        cmbCategory.AddItem RSAllCategories("CategoryName")
        cmbCategory.ItemData(cmbCategory.NewIndex) = _
            RSAllCategories("CategoryID")
        RSAllCategories.MoveNext
    Loop
End Sub
```

The procedure will need a Recordset object:

```
Dim RSAllCategories As ADODB.Recordset
```

which contains all the names and IDs of the categories:

```
Set RSAllCategories = MyConnection.Execute("Exec GetAllCategories")
```

You then start a loop so that you can process each of the records returned:

```
Do Until RSAllCategories.EOF
```

The name of the category is added to the combo box:

```
cmbCategory.AddItem RSAllCategories("CategoryName")
```

Then the item data for the entry is added, and the data that is not seen in the combo box is set to the ID of the category. So the user will see a list of categories, and you can retrieve the ID of the category that they selected:

```
cmbCategory.ItemData(cmbCategory.NewIndex) = _
      SAllCategories("CategoryID")
```

You then move on to process the next record:

```
RSAllCategories.MoveNext
Loop
```

When the form is first opened, you need to set up the grid columns and populate them. This is done in the Load event.

```
Private Sub Form_Load()
    Dim RSAllRecords As ADODB.Recordset
    Dim CurrentRow As Integer
    MyConnection.ConnectionString = "driver={SQL Server};" _
        & "server=MyServer;uid=" & SQLUserName _
        & ";pwd=" & SQLPassword & ";" _
        & "database=C4MoneyManager"
    MyConnection.Open
    Set RSAllRecords = MyConnection.Execute("Exec GetAllActivity")
    grdTrans.Row = 0
    grdTrans.Col = 0
    grdTrans.Text = ""
    grdTrans.ColWidth(0) = 300
    grdTrans.ColAlignment(0) = flexAlignCenterCenter
    grdTrans.Col = 1
    grdTrans.Text = "AccountTransactionID"
    grdTrans.ColWidth(1) = 0
    grdTrans.ColAlignment(1) = flexAlignCenterCenter
    grdTrans.Col = 2
    grdTrans.Text = "Date"
    grdTrans.ColWidth(2) = 1600
    grdTrans.ColAlignment(2) = flexAlignCenterCenter
    grdTrans.Col = 3
    grdTrans.Text = "Description"
    grdTrans.ColWidth(3) = 4500
    grdTrans.ColAlignment(3) = flexAlignLeftCenter
    grdTrans.Col = 4
    grdTrans.Text = "Category"
    grdTrans.ColWidth(4) = 2500
    grdTrans.ColAlignment(4) = flexAlignLeftCenter
    grdTrans.Col = 5
    grdTrans.Text = "Amount"
    grdTrans.ColWidth(5) = 2000
    grdTrans.ColAlignment(5) = flexAlignRightCenter
    CurrentRow = 1
    Do Until RSAllRecords.EOF
        grdTrans.Row = CurrentRow
        CurrentRow = CurrentRow + 1
        grdTrans.Rows = grdTrans.Rows + 1
        grdTrans.Col = 1
        grdTrans.Text = RSAllRecords("AccountTransactionID")
        grdTrans.Col = 2
        grdTrans.Text = RSAllRecords("TransactionDate")
```

```
        grdTrans.Col = 3
        grdTrans.Text = RSAllRecords("TransDescription")
        grdTrans.Col = 4
        grdTrans.Text = RSAllRecords("CategoryName")
        grdTrans.Col = 5
        grdTrans.Text = FormatCurrency(RSAllRecords("Amount"))
        If RSAllRecords("Amount") >= 0 Then
            grdTrans.CellBackColor = &HC0FFC0
        Else
            grdTrans.CellBackColor = &HC0C0FF
        End If
        RSAllRecords.MoveNext
    Loop
    CalcBalance
    UpdateCombo
    grdTrans_Click
End Sub
```

The form needs a Recordset object that will be used to retrieve all the transaction records:

```
Dim RSAllRecords As ADODB.Recordset
```

It also needs a variable that will be used to store the current row number:

```
Dim CurrentRow As Integer
```

You then open a connection to your SQL Server database, using the login information supplied by the user when the application first started:

```
MyConnection.ConnectionString = "driver={SQL Server};" _
& "server=MyServer;uid=" & SQLUserName _
& ";pwd=" & SQLPassword & ";" _
& "database=C4MoneyManager"
```

You then open that connection:

```
MyConnection.Open
```

and retrieve all the transactions from the database through the GetAllActivity stored procedure:

```
Set RSAllRecords = MyConnection.Execute("Exec GetAllActivity")
```

Now you need to create the columns and headers for the grid. You start by moving to the first cell in the first row:

```
grdTrans.Row = 0
grdTrans.Col = 0
```

and clear any text in this cell:

```
grdTrans.Text = ""
```

You then set the width to a small size. This is the column that contains the gray boxes to the left of a record:

```
grdTrans.ColWidth(0) = 300
```

You center the alignment for that column:

```
grdTrans.ColAlignment(0) = flexAlignCenterCenter
```

and move on to the next column:

```
grdTrans.Col = 1
```

which will store the ID of the transaction:

```
grdTrans.Text = "AccountTransactionID"
```

You then set the width for the column to 0. You need the data in your code, but the user does not need to see it:

```
grdTrans.ColWidth(1) = 0
grdTrans.ColAlignment(1) = flexAlignCenterCenter
```

The next column will contain the transaction date:

```
grdTrans.Col = 2
grdTrans.Text = "Date"
```

the width for the date is set to a medium size,

```
grdTrans.ColWidth(2) = 1600
```

and the text in that column will be centered:

```
grdTrans.ColAlignment(2) = flexAlignCenterCenter
```

The next column will store the description of the transaction:

```
grdTrans.Col = 3
grdTrans.Text = "Description"
```

Therefore, it needs to be wider:

```
grdTrans.ColWidth(3) = 4500
```

and have a left alignment:

```
grdTrans.ColAlignment(3) = flexAlignLeftCenter
```

Column four will store the category of the transaction activity:

```
grdTrans.Col = 4
grdTrans.Text = "Category"
```

It is set to a medium width that is left aligned:

```
grdTrans.ColWidth(4) = 2500
grdTrans.ColAlignment(4) = flexAlignLeftCenter
```

The last column will contain the dollar amount of the transaction:

```
grdTrans.Col = 5
grdTrans.Text = "Amount"
```

The width is set to a medium length:

```
grdTrans.ColWidth(5) = 2000
```

and is right aligned:

```
grdTrans.ColAlignment(5) = flexAlignRightCenter
```

Now, you are ready to add records to the grid. You set the row pointer to the first data row in the grid, after the header row:

```
CurrentRow = 1
```

and start a loop so that you can process each transaction record:

```
Do Until RSAllRecords.EOF
```

You move the grid so that you are pointing to the current row that data will be placed in:

```
grdTrans.Row = CurrentRow
```

and then iterate your row counter:

```
CurrentRow = CurrentRow + 1
```

and add an extra row. This way, you will be left with a blank row at the bottom of the grid:

```
grdTrans.Rows = grdTrans.Rows + 1
```

The first piece of that is placed in the first column:

```
grdTrans.Col = 1
```

That column is not visible, since its width is set to 0. The ID of the transaction is placed there:

```
grdTrans.Text = RSAllRecords("AccountTransactionID")
```

In the next column:

```
grdTrans.Col = 2
```

place the date of the transaction:

```
grdTrans.Text = RSAllRecords("TransactionDate")
```

After that comes the description:

```
grdTrans.Col = 3
grdTrans.Text = RSAllRecords("TransDescription")
```

and the category that the transaction is in:

```
grdTrans.Col = 4
grdTrans.Text = RSAllRecords("CategoryName")
```

The last column contains the amount for the transaction, which is formatted so that it appears as currency:

```
grdTrans.Col = 5
grdTrans.Text = FormatCurrency(RSAllRecords("Amount"))
```

If the amount of the transaction is zero or positive:

```
If RSAllRecords("Amount") >= 0 Then
```

the background color for the cell is set to a light green:

```
grdTrans.CellBackColor = &HC0FFC0
```

Otherwise, it is set to a light red:

```
grdTrans.CellBackColor = &HC0C0FF
```

You then move on to process the next transaction record:

```
RSAllRecords.MoveNext
Loop
```

After the records are all added to the grid, you need to update your total labels:

```
CalcBalance
```

populate the combo box:

```
UpdateCombo
```

and update the text boxes at the bottom of the form so that they contain the values of the current selected record:

```
grdTrans_Click
```

The next procedure fires when the form is closed.

```
Private Sub Form_Unload(Cancel As Integer)
    frmMenu.Show
    Set frmAccountTransactions = Nothing
End Sub
```

The code displays the Menu form:

```
frmMenu.Show
```

and releases all the resources of this form:

```
Set frmAccountTransactions = Nothing
```

In code, as well as when the user clicks the grid, you need to update the combo box and the text boxes at the bottom of the form so that they contain the full data for the record selected. This is done through the Click event of the grid.

```
Private Sub grdTrans_Click()
    Dim RSTrans As ADODB.Recordset
    Dim CurrentID As Long
    Dim I As Long
    grdTrans.Col = 1
    If IsNumeric(grdTrans.Text) Then
        CurrentID = grdTrans.Text
        Set RSTrans = MyConnection.Execute("Exec GetTransactionRecord " _
            & CurrentID)
        If Not RSTrans.EOF Then
            txtTransactionDate.Text = RSTrans("TransactionDate")
            txtTransDescription.Text = RSTrans("TransDescription")
            txtAmount.Text = FormatCurrency(RSTrans("Amount"), , , False)
            txtTransNote.Text = RSTrans("TransNote")
            For I = 0 To cmbCategory.ListCount - 1
                If cmbCategory.ItemData(I) = RSTrans("CategoryID") Then
                    cmbCategory.ListIndex = I
                    Exit For
                End If
            Next
        Else
            txtTransactionDate.Text = ""
            txtTransDescription.Text = ""
            txtAmount.Text = ""
            txtTransNote.Text = ""
        End If
    Else
        txtTransactionDate.Text = ""
        txtTransDescription.Text = ""
        txtAmount.Text = ""
        txtTransNote.Text = ""
    End If
    grdTrans.Col = 2
End Sub
```

You will need a Recordset object that is used to retrieve the full contents of the current record in the grid:

```
Dim RSTrans As ADODB.Recordset
```

You will also need a variable to store the ID of the currently selected record:

```
Dim CurrentID As Long
```

and one that is used in an iterative loop:

```
Dim I As Long
```

You move to Column 1, the second column, which is where the ID field is stored:

```
grdTrans.Col = 1
```

You check to see if the value in that cell is a number, meaning that you are in a record with data and not in the blank row:

```
If IsNumeric(grdTrans.Text) Then
```

If that is the case, you store the ID in your local variable:

```
CurrentID = grdTrans.Text
```

and retrieve the full contents of that transaction record:

```
Set RSTrans = MyConnection.Execute("Exec GetTransactionRecord " _
      & CurrentID)
```

Then make sure that a record was found:

```
If Not RSTrans.EOF Then
```

If it was, you populate the text boxes in the bottom of the form using the values retrieved:

```
txtTransactionDate.Text = RSTrans("TransactionDate")
txtTransDescription.Text = RSTrans("TransDescription")
txtAmount.Text = FormatCurrency(RSTrans("Amount"), , , False)
txtTransNote.Text = RSTrans("TransNote")
```

You then need to loop through the Category combo box:

```
For I = 0 To cmbCategory.ListCount - 1
```

and look for the ID of the currently selected category:

```
If cmbCategory.ItemData(I) = RSTrans("CategoryID") Then
```

Once you find it, you set the combo box up so that it is the currently selected item in the list:

```
cmbCategory.ListIndex = I
```

and abort the rest of the For structure:

```
Exit For
```

If the code flows to this point, it means that the record selected is no longer available:

```
Else
```

In that case, you clear the text boxes:

```
txtTransactionDate.Text = ""
txtTransDescription.Text = ""
txtAmount.Text = ""
txtTransNote.Text = ""
```

If the code flows here, it means the record that has been selected is the blank record at the bottom of the grid:

```
Else
```

In that case, you also need to clear the text boxes on the form:

```
txtTransactionDate.Text = ""
txtTransDescription.Text = ""
txtAmount.Text = ""
txtTransNote.Text = ""
```

Move the column pointer to the next cell in the row so that it will be selected, since the column you are currently working with is invisible:

```
grdTrans.Col = 2
```

The next code block fires when the Add button is clicked.

```
Private Sub cmdAdd_Click()
    Dim RSAddNew As ADODB.Recordset
    Set RSAddNew = MyConnection.Execute("Exec AccountTransactionsAdd '" _
        & txtTransactionDate.Text & "', '" & txtTransDescription.Text _
        & "', " & cmbCategory.ItemData(cmbCategory.ListIndex) _
        & ", " & txtAmount.Text & ", '" _
        & txtTransNote.Text & "'")
    grdTrans.Row = grdTrans.Rows - 1
    grdTrans.Col = 1
    grdTrans.Text = RSAddNew("TheNewID")
    grdTrans.Col = 2
    grdTrans.Text = txtTransactionDate.Text
    grdTrans.Col = 3
    grdTrans.Text = txtTransDescription.Text
    grdTrans.Col = 4
    grdTrans.Text = cmbCategory.Text
    grdTrans.Col = 5
    grdTrans.Text = FormatCurrency(txtAmount.Text)
    If CCur(txtAmount.Text) >= 0 Then
        grdTrans.CellBackColor = &HC0FFC0
    Else
        grdTrans.CellBackColor = &HC0C0FF
    End If
    grdTrans.Rows = grdTrans.Rows + 1
    grdTrans.Row = grdTrans.Rows - 1
    grdTrans_Click
    CalcBalance
End Sub
```

The procedure will need a Recordset object:

```
Dim RSAddNew As ADODB.Recordset
```

which is set to the ID of the record that you are adding. Passed to the call are the values for the record being added:

```
Set RSAddNew = MyConnection.Execute("Exec AccountTransactionsAdd '" _
      & txtTransactionDate.Text & "', '" & txtTransDescription.Text _
      & "', " & cmbCategory.ItemData(cmbCategory.ListIndex) _
      & ", " & txtAmount.Text & ", '" _
      & txtTransNote.Text & "'")
```

You then move to the bottom, blank row in the grid so that you can add the item just entered into the grid:

```
grdTrans.Row = grdTrans.Rows - 1
```

Populate the record inserted into the grid. You use the ID of the record that was returned from the call to the stored procedure:

```
grdTrans.Col = 1
grdTrans.Text = RSAddNew("TheNewID")
```

You also place in the date of the transaction:

```
grdTrans.Col = 2
grdTrans.Text = txtTransactionDate.Text
```

as well as the description, category, and amount:

```
grdTrans.Col = 3
grdTrans.Text = txtTransDescription.Text
grdTrans.Col = 4
grdTrans.Text = cmbCategory.Text
grdTrans.Col = 5
grdTrans.Text = FormatCurrency(txtAmount.Text)
```

You also need to set the background of the cell for the amount according to whether it is positive or negative:

```
If CCur(txtAmount.Text) >= 0 Then
```

If it is 0 or positive, you set the color to a light green:

```
grdTrans.CellBackColor = &HC0FFC0
```

Otherwise, it is set to a light red:

```
grdTrans.CellBackColor = &HC0C0FF
```

Add another row to the grid:

```
grdTrans.Rows = grdTrans.Rows + 1
```

move to that row:

```
grdTrans.Row = grdTrans.Rows - 1
```

clear out the text boxes for that blank row:

```
grdTrans_Click
```

and recalculate the total labels:

```
CalcBalance
```

The next procedure fires when the user clicks the Update button.

```
Private Sub cmdUpdate_Click()
    Dim RSUpdate As ADODB.Recordset
    grdTrans.Col = 1
    If Not IsNumeric(grdTrans.Text) Then
        cmdAdd_Click
        Exit Sub
    End If
    Set RSUpdate = MyConnection.Execute("Exec AccountTransactionsUpdate " _
        & grdTrans.Text & ", '" _
        & txtTransactionDate.Text & "', '" & txtTransDescription.Text _
        & "', " & cmbCategory.ItemData(cmbCategory.ListIndex) _
        & ", " & txtAmount.Text & ", '" _
        & txtTransNote.Text & "'")
    grdTrans.Col = 2
    grdTrans.Text = txtTransactionDate.Text
    grdTrans.Col = 3
    grdTrans.Text = txtTransDescription.Text
    grdTrans.Col = 4
    grdTrans.Text = cmbCategory.Text
    grdTrans.Col = 5
    grdTrans.Text = FormatCurrency(txtAmount.Text)
    If CCur(txtAmount.Text) >= 0 Then
        grdTrans.CellBackColor = &HC0FFC0
    Else
        grdTrans.CellBackColor = &HC0C0FF
    End If
    grdTrans.Row = grdTrans.Rows - 1
    grdTrans_Click
    CalcBalance
End Sub
```

The procedure uses a Recordset object:

```
Dim RSUpdate As ADODB.Recordset
```

Then move to Column 1, the one that contains the ID of the record being edited:

```
grdTrans.Col = 1
```

and make sure that the ID is a number:

```
If Not IsNumeric(grdTrans.Text) Then
```

If it isn't, the user is editing the blank row and really needs to add a new record. So you call that procedure:

```
cmdAdd_Click
```

and leave this procedure:

```
Exit Sub
```

Otherwise, you can update the desired record:

```
Set RSUpdate = MyConnection.Execute("Exec AccountTransactionsUpdate " _
    & grdTrans.Text & ", '" _
    & txtTransactionDate.Text & "', '" & txtTransDescription.Text _
    & "', " & cmbCategory.ItemData(cmbCategory.ListIndex) _
    & ", " & txtAmount.Text & ", '" _
    & txtTransNote.Text & "'")
```

Then you need to update the grid with the data entered by the user:

```
grdTrans.Col = 2
grdTrans.Text = txtTransactionDate.Text
grdTrans.Col = 3
grdTrans.Text = txtTransDescription.Text
grdTrans.Col = 4
grdTrans.Text = cmbCategory.Text
grdTrans.Col = 5
grdTrans.Text = FormatCurrency(txtAmount.Text)
If CCur(txtAmount.Text) >= 0 Then
    grdTrans.CellBackColor = &HC0FFC0
Else
    grdTrans.CellBackColor = &HC0C0FF
End If
```

Move to the last row in the grid:

```
    grdTrans.Row = grdTrans.Rows - 1
```

clear the text boxes at the bottom of the form:

```
grdTrans_Click
```

and recalculate the total labels:

```
CalcBalance
```

When the user clicks the Delete button, the next code block fires.

```
Private Sub cmdDelete_Click()
    grdTrans.Col = 1
    If Not IsNumeric(grdTrans.Text) Then
        cmdClear_Click
    Else
        MyConnection.Execute "AccountTransactionsDelete " _
            & grdTrans.Text
        grdTrans.RemoveItem grdTrans.Row
        CalcBalance
        grdTrans.Row = grdTrans.Rows - 1
        grdTrans_Click
    End If
End Sub
```

You move to column 1 of the current record in the grid, since that contains the ID of the record to be deleted:

```
grdTrans.Col = 1
```

If the value in that cell is not a number, it means the user is on the blank record:

```
If Not IsNumeric(grdTrans.Text) Then
```

and you just need to clear the text boxes on the form:

```
cmdClear_Click
```

Otherwise, you delete the offending record from the database:

```
MyConnection.Execute "AccountTransactionsDelete " _
    & grdTrans.Text
```

as well as from the grid:

```
grdTrans.RemoveItem grdTrans.Row
```

update your total labels:

```
CalcBalance
```

move to the last record:

```
grdTrans.Row = grdTrans.Rows - 1
```

and clear the text boxes:

```
grdTrans_Click
```

The next procedure fires when the Clear button is clicked.

```
Private Sub cmdClear_Click()
    grdTrans.Row = grdTrans.Rows - 1
    grdTrans_Click
End Sub
```

In that case, the user wants to clear the text boxes at the bottom of the form. So you move to the blank record in the grid:

```
grdTrans.Row = grdTrans.Rows - 1
```

and let the Click procedure of the grid clean up the text boxes for you:

```
    grdTrans_Click
```

The code behind the Add Category button is used to add a new category to the database when the Add Category button is clicked.

```
Private Sub cmdAddCategory_Click()
    Dim RSNewCategory As ADODB.Recordset
    Dim NewName As String
    NewName = InputBox("Eneter the name for the new category")
    If NewName <> "" Then
        Set RSNewCategory = MyConnection.Execute("CategoryAdd '" _
            & NewName & "'")
        If RSNewCategory("TheNewID") <> 0 Then
            cmbCategory.AddItem NewName
            cmbCategory.ItemData(cmbCategory.NewIndex) = _
                RSNewCategory("TheNewID")
        End If
    End If
End Sub
```

You will need a Recordset object in this procedure:

```
Dim RSNewCategory As ADODB.Recordset
```

and a string to store the name for the new category:

```
Dim NewName As String
```

Prompt the user for the name of the new category:

```
NewName = InputBox("Enter the name for the new category")
```

If the name entered is blank, the user clicked the Cancel button in the dialog box or doesn't want to add a new category:

```
If NewName <> "" Then
```

If that is not the case, you call the CategoryAdd stored procedure to add the new category:

```
Set RSNewCategory = MyConnection.Execute("CategoryAdd '" _
    & NewName & "'")
```

and check the return value. If it is not 0, the record was not a repeat but was added:

```
If RSNewCategory("TheNewID") <> 0 Then
```

So you add it to the combo box:

```
cmbCategory.AddItem NewName
```

as well as adding the ID for that category to the combo box:

```
cmbCategory.ItemData(cmbCategory.NewIndex) = _
    RSNewCategory("TheNewID")
```

The other procedure on this form closes the form when the Close button is clicked:

```
Private Sub cmdClose_Click()
    Unload Me
End Sub
```

frmReport Form

The Report form provides the code needed to preview and print reports by a category or a date range. The form displays the preview in a label. The font for the label is set to a fixed-width font to make it easier to line up the columns of information.

In the General Declarations of the form, you will find these two lines of code:

```
Option Explicit
Private MyConnection As New ADODB.Connection
```

The first tells the compiler that you will declare your variables:

```
Option Explicit
```

The other declares a Connection object that you will use throughout this form:

```
Private MyConnection As New ADODB.Connection
```

The form has a single user-defined procedure. The function sizes a string to a specific width. It is used to size the data to the width of the column that the data is in.

```
Public Function SizeIt(String2Size As String, TheLength As Integer) As String
    If Len(String2Size) >= TheLength Then
        SizeIt = Left(String2Size, TheLength)
    Else
        Do Until Len(String2Size) = TheLength
            String2Size = String2Size & " "
        Loop
        SizeIt = String2Size
    End If
End Function
```

The function requires two parameters, the string to size and the length that the string is to be changed to. The function returns the sized string:

```
Public Function SizeIt(String2Size As String, TheLength As Integer) As String
```

You first check to see whether the string to modify is too long:

```
If Len(String2Size) >= TheLength Then
```

In that case, you merely return the portion of the string up to the size that the string is to be:

```
SizeIt = Left(String2Size, TheLength)
```

Otherwise, you enter a loop that will run until the string is of the size desired:

```
Do Until Len(String2Size) = TheLength
```

Pad the string with a space:

```
String2Size = String2Size & " "
```

and check the length again:

```
Loop
```

After the loop, you return the sized string:

```
SizeIt = String2Size
```

When the form first loads, the Load event populates the Category combo box.

```
Private Sub Form_Load()
    Dim RSAllCategories As ADODB.Recordset
    MyConnection.ConnectionString = "driver={SQL Server};" _
        & "server=MyServer;uid=" & SQLUserName _
        & ";pwd=" & SQLPassword & ";" _
        & "database=C4MoneyManager"
    MyConnection.Open
    Set RSAllCategories = MyConnection.Execute("Exec GetAllCategories")
    Do Until RSAllCategories.EOF
        cmbCategory.AddItem RSAllCategories("CategoryName")
        cmbCategory.ItemData(cmbCategory.NewIndex) = _
            RSAllCategories("CategoryID")
        RSAllCategories.MoveNext
    Loop
End Sub
```

The procedure will need a Recordset object to do that:

```
Dim RSAllCategories As ADODB.Recordset
```

But you must first set up and connect to your back-end database:

```
MyConnection.ConnectionString = "driver={SQL Server};" _
    & "server=MyServer;uid=" & SQLUserName _
    & ";pwd=" & SQLPassword & ";" _
    & "database=C4MoneyManager"
MyConnection.Open
```

Then you can retrieve the category records:

```
Set RSAllCategories = MyConnection.Execute("Exec GetAllCategories")
```

You enter a loop so that you can process each record:

```
Do Until RSAllCategories.EOF
```

Each record is added to the Category combo box:

```
cmbCategory.AddItem RSAllCategories("CategoryName")
cmbCategory.ItemData(cmbCategory.NewIndex) = _
    RSAllCategories("CategoryID")
```

before moving on to process the next record:

```
RSAllCategories.MoveNext
Loop
```

The next code block fires when the form is closed.

```
Private Sub Form_Unload(Cancel As Integer)
    frmMenu.Show
    Set frmReport = Nothing
End Sub
```

You display the Menu form:

```
frmMenu.Show
```

and then release the resources being used by this form:

```
Set frmReport = Nothing
```

When the Preview button is clicked, the label is set to contain the contents of the report.

```
Private Sub cmdPreview_Click()
    Dim RSReportContents As ADODB.Recordset
    Dim TheTotal As Currency
    lblPreview.Caption = "Date                " _
        & "Description                          " _
        & "Category                 " _
        & "Amount" & vbNewLine
    lblPreview.Caption = lblPreview.Caption & "----                " _
        & "-----------                          " _
        & "--------                 " _
```

```
        & "------"
    If optCategory.Value = True Then
        Set RSReportContents = MyConnection.Execute _
            ("Exec GetAllActivityInCategory " _
            & cmbCategory.ItemData(cmbCategory.ListIndex))
    Else
        Set RSReportContents = MyConnection.Execute _
            ("Exec GetAllActivityInDateRange '" _
            & txtFrom.Text & "', '" _
            & txtTo.Text & "'")
    End If
    Do Until RSReportContents.EOF
        lblPreview.Caption = lblPreview.Caption & vbNewLine _
        & SizeIt(RSReportContents("TransactionDate"), 14) _
        & SizeIt(RSReportContents("TransDescription"), 42) _
        & SizeIt(RSReportContents("CategoryName"), 30) _
        & FormatCurrency(RSReportContents("Amount"))
        TheTotal = TheTotal + RSReportContents("Amount")
        RSReportContents.MoveNext
    Loop
    lblPreview.Caption = lblPreview.Caption & vbNewLine & vbNewLine _
        & "Total: " & FormatCurrency(TheTotal)
End Sub
```

The procedure will need a Recordset object:

```
Dim RSReportContents As ADODB.Recordset
```

as well as a variable to store the total dollar amount of the records retrieved:

```
Dim TheTotal As Currency
```

The first row of the report contains the column headers:

```
lblPreview.Caption = "Date          " _
    & "Description                                " _
    & "Category                      " _
    & "Amount" & vbNewLine
```

The second row contains underlines for those column headers:

```
lblPreview.Caption = lblPreview.Caption & "----          " _
    & "-----------                                " _
```

```
    & "--------                              " _
    & "------"
```

If the Category option is selected, the user wants to display a report based on the category selected:

```
If optCategory.Value = True Then
```

In that case, you retrieve records through the GetAllActivityInCategory stored procedure:

```
Set RSReportContents = MyConnection.Execute _
    ("Exec GetAllActivityInCategory " _
    & cmbCategory.ItemData(cmbCategory.ListIndex))
```

Otherwise, you retrieve records through the GetAllActivityInDateRange stored procedure:

```
Set RSReportContents = MyConnection.Execute _
    ("Exec GetAllActivityInDateRange '" _
    & txtFrom.Text & "', '" _
    & txtTo.Text & "'")
```

Either way, after the If statement, you enter a loop so that you can process each of the records that matched the user's criteria:

```
Do Until RSReportContents.EOF
```

Each record retrieved is placed on its own line in the preview label. Each field is sized according to the size of that column:

```
lblPreview.Caption = lblPreview.Caption & vbNewLine _
    & SizeIt(RSReportContents("TransactionDate"), 14) _
    & SizeIt(RSReportContents("TransDescription"), 42) _
    & SizeIt(RSReportContents("CategoryName"), 30) _
    & FormatCurrency(RSReportContents("Amount"))
```

Add the amount in the current record to your tally:

```
TheTotal = TheTotal + RSReportContents("Amount")
```

and move on to process the next record:

```
RSReportContents.MoveNext
```

After the loop, you add another line to the label for the amount total:

```
lblPreview.Caption = lblPreview.Caption & vbNewLine & vbNewLine _
    & "Total: " & FormatCurrency(TheTotal)
```

The other procedure writes the report to the printer when the Print button is clicked.

```
Private Sub cmdPrint_Click()
    Printer.Font = "Courier New"
    Printer.FontSize = 10
    Printer.Print lblPreview.Caption
    Printer.EndDoc
End Sub
```

Set the printer font to a fixed-width font to make the columns line up:

```
Printer.Font = "Courier New"
```

and also set the size so that a row on the label will fit on the paper:

```
Printer.FontSize = 10
```

Then send the text in the label to the default printer:

```
Printer.Print lblPreview.Caption
```

and print the report:

```
Printer.EndDoc
```

CHAPTER

5

Personal Information Manager (PIM)

IN THIS CHAPTER:

C5SQLObjects.sql

Contacts.txt

ContactPhones.txt

Reminders.txt

Chapter5PIM.vbp

In this chapter, you will look at a solution that allows the user to manage their contacts and reminders. The solution uses a SQL Server database back end that is connected to through a Visual Basic 6 front end.

Personal Information Manager

As you read through this solution, pay close attention to the Data Environment and Data Reports objects, which are used to generate reports for the user. One report is based on a view, the other a stored procedure.

Application Walk-Through

When the user first enters the application, they are prompted for their user name and password for the SQL Server database. If they enter a valid login, they see the Menu form displayed in Figure 5-1.

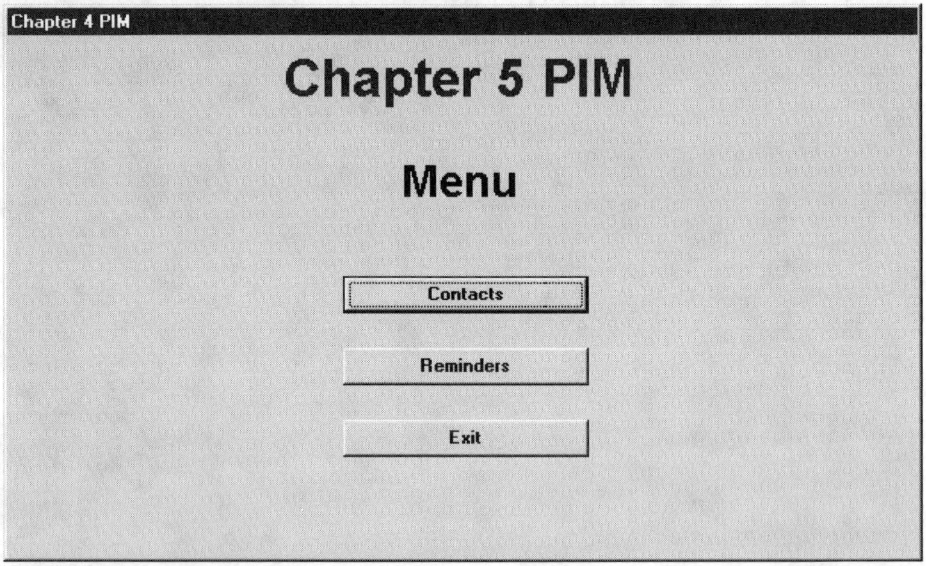

Figure 5-1 *Menu form*

The Menu form provides access to the rest of the application. But it also contains a timer control that fires every minute and checks to see whether the user has any reminders that they are due to be prompted for. If so, the user sees a message with their reminder like the one displayed in Figure 5-2.

The user will see each of the alarms that are set to go off in turn. The application will continue to prompt the user until they turn off the reminder.

If the user wishes to work with their contacts, they click Contacts on the Menu form. When they do that, they see the form displayed in Figure 5-3.

In the Contacts form, the user can view, add, edit, and delete their contacts. They use the combo box to navigate to the desired contact. Note the Phone Numbers frame. The user can add as many phone numbers to a contact as they like by clicking Add in that frame.

If the user wishes to view a report for this customer, they click View Report. They would then see a report like the one displayed in Figure 5-4.

The report displays all the information for the contact including all of their phone numbers. As you will see when you look at the code, the report uses the Visual Basic

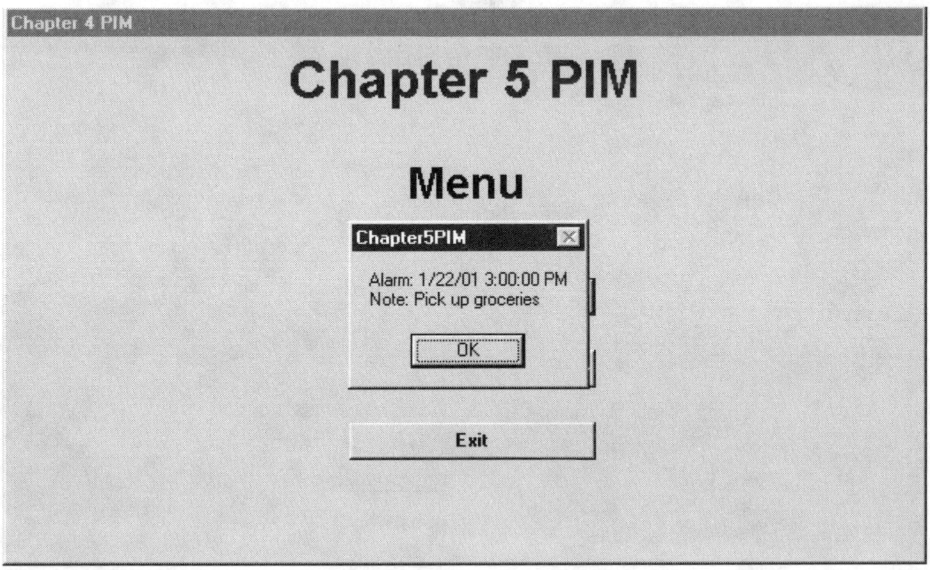

Figure 5-2 *Reminder alarm*

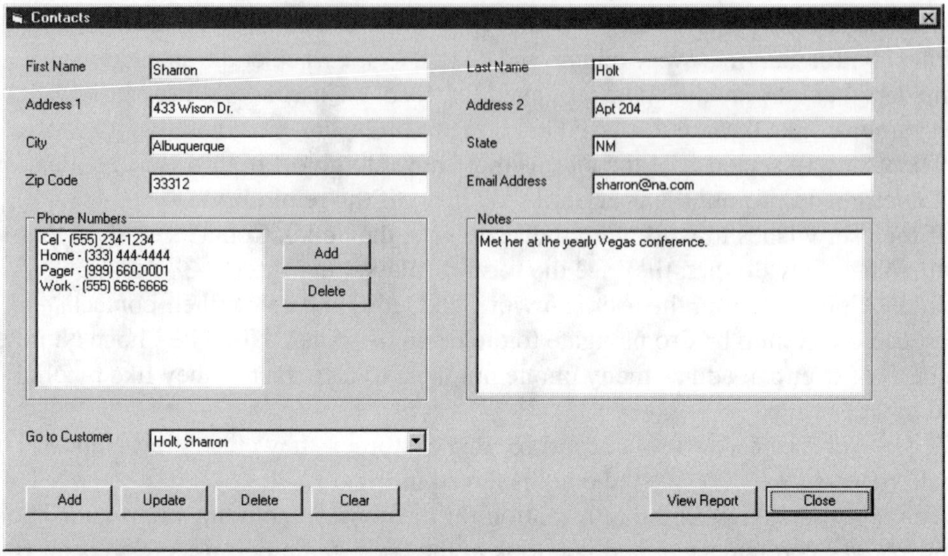

Figure 5-3 *Contacts form*

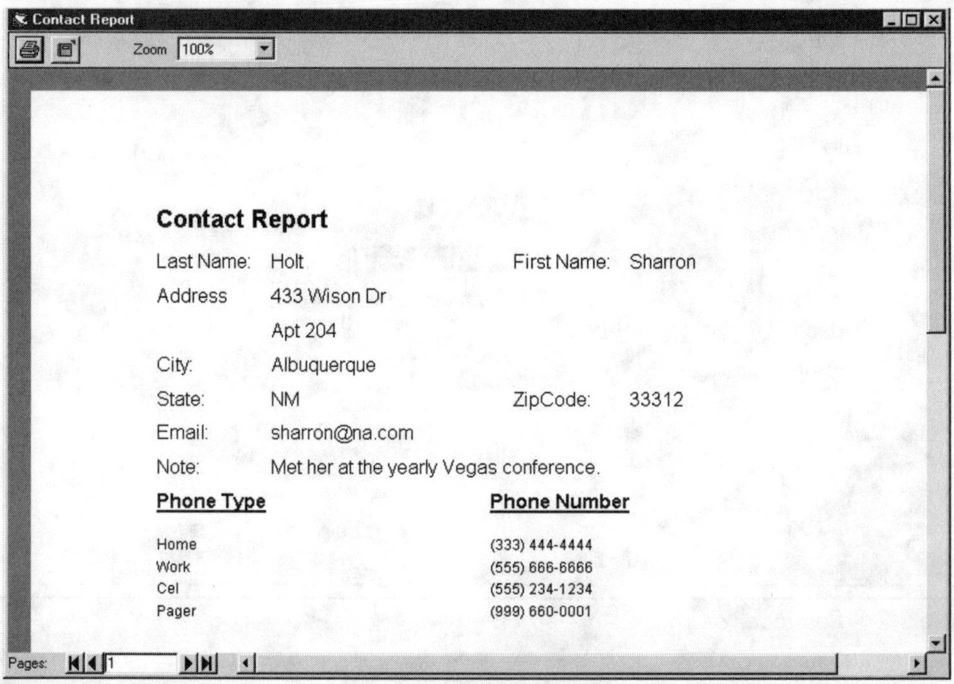

Figure 5-4 *Contact report*

Data Report tool through the Data Environment. The buttons at the top left of the form allow the user to print or export the report.

If the user wished to manage their reminders, they would click Reminder on the Menu form. When they do that, the Reminders form is displayed, as is shown in Figure 5-5.

Like the Contacts form, the Reminders form allows the user to view, add, edit, or delete their reminders. The Alarm Time text box is used to indicate the time that the user wants to sound an alarm for this reminder. The check box beneath that is used to indicate whether the user wants to see a reminder for this item.

When the user clicks the View Reminders Not Clear Report button, they see the report displayed in Figure 5-6.

The report shows all the reminders that have their alarm turned on regardless of whether the alarm time has passed. The report is a Visual Basic Data Report that uses a view from your SQL Server database back end.

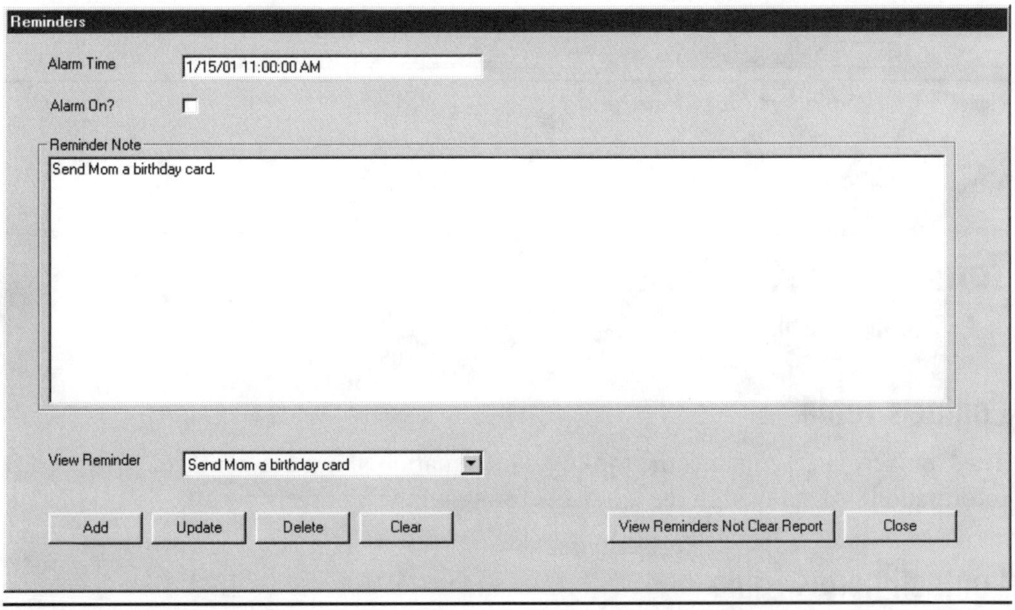

Figure 5-5 *Reminders form*

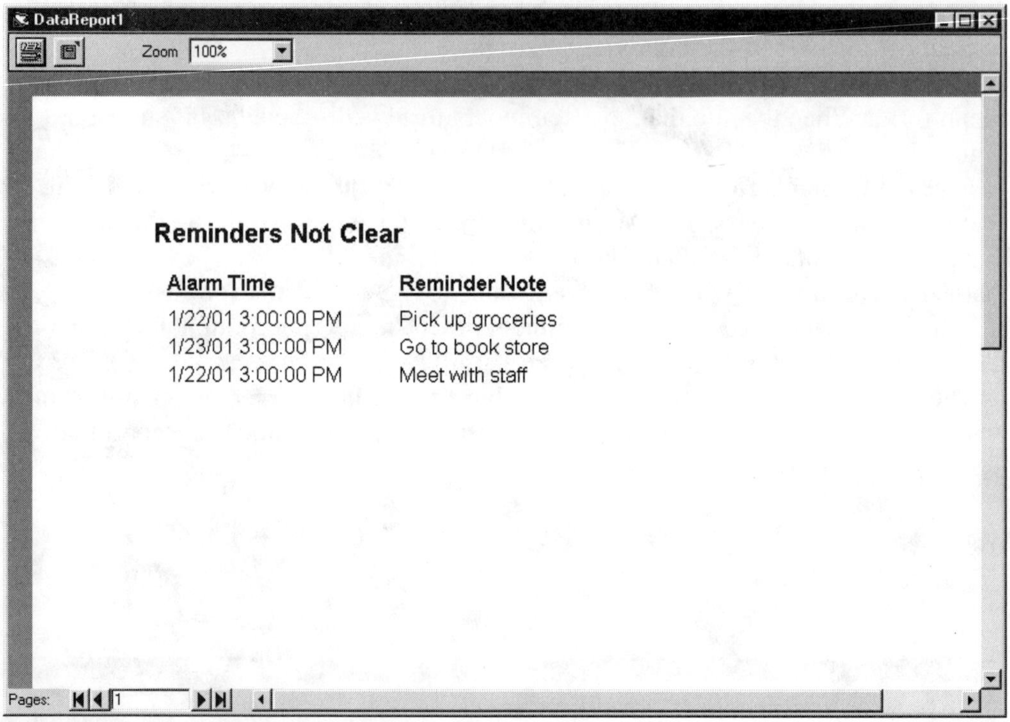

Figure 5-6 *Reminders Not Clear report*

Tables and Relationships

C5SQLObjects.sql

Contacts Table

The Contacts table contains the top-level information about the contacts. This information is displayed in the Contacts form and the Contacts report.

ContactPhones Table

The ContactPhones table stores the phone numbers information for the contacts. The table is in a one-to-many relationship with the Contacts table. Each contact can have many phone numbers.

Reminders Table

The Reminders table stores the user's reminder notes. The data is used on the Reminders form, as well as for prompting the user when one of their reminder alarms goes off.

Contacts Table

Contacts.txt

The field specifications for the Contacts table are displayed in Table 5-1.

The ContactID field is the primary key in the table. Since it is an identity column, it is automatically populated when a new record is added. The rest of the fields store the data about the contact.

ContactPhones Table

ContactPhones.txt

The field specifications for the ContactPhones table are displayed in Table 5-2.

The ContactPhoneID field is the primary key in this table. The ContactID field is a foreign key that links this table to the Contacts table.

Reminders Table

Reminders.txt

The field specifications for the Reminders table are displayed in Table 5-3.

Field Name	Field Type	Notes
ContactID	int	Primary Key, Identity Column
FirstName	varchar	Length = 50
LastName	varchar	Length = 50
Address1	varchar	Length = 100
Address2	varchar	Length = 100
City	varchar	Length = 50
State	varchar	Length = 2
ZipCode	varchar	Length = 10
EmailAddress	varchar	Length = 50
ContactNote	varchar	Length = 500

Table 5-1 *Contacts Table Field Specifications*

Field Name	Field Type	Notes
ContactPhoneID	int	Primary Key, Identity Column
ContactID	int	Primary Key
PhoneType	varchar	Length = 50
PhoneNumber	varchar	Length = 50

Table 5-2 *ContactPhones Table Field Specifications*

The ReminderID field is the primary key in the Reminder table. The AlarmOn field is a Boolean field that stores whether an alarm should ring for this reminder. The AlarmTime field stores when the Alarm should go off.

Triggers

DeleteContacts Trigger

When a user deletes a contact record, you want to delete all the phone numbers that go with that contact. One of the ways that you can accomplish this is with a Delete trigger.

```
CREATE TRIGGER DeleteContacts ON dbo.Contacts
AFTER DELETE
AS
BEGIN
      Delete from ContactPhones Where
            ContactID = (Select ContactID from Deleted)
END
```

Field Name	Field Type	Notes
ReminderID	int	Primary Key, Identity Column
AlarmOn	bit	
AlarmTime	datetime	
ReminderNote	varchar	Length = 1000

Table 5-3 *Reminders Table Field Specifications*

The trigger runs whenever a record is deleted from the Contacts table:

```
AFTER DELETE
```

It then deletes all the records from the ContactPhones table that are for the deleted contact record, as determined by the ContactID. Note that you retrieve the ContactID from the special table called "Deleted" that provides you with the data in the deleted record in a trigger:

```
Delete from ContactPhones Where
      ContactID = (Select ContactID from Deleted)
```

Stored Procedures

ContactAdd Stored Procedure

The ContactAdd stored procedure provides the mechanism for the calling application to add a record to the Contacts table.

```
CREATE PROCEDURE ContactAdd
@FirstName varchar(50),
@LastName varchar(50),
@Address1 varchar(100),
@Address2 varchar(100),
@City varchar(50),
@State varchar(2),
@ZipCode varchar(10),
@EmailAddress varchar(50),
@ContactNote varchar(5000)
AS
      BEGIN
            Insert Into Contacts
                  (FirstName, LastName, Address1,
                  Address2, City, State, ZipCode,
                  EmailAddress, ContactNote) values
                  (@FirstName, @LastName, @Address1,
                  @Address2, @City, @State, @ZipCode,
                  @EmailAddress, @ContactNote)
            Select @@Identity as TheNewID
      END
GO
```

The procedure requires parameters for each of the data fields in the record:

```
@FirstName varchar(50),
@LastName varchar(50),
@Address1 varchar(100),
@Address2 varchar(100),
@City varchar(50),
@State varchar(2),
@ZipCode varchar(10),
@EmailAddress varchar(50),
@ContactNote varchar(5000)
```

You then use the data passed into those parameters in a SQL Insert statement to add the record to the Contacts table:

```
Insert Into Contacts
      (FirstName, LastName, Address1,
      Address2, City, State, ZipCode,
      EmailAddress, ContactNote) values
      (@FirstName, @LastName, @Address1,
      @Address2, @City, @State, @ZipCode,
      @EmailAddress, @ContactNote)
```

The one field you didn't supply in the Insert statement is the ContactID field. That is because it is an identity column and is automatically added. You can retrieve the value for that field through the @@Identity global variable. That value is returned from this stored procedure:

```
Select @@Identity as TheNewID
```

ContactUpdate Stored Procedure

The ContactUpdate stored procedure allows for editing an existing contact record.

```
CREATE PROCEDURE ContactUpdate
@ContactID integer,
@FirstName varchar(50),
@LastName varchar(50),
@Address1 varchar(100),
@Address2 varchar(100),
@City varchar(50),
@State varchar(2),
@ZipCode varchar(10),
```

```
@EmailAddress varchar(50),
@ContactNote varchar(5000)
AS
      BEGIN
            Update Contacts set
                  FirstName = @FirstName,
                  LastName = @LastName,
                  Address1 = @Address1,
                  Address2 = @Address2,
                  City = @City,
                  State = @State,
                  ZipCode = @ZipCode,
                  EmailAddress = @EmailAddress,
                  ContactNote = @ContactNote
                  Where ContactID = @ContactID
      END
GO
```

The first parameter sent to this procedure is the ID of the record to be updated:

```
@ContactID integer,
```

The rest of the parameters store the new values for the record:

```
@FirstName varchar(50),
@LastName varchar(50),
@Address1 varchar(100),
@Address2 varchar(100),
@City varchar(50),
@State varchar(2),
@ZipCode varchar(10),
@EmailAddress varchar(50),
@ContactNote varchar(5000)
```

You then use an Update statement to update the desired record:

```
Update Contacts set
      FirstName = @FirstName,
      LastName = @LastName,
      Address1 = @Address1,
      Address2 = @Address2,
      City = @City,
      State = @State,
```

```
        ZipCode = @ZipCode,
        EmailAddress = @EmailAddress,
        ContactNote = @ContactNote
        Where ContactID = @ContactID
```

DeleteContact Stored Procedure

When the calling application wants to delete a record from the Contacts table, the DeleteContact stored procedure is called.

```
CREATE PROCEDURE ContactDelete
@ContactID integer
AS
        BEGIN
                Delete from  Contacts
                        Where ContactID = @ContactID
        END
GO
```

The procedure requires a single parameter, the ID of the record to be deleted.

```
@ContactID integer
```

The offending record is then deleted from the Contacts table through this SQL statement:

```
Delete from  Contacts
        Where ContactID = @ContactID
```

ContactRecord Stored Procedure

On the Contacts form in the Visual Basic front end, you need to display the contents of a Contacts record. All the fields in a single record are retrieved through the ContactRecord stored procedure.

```
CREATE PROCEDURE ContactRecord
@ContactID integer
AS
BEGIN
        If @ContactID = 0
                BEGIN
                        Select * from Contacts Where
                                ContactID = (Select Min(ContactID)
```

```
                        from Contacts)
            END
      Else
            BEGIN
                  Select * from Contacts Where
                        ContactID = @ContactID
            END
END
GO
```

Passed into the procedure is the ID of the contact whose data is to be retrieved:

```
@ContactID integer
```

You check to see if the ID is 0, which has special meaning:

```
If @ContactID = 0
```

If that is the case, the calling application is requesting the first record in the Contacts table. Therefore, you retrieve that record in a Select statement that has a subquery that retrieves the lowest value in the ContactID field:

```
Select * from Contacts Where
      ContactID = (Select Min(ContactID)
      from Contacts)
```

If the ContactID parameter was not 0, you simply retrieve the record corresponding to the value passed in:

```
Select * from Contacts Where
      ContactID = @ContactID
```

ContactList Stored Procedure

On the Contacts form in the Visual Basic application, a combo box lists the names of all the contacts. That list is populated through the return of the ContactList stored procedure.

```
CREATE PROCEDURE ContactList
AS
BEGIN
      Select ContactID, LastName + ', ' + FirstName as TheName
             from Contacts Order By LastName + ', ' + FirstName
END
GO
```

The procedure returns all the IDs and the name of the contact, which is a concatenation of the contact's first and last names. The return also is sorted by the contact name:

```
Select ContactID, LastName + ', ' + FirstName as TheName
       from Contacts Order By LastName + ', ' + FirstName
```

ContactReport Stored Procedure

The ContactReport stored procedure is used by the Contact Data report in the Visual Basic application. The stored procedure returns all the information for the desired contact.

```
CREATE PROCEDURE ContactReport
@ContactID as integer
 AS
      Select Contacts.FirstName, Contacts.LastName, Contacts.Address1,
            Contacts.Address2, Contacts.City, Contacts.State,
            Contacts.ZipCode, Contacts.EmailAddress,
            Contacts.ContactNote, ContactPhones.PhoneType,
            ContactPhones.PhoneNumber
            FROM Contacts LEFT OUTER JOIN
            ContactPhones ON Contacts.ContactID = ContactPhones.ContactID
            WHERE Contacts.ContactID = @ContactID
GO
```

Passed into the procedure is the ID of the contact whose data is to be retrieved:

```
@ContactID as integer
```

You then return all the data for that contact from both the Contacts table and the ContactPhones table. Note that the tables are joined with a left outer join. That means that all the records will be included from the Contacts table, instead of just matching records. This allows you to see the contact data for contacts that do not have a phone number listed:

```
SELECT Contacts.FirstName, Contacts.LastName, Contacts.Address1,
      Contacts.Address2, Contacts.City, Contacts.State,
      Contacts.ZipCode, Contacts.EmailAddress,
      Contacts.ContactNote, ContactPhones.PhoneType,
      ContactPhones.PhoneNumber
      FROM Contacts LEFT OUTER JOIN
      ContactPhones ON Contacts.ContactID = ContactPhones.ContactID
      WHERE Contacts.ContactID = @ContactID
```

ContactPhoneAdd Stored Procedure

The ContactPhoneAdd stored procedure provides the mechanism for adding a record to the ContactPhones table.

```
CREATE PROCEDURE ContactPhoneAdd
@ContactID integer,
@PhoneType varchar(50),
@PhoneNumber varchar(50)
AS
      BEGIN
            Insert Into ContactPhones
                  (ContactID, PhoneType, PhoneNumber) values
                  (@ContactID, @PhoneType, @PhoneNumber)
      END
GO
```

The values for the record being added are passed into the procedure:

```
@ContactID integer,
@PhoneType varchar(50),
@PhoneNumber varchar(50)
```

Those values are then used in a SQL Insert statement:

```
Insert Into ContactPhones
      (ContactID, PhoneType, PhoneNumber) values
      (@ContactID, @PhoneType, @PhoneNumber)
```

ContactPhoneDelete Stored Procedure

Another stored procedure for the ContactPhones table is the ContactPhoneDelete stored procedure. It allows the calling application to delete a record from that table.

```
CREATE PROCEDURE ContactPhoneDelete
@ContactPhoneID integer
AS
      BEGIN
            Delete from  ContactPhones
                  Where ContactPhoneID = @ContactPhoneID
      END
GO
```

Passed into the procedure is the ID of the record to be deleted:

```
@ContactPhoneID integer
```

You then delete the record matching the ID passed into this procedure:

```
Delete from  ContactPhones
      Where ContactPhoneID = @ContactPhoneID
```

ContactPhoneList Stored Procedure

The ContactPhoneList stored procedure returns all the phone records for a specific contact so that they can be displayed in a list box on the Contacts form in the Visual Basic application.

```
CREATE PROCEDURE ContactPhoneList
@ContactID integer
AS
BEGIN
      Select ContactPhoneID, PhoneType + ' - ' + PhoneNumber as ThePhone
             from ContactPhones Where ContactID = @ContactID
            Order By PhoneType + ' - ' + PhoneNumber
END
GO
```

The ID of the contact whose phone list is to be retrieved is passed into the procedure:

```
@ContactID integer
```

The first field output in the Select statement is the ID of the phone record. The other field returned, called ThePhone, is a concatenation of the type and number of the phone:

```
Select ContactPhoneID, PhoneType + ' - ' + PhoneNumber as ThePhone
 from ContactPhones Where ContactID = @ContactID
      Order By PhoneType + ' - ' + PhoneNumber
```

ReminderAdd Stored Procedure

The ReminderAdd stored procedure provides the mechanism for the calling application to add a record to the Reminders table.

```
CREATE PROCEDURE ReminderAdd
@AlarmOn bit,
@AlarmTime datetime,
@ReminderNote varchar(1000)
AS
      BEGIN
            Insert Into Reminders
                  (AlarmOn, AlarmTime, ReminderNote) values
                  (@AlarmOn, @AlarmTime, @ReminderNote)
            Select @@Identity as TheNewID
      END
GO
```

The data for the record to be added is passed into the procedure:

```
@AlarmOn bit,
@AlarmTime datetime,
@ReminderNote varchar(1000)
```

That data is then added to the Reminders table:

```
Insert Into Reminders
      (AlarmOn, AlarmTime, ReminderNote) values
      (@AlarmOn, @AlarmTime, @ReminderNote)
```

and the ID for the new record is returned from the stored procedure:

```
Select @@Identity as TheNewID
```

ReminderUpdate Stored Procedure

The ReminderUpdate stored procedure allows for the editing of an existing reminder record.

```
CREATE PROCEDURE ReminderUpdate
@ReminderID integer,
@AlarmOn bit,
@AlarmTime datetime,
@ReminderNote varchar(1000)
AS
      BEGIN
            Update Reminders set
                  AlarmOn = @AlarmOn,
```

```
                    AlarmTime = @AlarmTime,
                    ReminderNote = @ReminderNote
                    Where ReminderID = @ReminderID
          END
GO
```

The first parameter passed in is the ID of the record to be updated:

```
@ReminderID integer,
```

The rest of the parameters passed in provide the new values for the fields in the edited record:

```
@AlarmOn bit,
@AlarmTime datetime,
@ReminderNote varchar(1000)
```

An Update statement is then used to update the desired record:

```
Update Reminders set
          AlarmOn = @AlarmOn,
          AlarmTime = @AlarmTime,
          ReminderNote = @ReminderNote
          Where ReminderID = @ReminderID
```

ReminderDelete Stored Procedure

The ReminderDelete stored procedure is used to remove a record from the Reminders table.

```
CREATE PROCEDURE ReminderDelete
@ReminderID integer
AS
          BEGIN
                    Delete from  Reminders
                              Where ReminderID = @ReminderID
          END
GO
```

The procedure requires a single input parameter, the ID of the record to be deleted:

```
@ReminderID integer
```

The record corresponding to that ID is then deleted from the Reminders table:

```
Delete from  Reminders
      Where ReminderID = @ReminderID
```

ReminderRecord Stored Procedure

The ReminderRecord stored procedure returns the contents of a single reminder record.

```
CREATE PROCEDURE ReminderRecord
@ReminderID integer
AS
BEGIN
      If @ReminderID = 0
            BEGIN
                  Select * from Reminders Where
                        ReminderID = (Select Min(ReminderID)
                        from Reminders)
            END
      Else
            BEGIN
                  Select * from Reminders Where
                        ReminderID = @ReminderID
            END
END
GO
```

The ID of the record to be retrieved is passed into the procedure:

```
@ReminderID integer
```

You first check to see whether the ID passed in is 0, which has special meaning:

```
If @ReminderID = 0
```

If it is, you need to return the first record in the table. A subquery is used to return the lowest value in the ReminderID field:

```
Select * from Reminders Where
      ReminderID = (Select Min(ReminderID)
      from Reminders)
```

Any other number passed into the parameter means that you need to return the record matching that ID:

```
Select * from Reminders Where
      ReminderID = @ReminderID
```

ReminderList Stored Procedure

On the Reminders form in the Visual Basic front-end application, the user selects a reminder that they want to view from a combo box. That list is populated through the ReminderList stored procedure.

```
CREATE PROCEDURE ReminderList
AS
BEGIN
      Select ReminderID, Left(ReminderNote, 30) as TheNote
             from Reminders Order By ReminderNote
END
GO
```

To populate that list, you return the ReminderID field as well as the first 30 characters in the reminder note to help the user cue into the specific record that they want to view:

```
Select ReminderID, Left(ReminderNote, 30) as TheNote
       from Reminders Order By ReminderNote
```

Views

ReminderAlarms View

The ReminderAlarms view returns all the records from the Reminders table with alarms that are going off, which is based on the alarm being on and the alarm time having passed. These records are then used to prompt the user in the Visual Basic application. Note the use of the GetDate function in the Where clause, which returns the current system date and time:

```
Select AlarmTime, ReminderNote
FROM Reminders
Where (AlarmTime <= GETDATE()) AND (AlarmOn = 1)
```

RemindersNotClear View

The report available through the Reminders form displays all the reminders with their alarm on. The data for that report comes from the RemindersNotClear view.

```
SELECT AlarmTime, ReminderNote
FROM Reminders
WHERE AlarmOn = 1
```

Using a Data Environment

The Visual Basic front-end application used in this solution includes Data Reports. In this solution, you use a data environment, which contains a Connection object that points to your SQL Server database. The Connection object contains two Command objects, which point to a view and a stored procedure in your database. The data reports use these Command objects.

To use this scenario, first a data environment was added to your Visual Basic project. You do this by selecting Project | More ActiveX Designers | Date Environment from the Visual Basic menu. When you do that, a data environment is added to your project. Figure 5-7 shows the data environment used in this Visual Basic application.

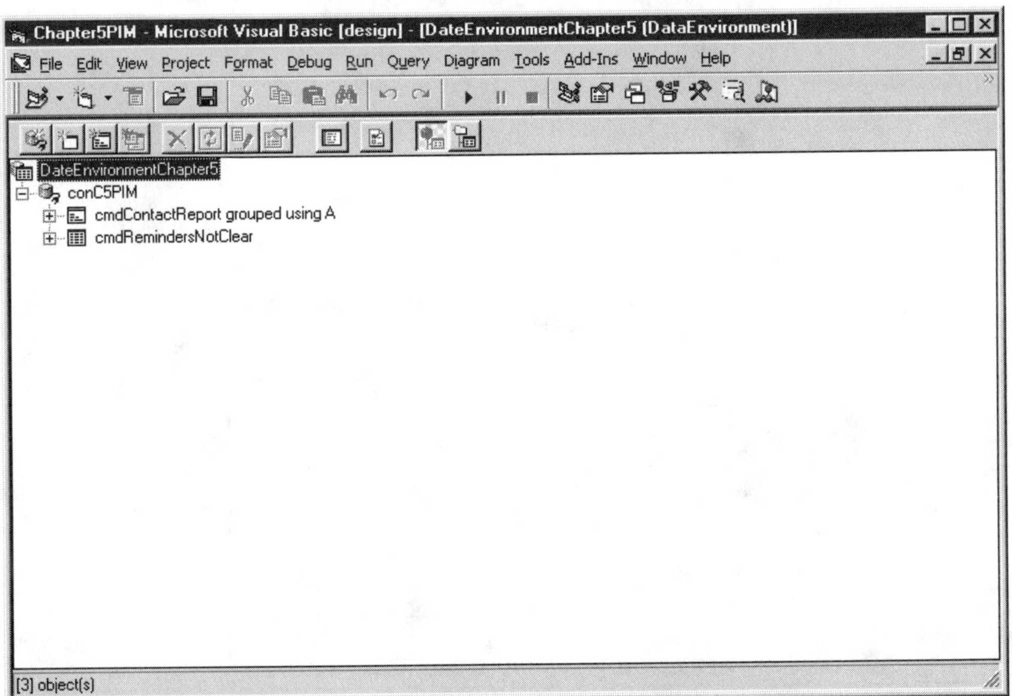

Figure 5-7 *Data environment*

If you select the Data Environment object in this tree view and press F4, you can view the properties for the object. This is where you can change the name of the Data Environment object.

Next, you need to add a Connection object to your data environment. A Connection object links to a database. Right-click the Data Environment object and select Add Connection. A Connection object will be added to the Data Environment tree view. Next, you need to point the Connection object to your database. Right-click the connection object and select properties to build your connection. Figure 5-8 shows the Properties dialog box.

On the first page, you select the type of database that you wish to connect to. In this case, you want to connect to a SQL Server database, so you select that option. Now click Next to see the dialog box displayed in Figure 5-9. Here, you enter the name of your SQL Server, your login information, and the name of the database that you want to connect to. You can then click the Test Connection button to make sure that the information you entered is correct. If it is, click OK to close the dialog box. As with the Data Environment object, press F4 while the Connection object is

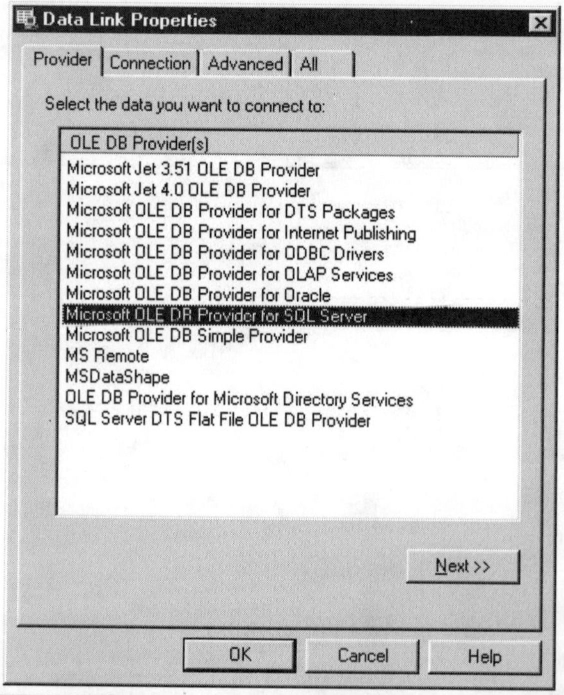

Figure 5-8 *Connection Properties dialog box*

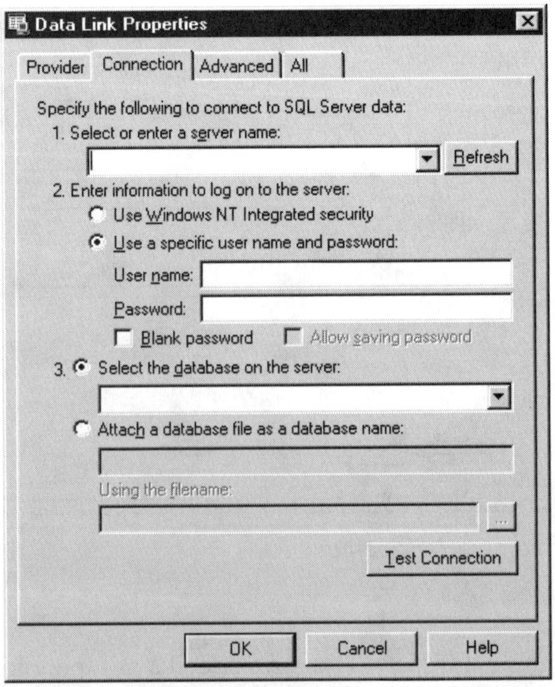

Figure 5-9 *Connection tab for data link properties*

selected to view the standard properties dialog box so that you can give the object a name and set other properties of the object.

Now you need to add Command objects to your Connection object. A Command object allows you to link to a specific object in the database, such as a table, view, or stored procedure. To add a Command object, right-click the Connection object and select Add Command. Back in Figure 5-7, you can see that I have added two Command objects.

Right-click the newly created Command object and select Properties. You may then be prompted to log into the database; you should then see the Command object properties displayed in Figure 5-10.

On the General tab, you can give your Command object a name. Then select the type of database object you want to use and then the object itself from the list. Here you are linking to the ContactReport stored procedure.

As you may recall from the "Stored Procedures" section, this report displays information about a contact and then lists all of the telephone numbers beneath that. This was possible because the Grouping tab was utilized. Take a look at the

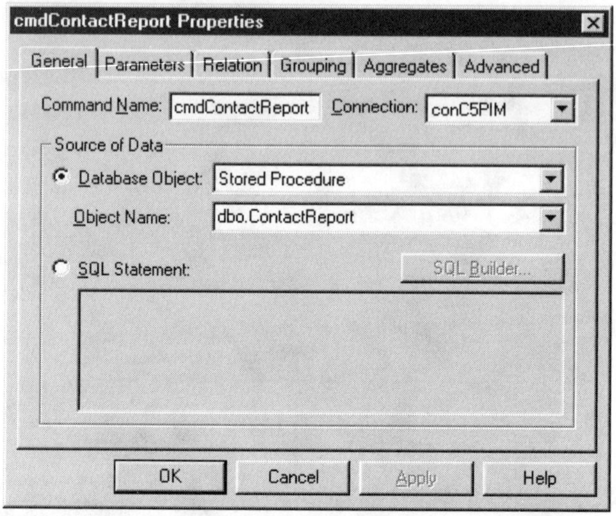

Figure 5-10 *Command object properties*

Grouping tab in Figure 5-11. Here, you have added a grouping level. All the data from the Contacts table is placed at the top level. Left for the detail section of the report is the telephone number information.

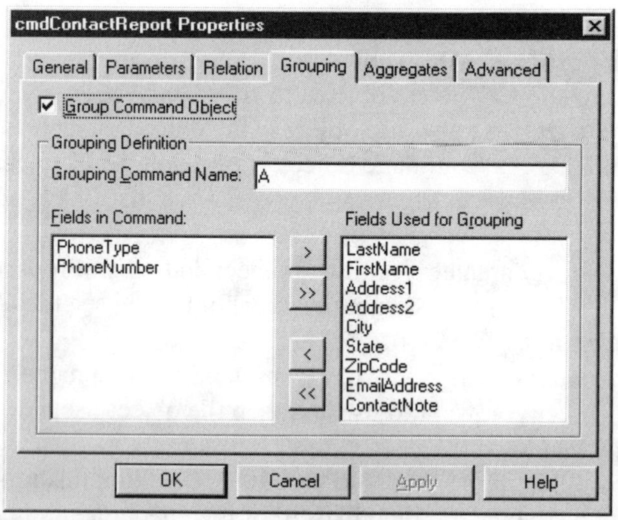

Figure 5-11 *Grouping tab of the command object properties*

Once you have set up your Command objects, you can add a Data Report to your Visual Basic project. You can do this by selecting Add Data Report from the Add menu. Then, on the properties for the Data Report, you set the DataSouce property so that it points to your Data Environment object and you set the DataMember property so that it points to the Command object you wish to use. You can then drag the field names in the Command object and drop them onto the Data Report.

Modules

Chapter5PIM.vbp

modPublicProcs Module

The Visual Basic front-end application contains a single module called modPublicProcs. In the General Declarations section of that module, you will find this code.

```
Option Explicit
Public SQLUserName As String
Public SQLPassword As String
```

The first line tells the compiler that variable declaration is required:

```
Option Explicit
```

The other two lines declare variables that store the user's name and password that have a Public scope, which means they are available throughout the application:

```
Public SQLUserName As String
Public SQLPassword As String
```

When the application first starts, the procedure Main runs.

```
Public Sub Main()
    SQLUserName = InputBox("Please enter your user name.")
    SQLPassword = InputBox("Please enter your password.")
    frmMenu.Show
End Sub
```

The procedure prompts the user for their name:

```
SQLUserName = InputBox("Please enter your user name.")
```

and password through input boxes, which are stored in the Public variables:

```
SQLPassword = InputBox("Please enter your password.")
```

Then display the menu form:

```
frmMenu.Show
```

Forms

frmMenu Form

The code on the Menu form allows the user to access the different parts of the application. It also contains a Timer control, which prompts the user with any alarming reminders. The form has this code in the General Declarations section.

```
Option Explicit
Private MyConnection As New ADODB.Connection
```

You first tell the compiler that you will declare your variables:

```
Option Explicit
```

Then declare a Connection object that will be used to connect to your SQL Server database:

```
Private MyConnection As New ADODB.Connection
```

The Load event fires when the form is first loaded.

```
Private Sub Form_Load()
    MyConnection.ConnectionString = "driver={SQL Server};" _
        & "server=MyServer;uid=" & SQLUserName _
        & ";pwd=" & SQLPassword & ";" _
        & "database=C5PIM"
    MyConnection.Open
End Sub
```

The first line of code sets the connect string up for the Connection object so that it points to your SQL Server database, and it uses the login information supplied by the user:

```
MyConnection.ConnectionString = "driver={SQL Server};" _
      & "server=MyServer;uid=" & SQLUserName _
      & ";pwd=" & SQLPassword & ";" _
      & "database=C5PIM"
```

You then open that connection:

```
MyConnection.Open
```

As previously mentioned, this form contains a Timer control. The Timer control fires every minute. When it does, the code in the Timer event fires.

```
Private Sub timAlarms_Timer()
    Dim RSAlarms As ADODB.Recordset
    Set RSAlarms = MyConnection.Execute("ReminderAlarms")
    Do Until RSAlarms.EOF
        MsgBox "Alarm: " & RSAlarms("AlarmTime") _
            & vbNewLine & "Note: " & RSAlarms("ReminderNote")
        RSAlarms.MoveNext
    Loop
End Sub
```

The code needs a Recordset object:

```
Dim RSAlarms As ADODB.Recordset
```

which opens your ReminderAlarms view:

```
Set RSAlarms = MyConnection.Execute("ReminderAlarms")
```

If the Recordset returns any records, the user has Reminders that they need to be prompted for. So you enter a loop to prompt them with the reminder:

```
Do Until RSAlarms.EOF
```

The contents of the reminder are displayed in a message box:

```
MsgBox "Alarm: " & RSAlarms("AlarmTime") _
     & vbNewLine & "Note: " & RSAlarms("ReminderNote")
```

before you move on to the next record:

```
RSAlarms.MoveNext
```

When the user clicks Contacts, the Contacts form is displayed using the Show method of the Form object:

```
Private Sub cmdContacts_Click()
    frmContacts.Show
End Sub
```

Similarly, the Reminders form is opened when the Reminders button is clicked:

```
Private Sub cmdReminders_Click()
    frmReminders.Show
End Sub
```

The other button on the form, Exit, closes the application:

```
Private Sub cmdExit_Click()
    End
End Sub
```

FrmContacts Form

The code on the Contacts form allows the user to manipulate the Contacts records. In the General Declarations section of the form, you will find the following code.

```
Option Explicit
Private MyConnection As New ADODB.Connection
Private CurrentID As Long
```

The first line indicates that all your variables will be declared:

```
Option Explicit
```

The next line declares a Connection object that you can use throughout the procedures on this form:

```
Private MyConnection As New ADODB.Connection
```

This other variable is also available throughout the form and stores the ID of the current contact:

```
Private CurrentID As Long
```

The form has three procedures of its own, which are called from other Event procedures. The first displays a Contact record on the form.

```
Public Sub DisplayContact(ID2Use As Long)
    Dim RSContact As ADODB.Recordset
    Set RSContact = MyConnection.Execute("Exec ContactRecord " _
        & ID2Use)
    If RSContact.EOF Then
        cmdClear_Click
    Else
        CurrentID = RSContact("ContactID")
        txtFirstName.Text = RSContact("FirstName")
        txtLastName.Text = RSContact("LastName")
        txtAddress1.Text = RSContact("Address1")
        txtAddress2.Text = RSContact("Address2")
        txtCity.Text = RSContact("City")
        txtState.Text = RSContact("State")
        txtZipCode.Text = RSContact("ZipCode")
        txtEmailAddress.Text = RSContact("EmailAddress")
        txtContactNote.Text = RSContact("ContactNote")
        DisplayPhoneList
    End If
End Sub
```

The procedure expects a single parameter, the ID of the Contact whose record is to be retrieved:

```
Public Sub DisplayContact(ID2Use As Long)
```

You will need a Recordset object:

```
Dim RSContact As ADODB.Recordset
```

which calls your ContactRecord stored procedure that will retrieve a record from the Contacts table:

```
Set RSContact = MyConnection.Execute("Exec ContactRecord " _
      & ID2Use)
```

If no records are returned, EOF will be set:

```
If RSContact.EOF Then
```

Either you have no records or the record selected was not found. In that case, you simply need to clear the form:

```
cmdClear_Click
```

Otherwise, a record was returned and you can store the ID of the Contact in your form-wide variable:

```
CurrentID = RSContact("ContactID")
```

and populate the rest of the fields in the text boxes:

```
txtFirstName.Text = RSContact("FirstName")
txtLastName.Text = RSContact("LastName")
txtAddress1.Text = RSContact("Address1")
txtAddress2.Text = RSContact("Address2")
txtCity.Text = RSContact("City")
txtState.Text = RSContact("State")
txtZipCode.Text = RSContact("ZipCode")
txtEmailAddress.Text = RSContact("EmailAddress")
txtContactNote.Text = RSContact("ContactNote")
```

You then call the procedure that lists all the phone numbers:

```
DisplayPhoneList
```

This procedure populates the list box on the form with all the phone number records for the current Contact.

```
Public Sub DisplayPhoneList()
        Dim RSPhoneList As ADODB.Recordset
        lstPhoneNumbers.Clear
        Set RSPhoneList = MyConnection.Execute("Exec ContactPhoneList " _
            & CurrentID)
        Do Until RSPhoneList.EOF
            lstPhoneNumbers.AddItem RSPhoneList("ThePhone")
            lstPhoneNumbers.ItemData(lstPhoneNumbers.NewIndex) = _
                RSPhoneList("ContactPhoneID")
            RSPhoneList.MoveNext
```

```
        Loop
End Sub
```

The procedure requires a Recordset object:

```
Dim RSPhoneList As ADODB.Recordset
```

First, though, you need to clear the contents of the list box:

```
lstPhoneNumbers.Clear
```

Then you can retrieve the phone numbers of the current contact through the ContactPhoneList stored procedure:

```
Set RSPhoneList = MyConnection.Execute("Exec ContactPhoneList " _
      & CurrentID)
```

You then enter a loop so that you can process each of the phone number records:

```
Do Until RSPhoneList.EOF
```

The type and number of the phone are added to the list so that they are visible to the user:

```
lstPhoneNumbers.AddItem RSPhoneList("ThePhone")
```

but the ID of the phone number is placed in the ItemData property for the item just added. So the user sees the phone number, but you have the ID stored so that you know the primary-key value for that phone number in your code:

```
lstPhoneNumbers.ItemData(lstPhoneNumbers.NewIndex) = _
      RSPhoneList("ContactPhoneID")
```

You then move on to process the next record:

```
      RSPhoneList.MoveNext
Loop
```

The other user-defined procedure populates the combo box with a list of all the Contacts.

```
Public Sub UpdateNameCombo()
    Dim RSNames As ADODB.Recordset
```

```
    Set RSNames = MyConnection.Execute("Exec ContactList")
    cmbContacts.Clear
    Do Until RSNames.EOF
        cmbContacts.AddItem RSNames("TheName")
        cmbContacts.ItemData(cmbContacts.NewIndex) = _
            RSNames("ContactID")
        RSNames.MoveNext
    Loop
End Sub
```

To perform that task, a Record object is needed:

```
Dim RSNames As ADODB.Recordset
```

That Recordset is set to the return of a call to your ContactList stored procedure:

```
Set RSNames = MyConnection.Execute("Exec ContactList")
```

Then clear the combo box:

```
cmbContacts.Clear
```

and enter a loop so that each Contact can be added to the combo box:

```
Do Until RSNames.EOF
```

The name of the Contact is added to the list portion of the combo box:

```
cmbContacts.AddItem RSNames("TheName")
```

and the ID of the contact is placed in the ItemData property:

```
cmbContacts.ItemData(cmbContacts.NewIndex) = _
    RSNames("ContactID")
```

You then move on to process the next record:

```
    RSNames.MoveNext
Loop
```

When the form first opens, the Load event runs.

```
Private Sub Form_Load()
    MyConnection.ConnectionString = "driver={SQL Server};" _
```

```
        & "server=MyServer;uid=" & SQLUserName _
        & ";pwd=" & SQLPassword & ";" _
        & "database=C5PIM"
    MyConnection.Open
    DisplayContact 0
    UpdateNameCombo
End Sub
```

First, you set up the connect string for your Connection object:

```
MyConnection.ConnectionString = "driver={SQL Server};" _
      & "server=MyServer;uid=" & SQLUserName _
      & ";pwd=" & SQLPassword & ";" _
      & "database=C5PIM"
```

then open that connection:

```
MyConnection.Open
```

Next, you call your procedure so that the first record is displayed on the form:

```
DisplayContact 0
```

and you update the combo box that lists all the contact names:

```
UpdateNameCombo
```

When the user selects a name in that combo box, the Click() event fires. The code simply calls your DisplayContact procedure so that the contact selected in the combo box is displayed:

```
Private Sub cmbContacts_Click()
    DisplayContact cmbContacts.ItemData(cmbContacts.ListIndex)
End Sub
```

When the form is closed, the Unload event fires. It simply releases the resources of the form:

```
Private Sub Form_Unload(Cancel As Integer)
    frmMenu.Show
    Set frmContacts = Nothing
End Sub
```

The next code block fires when the Add button on the bottom of the form is clicked.

```
Private Sub cmdAdd_Click()
    Dim RSAddNew As ADODB.Recordset
    Set RSAddNew = MyConnection.Execute("Exec ContactAdd " _
        & "'" & txtFirstName.Text & "', " _
        & "'" & txtLastName.Text & "', " _
        & "'" & txtAddress1.Text & "', " _
        & "'" & txtAddress2.Text & "', " _
        & "'" & txtCity.Text & "', " _
        & "'" & txtState.Text & "', " _
        & "'" & txtZipCode.Text & "', " _
        & "'" & txtEmailAddress.Text & "', " _
        & "'" & txtContactNote.Text & "'")
    CurrentID = RSAddNew("TheNewID")
    cmbContacts.AddItem txtLastName.Text & ", " _
        & txtFirstName.Text
    cmbContacts.ItemData(cmbContacts.NewIndex) = _
        RSAddNew("TheNewID")
End Sub
```

The procedure needs to add a new record to the Contacts table. A Recordset object is needed to perform this task:

```
Dim RSAddNew As ADODB.Recordset
```

That object calls your ContactAdd stored procedure, passing to it the values of the fields for the record to be added:

```
Set RSAddNew = MyConnection.Execute("Exec ContactAdd " _
      & "'" & txtFirstName.Text & "', " _
      & "'" & txtLastName.Text & "', " _
      & "'" & txtAddress1.Text & "', " _
      & "'" & txtAddress2.Text & "', " _
      & "'" & txtCity.Text & "', " _
      & "'" & txtState.Text & "', " _
      & "'" & txtZipCode.Text & "', " _
      & "'" & txtEmailAddress.Text & "', " _
      & "'" & txtContactNote.Text & "'")
```

The stored procedure returns the ID of the record you just added, which you store in the CurrentID formwide variable:

```
CurrentID = RSAddNew("TheNewID")
```

Then add the name just added to the Contacts combo box:

```
cmbContacts.AddItem txtLastName.Text & ", " _
      & txtFirstName.Text
```

and the ID of the contact to the ItemData property:

```
cmbContacts.ItemData(cmbContacts.NewIndex) = _
      RSAddNew("TheNewID")
```

When the Update button is clicked, the current Contacts record needs to be updated.

```
Private Sub cmdUpdate_Click()
    If CurrentID = 0 Then
        cmdAdd_Click
    Else
        MyConnection.Execute "Exec ContactUpdate " _
            & CurrentID & ", " _
            & "'" & txtFirstName.Text & "', " _
            & "'" & txtLastName.Text & "', " _
            & "'" & txtAddress1.Text & "', " _
            & "'" & txtAddress2.Text & "', " _
            & "'" & txtCity.Text & "', " _
            & "'" & txtState.Text & "', " _
            & "'" & txtZipCode.Text & "', " _
            & "'" & txtEmailAddress.Text & "', " _
            & "'" & txtContactNote.Text & "'"
        UpdateNameCombo
    End If
End Sub
```

First, you make sure you are not in Add mode:

```
If CurrentID = 0 Then
```

If you are, you don't need to update, you need to add. Therefore, you call that procedure:

```
cmdAdd_Click
```

Otherwise, you can call the ContactUpdate stored procedure to update the current record:

```
MyConnection.Execute "Exec ContactUpdate " _
      & CurrentID & ", " _
      & "'" & txtFirstName.Text & "', " _
      & "'" & txtLastName.Text & "', " _
      & "'" & txtAddress1.Text & "', " _
      & "'" & txtAddress2.Text & "', " _
      & "'" & txtCity.Text & "', " _
      & "'" & txtState.Text & "', " _
      & "'" & txtZipCode.Text & "', " _
      & "'" & txtEmailAddress.Text & "', " _
      & "'" & txtContactNote.Text & "'"
```

then update the Contacts combo box by calling your procedure:

```
UpdateNameCombo
```

When the Delete button on the bottom of the form is clicked, you need to delete the current record.

```
Private Sub cmdDelete_Click()
    If CurrentID = 0 Then
        cmdClear_Click
    Else
        MyConnection.Execute "Exec ContactDelete " _
            & CurrentID
        UpdateNameCombo
        DisplayContact 0
    End If
End Sub
```

First, you check to see whether you are in Add mode:

```
If CurrentID = 0 Then
```

If that is the case, you just need to clear the form:

```
cmdClear_Click
```

Otherwise, you can delete the current record:

```
MyConnection.Execute "Exec ContactDelete " _
      & CurrentID
```

You then need to update the Contacts combo box:

```
UpdateNameCombo
```

and display another record on the form:

```
DisplayContact 0
```

The next procedure fires when the Clear button is clicked.

```
Private Sub cmdClear_Click()
    CurrentID = 0
    txtFirstName.Text = ""
    txtLastName.Text = ""
    txtAddress1.Text = ""
    txtAddress2.Text = ""
    txtCity.Text = ""
    txtState.Text = ""
    txtZipCode.Text = ""
    txtEmailAddress.Text = ""
    txtContactNote.Text = ""
    lstPhoneNumbers.Clear
End Sub
```

First, you clear the ID of the current contact, putting you in Add mode:

```
CurrentID = 0
```

then you clear the text boxes on the form:

```
txtFirstName.Text = ""
txtLastName.Text = ""
txtAddress1.Text = ""
txtAddress2.Text = ""
txtCity.Text = ""
txtState.Text = ""
txtZipCode.Text = ""
txtEmailAddress.Text = ""
txtContactNote.Text = ""
```

You also need to clear the Phone Number list box:

```
lstPhoneNumbers.Clear
```

When the user clicks the View Report button, they need to see a Data Report that displays all the data for the current contact.

```
Private Sub cmdViewReport_Click()
    DateEnvironmentChapter5.conC5PIM.ConnectionString = _
        "driver={SQL Server};" _
        & "server=MyServer;uid=" & SQLUserName _
        & ";pwd=" & SQLPassword & ";" _
        & "database=C5PIM"
    DateEnvironmentChapter5.Commands(1).Parameters(1).Value = CurrentID
    drContactReport.Show 1
    Set DateEnvironmentChapter5 = Nothing
End Sub
```

To do that, you need to enter the user name and password supplied by the user in your Connection object. If you don't do this, the user will be asked for their user name and password again:

```
DateEnvironmentChapter5.conC5PIM.ConnectionString = _
      "driver={SQL Server};" _
      & "server=MyServer;uid=" & SQLUserName _
      & ";pwd=" & SQLPassword & ";" _
      & "database=C5PIM"
```

The Command object that the data reports use needs to know the ID of the contact you want to view so that the correct record is displayed. You do that by setting the Value property of the first Parameter object in the Parameters collection to the current ID:

```
DateEnvironmentChapter5.Commands(1).Parameters(1).Value = CurrentID
```

Now you can show your data report modally:

```
drContactReport.Show 1
```

After the user closes the report, you release its resources:

```
Set DateEnvironmentChapter5 = Nothing
```

When the Close button is clicked, the form is simply unloaded:

```
Private Sub cmdClose_Click()
    Unload Me
End Sub
```

Another Add button is present in the Phone Numbers frame. The next code block fires when that button is clicked.

```
Private Sub cmdAddPhone_Click()
    Dim PhoneType As String
    Dim PhoneNumber As String
    If CurrentID = 0 Then
        MsgBox "First save the new record or " _
            & "select an existing record to add a phone number to."
    Else
        PhoneType = InputBox("Enter the type for the phone number:")
        PhoneNumber = InputBox("Enter the new phone number:")
        If PhoneType <> "" And PhoneNumber <> "" Then
            MyConnection.Execute "Exec ContactPhoneAdd " _
                & CurrentID & ", " _
                & "'" & PhoneType & "', " _
                & "'" & PhoneNumber & "'"
            DisplayPhoneList
        End If
    End If
End Sub
```

The procedure needs to add a new phone number for the current contact. So you will need variables to store the type and number for the phone:

```
Dim PhoneType As String
Dim PhoneNumber As String
```

First, you make sure that you are on a valid current record:

```
If CurrentID = 0 Then
```

If you are not, you inform the user of the problem:

```
MsgBox "First save the new record or " _
    & "select an existing record to add a phone number to."
```

Otherwise, you prompt the user for the type of phone being added:

```
PhoneType = InputBox("Enter the type for the phone number:")
```

and the number for that phone:

```
PhoneNumber = InputBox("Enter the new phone number:")
```

Then make sure they entered information into those two variables:

```
If PhoneType <> "" And PhoneNumber <> "" Then
```

If they did, you call the ContactPhoneAdd stored procedure to add the phone number record:

```
MyConnection.Execute "Exec ContactPhoneAdd " _
      & CurrentID & ", " _
      & "'" & PhoneType & "', " _
      & "'" & PhoneNumber & "'"
```

and then update the Phone Number list box:

```
DisplayPhoneList
```

The other procedure on the form fires when the Delete button in the Phone Number frame is clicked. The procedure needs to delete the selected phone number.

```
Private Sub cmdDeletePhone_Click()
    If lstPhoneNumbers.ListIndex = -1 Then
        MsgBox "First, select and item to delete."
    Else
            MyConnection.Execute "Exec ContactPhoneDelete " _
                & lstPhoneNumbers.ItemData(lstPhoneNumbers.ListIndex)
            DisplayPhoneList
    End If
End Sub
```

First, you check to see if the user has selected an item in the list box:

```
If lstPhoneNumbers.ListIndex = -1 Then
```

If they haven't, you display an error message:

```
MsgBox "First, select and item to delete."
```

Otherwise, you can call the stored procedure to delete the selected phone number:

```
MyConnection.Execute "Exec ContactPhoneDelete " _
      & lstPhoneNumbers.ItemData(lstPhoneNumbers.ListIndex)
```

and then update the Phone Number list box:

```
DisplayPhoneList
```

frmReminders Form

The code on the Reminders form allows the user to manipulate the reminder records. Most of the code is identical in structure to the code on the Contacts form except for the procedure noted here.

The form contains a check box that indicates whether the alarm for the reminder is on or off. The Visual Basic check box has three states: checked, unchecked, or grayed. But you need to store the value in a bit field that has a value of True or False. So you need to skip the grayed-out state of the check box. You do that in the Click event of the check box.

```
Private Sub chkAlarmOn_Click()
    If chkAlarmOn.Value = 2 Then
        chkAlarmOn.Value = 0
    End If
End Sub
```

You check to see whether the value of the check box is grayed:

```
If chkAlarmOn.Value = 2 Then
```

If it is, you set it to unchecked:

```
chkAlarmOn.Value = 0
```

CHAPTER

6

Help Desk

IN THIS CHAPTER:

C6SQLObjects.sql

SupportPeople.txt

ProblemCategories.txt

Cases.txt

ProgressNotes.txt

Chapter6HelpDesk.vbproj

In this chapter, you will look at a solution that allows the user to manage Help requests. The requests are stored as *cases* to which an employee is assigned. Each case has a status and has progress notes that go along with it. Each case also belongs to a specific problem category.

Managing Support Requests

The back-end SQL Server database is accessed through a VB.net front end. As you review this example, note that the solution was developed with VisualStudio.net Beta 1. So some of the code and techniques used may need to be changed as Microsoft moves toward the final release of the product.

Application Walk-Through

When the user first launches the VB.net application, they are asked for their SQL Server user name and password. The user then sees the menu for the project, which is displayed in Figure 6-1.

Figure 6-1 *Menu form*

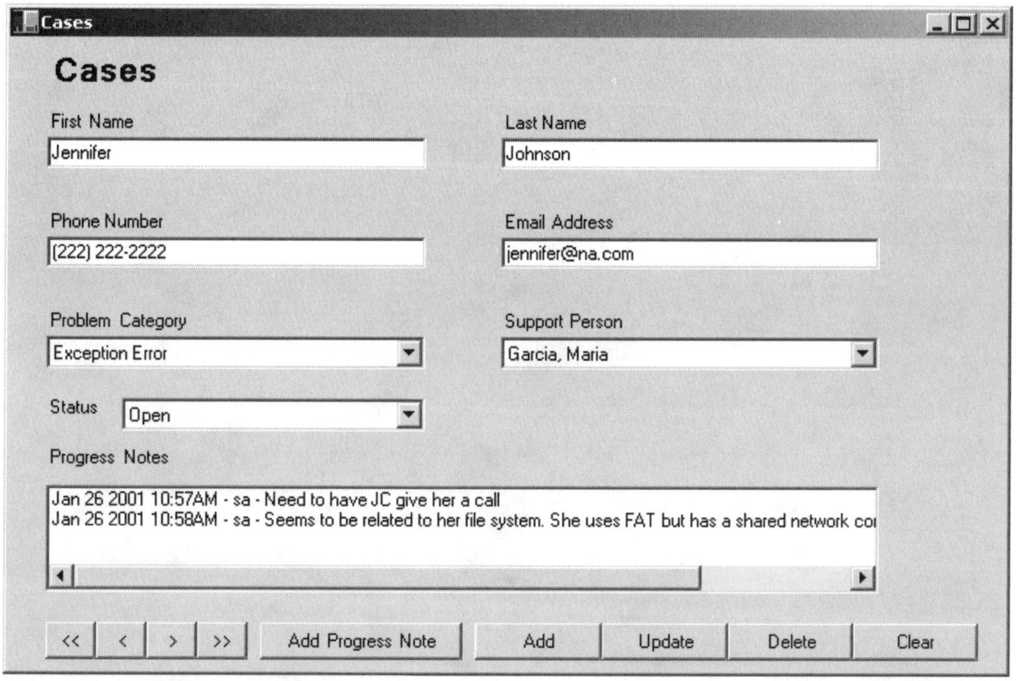

Figure 6-2 *Cases form*

From the Menu form the user can access any of the other forms in the application. The main part of the application is on the Cases form, which is displayed in Figure 6-2.

The cases are individual help requests. A customer or employee makes the requests. Each request belongs in a specific category and is managed by a specific support person.

The progress in resolving the help request is tracked through progress notes that are displayed in a list box on the form. The user can add a progress note by clicking the Add Progress Note button. When they do that, they see the dialog displayed in Figure 6-3.

The user enters the message for their note and clicks OK. When they do that, the new note is added to the list, as displayed in Figure 6-4.

Note that the user's text now appears in the list box. Also added to the note is the date and time that the note was entered and the name of the person who entered the note, taken from their database login.

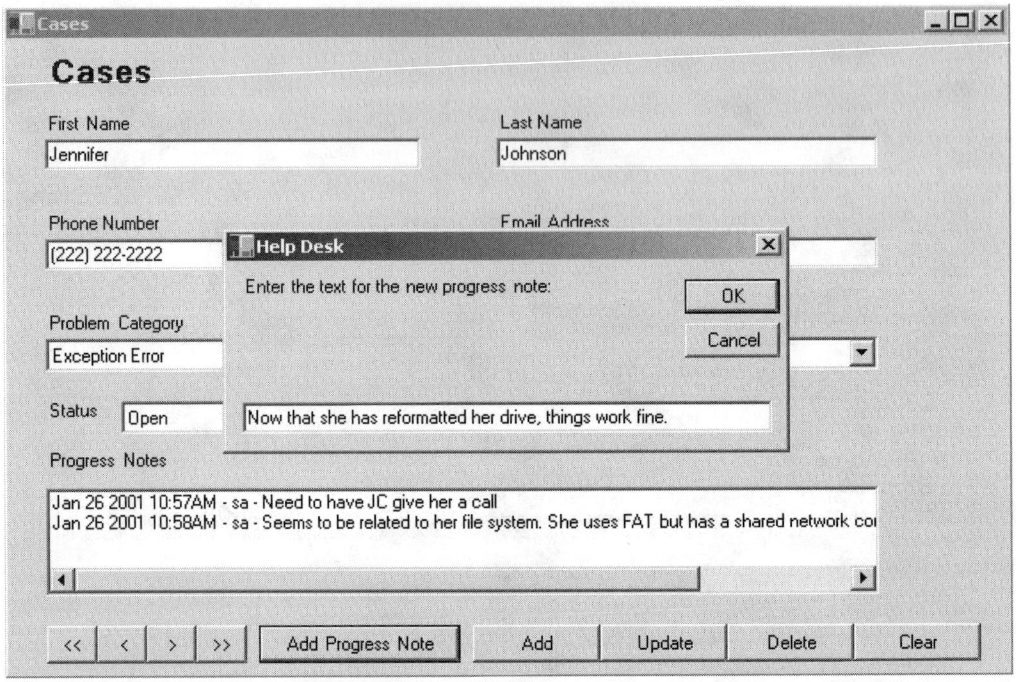

Figure 6-3 *Add Progress Note dialog box*

Back on the Menu form, the user can click the Support People button to see the Support People form, which is displayed in Figure 6-5.

Each help request or case is managed by a specific support person. The Support People form provides the user with the mechanism to manage the support staff.

The other form in this front-end VB.net application is the Problem Category form. That form is displayed in Figure 6-6.

Each case is grouped into a problem category to help the support person manage the problem. The Problem Category form provides the user with the method of adding and deleting those categories.

Tables and Relationships

C6SQLObjects.sql

SupportPeople Table

The SupportPeople table contains all the information about the employees who manage cases. The table is then used in a relationship with the Cases table.

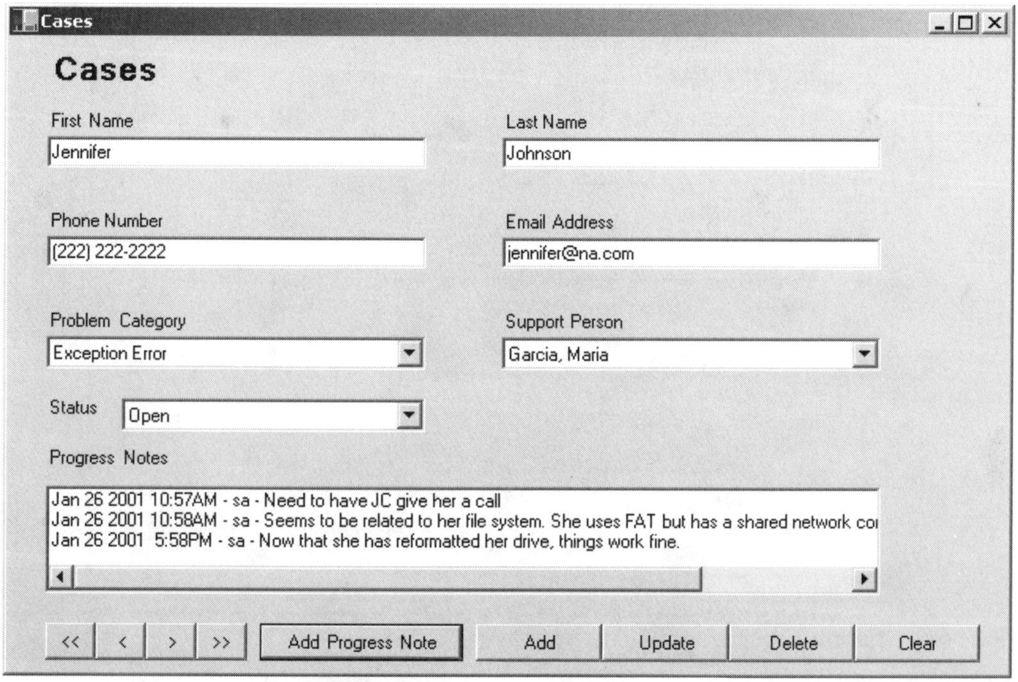

Figure 6-4 *Cases form with new progress note*

ProblemCategories Table

Problem categories are titles or groupings placed on help requests. The Problem-Categories table stores that information.

Cases Table

The main table in this solution is the Cases table. This table stores information about the help requests that have been made. The table is in a one-to-many relationship with the SupportPeople table. Each case is assigned to a specific support person, but each support person can manage many cases.

The table is also in a one-to-many relationship with the ProblemCategories table. Each of the cases goes in a specific category, but many cases may be in a single category.

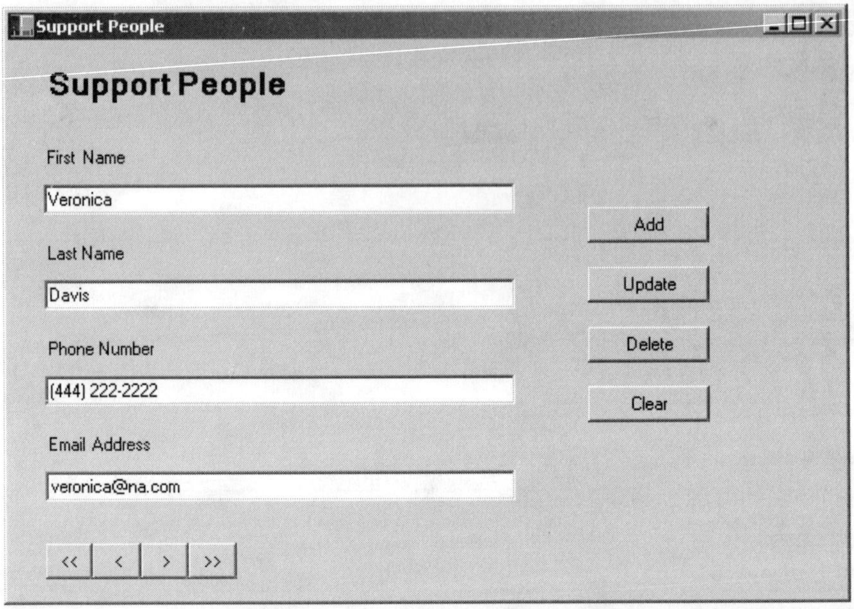

Figure 6-5 *Support People form*

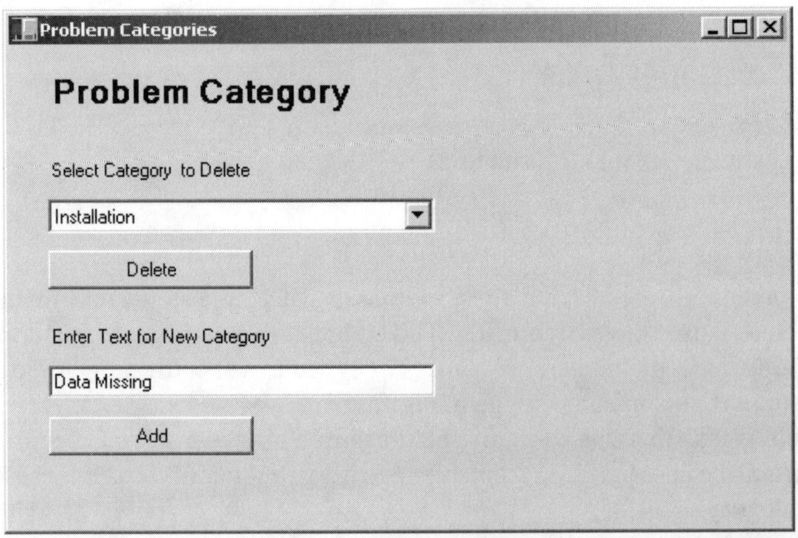

Figure 6-6 *Problem Category form*

ProgressNotes Table

The ProgressNotes table stores the log of progress for each of the cases. The table is in a one-to-many relationship with the Cases table. Each note goes with a single case, but each case can have many notes.

SupportPeople Table

SupportPeople.txt

The field specifications for the SupportPeople table are displayed in Table 6-1.

The primary key for this table is the SupportPersonID field. The field is implemented as an identity column, so the field is automatically populated when a new record is added. The rest of the fields store information about the support person.

ProblemCategories Table

ProblemCategories.txt

The field specification for the ProblemCategories table is displayed in Table 6-2.

The table contains just a single field. That field is the primary key and contains the text of the category.

Cases Table

Cases.txt

The field specifications for the Cases table are displayed in Table 6-3.

The CaseID field is the primary key for this table. The SupportPersonID field is a foreign key that links this table to the SupportPeople table. A combo box on the Cases form limits the Status field to the values Open and Closed. The other fields store information about the person requesting help.

Field Name	Field Type	Notes
SupportPersonID	int	Primary Key, Identity Column
FirstName	varchar	Length = 50
LastName	varchar	Length = 50
PhoneNumber	varchar	Length = 50
EmailAddress	varchar	Length = 50

Table 6-1 *SupportPeople Table Field Specifications*

Field Name	Field Type	Notes
ProblemCategory	varchar	Length = 50, Primary Key

Table 6-2 *ProblemCategories Table Field Specification*

ProgressNotes Table

ProgressNotes.txt

The field specifications for the ProgressNotes table are displayed in Table 6-4.

The primary key in this table is the ProgressNoteID field. The CaseID field links this table with the Cases table. The DateEntered field stores the date and time that the entry was made. The EnteredBy field stores the name of the person who made the entry. The ProgressNote field stores the contents of the progress note.

Stored Procedures

SupportPersonAdd Stored Procedure

The SupportPersonAdd stored procedure provides the mechanism for adding a new support person to the SupportPeople table.

Field Name	Field Type	Notes
CaseID	int	Primary Key, Identity Column
ProblemCategory	varchar	Length = 50
SupportPersonID	int	Foreign Key
Status	varchar	Length = 50
FirstName	varchar	Length = 50
LastName	varchar	Length = 50
PhoneNumber	varchar	Length = 50
EmailAddress	varchar	Length = 50

Table 6-3 *Cases Table Field Specifications*

Field Name	Field Type	Notes
ProgressNoteID	int	Primary Key, Identity Column
CaseID	varchar	Foreign Key
DateEntered	int	
EnteredBy	varchar	Length = 50
ProgressNote	varchar	Length = 1000

Table 6-4 *ProgressNotes Table Field Specifications*

```
CREATE PROCEDURE SupportPersonAdd
@FirstName varchar(50),
@LastName varchar(50),
@PhoneNumber varchar(50),
@EmailAddress varchar(50)
AS
      BEGIN
            Insert Into SupportPeople
                  (FirstName, LastName, PhoneNumber,
                  EmailAddress) values
                  (@FirstName, @LastName, @PhoneNumber,
                  @EmailAddress)
            Select @@Identity as TheNewID
      END
GO
```

The procedure needs parameters passed in for the values for each of the fields in the new record:

```
@FirstName varchar(50),
@LastName varchar(50),
@PhoneNumber varchar(50),
@EmailAddress varchar(50)
```

Those values are then used in a SQL Insert statement:

```
Insert Into SupportPeople
      (FirstName, LastName, PhoneNumber,
```

```
      EmailAddress) values
      (@FirstName, @LastName, @PhoneNumber,
      @EmailAddress)
```

You then return the ID of the record just added to the SupportPeople table through the global variable @@Identity:

```
Select @@Identity as TheNewID
```

SupportPersonUpdate Stored Procedure

The next stored procedure, SupportPersonUpdate, allows the calling application to update an existing record in the SupportPeople table.

```
CREATE PROCEDURE SupportPersonUpdate
@SupportPersonID integer,
@FirstName varchar(50),
@LastName varchar(50),
@PhoneNumber varchar(50),
@EmailAddress varchar(50)
AS
      BEGIN
            Update SupportPeople set
                  FirstName = @FirstName,
                  LastName = @LastName,
                  PhoneNumber = @PhoneNumber,
                  EmailAddress = @EmailAddress
                  Where SupportPersonID = @SupportPersonID
      END
GO
```

The procedure requires a single parameter, the ID of the record being updated:

```
@SupportPersonID integer,
```

Also passed into the procedure through its parameters are the values for the fields being updated:

```
@FirstName varchar(50),
@LastName varchar(50),
@PhoneNumber varchar(50),
@EmailAddress varchar(50)
```

Those values are then used in the Update statement, and the ID is used in the Where clause:

```
Update SupportPeople set
      FirstName = @FirstName,
      LastName = @LastName,
      PhoneNumber = @PhoneNumber,
      EmailAddress = @EmailAddress
      Where SupportPersonID = @SupportPersonID
```

SupportPersonDelete Stored Procedure

When the calling application needs to delete a record from the SupportPeople table, the SupportPersonDelete stored procedure is called.

```
CREATE PROCEDURE SupportPersonDelete
@SupportPersonID integer
AS
      BEGIN
            Delete from  SupportPeople
                  Where SupportPersonID = @SupportPersonID
      END
GO
```

The ID of the record to be deleted is passed in to the procedure:

```
@SupportPersonID integer
```

That ID is then used in the Where clause of a Delete statement:

```
Delete from  SupportPeople
      Where SupportPersonID = @SupportPersonID
```

SupportPersonRecord Stored Procedure

On the Support People form, the user clicks navigational buttons to move themselves through the records in the SupportPeople table. The VB.net application calls the SupportPersonRecord stored procedure to return a record that is chosen through navigational movement within the records in the table.

```
CREATE PROCEDURE SupportPersonRecord
@MoveDirection varchar(8),
@LastPosition integer = 0
```

```
AS
Declare @ID2Use integer
If @MoveDirection = 'FIRST'
      BEGIN
            Select @ID2Use = Min(SupportPersonID)
                  from SupportPeople
            Select * from SupportPeople
                  Where SupportPersonID = @ID2Use
      END
Else
      If (@MoveDirection) = 'LAST'
            BEGIN
                  Select @ID2Use = Max(SupportPersonID)
                        from SupportPeople
                  Select * from SupportPeople
                        Where SupportPersonID = @ID2Use
            END
      Else
            If (@MoveDirection) = 'NEXT'
                  BEGIN
                        Select Top 1 * from SupportPeople
                              Where SupportPersonID > @LastPosition
                              Order By SupportPersonID
                  END
            Else
                  BEGIN
                        Select Top 1 * from SupportPeople
                              Where SupportPersonID < @LastPosition
                              Order By SupportPersonID DESC
                  END
GO
```

Two parameters are passed into the procedure. The first is the navigational direction of the record to be returned: the first one, the last one, the next one, or the previous one:

```
@MoveDirection varchar(8),
```

If the direction is next or previous, the procedure needs to know next or previous from what position. That position is based on the ID passed into the second option parameter:

```
@LastPosition integer = 0
```

Within the procedure, you will store the ID of the record that is to be retrieved in this variable:

```
Declare @ID2Use integer
```

Then you check to see if the calling application wants the first record in the table:

```
If @MoveDirection = 'FIRST'
```

If so, you retrieve the lowest ID in the SupportPeople table and place that value in the local variable:

```
Select @ID2Use = Min(SupportPersonID)
      from SupportPeople
```

You then return all the fields for the record based on that ID:

```
Select * from SupportPeople
      Where SupportPersonID = @ID2Use
```

Next, you check to see if the calling application wants the last record in the table:

```
If (@MoveDirection) = 'LAST'
```

If so, you retrieve the highest value in the ID field and place it in your local variable:

```
Select @ID2Use = Max(SupportPersonID)
      from SupportPeople
```

That ID is then used to return the contents of the last record:

```
Select * from SupportPeople
      Where SupportPersonID = @ID2Use
```

The next condition you check for is when the calling application wants to return the next record:

```
If (@MoveDirection) = 'NEXT'
```

So you return a single record that has an ID greater than the one passed into this procedure:

```
Select Top 1 * from SupportPeople
      Where SupportPersonID > @LastPosition
      Order By SupportPersonID
```

The Else condition means that the calling application wants the previous record returned:

```
Else
```

Then you return the contents of the record that is found just before the ID of the record that is used as the pointer:

```
Select Top 1 * from SupportPeople
      Where SupportPersonID < @LastPosition
      Order By SupportPersonID DESC
```

SupportPersonList Form

On the Cases form in the VB.net application, there is a list of the support people that is used to select the support person in charge of the case. The user selects the name of the support person, but you need to store the ID of that person. The calling application uses the SupportPersonList stored procedure to return the names formatted to be displayed in that combo box.

```
CREATE PROCEDURE SupportPersonList
AS
BEGIN
      Select SupportPersonID, convert(char(100), LastName + ', ' + FirstName)
            as TheName from SupportPeople
            Order By LastName + ', ' + FirstName
END
GO
```

The procedure returns two fields. The first is the ID of the support person. The second is the full name of the support person concatenated together. Note that the latter field is returned with a length of 100, since it is a fixed character field. As you will see when you look at the VB.net code, that allows you to display to the user the full name of the person and then place the ID of the person in the viewable area of the combo box:

```
Select SupportPersonID, convert(char(100), LastName + ', ' + FirstName)
      as TheName from SupportPeople
      Order By LastName + ', ' + FirstName
```

ProblemCategoryAdd Stored Procedure

On the Problem Categories form in the VB.net application, you allow the user to add and delete problem categories. The ProblemCategoryAdd stored procedure is used on that form to add a new record to the ProblemCategories table.

```
CREATE PROCEDURE ProblemCategoryAdd
@ProblemCategory varchar(50)
AS
      BEGIN
            Insert Into ProblemCategories
                  (ProblemCategory) values
                  (@ProblemCategory)
      END
GO
```

The name of the new category is passed into the procedure:

```
@ProblemCategory varchar(50)
```

That value is then added to the ProblemCategories table:

```
Insert Into ProblemCategories
      (ProblemCategory) values
      (@ProblemCategory)
```

ProblemCategoryDelete Stored Procedure

The ProblemCategoryDelete stored procedure allows the calling application to delete a problem category.

```
CREATE PROCEDURE ProblemCategoryDelete
@ProblemCategory varchar(50)
AS
      BEGIN
            Delete from  ProblemCategories
                  Where ProblemCategory = @ProblemCategory
      END
GO
```

Passed into the procedure is the name of the category to be deleted:

```
@ProblemCategory varchar(50)
```

That value is then used in the Where clause of a Delete statement:

```
Delete from  ProblemCategories
      Where ProblemCategory = @ProblemCategory
```

ProblemCategoryList Stored Procedure

On the Cases form, as well as on the Problem Categories form, you need to display a list of all the problem categories. The ProblemCategoryList stored procedure returns the contents for that list.

```
CREATE PROCEDURE ProblemCategoryList
AS
BEGIN
      Select * from ProblemCategories
            Order By ProblemCategory
END
GO
```

It simply returns all the category names sorted by the category name:

```
Select * from ProblemCategories
      Order By ProblemCategory
```

CaseAdd Stored Procedure

The CaseAdd stored procedure provides the calling application with the mechanism for adding records to the Cases table.

```
CREATE PROCEDURE CaseAdd
@ProblemCategory varchar(50),
@SupportPersonID integer,
@Status varchar(50),
@FirstName varchar(50),
@LastName varchar(50),
@PhoneNumber varchar(50),
@EmailAddress varchar(50)
AS
      BEGIN
```

```
            Insert Into Cases
                  (ProblemCategory, SupportPersonID, Status,
                  FirstName, LastName, PhoneNumber,
                  EmailAddress) values
                  (@ProblemCategory, @SupportPersonID, @Status,
                  @FirstName, @LastName, @PhoneNumber,
                  @EmailAddress)
            Select @@Identity as TheNewID
      END
GO
```

You pass into the procedure the values for each of the fields being inserted into the new record:

```
@ProblemCategory varchar(50),
@SupportPersonID integer,
@Status varchar(50),
@FirstName varchar(50),
@LastName varchar(50),
@PhoneNumber varchar(50),
@EmailAddress varchar(50)
```

Those values are then used in a SQL Insert statement:

```
Insert Into Cases
      (ProblemCategory, SupportPersonID, Status,
      FirstName, LastName, PhoneNumber,
      EmailAddress) values
      (@ProblemCategory, @SupportPersonID, @Status,
      @FirstName, @LastName, @PhoneNumber,
      @EmailAddress)
```

You then return the ID of the record just added to the calling application:

```
Select @@Identity as TheNewID
```

CaseUpdate Stored Procedure

The CaseUpdate stored procedure is used by the calling application to update an existing case record.

```
CREATE PROCEDURE CaseUpdate
@CaseID integer,
```

```
@ProblemCategory varchar(50),
@SupportPersonID integer,
@Status varchar(50),
@FirstName varchar(50),
@LastName varchar(50),
@PhoneNumber varchar(50),
@EmailAddress varchar(50)AS
      BEGIN
            Update Cases set
                  ProblemCategory = @ProblemCategory,
                  SupportPersonID = @SupportPersonID,
                  Status   = @Status,
                  FirstName = @FirstName,
                  LastName = @LastName,
                  PhoneNumber = @PhoneNumber,
                  EmailAddress = @EmailAddress
                  Where CaseID = @CaseID
      END
GO
```

The first parameter passed in is the ID of the record to be updated:

```
@CaseID integer,
```

The rest of the parameters are for the fields in the record being updated:

```
@ProblemCategory varchar(50),
@SupportPersonID integer,
@Status varchar(50),
@FirstName varchar(50),
@LastName varchar(50),
@PhoneNumber varchar(50),
@EmailAddress varchar(50)AS
```

Those values are then used in the Update statement:

```
Update Cases set
      ProblemCategory = @ProblemCategory,
      SupportPersonID = @SupportPersonID,
      Status   = @Status,
      FirstName = @FirstName,
      LastName = @LastName,
      PhoneNumber = @PhoneNumber,
```

```
      EmailAddress = @EmailAddress
      Where CaseID = @CaseID
```

CaseDelete Stored Procedure

The CaseDelete stored procedure allows the caller to delete a record from the Cases table.

```
CREATE PROCEDURE CaseDelete
@CaseID integer
AS
      BEGIN
            Delete from  Cases
                  Where CaseID = @CaseID
      END
GO
```

Passed into the procedure is the ID of the record to be deleted:

```
@CaseID integer
```

That ID is then used in a Delete statement:

```
Delete from  Cases
      Where CaseID = @CaseID
```

CaseRecord Stored Procedure

On the Cases form in the VB.net application, you provide buttons for the user to navigate through the case records. The code calls the CaseRecord stored procedure to return a record based on that navigational movement.

```
CREATE PROCEDURE CaseRecord
@MoveDirection varchar(8),
@LastPosition integer = 0
AS
Declare @ID2Use integer
If @MoveDirection = 'FIRST'
      BEGIN
            Select @ID2Use = Min(CaseID)
                  from Cases
            Select Cases.*,
                  Convert(char(100), SupportPeople.LastName + ', ' +
```

```
SupportPeople.FirstName)
                  AS SupportName From Cases Left Outer Join
                  SupportPeople On Cases.SupportPersonID =
SupportPeople.SupportPersonID
                  Where CaseID = @ID2Use
      END
Else
      If (@MoveDirection) = 'LAST'
            BEGIN
                  Select @ID2Use = Max(CaseID)
                        from Cases
                  Select Cases.*,
                        Convert(char(100), SupportPeople.LastName + ', ' +
SupportPeople.FirstName)
                        AS SupportName From Cases Left Outer Join
                        SupportPeople On Cases.SupportPersonID =
SupportPeople.SupportPersonID
                        Where CaseID = @ID2Use
            END
      Else
            If (@MoveDirection) = 'NEXT'
                  BEGIN
                        Select Top 1 Cases.*,
                              Convert(char(100), SupportPeople.LastName + ', '
+ SupportPeople.FirstName)
                              AS SupportName From Cases Left Outer Join
                              SupportPeople On Cases.SupportPersonID =
SupportPeople.SupportPersonID
                              Where CaseID > @LastPosition
                              Order By CaseID
                  END
            Else
                  BEGIN
                        Select Top 1 Cases.*,
                              Convert(char(100), SupportPeople.LastName + ', '
+ SupportPeople.FirstName)
                              AS SupportName From Cases Left Outer Join
                              SupportPeople On Cases.SupportPersonID =
SupportPeople.SupportPersonID
                              Where CaseID < @LastPosition
                              Order By CaseID DESC
                  END
GO
```

Passed into the procedure first is the direction of the record to return: the first, last, next, or previous record:

```
@MoveDirection varchar(8),
```

Also passed into the procedure is the ID of the record to base that movement on. This value is used if the navigational direction is previous or next, so you know previous or next in relation to what record:

```
@LastPosition integer = 0
```

You then declare a local variable that will be used in some of the cases to store the ID of the case being retrieved:

```
Declare @ID2Use integer
```

First, you test to see if the calling application wants the first record:

```
If @MoveDirection = 'FIRST'
```

If so, you need to retrieve the lowest ID of any case record:

```
Select @ID2Use = Min(CaseID)
      from Cases
```

That value is then used in the Where clause of a Select statement to return the first record in the table. Note that you return all the fields from the Cases table. But you also return the name of the support person that is responsible for this case so that it can be displayed with the ID in the combo box on the Cases form:

```
Select Cases.*,
      Convert(char(100), SupportPeople.LastName + ', ' + SupportPeople.FirstName)
      AS SupportName From Cases Left Outer Join
      SupportPeople On Cases.SupportPersonID = SupportPeople.SupportPersonID
      Where CaseID = @ID2Use
```

The next condition you test for is whether the calling application wants the last record:

```
      If (@MoveDirection) = 'LAST'
```

In that case, you retrieve the highest ID in the CaseID field in the Cases table:

```
Select @ID2Use = Max(CaseID)
      from Cases
```

and use it in the Where clause of your Select statement, so you return the contents of the last record:

```
Select Cases.*,
      Convert(char(100), SupportPeople.LastName + ', ' + SupportPeople.FirstName)
```

```
        AS SupportName From Cases Left Outer Join
        SupportPeople On Cases.SupportPersonID = SupportPeople.SupportPersonID
        Where CaseID = @ID2Use
```

The next condition you test for is whether the calling application wants the next record returned:

```
If (@MoveDirection) = 'NEXT'
```

In that case, you return a single record. The record has to be greater than the ID of the record in the last position. And the records are sorted by the ID, so the record returned is the next one in accordance with the value of the ID field:

```
Select Top 1 Cases.*,
        Convert(char(100), SupportPeople.LastName + ', ' + SupportPeople.FirstName)
        AS SupportName From Cases Left Outer Join
        SupportPeople On Cases.SupportPersonID = SupportPeople.SupportPersonID
        Where CaseID > @LastPosition
        Order By CaseID
```

The Else condition means that the calling application wants the previous record:

```
Else
```

In that case, you return the single record that occurs just before the last-position record relative to the CaseID field:

```
Select Top 1 Cases.*,
        Convert(char(100), SupportPeople.LastName + ', ' + SupportPeople.FirstName)
        AS SupportName From Cases Left Outer Join
        SupportPeople On Cases.SupportPersonID = SupportPeople.SupportPersonID
        Where CaseID < @LastPosition
        Order By CaseID DESC
```

ProgressNoteAdd Stored Procedure

On the Cases form, you need to be able to add records to the ProgressNotes table. The ProgressNoteAdd stored procedure provides that functionality.

```
CREATE PROCEDURE ProgressNoteAdd
@CaseID integer,
@DateEntered datetime,
@EnteredBy varchar(50),
@ProgressNote varchar(1000)
AS
        BEGIN
```

```
            Insert Into ProgressNotes
                  (CaseID, DateEntered, EnteredBy,
                  ProgressNote) values
                  (@CaseID, @DateEntered, @EnteredBy,
                  @ProgressNote)
            Select @@Identity as TheNewID
      END
GO
```

Passed into the procedure are the values for the fields in the record being added:

```
@CaseID integer,
@DateEntered datetime,
@EnteredBy varchar(50),
@ProgressNote varchar(1000)
```

Those values are then used in a SQL Insert statement:

```
Insert Into ProgressNotes
      (CaseID, DateEntered, EnteredBy,
      ProgressNote) values
      (@CaseID, @DateEntered, @EnteredBy,
      @ProgressNote)
```

You then return the ID of the record just added:

```
Select @@Identity as TheNewID
```

ProgressNoteList Stored Procedure

On the Cases form in the VB.net application, there is a list box that displays all the notes for this case. The ProgressNoteList stored procedure returns the contents of that list.

```
CREATE PROCEDURE ProgressNoteList
@CaseID integer
AS
BEGIN
      Select convert(varchar(50), DateEntered) + ' - ' + EnteredBy + ' - ' +
ProgresssNote
            As TheNote From ProgressNotes
            Where CaseID = @CaseID
            Order By DateEntered
END
GO
```

Passed into the procedure is the ID of the case for which you want the notes returned:

```
@CaseID integer
```

You then return the content of the notes for that case concatenated into a single field called TheNote for just the records that match the ID passed in. The records are sorted by the date that they were entered:

```
Select convert(varchar(50), DateEntered) + ' - ' + EnteredBy + ' - ' +
ProgressNote
      As TheNote From ProgressNotes
      Where CaseID = @CaseID
      Order By DateEntered
```

Application Notes

Chapter6HelpDesk.vbproj

The easiest way to navigate around the front-end VB.net solution is through the Solution Explorer. You can view the Solution Explorer by selecting it through the View menu. Take a look at the Solution Explorer for this solution; it is displayed in Figure 6-7.

From the Solution Explorer, you can view any of the forms, modules, or other files that are part of this solution. Once you have opened a code view or a form's design view, it is part of the tabbed dialog box until you close it. So it is pretty easy to jump from code window to code window when you want to copy and paste or refer back to code on another form.

To view the properties for the project, right-click the project and select Properties. The dialog box displayed is shown in Figure 6-8.

The left side of the dialog box lists the different pages available. Here, you are looking at the General property page. From this page, you can set the name and type of the application, the procedure that should be started when the application is launched, and the Root namespace.

Back in the Solution Explorer windows, you can see that the solution includes four forms and a single module. You can also see the objects that the solution references. The only reference that was added to this solution was the ADO reference. You add references like this by right-clicking the References folder

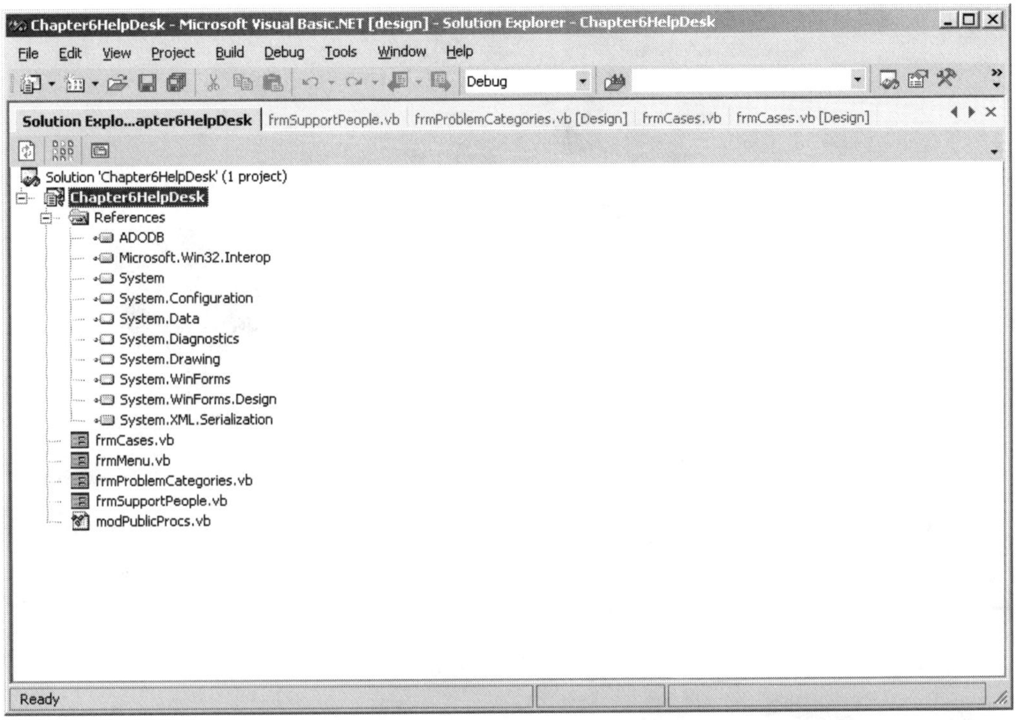

Figure 6-7 *VB.net Solution Explorer*

in the Solution Explorer and clicking Add. You should then see the dialog box displayed in Figure 6-9.

Objects such as ADO and other libraries you may have used in previous versions of Visual Basic are likely to be located on the COM tab.

Modules

modPublicProcs Module

Probably the easiest coding object to make the transition to from earlier versions of VB is the code module. Unlike forms where line after line of never-before-seen code by the VB developer is now exposed, the module code hardly changes. The Help

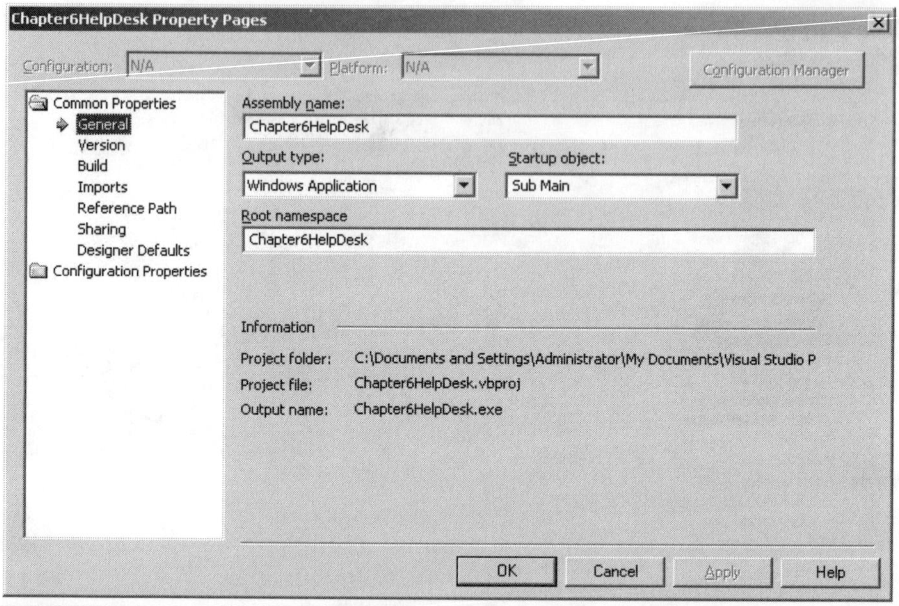

Figure 6-8 *Project Properties*

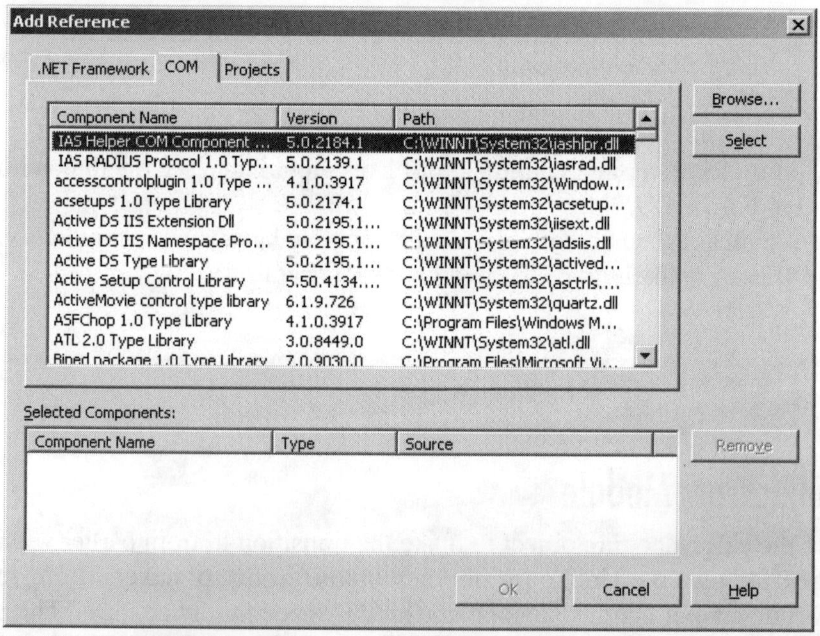

Figure 6-9 *Add Reference dialog box*

Desk front-end VB.net solution includes a single module called modPublicProcs. All the code in that module is as follows:

```
Module modPublicProcs
    Public SQLUserName As String
    Public SQLPassword As String
    Public instfrmMenu As New frmMenu()
    Public Sub Main()
        SQLUserName = InputBox("Please enter your user name.", _
            "Help Desk")
        If SQLUserName = "" Then
            End
        End If
        SQLPassword = InputBox("Please enter your password.", _
            "Help Desk")
        If SQLPassword = "" Then
            End
        End If
        instfrmMenu.ShowDialog()
    End Sub
End Module
```

Start with the opening header of the module:

```
Module modPublicProcs
```

In modules as well as forms, you no longer have a General Declarations section where you can define form- or application-wide variables. You can do that outside of any procedure definition, as we have done here. First, you declare an application-wide variable that will store the name of the user:

```
Public SQLUserName As String
```

and one that will store the password of the user:

```
Public SQLPassword As String
```

You also need an object variable so that you can create an instance of your menu form, which will be called from this module:

```
Public instfrmMenu As New frmMenu()
```

Back in the Project Properties dialog box displayed in Figure 6-8, note that the startup object is set to a procedure called Main. That procedure is defined in this module:

```
Public Sub Main()
```

Within that procedure, you prompt the user for their SQL name:

```
SQLUserName = InputBox("Please enter your user name.", _
      "Help Desk")
```

If they left it blank or clicked Cancel, your string would be empty:

```
If SQLUserName = "" Then
```

and you exit the application:

```
End
```

Otherwise, you prompt the user for their password:

```
SQLPassword = InputBox("Please enter your password.", _
      "Help Desk")
```

Again, you check to see whether they clicked Cancel:

```
If SQLPassword = "" Then
```

and exit if they did:

```
End
```

Otherwise, you can open and display the menu form:

```
instfrmMenu.ShowDialog()
```

frmMenu Form

Differing from modules greatly, VB.net exposes the developer to huge amounts of code that you never saw before. In this section, you will review all the code that you added to a form, as well as the code that the compiler automatically added on its own.

You do this on a simple form, the Menu form, which has far fewer objects on it than any of the forms in this application. Here is all the code for the Menu form:

```
Option Explicit On
Option Strict Off
Imports System.Drawing
Imports System.WinForms
Imports System.ComponentModel
Public Class frmMenu
    Inherits System.WinForms.Form
    Public Sub New()
        MyBase.New
        frmMenu = Me
        'This call is required by the Win Form Designer.
        InitializeComponent()
       'TODO: Add any initialization after the InitializeComponent() call
    End Sub
    'Form overrides dispose to clean up the component list.
    Overrides Public Sub Dispose()
        MyBase.Dispose
        components.Dispose
    End Sub
#Region " Windows Form Designer generated code "
    'Required by the Windows Form Designer
    Private components As System.ComponentModel.Container
    Private WithEvents cmdProductCategories As System.WinForms.Button
    Private WithEvents cmdExit As System.WinForms.Button
    Private WithEvents cmdSupportPeople As System.WinForms.Button
    Private WithEvents cmdCases As System.WinForms.Button
        Private WithEvents Label2 As System.WinForms.Label
        Private WithEvents Label1 As System.WinForms.Label
    Dim WithEvents frmMenu As System.WinForms.Form
    'NOTE: The following procedure is required by the Windows Form Designer
    'It can be modified using the Windows Form Designer.
    'Do not modify it using the code editor.
    Private Sub InitializeComponent()
        Me.components = New System.ComponentModel.Container()
        Me.Label2 = New System.WinForms.Label()
        Me.cmdProductCategories = New System.WinForms.Button()
        Me.cmdSupportPeople = New System.WinForms.Button()
        Me.cmdCases = New System.WinForms.Button()
        Me.Label1 = New System.WinForms.Label()
        Me.cmdExit = New System.WinForms.Button()
        '@design Me.TrayHeight = 0
        '@design Me.TrayLargeIcon = False
        '@design Me.TrayAutoArrange = True
        Label2.Location = New System.Drawing.Point(8, 88)
        Label2.Text = "Menu"
        Label2.Size = New System.Drawing.Size(585, 49)
```

```
        Label2.RightToLeft = System.WinForms.RightToLeft.No
        Label2.ForeColor = System.Drawing.SystemColors.MenuText
        Label2.Font = New System.Drawing.Font("Arial", 21.75!,
System.Drawing.FontStyle.Bold)
        Label2.TabIndex = 1
        Label2.BackColor = System.Drawing.SystemColors.Control
        Label2.TextAlign = System.WinForms.HorizontalAlignment.Center
        cmdProductCategories.Location = New System.Drawing.Point(224, 248)
        cmdProductCategories.BackColor = System.Drawing.SystemColors.Control
        cmdProductCategories.Size = New System.Drawing.Size(161, 25)
        cmdProductCategories.TabIndex = 5
        cmdProductCategories.RightToLeft = System.WinForms.RightToLeft.No
        cmdProductCategories.Text = "Problem Categories"
        cmdSupportPeople.Location = New System.Drawing.Point(224, 200)
        cmdSupportPeople.BackColor = System.Drawing.SystemColors.Control
        cmdSupportPeople.Size = New System.Drawing.Size(161, 25)
        cmdSupportPeople.TabIndex = 3
        cmdSupportPeople.RightToLeft = System.WinForms.RightToLeft.No
        cmdSupportPeople.Text = "Support People"
        cmdCases.Location = New System.Drawing.Point(224, 152)
        cmdCases.BackColor = System.Drawing.SystemColors.Control
        cmdCases.Size = New System.Drawing.Size(161, 25)
        cmdCases.TabIndex = 2
        cmdCases.RightToLeft = System.WinForms.RightToLeft.No
        cmdCases.Text = "Cases"
        Label1.Location = New System.Drawing.Point(8, 16)
        Label1.Text = "Chapter 6 Help Desk"
        Label1.Size = New System.Drawing.Size(585, 49)
        Label1.RightToLeft = System.WinForms.RightToLeft.No
        Label1.ForeColor = System.Drawing.SystemColors.Highlight
        Label1.Font = New System.Drawing.Font("Arial", 26.25!,
System.Drawing.FontStyle.Bold)
        Label1.TabIndex = 0
        Label1.BackColor = System.Drawing.SystemColors.Control
        Label1.TextAlign = System.WinForms.HorizontalAlignment.Center
        cmdExit.Location = New System.Drawing.Point(224, 296)
        cmdExit.BackColor = System.Drawing.SystemColors.Control
        cmdExit.Size = New System.Drawing.Size(161, 25)
        cmdExit.TabIndex = 4
        cmdExit.RightToLeft = System.WinForms.RightToLeft.No
        cmdExit.Text = "Exit"
        Me.Text = "frmMenu"
        Me.StartPosition = System.WinForms.FormStartPosition.CenterScreen
        Me.AutoScaleBaseSize = New System.Drawing.Size(5, 13)
        Me.BorderStyle = System.WinForms.FormBorderStyle.FixedDialog
        Me.ControlBox = False
```

```
        Me.ClientSize = New System.Drawing.Size(610, 335)
        Me.Controls.Add(cmdProductCategories)
        Me.Controls.Add(cmdExit)
        Me.Controls.Add(cmdSupportPeople)
        Me.Controls.Add(cmdCases)
        Me.Controls.Add(Label2)
        Me.Controls.Add(Label1)
    End Sub
#End Region
    Protected Sub cmdProductCategories_Click(ByVal sender As Object, ByVal e As
System.EventArgs)
        Dim MyForm As New frmProductCategories()
        MyForm.show()
        Me.Hide()
    End Sub
    Protected Sub cmdSupportPeople_Click(ByVal sender As Object, ByVal e As
System.EventArgs)
        Dim MyForm As New frmSupportPeople()
        MyForm.show()
        Me.Hide()
    End Sub
    Protected Sub cmdCases_Click(ByVal sender As Object, ByVal e As
System.EventArgs)
        Dim MyForm As New frmCases()
        MyForm.show()
        Me.Hide()
    End Sub
    Protected Sub cmdExit_Click(ByVal sender As Object, ByVal e As
System.EventArgs)
        End
    End Sub
End Class
```

You actually start out with two lines of your own. The first one is very familiar. You start by telling the compiler that you will declare all your variables:

```
Option Explicit On
```

The next compiler option is new. Vb.net is picky about allowing you to do type conversions. For example, when you concatenate a number, a string, and a date into a single string, you are doing type conversions. By default Vb.net does not allow most of those conversions. I prefer to still do them that way, so I turn off the strict conversion rules:

```
Option Strict Off
```

Now you leave your code and start looking at the code added by the compiler. First, the compiler notes libraries that are linked to this form. That means their code is accessible from your form:

```
Imports System.Drawing
Imports System.WinForms
Imports System.ComponentModel
```

Now you enter the contents of the code for this form, which, like all forms, is defined as a class:

```
Public Class frmMenu
```

The form is based on the template of a standard Windows form:

```
Inherits System.WinForms.Form
```

Note that this point in the code is like your old General Declarations section. So here you would place any form-wide Private variables.

When the component is first instantiated, that is, when the form is first opened, the New procedure fires. This is similar to the Load event from previous versions of Visual Basic. So, here you will place code that you want to run when the form is first called, such as setting up database connections:

```
Public Sub New()
      MyBase.New
      frmMenu = Me
      'This call is required by the Win Form Designer.
      InitializeComponent()
      'TODO: Add any initialization after the InitializeComponent() call
End Sub
```

This clean-up procedure fires instead of the one inherited from the base class:

```
'Form overrides dispose to clean up the component list.
Overrides Public Sub Dispose()
      MyBase.Dispose
      components.Dispose
End Sub
```

A region can be used in the design environment to break the code into a logical group that you can expand and contract through the code hierarchy:

```
#Region " Windows Form Designer generated code "
```

Next, the compiler instantiates objects that will be placed on this form:

```
'Required by the Windows Form Designer
Private components As System.ComponentModel.Container
Private WithEvents cmdProductCategories As System.WinForms.Button
Private WithEvents cmdExit As System.WinForms.Button
Private WithEvents cmdSupportPeople As System.WinForms.Button
Private WithEvents cmdCases As System.WinForms.Button
Private WithEvents Label2 As System.WinForms.Label
Private WithEvents Label1 As System.WinForms.Label
Dim WithEvents frmMenu As System.WinForms.Form
'NOTE: The following procedure is required by the Windows Form Designer
'It can be modified using the Windows Form Designer.
'Do not modify it using the code editor.
Private Sub InitializeComponent()
Me.components = New System.ComponentModel.Container()
Me.Label2 = New System.WinForms.Label()
Me.cmdProductCategories = New System.WinForms.Button()
Me.cmdSupportPeople = New System.WinForms.Button()
Me.cmdCases = New System.WinForms.Button()
Me.Label1 = New System.WinForms.Label()
Me.cmdExit = New System.WinForms.Button()
```

Then it goes through each of those objects placed on the form and applies properties to them that are different than those inherited when they are instantiated:

```
Label2.Location = New System.Drawing.Point(8, 88)
Label2.Text = "Menu"
Label2.Size = New System.Drawing.Size(585, 49)
Label2.RightToLeft = System.WinForms.RightToLeft.No
Label2.ForeColor = System.Drawing.SystemColors.MenuText
Label2.Font = New System.Drawing.Font("Arial", 21.75!,
System.Drawing.FontStyle.Bold)
Label2.TabIndex = 1
Label2.BackColor = System.Drawing.SystemColors.Control
Label2.TextAlign = System.WinForms.HorizontalAlignment.Center
cmdProductCategories.Location = New System.Drawing.Point(224, 248)
cmdProductCategories.BackColor = System.Drawing.SystemColors.Control
cmdProductCategories.Size = New System.Drawing.Size(161, 25)
cmdProductCategories.TabIndex = 5
cmdProductCategories.RightToLeft = System.WinForms.RightToLeft.No
cmdProductCategories.Text = "Problem Categories"
cmdSupportPeople.Location = New System.Drawing.Point(224, 200)
cmdSupportPeople.BackColor = System.Drawing.SystemColors.Control
```

```
cmdSupportPeople.Size = New System.Drawing.Size(161, 25)
cmdSupportPeople.TabIndex = 3
cmdSupportPeople.RightToLeft = System.WinForms.RightToLeft.No
cmdSupportPeople.Text = "Support People"
cmdCases.Location = New System.Drawing.Point(224, 152)
cmdCases.BackColor = System.Drawing.SystemColors.Control
cmdCases.Size = New System.Drawing.Size(161, 25)
cmdCases.TabIndex = 2
cmdCases.RightToLeft = System.WinForms.RightToLeft.No
cmdCases.Text = "Cases"
Label1.Location = New System.Drawing.Point(8, 16)
Label1.Text = "Chapter 6 Help Desk"
Label1.Size = New System.Drawing.Size(585, 49)
Label1.RightToLeft = System.WinForms.RightToLeft.No
Label1.ForeColor = System.Drawing.SystemColors.Highlight
Label1.Font = New System.Drawing.Font("Arial", 26.25!,
System.Drawing.FontStyle.Bold)
Label1.TabIndex = 0
Label1.BackColor = System.Drawing.SystemColors.Control
Label1.TextAlign = System.WinForms.HorizontalAlignment.Center
cmdExit.Location = New System.Drawing.Point(224, 296)
cmdExit.BackColor = System.Drawing.SystemColors.Control
cmdExit.Size = New System.Drawing.Size(161, 25)
cmdExit.TabIndex = 4
cmdExit.RightToLeft = System.WinForms.RightToLeft.No
cmdExit.Text = "Exit"
```

It also sets up properties of the form that differ from those that were inherited:

```
Me.Text = "frmMenu"
Me.StartPosition = System.WinForms.FormStartPosition.CenterScreen
Me.AutoScaleBaseSize = New System.Drawing.Size(5, 13)
Me.BorderStyle = System.WinForms.FormBorderStyle.FixedDialog
Me.ControlBox = False
Me.ClientSize = New System.Drawing.Size(610, 335)
```

and places the controls on the form:

```
Me.Controls.Add(cmdProductCategories)
Me.Controls.Add(cmdExit)
Me.Controls.Add(cmdSupportPeople)
Me.Controls.Add(cmdCases)
Me.Controls.Add(Label2)
Me.Controls.Add(Label1)
```

You then end this compiler-created region:

```
    End Sub
#End Region
```

and finally enter the section that contains your own procedures. This code block fires when the Product Categories button is clicked:

```
Protected Sub cmdProductCategories_Click(ByVal sender As Object,
ByVal e As System.EventArgs)
```

It first instantiates the Categories form:

```
Dim MyForm As New frmProductCategories()
```

and then displays it:

```
MyForm.show()
```

You then hide the Menu form:

```
Me.Hide()
```

This procedure fires when the Support People button is clicked:

```
Protected Sub cmdSupportPeople_Click(ByVal sender As Object,
ByVal e As System.EventArgs)
```

It instantiates a copy of your Support People form:

```
Dim MyForm As New frmSupportPeople()
```

displays that form:

```
MyForm.show()
```

and hides the Menu form:

```
Me.Hide()
```

This procedure fires when the Cases button is clicked:

```
Protected Sub cmdCases_Click(ByVal sender As Object,
ByVal e As System.EventArgs)
```

It creates a copy of the Cases form:

```
Dim MyForm As New frmCases()
```

then shows that form:

```
MyForm.show()
```

and hides this form:

```
Me.Hide()
```

The last procedure ends the application when the Exit button is clicked:

```
Protected Sub cmdExit_Click(ByVal sender As Object,
ByVal e As System.EventArgs)
        End
End Sub
```

frmCases Form

The code on the Cases form allows the user to manipulate the case records. At the top of the class, two compiler options are set. The first tells the compiler that you will declare all your variables:

```
Option Explicit On
```

The other tells the compiler that you do not wish to use the strict conversion rules of VB.net:

```
Option Strict Off
```

Right after the class definition, you enter the section of the code where you can define form-wide variables that were pointed out in the preceding section of this chapter. Here you will find this code:

```
Private MyConnection As New ADODB.Connection()
Private CurrentID As Long = 0
```

You need a form-wide database connection so that you can make the calls to the server:

```
Private MyConnection As New ADODB.Connection()
```

And a variable that will store the ID of the current case number, which is set to a default value of 0:

```
Private CurrentID As Long = 0
```

The form contains a few user-defined procedures that you call from other locations in your code. The first populates the Problem Categories combo box so that it contains a list of all the problem categories.

```
Public Sub UpdatePCCombo()
    Dim RSAllCategories As ADODB.Recordset
    RSAllCategories = MyConnection.Execute("Exec ProblemCategoryList")
    cmbCategory.Items.Clear()
    Do Until RSAllCategories.EOF
        cmbCategory.Items.Add
(RSAllCategories.Fields("ProblemCategory").Value)
        RSAllCategories.MoveNext()
    Loop
End Sub
```

To do that, you will need a Recordset object:

```
Dim RSAllCategories As ADODB.Recordset
```

which is set to the return of a call to your ProblemCategoryList stored procedure:

```
RSAllCategories = MyConnection.Execute("Exec ProblemCategoryList")
```

You then clear the contents of your combo box:

```
cmbCategory.Items.Clear()
```

and enter a loop so that you can process each record:

```
Do Until RSAllCategories.EOF
```

The name of each problem category is added to the list:

```
cmbCategory.Items.Add (RSAllCategories.Fields("ProblemCategory").Value)
```

before you move on to process the next record:

```
RSAllCategories.MoveNext()
Loop
```

The next user-defined procedure populates the Support Person combo box.

```
Public Sub UpdateSPCombo()
    Dim RSAllSupportPeople As ADODB.Recordset
    RSAllSupportPeople = MyConnection.Execute("Exec SupportPersonList")
    cmbSupportPerson.Items.Clear()
    Do Until RSAllSupportPeople.EOF
        cmbSupportPerson.Items.Add (RSAllSupportPeople.Fields("TheName").Value _
            & RSAllSupportPeople.Fields("SupportPersonID").Value)
        RSAllSupportPeople.MoveNext()
    Loop
End Sub
```

The procedure requires a Recordset object:

```
Dim RSAllSupportPeople As ADODB.Recordset
```

which is set to the return of the call to the SupportPersonList stored procedure:

```
RSAllSupportPeople = MyConnection.Execute("Exec SupportPersonList")
```

After the call, you clear the contents of the combo box:

```
cmbSupportPerson.Items.Clear()
```

and enter a loop so that each of the Support People records can be processed:

```
Do Until RSAllSupportPeople.EOF
```

You add each of the records to the combo box. Remember that the name of the support person is set to a length of 100. So, even though the ID is concatenated to the entry in the list, it will not be seen because it is off the edge of the viewable portion of the list. But in code you will be able to retrieve that number:

```
cmbSupportPerson.Items.Add
(RSAllSupportPeople.Fields("TheName").Value _
      & RSAllSupportPeople.Fields("SupportPersonID").Value)
```

You then move on to process the next record:

```
      RSAllSupportPeople.MoveNext()
Loop
```

The next procedure is used to update the contents of the Progress Notes list box on the bottom of the form.

```
Public Sub UpdatePNList()
    Dim RSPN As ADODB.Recordset
    RSPN = MyConnection.Execute("Exec ProgressNoteList " _
        & CurrentID)
    lstProgressNotes.Items.Clear()
    Do Until RSPN.EOF
        lstProgressNotes.Items.Add (RSPN.Fields("TheNote").Value)
        RSPN.MoveNext()
    Loop
End Sub
```

The procedure requires a Recordset object:

```
Dim RSPN As ADODB.Recordset
```

which will contain all the notes for the current case:

```
RSPN = MyConnection.Execute("Exec ProgressNoteList " _
      & CurrentID)
```

You then clear the list box:

```
lstProgressNotes.Items.Clear()
```

and enter a loop to process each of the records returned from the stored procedure:

```
Do Until RSPN.EOF
```

Each record is added as an Item to the Items collection of the list box control:

```
lstProgressNotes.Items.Add (RSPN.Fields("TheNote").Value)
```

before you move on to process the next record:

```
    RSPN.MoveNext()
Loop
```

The next procedure is used to clear the contents of the form.

```
Public Sub ClearForm()
    CurrentID = 0
    txtFirstName.Text = ""
    txtLastName.Text = ""
    txtPhoneNumber.Text = ""
    txtEmailAddress.Text = ""
    lstProgressNotes.Items.Clear()
End Sub
```

First, you clear the ID of the current record:

```
CurrentID = 0
```

then you clear the contents of the text boxes:

```
txtFirstName.Text = ""
txtLastName.Text = ""
txtPhoneNumber.Text = ""
txtEmailAddress.Text = ""
```

as well as the list box:

```
lstProgressNotes.Items.Clear()
```

The next procedure is used to populate the form with a record from the Cases table.

```
Public Sub PopulateSPRecord(ByVal TheDirection As String)
    Dim RSCase As New ADODB.Recordset()
    RSCase = MyConnection.Execute("Exec CaseRecord '" _
        & TheDirection & "', " & CurrentID)
    If RSCase.EOF Then
        RSCase = MyConnection.Execute("Exec CaseRecord '" _
            & "FIRST" & "', " & CurrentID)
        If RSCase.EOF Then
            ClearForm()
        Else
            CurrentID = RSCase.Fields("CaseID").Value
            cmbSupportPerson.Text = RSCase.Fields("SupportName").Value _
                & RSCase.Fields("SupportPersonID").Value
            cmbCategory.Text = RSCase.Fields("ProblemCategory").Value
            cmbStatus.Text = RSCase.Fields("Status").Value
            txtFirstName.Text = RSCase.Fields("FirstName").Value
            txtLastName.Text = RSCase.Fields("LastName").Value
            txtPhoneNumber.Text = RSCase.Fields("PhoneNumber").Value
            txtEmailAddress.Text = RSCase.Fields("EmailAddress").Value
            UpdatePNList()
        End If
    Else
        CurrentID = RSCase.Fields("CaseID").Value
        cmbSupportPerson.Text = RSCase.Fields("SupportName").Value _
            & RSCase.Fields("SupportPersonID").Value
        cmbCategory.Text = RSCase.Fields("ProblemCategory").Value
        cmbStatus.Text = RSCase.Fields("Status").Value
        txtFirstName.Text = RSCase.Fields("FirstName").Value
        txtLastName.Text = RSCase.Fields("LastName").Value
        txtPhoneNumber.Text = RSCase.Fields("PhoneNumber").Value
```

```
        txtEmailAddress.Text = RSCase.Fields("EmailAddress").Value
        UpdatePNList()
    End If
End Sub
```

The procedure requires a single parameter, the direction for the record move:

```
Public Sub PopulateSPRecord(ByVal TheDirection As String)
```

The procedure requires a Recordset object:

```
    Dim RSCase As New ADODB.Recordset()
```

which you use to retrieve the contents of the desired record:

```
RSCase = MyConnection.Execute("Exec CaseRecord '" _
      & TheDirection & "', " & CurrentID)
```

If no record was found through the request, EOF will be set:

```
If RSCase.EOF Then
```

In that case, you attempt to retrieve the first record in the table:

```
RSCase = MyConnection.Execute("Exec CaseRecord '" _
      & "FIRST" & "', " & CurrentID)
```

If EOF is again set:

```
If RSCase.EOF Then
```

there are no Case records. Therefore, you simply clear the form:

```
ClearForm()
```

Otherwise, you have a valid record, the first record. So you set the ID to that returned from the procedure:

```
CurrentID = RSCase.Fields("CaseID").Value
```

and display the values of the fields on the form:

```
cmbSupportPerson.Text = RSCase.Fields("SupportName").Value _
      & RSCase.Fields("SupportPersonID").Value
cmbCategory.Text = RSCase.Fields("ProblemCategory").Value
cmbStatus.Text = RSCase.Fields("Status").Value
txtFirstName.Text = RSCase.Fields("FirstName").Value
txtLastName.Text = RSCase.Fields("LastName").Value
```

```
txtPhoneNumber.Text = RSCase.Fields("PhoneNumber").Value
txtEmailAddress.Text = RSCase.Fields("EmailAddress").Value
```

You also need to update the Progress Notes list box:

```
UpdatePNList()
```

If the code flows here, the initial request for a record was successful:

```
Else
```

So, again you store the ID of the record returned:

```
CurrentID = RSCase.Fields("CaseID").Value
```

populate the controls on the form:

```
cmbSupportPerson.Text = RSCase.Fields("SupportName").Value _
      & RSCase.Fields("SupportPersonID").Value
cmbCategory.Text = RSCase.Fields("ProblemCategory").Value
cmbStatus.Text = RSCase.Fields("Status").Value
txtFirstName.Text = RSCase.Fields("FirstName").Value
txtLastName.Text = RSCase.Fields("LastName").Value
txtPhoneNumber.Text = RSCase.Fields("PhoneNumber").Value
txtEmailAddress.Text = RSCase.Fields("EmailAddress").Value
```

and update the list box:

```
UpdatePNList()
```

When the form is first instantiated, the New procedure fires. The following code was added to that compiler-added procedure.

```
MyConnection.ConnectionString = "driver={SQL Server};" _
      & "server=MyServer;uid=" & SQLUserName _
      & ";pwd=" & SQLPassword & ";" & "database=C6HelpDesk"
MyConnection.Open()
UpdatePCCombo()
UpdateSPCombo()
PopulateSPRecord ("FIRST")
```

Since the code fires when the form is first instantiated, you need to set up your connection object. You first set the connect string:

```
MyConnection.ConnectionString = "driver={SQL Server};" _
     & "server=MyServer;uid=" & SQLUserName _
     & ";pwd=" & SQLPassword & ";" & "database=C6HelpDesk"
```

and then open the connection to the database:

```
MyConnection.Open()
```

You then populate the Problem Categories combo box:

```
UpdatePCCombo()
```

likewise populate the Support Person combo box:

```
UpdateSPCombo()
```

and display the first record on the form:

```
PopulateSPRecord ("FIRST")
```

When the form is closed, the Close event fires.

```
Public Sub frmCases_Closed(ByVal sender As Object,
      ByVal e As System.EventArgs) Handles frmCases.Closed
    MyConnection = Nothing
    instfrmMenu.Show()
End Sub
```

You use that procedure to release your connection object:

```
MyConnection = Nothing
```

and to display the Menu form:

```
instfrmMenu.Show()
```

The next procedure fires when the Move First button is clicked.

```
Public Sub cmdMoveFirst_Click(ByVal sender As Object,
      ByVal e As System.EventArgs) Handles cmdMoveFirst.Click
    PopulateSPRecord ("FIRST")
End Sub
```

The procedure calls your procedure to populate the form with the first record:

```
PopulateSPRecord ("FIRST")
```

When the Move Previous button is clicked, this procedure fires.

```
Public Sub cmdMovePrevious_Click(ByVal sender As Object,
      ByVal e As System.EventArgs) Handles cmdMovePrevious.Click
    PopulateSPRecord ("PREVIOUS")
End Sub
```

It calls your procedure to move you to the previous record:

```
PopulateSPRecord ("PREVIOUS")
```

Similarly, you call the procedure to display the next record when the Move Next button is clicked:

```
Public Sub cmdMoveNext_Click(ByVal sender As Object,
      ByVal e As System.EventArgs) Handles cmdMoveNext.Click
    PopulateSPRecord ("NEXT")
End Sub
```

and do the same for the Move Last button:

```
Public Sub cmdMoveLast_Click(ByVal sender As Object,
      ByVal e As System.EventArgs) Handles cmdMoveLast.Click
    PopulateSPRecord ("LAST")
End Sub
```

The next procedure fires when the Add Progress Note button is clicked. It adds a record to the ProgressNotes table.

```
Protected Sub cmdAddProgressNote_Click(ByVal sender As Object,
      ByVal e As System.EventArgs)
    Dim TheNewNote As String
    TheNewNote = InputBox("Enter the text for the new progress note:", _
        "Help Desk")
    If TheNewNote <> "" Then
        TheNewNote = Replace(TheNewNote, "'", "''")
        MyConnection.Execute ("Exec ProgressNoteAdd " _
            & CurrentID & ", " _
            & "'" & Now & "', " _
            & "'" & SQLUserName & "', " _
            & "'" & TheNewNote & "'")
        UpdatePNList()
    End If
End Sub
```

You need a variable to store the note supplied by the user:

```
Dim TheNewNote As String
```

You then prompt the user for the note:

```
TheNewNote = InputBox("Enter the text for the new progress note:", _
      "Help Desk")
```

If the user did not click Cancel:

```
If TheNewNote <> "" Then
```

you can add the new note. You start by replacing any ' characters with '' so that they will be stored properly in the database:

```
TheNewNote = Replace(TheNewNote, "'", "''")
```

Then you call your stored procedure to add a new progress record:

```
MyConnection.Execute ("Exec ProgressNoteAdd " _
      & CurrentID & ", " _
      & "'" & Now & "', " _
      & "'" & SQLUserName & "', " _
      & "'" & TheNewNote & "'")
```

and call your procedure to repopulate the list box:

```
UpdatePNList()
```

When the Add button is clicked, this code block fires.

```
Public Sub cmdAdd_Click(ByVal sender As Object,
      ByVal e As System.EventArgs) Handles cmdAdd.Click
    Dim RSNewID As ADODB.Recordset
    Dim TheFirstName As String
    Dim TheLastName As String
    Dim ThePhoneNumber As String
    Dim TheEmailAddress As String
    Dim TheStatus As String
    Dim TheProblemCategory As String
    TheFirstName = Replace(txtFirstName.Text, "'", "''")
    TheLastName = Replace(txtLastName.Text, "'", "''")
    ThePhoneNumber = Replace(txtPhoneNumber.Text, "'", "''")
    TheEmailAddress = Replace(txtEmailAddress.Text, "'", "''")
```

```
    TheStatus = Replace(cmbStatus.Text, "'", "''")
    TheProblemCategory = Replace(cmbCategory.Text, "'", "''")
    RSNewID = MyConnection.Execute("Exec CaseAdd " _
        & "'" & TheProblemCategory & "', " _
        & "'" & Mid(cmbSupportPerson.Text, 101) & "', " _
        & "'" & TheStatus & "', " _
        & "'" & TheFirstName & "', " _
        & "'" & TheLastName & "', " _
        & "'" & ThePhoneNumber & "', " _
        & "'" & TheEmailAddress & "'")
    CurrentID = RSNewID.Fields("TheNewID").Value
End Sub
```

You will need a Recordset object:

```
Dim RSNewID As ADODB.Recordset
```

as well as strings to store the contents in the text boxes:

```
Dim TheFirstName As String
Dim TheLastName As String
Dim ThePhoneNumber As String
Dim TheEmailAddress As String
Dim TheStatus As String
Dim TheProblemCategory As String
```

You then set up those variables so that they contain the values from the text boxes with the ' character converted to a '':

```
TheFirstName = Replace(txtFirstName.Text, "'", "''")
TheLastName = Replace(txtLastName.Text, "'", "''")
ThePhoneNumber = Replace(txtPhoneNumber.Text, "'", "''")
TheEmailAddress = Replace(txtEmailAddress.Text, "'", "''")
TheStatus = Replace(cmbStatus.Text, "'", "''")
TheProblemCategory = Replace(cmbCategory.Text, "'", "''")
```

The call is then made to your stored procedure to add a new case record:

```
RSNewID = MyConnection.Execute("Exec CaseAdd " _
    & "'" & TheProblemCategory & "', " _
    & "'" & Mid(cmbSupportPerson.Text, 101) & "', " _
    & "'" & TheStatus & "', " _
```

```
    & "'" & TheFirstName & "', " _
    & "'" & TheLastName & "', " _
    & "'" & ThePhoneNumber & "', " _
    & "'" & TheEmailAddress & "'")
```

The ID of the new record is returned from the stored procedure and is placed in your form-wide variable:

```
CurrentID = RSNewID.Fields("TheNewID").Value
```

When the Update button is clicked, this event fires.

```
Public Sub cmdUpdate_Click(ByVal sender As Object,
      ByVal e As System.EventArgs) Handles cmdUpdate.Click
    Dim TheFirstName As String
    Dim TheLastName As String
    Dim ThePhoneNumber As String
    Dim TheEmailAddress As String
    Dim TheStatus As String
    Dim TheProblemCategory As String
    TheFirstName = Replace(txtFirstName.Text, "'", "''")
    TheLastName = Replace(txtLastName.Text, "'", "''")
    ThePhoneNumber = Replace(txtPhoneNumber.Text, "'", "''")
    TheEmailAddress = Replace(txtEmailAddress.Text, "'", "''")
    TheStatus = Replace(cmbStatus.Text, "'", "''")
    TheProblemCategory = Replace(cmbCategory.Text, "'", "''")
    If CurrentID = 0 Then
        MsgBox("You are not in an active record!", _
            Microsoft.VisualBasic.MsgBoxStyle.Exclamation, "Help
Desk")
    Else
        MyConnection.Execute ("Exec CaseUpdate " _
            & CurrentID & ", " _
            & "'" & TheProblemCategory & "', " _
            & "'" & Mid(cmbSupportPerson.Text, 101) & "', " _
            & "'" & TheStatus & "', " _
            & "'" & TheFirstName & "', " _
            & "'" & TheLastName & "', " _
            & "'" & ThePhoneNumber & "', " _
            & "'" & TheEmailAddress & "'")
    End If
End Sub
```

You start by declaring variables that will store the values for the updated fields:

```
Dim TheFirstName As String
Dim TheLastName As String
Dim ThePhoneNumber As String
Dim TheEmailAddress As String
Dim TheStatus As String
Dim TheProblemCategory As String
```

Into those variables you place the contents of the text boxes with any ' characters converted:

```
TheFirstName = Replace(txtFirstName.Text, "'", "''")
TheLastName = Replace(txtLastName.Text, "'", "''")
ThePhoneNumber = Replace(txtPhoneNumber.Text, "'", "''")
TheEmailAddress = Replace(txtEmailAddress.Text, "'", "''")
TheStatus = Replace(cmbStatus.Text, "'", "''")
TheProblemCategory = Replace(cmbCategory.Text, "'", "''")
```

But before updating the record, you make sure that you are on a current record:

```
If CurrentID = 0 Then
```

If not, you display an error message to the user:

```
MsgBox("You are not in an active record!", _
      Microsoft.VisualBasic.MsgBoxStyle.Exclamation, "Help Desk")
```

Otherwise, you can update the desired record:

```
MyConnection.Execute ("Exec CaseUpdate " _
      & CurrentID & ", " _
      & "'" & TheProblemCategory & "', " _
      & "'" & Mid(cmbSupportPerson.Text, 101) & "', " _
      & "'" & TheStatus & "', " _
      & "'" & TheFirstName & "', " _
      & "'" & TheLastName & "', " _
      & "'" & ThePhoneNumber & "', " _
      & "'" & TheEmailAddress & "'")
```

When the Delete button is clicked, this code block fires.

```
Public Sub cmdDelete_Click(ByVal sender As Object,
      ByVal e As System.EventArgs) Handles cmdDelete.Click
    If CurrentID = 0 Then
        ClearForm()
    Else
        MyConnection.Execute ("Exec CaseDelete " _
            & CurrentID)
        PopulateSPRecord ("FIRST")
    End If
End Sub
```

First, you make sure you are not in Add mode:

```
If CurrentID = 0 Then
```

If you are, you simply need to clear the form:

```
ClearForm()
```

Otherwise, you can delete the current record:

```
MyConnection.Execute ("Exec CaseDelete " _
      & CurrentID)
```

and display another record on the form:

```
PopulateSPRecord ("FIRST")
```

frmSupportPeople Form and frmProblemCategories Form

The code on the Support People form and on the Problem Categories form is nearly identical to the code on the Cases form. Refer to the "frmCases Form" section when reviewing these forms.

CHAPTER

7

Network Management

IN THIS CHAPTER:

C7SQLObjects.sql

Computers.txt

HardwareItems.txt

ComputerHardware.txt

DeviceTypes.txt

Devices.txt

Chapter7NetworkManagement.vbproj

In this chapter, you will look at another solution that uses SQL Server as the back end and Visual Basic.Net as the front end. The solution allows the user to track information about computers in their network.

Tracking Computers, Hardware, and Network Devices

As you review examples using SQL Server and Visual Basic.Net, note that the front-end portion of the solution was developed with Visual Studio.Net Beta 1. So some of the code and techniques used may need to be changed as Microsoft moves toward the final release of the product.

Application Walk-Through

When the user first launches the front-end application, they are asked to enter their user name and password. This information is used to log them into the SQL Server database. If the user enters this information, they are then presented with the menu displayed in Figure 7-1.

From the Menu form, the user can access the other four major areas of the site. As you will see when you look at the code, each time one of the buttons is clicked, a new instance of that form is displayed. Therefore, the user can actually open more than one copy of the same form, allowing them to compare information across records easily.

When the user clicks Computers, they are presented with the form displayed in Figure 7-2.

The user manages the computers on their network with the Computers form. The arrow buttons on the bottom of the form allow the user to navigate through the different computer records. The other buttons at the bottom of the form allow the user to add, update, or delete the current record, as well as clear the contents of the form in preparation for adding a new record.

Toward the bottom of the form, the user is presented with a list of hardware that the current computer contains. If the user wants to see the full description of a given hardware item, they can double-click it in the list. When they do that, they see the description of the item as is displayed in Figure 7-3.

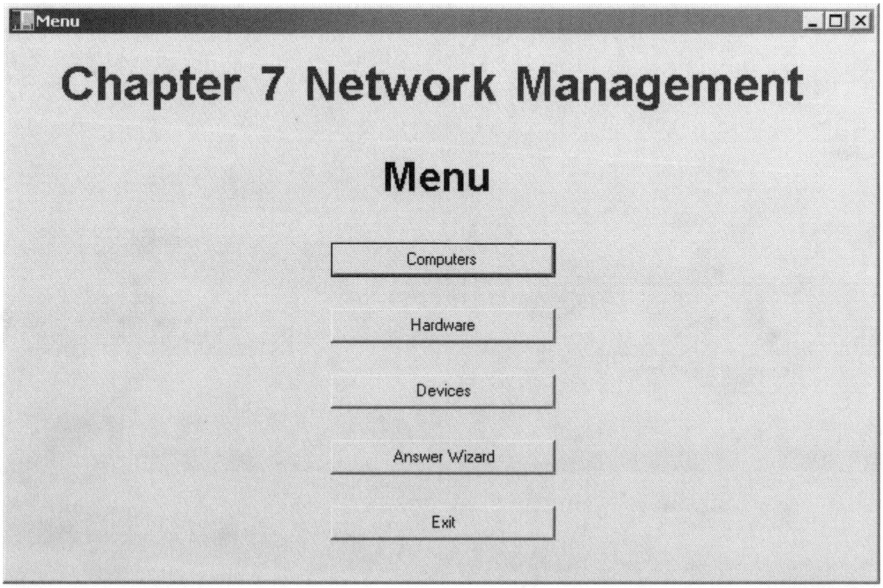

Figure 7-1 *Menu form*

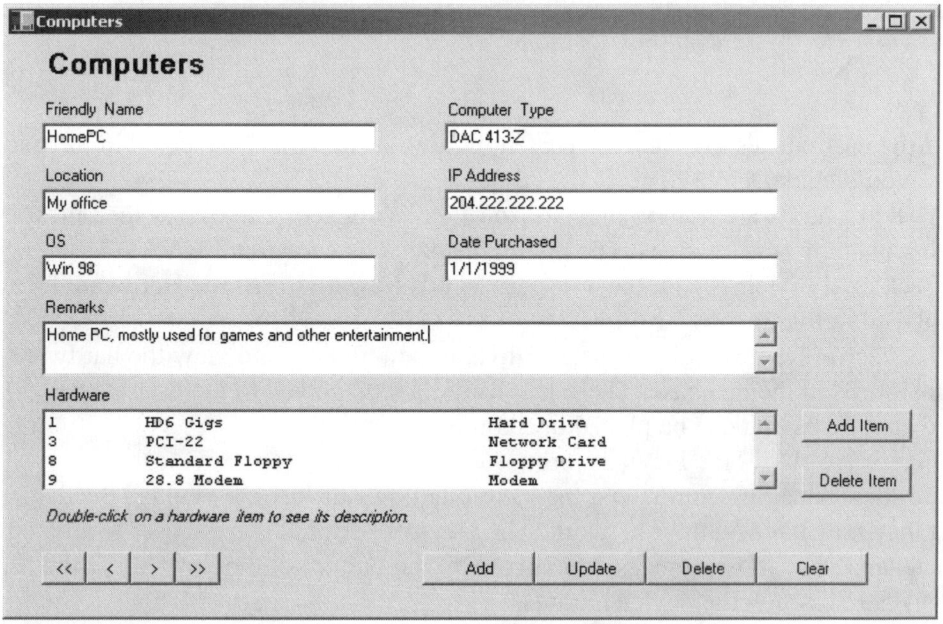

Figure 7-2 *Computers form*

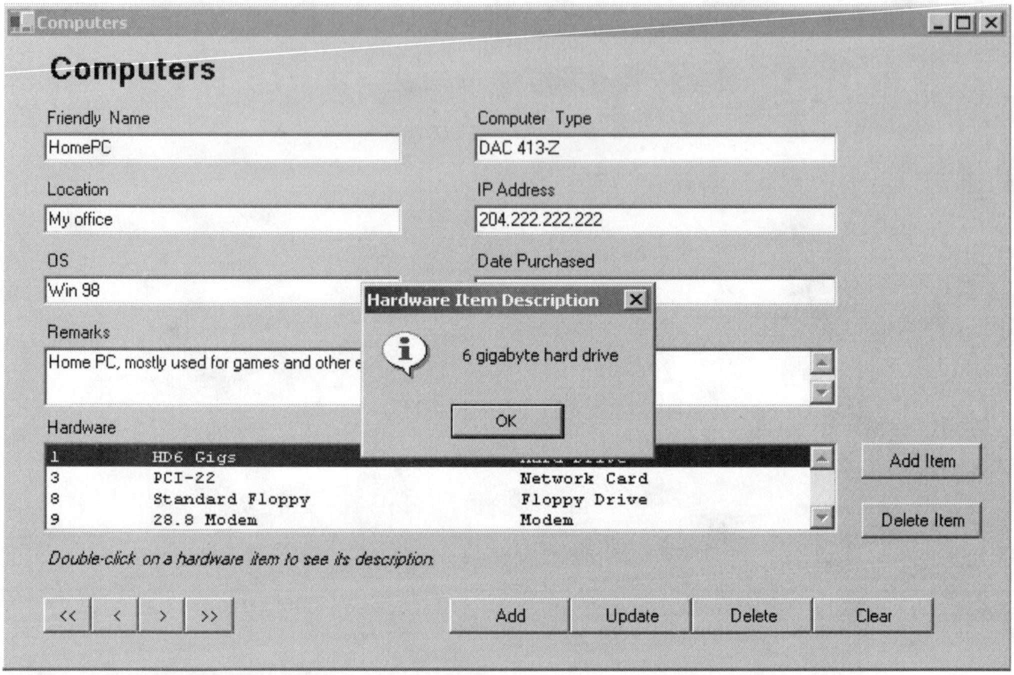

Figure 7-3 *Hardware item description*

If the user wishes to delete the current hardware item that is selected in the list, they would click Delete Item.

To add a hardware item to the list, Add Item is clicked. The user is then presented with a list of hardware items. The dialog displayed is shown in Figure 7-4.

Back on the Main menu, the user can click Hardware to see the Hardware form displayed in Figure 7-5.

The Hardware form allows the user to add, edit, delete, and view the hardware items stored in the database. These items are then displayed to the user as the hardware items that can be placed in a computer.

Figure 7-6 shows the Devices form.

Besides managing computers, the solution allows the user to manage the devices that they may have on their network. The Devices form allows the user to add, edit, delete, and view those devices. The arrows at the bottom of the form allow the user to navigate through the device records.

Note the "+" button on the form. When it is clicked, the user sees the dialog box displayed in Figure 7-7.

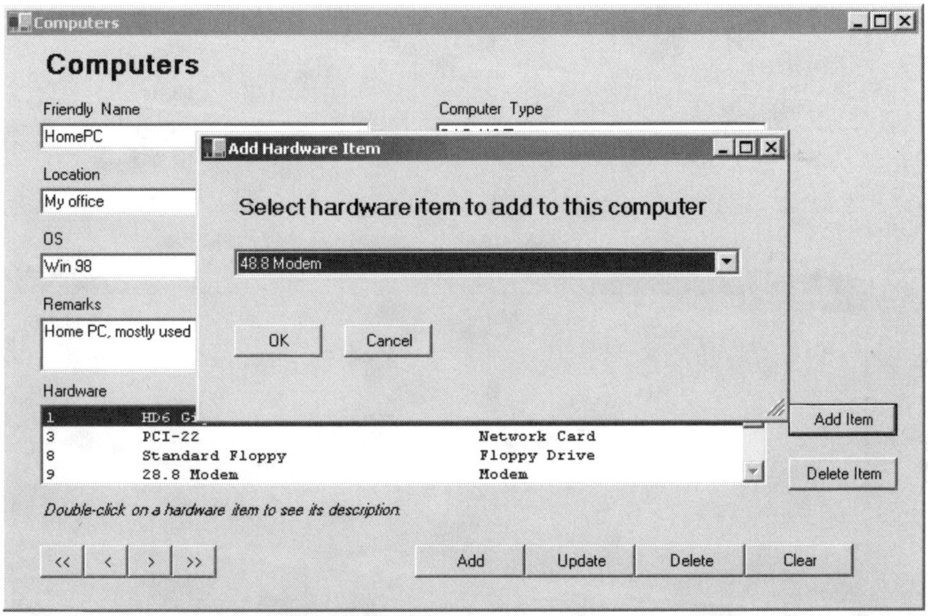

Figure 7-4 *Add Hardware Item dialog box*

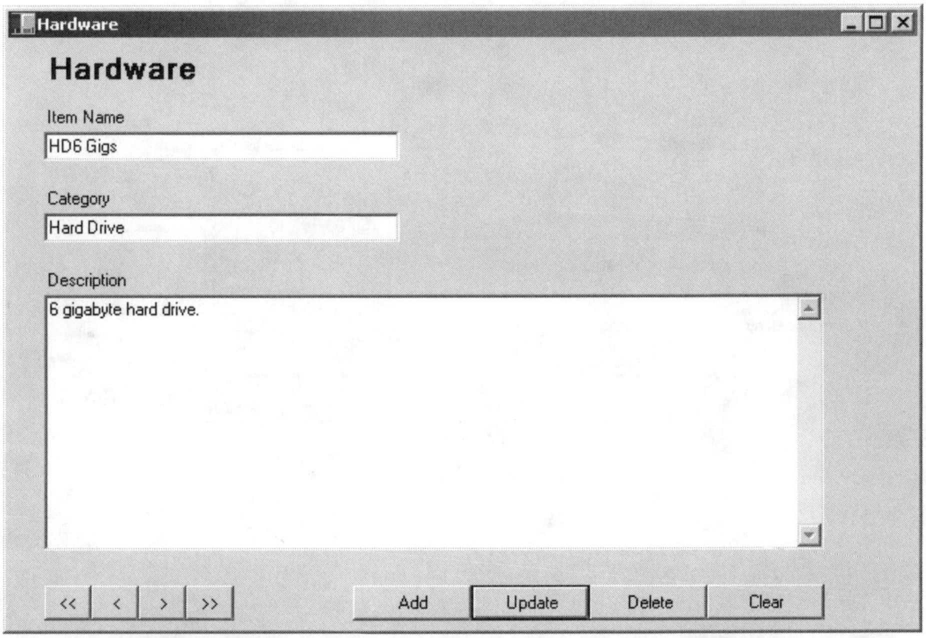

Figure 7-5 *Hardware form*

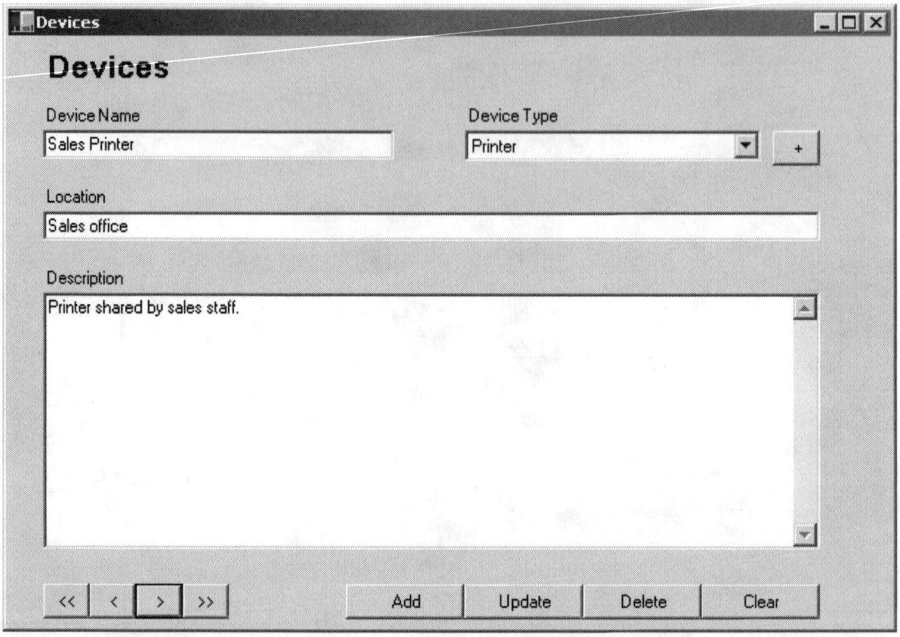

Figure 7-6 *Devices form*

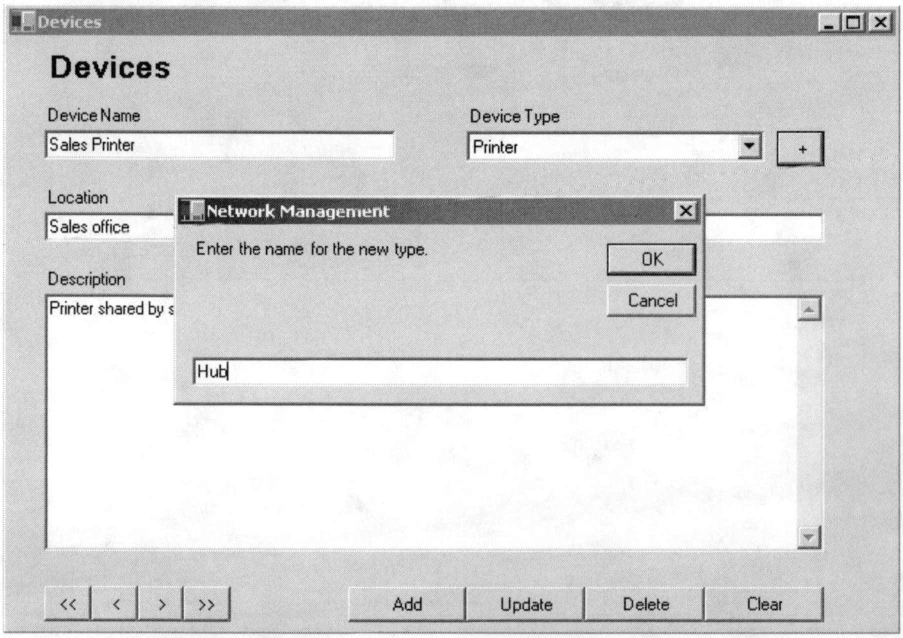

Figure 7-7 *Device Type dialog box*

Each of the devices is of a specific type. The Device Type list displays those different types. This dialog allows the user to add a new device type that is then displayed in the list.

The other form that is part of this application is the Answer Wizard form. That form is displayed in Figure 7-8.

The Answer Wizard is really a reporting tool. It provides a way for you to report summary information about the network to the user. The Wizard can display one of three reports.

The user selects the report from the list and then sees the results of that report when the Ask button is clicked. The reports display the results of the Group By Views query.

In this example the user sees the number of computers of each operating system that they have on their network. Another report is displayed in Figure 7-9.

In this report the user sees the number of devices of each type that they have on their network. A third report shows the number of computers of each type that they have on their network. As you will see when you look at the code, the Column names are actually the names of the output fields in the view.

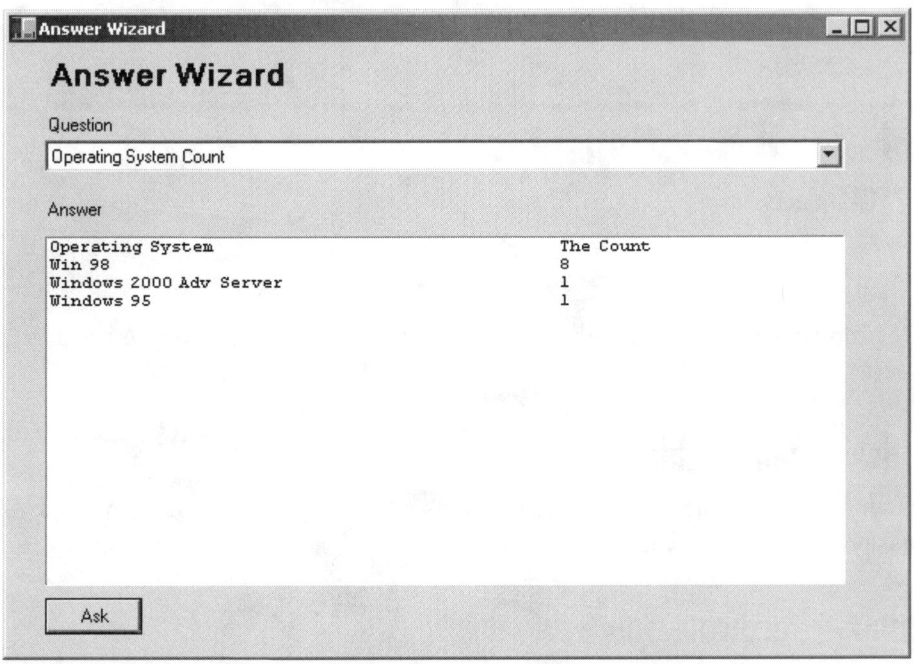

Figure 7-8 *Answer Wizard with Operating System Count report*

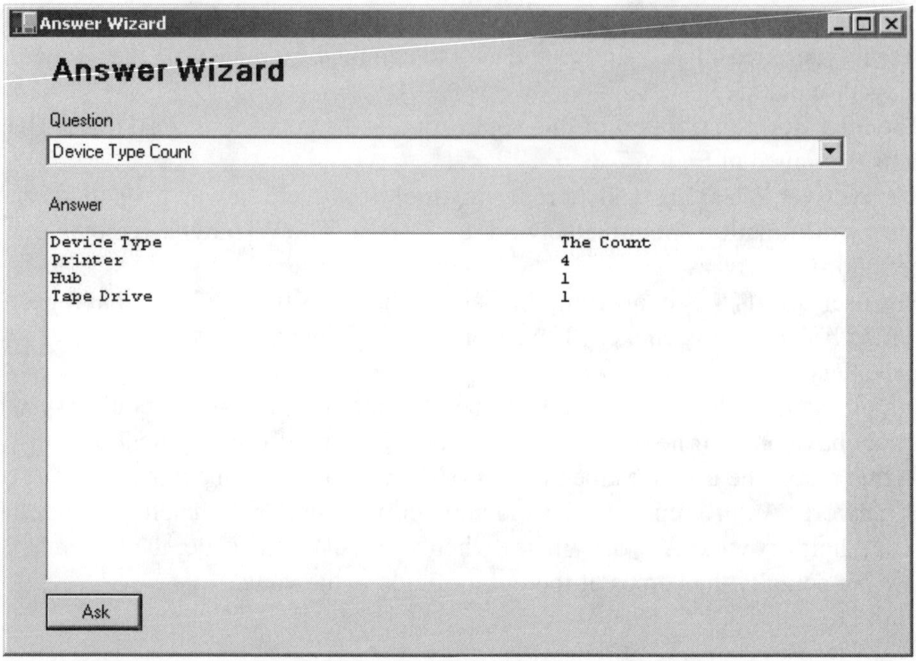

Figure 7-9 *Answer Wizard Device Type Count report*

Tables and Relationships

C7SQLObjects.sql

Computers Table

The Computers table stores the top-level information about the computers on the network.

HardwareItems Table

Another top-level table is the HardwareItems table. It stores the different hardware items and their descriptions.

ComputerHardware Table

The Computers table and the HardwareItems table are in a many-to-many relationship. Each computer can have many pieces of hardware, and each piece of hardware can be used in many different computers. Therefore, you need a middle table to satisfy that relationship. The ComputerHardware table fills that role. It is in a one-to-many relationship with the Computers table and is in a one-to-many relationship with the HardwareItems table.

DeviceTypes Table

Each device can be of a certain type. Those different types are stored in the DeviceTypes table.

Devices Table

The Devices table stores the data about the individual devices that the user has on their network. The table is in a one-to-many relationship with the DeviceTypes table. Each device is of a specific type, but each type can be used by many devices.

Field Specifications

Computers Table

Computers.txt

The field specifications for the Computers table are displayed in Table 7-1.

Field Name	Field Type	Notes
ComputerID	int	Primary Key, Identity Column
FriendlyName	varchar	Length = 50
ComputerType	varchar	Length = 50
Location	varchar	Length = 200
PhoneNumber	varchar	Length = 50
IPAddress	varchar	Length = 50
OS	varchar	Length = 50
DatePurchased	datetime	
Remarks	varchar	Length = 2000

Table 7-1 *Computers Table Field Specifications*

Field Name	Field Type	Notes
HardwareItemID	int	Primary Key, Identity Column
ItemName	varchar	Length = 50
Category	varchar	Length = 50
TheDescription	varchar	Length = 2000

Table 7-2 *HardwareItems Table Field Specifications*

The ComputerID field is the primary key in this table. Since it is an identity column, a unique value is automatically generated for this field when a new record is added. The rest of the fields store information about the computer.

HardwareItems Table

HardwareItems.txt

The field specifications for the HardwareItems table are displayed in Table 7-2.

The primary key for the HardwareItems table is the HardwareItemID field. The other fields store the data about the hardware item.

ComputerHardware Table

ComputerHardware.txt

The field specifications for the ComputerHardware table are displayed in Table 7-3.

The ComputerHardwareID field is the primary key in this table. The ComputerID field is a foreign key that links this table to the Computers table. The HardwareItems table is also linked to this table through the HardwareItemID field. Those two fields

Field Name	Field Type	Notes
ComputerHardwareID	int	Primary Key, Identity Column
ComputerID	int	Foreign
HardwareItemID	int	Foreign

Table 7-3 *ComputerHardware Table Field Specifications*

Field Name	Field Type	Notes
DeviceTypeID	int	Primary Key, Identity Column
DeviceType	varchar	Length = 50
TheDescription	varchar	Length = 500

Table 7-4 *DeviceTypes Table Field Specifications*

satisfy the many-to-many relationship between the Computers table and the HardwareItems table.

DeviceTypes Table

DeviceTypes.txt

The field specifications for the DeviceTypes table are displayed in Table 7-4.

This primary key in this table is the DeviceTypeID field. The two other fields store the information about the device type.

Devices Table

Devices.txt

The field specifications for the Devices table are displayed in Table 7-5.x

The DeviceID field is the unique identifier in this table. The DeviceTypeID provides the linkage to the DeviceTypes table.

Field Name	Field Type	Notes
DeviceID	int	Primary Key, Identity Column
DeviceName	varchar	Length = 50
DeviceTypeID	int	Foreign Key
Location	varchar	Length = 200
TheDescription	varchar	Length = 2000

Table 7-5 *Devices Field Specifications*

Stored Procedures

ComputerAdd Stored Procedure

The ComputerAdd stored procedure provides the calling application with the method of adding records to the Computers table.

```
CREATE PROCEDURE ComputerAdd
@FriendlyName varchar(50),
@ComputerType varchar(50),
@Location varchar(200),
@IPAddress varchar(50),
@OS varchar(50),
@DatePurchased datetime,
@Remarks varchar(50)
AS
      BEGIN
            Insert Into Computers
                  (FriendlyName, ComputerType, Location,
                  IPAddress, OS, DatePurchased,
                  Remarks) values
                  (@FriendlyName, @ComputerType, @Location,
                  @IPAddress, @OS, @DatePurchased,
                  @Remarks)
            Select @@Identity as TheNewID
      END
GO
```

Passed into the procedure are the values for the fields in the new record:

```
@FriendlyName varchar(50),
@ComputerType varchar(50),
@Location varchar(200),
@IPAddress varchar(50),
@OS varchar(50),
@DatePurchased datetime,
@Remarks varchar(50)
```

Those values are then used in the value list of an Insert statement:

```
Insert Into Computers
      (FriendlyName, ComputerType, Location,
```

```
IPAddress, OS, DatePurchased,
Remarks) values
(@FriendlyName, @ComputerType, @Location,
@IPAddress, @OS, @DatePurchased,
@Remarks)
```

After a SQL Insert statement, the SQL public variable @@Identity is set to the value of the identity column in the record just added. Therefore, this line returns the ComputerID of the computer just added:

```
Select @@Identity as TheNewID
```

ComputerUpdate Stored Procedure

The ComputerUpdate stored procedure allows for editing of existing computer records.

```
CREATE PROCEDURE ComputerUpdate
@ComputerID integer,
@FriendlyName varchar(50),
@ComputerType varchar(50),
@Location varchar(200),
@IPAddress varchar(50),
@OS varchar(50),
@DatePurchased datetime,
@Remarks varchar(50)
AS
      BEGIN
            Update Computers set
                  FriendlyName = @FriendlyName,
                  ComputerType = @ComputerType,
                  Location = @Location,
                  IPAddress = @IPAddress,
                  OS = @OS,
                  DatePurchased = @DatePurchased,
                  Remarks = @Remarks
                  Where ComputerID = @ComputerID
      END
GO
```

Passed into the procedure is the ID of the computer to be edited:

```
@ComputerID integer,
```

Also passed in are the new values for the existing record:

```
@FriendlyName varchar(50),
@ComputerType varchar(50),
@Location varchar(200),
@IPAddress varchar(50),
@OS varchar(50),
@DatePurchased datetime,
@Remarks varchar(50)
```

Those values are paired with the field names of the fields that they are being placed in:

```
Update Computers set
      FriendlyName = @FriendlyName,
      ComputerType = @ComputerType,
      Location = @Location,
      IPAddress = @IPAddress,
      OS = @OS,
      DatePurchased = @DatePurchased,
      Remarks = @Remarks
      Where ComputerID = @ComputerID
```

ComputerDelete Stored Procedure

The ComputerDelete stored procedure allows the calling application to delete a record from the Computers table.

```
CREATE PROCEDURE ComputerDelete
@ComputerID integer
AS
      BEGIN
            Delete from  Computers
                  Where ComputerID = @ComputerID
      END
GO
```

Passed into the procedure is the ID of the computer to be deleted:

```
@ComputerID integer
```

You then delete the offending record:

```
Delete from  Computers
      Where ComputerID = @ComputerID
```

ComputerRecord Stored Procedure

On the Computers form you need to display a computer record when a user navigates through the records and at other times. The ComputerRecord stored procedure returns a record from the Computers table chosen by navigational movement.

```
CREATE PROCEDURE ComputerRecord
@MoveDirection varchar(8),
@LastPosition integer = 0
AS
If @MoveDirection = 'FIRST'
      BEGIN
            Select * from Computers
                  Where ComputerID =
                  (Select Min(ComputerID) from Computers)
      END
Else
      If (@MoveDirection) = 'LAST'
            BEGIN
            Select * from Computers
                  Where ComputerID =
                  (Select Max(ComputerID) from Computers)
            END
      Else
            If (@MoveDirection) = 'NEXT'
                  BEGIN
                        Select Top 1 * from Computers
                              Where ComputerID > @LastPosition
                              Order By ComputerID
                  END
            Else
                  BEGIN
                        Select Top 1 * from Computers
                              Where ComputerID < @LastPosition
                              Order By ComputerID DESC
                  END
GO
```

The first parameter contains the direction of the move, either First, Last, Next, or Previous:

```
@MoveDirection varchar(8),
```

If the move direction is Next or Previous, you need to know next or previous from which record. The next parameter indicates that position:

```
@LastPosition integer = 0
```

You then check to see if the calling application wants the first record:

```
If @MoveDirection = 'FIRST'
```

If so, you return the first computer. Note the subquery used to retrieve the lowest value in the ComputerID field:

```
Select * from Computers
      Where ComputerID =
      (Select Min(ComputerID) from Computers)
```

You then check to see if the calling application wants the last record:

```
If (@MoveDirection) = 'LAST'
```

If so, you return the last record as given by the highest ComputerID value returned from the subquery:

```
Select * from Computers
      Where ComputerID =
      (Select Max(ComputerID) from Computers)
```

The next condition you test for is if the calling application wants the next record:

```
If (@MoveDirection) = 'NEXT'
```

If that is the case, you return a single record: the record that has the next value for a ComputerID in terms of the last position:

```
Select Top 1 * from Computers
      Where ComputerID > @LastPosition
      Order By ComputerID
```

The Else condition means you need to return the preceding record:

```
Else
```

So you retrieve the preceding record relative to the last position parameter:

```
Select Top 1 * from Computers
      Where ComputerID < @LastPosition
      Order By ComputerID DESC
```

ComputerHardwareAdd Stored Procedure

The ComputerHardwareAdd stored procedure provides the mechanism for adding a hardware item to a specific computer.

```
CREATE PROCEDURE ComputerHardwareAdd
@ComputerID integer,
@HardwareItemID integer
AS
      BEGIN
            Insert Into ComputerHardware
                  (ComputerID, HardwareItemID) values
                  (@ComputerID, @HardwareItemID)
      END
GO
```

Passed into the procedure is the ID of the computer and the ID of the hardware item:

```
@ComputerID integer,
@HardwareItemID integer
```

Those values are then used in a SQL Insert statement:

```
Insert Into ComputerHardware
      (ComputerID, HardwareItemID) values
      (@ComputerID, @HardwareItemID)
```

ComputerHardwareDelete Stored Procedure

On the Computers form, the user can delete a hardware item from a computer record. The ComputerHardwareDelete stored procedure provides this capability.

```
CREATE PROCEDURE ComputerHardwareDelete
@ComputerHardwareID integer
AS
      BEGIN
            Delete from  ComputerHardware
                  Where ComputerHardwareID
                  = @ComputerHardwareID
      END
GO
```

Passed into the procedure is the ID for the computer's hardware item that is to be deleted:

```
@ComputerHardwareID integer
```

That value is then used in a SQL Delete statement:

```
Delete from  ComputerHardware
      Where ComputerHardwareID
      = @ComputerHardwareID
```

HardwareInComputer Stored Procedure

Also on the Computers form there is a list that displays all the hardware items in the computer. The HardwareInComputer stored procedure returns the list.

```
CREATE PROCEDURE HardwareInComputer
@ComputerID integer
AS
BEGIN
      Select ComputerHardware.ComputerHardwareID, HardwareItems.ItemName,
            HardwareItems.Category, HardwareItems.TheDescription
            From ComputerHardware Left Outer Join
            HardwareItems ON
            ComputerHardware.HardwareItemID = HardwareItems.HardwareItemID
            Where ComputerHardware.ComputerID = @ComputerID
END
GO
```

Passed into the procedure is the ID of the computer from which the calling application wants the hardware items retrieved:

```
@ComputerID integer
```

Then in a Select statement, you need to combine information from the ComputerHardware table and the HardwareItems table. Therefore, the two tables are joined and you return the ID of the item in the computer along with the details about the item:

```
Select ComputerHardware.ComputerHardwareID, HardwareItems.ItemName,
      HardwareItems.Category, HardwareItems.TheDescription
      From ComputerHardware Left Outer Join
      HardwareItems ON
      ComputerHardware.HardwareItemID = HardwareItems.HardwareItemID
      Where ComputerHardware.ComputerID = @ComputerID
```

HardwareItemAdd Stored Procedure

The HardwareItemAdd stored procedure provides the mechanism for adding records to the HardwareItems table.

```
CREATE PROCEDURE HardwareItemAdd
@ItemName varchar(50),
@Category varchar(50),
@TheDescription varchar(2000)
AS
      BEGIN
            Insert Into HardwareItems
                  (ItemName, Category,
                  TheDescription) values
                  (@ItemName, @Category,
                  @TheDescription)
            Select @@Identity as TheNewID
      END
GO
```

Passed into the procedure are the values for the fields in the new hardware item record:

```
@ItemName varchar(50),
@Category varchar(50),
@TheDescription varchar(2000)
```

Those values are then used in a SQL Insert statement:

```
Insert Into HardwareItems
      (ItemName, Category,
      TheDescription) values
      (@ItemName, @Category,
      @TheDescription)
```

You then return the ID of the record just added to the calling application:

```
Select @@Identity as TheNewID
```

HardwareItemUpdate Stored Procedure

To update a HardwareItems record, the calling application calls the HardwareItemUpdate stored procedure.

```
CREATE PROCEDURE HardwareItemUpdate
@HardwareItemID integer,
@ItemName varchar(50),
@Category varchar(50),
@TheDescription varchar(2000)
AS
      BEGIN
            Update HardwareItems set
                  ItemName = @ItemName,
                  Category = @Category,
                  TheDescription = @TheDescription
                  Where HardwareItemID = @HardwareItemID
      END
GO
```

Passed into the procedure is the ID of the record to be edited:

```
@HardwareItemID integer,
```

Also passed in are the values for the fields for the record being edited:

```
@ItemName varchar(50),
@Category varchar(50),
@TheDescription varchar(2000)
```

The ID is used in the Where clause of an Update statement, and the values for the fields are paired with the field names:

```
Update HardwareItems set
      ItemName = @ItemName,
      Category = @Category,
      TheDescription = @TheDescription
      Where HardwareItemID = @HardwareItemID
```

HardwareItemDelete Stored Procedure

The HardwareItemDelete stored procedure provides the mechanism for deleting a hardware item record.

```
CREATE PROCEDURE HardwareItemDelete
@HardwareItemID integer
AS
      BEGIN
            Delete from  HardwareItems
                  Where HardwareItemID = @HardwareItemID
      END
GO
```

The calling application needs to pass in the ID of the record being deleted:

```
@HardwareItemID integer
```

That value is then used in the Where clause of a Delete statement:

```
Delete from  HardwareItems
      Where HardwareItemID = @HardwareItemID
```

HardwareItemRecord Stored Procedure

For navigational purposes and for other reasons, you need to display a single record on the Hardware form in the Visual Basic.Net front-end application. The HardwareItemRecord stored procedure returns a single record chosen in terms of navigational movement.

```
CREATE PROCEDURE HardwareItemRecord
@MoveDirection varchar(8),
@LastPosition integer = 0
AS
If @MoveDirection = 'FIRST'
      BEGIN
            Select * from HardwareItems
                  Where HardwareItemID =
                  (Select Min(HardwareItemID) from HardwareItems)
      END
Else
      If (@MoveDirection) = 'LAST'
            BEGIN
            Select * from HardwareItems
                  Where HardwareItemID =
                  (Select Max(HardwareItemID) from HardwareItems)
            END
      Else
            If (@MoveDirection) = 'NEXT'
                  BEGIN
                        Select Top 1 * from HardwareItems
                              Where HardwareItemID > @LastPosition
                              Order By HardwareItemID
                  END
            Else
                  BEGIN
                        Select Top 1 * from HardwareItems
                              Where HardwareItemID < @LastPosition
                              Order By HardwareItemID DESC
                  END
GO
```

Passed into the first parameter is the direction of the record movement:

```
@MoveDirection varchar(8),
```

If that movement is next or previous, you need to know the position that the record returned should be relative to. That value is passed into the second parameter:

```
@LastPosition integer = 0
```

First, you check to see if the calling application wants the first record:

```
If @MoveDirection = 'FIRST'
```

If so, a subquery is used to retrieve the ID of the first record in the HardwareItems table. That record is then selected:

```
Select * from HardwareItems
      Where HardwareItemID =
      (Select Min(HardwareItemID) from HardwareItems)
```

Next, you check to see if the calling application wants the last record:

```
If (@MoveDirection) = 'LAST'
```

If so, you return the last record in terms of the highest ID returned from the subquery:

```
Select * from HardwareItems
      Where HardwareItemID =
      (Select Max(HardwareItemID) from HardwareItems)
```

The third condition you check for is if the calling application wants the next record:

```
If (@MoveDirection) = 'NEXT'
```

If so, you return the next record relative to the last record returned. Note that the Top 1 is used to return a single record:

```
Select Top 1 * from HardwareItems
      Where HardwareItemID > @LastPosition
      Order By HardwareItemID
```

Your last condition means that the calling application wants the preceding record relative to the last position record:

```
Select Top 1 * from HardwareItems
      Where HardwareItemID < @LastPosition
      Order By HardwareItemID DESC
```

HardwareItemList Stored Procedure

When the user wants to add a hardware item to a computer on the Computers form, you show a dialog form that displays a list of all the hardware items. The HardwareItemList stored procedure is used to return that list.

```
CREATE PROCEDURE HardwareItemsList
AS
BEGIN
      Select HardwareItemID, ItemName from
            HardwareItems Order By
            ItemName
END
GO
```

A Select statement is used to return the name and ID of the hardware items sorted by their name:

```
Select HardwareItemID, ItemName from
      HardwareItems Order By
      ItemName
```

DeviceAdd Stored Procedure

The DeviceAdd stored procedure is used by the calling application to add a record to the Devices table.

```
CREATE PROCEDURE DeviceAdd
@DeviceName varchar(50),
@DeviceTypeID integer,
@Location varchar(200),
@TheDescription varchar(2000)
AS
      BEGIN
            Insert Into Devices
                  (DeviceName, DeviceTypeID, Location,
                  TheDescription) values
                  (@DeviceName, @DeviceTypeID, @Location,
                  @TheDescription)
            Select @@Identity as TheNewID
      END
GO
```

Passed into the stored procedure are the values for the fields in the new record:

```
@DeviceName varchar(50),
@DeviceTypeID integer,
@Location varchar(200),
@TheDescription varchar(2000)
```

You then add a new record to the Devices table using a SQL Insert statement:

```
Insert Into Devices
      (DeviceName, DeviceTypeID, Location,
      TheDescription) values
      (@DeviceName, @DeviceTypeID, @Location,
      @TheDescription)
```

The ID of the record just added is returned to the calling application:

```
Select @@Identity as TheNewID
```

DeviceUpdate Stored Procedure

The DeviceUpdate stored procedure provides the mechanism for updating records in the Devices table.

```
CREATE PROCEDURE DeviceUpdate
@DeviceID integer,
@DeviceName varchar(50),
@DeviceTypeID integer,
@Location varchar(200),
@TheDescription varchar(2000)
AS
      BEGIN
            Update Devices set
                  DeviceName = @DeviceName,
                  DeviceTypeID = @DeviceTypeID,
                  Location = @Location,
                  TheDescription = @TheDescription
                  Where DeviceID = @DeviceID
      END
GO
```

The first parameter is set to the ID of the record being updated:

```
@DeviceID integer,
```

The other parameters are set to the values of the fields in the record being updated:

```
@DeviceName varchar(50),
@DeviceTypeID integer,
@Location varchar(200),
@TheDescription varchar(2000)
```

Those values are then used in an Update statement:

```
Update Devices set
      DeviceName = @DeviceName,
      DeviceTypeID = @DeviceTypeID,
      Location = @Location,
      TheDescription = @TheDescription
      Where DeviceID = @DeviceID
```

DeviceDelete Stored Procedure

The DeviceDelete stored procedure provides the mechanism to the calling application for deleting records from the Devices table.

```
CREATE PROCEDURE DeviceDelete
@DeviceID integer
AS
      BEGIN
            Delete from  Devices
                  Where DeviceID = @DeviceID
      END
GO
```

Passed into the procedure is the ID of the record that is to be deleted:

```
@DeviceID integer
```

The offending record is then deleted:

```
Delete from  Devices
      Where DeviceID = @DeviceID
```

DeviceRecord Stored Procedure

The DeviceRecord stored procedure returns the contents of a single device record according to a navigational direction.

```
CREATE PROCEDURE DeviceRecord
@MoveDirection varchar(8),
@LastPosition integer = 0
AS
If @MoveDirection = 'FIRST'
      BEGIN
            Select * from Devices
                  Where DeviceID =
                  (Select Min(DeviceID) from Devices)
      END
Else
      If (@MoveDirection) = 'LAST'
            BEGIN
            Select * from Devices
                  Where DeviceID =
                  (Select Max(DeviceID) from Devices)
            END
      Else
            If (@MoveDirection) = 'NEXT'
                  BEGIN
                        Select Top 1 * from Devices
                              Where DeviceID > @LastPosition
                              Order By DeviceID
                  END
            Else
                  BEGIN
                        Select Top 1 * from Devices
                              Where DeviceID < @LastPosition
                              Order By DeviceID DESC
                  END
GO
```

The first parameter is set to the direction of the move within the table:

```
@MoveDirection varchar(8),
```

The second parameter is set to the ID of the device that the move is relative to:

```
@LastPosition integer = 0
```

You first check to see if the calling application wants the first record:

```
If @MoveDirection = 'FIRST'
```

If so, you return the first record in the devices table, that is, the record with the lowest DeviceID:

```
Select * from Devices
      Where DeviceID =
      (Select Min(DeviceID) from Devices)
```

Next, you check to see if the calling application wants the last record:

```
If (@MoveDirection) = 'LAST'
```

If so, you return the record with the highest DeviceID:

```
Select * from Devices
      Where DeviceID =
      (Select Max(DeviceID) from Devices)
```

Your next block of code runs if the calling application wants the next record:

```
If (@MoveDirection) = 'NEXT'
```

If so, the next record is returned relative to the last position record:

```
Select Top 1 * from Devices
      Where DeviceID > @LastPosition
      Order By DeviceID
```

Otherwise, you return the preceding record in terms of the last position record:

```
Select Top 1 * from Devices
      Where DeviceID < @LastPosition
      Order By DeviceID DESC
```

DeviceTypeAdd Stored Procedure

On the Devices form in the Visual Basic.Net application, you allow the user to add new device types by clicking the "+" button. The DeviceTypeAdd stored procedure provides the mechanism for that action.

```
CREATE PROCEDURE DeviceTypeAdd
@DeviceType varchar(50),
@TheDescription varchar(500)
AS
      BEGIN
            Insert Into DeviceTypes
                  (DeviceType, TheDescription) values
                  (@DeviceType, @TheDescription)
      END
GO
```

Passed into the procedure are the values for the fields in the new record:

```
@DeviceType varchar(50),
@TheDescription varchar(500)
```

Those values are then used in an Insert statement:

```
Insert Into DeviceTypes
      (DeviceType, TheDescription) values
      (@DeviceType, @TheDescription)
```

DeviceTypeList Stored Procedure

You also need to display the list of device types on the Devices form. The DeviceTypeList stored procedure provides the list.

```
CREATE PROCEDURE DeviceTypeList
AS
BEGIN
      Select DeviceTypeID, DeviceType from
            DeviceTypes Order By
            DeviceType
END
GO
```

It simply returns all the names and IDs of the device types sorted by their name:

```
Select DeviceTypeID, DeviceType from
      DeviceTypes Order By
      DeviceType
```

Views

ComputerTypeCount View

In the Visual Basic.Net application, you have a form called Answer Wizard that displays the results of summary queries. Those results are returned through three views.

The first view is the ComputerTypeCount view. It returns the count of each of the different computers. It does this by grouping by the ComputerType field and counting the number of records in each of those groups:

```
SELECT TOP 100 PERCENT ComputerType AS [Computer Type],
COUNT(ComputerID) AS [Count] FROM dbo.Computers
GROUP BY ComputerType
ORDER BY COUNT(ComputerID) DESC
```

DeviceTypeCount View

The DeviceTypeCount returns the number of devices of each type that are stored in the Devices table. Since only the ID is stored in that table, you join it together with the DeviceTypes table to retrieve the name of the type:

```
SELECT TOP 100 PERCENT dbo.DeviceTypes.DeviceType AS [Device Type],
COUNT(dbo.Devices.DeviceID) AS [The Count]
FROM dbo.Devices INNER JOIN dbo.DeviceTypes ON
dbo.Devices.DeviceTypeID = dbo.DeviceTypes.DeviceTypeID
GROUP BY dbo.DeviceTypes.DeviceType
ORDER BY COUNT(dbo.Devices.DeviceID) DESC
```

OSCount View

The OSCount view returns the total number of computers in the Computers table with each type of operating system. The data is grouped by the OS field. Note the use of aliasing on the output fields. In your code, you will use these names to display column headers on your Answer Wizard form:

```
SELECT TOP 100 PERCENT OS AS [Operating System],
COUNT(ComputerID) AS [The Count]
FROM dbo.Computers
GROUP BY OS
ORDER BY COUNT(ComputerID) DESC
```

Modules

Chapter7NetworkManagement.vbproj

modPublicProcs Module

The Visual Basic.Net front-end application contains a single module called modPublicProcs. That module contains the following declarations:

```
Module modPublicProcs
    Public SQLUserName As String
    Public SQLPassword As String
    Public PassedID As Long
End Module
```

All the variables have public scope, so they are available throughout the application to any procedure. The first variable stores the user's SQL Server name:

```
Public SQLUserName As String
```

The next one stores their password:

```
Public SQLPassword As String
```

The third variable stores the current ID and is used to pass a value between two forms:

```
Public PassedID As Long
```

Forms

frmMenu Form

The Menu form is the start-up object. Therefore, it appears when the application starts. At the top of the code window of this form, you set the following options.

```
Option Explicit On
Option Strict Off
```

The first tells the compiler that you will declare your variables:

```
Option Explicit On
```

The second turns off the Visual Basic.Net conversion checking:

```
Option Strict Off
```

The next code block was placed at the end of the New procedure. That means it will fire whenever the form is first instantiated.

```
SQLUserName = InputBox("Please enter your user name.", _
      "Network Management")
If SQLUserName = "" Then
      End
End If
SQLPassword = InputBox("Please enter your password.", _
      "Network Management")
If SQLPassword = "" Then
      End
End If
```

First, you prompt the user for their user name and store it in a public variable:

```
SQLUserName = InputBox("Please enter your user name.", _
      "Network Management")
```

If the user clicks Cancel when prompted for their name, you exit the application:

```
If SQLUserName = "" Then
      End
End If
```

Otherwise, you prompt the user for their password:

```
SQLPassword = InputBox("Please enter your password.", _
      "Network Management")
```

Again, you make sure that they enter something:

```
If SQLPassword = "" Then
```

If they don't, you close the application:

```
End
```

The next code block fires when the Computers button is clicked.

```
Protected Sub cmdComputers_Click(ByVal sender As Object,
      ByVal e As System.EventArgs)
      Dim MyfrmComputers As New frmComputers()
      MyfrmComputers.show()
End Sub
```

You declare an instance of the Computers form:

```
Dim MyfrmComputers As New frmComputers()
```

and display it:

```
MyfrmComputers.show()
```

When the Hardware button is clicked, you instantiate the Hardware form and display it:

```
Public Sub cmdHardware_Click(ByVal sender As Object,
      ByVal e As System.EventArgs) Handles cmdHardware.Click
      Dim MyfrmHardware As New frmHardware()
      MyfrmHardware.show()
End Sub
```

Similarly, the Devices form is displayed when the Devices button is clicked:

```
Public Sub cmdDevices_Click(ByVal sender As Object,
      ByVal e As System.EventArgs) Handles cmdDevices.Click
Dim MyfrmDevices As New frmDevices()
```

```
      MyfrmDevices.show()
End Sub
```

The same is true for the Answer Wizard button:

```
Public Sub cmdAnswerWizard_Click(ByVal sender As Object,
      ByVal e As System.EventArgs) Handles cmdAnswerWizard.Click
      Dim MyfrmAnswerWizard As New frmAnswerWizard()
      MyfrmAnswerWizard.show()
End Sub
```

and when the Exit button is clicked, the application is closed:

```
Public Sub cmdExit_Click(ByVal sender As Object,
      ByVal e As System.EventArgs) Handles cmdExit.Click
      End
End Sub
```

frmComputers Form

The code on the Computers form allows the user to add, edit, delete, and navigate through the computers and their hardware.

At the top of the code window you start by telling the compiler that you will declare your variables on this form and that you do not want strict type checking:

```
Option Explicit On
Option Strict Off
```

Before any procedures, at the top of the Class definition for the form, you can declare variables that are accessible to any procedure throughout the form.

```
Private MyConnection As New ADODB.Connection()
Private CurrentID As Long = 0
```

The first is a connection object that is used throughout the form to connect to your SQL Server database:

```
Private MyConnection As New ADODB.Connection()
```

The other stores the ID of the current computer record:

```
Private CurrentID As Long = 0
```

The form has its own procedure declared that you call from other procedures. The first populates a record on the form.

```
Public Sub PopulateRecord(ByVal TheDirection As String)
    Dim RSComputer As New ADODB.Recordset()
    RSComputer = MyConnection.Execute("Exec ComputerRecord '" _
        & TheDirection & "', " & CurrentID)
    If RSComputer.EOF Then
        RSComputer = MyConnection.Execute("Exec ComputerRecord '" _
            & "FIRST" & "', " & CurrentID)
        If RSComputer.EOF Then
            ClearForm()
        Else
            CurrentID = RSComputer.Fields("ComputerID").Value
            txtFriendlyName.Text = RSComputer.Fields("FriendlyName").Value
            txtComputerType.Text = RSComputer.Fields("ComputerType").Value
            txtLocation.Text = RSComputer.Fields("Location").Value
            txtIPAddress.Text = RSComputer.Fields("IPAddress").Value
            txtOS.Text = RSComputer.Fields("OS").Value
            txtDatePurchased.Text = RSComputer.Fields("DatePurchased").Value
            txtRemarks.Text = RSComputer.Fields("Remarks").Value
            PopulateList()
        End If
    Else
        CurrentID = RSComputer.Fields("ComputerID").Value
        txtFriendlyName.Text = RSComputer.Fields("FriendlyName").Value
        txtComputerType.Text = RSComputer.Fields("ComputerType").Value
        txtLocation.Text = RSComputer.Fields("Location").Value
        txtIPAddress.Text = RSComputer.Fields("IPAddress").Value
        txtOS.Text = RSComputer.Fields("OS").Value
        txtDatePurchased.Text = RSComputer.Fields("DatePurchased").Value
        txtRemarks.Text = RSComputer.Fields("Remarks").Value
        PopulateList()
    End If
End Sub
```

The procedure requires a single parameter, the direction of the navigational movement for the next record:

```
Public Sub PopulateRecord(ByVal TheDirection As String)
```

You will need a Recordset object:

```
Dim RSComputer As New ADODB.Recordset()
```

which you use to retrieve the desired record:

```
RSComputer = MyConnection.Execute("Exec ComputerRecord '" _
     & TheDirection & "', " & CurrentID)
```

You then make sure a record was found:

```
If RSComputer.EOF Then
```

If it wasn't, you attempt to retrieve the first record in the table:

```
RSComputer = MyConnection.Execute("Exec ComputerRecord '" _
     & "FIRST" & "', " & CurrentID)
```

If you still didn't find a record:

```
If RSComputer.EOF Then
```

the table is empty and you clear out the form:

```
ClearForm()
```

Otherwise, you have a valid record. You set the ID variable to the ID of the record retrieved:

```
CurrentID = RSComputer.Fields("ComputerID").Value
```

and then set the text boxes on the form to their corresponding fields:

```
txtFriendlyName.Text = RSComputer.Fields("FriendlyName").Value
txtComputerType.Text = RSComputer.Fields("ComputerType").Value
txtLocation.Text = RSComputer.Fields("Location").Value
txtIPAddress.Text = RSComputer.Fields("IPAddress").Value
txtOS.Text = RSComputer.Fields("OS").Value
txtDatePurchased.Text = RSComputer.Fields("DatePurchased").Value
txtRemarks.Text = RSComputer.Fields("Remarks").Value
```

You also need to populate the list box that shows the hardware items for this computer:

```
PopulateList()
```

If the code flows here, the first attempt to retrieve a record was successful. So you need to set the ID:

```
CurrentID = RSComputer.Fields("ComputerID").Value
```

set the text boxes on the form:

```
txtFriendlyName.Text = RSComputer.Fields("FriendlyName").Value
txtComputerType.Text = RSComputer.Fields("ComputerType").Value
txtLocation.Text = RSComputer.Fields("Location").Value
txtIPAddress.Text = RSComputer.Fields("IPAddress").Value
txtOS.Text = RSComputer.Fields("OS").Value
txtDatePurchased.Text = RSComputer.Fields("DatePurchased").Value
txtRemarks.Text = RSComputer.Fields("Remarks").Value
```

and populate the list box:

```
PopulateList()
```

The next procedure is used to populate the list box. It displays all the hardware items for the current computer.

```
Public Sub PopulateList()
    Dim RSList As ADODB.Recordset
    Dim CurrentPad As Integer
    Dim TempItem As String
    lstHardware.Items.Clear()
    If CurrentID <> 0 Then
        RSList = MyConnection.Execute("Exec HardwareInComputer " _
            & CurrentID)
        Do Until RSList.EOF
            CurrentPad = 10 - Len(RSList.Fields("ComputerHardwareID").Value)
TempItem = RSList.Fields("ComputerHardwareID").Value _
                & Space(CurrentPad)
            CurrentPad = 35 - Len(RSList.Fields("ItemName").Value)
            TempItem = TempItem & RSList.Fields("ItemName").Value _
                & Space(CurrentPad)
```

```
            CurrentPad = 100 - Len(RSList.Fields("Category").Value)
            TempItem = TempItem & RSList.Fields("Category").Value _
                & Space(CurrentPad)
            TempItem = TempItem & RSList.Fields("TheDescription").Value
            lstHardware.Items.Add (TempItem)
            RSList.MoveNext()
        Loop
    End If
End Sub
```

You will need a Recordset object:

```
Dim RSList As ADODB.Recordset
```

a number to store the amount of space padding that you need:

```
Dim CurrentPad As Integer
```

and a string to store the item for the list as it is being built:

```
Dim TempItem As String
```

First, though, you clear the list box:

```
    lstHardware.Items.Clear()
```

and make sure that you are in a valid computer record:

```
If CurrentID <> 0 Then
```

If so, you can retrieve all the hardware items for the current computer:

```
RSList = MyConnection.Execute("Exec HardwareInComputer " _
    & CurrentID)
```

and enter a loop so that you can process each record returned:

```
Do Until RSList.EOF
```

The list box uses a fixed-width font. That allows you to display the hardware items in a columar format. Therefore, you need to display each field in the record at a specific position in the list box. The ID takes up the first ten characters. So you figure out how many spaces you will need after the ID:

```
CurrentPad = 10 - Len(RSList.Fields("ComputerHardwareID").Value)
```

You then place in your temporary string the ID of the item, along with the number of spaces to size it to a width of ten characters:

```
TempItem = RSList.Fields("ComputerHardwareID").Value _
      & Space(CurrentPad)
```

The name of the item takes the next 35 characters. Again, you need to figure out how many spaces you will need:

```
CurrentPad = 35 - Len(RSList.Fields("ItemName").Value)
```

and then place the name of the item with a space pad into your temporary string:

```
TempItem = TempItem & RSList.Fields("ItemName").Value _
      & Space(CurrentPad)
```

The category takes up the next 100 characters:

```
CurrentPad = 100 - Len(RSList.Fields("Category").Value)
TempItem = TempItem & RSList.Fields("Category").Value _
      & Space(CurrentPad)
```

The description is then placed at the end of the entry. It is actually too far off the list to be seen. This is done on purpose. As you will see when you look at code later in this section, when the user double-clicks on an entry in the list box you display the description:

```
TempItem = TempItem & RSList.Fields("TheDescription").Value
```

You then place the string you just built into the list box:

```
lstHardware.Items.Add (TempItem)
```

and move on to process the next record:

```
      RSList.MoveNext()
Loop
```

The other user-defined procedure on this form clears its contents.

```
Public Sub ClearForm()
    CurrentID = 0
    txtFriendlyName.Text = ""
    txtComputerType.Text = ""
    txtLocation.Text = ""
    txtIPAddress.Text = ""
    txtOS.Text = ""
    txtDatePurchased.Text = ""
    txtRemarks.Text = ""
    lstHardware.Items.Clear()
End Sub
```

You start by clearing the ID of the current record:

```
CurrentID = 0
```

then you clear the text boxes on the form:

```
txtFriendlyName.Text = ""
txtComputerType.Text = ""
txtLocation.Text = ""
txtIPAddress.Text = ""
txtOS.Text = ""
txtDatePurchased.Text = ""
txtRemarks.Text = ""
```

as well as the list box:

```
lstHardware.Items.Clear()
```

The next code is placed in the New procedure. Therefore, it fires when the form is first instantiated.

```
MyConnection.ConnectionString = "driver={SQL Server};" _
      & "server=MyServer;uid=" & SQLUserName _
      & ";pwd=" & SQLPassword & ";" & "database=C7NetworkManagement"
MyConnection.Open()
PopulateRecord ("FIRST")
```

You start by setting the connect string for your Connection object. Note that if you call your database something different, you would need to change the connect string to match your database name:

```
MyConnection.ConnectionString = "driver={SQL Server};" _
      & "server=MyServer;uid=" & SQLUserName _
      & ";pwd=" & SQLPassword & ";" & "database=C7NetworkManagement"
```

You then open the connection:

```
MyConnection.Open()
```

and call your procedure to display the first record:

```
PopulateRecord ("FIRST")
```

When the user clicks the "<<", you call your procedure to move to the first record:

```
Protected Sub cmdMoveFirst_Click(ByVal sender As Object,
      ByVal e As System.EventArgs)
      PopulateRecord ("FIRST")
End Sub
```

When the "<" button is clicked, you call your PopulateRecord procedure, having it move to the preceding record:

```
Protected Sub cmdMovePrevious_Click(ByVal sender As Object,
      ByVal e As System.EventArgs)
      PopulateRecord ("PREVIOUS")
End Sub
```

The ">" button uses your procedure to move to the next record:

```
Public Sub cmdMoveNext_Click(ByVal sender As Object,
      ByVal e As System.EventArgs) Handles cmdMoveNext.Click
      PopulateRecord ("NEXT")
End Sub
```

And the ">>" button, when clicked, moves the form to the last record:

```
Public Sub cmdMoveLast_Click(ByVal sender As Object,
      ByVal e As System.EventArgs) Handles cmdMoveLast.Click
      PopulateRecord ("LAST")
End Sub
```

The next code block fires when the Add button is clicked.

```
Public Sub cmdAdd_Click(ByVal sender As Object, _
    ByVal e As System.EventArgs) Handles cmdAdd.Click
    Dim RSNewID As ADODB.Recordset
    Dim TheFriendlyName As String
    Dim TheComputerType As String
    Dim TheLocation As String
    Dim TheIPAddress As String
    Dim TheOS As String
    Dim TheRemarks As String
    TheFriendlyName = Replace(txtFriendlyName.Text, "'", "''")
    TheComputerType = Replace(txtComputerType.Text, "'", "''")
    TheLocation = Replace(txtLocation.Text, "'", "''")
    TheIPAddress = Replace(txtIPAddress.Text, "'", "''")
    TheOS = Replace(txtOS.Text, "'", "''")
    TheRemarks = Replace(txtRemarks.Text, "'", "''")
    RSNewID = MyConnection.Execute("Exec ComputerAdd " _
        & "'" & TheFriendlyName & "', " _
        & "'" & TheComputerType & "', " _
        & "'" & TheLocation & "', " _
        & "'" & TheIPAddress & "', " _
        & "'" & TheOS & "', " _
        & "'" & txtDatePurchased.Text & "', " _
        & "'" & TheRemarks & "'")
    CurrentID = RSNewID.Fields("TheNewID").Value
End Sub
```

The procedure will need a Recordset object:

```
Dim RSNewID As ADODB.Recordset
```

as well as strings to store the values for the text fields entered into the text boxes:

```
Dim TheFriendlyName As String
Dim TheComputerType As String
Dim TheLocation As String
Dim TheIPAddress As String
Dim TheOS As String
Dim TheRemarks As String
```

You then set those string variables to their corresponding text boxes, replacing any ' characters with two ' characters. This makes them acceptable to the SQL call:

```
TheFriendlyName = Replace(txtFriendlyName.Text, "'", "''")
TheComputerType = Replace(txtComputerType.Text, "'", "''")
TheLocation = Replace(txtLocation.Text, "'", "''")
TheIPAddress = Replace(txtIPAddress.Text, "'", "''")
TheOS = Replace(txtOS.Text, "'", "''")
TheRemarks = Replace(txtRemarks.Text, "'", "''")
```

You then use your stored procedure to add the new computer record:

```
RSNewID = MyConnection.Execute("Exec ComputerAdd " _
      & "'" & TheFriendlyName & "', " _
      & "'" & TheComputerType & "', " _
      & "'" & TheLocation & "', " _
      & "'" & TheIPAddress & "', " _
      & "'" & TheOS & "', " _
      & "'" & txtDatePurchased.Text & "', " _
      & "'" & TheRemarks & "'")
```

The stored procedure returns the ID of the record you just added. That value is placed in your form-wide variable:

```
CurrentID = RSNewID.Fields("TheNewID").Value
```

The next code block fires when the Update button is clicked.

```
Public Sub cmdUpdate_Click(ByVal sender As Object, _
    ByVal e As System.EventArgs) Handles cmdUpdate.Click
    Dim TheFriendlyName As String
    Dim TheComputerType As String
    Dim TheLocation As String
    Dim TheIPAddress As String
    Dim TheOS As String
    Dim TheRemarks As String
    TheFriendlyName = Replace(txtFriendlyName.Text, "'", "''")
    TheComputerType = Replace(txtComputerType.Text, "'", "''")
    TheLocation = Replace(txtLocation.Text, "'", "''")
    TheIPAddress = Replace(txtIPAddress.Text, "'", "''")
    TheOS = Replace(txtOS.Text, "'", "''")
    TheRemarks = Replace(txtRemarks.Text, "'", "''")
    If CurrentID = 0 Then
        MsgBox("You are not in an active record!", _
```

```
                Microsoft.VisualBasic.MsgBoxStyle.Exclamation, _
                "Network Management")
        Else
            MyConnection.Execute ("Exec ComputerUpdate " _
                & CurrentID & ", " _
                & "'" & TheFriendlyName & "', " _
                & "'" & TheComputerType & "', " _
                & "'" & TheLocation & "', " _
                & "'" & TheIPAddress & "', " _
                & "'" & TheOS & "', " _
                & "'" & txtDatePurchased.Text & "', " _
                & "'" & TheRemarks & "'")
        End If
End Sub
```

The procedure needs strings to store the values entered into the text boxes:

```
Dim TheFriendlyName As String
Dim TheComputerType As String
Dim TheLocation As String
Dim TheIPAddress As String
Dim TheOS As String
Dim TheRemarks As String
```

Those strings are set to the converted text in the text boxes:

```
TheFriendlyName = Replace(txtFriendlyName.Text, "'", "''")
TheComputerType = Replace(txtComputerType.Text, "'", "''")
TheLocation = Replace(txtLocation.Text, "'", "''")
TheIPAddress = Replace(txtIPAddress.Text, "'", "''")
TheOS = Replace(txtOS.Text, "'", "''")
TheRemarks = Replace(txtRemarks.Text, "'", "''")
```

But before making the call, you make sure that you are in an active record:

```
If CurrentID = 0 Then
```

If you aren't, you display a message to the user:

```
MsgBox("You are not in an active record!", _
      Microsoft.VisualBasic.MsgBoxStyle.Exclamation, _
      "Network Management")
```

Otherwise, you can update the desired record:

```
MyConnection.Execute ("Exec ComputerUpdate " _
      & CurrentID & ", " _
      & "'" & TheFriendlyName & "', " _
      & "'" & TheComputerType & "', " _
      & "'" & TheLocation & "', " _
      & "'" & TheIPAddress & "', " _
      & "'" & TheOS & "', " _
      & "'" & txtDatePurchased.Text & "', " _
      & "'" & TheRemarks & "'")
```

When the Delete button is clicked, this code runs.

```
Public Sub cmdDelete_Click(ByVal sender As Object,
    ByVal e As System.EventArgs) Handles cmdDelete.Click
    If CurrentID = 0 Then
        ClearForm()
    Else
        MyConnection.Execute ("Exec ComputerDelete " _
            & CurrentID)
        PopulateRecord ("FIRST")
    End If
End Sub
```

If you are in a new record:

```
If CurrentID = 0 Then
```

you just need to clear the form:

```
ClearForm()
```

Otherwise, you delete the offending record:

```
MyConnection.Execute ("Exec ComputerDelete " _
      & CurrentID)
```

and display another record on the form:

```
PopulateRecord ("FIRST")
```

When the Clear button is clicked, you simply call your Clear procedure:

```
Public Sub cmdClear_Click(ByVal sender As Object,
    ByVal e As System.EventArgs) Handles cmdClear.Click
```

```
    ClearForm()
End Sub
```

The next procedure fires when the list box is double-clicked. It displays the description of the hardware item that was in the list when it was double-clicked.

```
Public Sub lstHardware_DoubleClick(ByVal sender As Object,
    ByVal e As System.EventArgs) Handles lstHardware.DoubleClick
    If lstHardware.SelectedIndex <> -1 Then
        msgbox(mid(lstHardware.Text, 145), _
            Microsoft.VisualBasic.MsgBoxStyle.Information, _
            "Hardware Item Description")
    End If
End Sub
```

First, you check to see if an item in the list is highlighted:

```
If lstHardware.SelectedIndex <> -1 Then
```

If so, you display the description portion of that item, which starts at character position 145:

```
msgbox(mid(lstHardware.Text, 145), _
    Microsoft.VisualBasic.MsgBoxStyle.Information, _
    "Hardware Item Description")
```

The next procedure fires when the Add Hardware button is clicked.

```
Public Sub cmdAddHardware_Click(ByVal sender As Object,
    ByVal e As System.EventArgs) Handles cmdAddHardware.Click
    Dim MyAddHWForm As New frmAddHardwareItem()
    PassedID = CurrentID
    MyAddHWForm.ShowDialog()
    PopulateList()
End Sub
```

You instantiate the Add Hardware Item form:

```
Dim MyAddHWForm As New frmAddHardwareItem()
```

Place the ID of the current computer into a public variable so that it will be available to the Add Hardware Item form:

```
PassedID = CurrentID
```

You then show the form as a dialog so that it retains the focus:

```
MyAddHWForm.ShowDialog()
```

After the user is done with that form, you repopulate the hardware list box:

```
PopulateList()
```

The last procedure on the form fires when the Delete Hardware Item button is clicked.

```
Public Sub cmdDeleteHardware_Click(ByVal sender As Object,
    ByVal e As System.EventArgs) Handles cmdDeleteHardware.Click
    If lstHardware.SelectedIndex <> -1 Then
        If MsgBox("Are you sure you want to delete the selected Hardware Item?", _
            Microsoft.VisualBasic.MsgBoxStyle.YesNo, "Confirm Delete") = _
            Microsoft.VisualBasic.MsgBoxResult.Yes Then
            MyConnection.Execute ("Exec ComputerHardwareDelete " _
                & Trim(Mid(lstHardware.Text, 1, 10)))
            PopulateList()
        End If
    End If
End Sub
```

First, you make sure an item in the list has been selected:

```
If lstHardware.SelectedIndex <> -1 Then
```

If so, you ask the user to confirm that they want to delete the current record:

```
If MsgBox("Are you sure you want to delete the selected Hardware Item?", _
      Microsoft.VisualBasic.MsgBoxStyle.YesNo, "Confirm Delete") = _
      Microsoft.VisualBasic.MsgBoxResult.Yes Then
```

If they respond yes, you delete the selected record:

```
MyConnection.Execute ("Exec ComputerHardwareDelete " _
      & Trim(Mid(lstHardware.Text, 1, 10)))
```

and then repopulate the list box:

```
PopulateList()
```

frmAddHardwareItem Form

The Add Hardware Item form is called from the Computers form and is used to add a hardware item to a computer profile.

The form declares one form-wide variable that provides a connection to the database:

```
Private MyConnection As New ADODB.Connection()
```

The next block of code was placed into the New procedure so that it fires when the form is first loaded.

```
Dim RSList As ADODB.Recordset
MyConnection.ConnectionString = "driver={SQL Server};" _
           & "server=MyServer;uid=" & SQLUserName _
           & ";pwd=" & SQLPassword & ";" & "database=C7NetworkManagement"
MyConnection.Open()
RSList = MyConnection.Execute("Exec HardwareItemsList")
Do Until RSList.EOF
    cmbHardwareItem.Items.Add (RSList.Fields("ItemName").Value _
        & Space(120 - Len(RSList.Fields("ItemName").Value)) _
        & RSList.Fields("HardwareItemID").Value)
    RSList.MoveNext()
Loop
```

You will need a Recordset object:

```
Dim RSList As ADODB.Recordset
```

But first you need to set up your connection object:

```
MyConnection.ConnectionString = "driver={SQL Server};" _
     & "server=MyServer;uid=" & SQLUserName _
     & ";pwd=" & SQLPassword & ";" & "database=C7NetworkManagement"
```

and open the connection to your database:

```
MyConnection.Open()
```

You then retrieve the names of all the hardware items so that they can be placed in the combo box on the form:

```
RSList = MyConnection.Execute("Exec HardwareItemsList")
```

Next, you enter a loop so that you can process each record returned from the stored procedure:

```
Do Until RSList.EOF
```

Each item is added to the combo box on the form:

```
cmbHardwareItem.Items.Add (RSList.Fields("ItemName").Value _
      & Space(120 - Len(RSList.Fields("ItemName").Value)) _
      & RSList.Fields("HardwareItemID").Value)
```

before you move on to the next record:

```
      RSList.MoveNext()
Loop
```

If the user clicks Cancel, you just need to close the current form:

```
Public Sub cmdCancel_Click(ByVal sender As Object,
    ByVal e As System.EventArgs) Handles cmdCancel.Click
    Me.Close()
End Sub
```

The other code block on the form fires if the OK button is clicked.

```
Public Sub cmdOK_Click(ByVal sender As Object,
    ByVal e As System.EventArgs) Handles cmdOK.Click
    If cmbHardwareItem.SelectedIndex = -1 Then
        msgbox("Please select an item that you wish to add.", _
            Microsoft.VisualBasic.MsgBoxStyle.Exclamation, _
            "Network Management")
    Else
        MyConnection.Execute ("Exec ComputerHardwareAdd " _
            & PassedID & ", " _
            & Mid(cmbHardwareItem.Text, 120))
        Me.Close()
    End If
End Sub
```

First, you check to see if the user selected a hardware item in the combo box:

```
If cmbHardwareItem.SelectedIndex = -1 Then
```

If they didn't, you inform them of the problem:

```
msgbox("Please select an item that you wish to add.", _
      Microsoft.VisualBasic.MsgBoxStyle.Exclamation, _
      "Network Management")
```

Otherwise, you can add the hardware item to the computer that was current when this form was called from the Computers form:

```
MyConnection.Execute ("Exec ComputerHardwareAdd " _
      & PassedID & ", " _
      & Mid(cmbHardwareItem.Text, 120))
```

Finally, you close this form and send control back to the Computers form:

```
Me.Close()
```

frmHardware and frmDevics Forms

The Hardware form and the Devices form borrows code from the Computers form. Refer to that section when reviewing those forms.

frmAnswerWizard Form

The Answer Wizard form displays the results of calls to summary views when the user clicks Ask.

The form declares one variable that is accessible by any procedure on the form. It is a Connection object:

```
Private MyConnection As New ADODB.Connection()
```

The next code comes from the New procedure. Therefore, it fires when the form is first loaded.

```
MyConnection.ConnectionString = "driver={SQL Server};" _
    & "server=MyServer;uid=" & SQLUserName _
    & ";pwd=" & SQLPassword & ";" & "database=C7NetworkManagement"
MyConnection.Open()
```

It is used to connect to the SQL Server database. First, the connect string is set:

```
MyConnection.ConnectionString = "driver={SQL Server};" _
      & "server=MyServer;uid=" & SQLUserName _
      & ";pwd=" & SQLPassword & ";" & "database=C7NetworkManagement"
```

You then open the connection to the database:

```
MyConnection.Open()
```

The other procedure on the form fires when the Ask button is clicked. It displays the results of the summary report based on the summary report selected by the user.

```
Protected Sub cmdAsk_Click(ByVal sender As Object,
    ByVal e As System.EventArgs)
    Dim RSAnswer As ADODB.Recordset
    Dim CurrentPadSize As Integer
    lblAnswer.Text = ""
    If cmbQuestion.Text = "Operating System Count" Then
        RSAnswer = MyConnection.Execute("OSCount")
    ElseIf cmbQuestion.Text = "Computer Type Count" Then
        RSAnswer = MyConnection.Execute("ComputerTypeCount")
    ElseIf cmbQuestion.Text = "Device Type Count" Then
        RSAnswer = MyConnection.Execute("DeviceTypeCount")
    Else
        msgbox("Please select a question to view its answer.", _
            Microsoft.VisualBasic.MsgBoxStyle.Information, _
            "Network Management")
        Exit Sub
    End If
    CurrentPadSize = 51 - Len(RSAnswer.Fields(0).Name)
    lblAnswer.Text = RSAnswer.Fields(0).Name & Space(CurrentPadSize)
    lblAnswer.Text = lblAnswer.Text & RSAnswer.Fields(1).Name
    lblAnswer.Text = lblAnswer.Text & Chr(13) & Chr(10)
    Do Until RSAnswer.EOF
        CurrentPadSize = 51 - Len(RSAnswer.Fields(0).Value)
        lblAnswer.Text = lblAnswer.Text _
            & RSAnswer.Fields(0).Value & Space(CurrentPadSize)
        lblAnswer.Text = lblAnswer.Text & RSAnswer.Fields(1).Value
        lblAnswer.Text = lblAnswer.Text & Chr(13) & Chr(10)
        RSAnswer.MoveNext()
    Loop
End Sub
```

You will need a Recordset object:

```
Dim RSAnswer As ADODB.Recordset
```

as well as a variable to store the number of spaces needed to display the text of the summary report in columnar format:

```
Dim CurrentPadSize As Integer
```

The report is displayed on a label on the form. First, you clear the contents of that label:

```
lblAnswer.Text = ""
```

You then check to see which report the user selected. Having ascertained that section, you grab the data from one of the three views that you reviewed earlier in this chapter:

```
If cmbQuestion.Text = "Operating System Count" Then
      RSAnswer = MyConnection.Execute("OSCount")
ElseIf cmbQuestion.Text = "Computer Type Count" Then
      RSAnswer = MyConnection.Execute("ComputerTypeCount")
ElseIf cmbQuestion.Text = "Device Type Count" Then
      RSAnswer = MyConnection.Execute("DeviceTypeCount")
```

If the user didn't select a report, the code flows here:

```
Else
```

and you tell them that they need to select a report:

```
msgbox("Please select a question to view its answer.", _
      Microsoft.VisualBasic.MsgBoxStyle.Information, _
      "Network Management")
```

and exit this procedure:

```
Exit Sub
```

Otherwise, you can display the contents of the summary report. Regardless of which view was selected, it contains two fields. The first is the field that is used for grouping. The second is the number of items in that grouping. The names that you use as the first row in the summary report are the column headers, which come from the names of the fields returned from the view. The first column needs to be sized to 51 so that all the rows will line up:

```
CurrentPadSize = 51 - Len(RSAnswer.Fields(0).Name)
```

You then display that column name and its padding:

```
lblAnswer.Text = RSAnswer.Fields(0).Name & Space(CurrentPadSize)
```

After that, you display the name of the second column:

```
lblAnswer.Text = lblAnswer.Text & RSAnswer.Fields(1).Name
```

and move on to the second row, where the data will appear:

```
lblAnswer.Text = lblAnswer.Text & Chr(13) & Chr(10)
```

You then enter a loop so that you can process each record returned from the view:

```
Do Until RSAnswer.EOF
```

The first field in the record, the Grouped-by field, is also sized to 51:

```
CurrentPadSize = 51 - Len(RSAnswer.Fields(0).Value)
```

and displayed in the label:

```
lblAnswer.Text = lblAnswer.Text _
      & RSAnswer.Fields(0).Value & Space(CurrentPadSize)
```

as is the value for that record:

```
lblAnswer.Text = lblAnswer.Text & RSAnswer.Fields(1).Value
```

You then move on to the next line in the label:

```
lblAnswer.Text = lblAnswer.Text & Chr(13) & Chr(10)
```

and move on to process the next record before looping:

```
      RSAnswer.MoveNext()
Loop
```

CHAPTER 8

Code Library

IN THIS CHAPTER:

C8SQLObjects.sql

CodeBlocks.txt

OldCodeBlocks.txt

Languages.txt

Chapter8CodeLibrary.vbproj

In this chapter, you will look at a solution that allows the user to store and retrieve blocks of code. The solution is made up of a SQL Server back-end database with three tables and a Visual Basic.Net front end. Note that the front-end portion of the solution was developed with Visual Studio.Net Beta 1. Therefore, some of the code and techniques used may need to be changed as Microsoft moves toward the final release of the product.

As you review this solution, pay close attention to the triggers. Triggers are used to automatically archive old versions of code blocks and to maintain a date stamp field.

Application Walk-Through

The solution uses SQL Server Security to log the user into the database through ADO Connection objects. Therefore, when the application starts, the user needs to supply their user name and password. After that, they are presented with the Menu form displayed in Figure 8-1.

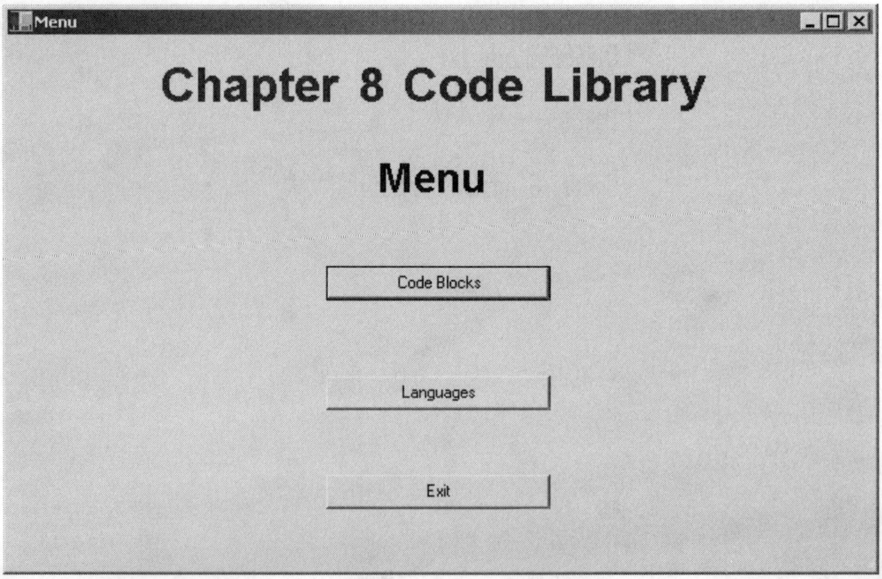

Figure 8-1 *Menu form*

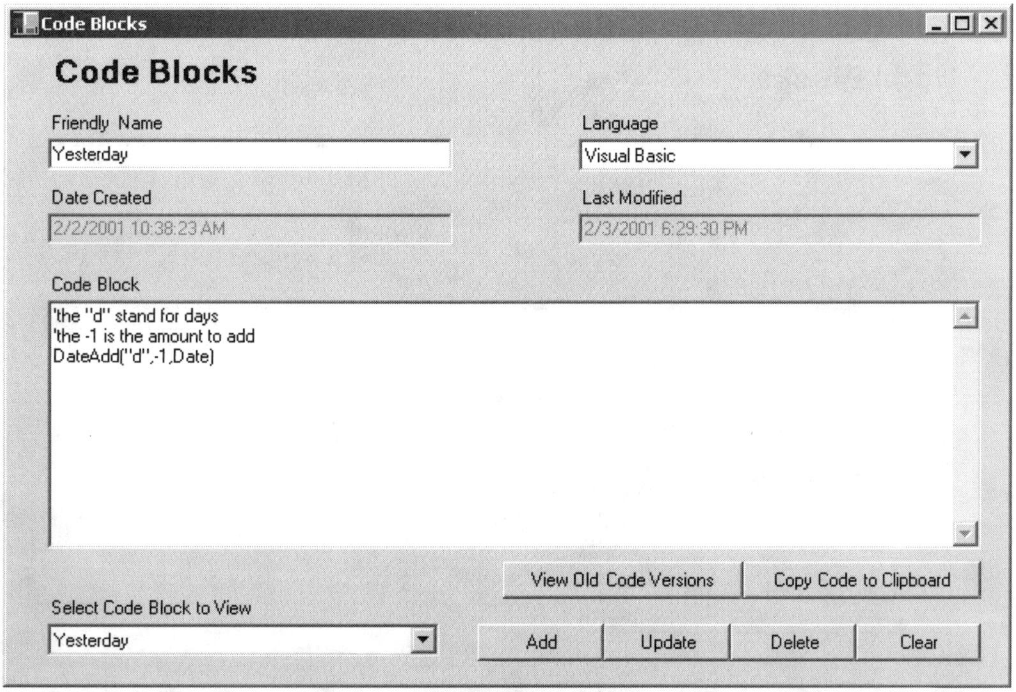

Figure 8-2 *Code Blocks form*

The main part of the application is accessed through the Code Blocks form. The user enters that form by clicking the Code Blocks button on the Menu form.

When they do that, they see the form displayed in Figure 8-2.

The Code Blocks form allows the user to add, edit, delete, and view any of the code block records. The navigational device on this form is the combo box at the bottom left of the form. The combo box lists all the code blocks. When the user selects a code block from the list, the record is displayed on the form.

Note that the two date fields are disabled. This is because they are initially set by default field values. The Last Modified field also automatically changes when the record is updated. Take a look at Figure 8-3.

The code in the Code Block text box has been updated. When the record is updated, the Last Modified field is automatically set to the current system time through a trigger. So the field is always up to date as new versions of the code are applied.

The user can copy the text of the code block onto the clipboard by clicking the Copy Code to Clipboard button.

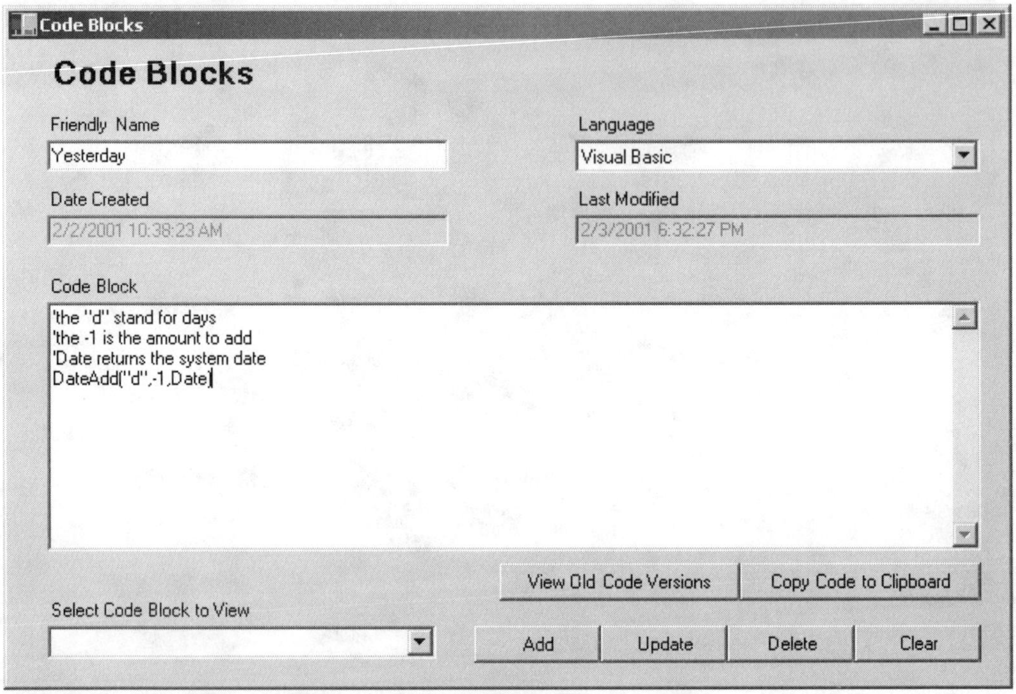

Figure 8-3 *Code Blocks form with modified date*

When they click the View Old Code Versions button, they see the form displayed in Figure 8-4.

The Old Code Blocks form displays all the previous versions of the current code block on the Code Blocks form. Every time the Code Block record is edited, a trigger copies the old version into an Old Code Block record. Therefore, the user has a history of code changes made to the code block in case they need to revert to a previous version.

Back on the Menu form the user can access the other form in this application, the Languages form. When they click the Languages button, they see the form displayed in Figure 8-5.

Each of the code blocks is categorized by the language that it is designed for. The Languages form is used to manage those languages. As with the Code Blocks form, the user selects the record that they want to work with through the combo box.

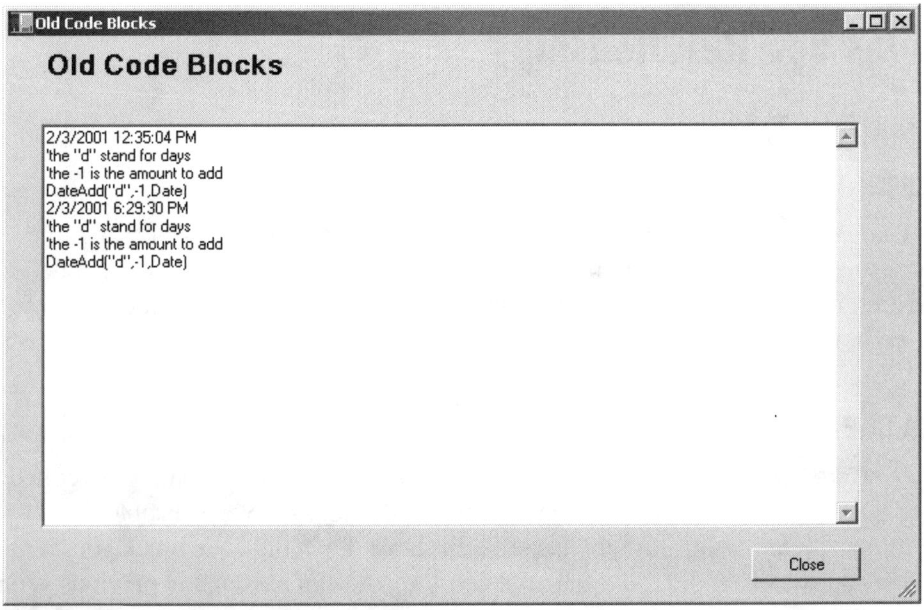

Figure 8-4 *Old Code Blocks form*

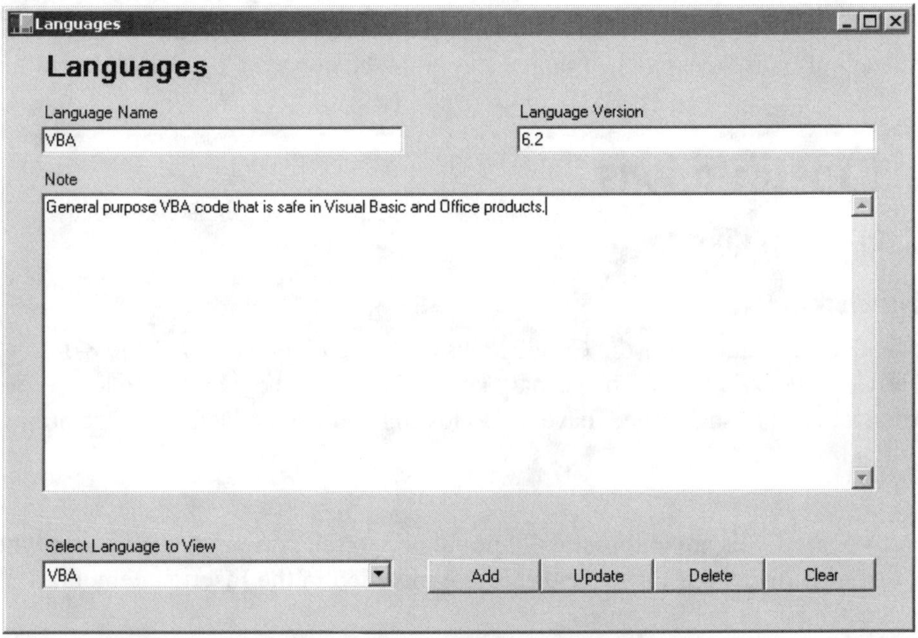

Figure 8-5 *Languages form*

Tables and Relationships

CodeBlocks Table

C8SQLObjects.sql

The CodeBlocks table stores the data on the code blocks themselves. The table relates to the Languages table in a one-to-many relationship. Each of the code blocks is written in a specific language, but each language can have many code blocks written in it.

OldCodeBlocks Table

The OldCodeBlocks table stores previous versions of code blocks as they are edited. The table is populated through a trigger on the CodeBlocks table. The table is in a one-to-many relationship with the CodeBlocks table. Each old code block goes with a specific code block record, but each code block record can have many previous versions.

Languages Table

The Languages table stores the Languages data that is displayed on the Languages form. The data is also displayed in the Languages combo box on the Code Blocks form.

Field Specifications

CodeBlocks Table

CodeBlocks.txt

The field specifications for the CodeBlocks table are displayed in Table 8-1.

The CodeBlockID field is the primary key in the table. The two date fields, DateCreated and LastModified, have the following code in the Default Value property:

```
GetDate()
```

Therefore, the fields are automatically populated to the system date and time when a new record is inserted if those fields are not included in the Insert statement.

Field Name	Field Type	Notes
CodeBlockID	int	Primary Key, Identity Column
FriendlyName	varchar	Length = 50
LanguageName	varchar	Length = 50
DateCreated	datetime	
LastModified	datetime	
CodeBlock	varchar	

Table 8-1 *CodeBlocks Table Field Specifications*

OldCodeBlocks Table

OldCodeBlocks.txt

The field specifications for the OldCodeBlocks table are displayed in Table 8-2.

The primary key in this table is the OldCodeBlockID field. The CodeBlockID field is a foreign key that links this table to the CodeBlocks table. The other fields store the value for the old version of the code block.

Languages Table

Languages.txt

The field specifications for the Languages table are displayed in Table 8-3.

The LanguageID field is the primary key in this table. The other fields store the data about the language.

Field Name	Field Type	Notes
OldCodeBlockID	int	Primary Key, Identity Column
CodeBlockID	int	Foreign Key
WhenEntered	datetime	
CodeBlock	varchar	Length = 5000

Table 8-2 *OldCodeBlocks Table Field Specifications*

Field Name	Field Type	Notes
LanguageID	int	Primary Key, Identity Column
LanguageName	varchar	Length = 50
LanguageVersion	varchar	Length = 50
TheNote	varchar	Length = 1000

Table 8-3 *Languages Table Field Specifications*

Stored Procedures

CodeBlockAdd Stored Procedure

The CodeBlockAdd stored procedure provides the mechanism for adding records to the CodeBlocks table.

```
CREATE PROCEDURE CodeBlockAdd
@FriendlyName varchar(50),
@LanguageName varchar(50),
@CodeBlock varchar(5000)
AS
      BEGIN
            Insert Into CodeBlocks
                  (FriendlyName, LanguageName,
                  CodeBlock) values
                  (@FriendlyName, @LanguageName,
                  @CodeBlock)
            Select @@Identity as TheNewID
      END
GO
```

The calling application passes into the stored procedure the values for the fields being inserted into the new record:

```
@FriendlyName varchar(50),
@LanguageName varchar(50),
@CodeBlock varchar(5000)
```

Those values are then used in the Insert statement:

```
Insert Into CodeBlocks
      (FriendlyName, LanguageName,
      CodeBlock) values
      (@FriendlyName, @LanguageName,
      @CodeBlock)
```

The ID of the new record is then returned to the calling application:

```
Select @@Identity as TheNewID
```

CodeBlockUpdate Stored Procedure

The CodeBlockUpdate stored procedure provides the calling application with the mechanism to update an existing code block record.

```
CREATE PROCEDURE CodeBlockUpdate
@CodeBlockID integer,
@FriendlyName varchar(50),
@LanguageName varchar(50),
@CodeBlock varchar(5000)
AS
      BEGIN
            Update CodeBlocks set
                  FriendlyName = @FriendlyName,
                  LanguageName = @LanguageName,
                  CodeBlock = @CodeBlock
                  Where CodeBlockID = @CodeBlockID
      END
GO
```

The first parameter passed into this procedure is the ID of the code block that is to be edited:

```
@CodeBlockID integer,
```

You also pass in the values for the editable fields in the table:

```
@FriendlyName varchar(50),
@LanguageName varchar(50),
@CodeBlock varchar(5000)
```

Those values are then paired with their corresponding field names in a SQL Update statement:

```
Update CodeBlocks set
      FriendlyName = @FriendlyName,
      LanguageName = @LanguageName,
      CodeBlock = @CodeBlock
      Where CodeBlockID = @CodeBlockID
```

Note that the two date fields in this table are not part of the Add or Update stored procedures. That is because their initial values are set with default values. And the updated value for the LastModified field is supplied through a trigger.

CodeBlockDelete Stored Procedure

The CodeBlockDelete stored procedure provides the mechanism for removing records from the CodeBlocks table.

```
CREATE PROCEDURE CodeBlockDelete
@CodeBlockID integer
AS
      BEGIN
            Delete from  CodeBlocks
                  Where CodeBlockID = @CodeBlockID
      END
GO
```

The procedure requires one parameter, the ID of the record that is to be deleted:

```
@CodeBlockID integer
```

You then remove that record from the CodeBlocks table:

```
Delete from  CodeBlocks
      Where CodeBlockID = @CodeBlockID
```

CodeBlockRecord Stored Procedure

When the user first opens the Code Blocks form, as well as when they select an item from the Code Block combo box, you need to display a record on that form. The CodeBlockRecord stored procedure returns a single record for that purpose.

```
CREATE PROCEDURE CodeBlockRecord
@CodeBlockID integer = 0
AS
If @CodeBlockID = 0
      BEGIN
            Select * from CodeBlocks
                  Where CodeBlockID =
                  (Select Min(CodeBlockID) from CodeBlocks)
      END
Else
      BEGIN
            Select * from CodeBlocks
                  Where CodeBlockID = @CodeBlockID
      END
GO
```

Passed into the procedure is the ID of the code block that is to be retrieved. It has a default value of 0:

```
@CodeBlockID integer = 0
```

If the ID was set to 0 or it was omitted, the code would flow into the True portion of the If statement:

```
If @CodeBlockID = 0
```

In that case, the calling application wants the first record in the CodeBlocks table. So you retrieve the first record by looking for the lowest ID, which is determined through a subquery:

```
Select * from CodeBlocks
      Where CodeBlockID =
      (Select Min(CodeBlockID) from CodeBlocks)
```

Otherwise, you return the contents of the record matching the ID passed into the procedure:

```
Select * from CodeBlocks
      Where CodeBlockID = @CodeBlockID
```

CodeBlockList Stored Procedure

On the Code Blocks form, you need to populate the Code Blocks combo box with the name and ID of each code block so that the user can select an item, which you then display on the form. The CodeBlockList stored procedure provides that capability.

```
CREATE PROCEDURE CodeBlockList
AS
BEGIN
      Select Convert(char(100), FriendlyName) +
            Convert(varchar(12), CodeBlockID)
            as TheListItem from
            CodeBlocks Order By
            FriendlyName
END
GO
```

The procedure simply returns one field through a Select statement. The field is the concatenation of the name of the code block and the ID of the code block. Note that the name of the code block is sized to a fixed width of 100 characters. This sets up the combo box so that the user sees the friendly name but does not see the ID of the code block:

```
Select Convert(char(100), FriendlyName) +
      Convert(varchar(12), CodeBlockID)
      as TheListItem from
      CodeBlocks Order By
      FriendlyName
```

OldCodeBlockList Stored Procedure

When the user opens the Old Code Blocks form, they need to be presented with all the old versions of the code for the current code block on the Code Blocks form. The OldCodeBlockList stored procedure returns those archived entries.

```
CREATE PROCEDURE OldCodeBlockList
@CodeBlockID integer
AS
BEGIN
      Select WhenEntered, CodeBlock
            from OldCodeBlocks
```

```
            Where CodeBlockID = @CodeBlockID
            Order By WhenEntered
END
GO
```

Passed into the procedure is the ID of the code block for which the archived entries are to be retrieved:

```
@CodeBlockID integer
```

The code and the dates the entries were originally made is returned through a Select statement sorted by date:

```
Select WhenEntered, CodeBlock
      from OldCodeBlocks
      Where CodeBlockID = @CodeBlockID
      Order By WhenEntered
```

LanguageAdd Stored Procedure

The LanguageAdd stored procedure provides the mechanism for adding new records to the Languages table.

```
CREATE PROCEDURE LanguageAdd
@LanguageName varchar(50),
@LanguageVersion varchar(50),
@TheNote varchar(1000)
AS
      BEGIN
            Insert Into Languages
                  (LanguageName, LanguageVersion,
                  TheNote) values
                  (@LanguageName, @LanguageVersion,
                  @TheNote)
            Select @@Identity as TheNewID
      END
GO
```

Passed into the procedure are the values for the three data fields in the table:

```
@LanguageName varchar(50),
@LanguageVersion varchar(50),
@TheNote varchar(1000)
```

Those values are then used in the value-list portion of a SQL Insert statement:

```
Insert Into Languages
      (LanguageName, LanguageVersion,
      TheNote) values
      (@LanguageName, @LanguageVersion,
      @TheNote)
```

Returned from the procedure is the ID of the language that was just added, since the LanguageID field is an identity column:

```
Select @@Identity as TheNewID
```

LanguageUpdate Stored Procedure

When the calling application needs to update a language record, the LanguageUpdate stored procedure is called.

```
CREATE PROCEDURE LanguageUpdate
@LanguageID integer,
@LanguageName varchar(50),
@LanguageVersion varchar(50),
@TheNote varchar(1000)
AS
      BEGIN
            Update Languages set
                  LanguageName = @LanguageName,
                  LanguageVersion = @LanguageVersion,
                  TheNote = @TheNote
                  Where LanguageID = @LanguageID
      END
GO
```

The first parameter is used to pass in the ID of the language that is to be edited, which is used in the Where clause of an Update statement:

```
@LanguageID integer,
```

The other parameters store the values for the fields being updated:

```
@LanguageName varchar(50),
@LanguageVersion varchar(50),
@TheNote varchar(1000)
```

Those values are then paired with their field names in the Update statement:

```
Update Languages set
      LanguageName = @LanguageName,
      LanguageVersion = @LanguageVersion,
      TheNote = @TheNote
      Where LanguageID = @LanguageID
```

LanguageDelete Stored Procedure

The LanguageDelete stored procedure is called when a record needs to be deleted from the Languages table.

```
CREATE PROCEDURE LanguageDelete
@LanguageID integer
AS
      BEGIN
            Delete from  Languages
                  Where LanguageID = @LanguageID
      END
GO
```

The calling application passes in the ID of the record to be deleted:

```
@LanguageID integer
```

That value is then used in the Where clause of the Delete statement:

```
Delete from  Languages
      Where LanguageID = @LanguageID
```

LanguageRecord Stored Procedure

On the Languages form, you need to display the contents of a specific language record. This is done by calling the LanguageRecord stored procedure.

```
CREATE PROCEDURE LanguageRecord
@LanguageID integer = 0
AS
If @LanguageID = 0
      BEGIN
            Select * from Languages
                  Where LanguageID =
```

```
                    (Select Min(LanguageID) from Languages)
        END
Else
        BEGIN
                Select * from Languages
                        Where LanguageID = @LanguageID
        END
GO
```

Passed into the procedure is the ID of the record that is to be retrieved:

```
@LanguageID integer = 0
```

If 0 was passed in, or the parameter was omitted, the code flows here:

```
If @LanguageID = 0
```

In that case, the calling application wants the first record in the table. As you will see when you look at the code in the Visual Basic.Net front-end application, you do this when the form is first opened or after a record has been deleted to populate the form with a default record:

```
Select * from Languages
        Where LanguageID =
        (Select Min(LanguageID) from Languages)
```

If the value passed in was not 0, you return the contents of the record requested:

```
Select * from Languages
        Where LanguageID = @LanguageID
```

LanguageList Stored Procedure

The LanguageList stored procedure is called to populate the Language List combo box on the Languages form. That combo box is used to navigate through the Languages records.

```
CREATE PROCEDURE LanguageList
AS
BEGIN
```

```
      Select Convert(char(100), LanguageName) +
            Convert(varchar(12), LanguageID)
            as TheListItem from
            Languages Order By
            LanguageName
END
GO
```

The procedure returns a single field, an output field that is made up of the name of the language and the ID of the language. The name of the language is sized wide enough so that the user only sees the name without seeing the ID. The records returned are sorted by the name of the language:

```
Select Convert(char(100), LanguageName) +
      Convert(varchar(12), LanguageID)
      as TheListItem from
      Languages Order By
      LanguageName
```

LanguageOnlyList Stored Procedure

Back on the Code Blocks form, you have a second combo box that allows the user to select a language that the code block is written in. The LanguageOnlyList stored procedure returns the contents for that list.

```
CREATE PROCEDURE LanguageOnlyList
AS
BEGIN
      Select LanguageName
            From Languages
            Order By LanguageName
END
GO
```

The procedure returns the name of the language sorted by the name:

```
Select LanguageName
      From Languages
      Order By LanguageName
```

Triggers

UpdateCodeBlock Trigger

When a code block record is updated, you need to change the LastModified date and archive the old version of the code block into the OldCodeBlocks table. The UpdateCodeBlock trigger accomplishes those tasks.

```
CREATE TRIGGER UpdateCodeBlocks ON dbo.CodeBlocks
AFTER UPDATE
AS
BEGIN
      DECLARE
      @UpdatedID integer,
      @UpdatedWhen datetime,
      @UpdatedCodeBlock varchar(5000)
      Select @UpdatedID = CodeBlockID from Deleted
      Select @UpdatedWhen = LastModified from Deleted
      Select @UpdatedCodeBlock = CodeBlock from Deleted
      Insert Into OldCodeBlocks
            (CodeBlockID, WhenEntered, CodeBlock)
            Values (@UpdatedID,
            @UpdatedWhen, @UpdatedCodeBlock)
      Update CodeBlocks
            Set LastModified = GetDate()
            Where CodeBlockID = (Select CodeBlockID
            From Deleted)
END
```

The trigger is for the CodeBlocks table:

```
CREATE TRIGGER UpdateCodeBlocks ON dbo.CodeBlocks
```

and fires after an existing record has been modified:

```
AFTER UPDATE
```

You will need three variables in this trigger:

```
DECLARE
@UpdatedID integer,
```

```
@UpdatedWhen datetime,
@UpdatedCodeBlock varchar(5000)
```

Those variables are set to the old values of the fields in the table. This is done by retrieving values from the Deleted table, which is a special table in a trigger that gives you access to the previous values in a field prior to an Update or a Delete:

```
Select @UpdatedID = CodeBlockID from Deleted
Select @UpdatedWhen = LastModified from Deleted
Select @UpdatedCodeBlock = CodeBlock from Deleted
```

Those values are then placed into a new record in the OldCodeBlocks table, which has the effect of creating an archived copy of the old code block:

```
Insert Into OldCodeBlocks
      (CodeBlockID, WhenEntered, CodeBlock)
      Values (@UpdatedID,
      @UpdatedWhen, @UpdatedCodeBlock)
```

You also need to update the LastModified field for the current code block record, since it has just been modified. You do that through an Update statement:

```
Update CodeBlocks
      Set LastModified = GetDate()
      Where CodeBlockID = (Select CodeBlockID
      From Deleted)
```

DeleteCodeBlocks Trigger

When a code block is deleted, you need to delete all the archived versions of the code block in the OldCodeBlocks table. That is done through the DeleteCodeBlocks trigger.

```
CREATE TRIGGER DeleteCodeBlocks ON dbo.CodeBlocks
AFTER DELETE
AS
BEGIN
      Delete from OldCodeBlocks Where
            CodeBlockID = (Select CodeBlockID from Deleted)
END
```

The trigger works on the CodeBlocks table:

```
CREATE TRIGGER DeleteCodeBlocks ON dbo.CodeBlocks
```

and fires after a record is deleted from that table:

```
AFTER DELETE
```

The trigger then deletes all the records from the OldCodeBlocks table that relate to the deleted code block record:

```
Delete from OldCodeBlocks Where
     CodeBlockID = (Select CodeBlockID from Deleted)
```

Modules

Chapter8CodeLibrary.vbproj

modPublicProcs Module

The front-end application contains a single code module called modPublicProcs. That module contains the following declarations:

```
Public SQLUserName As String
Public SQLPassword As String
Public ID2Use As Long
```

All three variables are declared with Public scope so that they are available to any procedure on any form in the application. The first is used to store the SQL Server user name of the person using the application:

```
Public SQLUserName As String
```

The next variable stores their SQL Server password:

```
Public SQLPassword As String
```

and the third Public variable stores an ID that is passed between the Code Blocks form and the Old Code Blocks form:

```
Public ID2Use As Long
```

Forms

frmMenu Form

The code on the Menu form prompts the user for their login information and connects the user to two of the other forms in the application.

This first block of code is placed within the New procedure so that it fires when the form is first opened.

```
SQLUserName = InputBox("Please enter your user name.", _
      "Network Management", "")
If SQLUserName = "" Then
      End
End If
SQLPassword = InputBox("Please enter your password.", _
      "Network Management", "")
If SQLPassword = "" Then
      End
End If
```

The code prompts the user for their name and places it in one of the Public variables:

```
SQLUserName = InputBox("Please enter your user name.", _
      "Network Management", "")
```

You then make sure that the user supplied a name:

```
If SQLUserName = "" Then
```

If they didn't, you exit the application:

```
End
```

Next, you prompt the user for their SQL Server password:

```
SQLPassword = InputBox("Please enter your password.", _
      "Network Management", "")
```

and you make sure that they didn't click the Cancel button:

```
If SQLPassword = "" Then
```

If they did, you exit the application:

```
End
```

The next code block fires when the Code Blocks button is clicked:

```
Public Sub cmdCodeBlocks_Click(ByVal sender As Object, _
      ByVal e As System.EventArgs) Handles cmdCodeBlocks.Click
      Dim MyfrmCodeBlocks As New frmCodeBlocks()
      MyfrmCodeBlocks.Show()
End Sub
```

The procedure creates an instance of the Code Blocks form:

```
Dim MyfrmCodeBlocks As New frmCodeBlocks()
```

which is then opened:

```
MyfrmCodeBlocks.Show()
```

When the Languages button is clicked, similar code fires.

```
Public Sub cmdLanguages_Click(ByVal sender As Object, _
    ByVal e As System.EventArgs) Handles cmdLanguages.Click
    Dim MyfrmLanguages As New frmLanguages()
    MyfrmLanguages.show()
End Sub
```

You create an instance of the Languages form:

```
Dim MyfrmLanguages As New frmLanguages()
```

and display that form:

```
MyfrmLanguages.show()
```

When the Exit button is clicked, you close the application:

```
Public Sub cmdExit_Click(ByVal sender As Object, _
    ByVal e As System.EventArgs) Handles cmdExit.Click
    End
End Sub
```

frmCodeBlocks Form

The code on the Code Blocks form provides the user with the capability of managing the code block records.

At the very top of the form's code, you set two options.

```
Option Explicit On
Option Strict Off
```

The first tells the compiler that you will declare your variables:

```
Option Explicit On
```

The second tells the compiler that you do not want restrictions placed on data type conversions:

```
Option Strict Off
```

Right after the class is defined, you declare two variables.

```
Private MyConnection As New ADODB.Connection()
Private CurrentID As Long = 0
```

The variables have Private scope, which means they can be used by any procedure on this form. The first is a connection object that you will use to connect to the database:

```
Private MyConnection As New ADODB.Connection()
```

The second stores the ID of the current code block on the form:

```
Private CurrentID As Long = 0
```

The form declares four user-defined procedures that are called from other procedures and event procedures. The first clears the contents of the form.

```
Public Sub ClearForm()
    CurrentID = 0
    txtFriendlyName.Text = ""
    txtDateCreated.Text = ""
    txtLastModified.Text = ""
    txtCodeBlock.Text = ""
End Sub
```

First, you clear the ID of the current code block:

```
CurrentID = 0
```

and then you clear the contents of the text boxes on the form:

```
txtFriendlyName.Text = ""
txtDateCreated.Text = ""
txtLastModified.Text = ""
txtCodeBlock.Text = ""
```

The next procedure populates the Language combo box on the form.

```
Public Sub PopulateLanguageList()
    Dim RSList As ADODB.Recordset
    cmbLanguage.Items.Clear()
    RSList = MyConnection.Execute("Exec LanguageOnlyList")
    Do Until RSList.EOF
        cmbLanguage.Items.Add (RSList.Fields("LanguageName").Value)
        RSList.MoveNext()
    Loop
End Sub
```

The procedure requires a Recordset object:

```
Dim RSList As ADODB.Recordset
```

You first clear the contents of the combo box:

```
cmbLanguage.Items.Clear()
```

and then retrieve the contents for the list through the LanguageOnlyList stored procedure:

```
RSList = MyConnection.Execute("Exec LanguageOnlyList")
```

You then enter a loop so that you can process each of the records returned:

```
Do Until RSList.EOF
```

Each record is added as an Item to the combo box:

```
cmbLanguage.Items.Add (RSList.Fields("LanguageName").Value)
```

before you move on to process the next record:

```
RSList.MoveNext()
Loop
```

The next procedure populates the other combo box on the form. This one contains all the names of the code blocks.

```
Public Sub PopulateCodeBlockList()
    Dim RSList As ADODB.Recordset
    cmbCodeBlockID.Items.Clear()
    RSList = MyConnection.Execute("Exec CodeBlockList")
    Do Until RSList.EOF
        cmbCodeBlockID.Items.Add (RSList.Fields(0).Value)
        RSList.MoveNext()
    Loop
End Sub
```

The procedure requires a Recordset object:

```
Dim RSList As ADODB.Recordset
```

First, you need to clear the contents of the combo box:

```
cmbCodeBlockID.Items.Clear()
```

Next, you retrieve the contents for the list through the CodeBlockList stored procedure:

```
RSList = MyConnection.Execute("Exec CodeBlockList")
```

You then enter a loop so that each record can be processed:

```
Do Until RSList.EOF
```

Each record is added to the combo box:

```
cmbCodeBlockID.Items.Add (RSList.Fields(0).Value)
```

You then move the record pointer forward and loop:

```
RSList.MoveNext()
Loop
```

The next procedure is called throughout the form to display a record on the form.

```
Public Sub PopulateRecord(ByVal ID2Use As Long)
    Dim RSCodeBlock As New ADODB.Recordset()
    RSCodeBlock = MyConnection.Execute("Exec CodeBlockRecord " _
        & ID2Use)
    If RSCodeBlock.EOF Then
        ClearForm()
    Else
        CurrentID = RSCodeBlock.Fields("CodeBlockID").Value
        txtFriendlyName.Text = RSCodeBlock.Fields("FriendlyName").Value
        cmbLanguage.Text = RSCodeBlock.Fields("LanguageName").Value
        txtDateCreated.Text = RSCodeBlock.Fields("DateCreated").Value
        txtLastModified.Text = RSCodeBlock.Fields("LastModified").Value
        txtCodeBlock.Text = RSCodeBlock.Fields("CodeBlock").Value
    End If
End Sub
```

The procedure requires a Recordset object:

```
Dim RSCodeBlock As New ADODB.Recordset()
```

which is set to the return of a call to the CodeBlockRecord stored procedure passing to it the ID of the record to be retrieved:

```
RSCodeBlock = MyConnection.Execute("Exec CodeBlockRecord " _
      & ID2Use)
```

You then check to see if a record was found:

```
If RSCodeBlock.EOF Then
```

If it wasn't, you clear the contents of the form:

```
ClearForm()
```

Otherwise, you can set the CurrentID variable to the ID of the record retrieved:

```
CurrentID = RSCodeBlock.Fields("CodeBlockID").Value
```

and populate the text boxes and combo box on the form with the values in the record retrieved:

```
txtFriendlyName.Text = RSCodeBlock.Fields("FriendlyName").Value
cmbLanguage.Text = RSCodeBlock.Fields("LanguageName").Value
txtDateCreated.Text = RSCodeBlock.Fields("DateCreated").Value
txtLastModified.Text = RSCodeBlock.Fields("LastModified").Value
txtCodeBlock.Text = RSCodeBlock.Fields("CodeBlock").Value
```

The next code fires when the form is first opened, since it is to be found in the New procedure.

```
MyConnection.ConnectionString = "driver={SQL Server};" _
      & "server=MyServer;uid=" & SQLUserName _
      & ";pwd=" & SQLPassword & ";" & "database=C8CodeLibrary"
MyConnection.Open()
PopulateLanguageList()
PopulateCodeBlockList()
PopulateRecord (0)
```

First, you set the connect string property for your Connection object. Note that if you call your database something different than I have, you would need to change it here:

```
MyConnection.ConnectionString = "driver={SQL Server};" _
      & "server=MyServer;uid=" & SQLUserName _
      & ";pwd=" & SQLPassword & ";" & "database=C8CodeLibrary"
```

You then open the connection to the database:

```
MyConnection.Open()
```

You then call your procedure to populate the Language combo box:

```
PopulateLanguageList()
```

populate the Code Block combo box:

```
PopulateCodeBlockList()
```

and display a record on the form:

```
PopulateRecord (0)
```

The next procedure fires when the user selects one of the items in the Code Block combo box.

```
Public Sub cmbCodeBlockID_SelectedIndexChanged(ByVal sender As Object,
    ByVal e As System.EventArgs) Handles cmbCodeBlockID.SelectedIndexChanged
    If cmbCodeBlockID.SelectedIndex <> -1 Then
        PopulateRecord (Mid(cmbCodeBlockID.Text, 101))
    End If
End Sub
```

First, you make sure that the user has selected a valid item in the list:

```
If cmbCodeBlockID.SelectedIndex <> -1 Then
```

If so, you call your procedure so that the code block selected in the combo box is displayed on the form:

```
PopulateRecord (Mid(cmbCodeBlockID.Text, 101))
```

When the Add button is clicked, the next code block fires.

```
Public Sub cmdAdd_Click(ByVal sender As Object,
    ByVal e As System.EventArgs) Handles cmdAdd.Click
    Dim RSNewID As ADODB.Recordset
    Dim TheFriendlyName As String
    Dim TheCodeBlock As String
    TheFriendlyName = Replace(txtFriendlyName.Text, "'", "''")
    TheCodeBlock = Replace(txtCodeBlock.Text, "'", "''")
    RSNewID = MyConnection.Execute("Exec CodeBlockAdd " _
        & "'" & TheFriendlyName & "', " _
        & "'" & cmbLanguage.Text & "', " _
        & "'" & TheCodeBlock & "'")
    CurrentID = RSNewID.Fields("TheNewID").Value
    PopulateCodeBlockList()
    PopulateRecord (CurrentID)
End Sub
```

The procedure requires a Recordset object:

```
Dim RSNewID As ADODB.Recordset
```

as well as variables to store the converted values of some of the fields on the form:

```
Dim TheFriendlyName As String
Dim TheCodeBlock As String
```

You set those variables to their corresponding text boxes with the ' character converted so that it doesn't cause an error in your SQL statement in the stored procedure:

```
TheFriendlyName = Replace(txtFriendlyName.Text, "'", "''")
TheCodeBlock = Replace(txtCodeBlock.Text, "'", "''")
```

The stored procedure is then called to add a new code block record:

```
RSNewID = MyConnection.Execute("Exec CodeBlockAdd " _
      & "'" & TheFriendlyName & "', " _
      & "'" & cmbLanguage.Text & "', " _
      & "'" & TheCodeBlock & "'")
```

The stored procedure returns the ID of the record just added. You place that ID into your form-wide variable:

```
CurrentID = RSNewID.Fields("TheNewID").Value
```

You then update the Code Block combo box:

```
PopulateCodeBlockList()
```

and redisplay the record on the form so that the date fields will be updated:

```
PopulateRecord (CurrentID)
```

When the Update button is clicked, this code fires.

```
Public Sub cmdUpdate_Click(ByVal sender As Object,
    ByVal e As System.EventArgs) Handles cmdUpdate.Click
    Dim TheFriendlyName As String
    Dim TheCodeBlock As String
    TheFriendlyName = Replace(txtFriendlyName.Text, "'", "''")
    TheCodeBlock = Replace(txtCodeBlock.Text, "'", "''")
    If CurrentID = 0 Then
        MsgBox("You are not in an active record!", _
            Microsoft.VisualBasic.MsgBoxStyle.Exclamation, _
            "Code Library")
    Else
        MyConnection.Execute ("Exec CodeBlockUpdate " _
            & CurrentID & ", " _
            & "'" & TheFriendlyName & "', " _
```

```
            & "'" & cmbLanguage.Text & "', " _
            & "'" & TheCodeBlock & "'")
        PopulateCodeBlockList()
        PopulateRecord (CurrentID)
    End If
End Sub
```

The procedure needs two variables:

```
Dim TheFriendlyName As String
Dim TheCodeBlock As String
```

that are set to the converted values in their corresponding text boxes, as you did in the Add procedure:

```
TheFriendlyName = Replace(txtFriendlyName.Text, "'", "''")
TheCodeBlock = Replace(txtCodeBlock.Text, "'", "''")
```

But first you make sure you are in a valid record:

```
If CurrentID = 0 Then
```

If you aren't, you let the user know:

```
MsgBox("You are not in an active record!", _
      Microsoft.VisualBasic.MsgBoxStyle.Exclamation, _
      "Code Library")
```

Otherwise, you can update the current record:

```
MyConnection.Execute ("Exec CodeBlockUpdate " _
      & CurrentID & ", " _
      & "'" & TheFriendlyName & "', " _
      & "'" & cmbLanguage.Text & "', " _
      & "'" & TheCodeBlock & "'")
```

You then need to update the Code Block combo box:

```
PopulateCodeBlockList()
```

and repopulate the record on the form so that the date field is displayed correctly:

```
PopulateRecord (CurrentID)
```

When the user clicks the Delete button, the next code block fires.

```
Public Sub cmdDelete_Click(ByVal sender As Object,
    ByVal e As System.EventArgs) Handles cmdDelete.Click
    If CurrentID = 0 Then
        ClearForm()
    Else
        MyConnection.Execute ("Exec CodeBlockDelete " _
            & CurrentID)
        PopulateRecord (0)
        PopulateCodeBlockList()
    End If
End Sub
```

You first make sure you are not in Add mode:

```
If CurrentID = 0 Then
```

If you are, you just need to clear the form:

```
ClearForm()
```

Otherwise, you delete the current record:

```
MyConnection.Execute ("Exec CodeBlockDelete " _
      & CurrentID)
```

display a valid record:

```
PopulateRecord (0)
```

and update the Code Block combo box:

```
PopulateCodeBlockList()
```

When the user clicks the Clear button, this code block calls your procedure to clear the contents of the form:

```
Public Sub cmdClear_Click(ByVal sender As Object,
    ByVal e As System.EventArgs) Handles cmdClear.Click
    ClearForm()
End Sub
```

The next procedure fires when the View Old Code Versions button is clicked.

```
Public Sub cmdOldCode_Click(ByVal sender As Object,
    ByVal e As System.EventArgs) Handles cmdOldCode.Click
    Dim MyfrmOldCodeBlocks As New frmOldCodeBlocks()
    ID2Use = CurrentID
    MyfrmOldCodeBlocks.ShowDialog()
    MyfrmOldCodeBlocks = Nothing
End Sub
```

The procedure creates an instance of your Old Code Blocks form:

```
Dim MyfrmOldCodeBlocks As New frmOldCodeBlocks()
```

and sets the Public ID so that form can retrieve it:

```
ID2Use = CurrentID
```

You then open the Old Code Blocks form as a dialog box so that it retains the focus:

```
MyfrmOldCodeBlocks.ShowDialog()
```

After the user is done with that form, you release its resources:

```
MyfrmOldCodeBlocks = Nothing
```

The last code block fires when the Copy Code to Clipboard button is clicked.

```
Public Sub cmdCopyCodeToClipBoard_Click(ByVal sender As Object,
    ByVal e As System.EventArgs) Handles cmdCopyCodeToClipBoard.Click
    Clipboard.SetDataObject (txtCodeBlock.Text)
End Sub
```

It simply uses the SetDataObject method of the clipboard object to place the contents of the Code Block text box onto the Clipboard:

```
Clipboard.SetDataObject (txtCodeBlock.Text)
```

frmOldCodeBlocks Form

The code on the Old Code Blocks form displays the archived code blocks for the current code block on the Code Blocks form. At the top of the form, you set these two options:

```
Option Explicit On
Option Strict Off
```

The first tells the compiler that you will declare your variables:

```
Option Explicit On
```

The other tells the compiler not to use strict conversion checking:

```
Option Strict Off
```

You declare one variable with the scope of Private so that it is available to any procedure on this form. The variable will store your connection to the database:

```
Private MyConnection As New ADODB.Connection()
```

The first code block fires when the form is first loaded.

```
Dim RSOldCode As ADODB.Recordset
MyConnection.ConnectionString = "driver={SQL Server};" _
    & "server=MyServer;uid=" & SQLUserName _
    & ";pwd=" & SQLPassword & ";" & "database=C8CodeLibrary"
MyConnection.Open()
RSOldCode = MyConnection.Execute("Exec OldCodeBlockList " _
    & ID2Use)
Do Until RSOldCode.EOF
    txtCodeBlock.Text = txtCodeBlock.Text _
        & RSOldCode.Fields("WhenEntered").Value _
        & Chr(13) & Chr(10) _
        & RSOldCode.Fields("CodeBlock").Value _
        & Chr(13) & Chr(10)
    RSOldCode.MoveNext()
Loop
```

You will need a Recordset object:

```
Dim RSOldCode As ADODB.Recordset
```

First, you set your Connect String property:

```
MyConnection.ConnectionString = "driver={SQL Server};" _
      & "server=MyServer;uid=" & SQLUserName _
      & ";pwd=" & SQLPassword & ";" & "database=C8CodeLibrary"
```

and open the connection to the database:

```
MyConnection.Open()
```

You then use the OldCodeBlockList stored procedure to retrieve all the archived versions of the current code block on the Code Blocks form:

```
RSOldCode = MyConnection.Execute("Exec OldCodeBlockList " _
     & ID2Use)
```

You then enter a loop so that you can process each of the archived code blocks:

```
Do Until RSOldCode.EOF
```

Each one is added to the text box on this form:

```
txtCodeBlock.Text = txtCodeBlock.Text _
     & RSOldCode.Fields("WhenEntered").Value _
     & Chr(13) & Chr(10) _
     & RSOldCode.Fields("CodeBlock").Value _
     & Chr(13) & Chr(10)
```

You then move on to process the next record:

```
RSOldCode.MoveNext()
Loop
```

The other code block on this form closes the form when the Close button is clicked:

```
Public Sub cmdClose_Click(ByVal sender As Object,
    ByVal e As System.EventArgs) Handles cmdClose.Click
    Me.Close()
End Sub
```

frmLanguages Form

The code on the Languages form is almost identical to the code on the Code Blocks form. Refer to that code when reviewing the Languages form.

PART III

Access/SQL Server Applications

CHAPTER

9

Access as a Front End to SQL Server

In this section of the book, we will look at solutions that use Access as a front end to SQL Server. But first, in this chapter, we will discuss the advantages of using Access as a front end.

Using Access with SQL Server

We then look at upsizing from Access to SQL Server and linking from Access to SQL Server. Last, you will see how you include components within Access so that you can use ADO with Access.

Advantages of Using Access

When developing a solution that includes a SQL Server back end, many developers start their work in Access. This is because, with the wizards included in Access, creating a basic front end is relatively straightforward. Access includes wizards for creating forms, queries, and reports, sometimes with no code necessary.

Using Access in such an environment provides you with a quick start, but if the application is in heavy use, the slowness and inefficiency of linking tables through Access becomes apparent. At that point, the developer needs to create solutions such as those discussed in this section that use stored procedures for data manipulation.

That doesn't mean that you as the developer should abandon Access. If you create efficient views that retrieve only the specific records needed, you can still use the power of Access to generate reports. Besides, Access's simple drag-and–drop query environment often makes it much easier for managers and other individuals without development experience to mine the data in their database.

Another reason that Access is used as a front end to SQL Server is that many SQL Server databases start as Access databases. Many databases start as a single-user solution. A specific employee has a specific set of data that they need to track. Access frequently is a great solution in such an environment, but then, over time, the needs of the company grow and the needs of the solution grow with it. So instead of starting a database over from scratch, as you will see in the next section of this chapter, developers will upsize their Access database to SQL Server and then modify that database to make it more efficient.

A third reason to use Access as a front end is its availability. If you know that everyone you need to provide the solution to has Microsoft Office with Access, then you can simply give the users of your solution the front-end Access database without having to worry about creating an installation.

Upsizing to SQL Server

As mentioned in the preceding section, for a variety of reasons, you may end up with an Access database that you need to convert or upsize to a SQL Server database. Access comes with a wizard called the Upsizing Wizard that makes this procedure pretty painless.

You start the wizard by selecting Upsizing Wizard from the Tools/Database Utilities menu. When you do that, you see the first dialog of the wizard, displayed in Figure 9-1.

You can choose to place your Access tables into an existing SQL Server database, or you can use the Wizard to create a new database. In this example, we will create a new SQL Server database. So select that and click Next to see the second dialog of the wizard, displayed in Figure 9-2.

In this dialog box, select or type in the name of the SQL Server where you want to create the database. Then enter your user name and password for that SQL Server. Note that you need to have the privileges to create a database for this wizard to work. In the last box on this dialog, enter a name for the new database. Then click Next to see the next dialog of the wizard, displayed in Figure 9-3.

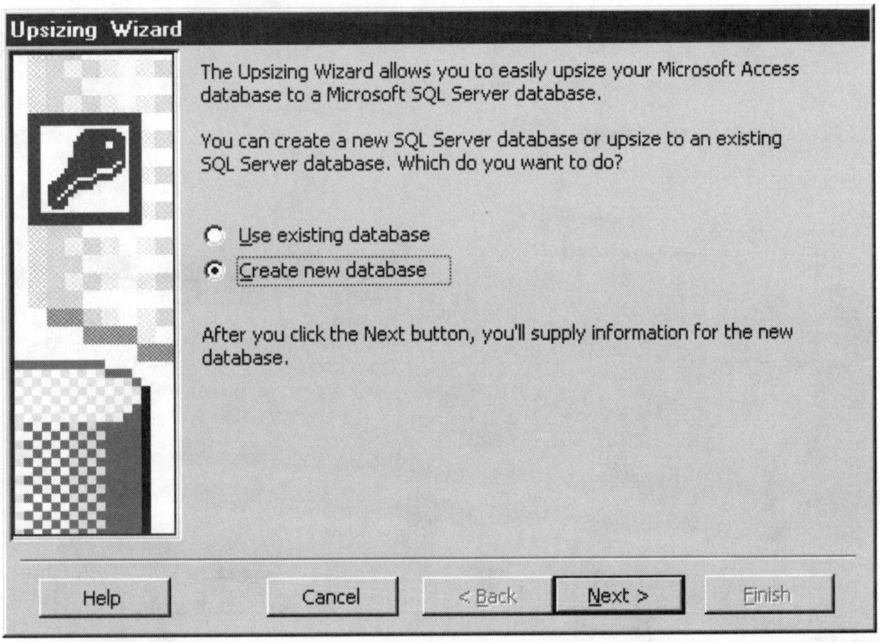

Figure 9-1 *Upsizing Wizard, step 1*

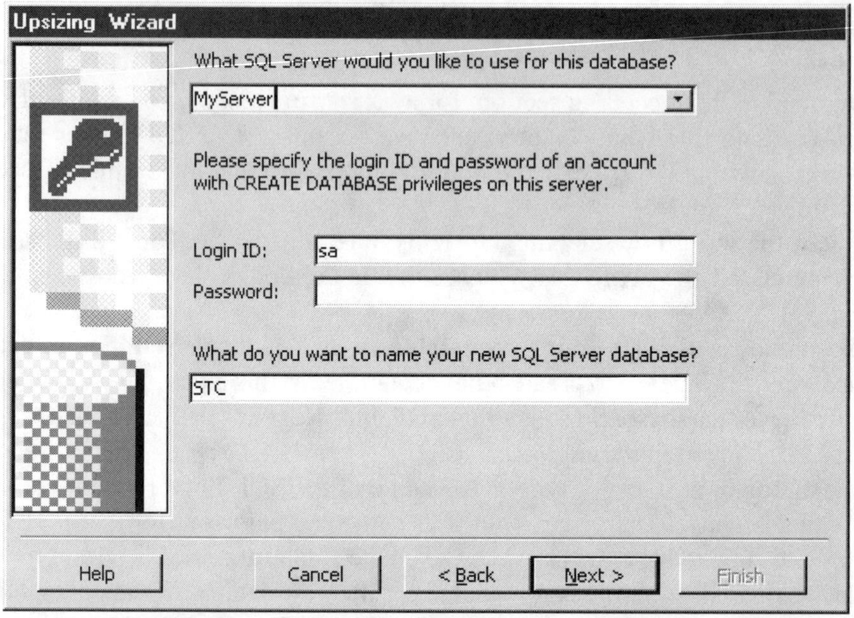

Figure 9-2 *Upsizing Wizard, step 2*

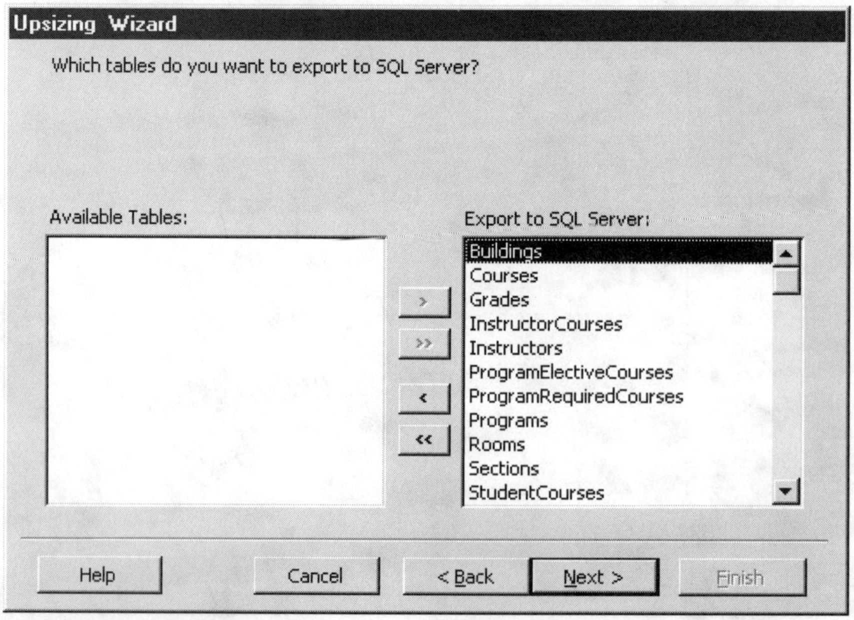

Figure 9-3 *Upsizing Wizard, step 3*

In this third step, you select the tables that you want to export to SQL Server. You don't have to export them all. In fact, some would more efficiently stay in the Access database. Any of the data that is shared by all should be upsized, but data that doesn't change, data that changes too infrequently, or data that is just for a single user can stay in the Access database. You would then give each user their own front-end Access database that contained any data they manage themselves. That Access database would then link to the SQL Server database where the shared data was located.

Click Next once you have selected the tables you want to export. You should see the dialog box displayed in Figure 9-4.

At the top of the fourth dialog, you select which field attributes you want to export to SQL Server. You can also decide whether you want the wizard to add timestamp fields to the SQL Server tables.

Timestamp fields are used to indicate whether a record has changed, not when it was changed. This information is then used by Access to determine whether a record that is being updated has changed.

You can also choose to only upsize the table structures without any data. Click Next to move on to the next step of the wizard, displayed in Figure 9-5.

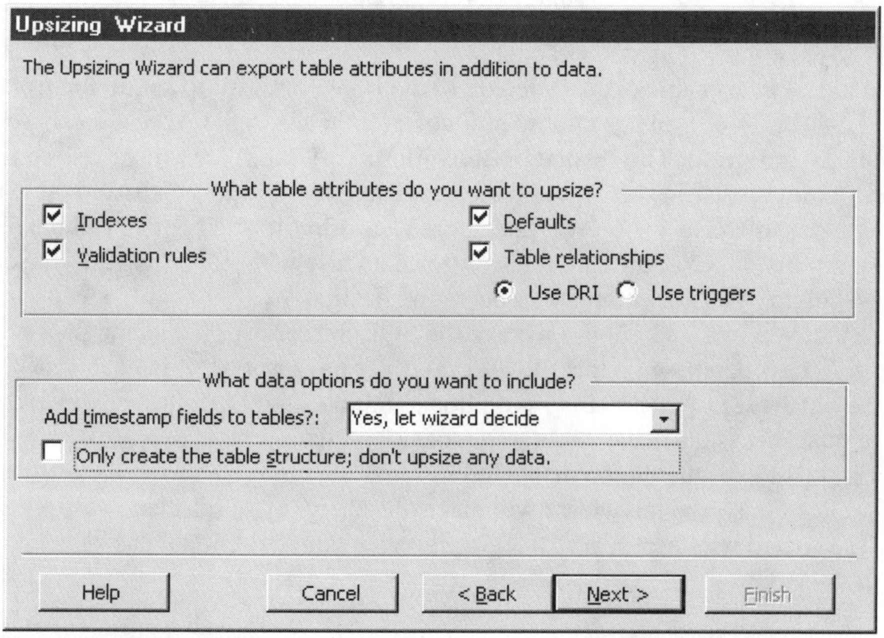

Figure 9-4 *Upsizing Wizard, step 4*

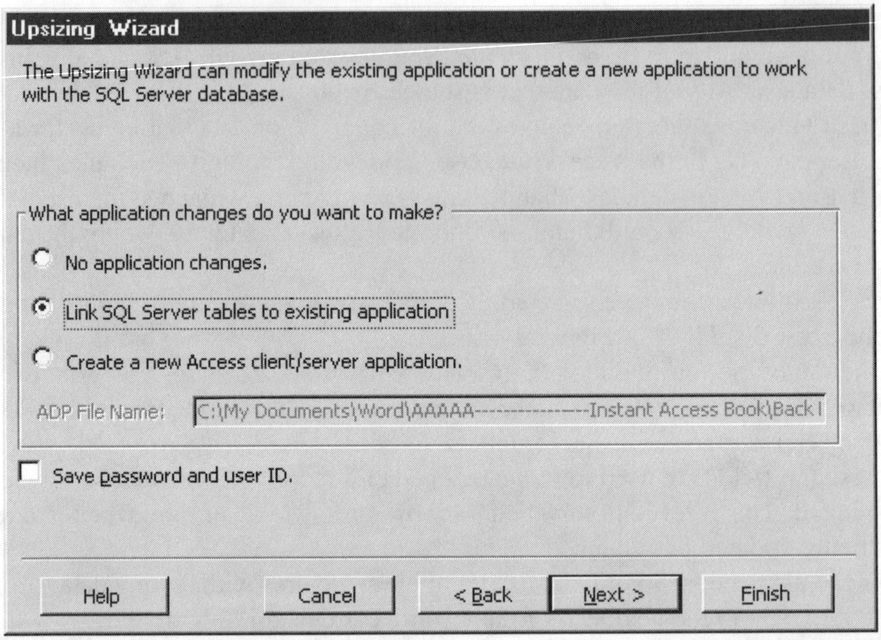

Figure 9-5 *Upsizing Wizard, step 5*

This dialog box enables you to decide if and how you want to set up the front end of the database. First, you can choose to make no changes to the Access database that you are upsizing from. The second option will modify the Access database so that the new tables appear in the Tables tab of the Database window as linked tables. The third option is to create a new Access database, an .adp file that contains all the forms, queries, reports, macros, and modules of this database with links to the SQL Server database, giving you a front-end and back-end design.

Note that you can also choose to save the SQL Server user name and password with the Access database so that the user does not have to type it in each time they open the database in Access. But doing this eliminates the SQL Server, since anyone can use this Access database to get to the back-end data.

Click Next to see the dialog displayed in Figure 9-6.

Now click Finish and the wizard will make the changes you selected in the previous steps. The wizard will then display a report showing you the action it has taken.

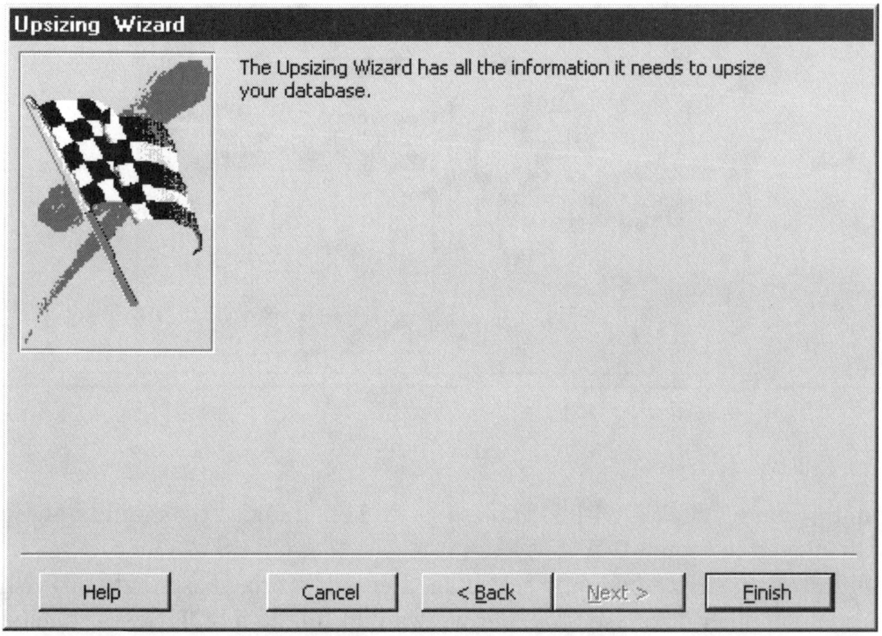

Figure 9-6 *Upsizing Wizard, step 6*

Linking Tables

As you will see with the solutions in this section of the book, we use stored procedures to provide for adding, editing, deleting, and viewing of data through forms. However, to use the simple report and query tools within Access, you will need to link to the SQL Server table or view that you wish to query or report on. Although you can link to tables, which you may want to do when you are just exploring with your data, once you have come up with a query that you wish to keep, it would be better to turn that query into a view within SQL Server and then link to that view.

In this section, you will see how you can link to your SQL Server tables and views.

Open up the Access database that you wish to link tables to, and from the database window select the Tables tab. Then click New to see the dialog box displayed in Figure 9-7.

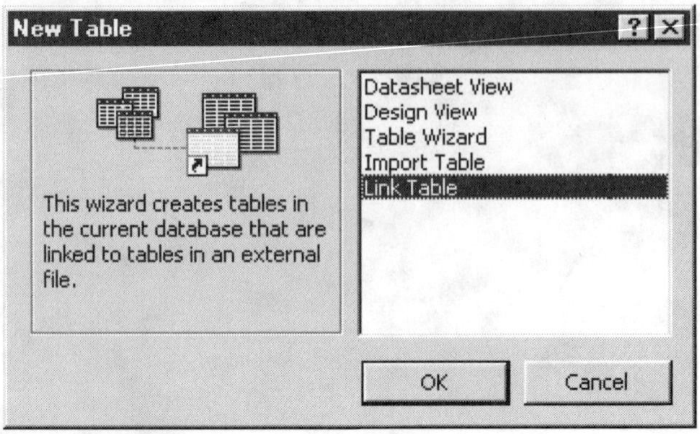

Figure 9-7 *New Table dialog box*

From this dialog click the Link Table item and click OK. You should now see the dialog displayed in Figure 9-8.

From this dialog box you could select another Access database that you wished to link to or some other database type, but we want to link to a SQL Server database.

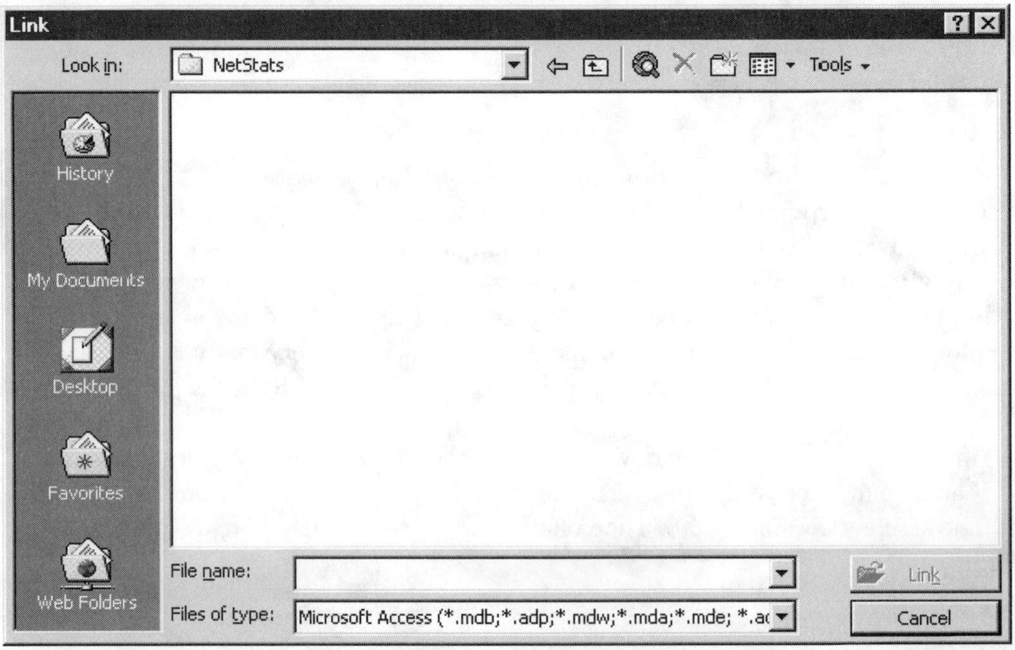

Figure 9-8 *File dialog box for linking tables and views*

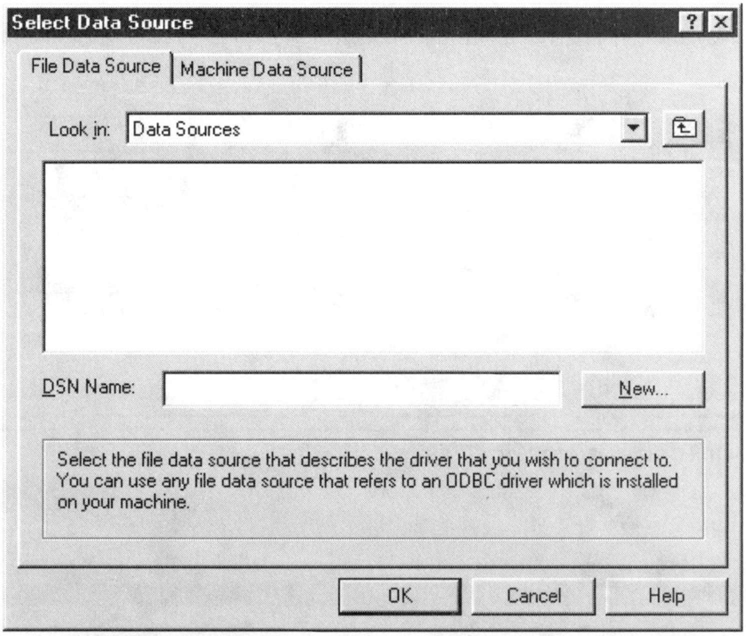

Figure 9-9 *Select Data Source dialog box*

Pull down the Files of Type combo box and select ODBC. You should then see the Select Data Source dialog box displayed in Figure 9-9.

From this dialog, you need to select the DSN that points to the SQL Server database that you wish to link to. To do that, you probably need to switch to the Machine Data Source tab. Select the correct database and click OK. You are then asked for your SQL Server user name and password. If successful, you should see the Link Tables dialog box displayed in Figure 9-10.

In the Link Tables dialog box, you should see a list of all the tables and views that are part of the SQL Server database. Note the Save Password check box. If you select this item, the user name and password that you entered when you linked to this database will be saved with the table definition. This enables you to view data in the tables again without having to enter a password when you reenter the Access database. Doing this is not recommended, since you would be allowing anyone to enter the SQL Server database without a password through your Access database.

Once you have selected the tables and views you wish to link to, click OK and they become part of your Access database just as if they were Access tables, as shown in Figure 9-11.

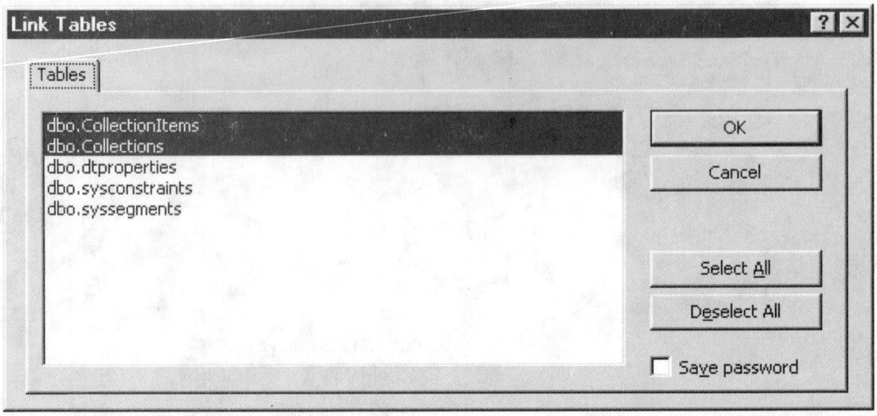

Figure 9-10 *Link Tables dialog box*

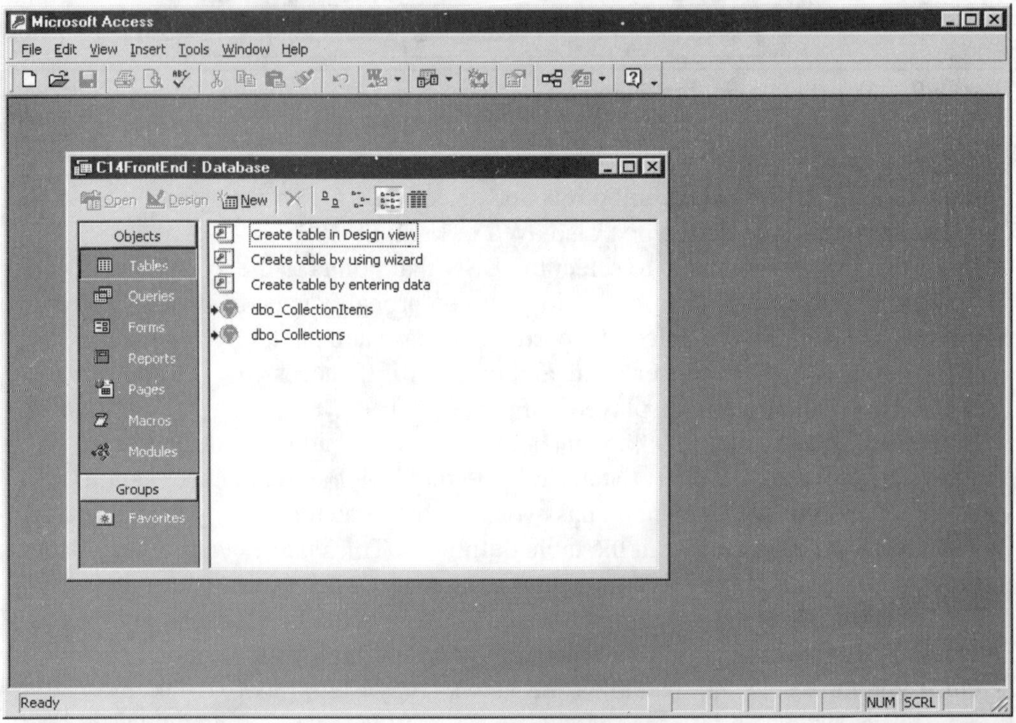

Figure 9-11 *Linked tables as seen through Access*

Note the tables have a different icon than a standard table icon so that you know that they are linked tables. Also note that when you delete the item from Access, you are not deleting the underlying table but merely the link to that table.

You can now use the linked tables and views in reports and queries. Note, though, that the data is not stored in Access; it is still stored in SQL Server. We are just linking to those tables. Also note that you cannot change the structure of the table through Access. When you look at the design view of a linked view or table, it will appear like any other Access table, as displayed in Figure 9-12.

In the design view, you can't change the names of the fields or their types. You would have to do that through SQL Server, but you can add Access properties to the linked table that are stored in Access, like captions. That way, when you create reports based on the table or view, they will have a viewable caption instead of the field name.

Look at what Access does with the field types in the linked table in Figure 9-12. It displays the types as if they were Access fields instead of SQL Server fields. So

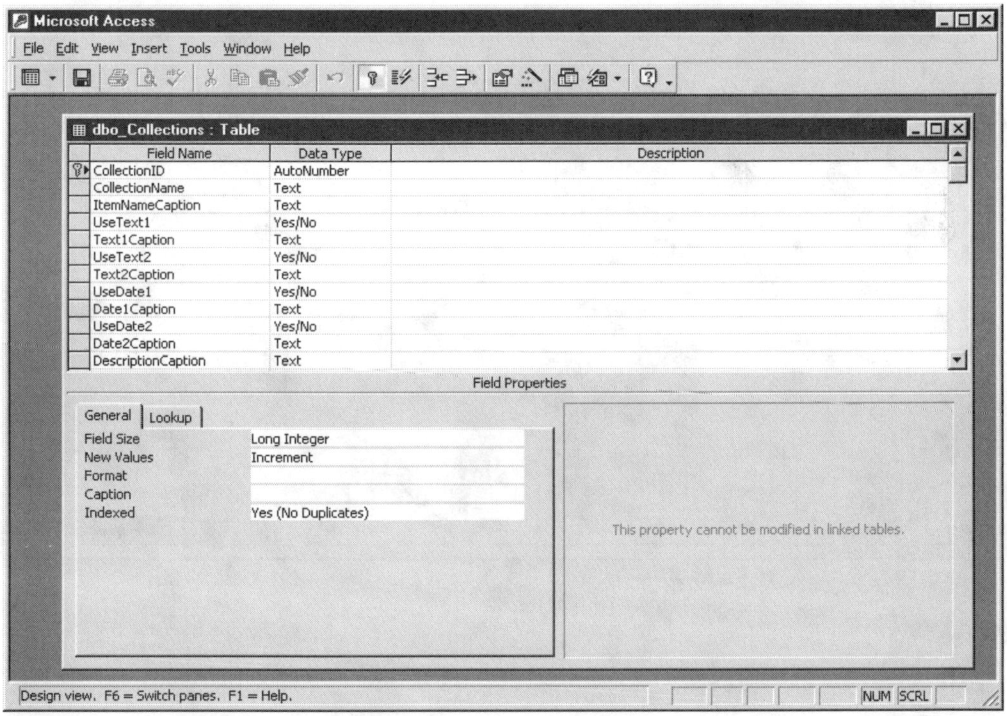

Figure 9-12 *Design view of a linked table*

instead of seeing an identity column, you see an AutoNumber field. Instead of seeing a varchar field, you see a Text field, and a bit field becomes a Yes/No field.

Once you have included all the tables that you wish to link to from one or more databases, you can use the Relationships feature of Access to show how the linked tables relate, as displayed in Figure 9-13.

This tool is accessible through the Relationships item in the Tools menu. The benefit of establishing relationships in Access is that once you do that, Access knows how to link parent and child tables together in subreports, as well as in the query designer.

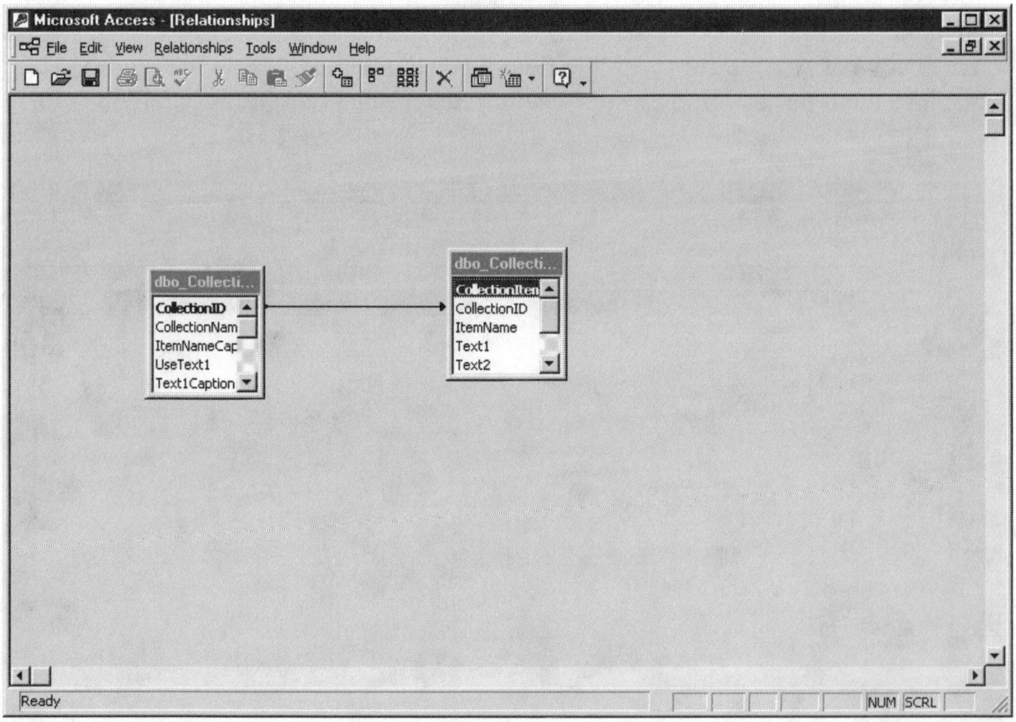

Figure 9-13 *Access Relationships tool*

Referencing ADO

All the database solutions presented in this section of the book use ADO to connect to the SQL Server database either through Connection and Command objects or through Connection and Recordset objects. For you to use ADO in the code of your Access database, the ADO library must be referenced. You reference a library through the Access Visual Basic Editor.

While you are in the design view of any form or report, right-click it and select Build Event. Then if you are presented with a dialog, select Code Builder to enter the Access Visual Basic Editor. This is where you write all your code that runs from your front-end Access database.

Next, to reference an object library, select References from the Tools menu to see the References dialog box displayed in Figure 9-14.

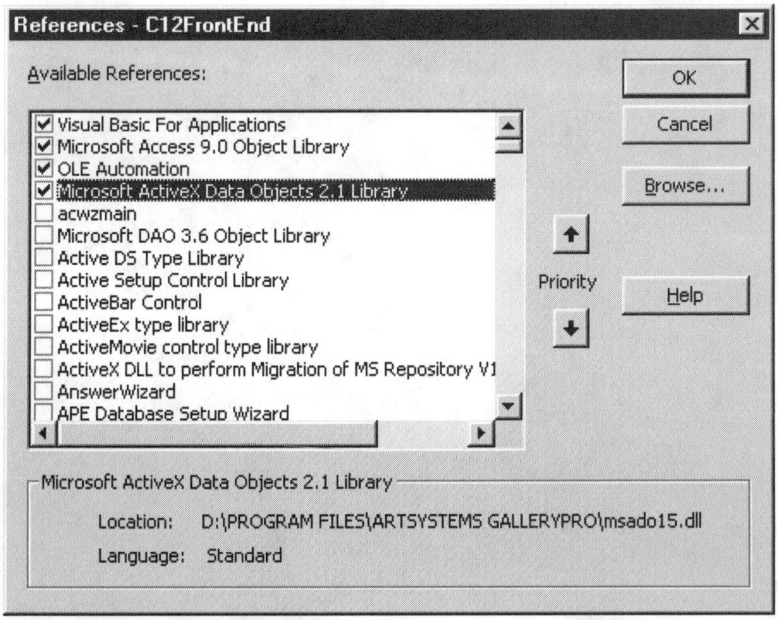

Figure 9-14 *References dialog box*

From this dialog box, locate the ADO library, check it as you see in Figure 9-14, and click OK. You can now instantiate and use the object of ADO within your Access database.

CHAPTER 10

Managing Employees

IN THIS CHAPTER:

C10FrontEnd.mdb

C10SQLObjects.sql

Departments.txt

Employees.txt

PayrollRecords.txt

SickHours.txt

VacationHours.txt

In this chapter, you will look at an application that provides the functionality needed to manage employees at a company.

Working with Employees, Departments, and Payroll Information

The application uses a SQL Server back-end database with an Access front end to supply the functionality needed to manage employees, departments, and payroll information. The application provides three different roles that each have their own functionality.

Solution Walk-Through

When the user first enters the application through the Access front-end database, they are prompted for their user name and password. If their login attempt is invalid, they are told why and the application closes.

If the user successfully logs into the front end, they will see a variety of menus based on their privileges. Figure 10-1 shows the most basic menu configuration.

Here, you have logged in as the user Julie. Julie is a standard employee, so all she sees is the Employee Activities menu, which is available for anyone who successfully enters the application.

From here, the user can view and manage their own personal information but cannot access information on any other employee. When the user clicks the Update Information button, they are taken to the form displayed in Figure 10-2.

The Employee Information form displays basic information about the user who logged into the application. They can edit any of the fields up to the e-mail address field by changing the information on this form and clicking the Update button. The other information on the form (User Name, Salary, Vacation Accrual, Sick Accrual) is read-only.

The user can also view any of three reports. If they click the Personal Payroll button on the Employee Activities menu, they will see the report displayed in Figure 10-3.

The Personal Payroll report displays all historical payroll activity for the employee who is logged into the application. At the bottom of the report, the user can see the total amount that they have been paid.

The next report accessible from the Employee Activities menu is the Personal Vacation Hours report displayed in Figure 10-4.

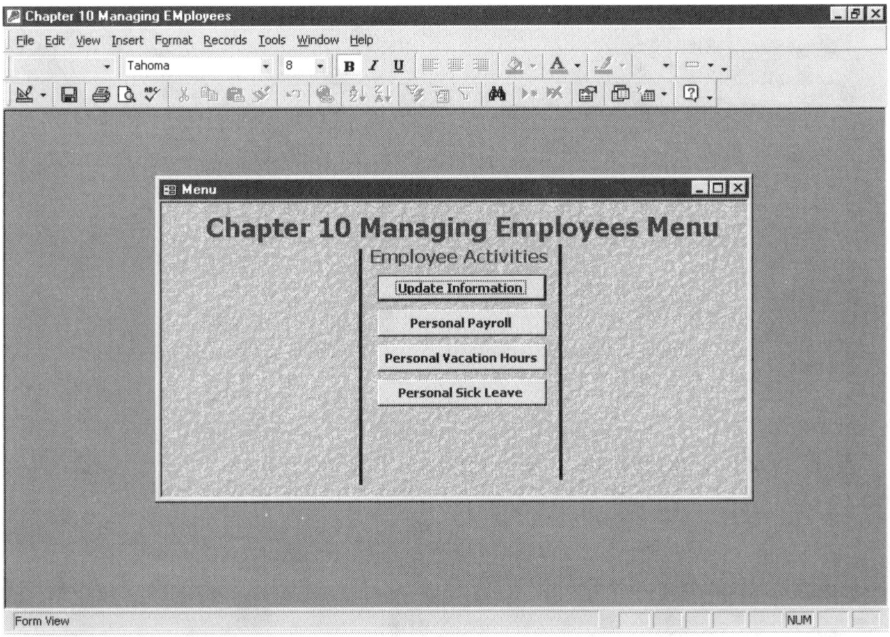

Figure 10-1 *Basic menu configuration*

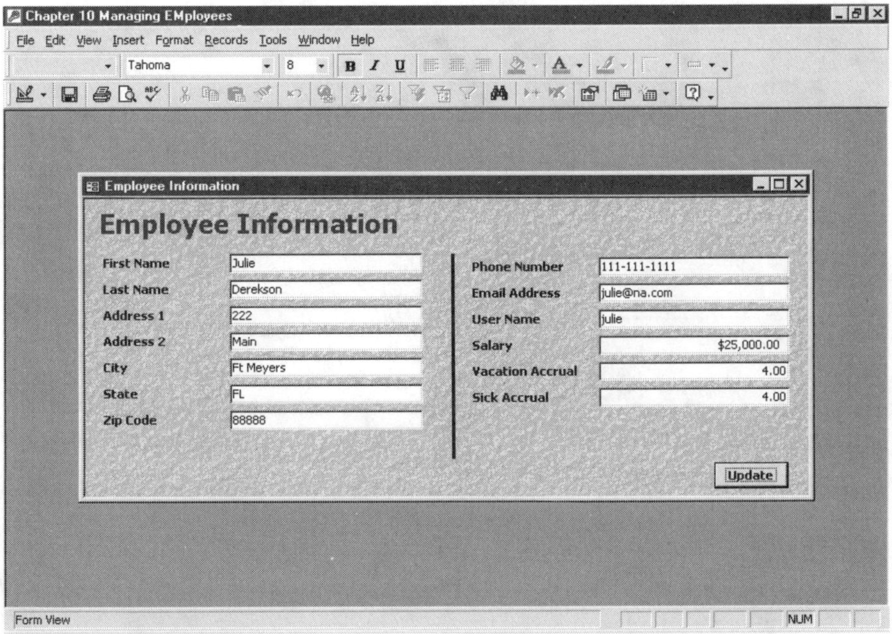

Figure 10-2 *Employee Information form*

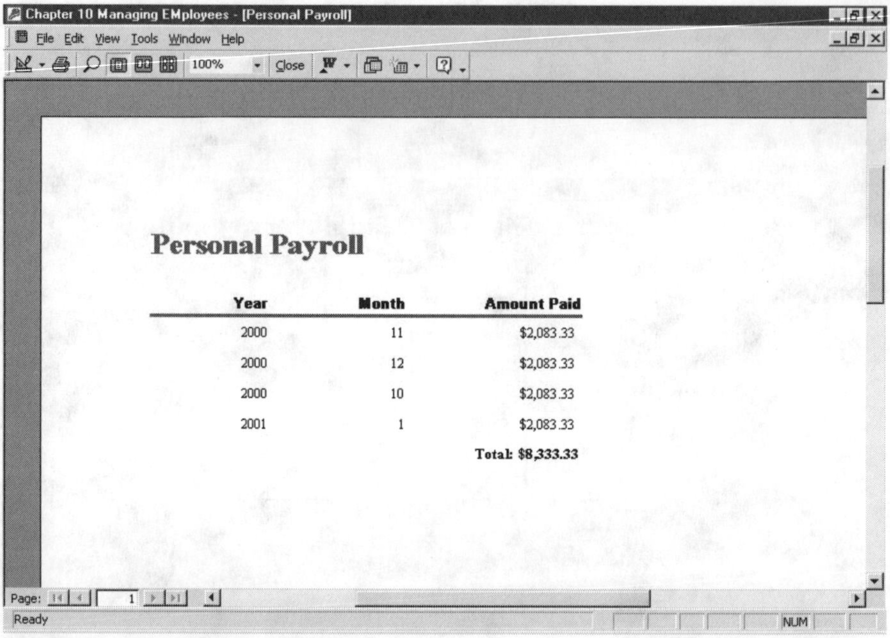

Figure 10-3 *Personal Payroll report*

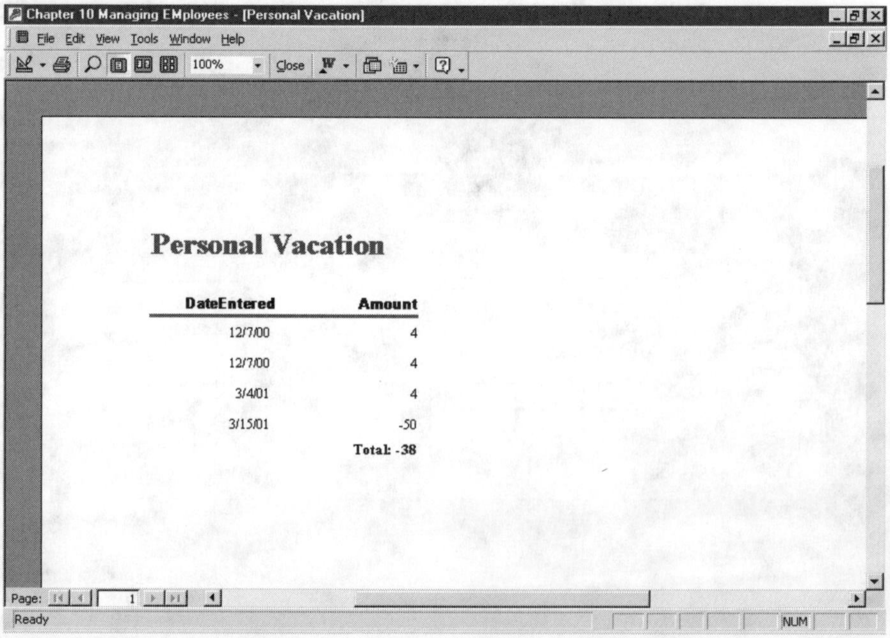

Figure 10-4 *Personal Vacation report*

The Personal Vacation report displays to the user all the historical activity with regard to their vacation time. The user sees the dates that they accrued vacation time and when they used it.

Figure 10-5 shows the other report that employees can access through the Employee Activities menu.

The Personal Sick Leave report shows the employee all the hours that they have earned or used in their Sick Hours account. At the bottom of the report, the user can see their current overall total.

If the user who enters the database is a manager, they see an additional menu like the one displayed in Figure 10-6 when they log into the database.

This time, you are logged into the database as Michelle. Michelle has the role of a manager, so she can also see the Manager Activities menu. This menu provides the functionality needed to manage the employees and employee activities in the database.

When the manager clicks the All Employees button, they see the form displayed in Figure 10-7.

The Employees form provides a way for the manager to change information on any employee, as well as add, edit, or delete employees. The two check boxes on the

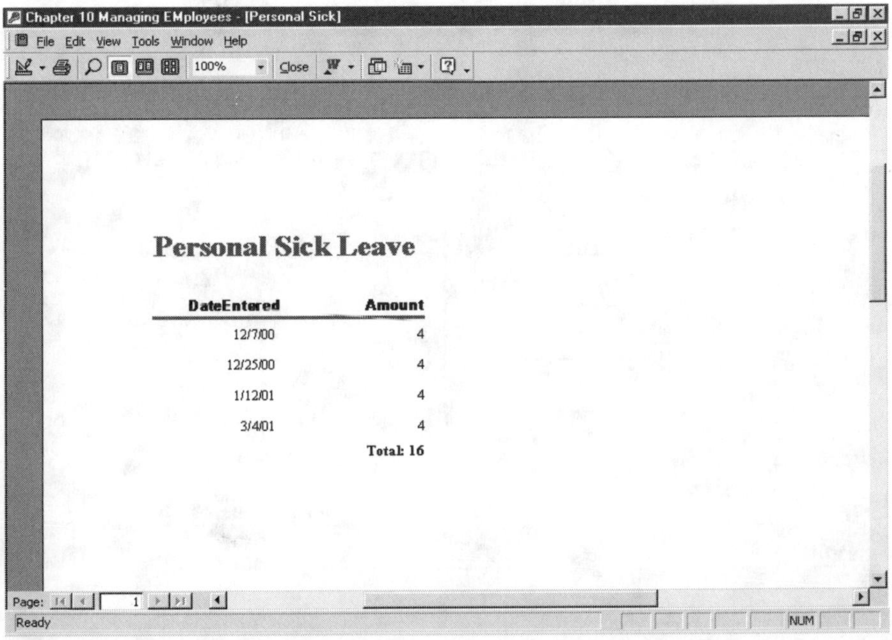

Figure 10-5 *Personal Sick Leave report*

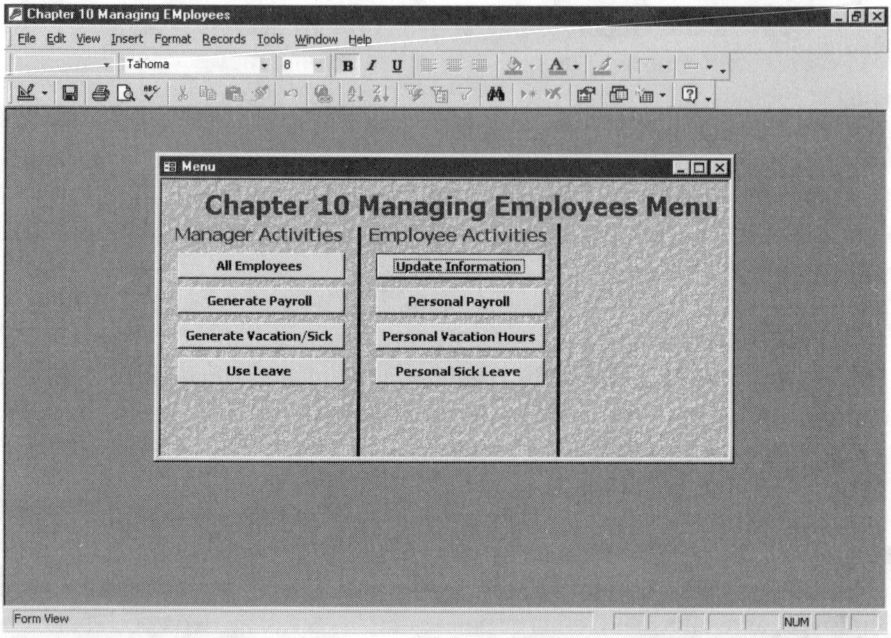

Figure 10-6 *Manager menu*

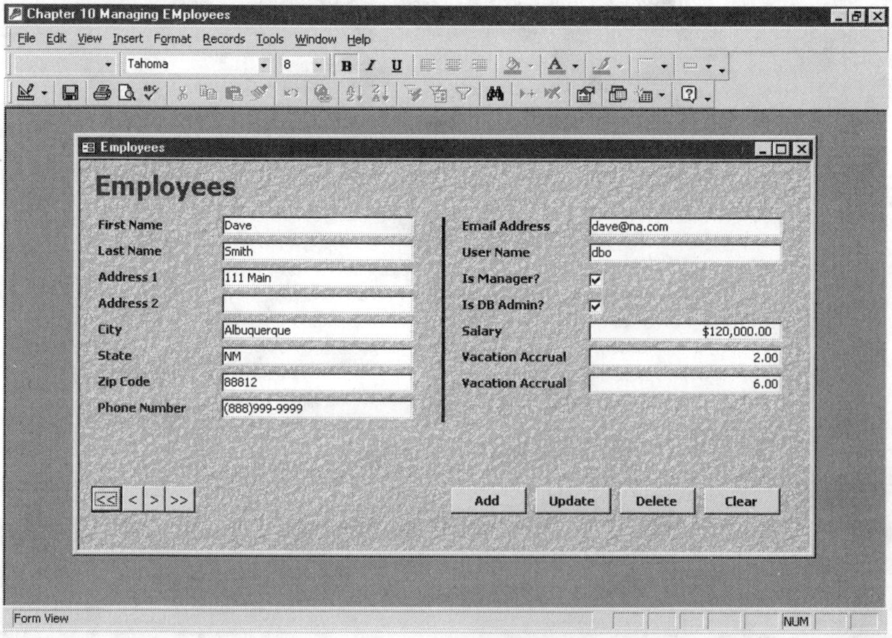

Figure 10-7 *Employees form*

form are used, in combination with SQL Server roles, in determining which of the menus the user sees when they enter the application.

When the manager clicks the Generate Payroll button on the Manager Activities menu, they see the form displayed in Figure 10-8.

The manager uses this form to generate payroll records. They enter the month and year of the payroll and click the Go button. The code then adds records to the Payroll table according to the employee salary, and the manager sees the report displayed in Figure 10-9.

The report shows the manager the records that they just added to the payroll table.

The next option on the Manager Activities menu is the General Vacation/Sick button. When the manager clicks that button, they see the Generate Vacation and Sick Leave form displayed in Figure 10-10.

This form provides the mechanism for the manager to accrue vacation and sick leave hours for each of the employees in the database. The manager enters the data to use for the records being added and clicks the Go button to the right of the type of hours that they want to add. The code then adds records to the database according to the accrual leave rate of the employee. The manager then sees the report displayed in Figure 10-11 that displays the records just added to the database.

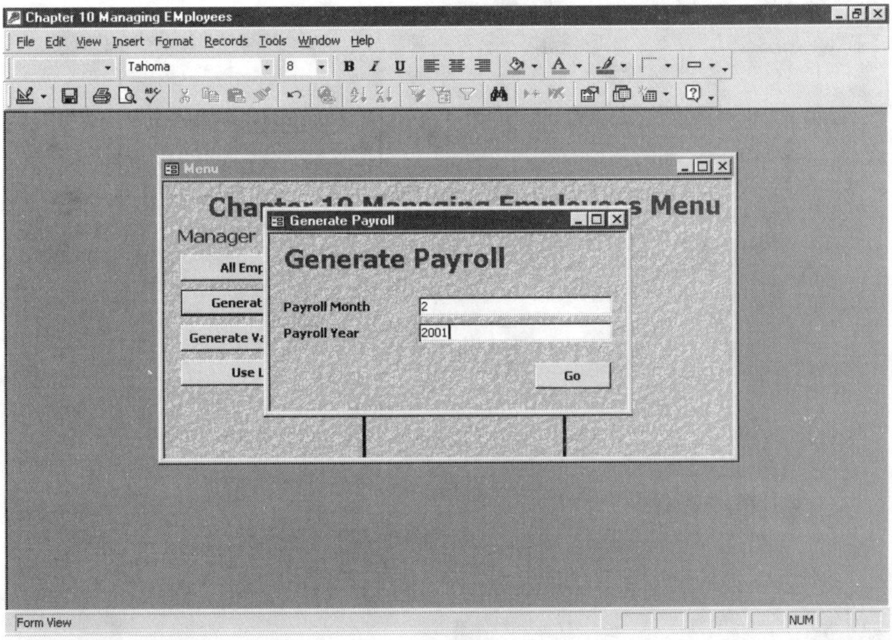

Figure 10-8 *Generate Payroll form*

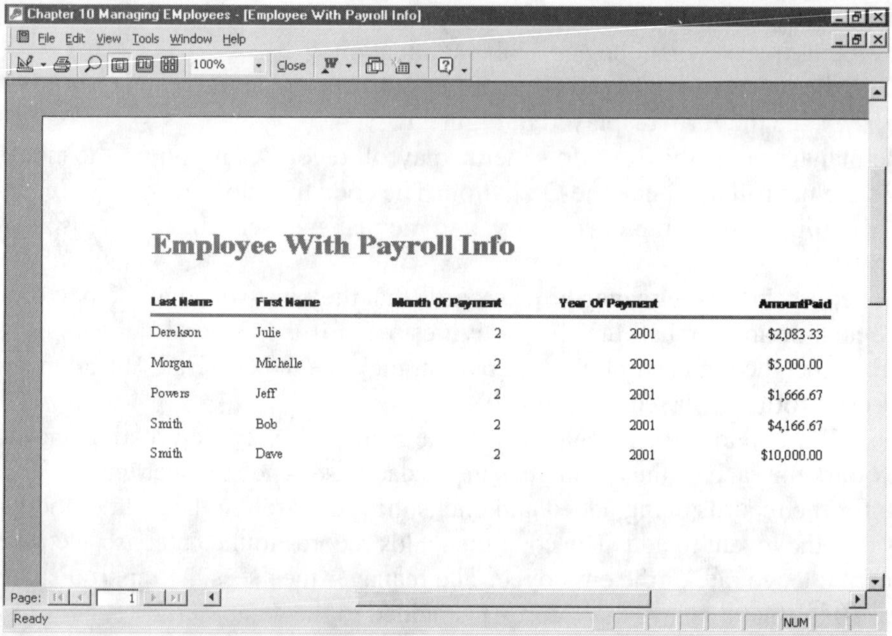

Figure 10-9 *Employee with Payroll Info report*

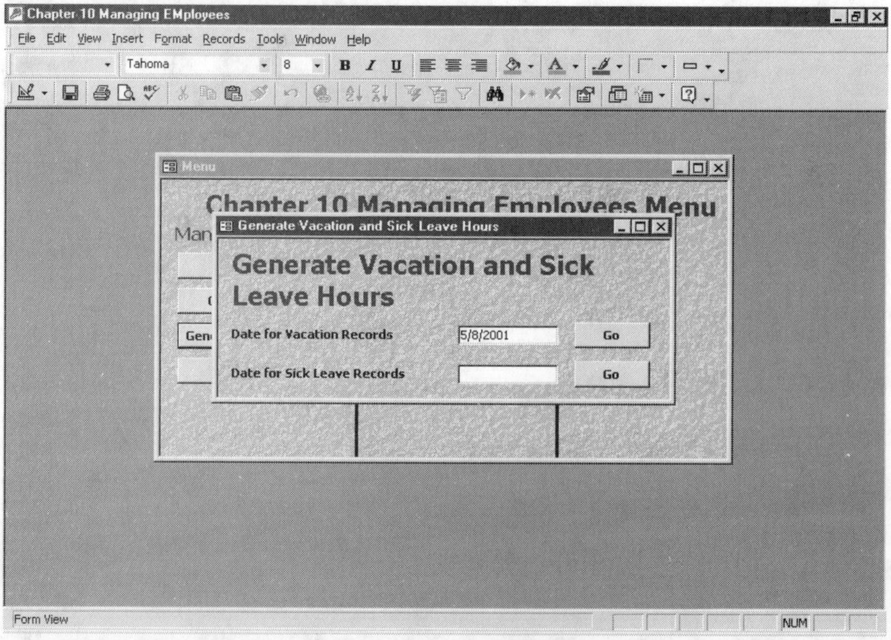

Figure 10-10 *Generate Vacation and Sick Leave Hours form*

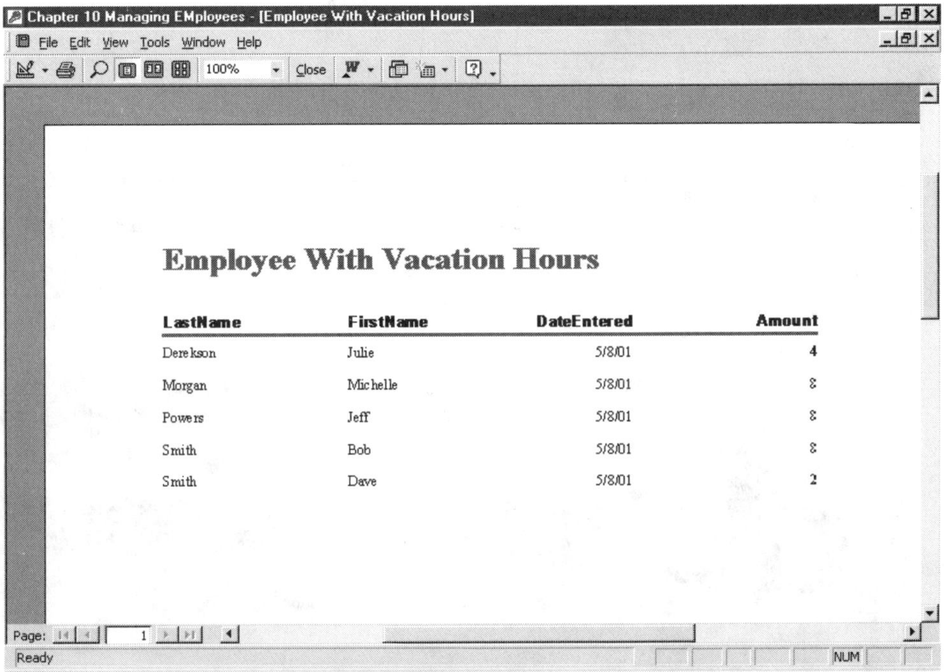

Figure 10-11 *Employee with Vacation Hours report*

When the manager needs to dock an employee for vacation or sick leave hours used, they click the Use Leave button to see the Use Leave form displayed in Figure 10-12.

Here, the manager enters the type of leave being used, Sick or Vacation; selects the employee who is using leave; and enters the date and amount for the leave.

If the user who enters the database is in the DB Admin role, they will see the menu displayed in Figure 10-13.

Here, you have logged into the application as Jeff. Jeff is a DB Admin, so he sees the appropriate menu. Note that a user can also be both a manager and a DB Admin. If that is the case, they see all three menus.

The DB Admin has just one additional option: they can enter the Departments form by clicking the Departments button. That form is displayed in Figure 10-14.

From this form, the DB Admin can add, edit, and delete the departments stored in the back-end database.

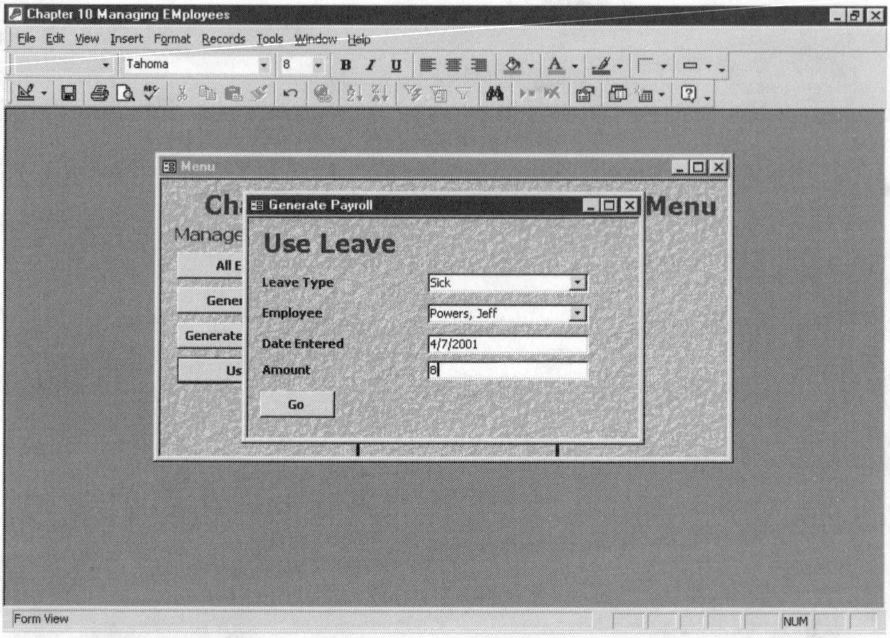

Figure 10-12 *Use Leave form*

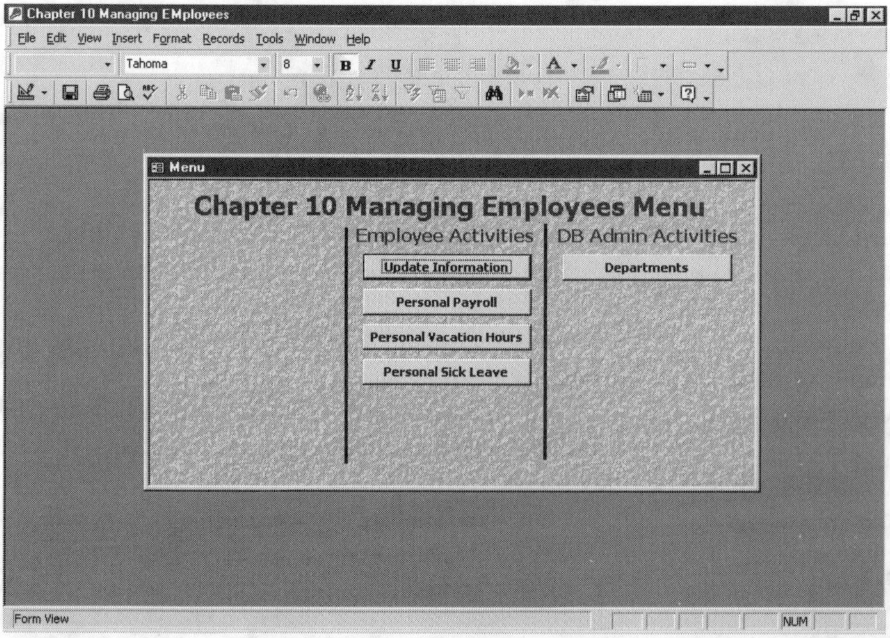

Figure 10-13 *DB Admin Activities menu*

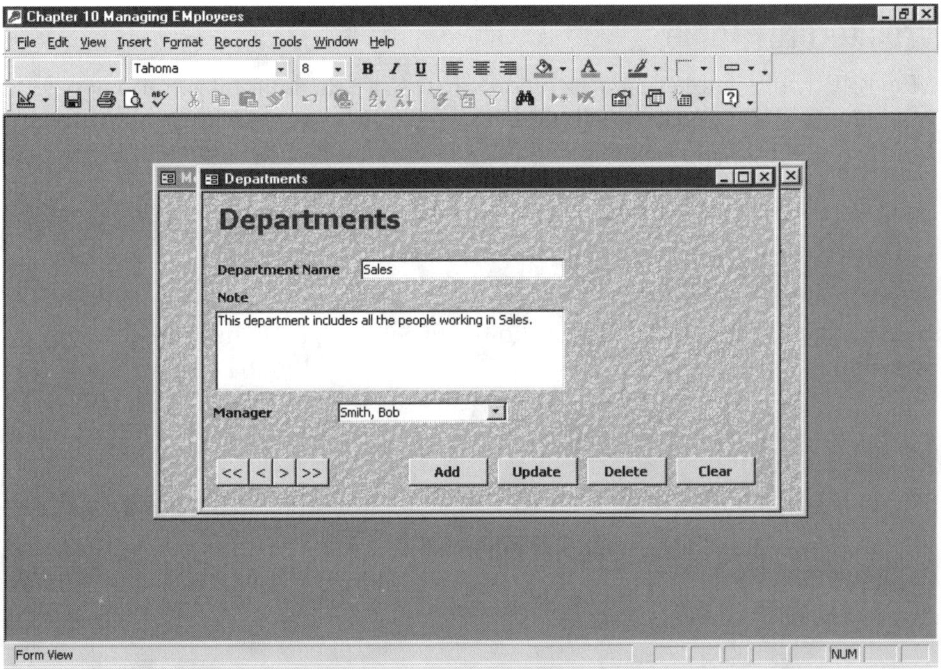

Figure 10-14 *Departments form*

Tables and Relationships

C10SQLObjects.sql

Employees Table

The top-level table in this SQL Server database is the Employees table. This table stores the basic information on the employees, which is also used to control the menus viewed in the Access front end. All the other tables link to this table.

Departments Table

The Departments table stores information about the departments. The table is in a one-to-many relationship with the Employees table. Each department has a single manager, but each manager can be the manager of many departments.

PayrollRecords Table

The PayrollRecords table contains records that store the amount of money paid to each employee during each pay period. The table links to the Employees table in a one-to-many relationship.

VacationHours Table

The VacationHours table stores information on vacation time earned and used by each employee. The table also relates to the Employees table in a one-to-many relationship.

SickHours Table

The SickHours table stores the number of sick hours earned and used by each employee. The table relates to the Employees table in a one-to-many relationship. Each SickHours record belongs to a single employee, but each employee can have many records in this table.

Field Specifications

Employees Table

Employees.txt

The field specifications for the Employees table are displayed in Table 10-1.

The EmployeeID field is the primary key in the table. It is an Identity column, so the field is automatically populated with a unique value when a new record is added to this table.

The UserName field must match the user name that is used by the user to log into the database. This allows the user to see their payroll and leave information on the reports.

The IsManager field is a Boolean field that controls whether the user can see the Manager Activities menu when they log into the database. But they must also be part of the Manager role to access that functionality.

The IsDBAdmin field is used to determine whether the user can see the DB Admin menu when they enter the database.

Field Name	Field Type	Notes
EmployeeID	int	Primary Key, Identity Column
FirstName	varchar	Length = 50
LastName	varchar	Length = 50
Address1	varchar	Length = 100
Address2	varchar	Length = 100
City	varchar	Length = 50
State	varchar	Length = 2
ZipCode	varchar	Length = 10
PhoneNumber	varchar	Length = 50
EmailAddress	varchar	Length = 50
UserName	varchar	Length = 50
IsManager	bit	
IsDBAdmin	bit	
Salary	money	
VacatAcc	float	
SickAcc	float	

Table 10-1 *Employees Table Field Specifications*

Departments Table

Departments.txt

The field specifications for the Departments table are displayed in Table 10-2.

The DepartmentID column is the primary key in this table. The DepartmentManagerID field is a foreign key that links this table to the Employees table in a one-to-many relationship.

Field Name	Field Type	Notes
DepartmentID	int	Primary Key, Identity Column
DepartmentManagerID	int	Foreign Key
DepartmentName	varchar	Length = 50
Note	text	

Table 10-2 *Departments Table Field Specifications*

Field Name	Field Type	Notes
PayrollRecordID	int	Primary Key, Identity Column
EmployeeID	int	Foreign Key
MonthOfPayment	int	
YearofPayment	int	
AmountPaid	money	

Table 10-3 *PayrollRecords Table Field Specifications*

PayrollRecords Table

PayrollRecords.txt

The field specifications for the PayrollRecords table are displayed in Table 10-3.

The PayrollRecordID is the primary key for the table. The EmployeeID field is a foreign key that links this table to the Employees table.

VacationHours Table

VacationHours.txt

The field specifications for the VacationHours table are displayed in Table 10-4.

The VacationHourID field is the primary key in this table. The EmployeeID column is a foreign key that links this table to the Employees table. The Amount field stores the number of vacation hours earned or used by the employee.

SickHours Table

SickHours.txt

The field specifications for the SickHours table are displayed in Table 10-5.

Field Name	Field Type	Notes
VacationHourID	int	Primary Key, Identity Column
EmployeeID	int	Foreign Key
DateEntered	datetime	
Amount	float	

Table 10-4 *VacationHours Table Field Specifications*

Field Name	Field Type	Notes
SickHourID	int	Primary Key, Identity Column
EmployeeID	int	Foreign Key
DateEntered	datetime	
Amount	float	

Table 10-5 *SickHours Table Field Specifications*

The primary key in this table is the SickHourID column. The EmployeeID field, like the other tables, links this table to the Employees table. The Amount field stores the number of sick leave hours used or earned by the employee.

User-Defined Function

DepartmentIDCheck Function

In numerous stored procedures, you need to determine whether the DepartmentID supplied is a valid ID. The DepartmentIDCheck function provides the answer to that question.

```
CREATE FUNCTION DepartmentIDCheck (@TheID int)
RETURNS Integer AS
BEGIN
      Declare @TheCount Integer
      Select @TheCount = Count(DepartmentID) from Departments
            Where DepartmentID = @TheID
      Return @TheCount
END
```

The function has a single parameter passed into it, the ID of the department to look for:

```
CREATE FUNCTION DepartmentIDCheck (@TheID int)
```

The function returns an integer indicating the result of the search for the ID:

```
RETURNS Integer AS
BEGIN
```

You then declare a variable that will store the number of matching records of the ID that you are searching for:

```
Declare @TheCount Integer
```

Next, you look for the ID in the Departments table:

```
Select @TheCount = Count(DepartmentID) from Departments
     Where DepartmentID = @TheID
```

and return the result:

```
Return @TheCount
END
```

EmployeeIDCheck Function

Similarly, in numerous locations, you need to determine whether an EmployeeID entered is valid. The EmployeeIDCheck function returns that information.

```
CREATE FUNCTION EmployeeIDCheck (@TheID int)
RETURNS Integer AS
BEGIN
     Declare @TheCount Integer
     Select @TheCount = Count(EmployeeID) from Employees
          Where EmployeeID = @TheID
     Return @TheCount
END
```

The function accepts a single parameter, the ID to look for:

```
CREATE FUNCTION EmployeeIDCheck (@TheID int)
```

and returns a count of the matching records:

```
RETURNS Integer AS
BEGIN
```

One variable will be needed in this function to store the number of matches found:

```
Declare @TheCount Integer
```

You then count the number of records that match the ID you are searching for:

```
Select @TheCount = Count(EmployeeID) from Employees
      Where EmployeeID = @TheID
```

and return that count:

```
Return @TheCount
END
```

Stored Procedures

EmployeeAdd Stored Procedure

The EmployeeAdd stored procedure adds a record to the Employees table.

```
CREATE PROCEDURE EmployeeAdd
@FirstName varchar(50),
@LastName varchar(50),
@Address1 varchar(100),
@Address2 varchar(100),
@City varchar(50),
@State varchar(2),
@ZipCode varchar(50),
@PhoneNumber varchar(50),
@EmailAddress varchar(50),
@UserName varchar(50),
@IsManager bit,
@IsDBAdmin bit,
@Salary money,
@VacatAcc float,
@SickAcc float
AS
If ((@Salary) < 20000) or ((@Salary) > 1000000)
      BEGIN
            Select 0 as ReturnValue, 'Salary must be in the range of '
                  + '$20,000 and $1,000,000!' as ReturnMessage
      END
Else
      If (@VacatAcc) < 0
            BEGIN
                  Select 0 as ReturnValue, 'The Vacation Accrual '
                        + 'rate must be '
                        + 'greater than zero!' as ReturnMessage
            END
```

```
      Else
            If (@SickAcc) < 0
                  BEGIN
                        Select 0 as ReturnValue, 'The Sick
                              + 'Accrual rate must be '
                              + 'greater than zero!' as ReturnMessage
                  END
            Else
                  BEGIN
                        Insert Into Employees (FirstName,
                              LastName, Address1, Address2, City,
                              State, ZipCode, PhoneNumber, EmailAddress,
                              UserName, IsManager, IsDBAdmin,
                              Salary, VacatAcc, SickAcc)
                              values (@FirstName, @LastName,
                              @Address1, @Address2, @City,
                              @State, @ZipCode, @PhoneNumber, @EmailAddress,
                              @UserName, @IsManager,
                              @IsDBAdmin, @Salary, @VacatAcc, @SickAcc)
                        Select 1 as ReturnValue, "No Errors" as ReturnMessage
                  END
GO
```

The procedure requires numerous parameters that each store a value for one of the fields in the new record:

```
@FirstName varchar(50),
@LastName varchar(50),
@Address1 varchar(100),
@Address2 varchar(100),
@City varchar(50),
@State varchar(2),
@ZipCode varchar(50),
@PhoneNumber varchar(50),
@EmailAddress varchar(50),
@UserName varchar(50),
@IsManager bit,
@IsDBAdmin bit,
@Salary money,
@VacatAcc float,
@SickAcc float
AS
```

After those parameters are declared, you check to make sure that the salary supplied is within your expected range:

```
If ((@Salary) < 20000) or ((@Salary) > 1000000)
```

If it isn't, you return an error to the calling application:

```
BEGIN
      Select 0 as ReturnValue, 'Salary must be in the range of '
            + '$20,000 and $1,000,000!' as ReturnMessage
END
```

Next, you check to see whether the vacation accrual rate is less than 0:

```
If (@VacatAcc) < 0
```

If it is, you send an error message back to the calling application and end this procedure:

```
BEGIN
      Select 0 as ReturnValue, 'The Vacation Accrual '
            + rate must be '
            + 'greater than zero!' as ReturnMessage
END
```

One more check is performed to make sure that the sick accrual rate is at least 0:

```
If (@SickAcc) < 0
```

If it isn't, you return an error message:

```
BEGIN
      Select 0 as ReturnValue, 'The Sick Accrual '
            + rate must be '
            + 'greater than zero!' as ReturnMessage
END
```

If the parameters pass the rules, then the record is added to the table:

```
BEGIN
      Insert Into Employees (FirstName, LastName, Address1,
            Address2, City,
            State, ZipCode, PhoneNumber, EmailAddress,
            UserName, IsManager, IsDBAdmin, Salary, VacatAcc, SickAcc)
            values (@FirstName, @LastName, @Address1, @Address2, @City,
            @State, @ZipCode, @PhoneNumber, @EmailAddress,
      @UserName, @IsManager, @IsDBAdmin, @Salary, @VacatAcc, @SickAcc)
```

And you return a success message to the calling application:

```
Select 1 as ReturnValue, "No Errors" as ReturnMessage
```

EmployeeEdit Stored Procedure

The EmployeeEdit stored procedure edits an existing employee record.

```
CREATE PROCEDURE EmployeeEdit
@UpdateID integer,
@FirstName varchar(50),
@LastName varchar(50),
@Address1 varchar(100),
@Address2 varchar(100),
@City varchar(50),
@State varchar(2),
@ZipCode varchar(50),
@PhoneNumber varchar(50),
@EmailAddress varchar(50),
@UserName varchar(50),
@IsManager bit,
@IsDBAdmin bit,
@Salary money,
@VacatAcc float,
@SickAcc float
AS
If (dbo.EmployeeIDCheck(@UpdateID)) = 0
      BEGIN
            Select 0 as ReturnValue, 'The EmployeeID being updated '
                  + 'was not found!' as ReturnMessage
      END
Else
      If ((@Salary) < 20000) or ((@Salary) > 1000000)
            BEGIN
                  Select 0 as ReturnValue, 'Salary must be in the range of '
                        + '$20,000 and $1,000,000!' as ReturnMessage
            END
      Else
            If (@VacatAcc) < 0
                  BEGIN
                        Select 0 as ReturnValue, 'The Vacation '
                              + 'Accrual rate must be '
                              + 'greater than zero!' as ReturnMessage
                  END
            Else
                  If (@SickAcc) < 0
```

```
            BEGIN
                  Select 0 as ReturnValue, 'The Sick '
                        + 'Accrual rate must be '
                        + 'greater than zero!' as ReturnMessage
            END
      Else

            BEGIN
                  Update Employees set
                  FirstName = @FirstName,
                  LastName = @LastName,
                  Address1 = @Address1,
                  Address2 = @Address2,
                  City = @City,
                  State = @State,
                  ZipCode = @ZipCode,
                  PhoneNumber = @PhoneNumber,
                  EmailAddress = @EmailAddress,
                  IsManager = @IsManager,
                  IsDBAdmin = @IsDBAdmin,
                  Salary = @Salary,
                  VacatAcc = @VacatAcc,
                  SickAcc = @SickAcc
                  Where EmployeeID = @UpdateID

                  Select 1 as ReturnValue,
                     "No Errors" as ReturnMessage
            END
GO
```

The procedure requires values for all the fields as parameters passed into it:

```
@UpdateID integer,
@FirstName varchar(50),
@LastName varchar(50),
@Address1 varchar(100),
@Address2 varchar(100),
@City varchar(50),
@State varchar(2),
@ZipCode varchar(50),
@PhoneNumber varchar(50),
@EmailAddress varchar(50),
@UserName varchar(50),
@IsManager bit,
@IsDBAdmin bit,
@Salary money,
```

```
@VacatAcc float,
@SickAcc float
```

Next, you call your function EmployeeIDCheck to make sure that the EmployeeID passed in is a valid ID:

```
If (dbo.EmployeeIDCheck(@UpdateID)) = 0
```

If it isn't, you return an error message:

```
BEGIN
      Select 0 as ReturnValue, 'The EmployeeID being updated '
            + 'was not found!' as ReturnMessage
END
```

Next, you make sure that the salary supplied to the procedure is in the valid range:

```
If ((@Salary) < 20000) or ((@Salary) > 1000000)
```

If it isn't, you return an error message:

```
BEGIN
      Select 0 as ReturnValue, 'Salary must be in the range of '
            + '$20,000 and $1,000,000!' as ReturnMessage
END
```

Then, you check to make sure that the vacation accrual rate is valid:

```
If (@VacatAcc) < 0
```

If it isn't, you return an error:

```
BEGIN
      Select 0 as ReturnValue, 'The Vacation Accrual rate must be '
            + 'greater than zero!' as ReturnMessage
END
```

You also need to make sure that the sick accrual rate is in the proper range:

```
If (@SickAcc) < 0
```

If it isn't, you return a different error message:

```
BEGIN
      Select 0 as ReturnValue, 'The Sick Accrual rate must be '
            + 'greater than zero!' as ReturnMessage
END
```

Otherwise, you edit the desired record:

```
Update Employees set
      FirstName = @FirstName,
      LastName = @LastName,
      Address1 = @Address1,
      Address2 = @Address2,
      City = @City,
      State = @State,
      ZipCode = @ZipCode,
      PhoneNumber = @PhoneNumber,
      EmailAddress = @EmailAddress,
      IsManager = @IsManager,
      IsDBAdmin = @IsDBAdmin,
      Salary = @Salary,
      VacatAcc = @VacatAcc,
      SickAcc = @SickAcc
      Where EmployeeID = @UpdateID
```

and return a success message:

```
Select 1 as ReturnValue, "No Errors" as ReturnMessage
```

EmployeeDelete Stored Procedure

The EmployeeDelete stored procedure is used to delete a record from the Employees table.

```
CREATE PROCEDURE EmployeeDelete
@DeleteID integer
AS
If (dbo.EmployeeIDCheck(@DeleteID)) = 0
      BEGIN
            Select 0 as ReturnValue, 'The EmployeeID being deleted '
                  + 'was not found!' as ReturnMessage
      END
Else
      BEGIN
            Delete from Employees
                  Where EmployeeID = @DeleteID
            Select 1 as ReturnValue, "No Errors" as ReturnMessage
      END
GO
```

The procedure requires a single parameter, the ID of the Employee to delete:

```
@DeleteID integer
```

First, you make sure that the ID is valid:

```
If (dbo.EmployeeIDCheck(@DeleteID)) = 0
```

If it isn't, you return an error message:

```
BEGIN
      Select 0 as ReturnValue, 'The EmployeeID being deleted '
            + 'was not found!' as ReturnMessage
END
```

Otherwise, you can delete the desired record:

```
BEGIN
      Delete from Employees
            Where EmployeeID = @DeleteID
```

and return a success message:

```
Select 1 as ReturnValue, "No Errors" as ReturnMessage
END
```

EmployeeMove Stored Procedure

The EmployeeMove stored procedure returns a single record to the calling application as determined by the movement through the records relative to the position of an ID passed into the procedure.

```
CREATE PROCEDURE EmployeeMove
@MoveDirection varchar(8),
@LastPosition integer = 0
AS
Declare @ID2Use integer
If (@MoveDirection) = 'FIRST'
      BEGIN
            Select @ID2Use = Min(EmployeeID) from Employees
            Select * from Employees Where EmployeeID = @ID2Use
      END
Else
```

```
    If (@MoveDirection) = 'LAST'
        BEGIN
            Select @ID2Use = Max(EmployeeID) from Employees
            Select * from Employees Where EmployeeID = @ID2Use
        END
    Else
        If (@MoveDirection) = 'NEXT'
            BEGIN
                Select Top 1 * from Employees
                    Where EmployeeID > @LastPosition
                    Order By EmployeeID
            END
        Else
            BEGIN
                Select Top 1 * from Employees
                    Where EmployeeID < @LastPosition
                    Order By EmployeeID DESC
            END
GO
```

The procedure requires two parameters passed in to it. The first is the direction of the movement:

```
@MoveDirection varchar(8),
```

The other is the record that is to be moved from:

```
@LastPosition integer = 0
```

The procedure will also use another variable that will hold the ID of the employee record to return:

```
Declare @ID2Use integer
```

You then check to see whether the caller wants the first employee record:

```
If (@MoveDirection) = 'FIRST'
```

If that is the case, you retrieve the lowest EmployeeID:

```
Select @ID2Use = Min(EmployeeID) from Employees
```

and return that record:

```
Select * from Employees Where EmployeeID = @ID2Use
```

Next, you check to see whether the calling application wants the last record retrieved:

```
If (@MoveDirection) = 'LAST'
```

If so, you retrieve the highest EmployeeID:

```
Select @ID2Use = Max(EmployeeID) from Employees
```

and then return that record:

```
Select * from Employees Where EmployeeID = @ID2Use
```

If Next is passed into the @MoveDirection parameter, the calling application wants the next record relative to the ID passed into the procedure:

```
If (@MoveDirection) = 'NEXT'
```

In that case, you retrieve the employee record of the next record that has an ID above the relative ID:

```
Select Top 1 * from Employees
      Where EmployeeID > @LastPosition
      Order By EmployeeID
```

The last block assumes that the calling application wants the preceding record. So you retrieve the data of the employee that is below the relative ID:

```
Select Top 1 * from Employees
      Where EmployeeID < @LastPosition
      Order By EmployeeID DESC
```

EmployeeComboList Stored Procedure

The EmployeeComboList stored procedure returns a list of employee names with IDs that are used in combo boxes on forms in the Access front end.

```
CREATE PROCEDURE EmployeeComboList
AS
```

```
Declare
@AllOfIt varchar(8000),
@CurrentID varchar(10),
@CurrentLastName varchar(50),
@CurrentFirstName varchar(50)
Declare CurEmps Cursor
For Select EmployeeID, LastName, FirstName from Employees
order by LastName, FirstName
Open CurEmps
Fetch CurEmps
Into @CurrentID, @CurrentLastName, @CurrentFirstName
Select @AllOfIt = ''
While @@Fetch_Status = 0
      BEGIN
            Select @AllOfIt = @AllOfIt + @CurrentID + ';'
                  + '"' + @CurrentLastName + ', '
                  + @CurrentFirstName + '";'
            Fetch CurEmps
                  Into @CurrentID, @CurrentLastName,
                  @CurrentFirstName
      END
Close CurEmps
Deallocate CurEmps
Select @AllOfIt
GO
```

The procedure declares a few parameters. The first is used to store the list as it is being built:

```
@AllOfIt varchar(8000),
```

The next three store the employee information as the record is being read:

```
@CurrentID varchar(10),
@CurrentLastName varchar(50),
@CurrentFirstName varchar(50)
```

You then declare a Cursor variable:

```
Declare CurEmps Cursor
```

that will be used to iterate through the employee records:

```
For Select EmployeeID, LastName, FirstName from Employees
      order by LastName, FirstName
```

You then open the cursor:

```
Open CurEmps
```

and retrieve the first record:

```
Fetch CurEmps
Into @CurrentID, @CurrentLastName, @CurrentFirstName
```

Next, you initialize your return variable:

```
Select @AllOfIt = ''
```

and enter a loop that will continue until you process each record:

```
While @@Fetch_Status = 0
```

The loop will run the code between the BEGIN and END statements with each record:

```
BEGIN
```

You append the data returned from each record into the return variable that is formatted so that it appears appropriately in a combo box in the Access front end:

```
Select @AllOfIt = @AllOfIt + @CurrentID + ';'
      + '"' + @CurrentLastName + ', '
      + @CurrentFirstName + '";'
```

You then retrieve the next record:

```
Fetch CurEmps
      Into @CurrentID, @CurrentLastName,
      @CurrentFirstName
```

and loop back up:

```
End
```

You then close the cursor:

```
Close CurEmps
```

and release its resources:

```
Deallocate CurEmps
```

before returning the Combo List text:

```
Select @AllOfIt
```

DepartmentAdd Stored Procedure

The DepartmentAdd stored procedure is used to add a new department to the Departments table.

```
CREATE PROCEDURE DepartmentAdd
@NewName varchar(50),
@NewNote text,
@NewEmployeeID integer
AS
If (dbo.EmployeeIDCheck(@NewEmployeeID)) = 0
      BEGIN
            Select 0 as ReturnValue, 'The EmployeeID being added '
                  + 'was not found!' as ReturnMessage
      END
Else
      BEGIN
            Insert Into Departments (DepartmentName, Note, DepartmentManagerID)
            values (@NewName, @NewNote, @NewEmployeeID)
            Select 1 as ReturnValue, "No Errors" as ReturnMessage
      END
GO
```

The procedure requires as parameters the values for each of the fields in the Departments table:

```
@NewName varchar(50),
@NewNote text,
@NewEmployeeID integer
```

You then make sure that the employee selected for the manager of this department is a valid ID:

```
If (dbo.EmployeeIDCheck(@NewEmployeeID)) = 0
```

If it isn't, you return an error record:

```
Select 0 as ReturnValue, 'The EmployeeID being added '
      + 'was not found!' as ReturnMessage
```

Otherwise, you insert the department and return a success message:

```
Insert Into Departments (DepartmentName, Note, DepartmentManagerID)
      values (@NewName, @NewNote, @NewEmployeeID)
Select 1 as ReturnValue, "No Errors" as ReturnMessage
```

DepartmentEdit Stored Procedure

The DepartmentEdit stored procedure is used to edit an existing department record.

```
CREATE PROCEDURE DepartmentEdit
@UpdateID integer,
@UpdateName varchar(50),
@UpdateNote text,
@UpdateEmployeeID integer
AS
If (dbo.DepartmentIDCheck(@UpdateID)) = 0
      BEGIN
            Select 0 as ReturnValue, 'The DepartmentID being updated '
                  + 'was not found!' as ReturnMessage
      END
Else
      If (dbo.EmployeeIDCheck(@UpdateEmployeeID)) = 0
            BEGIN
                  Select 0 as ReturnValue, 'The EmployeeID being updated '
                        + 'was not found!' as ReturnMessage
            END
      Else
            BEGIN
                  Update Departments set
                  DepartmentName = @UpdateName,
                  Note = @UpdateNote,
                  DepartmentManagerID = @UpdateEmployeeID
                  Where DepartmentID = @UpdateID

                  Select 1 as ReturnValue, "No Errors" as ReturnMessage
            END
GO
```

The procedure requires that all the fields in this table are passed in as parameters:

```
@UpdateID integer,
@UpdateName varchar(50),
@UpdateNote text,
@UpdateEmployeeID integer
```

You need to make sure that the record being edited is a valid department record:

```
If (dbo.DepartmentIDCheck(@UpdateID)) = 0
```

If it isn't, you return an error message:

```
Select 0 as ReturnValue, 'The DepartmentID being updated '
      + 'was not found!' as ReturnMessage
```

You also need to make sure that the manager selected for the department is a valid employee:

```
If (dbo.EmployeeIDCheck(@UpdateEmployeeID)) = 0
```

If not, you return an error message:

```
Select 0 as ReturnValue, 'The EmployeeID being updated '
      + 'was not found!' as ReturnMessage
```

Otherwise, you can update the desired record:

```
     Update Departments set
           DepartmentName = @UpdateName,
           Note = @UpdateNote,
           DepartmentManagerID = @UpdateEmployeeID
           Where DepartmentID = @UpdateID
```

and return a success message:

```
Select 1 as ReturnValue, "No Errors" as ReturnMessage
```

DepartmentDelete Stored Procedure

The DepartmentDelete stored procedure deletes a record from the Departments table.

```
CREATE PROCEDURE DepartmentDelete
@DeleteID integer
AS
If (dbo.DepartmentIDCheck(@DeleteID)) = 0
      BEGIN
            Select 0 as ReturnValue, 'The DepartmentID being deleted '
                  + 'was not found!' as ReturnMessage
      END
Else
      BEGIN
            Delete from Departments
            Where DepartmentID = @DeleteID
```

```
                Select 1 as ReturnValue, "No Errors" as ReturnMessage
        END
GO
```

The procedure requires a single parameter, the ID of the department to be deleted:

```
@DeleteID integer
```

You make sure that the ID passed in is a valid DepartmentID:

```
If (dbo.DepartmentIDCheck(@DeleteID)) = 0
```

If it isn't, an error record is returned from the procedure:

```
Select 0 as ReturnValue, 'The DepartmentID being deleted '
        + 'was not found!' as ReturnMessage
```

Otherwise, you delete the requested record:

```
Delete from Departments
        Where DepartmentID = @DeleteID
```

and return a success message:

```
Select 1 as ReturnValue, "No Errors" as ReturnMessage
```

DepartmentMove Stored Procedure

The DepartmentMove stored procedure returns the contents of a single record from the Departments table. The record returned is based on a navigational parameter and a relative parameter passed into the procedure.

```
CREATE PROCEDURE DepartmentMove
@MoveDirection varchar(8),
@LastPosition integer = 0
AS
Declare @ID2Use integer
If (@MoveDirection) = 'FIRST'
        BEGIN
                Select @ID2Use = Min(DepartmentID) from Departments
                Select * from Departments Where DepartmentID = @ID2Use
        END
Else
        If (@MoveDirection) = 'LAST'
```

```
            BEGIN
                  Select @ID2Use = Max(DepartmentID) from Departments
                  Select * from Departments Where DepartmentID = @ID2Use
            END
      Else
            If (@MoveDirection) = 'NEXT'
                  BEGIN
                        Select Top 1 * from Departments
                              Where DepartmentID > @LastPosition
                              Order By DepartmentID
                  END
            Else
                  BEGIN
                        Select Top 1 * from Departments
                              Where DepartmentID < @LastPosition
                              Order By DepartmentID DESC
                  END
GO
```

Those parameters are declared at the top of the procedure:

```
@MoveDirection varchar(8),
@LastPosition integer = 0
```

The procedure will also need a variable to store the ID of the record to be retrieved:

```
Declare @ID2Use integer
```

First, you check to see whether the calling application wants to retrieve the first record:

```
If (@MoveDirection) = 'FIRST'
```

If so, you retrieve the ID of the first record:

```
Select @ID2Use = Min(DepartmentID) from Departments
```

and return its contents:

```
Select * from Departments Where DepartmentID = @ID2Use
```

If the directional parameter contains the text “Last,” the calling application wants the last record in the Departments table:

```
If (@MoveDirection) = 'LAST'
```

so that ID is retrieved:

```
Select @ID2Use = Max(DepartmentID) from Departments
```

and the contents of that record are returned:

```
Select * from Departments Where DepartmentID = @ID2Use
```

Next, you check to see whether the calling application wants the Next record relative to the ID passed in:

```
If (@MoveDirection) = 'NEXT'
```

If so, you return that record:

```
Select Top 1 * from Departments
            Where DepartmentID > @LastPosition
            Order By DepartmentID
```

Otherwise, the calling application wants the preceding record. So that record is returned from the procedure:

```
Select Top 1 * from Departments
      Where DepartmentID < @LastPosition
      Order By DepartmentID DESC
```

GeneratePayrollRecords Stored Procedure

The GeneratePayrollRecords stored procedure adds payroll records to the database for each of the employees.

```
CREATE PROCEDURE GeneratePayrollRecords
@MonthToUse integer,
@YearToUse integer
AS
Declare
@CurrentID varchar(10),
@CurrentSalary money
If @MonthToUse < 1 or @MonthToUse > 12
      BEGIN
            Select 0 as ReturnValue, 'The month for payroll must be '
                  + 'between 1 and 12!' as ReturnMessage
      END
Else
      BEGIN
```

```
            Declare CurEmps Cursor
            For Select EmployeeID, Salary from Employees
            Open CurEmps
            Fetch CurEmps
                  Into @CurrentID, @CurrentSalary
            While @@Fetch_Status = 0
                  BEGIN
                        Set @CurrentSalary = @CurrentSalary / 12
                        Insert Into PayrollRecords
                              (EmployeeID, MonthOfPayment, YearOfPayment,
                              AmountPaid) values (
                              @CurrentID, @MonthToUse, @YearToUse,
                              @CurrentSalary)
                        Fetch CurEmps
                              Into @CurrentID, @CurrentSalary
                  END
            Close CurEmps
            Deallocate CurEmps
            Select 1 as ReturnValue, "No Errors" as ReturnMessage
      END
GO
```

The procedure expects two parameters. The first is the month to use for the payroll:

```
@MonthToUse integer,
```

and the year:

```
@YearToUse integer
```

The procedure also needs a variable to store the ID of the current employee and their salary:

```
Declare
@CurrentID varchar(10),
@CurrentSalary money
```

Next, you make sure the month supplied is in a valid range:

```
If @MonthToUse < 1 or @MonthToUse > 12
```

If not, you return an error record:

```
Select 0 as ReturnValue, 'The month for payroll must be '
      + 'between 1 and 12!' as ReturnMessage
```

Otherwise, you can process the request. You will need a Cursor object:

```
Declare CurEmps Cursor
```

and retrieve into that object employee information:

```
For Select EmployeeID, Salary from Employees
```

You then open that cursor:

```
Open CurEmps
```

and retrieve the first record:

```
Fetch CurEmps
      Into @CurrentID, @CurrentSalary
```

Next, you enter a loop that will take you through each of the records:

```
While @@Fetch_Status = 0
      BEGIN
```

The Salary stored in the Employees table is the yearly salary. So you need to calculate the monthly value:

```
Set @CurrentSalary = @CurrentSalary / 12
```

That value is used to create a new record in the PayrollRecords table:

```
Insert Into PayrollRecords
      (EmployeeID, MonthOfPayment, YearOfPayment,
      AmountPaid) values (
      @CurrentID, @MonthToUse, @YearToUse,
      @CurrentSalary)
```

You then retrieve the next record:

```
Fetch CurEmps
      Into @CurrentID, @CurrentSalary
```

and loop to process it:

```
END
```

After the loop, you close and release the resources of the cursor:

```
Close CurEmps
Deallocate CurEmps
```

and return a success record:

```
Select 1 as ReturnValue, "No Errors" as ReturnMessage
```

GenerateSickHours Stored Procedure

The GenerateSickHours stored procedure accrues sick hours for each employee at their own rate.

```
CREATE PROCEDURE GenerateSickHours
@DateToUse datetime
AS
Declare
@CurrentID varchar(10),
@CurrentSickAcc float
BEGIN
      Declare CurEmps Cursor
      For Select EmployeeID, SickAcc from Employees
      Open CurEmps
      Fetch CurEmps
            Into @CurrentID, @CurrentSickAcc
      While @@Fetch_Status = 0
            BEGIN
                  Insert Into SickHours
                        (EmployeeID, DateEntered, Amount)
                        values (@CurrentID, @DateToUse,
                        @CurrentSickAcc)
                  Fetch CurEmps
                        Into @CurrentID, @CurrentSickAcc
            END
      Close CurEmps
      Deallocate CurEmps
      Select 1 as ReturnValue, "No Errors" as ReturnMessage
END
GO
```

The procedure requires the date for the sick hour accrual:

```
@DateToUse datetime
```

The procedure will also need variables to store the EmployeeID and the rate of their accrual:

```
@CurrentID varchar(10),
@CurrentSickAcc float
```

as well as a cursor that will be used to retrieve employee information:

```
Declare CurEmps Cursor
      For Select EmployeeID, SickAcc from Employees
```

That cursor is opened:

```
Open CurEmps
```

and the first record retrieved:

```
Fetch CurEmps
      Into @CurrentID, @CurrentSickAcc
```

You then start a loop so that you can process each employee record:

```
While @@Fetch_Status = 0
```

and a record to the SickHours table for each of the employees:

```
Insert Into SickHours
      (EmployeeID, DateEntered, Amount)
      values (@CurrentID, @DateToUse,
      @CurrentSickAcc)
```

You then retrieve the next record:

```
Fetch CurEmps
      Into @CurrentID, @CurrentSickAcc
```

Close the cursor and release its resources:

```
Close CurEmps
Deallocate CurEmps
```

and return a success record:

```
Select 1 as ReturnValue, "No Errors" as ReturnMessage
```

GenerateVacationHours Stored Procedure

The GenerateVacationHours stored procedure provides the way for a manager to accrue vacation hours for all employees.

```
CREATE PROCEDURE GenerateVacationHours
@DateToUse datetime
AS
Declare
@CurrentID varchar(10),
@CurrentVacatAcc float
BEGIN
      Declare CurEmps Cursor
      For Select EmployeeID, VacatAcc from Employees
      Open CurEmps
      Fetch CurEmps
            Into @CurrentID, @CurrentVacatAcc
      While @@Fetch_Status = 0
            BEGIN
                  Insert Into VacationHours
                        (EmployeeID, DateEntered, Amount)
                        values (@CurrentID, @DateToUse,
                        @CurrentVacatAcc)
                  Fetch CurEmps
                        Into @CurrentID, @CurrentVacatAcc
            END
      Close CurEmps
      Deallocate CurEmps
      Select 1 as ReturnValue, "No Errors" as ReturnMessage
END
GO
```

The procedure takes a single parameter, the date to use for the entry in the VacationHours table:

```
@DateToUse datetime
```

The procedure will need variables to store the employee ID and accrual rate:

```
@CurrentID varchar(10),
@CurrentVacatAcc float
```

You will also need a Cursor variable:

```
Declare CurEmps Cursor
```

that will be used to retrieve the ID and accrual rate for each employee:

```
For Select EmployeeID, VacatAcc from Employees
```

The cursor is then opened:

```
Open CurEmps
```

and the first record retrieved:

```
Fetch CurEmps
      Into @CurrentID, @CurrentVacatAcc
```

You then start a loop to process each of the records:

```
While @@Fetch_Status = 0
```

Each Employee record is used to add a record to the VacationHours table:

```
Insert Into VacationHours
      (EmployeeID, DateEntered, Amount)
      values (@CurrentID, @DateToUse,
      @CurrentVacatAcc)
```

before retrieving the next record:

```
Fetch CurEmps
      Into @CurrentID, @CurrentVacatAcc
```

After the loop, the cursor is closed and released:

```
Close CurEmps
Deallocate CurEmps
```

and a success record is returned:

```
Select 1 as ReturnValue, "No Errors" as ReturnMessage
```

UseLeave Stored Procedure

The UseLeave stored procedure is used by the manager to charge an employee with vacation or sick leave hours.

```
CREATE PROCEDURE UseLeave
@EmployeeID integer,
@DateEntered datetime,
@Amount float,
@LeaveType varchar(8)
AS
If (dbo.EmployeeIDCheck(@EmployeeID)) = 0
      BEGIN
            Select 0 as ReturnValue, 'The EmployeeID entered '
                  + 'was not found!' as ReturnMessage
      END
Else
      If @LeaveType = 'Sick'
            BEGIN
                  Insert Into SickHours
                        (EmployeeID, DateEntered, Amount)
                        values (@EmployeeID, @DateEntered,
                        @Amount)
                  Select 1 as ReturnValue, "No Errors" as
ReturnMessage
            END
      Else
            BEGIN
                  Insert Into VacationHours
                        (EmployeeID, DateEntered, Amount)
                        values (@EmployeeID, @DateEntered,
                        @Amount)
                  Select 1 as ReturnValue, "No Errors" as
ReturnMessage
            END
GO
```

The procedure requires as parameters the ID of the employee who is using hours:

```
@EmployeeID integer,
```

the date used:

```
@DateEntered datetime,
```

the amount used:

```
@Amount float,
```

and the type of hours used, either Sick or Vacation:

```
@LeaveType varchar(8)
```

You then make sure that the ID of the employee supplied is valid:

```
If (dbo.EmployeeIDCheck(@EmployeeID)) = 0
```

If it isn't, you return an error message:

```
Select 0 as ReturnValue, 'The EmployeeID entered '
      + 'was not found!' as ReturnMessage
```

Otherwise, you check to see whether you are dealing with a sick hours request:

```
If @LeaveType = 'Sick'
```

If so, you insert a record into the SickHours table:

```
Insert Into SickHours
      (EmployeeID, DateEntered, Amount)
      values (@EmployeeID, @DateEntered,
      @Amount)
```

and return a success record:

```
Select 1 as ReturnValue, "No Errors" as ReturnMessage
```

If the code flows here, you assume that the calling application wants to use vacation hours:

```
Insert Into VacationHours
      (EmployeeID, DateEntered, Amount)
      values (@EmployeeID, @DateEntered,
      @Amount)
```

and return a success record:

```
Select 1 as ReturnValue, "No Errors" as ReturnMessage
```

EmployeePermissions Stored Procedure

The EmployeePermissions stored procedure returns the permissions of the current user to build the menu in the Access front end.

```
CREATE PROCEDURE EmployeePermissions
AS
Declare @CurrentUser varchar(50)
Set @CurrentUser = User_Name()
Select IsManager, IsDBAdmin from Employees
Where UserName = @CurrentUser
GO
```

The procedure declares one variable:

```
Declare @CurrentUser varchar(50)
```

which is set to the user who is logged into the database:

```
Set @CurrentUser = User_Name()
```

That user's privileges are returned from the procedure:

```
Select IsManager, IsDBAdmin from Employees
      Where UserName = @CurrentUser
```

EmployeePersonalRecord Stored Procedure

The EmployeePersonalRecord stored procedure simply returns the employee information of the employee who is logged into the database:

```
CREATE PROCEDURE EmployeePersonalRecord AS
Select * from Employees Where UserName = User_Name()
GO
```

EmployeePersonalRecordUpdate Stored Procedure

The EmployeePersonalRecordUpdate stored procedure is used to update the information that an employee can update on their own record.

```
CREATE PROCEDURE EmployeePersonalRecordUpdate
@UpdateID integer,
@FirstName varchar(50),
@LastName varchar(50),
@Address1 varchar(100),
@Address2 varchar(100),
@City varchar(50),
@State varchar(2),
@ZipCode varchar(50),
@PhoneNumber varchar(50),
@EmailAddress varchar(50)
AS
If (dbo.EmployeeIDCheck(@UpdateID)) = 0
      BEGIN
            Select 0 as ReturnValue, 'The EmployeeID being updated '
                  + 'was not found!' as ReturnMessage
      END
Else
      BEGIN
            Update Employees set
            FirstName = @FirstName,
            LastName = @LastName,
            Address1 = @Address1,
            Address2 = @Address2,
            City = @City,
            State = @State,
            ZipCode = @ZipCode,
            PhoneNumber = @PhoneNumber,
            EmailAddress = @EmailAddress
            Where EmployeeID = @UpdateID

            Select 1 as ReturnValue, "No Errors" as ReturnMessage
      END
GO
```

The procedure takes as parameters the values for the columns in the record that the employee can change:

```
@UpdateID integer,
@FirstName varchar(50),
@LastName varchar(50),
@Address1 varchar(100),
@Address2 varchar(100),
@City varchar(50),
@State varchar(2),
@ZipCode varchar(50),
@PhoneNumber varchar(50),
@EmailAddress varchar(50)
```

You make sure that the ID supplied is a valid ID:

```
If (dbo.EmployeeIDCheck(@UpdateID)) = 0
```

If it isn't, an error record is returned:

```
Select 0 as ReturnValue, 'The EmployeeID being updated '
      + 'was not found!' as ReturnMessage
```

Otherwise, you update the employee record:

```
Update Employees set
      FirstName = @FirstName,
      LastName = @LastName,
      Address1 = @Address1,
      Address2 = @Address2,
      City = @City,
      State = @State,
      ZipCode = @ZipCode,
      PhoneNumber = @PhoneNumber,
      EmailAddress = @EmailAddress
      Where EmployeeID = @UpdateID
```

and return a success record:

```
Select 1 as ReturnValue, "No Errors" as ReturnMessage
```

Views

EmployeeWithPayrollInfo View

The EmployeeWithPayrollInfo view returns employee information joined with payroll information that is used in the Access front end after payroll records are generated.

```
Select dbo.Employees.LastName, dbo.Employees.FirstName,
      dbo.PayrollRecords.MonthOfPayment, dbo.PayrollRecords.YearOfPayment,
      dbo.PayrollRecords.AmountPaid FROM dbo.Employees INNER JOIN
      dbo.PayrollRecords ON
      dbo.Employees.EmployeeID = dbo.PayrollRecords.EmployeeID
```

EmployeeWithSickHours View

The EmployeeWithSickHours view joins the employee information together with sick hour records. The view is used to show the manager the records that they have added to the SickHours table when sick hours are accrued.

```
Select dbo.Employees.LastName, dbo.Employees.FirstName,
      dbo.SickHours.DateEntered, dbo.SickHours.Amount
      FROM dbo.Employees INNER JOIN dbo.SickHours ON
      dbo.Employees.EmployeeID = dbo.SickHours.EmployeeID
```

EmployeeWithVacationHours View

The EmployeeWithVacationHours view joins employee record information with vacation hour information. The manager sees this view in an Access report when they have completed accruing vacation hours.

```
Select dbo.Employees.LastName, dbo.Employees.FirstName,
      dbo.VacationHours.DateEntered, dbo.VacationHours.Amount
      FROM dbo.Employees INNER JOIN  dbo.VacationHours ON
      dbo.Employees.EmployeeID = dbo.VacationHours.EmployeeID
```

PersonalPayroll View

The PersonalPayroll view displays all the payroll records for the employee who is currently logged into the database. The system function User_Name() is used in the Where clause to limit the rows to those that are for this employee:

```
Select dbo.PayrollRecords.YearOfPayment, dbo.PayrollRecords.MonthOfPayment,
      dbo.PayrollRecords.AmountPaid FROM dbo.Employees INNER JOIN
      dbo.PayrollRecords ON
      dbo.Employees.EmployeeID = dbo.PayrollRecords.EmployeeID
      WHERE (dbo.Employees.UserName = USER_NAME())
```

PersonalSick View

The PersonalSick view shows the logged-in employee all their sick leave records. This view is used as the basis for a report in the Access front end.

```
Select TOP 100 PERCENT dbo.SickHours.DateEntered, dbo.SickHours.Amount
      FROM dbo.Employees INNER JOIN dbo.SickHours ON
      dbo.Employees.EmployeeID = dbo.SickHours.EmployeeID
      WHERE (dbo.Employees.UserName = USER_NAME())
```

PersonalVacation View

The PersonalVacation view uses the User_Name() system function to show the logged-in user their vacation hours records.

```
Select TOP 100 PERCENT dbo.VacationHours.DateEntered,
      dbo.VacationHours.Amount
      FROM dbo.Employees INNER JOIN dbo.VacationHours ON
      dbo.Employees.EmployeeID = dbo.VacationHours.EmployeeID
      WHERE (dbo.Employees.UserName = USER_NAME())
      ORDER BY dbo.VacationHours.DateEntered
```

Roles

Employee Role

All of the users in this application should be members of the Employee role. The role provides the functionality to view and manipulate the employee personal information.

Manager Role

The Manager role provides the functionality needed to manage employees. This includes all the procedures to manipulate employee records and payroll information.

DB Admin Role

The DB Admin role has the additional functionality needed to manipulate department records.

Application Notes

C10FrontEnd.mdb

The Access database does not have any local tables. It also does not link to any of the underlying tables in the SQL Server database. It does, however, link to all the views in the SQL Server database. Those views are used for reports in the Access front end.

For the views to work correctly and for the code to run correctly, a DSN with the name of C10ManagingEmps needs to be installed on the client computer.

Modules

GeneralProcs Module

The GeneralProcs module contains some variables declared in the General Declarations section that are available throughout the Access database.

```
Public MyDB As New ADODB.Connection
Public SQLUserName As String
Public IsDBAdminMenu As Boolean
Public IsManagerMenu As Boolean
```

A connection object will be used throughout the application to connect to the SQL Server database:

```
Public MyDB As New ADODB.Connection
```

This variable will store the name of the user logging into the database:

```
Public SQLUserName As String
```

and these variables will store the user's permissions for displaying the menu:

```
Public IsDBAdminMenu As Boolean
Public IsManagerMenu As Boolean
```

When the user first enters the database, the AutoExec macro runs. That macro calls the StartUp function in the GeneralProcs module. That function logs the user into the database and loads the menu.

```
Public Function StartUp()
    On Error GoTo HandleError
    Dim SQLPassword As String
    Dim RSPermissions As ADODB.Recordset
    SQLUserName = InputBox("Please enter your user name.", "User Name")
    SQLPassword = InputBox("Please enter your user name.", "Password")
    MyDB.Open "DSN=C10ManagingEmps;UID=" & SQLUserName _
        & ";Password=" & SQLPassword
    Set RSPermissions = MyDB.Execute("Exec EmployeePermissions")
    IsDBAdminMenu = RSPermissions.Fields("IsDBAdmin")
    IsManagerMenu = RSPermissions.Fields("IsManager")
    DoCmd.OpenForm "frmMenu"
    Exit Function
HandleError:
    MsgBox Err.Number & ": " & Err.Description & _
        ". Closing application.", vbCritical, "Can't Start Application"
    Application.CloseCurrentDatabase
End Function
```

If the login attempt fails, the code will flow to an error handler:

```
On Error GoTo HandleError
```

The code will need a variable to store the user's database password and a Recordset object to retrieve their permissions:

```
Dim SQLPassword As String
Dim RSPermissions As ADODB.Recordset
```

You then prompt the user for their user name and password:

```
SQLUserName = InputBox("Please enter your user name.", "User Name")
SQLPassword = InputBox("Please enter your user name.", "Password")
```

You then attempt to connect to the database using the login supplied by the user:

```
MyDB.Open "DSN=C10ManagingEmps;UID=" & SQLUserName _
    & ";Password=" & SQLPassword
```

If you succeed in logging into the database, you next retrieve the user's permissions:

```
Set RSPermissions = MyDB.Execute("Exec EmployeePermissions")
```

and store those permissions in Public variables:

```
IsDBAdminMenu = RSPermissions.Fields("IsDBAdmin")
IsManagerMenu = RSPermissions.Fields("IsManager")
```

and open the menu form:

```
DoCmd.OpenForm "frmMenu"
```

If an error occurs, the code flows here:

```
HandleError:
```

You display the error to the user:

```
MsgBox Err.Number & ": " & Err.Description & _
      ". Closing application.", vbCritical, "Can't Start Application"
```

and close the database:

```
Application.CloseCurrentDatabase
```

frmMenu Form

The frmMenu form displays front-end options in accordance with the user's permissions. When the form is first opened, the code shows the buttons appropriate to their permissions.

```
Private Sub Form_Load()
    If IsManagerMenu = True Then
        lblManagerActivities.Visible = True
        cmdAllEmployees.Visible = True
        cmdGeneratePayroll.Visible = True
        cmdGenerateVacatSick.Visible = True
        cmdUseLeave.Visible = True
    End If
    If IsDBAdminMenu = True Then
        lblDBAdminActivities.Visible = True
        cmdDepartments.Visible = True
    End If
End Sub
```

If the user is a manager:

```
If IsManagerMenu = True Then
```

you display all the items on the Manager Activities menu:

```
lblManagerActivities.Visible = True
cmdAllEmployees.Visible = True
cmdGeneratePayroll.Visible = True
cmdGenerateVacatSick.Visible = True
cmdUseLeave.Visible = True
```

If the user is a DB Admin:

```
If IsDBAdminMenu = True Then
```

the DB Admin Activities menu is displayed:

```
lblDBAdminActivities.Visible = True
cmdDepartments.Visible = True
```

All the buttons on the form use the DoCmd object to open the form indicated by the button:

```
DoCmd.OpenForm "frmUseLeave"
```

Or, use the OpenReport method of the DoCmd object to open a report:

```
DoCmd.OpenReport "Personal Vacation", acViewPreview
```

Employees Form

The code on the Employees form provides for the functionality to add, edit, delete, and view employee records. When the form is first loaded, the first Employee record is retrieved.

```
Private Sub Form_Load()
    Dim RSCurrentRecord As ADODB.Recordset
    Set RSCurrentRecord = MyDB.Execute("Exec EmployeeMove 'First'")
    CurrentID = RSCurrentRecord.Fields("EmployeeID")
    [txtFirstName] = RSCurrentRecord.Fields("FirstName")
    [txtLastName] = RSCurrentRecord.Fields("LastName")
    [txtAddress1] = RSCurrentRecord.Fields("Address1")
    [txtAddress2] = RSCurrentRecord.Fields("Address2")
```

```
    [txtCity] = RSCurrentRecord.Fields("City")
    [txtState] = RSCurrentRecord.Fields("State")
    [txtZipCode] = RSCurrentRecord.Fields("ZipCode")
    [txtPhoneNumber] = RSCurrentRecord.Fields("PhoneNumber")
    [txtEmailAddress] = RSCurrentRecord.Fields("EmailAddress")
    [txtUserName] = RSCurrentRecord.Fields("UserName")
    [chkIsManager] = RSCurrentRecord.Fields("IsManager")
    [chkIsDBAdmin] = RSCurrentRecord.Fields("IsDBAdmin")
    [txtSalary] = RSCurrentRecord.Fields("Salary")
    [txtVacatAcc] = RSCurrentRecord.Fields("VacatAcc")
    [txtSickAcc] = RSCurrentRecord.Fields("SickAcc")
    txtFirstName.SetFocus
End Sub
```

A Recordset object will be needed:

```
Dim RSCurrentRecord As ADODB.Recordset
```

You then call the EmployeeMove stored procedure to retrieve the first record:

```
Set RSCurrentRecord = MyDB.Execute("Exec EmployeeMove 'First'")
```

store the ID of the employee in a form-wide variable:

```
CurrentID = RSCurrentRecord.Fields("EmployeeID")
```

and display the contents of that record:

```
[txtFirstName] = RSCurrentRecord.Fields("FirstName")
[txtLastName] = RSCurrentRecord.Fields("LastName")
[txtAddress1] = RSCurrentRecord.Fields("Address1")
[txtAddress2] = RSCurrentRecord.Fields("Address2")
[txtCity] = RSCurrentRecord.Fields("City")
[txtState] = RSCurrentRecord.Fields("State")
[txtZipCode] = RSCurrentRecord.Fields("ZipCode")
[txtPhoneNumber] = RSCurrentRecord.Fields("PhoneNumber")
[txtEmailAddress] = RSCurrentRecord.Fields("EmailAddress")
[txtUserName] = RSCurrentRecord.Fields("UserName")
[chkIsManager] = RSCurrentRecord.Fields("IsManager")
[chkIsDBAdmin] = RSCurrentRecord.Fields("IsDBAdmin")
[txtSalary] = RSCurrentRecord.Fields("Salary")
[txtVacatAcc] = RSCurrentRecord.Fields("VacatAcc")
[txtSickAcc] = RSCurrentRecord.Fields("SickAcc")
txtFirstName.SetFocus
```

When the user clicks one of the Move buttons, the code uses the EmployeeMove stored procedure to retrieve the appropriate record. Here, the Next button is clicked.

```
Private Sub cmdMoveNext_Click()
    Dim RSCurrentRecord As ADODB.Recordset
    Set RSCurrentRecord = MyDB.Execute("Exec EmployeeMove 'Next', " & CurrentID)
    If RSCurrentRecord.EOF Then
        cmdMoveLast_Click
    Else
        CurrentID = RSCurrentRecord.Fields("EmployeeID")
        [txtFirstName] = RSCurrentRecord.Fields("FirstName")
        [txtLastName] = RSCurrentRecord.Fields("LastName")
        [txtAddress1] = RSCurrentRecord.Fields("Address1")
        [txtAddress2] = RSCurrentRecord.Fields("Address2")
        [txtCity] = RSCurrentRecord.Fields("City")
        [txtState] = RSCurrentRecord.Fields("State")
        [txtZipCode] = RSCurrentRecord.Fields("ZipCode")
        [txtPhoneNumber] = RSCurrentRecord.Fields("PhoneNumber")
        [txtEmailAddress] = RSCurrentRecord.Fields("EmailAddress")
        [txtUserName] = RSCurrentRecord.Fields("UserName")
        [chkIsManager] = RSCurrentRecord.Fields("IsManager")
        [chkIsDBAdmin] = RSCurrentRecord.Fields("IsDBAdmin")
        [txtSalary] = RSCurrentRecord.Fields("Salary")
        [txtVacatAcc] = RSCurrentRecord.Fields("VacatAcc")
        [txtSickAcc] = RSCurrentRecord.Fields("SickAcc")
        txtFirstName.SetFocus
    End If
End Sub
```

You use a Recordset object:

```
Dim RSCurrentRecord As ADODB.Recordset
```

and set it to the return value of the EmployeeMove stored procedure:

```
Set RSCurrentRecord = MyDB.Execute("Exec EmployeeMove 'Next', " & CurrentID)
```

If no next record was found, you move to the last record:

```
If RSCurrentRecord.EOF Then
    cmdMoveLast_Click
```

Otherwise, you display the contents of the record:

```
Else
    CurrentID = RSCurrentRecord.Fields("EmployeeID")
    [txtFirstName] = RSCurrentRecord.Fields("FirstName")
    [txtLastName] = RSCurrentRecord.Fields("LastName")
    [txtAddress1] = RSCurrentRecord.Fields("Address1")
    [txtAddress2] = RSCurrentRecord.Fields("Address2")
```

```
    [txtCity] = RSCurrentRecord.Fields("City")
    [txtState] = RSCurrentRecord.Fields("State")
    [txtZipCode] = RSCurrentRecord.Fields("ZipCode")
    [txtPhoneNumber] = RSCurrentRecord.Fields("PhoneNumber")
    [txtEmailAddress] = RSCurrentRecord.Fields("EmailAddress")
    [txtUserName] = RSCurrentRecord.Fields("UserName")
    [chkIsManager] = RSCurrentRecord.Fields("IsManager")
    [chkIsDBAdmin] = RSCurrentRecord.Fields("IsDBAdmin")
    [txtSalary] = RSCurrentRecord.Fields("Salary")
    [txtVacatAcc] = RSCurrentRecord.Fields("VacatAcc")
    [txtSickAcc] = RSCurrentRecord.Fields("SickAcc")
    txtFirstName.SetFocus
```

When the Add button is clicked, the values entered on the form by the user are added to the database.

```
Private Sub cmdAdd_Click()
    Dim RSStatus As ADODB.Recordset
    Dim NewFirstName As String
    Dim NewLastName As String
    Dim NewAddress1 As String
    Dim NewAddress2 As String
    Dim NewCity As String
    Dim NewState As String
    Dim NewZipCode As String
    Dim NewPhoneNumber As String
    Dim NewEmailAddress As String
    Dim NewUserName As String
    NewFirstName = Replace([txtFirstName], "'", "''", 1, -1, vbTextCompare)
    NewLastName = Replace([txtLastName], "'", "''", 1, -1, vbTextCompare)
    NewAddress1 = Replace([txtAddress1], "'", "''", 1, -1, vbTextCompare)
    NewAddress2 = Replace([txtAddress2], "'", "''", 1, -1, vbTextCompare)
    NewCity = Replace([txtCity], "'", "''", 1, -1, vbTextCompare)
    NewState = Replace([txtState], "'", "''", 1, -1, vbTextCompare)
    NewZipCode = Replace([txtZipCode], "'", "''", 1, -1, vbTextCompare)
    NewPhoneNumber = Replace([txtPhoneNumber], "'", "''", 1, -1, vbTextCompare)
    NewEmailAddress = Replace([txtEmailAddress], "'", "''", 1, -1, vbTextCompare)
    NewUserName = Replace([txtUserName], "'", "''", 1, -1, vbTextCompare)
    Set RSStatus = MyDB.Execute("Exec EmployeeAdd " _
        & "'" & NewFirstName & "', "_
        & "'" & NewLastName & "', " _
        & "'" & NewAddress1 & "', "_
        & "'" & NewAddress2 & "', " _
        & "'" & NewCity & "', "_
        & "'" & NewState & "', " _
```

```
        & "'" & NewZipCode & "', " _
        & "'" & NewPhoneNumber & "', " _
        & "'" & NewEmailAddress & "', " _
        & "'" & NewUserName & "', " _
        & Abs([chkIsManager]) & ", " _
        & Abs([chkIsDBAdmin]) & ", " _
        & [txtSalary] & ", " _
        & [txtVacatAcc] & ", " _
        & [txtSickAcc])
    If RSStatus(0) = 1 Then
        cmdMoveLast_Click
    Else
        MsgBox RSStatus(1), vbExclamation, "Could not add record."
    End If
End Sub
```

The procedure will need a Recordset object:

```
Dim RSStatus As ADODB.Recordset
```

as well as variables that will need to store converted field values:

```
Dim NewFirstName As String
Dim NewLastName As String
Dim NewAddress1 As String
Dim NewAddress2 As String
Dim NewCity As String
Dim NewState As String
Dim NewZipCode As String
Dim NewPhoneNumber As String
Dim NewEmailAddress As String
Dim NewUserName As String
```

You then convert the "'" character to "''" characters to allow for the apostrophe to be inserted into the SQL statement for each of the string fields:

```
NewFirstName = Replace([txtFirstName], "'", "''", 1, -1, vbTextCompare)
NewLastName = Replace([txtLastName], "'", "''", 1, -1, vbTextCompare)
NewAddress1 = Replace([txtAddress1], "'", "''", 1, -1, vbTextCompare)
NewAddress2 = Replace([txtAddress2], "'", "''", 1, -1, vbTextCompare)
NewCity = Replace([txtCity], "'", "''", 1, -1, vbTextCompare)
NewState = Replace([txtState], "'", "''", 1, -1, vbTextCompare)
NewZipCode = Replace([txtZipCode], "'", "''", 1, -1, vbTextCompare)
NewPhoneNumber = Replace([txtPhoneNumber], "'", "''", 1, -1, vbTextCompare)
NewEmailAddress = Replace([txtEmailAddress], "'", "''", 1, -1, vbTextCompare)
NewUserName = Replace([txtUserName], "'", "''", 1, -1, vbTextCompare)
```

Next, you call the EmployeeAdd stored procedure to add the record to the database:

```
Set RSStatus = MyDB.Execute("Exec EmployeeAdd " _
      & "'" & NewFirstName & "', " _
      & "'" & NewLastName & "', " _
      & "'" & NewAddress1 & "', " _
      & "'" & NewAddress2 & "', " _
      & "'" & NewCity & "', " _
      & "'" & NewState & "', " _
      & "'" & NewZipCode & "', " _
      & "'" & NewPhoneNumber & "', " _
      & "'" & NewEmailAddress & "', " _
      & "'" & NewUserName & "', " _
```

Note the use of the absolute value function on the check boxes. A checked box is numerically represented as a –1 in Access. But you want to store that as a bit in the SQL Server database, so you need to make a –1 a 1:

```
& Abs([chkIsManager]) & ", " _
& Abs([chkIsDBAdmin]) & ", " _
& [txtSalary] & ", " _
& [txtVacatAcc] & ", " _
& [txtSickAcc])
```

You then check to see whether an error was returned by the procedure:

```
If RSStatus(0) = 1 Then
```

If it wasn't, you move to the record just added:

```
cmdMoveLast_Click
```

Otherwise, you display the error message:

```
MsgBox RSStatus(1), vbExclamation, "Could not add record."
```

When the Update button is clicked, the next code block fires.

```
Private Sub cmdUpdate_Click()
    Dim RSStatus As ADODB.Recordset
    Dim UpdateFirstName As String
    Dim UpdateLastName As String
    Dim UpdateAddress1 As String
    Dim UpdateAddress2 As String
```

```
    Dim UpdateCity As String
    Dim UpdateState As String
    Dim UpdateZipCode As String
    Dim UpdatePhoneNumber As String
    Dim UpdateEmailAddress As String
    Dim UpdateUserName As String
    If CurrentID = 0 Then
        cmdAdd_Click
        Exit Sub
    End If
    UpdateFirstName = Replace([txtFirstName], "'", "''", 1, -1, vbTextCompare)
    UpdateLastName = Replace([txtLastName], "'", "''", 1, -1, vbTextCompare)
    UpdateAddress1 = Replace([txtAddress1], "'", "''", 1, -1, vbTextCompare)
    UpdateAddress2 = Replace([txtAddress2], "'", "''", 1, -1, vbTextCompare)
    UpdateCity = Replace([txtCity], "'", "''", 1, -1, vbTextCompare)
    UpdateState = Replace([txtState], "'", "''", 1, -1, vbTextCompare)
    UpdateZipCode = Replace([txtZipCode], "'", "''", 1, -1, vbTextCompare)
    UpdatePhoneNumber = Replace([txtPhoneNumber], "'", "''", 1, -1, vbTextCompare)
    UpdateEmailAddress = Replace([txtEmailAddress], "'", "''", 1, -1, vbTextCompare)
    UpdateUserName = Replace([txtUserName], "'", "''", 1, -1, vbTextCompare)
    Set RSStatus = MyDB.Execute("Exec EmployeeEdit " _
        & CurrentID & ", " _
        & "'" & UpdateFirstName & "', " _
        & "'" & UpdateLastName & "', " _
        & "'" & UpdateAddress1 & "', " _
        & "'" & UpdateAddress2 & "', " _
        & "'" & UpdateCity & "', " _
        & "'" & UpdateState & "', " _
        & "'" & UpdateZipCode & "', " _
        & "'" & UpdatePhoneNumber & "', " _
        & "'" & UpdateEmailAddress & "', " _
        & "'" & UpdateUserName & "', " _
        & Abs([chkIsManager]) & ", " _
        & Abs([chkIsDBAdmin]) & ", " _
        & [txtSalary] & ", " _
        & [txtVacatAcc] & ", " _
        & [txtSickAcc])
    If RSStatus(0) = 0 Then
        MsgBox RSStatus(1), vbExclamation, "Could not update record."
    End If
End Sub
```

The procedure will need a Recordset object:

```
Dim RSStatus As ADODB.Recordset
```

and variables to store converted strings:

```
Dim UpdateFirstName As String
Dim UpdateLastName As String
Dim UpdateAddress1 As String
Dim UpdateAddress2 As String
Dim UpdateCity As String
Dim UpdateState As String
Dim UpdateZipCode As String
Dim UpdatePhoneNumber As String
Dim UpdateEmailAddress As String
Dim UpdateUserName As String
```

If the CurrentID is 0, that means the user is trying to add a new record instead of updating an existing record. Therefore, you call the Add procedure:

```
If CurrentID = 0 Then
      cmdAdd_Click
      Exit Sub
End If
```

Otherwise, you convert the string fields as you did with the Add statement:

```
UpdateFirstName = Replace([txtFirstName], "'", "''", 1, -1, vbTextCompare)
UpdateLastName = Replace([txtLastName], "'", "''", 1, -1, vbTextCompare)
UpdateAddress1 = Replace([txtAddress1], "'", "''", 1, -1, vbTextCompare)
UpdateAddress2 = Replace([txtAddress2], "'", "''", 1, -1, vbTextCompare)
UpdateCity = Replace([txtCity], "'", "''", 1, -1, vbTextCompare)
UpdateState = Replace([txtState], "'", "''", 1, -1, vbTextCompare)
UpdateZipCode = Replace([txtZipCode], "'", "''", 1, -1, vbTextCompare)
UpdatePhoneNumber = Replace([txtPhoneNumber], "'", "''", 1, -1, vbTextCompare)
UpdateEmailAddress = Replace([txtEmailAddress], "'", "''", 1, -1, vbTextCompare)
UpdateUserName = Replace([txtUserName], "'", "''", 1, -1, vbTextCompare)
```

and call the EmployeeEdit stored procedure:

```
Set RSStatus = MyDB.Execute("Exec EmployeeEdit " _
      & CurrentID & ", " _
      & "'" & UpdateFirstName & "', " _
      & "'" & UpdateLastName & "', " _
      & "'" & UpdateAddress1 & "', " _
      & "'" & UpdateAddress2 & "', " _
      & "'" & UpdateCity & "', " _
      & "'" & UpdateState & "', " _
      & "'" & UpdateZipCode & "', " _
```

```
& "'" & UpdatePhoneNumber & "', " _
& "'" & UpdateEmailAddress & "', " _
& "'" & UpdateUserName & "', " _
& Abs([chkIsManager]) & ", " _
& Abs([chkIsDBAdmin]) & ", " _
& [txtSalary] & ", " _
& [txtVacatAcc] & ", " _
& [txtSickAcc])
```

You then see whether the stored procedure returned an error record:

```
If RSStatus(0) = 0 Then
```

If it did, you display the error message to the user:

```
MsgBox RSStatus(1), vbExclamation, "Could not update record."
```

The next procedure fires when the Delete button is clicked.

```
Private Sub cmdDelete_Click()
    Dim RSStatus As ADODB.Recordset
    If CurrentID = 0 Then
        cmdClear_Click
        Exit Sub
    End If
    Set RSStatus = MyDB.Execute("Exec EmployeeDelete " _
        & CurrentID)
    If RSStatus(0) = 1 Then
        cmdMovePrevious_Click
    Else
        MsgBox RSStatus(1), vbExclamation, "Could not delete record."
    End If
End Sub
```

The procedure will need a Recordset object:

```
Dim RSStatus As ADODB.Recordset
```

You make sure you aren't in Add mode:

```
If CurrentID = 0 Then
```

If you are, you just clear out the record that the user was in the process of adding:

```
cmdClear_Click
```

Otherwise, you call the EmployeeDelete stored procedure to delete the current employee:

```
Set RSStatus = MyDB.Execute("Exec EmployeeDelete " _
      & CurrentID)
```

You then check the return status of the record deletion:

```
If RSStatus(0) = 1 Then
```

If the deletion was successful, you move to the preceding record:

```
cmdMovePrevious_Click
```

Otherwise, you display the error message returned by the stored procedure:

```
MsgBox RSStatus(1), vbExclamation, "Could not delete record."
```

When the Clear button is clicked, the last procedure on this form fires. The procedure simply clears out all the fields on the form:

```
Private Sub cmdClear_Click()
      [txtFirstName] = ""
      [txtLastName] = ""
      [txtAddress1] = ""
      [txtAddress2] = ""
      [txtCity] = ""
      [txtState] = ""
      [txtZipCode] = ""
      [txtPhoneNumber] = ""
      [txtEmailAddress] = ""
      [txtUserName] = ""
      [chkIsManager] = False
      [chkIsDBAdmin] = False
      [txtSalary] = 0
      [txtVacatAcc] = 0
      [txtSickAcc] = 0
      txtFirstName.SetFocus
      CurrentID = 0
End Sub
```

Departments Form

The Department form contains code that is nearly identical to that of the Employees form, except that the form calls the department stored procedures instead of the employee stored procedures. The only other major difference is in the Load event of that form.

```
Private Sub Form_Load()
    Dim RSCurrentRecord As ADODB.Recordset
    Dim RSEmpList As ADODB.Recordset
    Set RSEmpList = MyDB.Execute("Exec EmployeeComboList")
    cmbDepartmentManagerID.RowSource = RSEmpList.Fields(0)
    Set RSCurrentRecord = MyDB.Execute("Exec DepartmentMove 'First'")
    CurrentID = RSCurrentRecord.Fields("DepartmentID")
    [txtDepartmentName] = RSCurrentRecord.Fields("DepartmentName")
    [txtNote] = RSCurrentRecord.Fields("Note")
    [cmbDepartmentManagerID] = RSCurrentRecord.Fields("DepartmentManagerID")
    txtDepartmentName.SetFocus
End Sub
```

The event procedure needs one recordset that will retrieve the data for the first department record:

```
Dim RSCurrentRecord As ADODB.Recordset
```

and one that will be used to build the employee combo box:

```
Dim RSEmpList As ADODB.Recordset
```

You retrieve the text for the list portion of the combo box by calling the EmployeeComboList stored procedure:

```
Set RSEmpList = MyDB.Execute("Exec EmployeeComboList")
```

The return from that stored procedure is placed in the RowSource property of the combo box:

```
cmbDepartmentManagerID.RowSource = RSEmpList.Fields(0)
```

You then retrieve the value for the first department record:

```
Set RSCurrentRecord = MyDB.Execute("Exec DepartmentMove 'First'")
```

store the ID of the department into a form-level variable:

```
CurrentID = RSCurrentRecord.Fields("DepartmentID")
```

and populate the fields on the form:

```
[txtDepartmentName] = RSCurrentRecord.Fields("DepartmentName")
[txtNote] = RSCurrentRecord.Fields("Note")
[cmbDepartmentManagerID] =
RSCurrentRecord.Fields("DepartmentManagerID")
txtDepartmentName.SetFocus
```

Employee Form

The Employee form provides any employee with the ability to view and edit their personal information. When the form is first loaded, the Load event fires.

```
Private Sub Form_Load()
    Dim RSCurrentRecord As ADODB.Recordset
    Set RSCurrentRecord = MyDB.Execute("Exec EmployeePersonalRecord")
    CurrentID = RSCurrentRecord.Fields("EmployeeID")
    [txtFirstName] = RSCurrentRecord.Fields("FirstName")
    [txtLastName] = RSCurrentRecord.Fields("LastName")
    [txtAddress1] = RSCurrentRecord.Fields("Address1")
    [txtAddress2] = RSCurrentRecord.Fields("Address2")
    [txtCity] = RSCurrentRecord.Fields("City")
    [txtState] = RSCurrentRecord.Fields("State")
    [txtZipCode] = RSCurrentRecord.Fields("ZipCode")
    [txtPhoneNumber] = RSCurrentRecord.Fields("PhoneNumber")
    [txtEmailAddress] = RSCurrentRecord.Fields("EmailAddress")
    [txtUserName] = RSCurrentRecord.Fields("UserName")
    [txtSalary] = RSCurrentRecord.Fields("Salary")
    [txtVacatAcc] = RSCurrentRecord.Fields("VacatAcc")
    [txtSickAcc] = RSCurrentRecord.Fields("SickAcc")
    txtFirstName.SetFocus
End Sub
```

The procedure requires a Recordset object:

```
Dim RSCurrentRecord As ADODB.Recordset
```

You call the EmployeePersonalRecord stored procedure to retrieve the data for the current employee based on their SQL Server user name:

```
Set RSCurrentRecord = MyDB.Execute("Exec EmployeePersonalRecord")
```

Their ID is placed in a form-level variable:

```
CurrentID = RSCurrentRecord.Fields("EmployeeID")
```

and the rest of the fields are used to populate the controls on the form:

```
[txtFirstName] = RSCurrentRecord.Fields("FirstName")
[txtLastName] = RSCurrentRecord.Fields("LastName")
[txtAddress1] = RSCurrentRecord.Fields("Address1")
[txtAddress2] = RSCurrentRecord.Fields("Address2")
[txtCity] = RSCurrentRecord.Fields("City")
[txtState] = RSCurrentRecord.Fields("State")
[txtZipCode] = RSCurrentRecord.Fields("ZipCode")
[txtPhoneNumber] = RSCurrentRecord.Fields("PhoneNumber")
[txtEmailAddress] = RSCurrentRecord.Fields("EmailAddress")
[txtUserName] = RSCurrentRecord.Fields("UserName")
[txtSalary] = RSCurrentRecord.Fields("Salary")
[txtVacatAcc] = RSCurrentRecord.Fields("VacatAcc")
[txtSickAcc] = RSCurrentRecord.Fields("SickAcc")
txtFirstName.SetFocus
```

When the user clicks the Update button, the other procedure on the form fires.

```
Private Sub cmdUpdate_Click()
    Dim RSStatus As ADODB.Recordset
    Dim UpdateFirstName As String
    Dim UpdateLastName As String
    Dim UpdateAddress1 As String
    Dim UpdateAddress2 As String
    Dim UpdateCity As String
    Dim UpdateState As String
    Dim UpdateZipCode As String
    Dim UpdatePhoneNumber As String
    Dim UpdateEmailAddress As String
    Dim UpdateUserName As String
    UpdateFirstName = Replace([txtFirstName], "'", "''", 1, -1, _
        vbTextCompare)
    UpdateLastName = Replace([txtLastName], "'", "''", 1, -1, _
        vbTextCompare)
    UpdateAddress1 = Replace([txtAddress1], "'", "''", 1, -1, _
```

```
        vbTextCompare)
    UpdateAddress2 = Replace([txtAddress2], "'", "''", 1, -1, _
        vbTextCompare)
    UpdateCity = Replace([txtCity], "'", "''", 1, -1, _
        vbTextCompare)
    UpdateState = Replace([txtState], "'", "''", 1, -1, _
        vbTextCompare)
    UpdateZipCode = Replace([txtZipCode], "'", "''", 1, -1, _
        vbTextCompare)
    UpdatePhoneNumber = Replace([txtPhoneNumber], "'", "''", 1, -1, _
        vbTextCompare)
    UpdateEmailAddress = Replace([txtEmailAddress], "'", "''", 1, -1, _
        vbTextCompare)
    UpdateUserName = Replace([txtUserName], "'", "''", 1, -1, _
        vbTextCompare)
    Set RSStatus = MyDB.Execute _
        ("Exec EmployeePersonalRecordUpdate " _
        & CurrentID & ", " _
        & "'" & UpdateFirstName & "', " _
        & "'" & UpdateLastName & "', " _
        & "'" & UpdateAddress1 & "', " _
        & "'" & UpdateAddress2 & "', " _
        & "'" & UpdateCity & "', " _
        & "'" & UpdateState & "', " _
        & "'" & UpdateZipCode & "', " _
        & "'" & UpdatePhoneNumber & "', " _
        & "'" & UpdateEmailAddress & "'")
    If RSStatus(0) = 0 Then
        MsgBox RSStatus(1), vbExclamation, "Could not update record."
    End If
End Sub
```

The procedure requires a Recordset object:

```
Dim RSStatus As ADODB.Recordset
```

as well as variables to store the strings that need to be converted:

```
Dim UpdateFirstName As String
Dim UpdateLastName As String
Dim UpdateAddress1 As String
Dim UpdateAddress2 As String
Dim UpdateCity As String
Dim UpdateState As String
Dim UpdateZipCode As String
Dim UpdatePhoneNumber As String
```

```
Dim UpdateEmailAddress As String
Dim UpdateUserName As String
```

You then convert each string so that an apostrophe can be inserted into the database record:

```
UpdateFirstName = Replace([txtFirstName], "'", "''", 1, -1, _
        vbTextCompare)
UpdateLastName = Replace([txtLastName], "'", "''", 1, -1, _
        vbTextCompare)
UpdateAddress1 = Replace([txtAddress1], "'", "''", 1, -1, _
        vbTextCompare)
UpdateAddress2 = Replace([txtAddress2], "'", "''", 1, -1, _
        vbTextCompare)
UpdateCity = Replace([txtCity], "'", "''", 1, -1, _
        vbTextCompare)
UpdateState = Replace([txtState], "'", "''", 1, -1, _
        vbTextCompare)
UpdateZipCode = Replace([txtZipCode], "'", "''", 1, -1, _
        vbTextCompare)
UpdatePhoneNumber = Replace([txtPhoneNumber], "'", "''", 1, -1, _
        vbTextCompare)
UpdateEmailAddress = Replace([txtEmailAddress], "'", "''", 1, -1, _
        vbTextCompare)
UpdateUserName = Replace([txtUserName], "'", "''", 1, -1, _
        vbTextCompare)
```

You then call the EmployeePersonalRecordUpdate stored procedure to update the employee's record:

```
Set RSStatus = MyDB.Execute("Exec EmployeePersonalRecordUpdate " _
      & CurrentID & ", " _
      & "'" & UpdateFirstName & "', " _
      & "'" & UpdateLastName & "', " _
      & "'" & UpdateAddress1 & "', " _
      & "'" & UpdateAddress2 & "', " _
      & "'" & UpdateCity & "', " _
      & "'" & UpdateState & "', " _
      & "'" & UpdateZipCode & "', " _
      & "'" & UpdatePhoneNumber & "', " _
      & "'" & UpdateEmailAddress & "'")
```

If the stored procedure returns an error record, you display that message:

```
If RSStatus(0) = 0 Then
      MsgBox RSStatus(1), vbExclamation, "Could not update record."
End If
```

Generate Payroll Form

The Generate Payroll form provides the functionality for the manager to generate payroll records. These records are generated when the Go button is clicked.

```
Private Sub cmdGo_Click()
    Dim RSStatus As ADODB.Recordset
    Set RSStatus = MyDB.Execute("Exec GeneratePayrollRecords " _
        & [txtPayrollMonth] & ", " & [txtPayrollYear])
    If RSStatus(0) = 1 Then
        DoCmd.OpenReport "Employee With Payroll Info", _
            acViewPreview, , _
            "[MonthOfPayment] = " & [txtPayrollMonth] _
            & " and [YearOfPayment] = " & [txtPayrollYear]
        DoCmd.Close acForm, "frmGeneratePayroll"
    Else
        MsgBox RSStatus(1), vbExclamation, "Could not generate payroll."
    End If
End Sub
```

You will need a Recordset object:

```
Dim RSStatus As ADODB.Recordset
```

You then call the GeneratePayrollRecords stored procedure, passing to it the values entered on the form by the manager:

```
Set RSStatus = MyDB.Execute("Exec GeneratePayrollRecords " _
      & [txtPayrollMonth] & ", " & [txtPayrollYear])
```

You then make sure no errors were returned:

```
If RSStatus(0) = 1 Then
```

If they weren't, you open the Employee With Payroll Info report displaying the records that were just added:

```
DoCmd.OpenReport "Employee With Payroll Info", _
      acViewPreview, , _
      "[MonthOfPayment] = " & [txtPayrollMonth] _
      & " and [YearOfPayment] = " & [txtPayrollYear]
```

and close this form:

```
DoCmd.Close acForm, "frmGeneratePayroll"
```

Otherwise, you display the error record returned from the stored procedure call:

```
MsgBox RSStatus(1), vbExclamation, "Could not generate payroll."
```

Generate Vacation and Sick Leave Hours Form

The Generate Vacation and Sick Leave Hours form generates sick and vacation accrual records when either of the Go buttons are clicked. This code block fires when the Go Sick button is clicked.

```
Private Sub cmdGoSick_Click()
    Dim RSStatus As ADODB.Recordset
    Set RSStatus = MyDB.Execute("Exec GenerateSickHours '" _
        & [txtSickDate] & "'")
    If RSStatus(0) = 1 Then
        DoCmd.OpenReport "Employee With Sick Hours", _
            acViewPreview, , _
            "[DateEntered] = #" & [txtSickDate] & "#"
        DoCmd.Close acForm, "frmGenerateVacatandSick"
    Else
        MsgBox RSStatus(1), vbExclamation, "Could not generate report."
    End If
End Sub
```

The procedure requires a Recordset object:

```
Dim RSStatus As ADODB.Recordset
```

and then calls the GenerateSickHours stored procedure. If the user had clicked the other Go button, the GenerateVacationHours stored procedure would have been called:

```
Set RSStatus = MyDB.Execute("Exec GenerateSickHours '" _
      & [txtSickDate] & "'")
```

If the stored procedure runs correctly:

```
If RSStatus(0) = 1 Then
```

you open a report that will display the records that were just added:

```
DoCmd.OpenReport "Employee With Sick Hours", _
      acViewPreview, , _
      "[DateEntered] = #" & [txtSickDate] & "#"
```

and close this form:

```
DoCmd.Close acForm, "frmGenerateVacatandSick"
```

Otherwise, an error message is displayed:

```
MsgBox RSStatus(1), vbExclamation, "Could not generate report."
```

Use Leave Form

The Use Leave form provides a way for managers to charge employees for their Vacation or Sick Leave hours. When the form first loads, the following code block fires.

```
Private Sub Form_Load()
    Dim RSEmpList As ADODB.Recordset
    Set RSEmpList = MyDB.Execute("Exec EmployeeComboList")
    cmbEmployeeID.RowSource = RSEmpList.Fields(0)
End Sub
```

The procedure requires a Recordset object:

```
Dim RSEmpList As ADODB.Recordset
```

and uses it to call the EmployeeComboList stored procedure:

```
Set RSEmpList = MyDB.Execute("Exec EmployeeComboList")
```

The result of that call is used to populate the Employee combo box on the form:

```
cmbEmployeeID.RowSource = RSEmpList.Fields(0)
```

When the manager clicks the Go button, the next code block fires.

```
Private Sub cmdGo_Click()
    Dim RSStatus As ADODB.Recordset
    Set RSStatus = MyDB.Execute("Exec UseLeave " _
        & [cmbEmployeeID] & ", " _
        & "'" & [txtDateEntered] & "', " _
        & ([txtAmount] * -1) & ", " _
        & "'" & [cmbLeaveType] & "'")
    If RSStatus(0) = 1 Then
        MsgBox "Record Added."
    Else
        MsgBox RSStatus(1), vbExclamation, "Could not generate report."
    End If
End Sub
```

You will need a Recordset object:

```
Dim RSStatus As ADODB.Recordset
```

which is used to call the UseLeave stored procedure:

```
Set RSStatus = MyDB.Execute("Exec UseLeave " _
      & [cmbEmployeeID] & ", " _
      & "'" & [txtDateEntered] & "', " _
      & ([txtAmount] * -1) & ", " _
      & "'" & [cmbLeaveType] & "'")
```

If that stored procedure runs correctly, you display a success message to the manager:

```
If RSStatus(0) = 1 Then
      MsgBox "Record Added."
```

Otherwise, an error message is displayed:

```
MsgBox RSStatus(1), vbExclamation, "Could not generate report."
```

CHAPTER

11

Working with Customers

IN THIS CHAPTER:

C11SQLObjects.sql

Customer.txt

CustomerManagers.txt

CustomerNotes.txt

ZipCodes.txt

Chapter11FrontEnd.mdb

In this chapter, you will review an application that can be used to work with customers. The application would be used by a company to assign customers to specific managers and to track notes for those customers. The front-end database that provides the interface for the back-end SQL Server database was developed in Access 2000.

Solution Walk-Through

When the user first opens the application, they are asked to supply their SQL Server user name and password. If they enter an invalid account or there is some other problem, they will see a message box with an error message and are exited from the application.

If the user succeeds in logging into the database, they are taken to the Main menu, displayed in Figure 11-1.

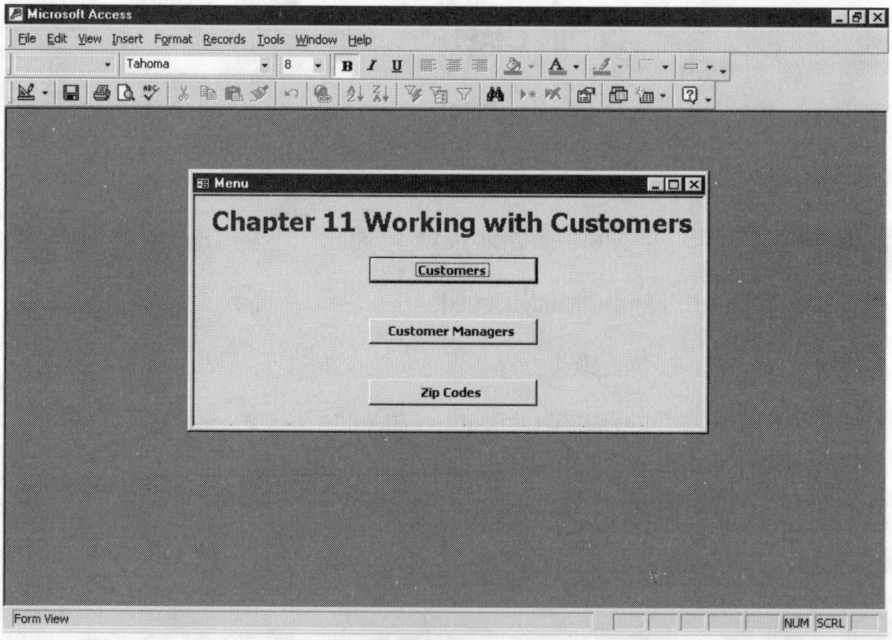

Figure 11-1 *Main menu*

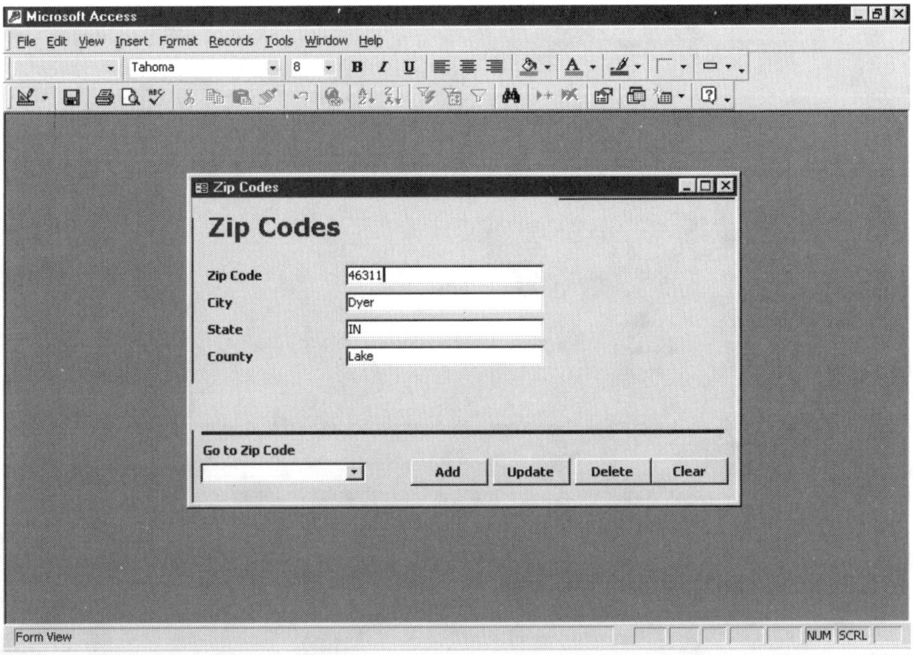

Figure 11-2 *Zip Codes form*

From the menu, the user can access any of the forms and reports in this application. One of the lower-level forms is the Zip Codes form. That form is displayed in Figure 11-2.

The Zip Codes form allows the user to manage ZIP codes that are used in the Customers form. This application shows you, through ZIP codes, how you can provide a lookup table that supplies the values of fields in terms of an entry in another field.

If the user clicks the Customer Managers button, they see the Customer Managers form displayed in Figure 11-3.

Each customer has a manager that is assigned to them. This person would be the primary person to contact the customer. The Customer Managers form allows the user to add, edit, delete, and view these people. Notice the combo box on the bottom of the form. The combo box lists all the customer managers in the database. When the user selects one of the items in the list, they are taken to that record. Such a mechanism is used on all the main forms in this application to navigate through the records.

When the user clicks the Customers button on the menu, they are taken to the Customers form displayed in Figure 11-4.

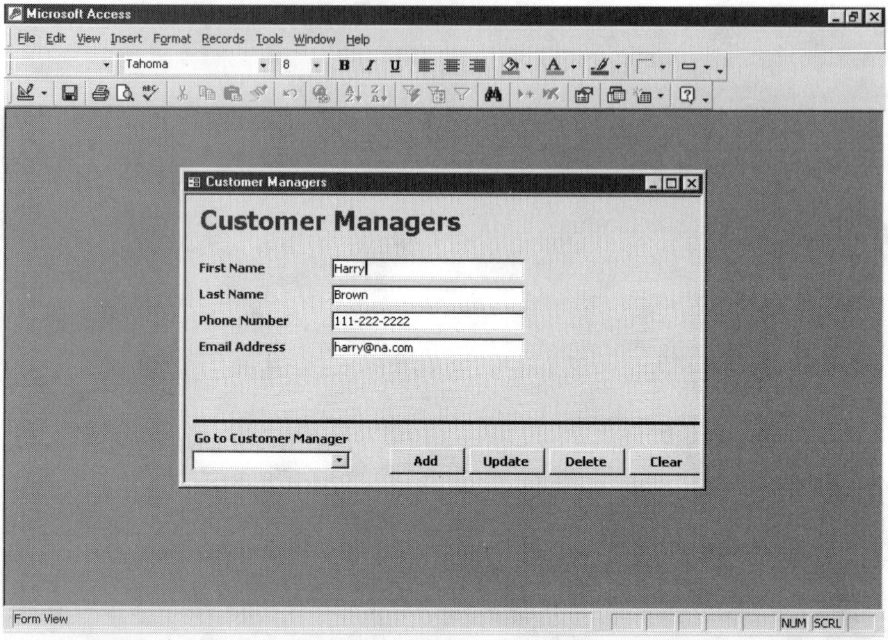

Figure 11-3 *Customer Managers form*

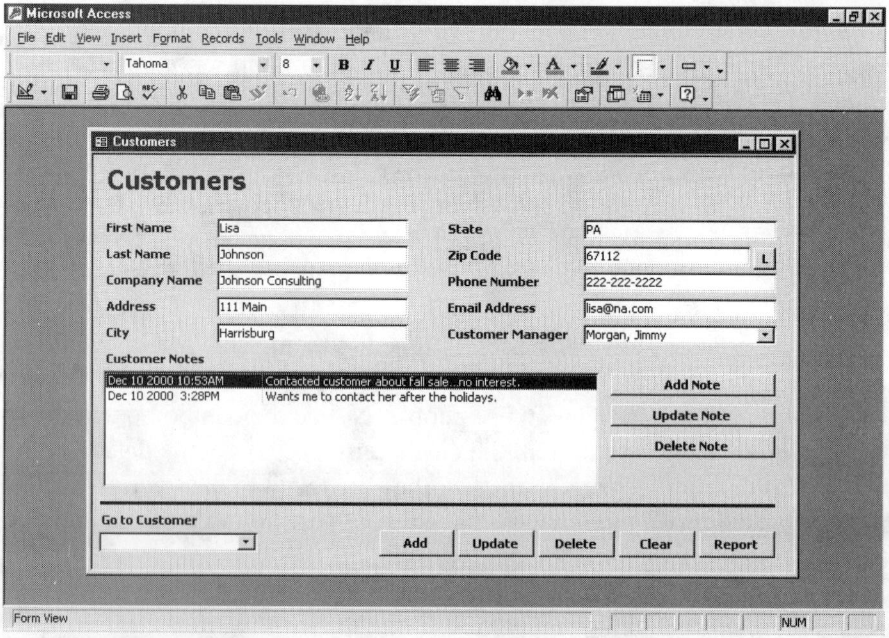

Figure 11-4 *Customers form*

The Customers form allows the user to work with the customer's data. Notice the "L" button to the right of the ZIP code. When clicked, the code calls a procedure that returns the city and state for the ZIP code, which is used in the text boxes on this form.

The form also contains a list box that acts like a subform. The Customer Notes section contains a list of all the notes made about this customer. The user can add a new record or edit a note by clicking the buttons to the right. When they do, a separate form opens, like the one displayed in Figure 11-5.

The user either edits the note or adds a new note on this form; and when they click the OK button, the list on the Customers form reflects their change. The date that the note was entered is automatically set to the current date and time.

The Customers form also contains a button labeled Report. When that button is clicked, the user sees the report displayed in Figure 11-6.

The report displays information about the currently selected customer on the Customers form. A view is used and filtered to achieve this report.

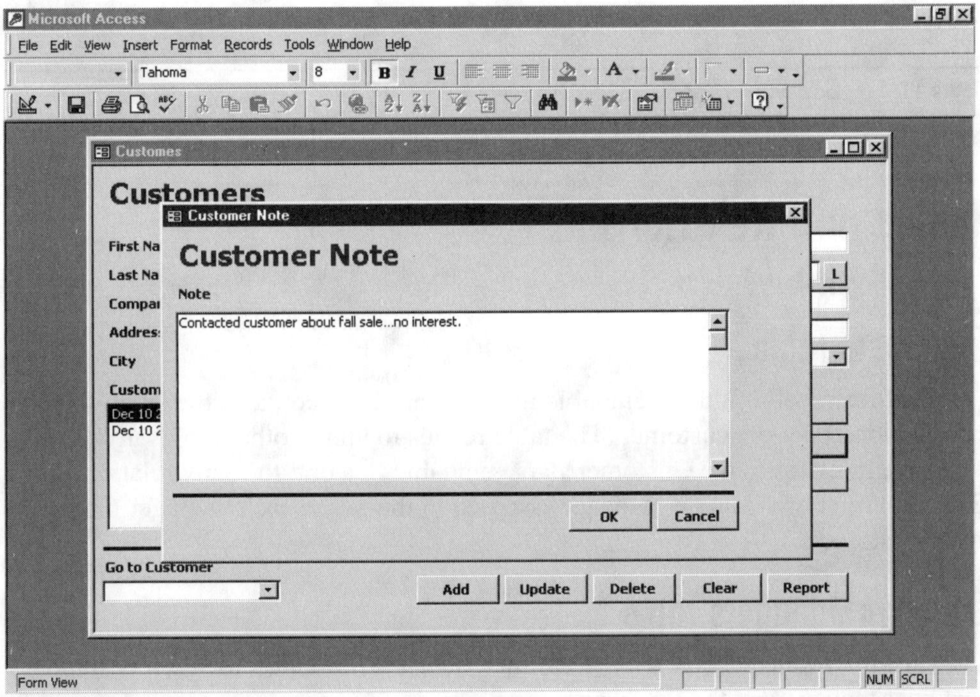

Figure 11-5 *Customer Note form*

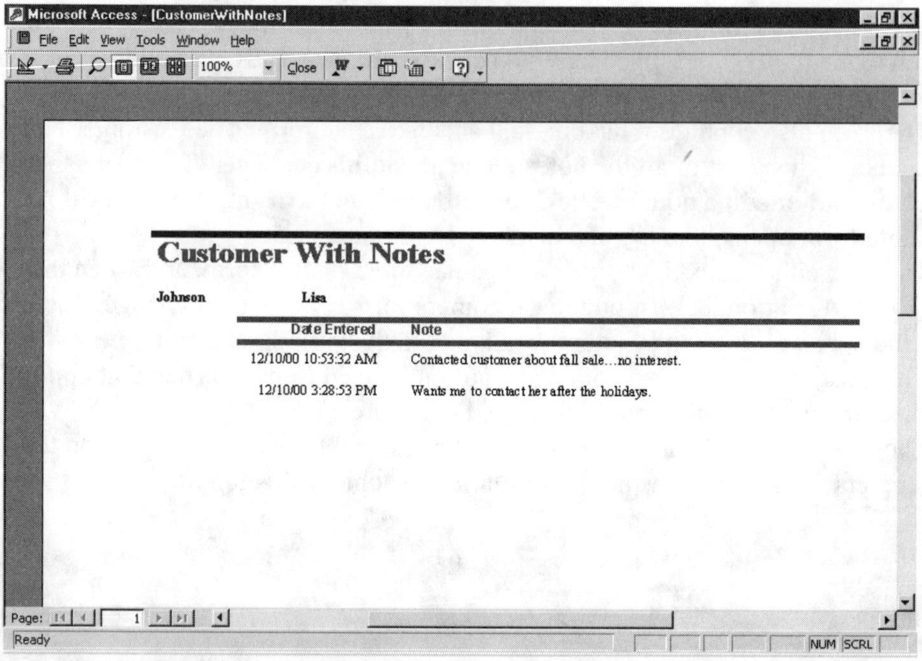

Figure 11-6 *Customer report*

Tables and Relationships

C11SQLObjects.sql

Customers Table

The Customers table is the main table in the database. It contains the singular information about the customer. The table relates to all the other tables in the database. It relates to the CustomerManagers table in a one-to-many relationship. Each customer has a single manager assigned to them, but each manager manages many customers.

CustomerManagers Table

The CustomerManagers table contains the contact information for each of the customer managers in the database.

CustomerNotes Table

The CustomerNotes table contains notes that are made about each customer. The table relates to the Customers table in a one-to-many relationship. Each note goes with a single customer, but each customer can have many notes made about them.

ZipCodes Table

The ZipCodes table contains the ZIP code data. That data is used on the Customers form to populate the customer's city and state.

Field Specifications

Customers Table

Customer.txt

The field specifications for the Customers table are displayed in Table 11-1.

Field Name	Field Type	Notes
CustomerID	int	Primary Key, Identity Column
CustomerManagerID	int	Foreign Key
FirstName	varchar	Length = 50
LastName	varchar	Length = 50
CompanyName	varchar	Length = 50
Address	varchar	Length = 100
City	varchar	Length = 75
State	varchar	Length = 2
ZipCode	varchar	Length = 10
EmailAddress	varchar	Length = 50
PhoneNumber	varchar	Length = 50

Table 11-1 *Customers Table Field Specifications*

The CustomerID field is the primary key for this table. It is set up as an identity column seeded and incremented by one. Therefore, when a new record is added to this table, it is automatically populated with a unique value that starts at one and increases by one with each new record.

The CustomerManagerID field is a foreign key that links this table to the CustomerManagers table.

CustomerManagers Table

CustomerManagers.txt

The field specifications for the CustomerManagers table are displayed in Table 11-2.

The CustomerManagerID field is the primary key in this table, uniquely identifying each record. The rest of the columns store information about the customer manager.

CustomerNotes Table

CustomerNotes.txt

The field specifications for the CustomerNotes table are displayed in Table 11-3.

The CustomerNoteID field is the primary key in this table. The CustomerID field is a foreign key and links this table to the Customers table.

The DateEntered field defaults to the current system date and time through the use of this T-SQL function:

```
GetDate()
```

Field Name	Field Type	Notes
CustomerManagerID	int	Primary Key, Identity Column
FirstName	varchar	Length = 50
LastName	varchar	Length = 50
EmailAddress	varchar	Length = 50
PhoneNumber	varchar	Length = 50

Table 11-2 *CustomerManagers Table Field Specifications*

Field Name	Field Type	Notes
CustomreNoteID	int	Primary Key, Identity Column
CustomerID	int	Foreign Key
DateEntered	datetime	
Note	text	

Table 11-3 *CustomerNotes Table Field Specifications*

ZipCodes Table

ZipCodes.txt

The field specifications for the ZipCodes table are displayed in Table 11-4.

The ZipCode field is the primary key in this table. The rest of the fields store information about the ZIP code.

User-Defined Functions

CustomerIDCheck Function

In a variety of stored procedures, you need to confirm that a CustomerID is valid. The CustomerIDCheck function performs that task.

Field Name	Field Type	Notes
ZipCode	varchar	Primary Key, Length = 10
City	varchar	Length = 75
State	varchar	Length = 2
County	varchar	Length = 50

Table 11-4 *ZipCodes Table Field Specifications*

```
CREATE FUNCTION CustomerIDCheck (@TheID integer)
RETURNS Integer AS
BEGIN
      Declare @TheCount Integer
      Select @TheCount = Count(CustomerID) from Customers
            Where CustomerID = @TheID
      Return @TheCount
END
```

The function takes a single parameter, the ID of the customer to check for:

```
CREATE FUNCTION CustomerIDCheck (@TheID integer)
```

and returns an integer value that indicates whether the ID was found:

```
RETURNS Integer AS
```

You declare a variable that will store the number of occurrences of the ID:

```
Declare @TheCount Integer
```

and set that variable to that count:

```
Select @TheCount = Count(CustomerID) from Customers
      Where CustomerID = @TheID
```

which is then returned from the function:

```
Return @TheCount
```

CustomerManagerIDCheck Function

The CustomerManagerID function returns 0 if the CustomerManagerID passed in does not exist; it returns a positive number if it does.

```
CREATE FUNCTION CustomerManagerIDCheck (@TheID int)
RETURNS Integer AS
BEGIN
      Declare @TheCount Integer
      Select @TheCount = Count(CustomerManagerID) from CustomerManagers
            Where CustomerManagerID = @TheID
      Return @TheCount
END
```

Passed into the function is the ID of the customer manager to check:

```
CREATE FUNCTION CustomerManagerIDCheck (@TheID int)
```

The return value will be of an integer type:

```
RETURNS Integer AS
```

The function needs a local variable to store the occurrences of the ID:

```
Declare @TheCount Integer
```

You then look in the CustomerManagers table for the ID requested:

```
Select @TheCount = Count(CustomerManagerID) from CustomerManagers
      Where CustomerManagerID = @TheID
```

and return that value to the calling procedure:

```
Return @TheCount
```

CustomerNoteIDCheck Function

The CustomerNoteIDCheck function checks for the existence of a CustomerNoteID.

```
CREATE FUNCTION CustomerNoteIDCheck (@TheID integer)
RETURNS Integer AS
BEGIN
      Declare @TheCount Integer
      Select @TheCount = Count(CustomerNoteID) from CustomerNotes
            Where CustomerNoteID = @TheID
      Return @TheCount
END
```

The function takes a single parameter, the ID of the note to check for:

```
CREATE FUNCTION CustomerNoteIDCheck (@TheID integer)
```

and returns an integer:

```
RETURNS Integer AS
```

The procedure declares a local variable:

```
Declare @TheCount Integer
```

which is set to the occurrences of the ID sought:

```
Select @TheCount = Count(CustomerNoteID) from CustomerNotes
      Where CustomerNoteID = @TheID
```

The occurrence count is returned from the function:

```
Return @TheCount
```

ZipCodeCheck Function

The ZipCodeCheck function checks to see whether a ZIP code exists in the ZipCodes table. If it does, the function returns a positive number; if it doesn't, the function returns 0.

```
CREATE FUNCTION ZipCodeCheck (@TheID varchar(10))
RETURNS Integer AS
BEGIN
      Declare @TheCount Integer
      Select @TheCount = Count(ZipCode) from ZipCodes
            Where ZipCode = @TheID
      Return @TheCount
END
```

The function expects one parameter, the ZIP code being sought:

```
CREATE FUNCTION ZipCodeCheck (@TheID varchar(10))
```

and returns an integer:

```
RETURNS Integer AS
```

The function declares a variable that is set to the number of occurrences of the ZIP code passed in:

```
Declare @TheCount Integer
Select @TheCount = Count(ZipCode) from ZipCodes
      Where ZipCode = @TheID
```

That variable is returned from the function:

```
Return @TheCount
```

Stored Procedures

CustomerAdd Stored Procedure

The CustomerAdd stored procedure provides the mechanism for adding a new customer to the database.

```
CREATE PROCEDURE CustomerAdd
@CustomerManagerID integer,
@FirstName varchar(50),
@LastName varchar(50),
@CompanyName varchar(50),
@Address varchar(100),
@City varchar(75),
@State varchar(2),
@ZipCode varchar(10),
@EmailAddress varchar(50),
@PhoneNumber varchar(50)
AS
If (dbo.CustomerManagerIDCheck(@CustomerManagerID)) = 0
      BEGIN
            Select 0 as ReturnValue, 'The CustomerManagerID entered '
                  + 'was not found!' as ReturnMessage
      END
Else
      BEGIN
            Insert Into Customers (CustomerManagerID, FirstName, LastName,
                  CompanyName, Address, City, State, ZipCode,
                  EmailAddress, PhoneNumber)
            values (@CustomerManagerID, @FirstName, @LastName,
                  @CompanyName, @Address, @City, @State, @ZipCode,
                  @EmailAddress, @PhoneNumber)
            Select 1 as ReturnValue, 'No Errors' as ReturnMessage, @@Identity
      END
GO
```

The function expects parameters to be passed in for each column in the Customers table except the ID field:

```
@CustomerManagerID integer,
@FirstName varchar(50),
@LastName varchar(50),
@CompanyName varchar(50),
@Address varchar(100),
@City varchar(75),
@State varchar(2),
@ZipCode varchar(10),
@EmailAddress varchar(50),
@PhoneNumber varchar(50)
```

Before you add the record, you need to make sure that the value entered in the CustomerManagerID field is a valid CustomerManagerID:

```
If (dbo.CustomerManagerIDCheck(@CustomerManagerID)) = 0
```

If it isn't, you return an error record to the calling application:

```
Select 0 as ReturnValue, 'The CustomerManagerID entered '
      + 'was not found!' as ReturnMessage
```

Otherwise, the new record is added to the Customers table using a T-SQL Insert statement:

```
Insert Into Customers (CustomerManagerID, FirstName, LastName,
      CompanyName, Address, City, State, ZipCode,
      EmailAddress, PhoneNumber)
      values (@CustomerManagerID, @FirstName, @LastName,
      @CompanyName, @Address, @City, @State, @ZipCode,
      @EmailAddress, @PhoneNumber)
```

and you return a success message to the calling application along with the ID of the customer that was just added:

```
Select 1 as ReturnValue, 'No Errors' as ReturnMessage, @@Identity
```

CustomerEdit Stored Procedure

The CustomerEdit stored procedure provides the ability to edit a record in the Customers table.

```
CREATE PROCEDURE CustomerEdit
@CustomerID integer,
```

```
@CustomerManagerID integer,
@FirstName varchar(50),
@LastName varchar(50),
@CompanyName varchar(50),
@Address varchar(100),
@City varchar(75),
@State varchar(2),
@ZipCode varchar(10),
@EmailAddress varchar(50),
@PhoneNumber varchar(50)
AS
If (dbo.CustomerIDCheck(@CustomerID)) = 0
      BEGIN
            Select 0 as ReturnValue, 'The CustomerID being updated '
                  + 'was not found!' as ReturnMessage
      END
Else
      If (dbo.CustomerManagerIDCheck(@CustomerManagerID)) = 0
            BEGIN
                  Select 0 as ReturnValue, 'The CustomerManagerID entered '
                        + 'does not exist!' as ReturnMessage
            END
      Else
            BEGIN
                  Update Customers set
                        CustomerManagerID = @CustomerManagerID,
                        FirstName = @FirstName,
                        LastName = @LastName,
                        CompanyName = @CompanyName,
                        Address = @Address,
                        City = @City,
                        State = @State,
                        ZipCode = @ZipCode,
                        EmailAddress = @EmailAddress,
                        PhoneNumber = @PhoneNumber
                        Where CustomerID = @CustomerID
                  Select 1 as ReturnValue, "No Errors" as ReturnMessage
            END
GO
```

The procedure expects that the calling application pass in the value for each of the fields, including the ID of the customer record that is being edited:

```
@CustomerID integer,
@CustomerManagerID integer,
@FirstName varchar(50),
@LastName varchar(50),
```

```
@CompanyName varchar(50),
@Address varchar(100),
@City varchar(75),
@State varchar(2),
@ZipCode varchar(10),
@EmailAddress varchar(50),
@PhoneNumber varchar(50)
```

First, you check to make sure that the ID of the customer record being edited exists:

```
If (dbo.CustomerIDCheck(@CustomerID)) = 0
```

If it doesn't, your function will return 0 and you send an error record back to the calling application:

```
Select 0 as ReturnValue, 'The CustomerID being updated '
      + 'was not found!' as ReturnMessage
```

Then you make sure that the CustomerManagerID being assigned to this customer is a valid ID:

```
If (dbo.CustomerManagerIDCheck(@CustomerManagerID)) = 0
```

If it isn't, the CustomerManagerIDCheck function will return 0 and you then return an error message:

```
Select 0 as ReturnValue, 'The CustomerManagerID entered '
      + 'does not exist!' as ReturnMessage
```

If both conditions are met, you can update the requested record:

```
Update Customers set
      CustomerManagerID = @CustomerManagerID,
      FirstName = @FirstName,
      LastName = @LastName,
      CompanyName = @CompanyName,
      Address = @Address,
      City = @City,
      State = @State,
      ZipCode = @ZipCode,
      EmailAddress = @EmailAddress,
      PhoneNumber = @PhoneNumber
      Where CustomerID = @CustomerID
```

and return a success record:

```
Select 1 as ReturnValue, "No Errors" as ReturnMessage
```

CustomerDelete Stored Procedure

The CustomerDelete stored procedure provides the functionality for deleting a customer record.

```
CREATE PROCEDURE CustomerDelete
@CustomerID integer
AS
If (dbo.CustomerIDCheck(@CustomerID)) = 0
      BEGIN
            Select 0 as ReturnValue, 'The Customer being deleted '
                  + 'was not found!' as ReturnMessage
      END
Else
      BEGIN
            Delete from Customers
            Where CustomerID = @CustomerID
            Select 1 as ReturnValue, "No Errors" as ReturnMessage
      END
GO
```

The procedure receives one parameter, the ID of the customer being deleted:

```
@CustomerID integer
```

You then make sure that the ID of the customer passed in is a valid ID:

```
If (dbo.CustomerIDCheck(@CustomerID)) = 0
```

If it isn't, you return an error record:

```
Select 0 as ReturnValue, 'The Customer being deleted '
      + 'was not found!' as ReturnMessage
```

Otherwise, you can delete the desired record in terms of the ID passed into this procedure:

```
Delete from Customers
      Where CustomerID = @CustomerID
```

and return a success record:

```
Select 1 as ReturnValue, "No Errors" as ReturnMessage
```

CustomerRecord Stored Procedure

The CustomerRecord stored procedure returns the contents of a single customer record to the calling application.

```
CREATE PROCEDURE CustomerRecord
@CustomerID integer = '0'
AS
If @CustomerID = '0'
      BEGIN
            Select * from Customers Where
                  CustomerID = (Select Min(CustomerID)
                        from Customers)
      END
ELSE
      BEGIN
            Select * from Customers Where
                  CustomerID = @CustomerID
      END
GO
```

The procedure has a single optional parameter. You know the parameter is optional, since it is assigned a value. The parameter is the ID of the customer to be returned. If the parameter is not entered, it is assigned a value of 0:

```
@CustomerID integer = '0'
```

You then check to see whether the parameter was not supplied or 0 was passed in, which has a special meaning:

```
If @CustomerID = '0'
```

If that is the case, the calling application simply wants the first record in the table. That is done through a subquery that selects the minimum customer ID; the main query then returns the contents of that record:

```
Select * from Customers Where
      CustomerID = (Select Min(CustomerID)
      from Customers)
```

If the ID is not 0, the calling application wants a specific customer record. The Select statement returns the contents of the customer record selected:

```
Select * from Customers Where
      CustomerID = @CustomerID
```

CustomerComboList Stored Procedure

The CustomerComboList stored procedure returns all of the customer names and IDs in a form that can be displayed in an Access combo box.

```
CREATE PROCEDURE CustomerComboList
AS
Declare
@AllOfIt varchar(8000),
@CustomerID varchar(10),
@FirstName varchar(50),
@LastName varchar(50)
Declare CurCustomers Cursor
For Select CustomerID, FirstName, LastName from Customers
Order By LastName, FirstName
Open CurCustomers
Fetch CurCustomers
      Into @CustomerID, @FirstName, @LastName
Select @AllOfIt = ''
While @@Fetch_Status = 0
      BEGIN
            Select @AllOfIt = @AllOfIt + @CustomerID + ';"'
                  + @LastName + ', ' + @FirstName + '";'
            Fetch CurCustomers
                  Into @CustomerID, @FirstName, @LastName
      END
Close CurCustomers
Deallocate CurCustomers
Select @AllOfIt
GO
```

A variable will be needed to store the contents of the return value as you are building it:

```
@AllOfIt varchar(8000),
```

This variable will store the ID of the customer being retrieved from the Customers table:

```
@CustomerID varchar(10),
```

and the other two will store the name of the customer:

```
@FirstName varchar(50),
@LastName varchar(50)
```

You will also need a Cursor object to retrieve the customer records that will be sorted by the name of the customer from the database:

```
Declare CurCustomers Cursor
      For Select CustomerID, FirstName, LastName from Customers
      Order By LastName, FirstName
```

The cursor is then opened:

```
Open CurCustomers
```

and the first record is retrieved, with the data retrieved being placed into your local variables:

```
Fetch CurCustomers
      Into @CustomerID, @FirstName, @LastName
```

You then initialize your return variable:

```
Select @AllOfIt = ''
```

Next, you enter a loop that will run until it runs out of records in the Cursor object:

```
While @@Fetch_Status = 0
```

Within that loop, the contents of the customer's record are formatted to appear correctly in an Access combo box:

```
Select @AllOfIt = @AllOfIt + @CustomerID + ';"'
      + @LastName + ', ' + @FirstName + '";'
```

Next, you retrieve another record into your local variables before looping back up:

```
Fetch CurCustomers
      Into @CustomerID, @FirstName, @LastName
```

After the loop, you close your Cursor object:

```
Close CurCustomers
```

and release its resources:

```
Deallocate CurCustomers
```

You then return the string you build in your loop to the calling application:

```
Select @AllOfIt
```

CustomerManagerAdd Stored Procedure

The CustomerManagerAdd stored procedure provides the mechanism for adding records to the CustomerManagers table.

```
CREATE PROCEDURE CustomerManagerAdd
@FirstName varchar(50),
@LastName varchar(50),
@PhoneNumber varchar(50),
@EmailAddress varchar(50)
AS
BEGIN
      Insert Into CustomerManagers (FirstName, LastName, PhoneNumber,
            EmailAddress)
            values (@FirstName, @LastName, @PhoneNumber,
            @EmailAddress)
      Select 1 as ReturnValue, 'No Errors' as ReturnMessage, @@Identity
END
GO
```

The procedure receives as parameters the values for the new record being added:

```
@FirstName varchar(50),
@LastName varchar(50),
```

```
@PhoneNumber varchar(50),
@EmailAddress varchar(50)
```

A T-SQL Insert statement is used to add the record:

```
Insert Into CustomerManagers (FirstName, LastName, PhoneNumber,
      EmailAddress)
      values (@FirstName, @LastName, @PhoneNumber,
      @EmailAddress)
```

You use the SQL Server global variable @@Identity to return the ID of the record just added in the previous Insert statement to the calling application:

```
      Select 1 as ReturnValue, 'No Errors' as ReturnMessage, @@Identity
```

CustomerManagerEdit Stored Procedure

The CustomerManagerEdit stored procedure is used to edit an existing customer manager record.

```
CREATE PROCEDURE CustomerManagerEdit
@CustomerManagerID integer,
@FirstName varchar(50),
@LastName varchar(50),
@PhoneNumber varchar(50),
@EmailAddress varchar(50)
AS
If (dbo.CustomerManagerIDCheck(@CustomerManagerID)) = 0
      BEGIN
            Select 0 as ReturnValue, 'The Customer Manager ID being updated '
                  + 'was not found!' as ReturnMessage
      END
Else
      BEGIN
            Update CustomerManagers set
            FirstName = @FirstName,
            LastName = @LastName,
            PhoneNumber = @PhoneNumber,
            EmailAddress = @EmailAddress
            Where CustomerManagerID = @CustomerManagerID
            Select 1 as ReturnValue, "No Errors" as ReturnMessage
      END
GO
```

The procedure expects parameters to be passed in for each of the columns in the Customer Managers table:

```
@CustomerManagerID integer,
@FirstName varchar(50),
@LastName varchar(50),
@PhoneNumber varchar(50),
@EmailAddress varchar(50)
```

But before you edit a record, you make sure that the record being edited exists:

```
If (dbo.CustomerManagerIDCheck(@CustomerManagerID)) = 0
```

If your User Defined Function CustomerManagerIDCheck returns 0, the ID does not exist. Therefore, you return an error record:

```
Select 0 as ReturnValue, 'The Customer Manager ID being updated '
      + 'was not found!' as ReturnMessage
```

Otherwise, you can update the requested record with reference to the ID passed in:

```
Update CustomerManagers set
      FirstName = @FirstName,
      LastName = @LastName,
      PhoneNumber = @PhoneNumber,
      EmailAddress = @EmailAddress
      Where CustomerManagerID = @CustomerManagerID
```

and return a success record:

```
Select 1 as ReturnValue, "No Errors" as ReturnMessage
```

CustomerManagerDelete Stored Procedure

The CustomerManagerDelete stored procedure is used to delete an existing customer manager record.

```
CREATE PROCEDURE CustomerManagerDelete
@CustomerManagerID integer
AS
If (dbo.CustomerManagerIDCheck(@CustomerManagerID)) = 0
      BEGIN
            Select 0 as ReturnValue, 'The Customer Manager being deleted '
                  + 'was not found!' as ReturnMessage
      END
Else
```

```
        BEGIN
                Delete from CustomerManagers
                Where CustomerManagerID = @CustomerManagerID
                Select 1 as ReturnValue, "No Errors" as ReturnMessage
        END
GO
```

The procedure requires a single parameter, the ID of the record being deleted:

```
@CustomerManagerID integer
```

You then make sure the record exists:

```
If (dbo.CustomerManagerIDCheck(@CustomerManagerID)) = 0
```

If it doesn't, you inform the calling application by passing back an error message:

```
Select 0 as ReturnValue, 'The Customer Manager being deleted '
        + 'was not found!' as ReturnMessage
```

Otherwise, you can delete the requested record and return a success record:

```
Delete from CustomerManagers
        Where CustomerManagerID = @CustomerManagerID
        Select 1 as ReturnValue, "No Errors" as ReturnMessage
```

CustomerManagerRecord Stored Procedure

The CustomerManagerRecord is used by the calling application to return either a specific record or the first record in the CustomerManagers table.

```
CREATE PROCEDURE CustomerManagerRecord
@CustomerManagerID integer = 0
AS
If @CustomerManagerID = 0
        BEGIN
                Select * from CustomerManagers Where
                        CustomerManagerID = (Select Min(CustomerManagerID)
                        From CustomerManagers)
        END
ELSE
        BEGIN
                Select * from CustomerManagers Where
                        CustomerManagerID = @CustomerManagerID
        END
GO
```

The procedure has a single optional parameter, the ID of the record to be retrieved. If the parameter is not passed, it is assigned the value of 0:

```
@CustomerManagerID integer = 0
```

If that happens, the code flows into this If block:

```
If @CustomerManagerID = 0
```

and you use a subquery to retrieve the ID for the first record in the table and then return the contents of that record:

```
Select * from CustomerManagers Where
      CustomerManagerID = (Select Min(CustomerManagerID)
      From CustomerManagers)
```

Otherwise, you return the contents of the customer manager requested using the ID passed in:

```
Select * from CustomerManagers Where
      CustomerManagerID = @CustomerManagerID
```

CustomerManagerComboList Stored Procedure

The CustomerManagerComboList stored procedure returns a list of customer managers with their IDs in the form that can be used in a combo list within Access.

```
CREATE PROCEDURE CustomerManagerComboList
AS
Declare
@AllOfIt varchar(8000),
@CustomerManagerID varchar(10),
@FirstName varchar(50),
@LastName varchar(50)
Declare CurCustomerManagers Cursor
For Select CustomerManagerID, FirstName, LastName from CustomerManagers
Order By LastName, FirstName
Open CurCustomerManagers
Fetch CurCustomerManagers
      Into @CustomerManagerID, @FirstName, @LastName
Select @AllOfIt = ''
While @@Fetch_Status = 0
      BEGIN
            Select @AllOfIt = @AllOfIt + @CustomerManagerID + ';"'
                  + @LastName + ', ' + @FirstName + '";'
```

```
            Fetch CurCustomerManagers
                  Into @CustomerManagerID, @FirstName, @LastName
      END
Close CurCustomerManagers
Deallocate CurCustomerManagers
Select @AllOfIt
GO
```

The procedure will need a variable to store the contents of the combo box list as you are building it in a loop:

```
@AllOfIt varchar(8000),
```

as well as variables that will contain the IDs and names of customer managers as they are retrieved from the CustomerManagers table:

```
@CustomerManagerID varchar(10),
@FirstName varchar(50),
@LastName varchar(50)
```

A Cursor object is needed to retrieve the data from the CustomerManagers table:

```
Declare CurCustomerManagers Cursor
      For Select CustomerManagerID, FirstName, LastName from CustomerManagers
      Order By LastName, FirstName
```

You then open your cursor object:

```
Open CurCustomerManagers
```

and retrieve the contents of the first record into the local variables:

```
Fetch CurCustomerManagers
      Into @CustomerManagerID, @FirstName, @LastName
```

Next, you initialize the return value:

```
Select @AllOfIt = ''
```

and enter a loop that will iterate through the records in the cursor:

```
While @@Fetch_Status = 0
```

You then concatenate the ID and name of the current customer manager onto your return value. Notice the use of semicolons. They are used in Access to divide the columns in the combo box:

```
Select @AllOfIt = @AllOfIt + @CustomerManagerID + ';"'
      + @LastName + ', ' + @FirstName + '";'
```

You then retrieve the next record and loop:

```
Fetch CurCustomerManagers
      Into @CustomerManagerID, @FirstName, @LastName
```

After the code is done looping through each of the records in the cursor, you close and release the resources used by it:

```
Close CurCustomerManagers
Deallocate CurCustomerManagers
```

and return the text that would be used in an Access combo box:

```
Select @AllOfIt
```

CustomerNoteAdd Stored Procedure

The CustomerNoteAdd stored procedure provides the mechanism for adding a note record to the CustomerNotes table.

```
CREATE PROCEDURE CustomerNoteAdd
@CustomerID integer,
@Note text
AS
If (dbo.CustomerIDCheck(@CustomerID)) = 0
      BEGIN
            Select 0 as ReturnValue, 'The CustomerID entered '
                  + 'does not exist!' as ReturnMessage
      END
Else
      BEGIN
            Insert Into CustomerNotes (CustomerID, Note)
            values (@CustomerID, @Note)
            Select 1 as ReturnValue, "No Errors" as ReturnMessage
      END
GO
```

The procedure requires the ID and the contents of the note to be passed in. The date field isn't passed in, since it is defaulted to the current system date and time:

```
@CustomerID integer,
@Note text
```

You need to make sure that the ID of the customer that the note is being associated with is a valid ID:

```
If (dbo.CustomerIDCheck(@CustomerID)) = 0
```

If it isn't, you return an error record:

```
Select 0 as ReturnValue, 'The CustomerID entered '
     + 'does not exist!' as ReturnMessage
```

Otherwise, an Insert statement is used to add the note to the CusotmerNotes table:

```
Insert Into CustomerNotes (CustomerID, Note)
     values (@CustomerID, @Note)
```

and a success message is returned:

```
Select 1 as ReturnValue, "No Errors" as ReturnMessage
```

CustomerNoteEdit Stored Procedure

The CustomerNoteEdit stored procedure is used to edit an existing record in the CustomerNotes table.

```
CREATE PROCEDURE CustomerNoteEdit
@CustomerNoteID integer,
@Note text
AS
If (dbo.CustomerNoteIDCheck(@CustomerNoteID)) = 0
     BEGIN
          Select 0 as ReturnValue, 'The Customer Note being updated '
               + 'was not found!' as ReturnMessage
     END
Else
     BEGIN
          Update CustomerNotes set
          Note = @Note
          Where CustomerNoteID = @CustomerNoteID
          Select 1 as ReturnValue, 'No Errors' as ReturnMessage
     END
GO
```

Passed into the procedure are the ID of the note being edited and the contents of that note:

```
@CustomerNoteID integer,
@Note text
```

But before editing, you make sure that the record requested to be edited exists:

```
If (dbo.CustomerNoteIDCheck(@CustomerNoteID)) = 0
```

If it doesn't, you return an error message:

```
Select 0 as ReturnValue, 'The Customer Note being updated '
      + 'was not found!' as ReturnMessage
```

Otherwise, an Update statement is used to modify the contents of the Note column for the requested record:

```
Update CustomerNotes set
      Note = @Note
      Where CustomerNoteID = @CustomerNoteID
```

You then return a success message:

```
Select 1 as ReturnValue, 'No Errors' as ReturnMessage
```

CustomerNoteDelete Stored Procedure

The CustomerNoteDelete stored procedure provides the calling application with a method for deleting a record from the CustomerNotes table.

```
CREATE PROCEDURE CustomerNoteDelete
@CustomerNoteID integer
AS
If (dbo.CustomerNoteIDCheck(@CustomerNoteID)) = 0
      BEGIN
            Select 0 as ReturnValue, 'The Customer Note being deleted '
                  + 'was not found!' as ReturnMessage
      END
Else
      BEGIN
            Delete from CustomerNotes
            Where CustomerNoteID= @CustomerNoteID
            Select 1 as ReturnValue, 'No Errors' as ReturnMessage
      END
GO
```

The procedure requires that the ID of the record being deleted be passed in as an input parameter:

```
@CustomerNoteID integer
```

You need to make sure that the ID being deleted exists. This is done by using your user-defined function:

```
If (dbo.CustomerNoteIDCheck(@CustomerNoteID)) = 0
```

If a matching record is not found, an error is returned:

```
Select 0 as ReturnValue, 'The Customer Note being deleted '
      + 'was not found!' as ReturnMessage
```

Otherwise, you can delete the offending record and return a success record:

```
Delete from CustomerNotes
      Where CustomerNoteID= @CustomerNoteID
Select 1 as ReturnValue, 'No Errors' as ReturnMessage
```

CustomerNoteRecord Stored Procedure

The CustomerNoteRecord stored procedure returns the contents of the specified note record from the CustomerNotes table.

```
CREATE PROCEDURE CustomerNoteRecord
@CustomerNoteID integer
AS
BEGIN
      Select Note from CustomerNotes Where
            CustomerNoteID = @CustomerNoteID
END
GO
```

The procedure receives a single input parameter:

```
@CustomerNoteID integer
```

That parameter is used in determining which note record to return:

```
Select Note from CustomerNotes Where
      CustomerNoteID = @CustomerNoteID
```

CustomerNoteListBox Stored Procedure

On the Customers form in your Access front end, the notes for a customer are displayed in a list box. This procedure returns the text of the notes fields formatted so that they can appear in a list box.

```
CREATE PROCEDURE CustomerNoteListBox
@CustomerID integer
AS
Declare
@AllOfIt varchar(8000),
@CustomerNoteID varchar(10),
@DateEntered varchar(50),
@Note varchar(50)
Declare CurCustomerNotes Cursor
For Select CustomerNoteID, DateEntered, Note from CustomerNotes
      Where CustomerID = @CustomerID
      Order By DateEntered
Open CurCustomerNotes
Fetch CurCustomerNotes
      Into @CustomerNoteID, @DateEntered, @Note
Select @AllOfIt = ''
While @@Fetch_Status = 0
      BEGIN
            Select @AllOfIt = @AllOfIt + @CustomerNoteID + ';'
                  + @DateEntered + ';"' + @Note + '";'
            Fetch CurCustomerNotes
                  Into @CustomerNoteID, @DateEntered, @Note
      END
Close CurCustomerNotes
Deallocate CurCustomerNotes
Select @AllOfIt
GO
```

The procedure expects, as a parameter, the ID of the customer whose notes you want to return:

```
@CustomerID integer
```

The procedure also needs its own local variables. The first will store the contents of the return value as it is being built:

```
Declare
@AllOfIt varchar(8000),
```

You will need to retrieve three fields from the notes table: the ID of the note, the date of the note, and the first 50 characters of the note text:

```
@CustomerNoteID varchar(10),
@DateEntered varchar(50),
@Note varchar(50)
```

You also need a Cursor object so that you can iterate through the Notes records:

```
Declare CurCustomerNotes Cursor
```

You set that cursor so that it will retrieve the fields you need to build the list box:

```
For Select CustomerNoteID, DateEntered, Note from CustomerNotes
      Where CustomerID = @CustomerID
      Order By DateEntered
```

The cursor is then opened:

```
Open CurCustomerNotes
```

and the first record is retrieved:

```
Fetch CurCustomerNotes
      Into @CustomerNoteID, @DateEntered, @Note
```

You then initialize your return variable:

```
Select @AllOfIt = ''
```

and enter a loop that will iterate through the Notes record so that you can process each record:

```
While @@Fetch_Status = 0
```

On the Customers form, the list box contains three columns. The first is the ID of the record, which is not shown in the list box. The second column contains the date of the note, and the third column contains the text of the note. Each column in the list box needs to be separated from the next by a semicolon:

```
Select @AllOfIt = @AllOfIt + @CustomerNoteID + ';'
      + @DateEntered + ';"' + @Note + '";'
```

You then move on to process the next record:

```
Fetch CurCustomerNotes
      Into @CustomerNoteID, @DateEntered, @Note
```

After the loop, the cursor is closed and its resources are released:

```
Close CurCustomerNotes
Deallocate CurCustomerNotes
```

Finally, you return the text for the list box:

```
Select @AllOfIt
```

ZipCodeAdd Stored Procedure

The ZipCodeAdd stored procedure provides the mechanism for adding a new record to the ZipCodes table.

```
CREATE PROCEDURE ZipCodeAdd
@ZipCode varchar(10),
@City varchar(75),
@State varchar(2),
@County varchar(50)
AS
If (dbo.ZipCodeCheck(@ZipCode)) >= 1
      BEGIN
            Select 0 as ReturnValue, 'The Zip Code entered '
                  + 'already exists!' as ReturnMessage
      END
Else
      BEGIN
            Insert Into ZipCodes (ZipCode, City, State, County)
            values (@ZipCode, @City, @State, @County)
            Select 1 as ReturnValue, "No Errors" as ReturnMessage
      END
GO
```

The procedure requires a parameter for each field to be inserted:

```
@ZipCode varchar(10),
@City varchar(75),
@State varchar(2),
@County varchar(50)
```

Since the ZipCode is the primary key in the table, you need to make sure that an entry does not already exist for it:

```
If (dbo.ZipCodeCheck(@ZipCode)) >= 1
```

If one does, you return an error message:

```
Select 0 as ReturnValue, 'The Zip Code entered '
     + 'already exists!' as ReturnMessage
```

Otherwise, you can insert the record into the ZipCodes table and return a success message:

```
Insert Into ZipCodes (ZipCode, City, State, County)
     values (@ZipCode, @City, @State, @County)
Select 1 as ReturnValue, "No Errors" as ReturnMessage
```

ZipCodeEdit Stored Procedure

The ZipCodeEdit stored procedure provides the functionality for editing an existing ZIP code record.

```
CREATE PROCEDURE ZipCodeEdit
@OldZipCode varchar(10),
@ZipCode varchar(10),
@City varchar(75),
@State varchar(2),
@County varchar(50)
AS
If (dbo.ZipCodeCheck(@OldZipCode)) = 0
     BEGIN
          Select 0 as ReturnValue, 'The Zip Code being updated '
               + 'was not found!' as ReturnMessage
     END
Else
     BEGIN
```

```
            Update ZipCodes set
            ZipCode = @ZipCode,
            City = @City,
            State = @State,
            County = @County
            Where ZipCode = @OldZipCode
            Select 1 as ReturnValue, "No Errors" as ReturnMessage
      END
GO
```

The procedure requires five parameters—one for each field in the table and one for the old ZIP code value:

```
@OldZipCode varchar(10),
@ZipCode varchar(10),
@City varchar(75),
@State varchar(2),
@County varchar(50)
```

Next, you need to make sure that a record exists with the ZIP code being edited:

```
If (dbo.ZipCodeCheck(@OldZipCode)) = 0
```

If it doesn't, you return an error message:

```
Select 0 as ReturnValue, 'The Zip Code being updated '
      + 'was not found!' as ReturnMessage
```

Otherwise, you can use a T-SQL Update statement that contains the ZIP code in the Where clause that you want to edit:

```
Update ZipCodes set
      ZipCode = @ZipCode,
      City = @City,
      State = @State,
      County = @County
      Where ZipCode = @OldZipCode
```

You then return a success record:

```
Select 1 as ReturnValue, "No Errors" as ReturnMessage
```

ZipCodeDelete Stored Procedure

The ZipCodeDelete stored procedure provides the mechanism for deleting a ZIP code record.

```
CREATE PROCEDURE ZipCodeDelete
@ZipCode varchar(10)
AS
If (dbo.ZipCodeCheck(@ZipCode)) = 0
      BEGIN
            Select 0 as ReturnValue, 'The Zip Code being deleted '
                  + 'was not found!' as ReturnMessage
      END
Else
      BEGIN
            Delete from ZipCodes
            Where ZipCode = @ZipCode

            Select 1 as ReturnValue, 'No Errors' as ReturnMessage
      END
GO
```

The procedure has a single parameter, the ZIP code to be deleted:

```
@ZipCode varchar(10)
```

You first make sure the ZIP code exists in the ZipCodes table:

```
If (dbo.ZipCodeCheck(@ZipCode)) = 0
```

If it doesn't, you return an error record:

```
Select 0 as ReturnValue, 'The Zip Code being deleted '
      + 'was not found!' as ReturnMessage
```

Otherwise, you can delete the offending record and return a success record:

```
Delete from ZipCodes
      Where ZipCode = @ZipCode
Select 1 as ReturnValue, 'No Errors' as ReturnMessage
```

ZipCodeRecord Stored Procedure

On the Zip Codes form and the Customers form, you need to return a specific ZIP code record or the first ZIP code record. The ZipCodeRecord stored procedure provides for that functionality.

```
CREATE PROCEDURE ZipCodeRecord
@ZipCode varchar(10) = '0'
AS
Declare @ZipCode2Use varchar(10)
If @ZipCode = '0'
      BEGIN
            Select @ZipCode2Use = Min(ZipCode) from ZipCodes
            Select * from ZipCodes Where
                  ZipCode = @ZipCode2Use
      END
ELSE
      BEGIN
            Select * from ZipCodes Where
                  ZipCode = @ZipCode
      END
GO
```

The procedure has a single optional parameter, the ZIP code for which you want to retrieve the record. If the parameter is not supplied, you set it to a special value of 0:

```
@ZipCode varchar(10) = '0'
```

The procedure also needs a local variable to store the first ZIP code:

```
Declare @ZipCode2Use varchar(10)
```

If the parameter wasn't passed in, that means that the calling application wants to receive the first record in the table:

```
If @ZipCode = '0'
```

In that case, you retrieve the value of the first ZIP code:

```
Select @ZipCode2Use = Min(ZipCode) from ZipCodes
```

and return its contents:

```
Select * from ZipCodes Where
      ZipCode = @ZipCode2Use
```

Otherwise, you return the contents of the desired ZIP code record:

```
Select * from ZipCodes Where
      ZipCode = @ZipCode
```

ZipCodeComboList Stored Procedure

On the Zip Code form there is a combo box that lists all the ZIP codes in the ZipCodes table. The combo box allows the user to navigate through the records by selecting one of the items in the list. The ZipCodeComboList stored procedure returns the text needed to populate the combo box.

```
CREATE PROCEDURE ZipCodeComboList
AS
Declare
@AllOfIt varchar(8000),
@ZipCode varchar(10)
Declare CurZipCodes Cursor
For Select ZipCode from ZipCodes
Open CurZipCodes
Fetch CurZipCodes
Into @ZipCode
Select @AllOfIt = ''
While @@Fetch_Status = 0
      BEGIN
            Select @AllOfIt = @AllOfIt + @ZipCode + ';'
            Fetch CurZipCodes
                  Into @ZipCode
      END
Close CurZipCodes
Deallocate CurZipCodes
Select @AllOfIt
GO
```

The procedure does not have any input parameters. It does, though, declare local variables that are used to store the return value as it is being built:

```
@AllOfIt varchar(8000),
```

and retrieve the text of the ZipCode field:

```
@ZipCode varchar(10)
```

You also need a Cursor object that retrieves the ZIP codes from the ZipCodes table:

```
Declare CurZipCodes Cursor
For Select ZipCode from ZipCodes
```

That cursor is opened:

```
Open CurZipCodes
```

and the first record is retrieved:

```
Fetch CurZipCodes
      Into @ZipCode
```

You need to initialize the return value:

```
Select @AllOfIt = ''
```

and enter a loop so that you can process each of the records:

```
While @@Fetch_Status = 0
```

Inside that loop, you use the text of the ZIP code as part of the return value concatenated with a semicolon for the combo box:

```
Select @AllOfIt = @AllOfIt + @ZipCode + ';'
```

You then retrieve the next record and loop:

```
      Fetch CurZipCodes
            Into @ZipCode
End
```

After the loop, the cursor is closed and released from memory:

```
Close CurZipCodes
Deallocate CurZipCodes
```

Finally, the return value is sent to the calling application:

```
Select @AllOfIt
```

Views

CustomerWithNotes View

The application includes just a single view, CustomerWithNotes. The view joins together the Customers table with the CustomerNotes table. That data is then used in the Access front end for the Customer report. The view uses a left join so that all the records from the Customers table are returned even if they don't have any matching records in the CustomerNotes table:

```
SELECT dbo.Customers.CustomerID, dbo.Customers.FirstName,
dbo.Customers.LastName, dbo.CustomerNotes.DateEntered,
dbo.CustomerNotes.Note FROM dbo.Customers LEFT OUTER JOIN
dbo.CustomerNotes ON
dbo.Customers.CustomerID = dbo.CustomerNotes.CustomerID
```

Application Notes

The code in the Access front end relies on an ADO connection object to point to the SQL Server database. That connection object locates the database through a DSN called:

```
C11WorkingWithCustomers
```

For the application to work correctly, you need to create the DSN. The Access front end does not have any local tables. It does, though, link to the CustomerWithNotes view discussed in the previous section, which is used to build the Customers report.

Modules

GeneralProcs Module

The Access front end contains a single module called GeneralProcs. In the General Declarations section of that module, you will find these declarations:

```
Public MyDB As New ADODB.Connection
```

The ADO Connection object is used throughout the code to call the 20 stored procedures in the back-end database:

When the user first enters the Access front end, an AutoExec macro fires. That macro calls the StartUp procedure.

```
Public Function StartUp()
    On Error GoTo HandleError
    Dim SQLUserName As String
    Dim SQLPassword As String
    SQLUserName = InputBox("Please enter your user name.", "User Name")
    SQLPassword = InputBox("Please enter your password.", "Password")
    MyDB.Open "DSN=C11WorkingWithCustomers;UID=" & SQLUserName _
        & ";Password=" & SQLPassword
    DoCmd.OpenForm "frmMenu"
    Exit Function
HandleError:
    MsgBox Err.Number & ": " & Err.Description & _
        ". Closing application.", vbCritical, "Can't Start Application"
    Application.CloseCurrentDatabase
End Function
```

The procedure includes an error handler that tells the compiler where to go if an error occurs, in this case, to the label called HandleError:

```
On Error GoTo HandleError
```

The procedure needs two local variables: one for the user name and the other for the password of their SQL Server login:

```
Dim SQLUserName As String
Dim SQLPassword As String
```

You then prompt the user for their user name and password:

```
SQLUserName = InputBox("Please enter your user name.", "User Name")
SQLPassword = InputBox("Please enter your password.", "Password")
```

You then use that information supplied to attempt a connection to the database:

```
MyDB.Open "DSN=C11WorkingWithCustomers;UID=" & SQLUserName _
    & ";Password=" & SQLPassword
```

If the connection succeeds, you open the Menu form:

```
DoCmd.OpenForm "frmMenu"
```

Otherwise, the code flows to the error handler:

```
HandleError:
```

In that handler, you display the error message:

```
MsgBox Err.Number & ": " & Err.Description & _
     ". Closing application.", vbCritical, "Can't Start Application"
```

and close the application:

```
Application.CloseCurrentDatabase
```

Forms

Menu Form

The code on the menu form provides the functionality to connect the user to the three main forms in the application.

When the user clicks the Customers button, they are taken to the Customers form through the OpenForm method of the DoCmd object:

```
DoCmd.OpenForm "frmCustomers"
```

When the Customer Managers button is clicked, the OpenForm method is also used to open the Customer Managers form. Here, you pass into the method the form name frmCustomerManagers, which is the name of the Customer Manager form:

```
DoCmd.OpenForm "frmCustomerManagers"
```

The other button uses the same procedure to open the Zip Codes form:

```
DoCmd.OpenForm "frmZipCodes"
```

Customers Form

The code on the Customers form provides the functionality to display and work with the customer data. In the General Declarations section, you declare a form-wide variable that is used to keep track of the ID of the current customer:

```
Private CurrentID As Long
```

The form contains two custom procedures. The first is called RefreshList. It is used to populate the Customer combo box on the form.

```
Public Sub RefreshList()
    Dim RSCustomerList As ADODB.Recordset
    Set RSCustomerList = MyDB.Execute("Exec CustomerComboList")
    cmbCustomerID.RowSource = RSCustomerList.Fields(0)
End Sub
```

The procedure needs a Recordset object:

```
Dim RSCustomerList As ADODB.Recordset
```

You then get the contents of the combo box from the CustomerComboList stored procedure:

```
Set RSCustomerList = MyDB.Execute("Exec CustomerComboList")
```

The value returned is then placed in the combo box:

```
cmbCustomerID.RowSource = RSCustomerList.Fields(0)
```

The other custom procedure populates the list box so that it contains all the notes for the current customer.

```
Public Sub DisplayCustomerNotes()
    Dim RSCN As ADODB.Recordset
    Set RSCN = MyDB.Execute("Exec CustomerNoteListBox " & CurrentID)
    lstCustomerNotes.RowSource = RSCN.Fields(0)
End Sub
```

The procedure requires a Recordset object:

```
Dim RSCN As ADODB.Recordset
```

which is used to get the return from the CustomerNoteListBox stored procedure:

```
Set RSCN = MyDB.Execute("Exec CustomerNoteListBox " & CurrentID)
```

That return is placed in the list box:

```
lstCustomerNotes.RowSource = RSCN.Fields(0)
```

When the form first loads, you need to display the first record and populate the Customer Managers combo box.

```
Private Sub Form_Load()
    Dim RSCurrentRecord As ADODB.Recordset
    Dim RSCustomerManagerList As ADODB.Recordset
    Set RSCustomerManagerList = MyDB.Execute("Exec CustomerManagerComboList")
    cmbCustomerManagerID.RowSource = RSCustomerManagerList.Fields(0)
    Set RSCurrentRecord = MyDB.Execute("Exec CustomerRecord")
    RefreshList
    If RSCurrentRecord.EOF Then
        CurrentID = 0
    Else
        CurrentID = RSCurrentRecord.Fields("CustomerID")
        DisplayCustomerNotes
        [txtFirstName] = RSCurrentRecord.Fields("FirstName")
        [txtLastName] = RSCurrentRecord.Fields("LastName")
        [txtCompanyName] = RSCurrentRecord.Fields("CompanyName")
        [txtAddress] = RSCurrentRecord.Fields("Address")
        [txtCity] = RSCurrentRecord.Fields("City")
        [txtState] = RSCurrentRecord.Fields("State")
        [txtZipCode] = RSCurrentRecord.Fields("ZipCode")
        [txtPhoneNumber] = RSCurrentRecord.Fields("PhoneNumber")
        [txtEmailAddress] = RSCurrentRecord.Fields("EmailAddress")
        [cmbCustomerManagerID] = RSCurrentRecord.Fields("CustomerManagerID")
        txtFirstName.SetFocus
    End If
End Sub
```

You need one recordset to retrieve the contents of the first record:

```
Dim RSCurrentRecord As ADODB.Recordset
```

and another that will be used to populate the Customer Manager combo box:

```
Dim RSCustomerManagerList As ADODB.Recordset
```

You then retrieve the Customer Manager combo box text:

```
Set RSCustomerManagerList = MyDB.Execute("Exec CustomerManagerComboList")
```

and place that text in the combo box:

```
cmbCustomerManagerID.RowSource = RSCustomerManagerList.Fields(0)
```

Next, you call the CustomerRecord stored procedure without passing it the optional parameter. So, the first record is retrieved from the Customers table:

```
Set RSCurrentRecord = MyDB.Execute("Exec CustomerRecord")
```

You then refresh the Customer combo box by calling your procedure:

```
RefreshList
```

If the table is empty, the EOF flag will be set:

```
If RSCurrentRecord.EOF Then
```

In that case, you simply set the CurrentID to 0, which places you in an Add mode:

```
CurrentID = 0
```

Otherwise, you can populate the ID variable and the fields on the form to reflect the contents of the record:

```
CurrentID = RSCurrentRecord.Fields("CustomerID")
DisplayCustomerNotes
[txtFirstName] = RSCurrentRecord.Fields("FirstName")
[txtLastName] = RSCurrentRecord.Fields("LastName")
[txtCompanyName] = RSCurrentRecord.Fields("CompanyName")
[txtAddress] = RSCurrentRecord.Fields("Address")
[txtCity] = RSCurrentRecord.Fields("City")
[txtState] = RSCurrentRecord.Fields("State")
[txtZipCode] = RSCurrentRecord.Fields("ZipCode")
[txtPhoneNumber] = RSCurrentRecord.Fields("PhoneNumber")
[txtEmailAddress] = RSCurrentRecord.Fields("EmailAddress")
[cmbCustomerManagerID] = RSCurrentRecord.Fields("CustomerManagerID")
```

and move the focus to the First Name:

```
txtFirstName.SetFocus
```

When the user changes the item in the Customers combo box, you need to move to the customer that they selected.

```
Private Sub cmbCustomerID_Change()
    Dim RSCurrentRecord As ADODB.Recordset
    Set RSCurrentRecord = MyDB.Execute("Exec CustomerRecord '" _
        & [cmbCustomerID] & "'")
    If RSCurrentRecord.EOF Then
        CurrentID = 0
    Else
        CurrentID = RSCurrentRecord.Fields("CustomerID")
        [txtFirstName] = RSCurrentRecord.Fields("FirstName")
        [txtLastName] = RSCurrentRecord.Fields("LastName")
        [txtCompanyName] = RSCurrentRecord.Fields("CompanyName")
```

```
        [txtAddress] = RSCurrentRecord.Fields("Address")
        [txtCity] = RSCurrentRecord.Fields("City")
        [txtState] = RSCurrentRecord.Fields("State")
        [txtZipCode] = RSCurrentRecord.Fields("ZipCode")
        [txtPhoneNumber] = RSCurrentRecord.Fields("PhoneNumber")
        [txtEmailAddress] = RSCurrentRecord.Fields("EmailAddress")
        [cmbCustomerManagerID] = RSCurrentRecord.Fields("CustomerManagerID")
        txtFirstName.SetFocus
    End If
    DisplayCustomerNotes
End Sub
```

The procedure needs a Recordset object so that you can retrieve the contents of the selected customer:

```
Dim RSCurrentRecord As ADODB.Recordset
```

You then retrieve the desired record through the CustomerRecord stored procedure:

```
Set RSCurrentRecord = MyDB.Execute("Exec CustomerRecord '" _
      & [cmbCustomerID] & "'")
```

If no matching record was found, EOF will be True:

```
If RSCurrentRecord.EOF Then
```

and you put yourself in Add mode:

```
CurrentID = 0
```

Otherwise, the record retrieved is valid. You place the ID of the record into the form-wide variable:

```
CurrentID = RSCurrentRecord.Fields("CustomerID")
```

and place the data from the records into the fields on the form:

```
[txtFirstName] = RSCurrentRecord.Fields("FirstName")
[txtLastName] = RSCurrentRecord.Fields("LastName")
[txtCompanyName] = RSCurrentRecord.Fields("CompanyName")
[txtAddress] = RSCurrentRecord.Fields("Address")
[txtCity] = RSCurrentRecord.Fields("City")
[txtState] = RSCurrentRecord.Fields("State")
[txtZipCode] = RSCurrentRecord.Fields("ZipCode")
[txtPhoneNumber] = RSCurrentRecord.Fields("PhoneNumber")
```

```
[txtEmailAddress] = RSCurrentRecord.Fields("EmailAddress")
[cmbCustomerManagerID] = RSCurrentRecord.Fields("CustomerManagerID")
```

You then set the focus back to the First Name field so that the user can start editing the data:

```
txtFirstName.SetFocus
```

You also need to reset the Notes list box:

```
DisplayCustomerNotes
```

When the user clicks the Add button, you need to add the record that they entered into the database.

```
Private Sub cmdAdd_Click()
    Dim RSStatus As ADODB.Recordset
    Dim NewFirstName As String
    Dim NewLastName As String
    Dim NewCompanyName As String
    Dim NewAddress As String
    Dim NewCity As String
    Dim NewState As String
    Dim NewZipCode As String
    Dim NewPhoneNumber As String
    Dim NewEmailAddress As String
    NewFirstName = Replace([txtFirstName], "'", "''", 1, -1, vbTextCompare)
    NewLastName = Replace([txtLastName], "'", "''", 1, -1, vbTextCompare)
    NewCompanyName = Replace([txtCompanyName], "'", "''", 1, -1, vbTextCompare)
    NewAddress = Replace([txtAddress], "'", "''", 1, -1, vbTextCompare)
    NewCity = Replace([txtCity], "'", "''", 1, -1, vbTextCompare)
    NewState = Replace([txtState], "'", "''", 1, -1, vbTextCompare)
    NewZipCode = Replace([txtZipCode], "'", "''", 1, -1, vbTextCompare)
    NewPhoneNumber = Replace([txtPhoneNumber], "'", "''", 1, -1, vbTextCompare)
    NewEmailAddress = Replace([txtEmailAddress], "'", "''", 1, -1, vbTextCompare)
    Set RSStatus = MyDB.Execute("Exec CustomerAdd " _
        & [cmbCustomerManagerID] & ", " _
        & "'" & NewFirstName & "', " _
        & "'" & NewLastName & "', " _
        & "'" & NewCompanyName & "', " _
        & "'" & NewAddress & "', " _
        & "'" & NewCity & "', " _
        & "'" & NewState & "', " _
        & "'" & NewZipCode & "', " _
        & "'" & NewPhoneNumber & "', " _
        & "'" & NewEmailAddress & "'")
    If RSStatus(0) = 1 Then
```

```
        CurrentID = RSStatus(2)
        RefreshList
        DisplayCustomerNotes
    Else
        MsgBox RSStatus(1), vbExclamation, "Could not add record."
    End If
    txtFirstName.SetFocus
End Sub
```

The procedure will need a Recordset object:

```
Dim RSStatus As ADODB.Recordset
```

You also need variables to store the values of the text fields being inserted into the database:

```
Dim NewFirstName As String
Dim NewLastName As String
Dim NewCompanyName As String
Dim NewAddress As String
Dim NewCity As String
Dim NewState As String
Dim NewZipCode As String
Dim NewPhoneNumber As String
Dim NewEmailAddress As String
```

Next, you convert each of the text fields so that each apostrophe becomes two apostrophes, which allows them to appear as a single apostrophe in the database:

```
NewFirstName = Replace([txtFirstName], "'", "''", 1, -1, vbTextCompare)
NewLastName = Replace([txtLastName], "'", "''", 1, -1, vbTextCompare)
NewCompanyName = Replace([txtCompanyName], "'", "''", 1, -1, vbTextCompare)
NewAddress = Replace([txtAddress], "'", "''", 1, -1, vbTextCompare)
NewCity = Replace([txtCity], "'", "''", 1, -1, vbTextCompare)
NewState = Replace([txtState], "'", "''", 1, -1, vbTextCompare)
NewZipCode = Replace([txtZipCode], "'", "''", 1, -1, vbTextCompare)
NewPhoneNumber = Replace([txtPhoneNumber], "'", "''", 1, -1, vbTextCompare)
NewEmailAddress = Replace([txtEmailAddress], "'", "''", 1, -1, vbTextCompare)
```

After that, you call the CustomerAdd stored procedure to insert the new record:

```
Set RSStatus = MyDB.Execute("Exec CustomerAdd " _
    & [cmbCustomerManagerID] & ", " _
    & "'" & NewFirstName & "', " _
    & "'" & NewLastName & "', " _
    & "'" & NewCompanyName & "', " _
    & "'" & NewAddress & "', " _
```

```
    & "'" & NewCity & "', " _
    & "'" & NewState & "', " _
    & "'" & NewZipCode & "', " _
    & "'" & NewPhoneNumber & "', " _
    & "'" & NewEmailAddress & "'")
```

If the call was successful, the code will flow here:

```
If RSStatus(0) = 1 Then
```

You then set the CurrentID variable to be the ID of the record just added. Remember that the ID is passed back from the stored procedure through @@Identity:

```
CurrentID = RSStatus(2)
```

You also need to refresh the combo box and the list box so that they contain the data for the current customer:

```
RefreshList
DisplayCustomerNotes
```

If the call returned an error, you display it to the user:

```
MsgBox RSStatus(1), vbExclamation, "Could not add record."
```

Finally, you set the focus back to the First Name field:

```
txtFirstName.SetFocus
```

When the user clicks the Update button, the code calls a stored procedure to update the current record.

```
Private Sub cmdUpdate_Click()
    Dim RSStatus As ADODB.Recordset
    Dim UpFirstName As String
    Dim UpLastName As String
    Dim UpCompanyName As String
    Dim UpAddress As String
    Dim UpCity As String
    Dim UpState As String
    Dim UpZipCode As String
    Dim UpPhoneNumber As String
    Dim UpEmailAddress As String
    If CurrentID = "0" Then
        cmdAdd_Click
        Exit Sub
```

```
    End If
    UpFirstName = Replace([txtFirstName], "'", "''", 1, -1, vbTextCompare)
    UpLastName = Replace([txtLastName], "'", "''", 1, -1, vbTextCompare)
    UpCompanyName = Replace([txtCompanyName], "'", "''", 1, -1, vbTextCompare)
    UpAddress = Replace([txtAddress], "'", "''", 1, -1, vbTextCompare)
    UpCity = Replace([txtCity], "'", "''", 1, -1, vbTextCompare)
    UpState = Replace([txtState], "'", "''", 1, -1, vbTextCompare)
    UpZipCode = Replace([txtZipCode], "'", "''", 1, -1, vbTextCompare)
    UpPhoneNumber = Replace([txtPhoneNumber], "'", "''", 1, -1, vbTextCompare)
    UpEmailAddress = Replace([txtEmailAddress], "'", "''", 1, -1, vbTextCompare)
    Set RSStatus = MyDB.Execute("Exec CustomerEdit " _
        & CurrentID & ", " _
        & [cmbCustomerManagerID] & ", " _
        & "'" & UpFirstName & "', " _
        & "'" & UpLastName & "', " _
        & "'" & UpCompanyName & "', " _
        & "'" & UpAddress & "', " _
        & "'" & UpCity & "', " _
        & "'" & UpState & "', " _
        & "'" & UpZipCode & "', " _
        & "'" & UpPhoneNumber & "', " _
        & "'" & UpEmailAddress & "'")
    RefreshList
    If RSStatus(0) = 0 Then
        MsgBox RSStatus(1), vbExclamation, "Could not update record."
    End If
End Sub
```

The procedure will need a Recordset object:

```
Dim RSStatus As ADODB.Recordset
```

and variables to store the text fields being updated:

```
Dim UpFirstName As String
Dim UpLastName As String
Dim UpCompanyName As String
Dim UpAddress As String
Dim UpCity As String
Dim UpState As String
Dim UpZipCode As String
Dim UpPhoneNumber As String
Dim UpEmailAddress As String
```

But before you Update the record, you make sure that you are not in Add mode:

```
If CurrentID = "0" Then
```

If you are, you call the Add procedure instead:

```
cmdAdd_Click
Exit Sub
```

Otherwise, you can convert the apostrophes that might be contained in the text fields:

```
UpFirstName = Replace([txtFirstName], "'", "''", 1, -1, vbTextCompare)
UpLastName = Replace([txtLastName], "'", "''", 1, -1, vbTextCompare)
UpCompanyName = Replace([txtCompanyName], "'", "''", 1, -1, vbTextCompare)
UpAddress = Replace([txtAddress], "'", "''", 1, -1, vbTextCompare)
UpCity = Replace([txtCity], "'", "''", 1, -1, vbTextCompare)
UpState = Replace([txtState], "'", "''", 1, -1, vbTextCompare)
UpZipCode = Replace([txtZipCode], "'", "''", 1, -1, vbTextCompare)
UpPhoneNumber = Replace([txtPhoneNumber], "'", "''", 1, -1, vbTextCompare)
UpEmailAddress = Replace([txtEmailAddress], "'", "''", 1, -1, vbTextCompare)
```

and then you can update the record:

```
Set RSStatus = MyDB.Execute("Exec CustomerEdit " _
      & CurrentID & ", " _
      & [cmbCustomerManagerID] & ", " _
      & "'" & UpFirstName & "', " _
      & "'" & UpLastName & "', " _
      & "'" & UpCompanyName & "', " _
      & "'" & UpAddress & "', " _
      & "'" & UpCity & "', " _
      & "'" & UpState & "', " _
      & "'" & UpZipCode & "', " _
      & "'" & UpPhoneNumber & "', " _
      & "'" & UpEmailAddress & "'")
```

Since the name of the customer might have changed, you need to update the Customer combo box:

```
RefreshList
```

If the call to the stored procedure returned an error record, you display that here:

```
If RSStatus(0) = 0 Then
      MsgBox RSStatus(1), vbExclamation, "Could not update record."
End If
```

The code behind the Delete button deletes the current customer before displaying another valid record on the form.

```
Private Sub cmdDelete_Click()
    Dim RSStatus As ADODB.Recordset
    Dim RSCurrentRecord As ADODB.Recordset
    If CurrentID = 0 Then
        cmdClear_Click
        Exit Sub
    End If
    Set RSStatus = MyDB.Execute("Exec CustomerDelete " _
        & CurrentID)
    If RSStatus(0) = 1 Then
        RefreshList
        Set RSCurrentRecord = MyDB.Execute("Exec CustomerRecord")
        If RSCurrentRecord.EOF Then
            CurrentID = 0
        Else
            CurrentID = RSCurrentRecord.Fields("CustomerID")
            [txtFirstName] = RSCurrentRecord.Fields("FirstName")
            [txtLastName] = RSCurrentRecord.Fields("LastName")
            [txtCompanyName] = RSCurrentRecord.Fields("CompanyName")
            [txtAddress] = RSCurrentRecord.Fields("Address")
            [txtCity] = RSCurrentRecord.Fields("City")
            [txtState] = RSCurrentRecord.Fields("State")
            [txtZipCode] = RSCurrentRecord.Fields("ZipCode")
            [txtPhoneNumber] = RSCurrentRecord.Fields("PhoneNumber")
            [txtEmailAddress] = RSCurrentRecord.Fields("EmailAddress")
            [cmbCustomerManagerID] = RSCurrentRecord.Fields("CustomerManagerID")
            txtFirstName.SetFocus
        End If
        DisplayCustomerNotes
    Else
        MsgBox RSStatus(1), vbExclamation, "Could not delete record."
    End If
End Sub
```

You will need a Recordset object for deleting the record:

```
Dim RSStatus As ADODB.Recordset
```

and one for retrieving a valid record after deleting the record:

```
Dim RSCurrentRecord As ADODB.Recordset
```

First, though, you check to see if you are in Add mode:

```
If CurrentID = 0 Then
```

If that is the case, you just need to clear the form. You do this by clicking the Clear button in your code:

```
cmdClear_Click
```

Otherwise, you can delete the current record:

```
Set RSStatus = MyDB.Execute("Exec CustomerDelete " _
      & CurrentID)
```

If the record deletion was successful:

```
If RSStatus(0) = 1 Then
```

you need to refresh the Customer combo box:

```
RefreshList
```

and retrieve a record to display, in this case, the first record:

```
Set RSCurrentRecord = MyDB.Execute("Exec CustomerRecord")
```

If a valid record is not found, you place yourself in Add mode:

```
If RSCurrentRecord.EOF Then
      CurrentID = 0
```

Otherwise, you can display the record:

```
CurrentID = RSCurrentRecord.Fields("CustomerID")
[txtFirstName] = RSCurrentRecord.Fields("FirstName")
[txtLastName] = RSCurrentRecord.Fields("LastName")
[txtCompanyName] = RSCurrentRecord.Fields("CompanyName")
[txtAddress] = RSCurrentRecord.Fields("Address")
[txtCity] = RSCurrentRecord.Fields("City")
[txtState] = RSCurrentRecord.Fields("State")
[txtZipCode] = RSCurrentRecord.Fields("ZipCode")
[txtPhoneNumber] = RSCurrentRecord.Fields("PhoneNumber")
[txtEmailAddress] = RSCurrentRecord.Fields("EmailAddress")
[cmbCustomerManagerID] = RSCurrentRecord.Fields("CustomerManagerID")
```

and move the focus back to the first name field:

```
txtFirstName.SetFocus
```

Next, you need to display the notes for this customer:

```
DisplayCustomerNotes
```

If the record deletion produced an error record from the stored procedure, you display it here:

```
MsgBox RSStatus(1), vbExclamation, "Could not delete record."
```

The code behind the Clear button simply clears out all the fields on the form, including the form-wide ID and the list box:

```
Private Sub cmdClear_Click()
    [txtFirstName] = ""
    [txtLastName] = ""
    [txtCompanyName] = ""
    [txtAddress] = ""
    [txtCity] = ""
    [txtState] = ""
    [txtZipCode] = ""
    [txtPhoneNumber] = ""
    [txtEmailAddress] = ""
    CurrentID = 0
    DisplayCustomerNotes
    txtFirstName.SetFocus
End Sub
```

The code behind the Report button displays the Customer with Notes report filtering so that just the information for the current customer is displayed if you are not in Add mode:

```
Private Sub cmdReport_Click()
    If CurrentID <> 0 Then
                  DoCmd.OpenReport "CustomerWithNotes", acViewPreview, _
             , "[CustomerID] = " & CurrentID
    End If
End Sub
```

Next to the Zip Code field is a button labeled *L*. This button looks up the ZIP code entered and uses it to populate the City and State fields.

```
Private Sub cmdZipLookup_Click()
    Dim RSZipCode As ADODB.Recordset
    Set RSZipCode = MyDB.Execute("Exec ZipCodeRecord '" _
        & [txtZipCode] & "'")
    If RSZipCode.EOF Then
        MsgBox "The Zip Code you entered was not found."
    Else
        [txtCity] = RSZipCode.Fields("City")
        [txtState] = RSZipCode.Fields("State")
    End If
End Sub
```

The procedure will need a Recordset object:

```
Dim RSZipCode As ADODB.Recordset
```

which is used to retrieve the City and State for the ZIP code entered:

```
Set RSZipCode = MyDB.Execute("Exec ZipCodeRecord '" _
      & [txtZipCode] & "'")
```

If the ZIP code was not found in the database:

```
If RSZipCode.EOF Then
```

you inform the user through a message box:

```
MsgBox "The Zip Code you entered was not found."
```

Otherwise, you use the values received to set the City and State fields:

```
[txtCity] = RSZipCode.Fields("City")
[txtState] = RSZipCode.Fields("State")
```

The form also contains buttons that allow the user to manipulate the Notes records either through this form or through another form. The first code block fires when the Add Note button is clicked.

```
Private Sub cmdAddNote_Click()
    DoCmd.OpenForm "frmCustomerNotes", acNormal, _
        , , , acDialog, "A" & CurrentID
    DisplayCustomerNotes
End Sub
```

The code displays the Customer Notes form. Notice that the form is displayed as a dialog box. This means that the line after it will not run until the user is done with the Customer Notes form. Also note that you are passing an *A* and the ID to that form through the last parameter. As you will see, that form uses that information to figure out the mode that it is in:

```
DoCmd.OpenForm "frmCustomerNotes", acNormal, _
, , , acDialog, "A" & CurrentID
```

Once the user is done with that form, you need to update the list box so that their changes are reflected:

```
DisplayCustomerNotes
```

The next code block fires when the Update Note button is clicked.

```
Private Sub cmdUpdateNote_Click()
    If Not IsNull([lstCustomerNotes]) Then
        DoCmd.OpenForm "frmCustomerNotes", acNormal, _
            , , , acDialog, "U" & [lstCustomerNotes]
        DisplayCustomerNotes
    End If
End Sub
```

First, you make sure the user has highlighted a record in the list box that they want to update:

```
If Not IsNull([lstCustomerNotes]) Then
```

If they have, as you did in the previous procedure, you open the Customer Notes form as a dialog box. Notice that you now pass to that form a *U* to indicate that you are in update mode and the ID of the record being updated:

```
DoCmd.OpenForm "frmCustomerNotes", acNormal, _
, , , acDialog, "U" & [lstCustomerNotes]
```

After the user is done with that form, you update the list box:

```
DisplayCustomerNotes
```

When the user clicks the Delete Note button, the code deletes the note that is highlighted.

```
Private Sub cmdDeleteNote_Click()
    Dim RSStatus As ADODB.Recordset
    If Not IsNull([lstCustomerNotes]) Then
        Set RSStatus = MyDB.Execute("Exec CustomerNoteDelete " _
```

```
            & [lstCustomerNotes])
        DisplayCustomerNotes
        If RSStatus(0) = 0 Then
            MsgBox RSStatus(1), vbExclamation, "Could not delete record."
        End If
    End If
End Sub
```

You will need a Recordset object:

```
Dim RSStatus As ADODB.Recordset
```

But before you use it, you need to make sure that the user has selected a note in the list box to delete:

```
If Not IsNull([lstCustomerNotes]) Then
```

If so, you can delete the offending record:

```
Set RSStatus = MyDB.Execute("Exec CustomerNoteDelete " _
      & [lstCustomerNotes])
```

and then update the list box:

```
DisplayCustomerNotes
```

If the stored procedure returned an error record, you display it to the user:

```
If RSStatus(0) = 0 Then
      MsgBox RSStatus(1), vbExclamation, "Could not delete record."
End If
```

Note that the code on the Customer Managers and Zip Codes forms is almost identical to the code contained in the events on this form. So, use the explanation contained in this section to review those forms.

Customer Notes Form

The Customer Notes form is called through the Customers form when the user elects to add or edit a note. The General Declarations section declares two form-wide variables. The first stores the ID of either the customer who you are adding the record for or the ID of the note being edited:

```
Private CurrentID As Long
```

The other variable stores the mode you are in, either an *A* for Add or a *U* for Update:

```
Private CurrentMode As String
```

When the form first loads, the Load event fires:

```
Private Sub Form_Load()
    Dim RSNote As ADODB.Recordset
    If Left(Me.OpenArgs, 1) = "A" Then
        CurrentMode = "Add"
    Else
        CurrentMode = "Update"
        Set RSNote = MyDB.Execute("Exec CustomerNoteRecord " _
            & Mid(Me.OpenArgs, 2))
        [txtNote] = RSNote(0)
    End If
    CurrentID = Mid(Me.OpenArgs, 2)
End Sub
```

The procedure may need a Recordset object:

```
Dim RSNote As ADODB.Recordset
```

When the form is called from the Customers form, you pass data into this form through the OpenArgs parameter. The first part of that parameter is either an *A* or a *U*. If it is an *A:*

```
If Left(Me.OpenArgs, 1) = "A" Then
```

you put yourself in Add mode:

```
CurrentMode = "Add"
```

Otherwise, you are in Update mode:

```
CurrentMode = "Update"
```

so you retrieve the text of the note being edited:

```
Set RSNote = MyDB.Execute("Exec CustomerNoteRecord " _
      & Mid(Me.OpenArgs, 2))
```

and place that text into the note text box on the form:

```
[txtNote] = RSNote(0)
```

You then save the ID passed into the procedure into a form-wide variable:

```
CurrentID = Mid(Me.OpenArgs, 2)
```

When the user clicks the Cancel button, you simply close this form:

```
Private Sub cmdCancel_Click()
    DoCmd.Close acForm, "frmCustomerNotes"
End Sub
```

If the user clicks the OK button, you need to either Add the new record or update the text of the existing note record.

```
Private Sub cmdOK_Click()
    Dim RSStatus As ADODB.Recordset
    Dim TheNote As String
    TheNote = Replace([txtNote], "'", "''", 1, -1, vbTextCompare)
    If CurrentMode = "Add" Then
        Set RSStatus = MyDB.Execute("Exec CustomerNoteAdd " _
            & CurrentID & ", '" & TheNote & "'")
        If RSStatus(0) = 1 Then
            DoCmd.Close acForm, "frmCustomerNotes"
        Else
            MsgBox RSStatus(1), vbExclamation, "Could not add record."
        End If
    Else
        Set RSStatus = MyDB.Execute("Exec CustomerNoteEdit " _
            & CurrentID & ", '" & TheNote & "'")
        If RSStatus(0) = 1 Then
            DoCmd.Close acForm, "frmCustomerNotes"
        Else
            MsgBox RSStatus(1), vbExclamation, "Could not add record."
        End If
    End If
End Sub
```

The procedure will need a Recordset object:

```
Dim RSStatus As ADODB.Recordset
```

Also, a variable is needed to store the text of the note:

```
Dim TheNote As String
```

You then convert any apostrophes in the note so that they are valid:

```
TheNote = Replace([txtNote], "'", "''", 1, -1, vbTextCompare)
```

Next, you check to see what mode you are in. If you are in Add mode:

```
If CurrsentMode = "Add" Then
```

you add the note through the CustomerAddNote stored procedure:

```
Set RSStatus = MyDB.Execute("Exec CustomerNoteAdd " _
      & CurrentID & ", '" & TheNote & "'")
```

If the note was added successfully:

```
If RSStatus(0) = 1 Then
```

you can close the form:

```
DoCmd.Close acForm, "frmCustomerNotes"
```

Otherwise, you inform the user of the problem:

```
MsgBox RSStatus(1), vbExclamation, "Could not add record."
```

The code flows to this block if you are in Update mode. If that is the case, you call the CustomerNoteEdit stored procedure:

```
Set RSStatus = MyDB.Execute("Exec CustomerNoteEdit " _
      & CurrentID & ", '" & TheNote & "'")
```

If it returns a success record:

```
If RSStatus(0) = 1 Then
```

you can close this form:

```
DoCmd.Close acForm, "frmCustomerNotes"
```

Otherwise, you display the error message:

```
MsgBox RSStatus(1), vbExclamation, "Could not add record."
```

CHAPTER

12

Working with Events

IN THIS CHAPTER:

C12SQLObjects.sql

Events.txt

Attendees.txt

EventAttendees.txt

C12FrontEnd.mdb

In this chapter, you will look at an application that allows the user to plan events, work with attendees, and manage attendees of events. The structure of the code on the front end and the back end takes a different approach than the last two solutions presented in the previous Access front-end chapters. In those chapters, you returned messages and records from stored procedures through Select statements into Recordset objects.

In this chapter, you will take a different approach. The stored procedures will use output parameters to return information. Those output parameters will be received by the front-end Access application through ADO Command objects.

Application Walk-Through

When the user first enters this application, they are asked for their SQL Server user name and password. After supplying that information, they are taken to the Menu form displayed in Figure 12-1.

Through this form, the user can enter any of the forms or reports in this application. If they click the Attendees button, they will see the Attendees form displayed in Figure 12-2.

On this form, the user can add, edit, delete, and view any of the attendees. Notice the combo box on the form. This object provides the user with navigation abilities. They find the attendee whose information they wish to view and select it. When the user does that, the Attendees information appears on the form. When the user wants to add an attendee, they can click the Clear button to clear the contents of the form and then click the Add button after filling in the form.

When the user clicks the Events button on the menu form, they see the Events form displayed in Figure 12-3.

The Events form is made up of a form and a subform. The main part of the form displays the event information. The user can add, edit, delete, and view events through this form. They navigate to different events through the combo box.

The subform is really a list box that lists all of the attendees for the event. The user can add an Attendee by clicking the Add Attendee button. When they do that, they see the dialog box form displayed in Figure 12-4.

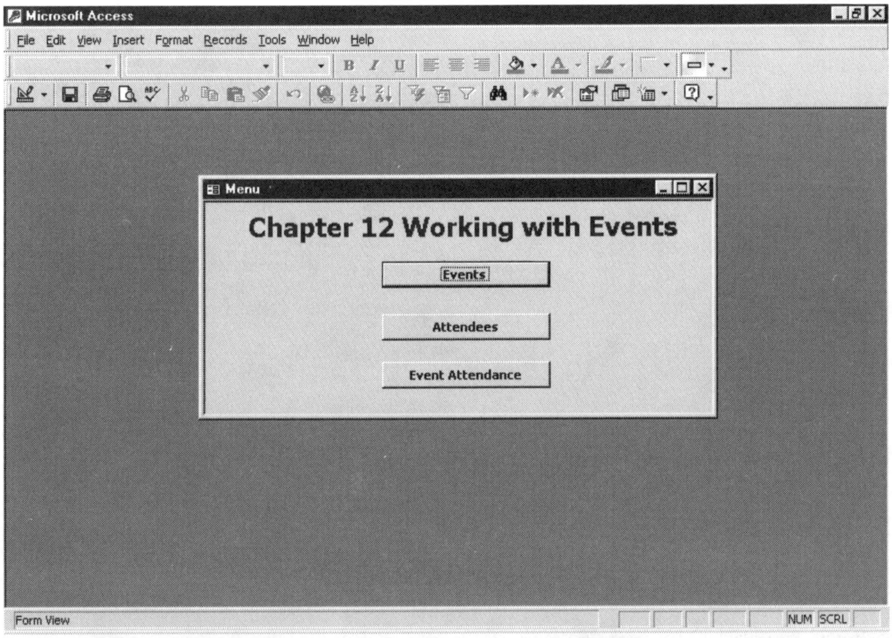

Figure 12-1 *Menu form*

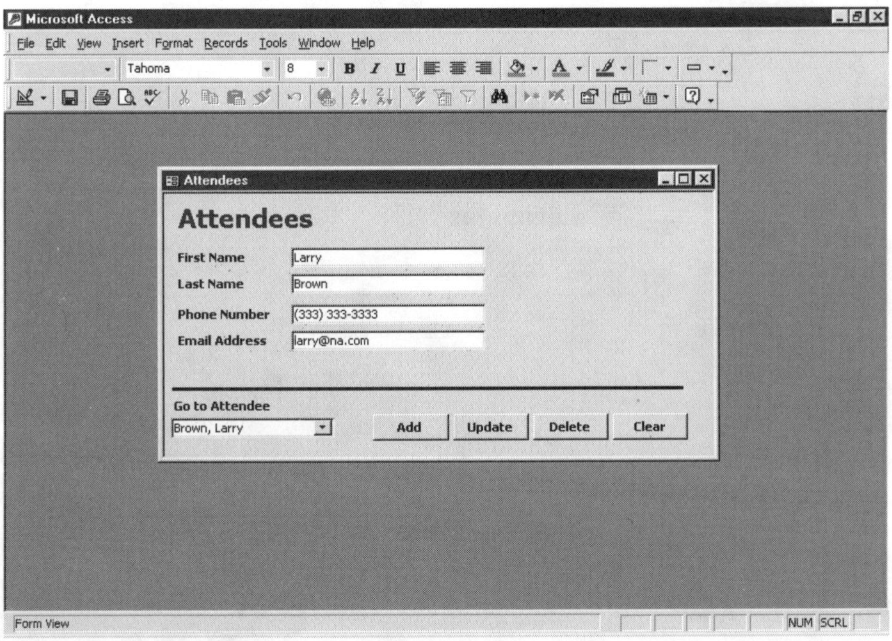

Figure 12-2 *Attendees form*

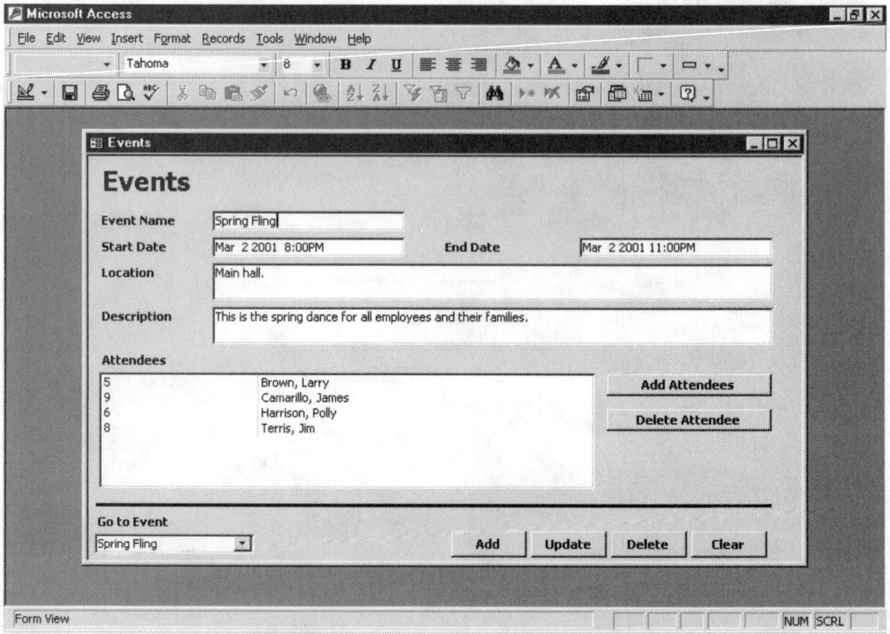

Figure 12-3 *Events form*

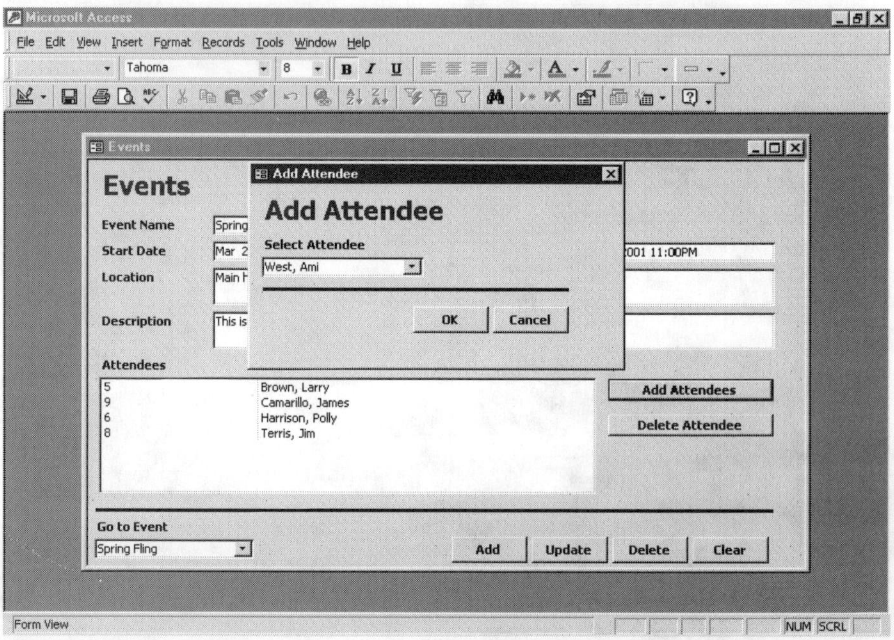

Figure 12-4 *Add Attendee form*

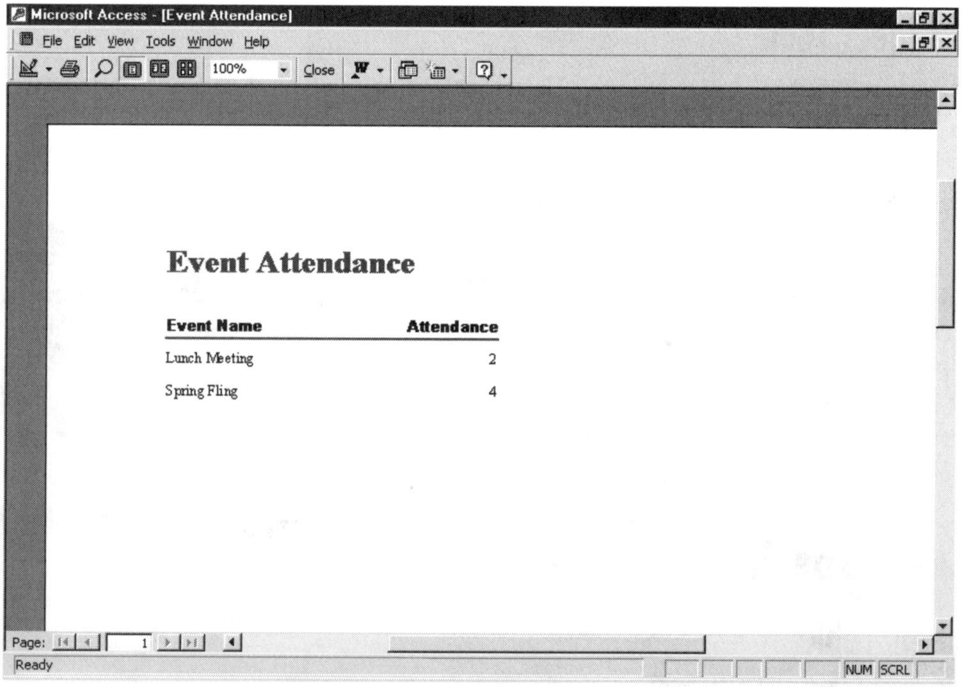

Figure 12-5 *Event Attendance report*

The user will select the attendee that they wish to add to this event and click the OK button. When they do that, they will see the name of the attendee they selected appear in the Attendees list.

The other button on the form is the Event Attendance button. When this button is clicked, the user sees the report displayed in Figure 12-5.

The Event Attendance report links to a SQL Server view that returns the total number of people that are listed as attendees for an event.

Tables and Relationships

C12SQLObjects.sql

Events Table

The Events table is one of the top-level tables in this database. It stores all the information about an event.

Attendees Table

The Attendees table is the other top-level table in the database. It stores the names and information about the people listed as attendees to an event.

EventAttendees Table

The two top-level tables are in a many-to-many relationship. Each of the attendees can attend many events, and each of the events can have many attendees. Since they are in such a relationship, you need a connecting table. The EventAttendees table satisfies that role. It is in a one-to-many relationship with both the Events table and the Attendees table. Each event can have many records listed in this table, and each attendee can have many records in this table.

Fields Specifications

Events Table

Events.txt

The field specifications for the Events table are displayed in Table 12-1.

The EventID field is the primary key in this table. It uniquely identifies each record. Since it is an identity column, the value is automatically inserted when a new record is added.

Field Name	Field Type	Notes
EventID	int	Primary Key, Identity Column
EventName	varchar	Length = 50
StartDate	datetime	
EndDate	datetime	
Location	varchar	Length = 1000
TheDescription	varchar	Length = 2000

Table 12-1 *Events Table Field Specifications*

Field Name	Field Type	Notes
AttendeeID	int	Primary Key, Identity Column
FirstName	varchar	Length = 50
LastName	varchar	Length = 50
PhoneNumber	varchar	Length = 50
EmailAddress	varchar	Length = 50

Table 12-2 *Attendees Table Field Specifications*

Through code in the stored procedures, a rule is enforced on the date fields. The EndDate field must be greater than the StartDate field.

Attendees Table

Attendees.txt

The field specifications for the Attendees table are displayed in Table 12-2.

The AttendeeID field is the primary key in this table. The other fields store the information about the attendee.

EventAttendees Table

EventAttendees.txt

The field specifications for the EventAttendees table are displayed in Table 12-3.

The EventAttendeeID field is the primary key for the table. The EventID field is a foreign key that links this table with the Events table. The AttendeeID field is another foreign key. It links this table to the Attendees table in a one-to-many relationship.

Field Name	Field Type	Notes
EventAttendeeID	int	Primary Key, Identity Column
EventID	int	Foreign Key
AttendeeID	int	Foreign Key

Table 12-3 *EventAttendees Table Field Specifications*

User-Defined Functions

EventIDCheck Function

In a variety of places, you need to confirm that an EventID exists or does not exist. The EventIDCheck function performs such a task.

```
CREATE FUNCTION EventIDCheck (@TheID integer)
RETURNS Integer AS
BEGIN
     Declare @TheCount Integer
     Select @TheCount = Count(EventID) from Events
          Where EventID = @TheID
     Return @TheCount
END
```

The function requires a single parameter, the ID of the event to check for to be passed in:

```
CREATE FUNCTION EventIDCheck (@TheID integer)
```

The function returns the number of times the ID was found through an integer return value:

```
RETURNS Integer AS
```

The procedure needs a local variable to store the return value:

```
Declare @TheCount Integer
```

which is set to the number of times the ID being sought was found:

```
Select @TheCount = Count(EventID) from Events
     Where EventID = @TheID
```

That value is then returned from the function:

```
Return @TheCount
```

AttendeeIDCheck Function

The AttendeeID check returns the number of occurrences that an AttendeeID was found. A return of 0 would indicate that the ID is not in use, while any other number would indicate that it is in use.

```
CREATE FUNCTION AttendeeIDCheck (@TheID integer)
RETURNS Integer AS
BEGIN
      Declare @TheCount Integer
      Select @TheCount = Count(AttendeeID) from Attendees
            Where AttendeeID = @TheID
      Return @TheCount
END
```

The function needs a single parameter, the ID of the attendee that you are checking:

```
CREATE FUNCTION AttendeeIDCheck (@TheID integer)
```

The function will return an integer:

```
RETURNS Integer AS
```

You then declare a variable:

```
Declare @TheCount Integer
```

that is set to the number of times that the AttendeeID was found in the Attendees table:

```
Select @TheCount = Count(AttendeeID) from Attendees
      Where AttendeeID = @TheID
```

That value is returned from the function:

```
Return @TheCount
```

EventAttendeeIDCheck Function

The other function in this SQL Server database returns the number of times an EventAttendeeID is found.

```
CREATE FUNCTION EventAttendeeIDCheck (@TheID integer)
RETURNS Integer AS
BEGIN
      Declare @TheCount Integer
      Select @TheCount = Count(EventAttendeeID) from EventAttendees
            Where EventAttendeeID = @TheID
      Return @TheCount
END
```

The function requires a single parameter, which is the ID being sought:

```
CREATE FUNCTION EventAttendeeIDCheck (@TheID integer)
```

and returns an integer:

```
RETURNS Integer AS
```

Within the code block of the procedure, you declare a variable:

```
Declare @TheCount Integer
```

that is set to the number of times that the ID being sought was found:

```
Select @TheCount = Count(EventAttendeeID) from EventAttendees
      Where EventAttendeeID = @TheID
```

That value is returned from the function:

```
Return @TheCount
```

Stored Procedures

EventAdd Stored Procedure

The EventAdd stored procedure provides the mechanism for adding an event to the Events table.

```
CREATE PROCEDURE EventAdd
@ReturnStatus integer OUTPUT,
@ReturnMessage varchar(50) OUTPUT,
@NewID integer OUTPUT,
@EventName varchar(50),
@StartDate datetime,
@EndDate datetime,
@Location varchar(1000),
@TheDescription varchar(2000)
AS
If @EndDate < @StartDate
      BEGIN
            set @ReturnStatus = 0
            set @ReturnMessage = 'End date menu be after start date!'
            set @NewID = 0
      END
```

```
Else
      BEGIN
            Insert Into Events
                  (EventName, StartDate, EndDate, Location, TheDescription)
                  values (@EventName, @StartDate, @EndDate, @Location, @TheDescription)
            set @ReturnStatus = 1
            set @ReturnMessage = 'Success'
            set @NewID = @@Identity
      END
GO
```

The first parameter is an Output parameter that will return the status of the stored procedure:

```
@ReturnStatus integer OUTPUT,
```

The next parameter is an output parameter and is used to return the message of the status:

```
@ReturnMessage varchar(50) OUTPUT,
```

This parameter will return the ID of the event that was just added:

```
@NewID integer OUTPUT,
```

The remaining parameters are all input parameters and are used to pass in the values for the columns being inserted into the Events table:

```
@EventName varchar(50),
@StartDate datetime,
@EndDate datetime,
@Location varchar(1000),
@TheDescription varchar(2000)
```

Before you insert a new record, you need to make sure that the end date is after the start date:

```
If @EndDate < @StartDate
```

If it isn't, you return an error status:

```
set @ReturnStatus = 0
```

and a message that can be used by the calling application:

```
set @ReturnMessage = 'End date menu be after start date!'
```

You also set the ID being returned to an invalid number:

```
set @NewID = 0
```

If the dates are correct, you can insert the record in the table:

```
Insert Into Events
      (EventName, StartDate, EndDate, Location, TheDescription)
      values (@EventName, @StartDate, @EndDate, @Location, @TheDescription)
```

and return a success code and success message:

```
set @ReturnStatus = 1
set @ReturnMessage = 'Success'
```

You also use the SQL Server global variable to return the ID of the record just added:

```
set @NewID = @@Identity
```

EventEdit Stored Procedure

The EventEdit stored procedure provides the mechanism for the calling application to edit a record in the Events table.

```
CREATE PROCEDURE EventEdit
@ReturnStatus integer OUTPUT,
@ReturnMessage varchar(50) OUTPUT,
@EventID integer,
@EventName varchar(50),
@StartDate datetime,
@EndDate datetime,
@Location varchar(1000),
@TheDescription varchar(2000)
AS
If (dbo.EventIDCheck(@EventID)) = 0
      BEGIN
            set @ReturnStatus = 0
            set @ReturnMessage = 'The Event ID entered ' +
                  'was not found.'
      END
Else
      If @EndDate < @StartDate
            BEGIN
                  set @ReturnStatus = 0
```

```
                set @ReturnMessage = 'End date menu be after start date!'
            END
      Else
            BEGIN
                  Update Events set
                        EventName = @EventName,
                        StartDate = @StartDate,
                        EndDate = @EndDate,
                        Location = @Location,
                        TheDescription = @TheDescription
                        Where EventID = @EventID
                  set @ReturnStatus = 1
                  set @ReturnMessage = 'Success.'
            END
GO
```

The procedure will return a status number and a message through output parameters:

```
@ReturnStatus integer OUTPUT,
@ReturnMessage varchar(50) OUTPUT,
```

and it requires as input parameters the values for each of the fields in the Events table:

```
@EventID integer,
@EventName varchar(50),
@StartDate datetime,
@EndDate datetime,
@Location varchar(1000),
@TheDescription varchar(2000)
```

First, you need to make sure that the ID supplied is a valid ID by calling your EventIDCheck function:

```
If (dbo.EventIDCheck(@EventID)) = 0
```

If the ID is not valid, you return an error status and message:

```
set @ReturnStatus = 0
set @ReturnMessage = 'The Event ID entered ' +
      'was not found.'
```

You also need to make sure that the EndDate field is after the StartDate field:

```
If @EndDate < @StartDate
```

If it is not, you return a different error message through the output parameters:

```
set @ReturnStatus = 0
set @ReturnMessage = 'End date menu be after start date!'
```

Otherwise, you can update the requested record:

```
Update Events set
      EventName = @EventName,
      StartDate = @StartDate,
      EndDate = @EndDate,
      Location = @Location,
      TheDescription = @TheDescription
      Where EventID = @EventID
```

and return a success value and message:

```
set @ReturnStatus = 1
set @ReturnMessage = 'Success.'
```

EventDelete Stored Procedure

The EventDelete stored procedure provides the mechanism for the calling application to delete a record from the Events table.

```
CREATE PROCEDURE EventDelete
@ReturnStatus integer OUTPUT,
@ReturnMessage varchar(50) OUTPUT,
@EventID integer
AS
If (dbo.EventIDCheck(@EventID)) = 0
      BEGIN
            set @ReturnStatus = 0
            set @ReturnMessage = 'The Event ID entered ' +
                  'was not found.'
      END
Else
      BEGIN
            Delete from Events
                  Where EventID = @EventID
            set @ReturnStatus = 1
            set @ReturnMessage = 'Success.'
      END
GO
```

The procedure will return a status number and a message through output parameters:

```
@ReturnStatus integer OUTPUT,
@ReturnMessage varchar(50) OUTPUT,
```

The procedure requires an input parameter that is the EventID of the record to delete:

```
@EventID integer
```

Before deleting, you make sure that the ID entered is valid:

```
If (dbo.EventIDCheck(@EventID)) = 0
```

If it isn't, you return an error status and message:

```
set @ReturnStatus = 0
set @ReturnMessage = 'The Event ID entered ' +
      'was not found.'
```

Otherwise, you can delete the requested record:

```
Delete from Events
      Where EventID = @EventID
```

and return a success message:

```
set @ReturnStatus = 1
set @ReturnMessage = 'Success.'
```

EventRecord Stored Procedure

The EventRecord stored procedure is used by the calling application to return the contents of a specified or first Events record.

```
CREATE PROCEDURE EventRecord
@ReturnStatus integer OUTPUT,
@ReturnMessage varchar(50) OUTPUT,
@EventID integer = 0 OUTPUT,
@EventName varchar(50) OUTPUT,
@StartDate varchar(50) OUTPUT,
@EndDate varchar(50) OUTPUT,
@Location varchar(1000) OUTPUT,
```

```
@TheDescription varchar(2000) OUTPUT
AS
If (dbo.EventIDCheck(@EventID)) = 0 and @EventID <> 0
      BEGIN
            set @ReturnStatus = 0
            set @ReturnMessage = 'The EventID entered ' +
                  'was not found.'
      END
Else
      If @EventID = 0
            BEGIN
                  Declare CurEvent Cursor
                  For Select EventID, EventName, StartDate, EndDate,
                        Location, TheDescription from Events
                        Where EventID = (Select Min(EventID)
                        from Events)
                  Open CurEvent
                  Fetch CurEvent
                        Into @EventID, @EventName, @StartDate, @EndDate,
                        @Location, @TheDescription
                  If @@Fetch_Status = 0
                        BEGIN
                              set @ReturnStatus = 1
                              set @ReturnMessage = 'Success'
                              Close CurEvent
                              Deallocate CurEvent
                        END
                  Else
                        BEGIN
                              set @ReturnStatus = 1
                              set @ReturnMessage = 'No records found'
                              set @EventName = ''
                              set @StartDate = ''
                              set @EndDate = ''
                              set @Location = ''
                              set @TheDescription = ''
                              Close CurEvent
                              Deallocate CurEvent
                        END
                  END
      Else
            BEGIN
                  Declare CurEvent Cursor
                  For Select EventName, StartDate, EndDate,
```

```
                    Location, TheDescription from Events
                    Where EventID = @EventID
              Open CurEvent
              Fetch CurEvent
                    Into @EventName, @StartDate, @EndDate,
                    @Location, @TheDescription
              set @ReturnStatus = 1
              set @ReturnMessage = 'Success'
              Close CurEvent
              Deallocate CurEvent
        END
GO
```

The procedure will return a status number and a message:

```
@ReturnStatus integer OUTPUT,
@ReturnMessage varchar(50) OUTPUT,
```

The EventID parameter is an input and output parameter. The calling application passes in the ID of the record to be returned, and the procedure returns that ID:

```
@EventID integer = 0 OUTPUT,
```

The rest of the parameters are all output parameters that return the values of all the fields in the requested record:

```
@EventName varchar(50) OUTPUT,
@StartDate varchar(50) OUTPUT,
@EndDate varchar(50) OUTPUT,
@Location varchar(1000) OUTPUT,
@TheDescription varchar(2000) OUTPUT
```

First, you check for the condition where the ID passed in is not 0 and also the ID was not found:

```
If (dbo.EventIDCheck(@EventID)) = 0 and @EventID <> 0
```

In that case, you have a request for a record that does not exist. Therefore, you return an error status and message:

```
set @ReturnStatus = 0
set @ReturnMessage = 'The EventID entered ' +
      'was not found.'
```

Next, you check to see whether the ID requested is 0:

```
If @EventID = 0
```

If that is the case, the caller wants the first record in the table. So you will need a Cursor object to return that record:

```
Declare CurEvent Cursor
```

You set that cursor so that it returns the first record in the table:

```
For Select EventID, EventName, StartDate, EndDate,
      Location, TheDescription from Events
      Where EventID = (Select Min(EventID)
      from Events)
```

You then open that cursor and retrieve the record into your output parameters:

```
Open CurEvent
Fetch CurEvent
      Into @EventID, @EventName, @StartDate, @EndDate,
      @Location, @TheDescription
```

You then make sure that there is a record in the table:

```
If @@Fetch_Status = 0
```

If so, you had a successful retrieval, and you pass a success message to the calling application:

```
set @ReturnStatus = 1
set @ReturnMessage = 'Success'
```

You then close the cursor and release its resources:

```
Close CurEvent
Deallocate CurEvent
```

If the code flows here, the table is empty. So you don't have an error, but you should inform the caller of the status:

```
set @ReturnStatus = 1
set @ReturnMessage = 'No records found'
```

In that case, you return empty values for each of the column output parameters:

```
set @EventName = ''
set @StartDate = ''
set @EndDate = ''
set @Location = ''
set @TheDescription = ''
```

You also need to close and release the cursor's resources:

```
Close CurEvent
Deallocate CurEvent
```

The next code would fire if the calling application passed in a valid EventID whose data you need to return. If this occurs, you will need a cursor:

```
Declare CurEvent Cursor
```

that is set to return the values in the requested record:

```
For Select EventName, StartDate, EndDate,
      Location, TheDescription from Events
      Where EventID = @EventID
```

You open that cursor and retrieve the record into your output parameters:

```
Open CurEvent
Fetch CurEvent
      Into @EventName, @StartDate, @EndDate,
      @Location, @TheDescription
```

You then set your status to success:

```
set @ReturnStatus = 1
set @ReturnMessage = 'Success'
```

and release the Cursor object:

```
Close CurEvent
Deallocate CurEvent
```

EventComboBox Stored Procedure

On the Events form, there is a combo box that contains the names and IDs of all the events. The user would use that combo box to navigate through the Events records. The EventComboBox stored procedure provides the contents of that combo box.

```
CREATE PROCEDURE EventComboBox
@TheList varchar(8000) OUTPUT
AS
Declare
@EventID varchar(10),
@EventName varchar(50)
Declare CurEvents Cursor
For Select EventID, EventName from Events
Order By EventName
Select @TheList = ''
Open CurEvents
Fetch CurEvents
      Into @EventID, @EventName
While @@Fetch_Status = 0
      BEGIN
            Select @TheList = @TheList + @EventID + ';"'
                  + @EventName + '";'
            Fetch CurEvents
                  Into @EventID, @EventName
      END
Close CurEvents
Deallocate CurEvents
GO
```

The procedure has a single output parameter, the list for the combo box:

```
@TheList varchar(8000) OUTPUT
```

Locally, the procedure will need a variable to store the IDs and names of events that are retrieved from the Events table:

```
Declare
@EventID varchar(10),
@EventName varchar(50)
```

The procedure will also need a Cursor object that will be used to retrieve all the IDs and names from the Events table:

```
Declare CurEvents Cursor
For Select EventID, EventName from Events
      Order By EventName
```

You need to initialize your return value:

```
Select @TheList = ''
```

Next, you open your Cursor object:

```
Open CurEvents
```

and retrieve the first record in the table:

```
Fetch CurEvents
      Into @EventID, @EventName
```

Next, you enter a loop so that you can process each record:

```
While @@Fetch_Status = 0
```

Within that loop, you append the ID and name of the event to the output parameter in the form that can be used by a combo box:

```
Select @TheList = @TheList + @EventID + ';"'
      + @EventName + '";'
```

You then retrieve the next record before looping:

```
Fetch CurEvents
      Into @EventID, @EventName
```

After the loop, you close and deallocate the Cursor object:

```
Close CurEvents
Deallocate CurEvents
```

AttendeeAdd Stored Procedure

The AttendeeAdd stored procedure provides the mechanism for adding records to the Attendees table.

```
CREATE PROCEDURE AttendeeAdd
@ReturnStatus integer OUTPUT,
@ReturnMessage varchar(50) OUTPUT,
@AttendeeID integer OUTPUT,
@FirstName varchar(50),
@LastName varchar(50),
@PhoneNumber varchar(50),
@EmailAddress varchar(50)
AS
BEGIN
      Insert Into Attendees
            (FirstName, LastName, PhoneNumber, EmailAddress)
            values (@FirstName, @LastName, @PhoneNumber, @EmailAddress)
      set @ReturnStatus = 1
      set @ReturnMessage = 'Success'
      set @AttendeeID = @@Identity
END
GO
```

The procedure has three output parameters. The first two return the status of the stored procedure:

```
@ReturnStatus integer OUTPUT,
@ReturnMessage varchar(50) OUTPUT,
```

The third returns the ID of the attendee just added:

```
@AttendeeID integer OUTPUT,
```

The other parameters are all input parameters. They are used to pass in the values for the columns being inserted:

```
@FirstName varchar(50),
@LastName varchar(50),
@PhoneNumber varchar(50),
@EmailAddress varchar(50)
```

You then use those parameters in a T-SQL Insert statement:

```
Insert Into Attendees
      (FirstName, LastName, PhoneNumber, EmailAddress)
      values (@FirstName, @LastName, @PhoneNumber, @EmailAddress)
```

The procedure returns a success message:

```
set @ReturnStatus = 1
set @ReturnMessage = 'Success'
```

as well as the ID of the attendee record just added, which is retrieved through the @@Identity global SQL Server variable. That variable always contains the value of the identity column for the record most recently inserted into the database:

```
set @AttendeeID = @@Identity
```

AttendeeEdit Stored Procedure

The AttendeeEdit stored procedure provides the calling application with the method to edit an existing record in the Attendees table.

```
CREATE PROCEDURE AttendeeEdit
@ReturnStatus integer OUTPUT,
@ReturnMessage varchar(50) OUTPUT,
@AttendeeID integer,
@FirstName varchar(50),
@LastName varchar(50),
@PhoneNumber varchar(50),
@EmailAddress varchar(50)
AS
If (dbo.AttendeeIDCheck(@AttendeeID)) = 0
      BEGIN
            set @ReturnStatus = 0
            set @ReturnMessage = 'The Event ID entered ' +
                  'was not found.'
      END
Else
      BEGIN
            Update Attendees set
                  FirstName = @FirstName,
                  LastName = @LastName,
                  PhoneNumber = @PhoneNumber,
                  EmailAddress = @EmailAddress
                  Where AttendeeID = @AttendeeID
```

```
            set @ReturnStatus = 1
            set @ReturnMessage = 'Success.'
      END
GO
```

The first two parameters are output parameters. They are used to return the status of the procedure call:

```
@ReturnStatus integer OUTPUT,
@ReturnMessage varchar(50) OUTPUT,
```

The next parameter is an input parameter. It is used to pass in the ID of the attendee to retrieve:

```
@AttendeeID integer,
```

The other parameters are all output parameters that return the value of the Attendee record retrieved:

```
@FirstName varchar(50),
@LastName varchar(50),
@PhoneNumber varchar(50),
@EmailAddress varchar(50)
```

Next, you make sure that the ID supplied is valid:

```
If (dbo.AttendeeIDCheck(@AttendeeID)) = 0
```

If it isn't, you return an error message:

```
set @ReturnStatus = 0
set @ReturnMessage = 'The Event ID entered ' +
      'was not found.'
```

Otherwise, you update the desired record:

```
Update Attendees set
      FirstName = @FirstName,
      LastName = @LastName,
      PhoneNumber = @PhoneNumber,
      EmailAddress = @EmailAddress
      Where AttendeeID = @AttendeeID
```

and return a success message:

```
set @ReturnStatus = 1
set @ReturnMessage = 'Success.'
```

AttendeeDelete Stored Procedure

The AttendeeDelete stored procedure is used to delete a record from the Attendees table.

```
CREATE PROCEDURE AttendeeDelete
@ReturnStatus integer OUTPUT,
@ReturnMessage varchar(50) OUTPUT,
@AttendeeID integer
AS
If (dbo.AttendeeIDCheck(@AttendeeID)) = 0
      BEGIN
            set @ReturnStatus = 0
            set @ReturnMessage = 'The Attendee ID entered ' +
                  'was not found.'
      END
Else
      BEGIN
            Delete from Attendees
                  Where AttendeeID = @AttendeeID
            set @ReturnStatus = 1
            set @ReturnMessage = 'Success.'
      END
GO
```

The procedure requires three parameters. The first two are used to return the status of the procedure call:

```
@ReturnStatus integer OUTPUT,
@ReturnMessage varchar(50) OUTPUT,
```

The third parameter contains the ID of the record to be deleted:

```
@AttendeeID integer
```

Before deleting, you make sure that the record being deleted exists by calling your AttendeeIDCheck function:

```
If (dbo.AttendeeIDCheck(@AttendeeID)) = 0
```

If that function returns 0, the ID passed in does not exist. In that case, you return an error message:

```
set @ReturnStatus = 0
set @ReturnMessage = 'The Attendee ID entered ' +
      'was not found.'
```

Otherwise, you can delete the offending record:

```
Delete from Attendees
      Where AttendeeID = @AttendeeID
```

and return a success message:

```
set @ReturnStatus = 1
set @ReturnMessage = 'Success.'
```

AttendeeRecord Stored Procedure

The AttendeeRecord stored procedure returns the contents of a specified Attendee record, or it returns the contents of the first record. If the table does not have any records, the procedure returns an empty record.

```
CREATE PROCEDURE AttendeeRecord
@ReturnStatus integer OUTPUT,
@ReturnMessage varchar(50) OUTPUT,
@AttendeeID integer = 0 OUTPUT,
@FirstName varchar(50) OUTPUT,
@LastName varchar(50) OUTPUT,
@PhoneNumber varchar(50) OUTPUT,
@EmailAddress varchar(50) OUTPUT
AS
If (dbo.AttendeeIDCheck(@AttendeeID)) = 0 and @AttendeeID <> 0
      BEGIN
            set @ReturnStatus = 0
            set @ReturnMessage = 'The AttendeeID entered ' +
                  'was not found.'
      END
Else
      If @AttendeeID = 0
            BEGIN
                  Declare CurAttendee Cursor
                  For Select AttendeeID, FirstName, LastName, PhoneNumber,
                        EmailAddress from Attendees
```

```
                Where AttendeeID = (Select Min(AttendeeID)
                from Attendees)
          Open CurAttendee
          Fetch CurAttendee
                Into @AttendeeID, @FirstName, @LastName,
                @PhoneNumber, @EmailAddress
          If @@Fetch_Status = 0
                BEGIN
                      set @ReturnStatus = 1
                      set @ReturnMessage = 'Success'
                      Close CurAttendee
                      Deallocate CurAttendee
                END
          Else
                BEGIN
                      set @ReturnStatus = 1
                      set @ReturnMessage = 'No records found'
                      set @FirstName = ''
                      set @LastName = ''
                      set @PhoneNumber = ''
                      set @EmailAddress = ''
                      Close CurAttendee
                      Deallocate CurAttendee
                END
          END
    Else
          BEGIN
                Declare CurAttendee Cursor
                For Select FirstName, LastName, PhoneNumber,
                      EmailAddress from Attendees
                      Where AttendeeID = @AttendeeID
                Open CurAttendee
                Fetch CurAttendee
                      Into @FirstName, @LastName, @PhoneNumber,
                      @EmailAddress
                set @ReturnStatus = 1
                set @ReturnMessage = 'Success'
                Close CurAttendee
                Deallocate CurAttendee
          END
GO
```

The first two parameters are used to return the status of the call to this procedure:

```
@ReturnStatus integer OUTPUT,
@ReturnMessage varchar(50) OUTPUT,
```

The next parameter is an option input/output parameter. If passed in, it contains the ID of the Attendee record to be retrieved. If it contains 0, that means the calling application wants the first record in the table. If omitted, the parameter is set to 0. The parameter returns the value of the ID retrieved from the Attendees table:

```
@AttendeeID integer = 0 OUTPUT,
```

The rest of the parameters are all output parameters that are used to return the values of the columns in the record retrieved:

```
@FirstName varchar(50) OUTPUT,
@LastName varchar(50) OUTPUT,
@PhoneNumber varchar(50) OUTPUT,
@EmailAddress varchar(50) OUTPUT
```

In the first condition, your user-defined function is called to make sure that the ID entered does not exist and that the ID entered is not a zero:

```
If (dbo.AttendeeIDCheck(@AttendeeID)) = 0 and @AttendeeID <> 0
```

In that case, the calling application is requesting a record that does not exist. If that is the case, you return an error value and message:

```
set @ReturnStatus = 0
set @ReturnMessage = 'The AttendeeID entered ' +
      'was not found.'
```

Next, you check to see whether the calling application wants the first record in the Attendees table:

```
If @AttendeeID = 0
```

In that case, you need a cursor object that is set to retrieve the contents of the first record based on the ID returned from the subquery:

```
Declare CurAttendee Cursor
For Select AttendeeID, FirstName, LastName, PhoneNumber,
      EmailAddress from Attendees
      Where AttendeeID = (Select Min(AttendeeID)
      from Attendees)
```

You then open the cursor and retrieve the contents of the first record into your output parameters:

```
Open CurAttendee
Fetch CurAttendee
      Into @AttendeeID, @FirstName, @LastName,
      @PhoneNumber, @EmailAddress
```

If a record was found in the table, the @@Fetch_Status global variable will be set to 0:

```
If @@Fetch_Status = 0
```

In that case, you return a success message:

```
set @ReturnStatus = 1
set @ReturnMessage = 'Success'
```

before closing and releasing the cursor:

```
Close CurAttendee
Deallocate CurAttendee
```

If the code flows to the next block, the table does not have any records, so you return such a message to the calling application:

```
set @ReturnStatus = 1
set @ReturnMessage = 'No records found'
```

and return empty strings for the output parameters:

```
set @FirstName = ''
set @LastName = ''
set @PhoneNumber = ''
set @EmailAddress = ''
```

You then close and release the Cursor object:

```
Close CurAttendee
Deallocate CurAttendee
```

The last code block fires when the caller is asking for a specific record that does exist. In that case, you will need a Cursor object:

```
Declare CurAttendee Cursor
```

that will retrieve the contents of the desired record:

```
For Select FirstName, LastName, PhoneNumber,
      EmailAddress from Attendees
      Where AttendeeID = @AttendeeID
```

You then open that record and retrieve its contents into the output parameters:

```
Open CurAttendee
Fetch CurAttendee
      Into @FirstName, @LastName, @PhoneNumber,
      @EmailAddress
```

return a success message:

```
set @ReturnStatus = 1
set @ReturnMessage = 'Success'
```

and release the cursor:

```
Close CurAttendee
Deallocate CurAttendee
```

AttendeeComboBox Stored Procedure

The AttendeeComboBox stored procedure returns text that can be used to populate a combo box so that it contains a list of all the attendees in the Attendees table.

```
CREATE PROCEDURE AttendeeComboBox
@TheList varchar(8000) OUTPUT
AS
Declare
@AttendeeID varchar(10),
@FirstName varchar(50),
@LastName varchar(50)
Declare CurAttendees Cursor
For Select AttendeeID, FirstName, LastName from Attendees
```

```
Order By LastName, FirstName
Select @TheList = ''
Open CurAttendees
Fetch CurAttendees
      Into @AttendeeID, @FirstName, @LastName
While @@Fetch_Status = 0
      BEGIN
            Select @TheList = @TheList + @AttendeeID + ';"'
                  + @LastName + ', ' + @FirstName + '";'
            Fetch CurAttendees
                  Into @AttendeeID, @FirstName, @LastName
      END
Close CurAttendees
Deallocate CurAttendees
GO
```

The procedure has a single output parameter. It is set to the text for the combo box:

```
@TheList varchar(8000) OUTPUT
```

Locally, the procedure needs three variables that are used to store the values of each of the attendee records:

```
@AttendeeID varchar(10),
@FirstName varchar(50),
@LastName varchar(50)
```

You also need a Cursor object:

```
Declare CurAttendees Cursor
```

which is set to connect to the Attendees table:

```
For Select AttendeeID, FirstName, LastName from Attendees
      Order By LastName, FirstName
```

Next, you initialize your return parameter:

```
Select @TheList = ''
```

open your cursor:

```
Open CurAttendees
```

and retrieve the values of the columns of the first record into your local variables:

```
Fetch CurAttendees
      Into @AttendeeID, @FirstName, @LastName
```

You then enter a loop so that you can process each record in the table:

```
While @@Fetch_Status = 0
```

Each record is concatenated to the output parameter, formatted so that it will appear correctly in a combo box:

```
Select @TheList = @TheList + @AttendeeID + ';"'
      + @LastName + ', ' + @FirstName + '";'
```

You then retrieve the next record before looping:

```
Fetch CurAttendees
      Into @AttendeeID, @FirstName, @LastName
```

After the loop, you close and release the resources of the Cursor object:

```
Close CurAttendees
Deallocate CurAttendees
```

EventAttendeeAdd Stored Procedure

The EventAttendeeAdd stored procedure is used to add a record to the EventAttendees table.

```
CREATE PROCEDURE EventAttendeeAdd
@ReturnStatus integer OUTPUT,
@ReturnMessage varchar(50) OUTPUT,
@EventID int,
@AttendeeID int
AS
BEGIN
      Insert Into EventAttendees
            (EventID, AttendeeID)
            values (@EventID, @AttendeeID)
      set @ReturnStatus = 1
      set @ReturnMessage = 'Success'
END
GO
```

The procedure takes four parameters. The first two are for the return message:

```
@ReturnStatus integer OUTPUT,
@ReturnMessage varchar(50) OUTPUT,
```

The next is used to pass in the ID of the event that is being added to:

```
@EventID int,
```

and the last is used to pass in the ID of the attendee who is attending the event:

```
@AttendeeID int
```

You then use those values to insert a record into the EventAttendees table:

```
Insert Into EventAttendees
      (EventID, AttendeeID)
      values (@EventID, @AttendeeID)
```

and return a success message:

```
set @ReturnStatus = 1
set @ReturnMessage = 'Success'
```

EventAttendeeDelete Stored Procedure

The EventAttendeeDelete stored procedure provides the mechanism for the calling application to delete a record from the EventAttendees table.

```
CREATE PROCEDURE EventAttendeeDelete
@ReturnStatus integer OUTPUT,
@ReturnMessage varchar(50) OUTPUT,
@EventAttendeeID integer
AS
BEGIN
      Delete from EventAttendees
            Where EventAttendeeID = @EventAttendeeID
      set @ReturnStatus = 1
      set @ReturnMessage = 'Success.'
END
GO
```

The procedure takes three parameters. The first two are for the return message from the procedure:

```
@ReturnStatus integer OUTPUT,
@ReturnMessage varchar(50) OUTPUT,
```

The third is used to pass in the ID of the record to be deleted:

```
@EventAttendeeID integer
```

You then delete the offending record:

```
Delete from EventAttendees
      Where EventAttendeeID = @EventAttendeeID
```

and return a success message:

```
set @ReturnStatus = 1
set @ReturnMessage = 'Success.'
```

EventAttendeeListBox Stored Procedure

The Events form in the Access front end contains a list box that displays the names of all the attendees for the event. The EventAttendeeListBox stored procedure returns the contents for that list box.

```
CREATE PROCEDURE EventAttendeesListBox
@EventID int,
@TheList varchar(8000) OUTPUT
AS
Declare
@EventAttendeeID varchar(10),
@TheName varchar(50)
Declare CurEventAttendees Cursor
For Select EventAttendeeID, TheName from EventsWithAttendees
Where EventID = @EventID
Order By TheName
Select @TheList = ''
Open CurEventAttendees
Fetch CurEventAttendees
      Into @EventAttendeeID, @TheName
While @@Fetch_Status = 0
      BEGIN
```

```
            Select @TheList = @TheList + @EventAttendeeID + ';"'
                  + @TheName + '";'
            Fetch CurEventAttendees
                  Into @EventAttendeeID, @TheName
      END
Close CurEventAttendees
Deallocate CurEventAttendees
GO
```

The first parameter indicates the ID of the event whose attendees you wish to return:

```
@EventID int,
```

The second parameter is an output parameter that returns the text of the list for the list box:

```
@TheList varchar(8000) OUTPUT
```

The procedure needs two local variables that will store the names and IDs of the attendees of the event:

```
@EventAttendeeID varchar(10),
@TheName varchar(50)
```

The procedure will also need a Cursor object to retrieve those names:

```
Declare CurEventAttendees Cursor
```

The list box needs to display the names of the attendees. But the EventAttendees table contains only the IDs of attendees. So the cursor is set to retrieve the data from a view that joins the EventAttendees table with the Attendees table:

```
For Select EventAttendeeID, TheName from EventsWithAttendees
      Where EventID = @EventID
      Order By TheName
```

You then initialize your return parameter:

```
Select @TheList = ''
```

open the cursor:

```
Open CurEventAttendees
```

and retrieve the first record from the view into your local variables:

```
Fetch CurEventAttendees
      Into @EventAttendeeID, @TheName
```

Next, you enter a loop so you can process each record:

```
While @@Fetch_Status = 0
```

The contents of each record are concatenated to the return parameter:

```
Select @TheList = @TheList + @EventAttendeeID + ';"'
      + @TheName + '";'
```

You then retrieve the next record before looping:

```
Fetch CurEventAttendees
      Into @EventAttendeeID, @TheName
```

Finally, you close and release the Cursor object:

```
Close CurEventAttendees
Deallocate CurEventAttendees
```

Views

EventsWithAttendees View

The EventsWithAttendees view is used by the EventAttendeeListBox stored procedure to produce a list of attendee names that are attending an event.

```
SELECT dbo.EventAttendees.EventAttendeeID,
dbo.EventAttendees.EventID, dbo.Attendees.LastName
+ ', ' + dbo.Attendees.FirstName AS TheName
FROM dbo.EventAttendees LEFT OUTER JOIN
dbo.Attendees ON
dbo.EventAttendees.AttendeeID = dbo.Attendees.AttendeeID
```

Notice that the view joins the EventAttendees table with the Attendees table in a left join so all the records will be returned from the EventAttendees table even if no match is found in the Attendees table.

Also note that the view outputs a field called TheName that is the concatenation of the attendees' first and last names.

Event Attendance View

The Event Attendance view is used by the Event Attendance report in the Access front end. It outputs the total number of attendees for each event.

```
SELECT TOP 100 PERCENT dbo.Events.EventName,
COUNT(dbo.EventAttendees.AttendeeID) AS Expr1
FROM dbo.Events LEFT OUTER JOIN
dbo.EventAttendees ON dbo.Events.EventID = dbo.EventAttendees.EventID
GROUP BY dbo.Events.EventName
ORDER BY dbo.Events.EventName
```

Note that the view joins the Events table to the EventAttendees table with a left join. So all the events are returned even if they have no attendees.

Application Notes

C12FrontEnd.mdb

The front-end Access application requires a DSN that points to the SQL Server back-end database to be present on the client computer. That DSN must be called:

```
C12WorkingWithEvents
```

The Access database does not have any local tables. It does, though, link to the Event Attendance view, which it uses for the Event Attendance report.

Modules

GeneralProcs Module

The Access application contains a single module called GeneralProcs. That module has the following declaration in the General Declarations section:

```
Public MyDB As New ADODB.Connection
```

The public variable MyDB is used throughout the application and provides access to the back-end database.

When the application is opened, the AutoExec macro automatically fires. That macro calls the following procedure that is in the GeneralProcs module.

```
Public Function StartUp()
    On Error GoTo HandleError
    Dim SQLUserName As String
    Dim SQLPassword As String
    SQLUserName = InputBox("Please enter your user name.", "User Name")
    SQLPassword = InputBox("Please enter your password.", "Password")
    MyDB.Open "DSN=C12WorkingWithEvents;UID=" & SQLUserName _
        & ";Password=" & SQLPassword
    DoCmd.OpenForm "frmMenu"
    Exit Function
HandleError:
    MsgBox Err.Number & ": " & Err.Description & _
        ". Closing application.", vbCritical, "Can't Start Application"
    Application.CloseCurrentDatabase
End Function
```

If an error were to occur in the procedure, the code would break to the line with the label HandleError:

```
On Error GoTo HandleError
```

Thc procedure needs two local variables. The first will store the user name entered by the user:

```
Dim SQLUserName As String
```

and the other will store their password:

```
Dim SQLPassword As String
```

You then use the InputBox function, which will display a small dialog box. You prompt the user through that dialog box to enter their user name:

```
SQLUserName = InputBox("Please enter your user name.", "User Name")
```

You then prompt the user for their password:

```
SQLPassword = InputBox("Please enter your password.", "Password")
```

Next, you attempt to connect to the database using the user name and password supplied by the user:

```
MyDB.Open "DSN=C12WorkingWithEvents;UID=" & SQLUserName _
      & ";Password=" & SQLPassword
```

If the connection was successful, you open the Menu form:

```
DoCmd.OpenForm "frmMenu"
```

and leave this procedure:

```
Exit Function
```

If the connection returned an error, the code would flow to this label:

```
HandleError:
```

You display the error to the user:

```
MsgBox Err.Number & ": " & Err.Description & _
      ". Closing application.", vbCritical, "Can't Start Application"
```

and exit the application:

```
Application.CloseCurrentDatabase
```

Forms

Menu Form

The code on the menu form allows the user to enter any of the forms and reports contained within the application. If the user clicks the Events button, the code uses the OpenForm method of the DoCmd object to display the Events form:

```
Private Sub cmdEvents_Click()
    DoCmd.OpenForm "frmEvents"
End Sub
```

Similarly, when the Attendees button is clicked, the code uses the OpenForm method to open the Attendees form, since that form name is passed to the method:

```
Private Sub cmdAttendees_Click()
    DoCmd.OpenForm "frmAttendees"
End Sub
```

When the user clicks the Event Attendance button, the OpenReport method of the DoCmd object is used to open the Event Attendance report. Note the second parameter in that call. This tells the method to display the report instead of printing it directly:

```
Private Sub cmdEventAttendance_Click()
    DoCmd.OpenReport "Event Attendance", acViewPreview
End Sub
```

Events Form

The code on the Events form allows the user to add, edit, delete, and view event records, as well as attendees to the event.

In the General Declarations section of the form, you will see the following variable declared:

```
Private CurrentID As Long
```

This variable is used to store the ID of the current event being viewed. Since it has Private scope, it is available to any procedure on this form.

The Events form contains the user-defined procedure. The first populates the combo box that contains a list of all the events.

```
Public Sub RefreshComboBox()
    Dim cmdList As New ADODB.Command
    Set cmdList.ActiveConnection = MyDB
    cmdList.CommandText = "EventComboBox"
    cmdList.CommandType = adCmdStoredProc
    cmdList.Parameters.Append cmdList.CreateParameter _
        ("TheList", adVarChar, adParamOutput, 8000)
    cmdList.Execute
    cmbEventID.RowSource = cmdList("TheList")
End Sub
```

The procedure needs a Command object to call a stored procedure:

```
Dim cmdList As New ADODB.Command
```

The Command object will use your public database connection:

```
Set cmdList.ActiveConnection = MyDB
```

It will call the EventsComboBox stored procedure:

```
cmdList.CommandText = "EventComboBox"
```

and the command type is set to stored procedure:

```
cmdList.CommandType = adCmdStoredProc
```

The Command object needs to pass one parameter to the stored procedure:

```
cmdList.Parameters.Append cmdList.CreateParameter _
      ("TheList", adVarChar, adParamOutput, 8000)
```

You then execute the Command object:

```
cmdList.Execute
```

and use the output parameter from the stored procedure to populate the combo box:

```
cmbEventID.RowSource = cmdList("TheList")
```

The other user-defined procedure on the Events form populates the list box with the name of the attendees to the current event.

```
Public Sub RefreshAttendeeList()
    Dim cmdList As New ADODB.Command
    Set cmdList.ActiveConnection = MyDB
    cmdList.CommandText = "EventAttendeesListBox"
    cmdList.CommandType = adCmdStoredProc
    cmdList.Parameters.Append cmdList.CreateParameter _
        ("EventID", adInteger, adParamInput, , CurrentID)
    cmdList.Parameters.Append cmdList.CreateParameter _
        ("TheList", adVarChar, adParamOutput, 8000)
    cmdList.Execute
    lstAttendees.RowSource = cmdList("TheList")
End Sub
```

The procedure will need a Command object:

```
Dim cmdList As New ADODB.Command
```

The connection for that object is set to your public connection:

```
Set cmdList.ActiveConnection = MyDB
```

The Command object will use the EventAttendeesListBox:

```
cmdList.CommandText = "EventAttendeesListBox"
```

which is a stored procedure:

```
cmdList.CommandType = adCmdStoredProc
```

The call to the stored procedure requires two parameters. The first is an input parameter that passes in the ID of the event whose Attendees you want returned. That value is retrieved through the CurrentID variable:

```
cmdList.Parameters.Append cmdList.CreateParameter _
    ("EventID", adInteger, adParamInput, , CurrentID)
```

The other parameter is an output parameter that you call The List. It is of type varchar and has a size of 8,000:

```
cmdList.Parameters.Append cmdList.CreateParameter _
    ("TheList", adVarChar, adParamOutput, 8000)
```

You then execute the Command object:

```
cmdList.Execute
```

and use the return parameter to populate the list box:

```
lstAttendees.RowSource = cmdList("TheList")
```

When the form first loads, the Load event fires.

```
Private Sub Form_Load()
    Dim cmdEvent As New ADODB.Command
    Set cmdEvent.ActiveConnection = MyDB
    cmdEvent.CommandText = "EventRecord"
    cmdEvent.CommandType = adCmdStoredProc
```

```
    cmdEvent.Parameters.Append cmdEvent.CreateParameter _
        ("ReturnStatus", adInteger, adParamOutput)
    cmdEvent.Parameters.Append cmdEvent.CreateParameter _
        ("ReturnMessage", adVarChar, adParamOutput, 50)
    cmdEvent.Parameters.Append cmdEvent.CreateParameter _
        ("EventID", adInteger, adParamInputOutput, , 0)
    cmdEvent.Parameters.Append cmdEvent.CreateParameter _
        ("EventName", adVarChar, adParamOutput, 50)
    cmdEvent.Parameters.Append cmdEvent.CreateParameter _
        ("StartDate", adVarChar, adParamOutput, 50)
    cmdEvent.Parameters.Append cmdEvent.CreateParameter _
        ("EndDate", adVarChar, adParamOutput, 50)
    cmdEvent.Parameters.Append cmdEvent.CreateParameter _
        ("Location", adVarChar, adParamOutput, 1000)
    cmdEvent.Parameters.Append cmdEvent.CreateParameter _
        ("TheDescription", adVarChar, adParamOutput, 8000)
    cmdEvent.Execute
    If cmdEvent("ReturnStatus") = 1 Then
        CurrentID = cmdEvent("EventID")
        [txtEventName] = cmdEvent("EventName")
        [txtStartDate] = cmdEvent("StartDate")
        [txtEndDate] = cmdEvent("EndDate")
        [txtLocation] = cmdEvent("Location")
        [txtTheDescription] = cmdEvent("TheDescription")
        RefreshComboBox
        RefreshAttendeeList
        txtEventName.SetFocus
    Else
        MsgBox cmdEvent("ReturnMessage")
    End If
End Sub
```

The procedure will need a Command object:

```
Dim cmdEvent As New ADODB.Command
```

The Command object will use your public database connection:

```
Set cmdEvent.ActiveConnection = MyDB
```

and will call the EventRecord stored procedure:

```
cmdEvent.CommandText = "EventRecord"
cmdEvent.CommandType = adCmdStoredProc
```

The call to EventRecord requires many parameters. The first two are output parameters, which will contain the status of the call:

```
cmdEvent.Parameters.Append cmdEvent.CreateParameter _
     ("ReturnStatus", adInteger, adParamOutput)
cmdEvent.Parameters.Append cmdEvent.CreateParameter _
     ("ReturnMessage", adVarChar, adParamOutput, 50)
```

The next parameter is an input/output parameter. You pass in 0, indicating that you want the first record in the table. What you will receive back through the parameter is the ID of the Event retrieved:

```
cmdEvent.Parameters.Append cmdEvent.CreateParameter _
     ("EventID", adInteger, adParamInputOutput, , 0)
```

The remaining parameters are all output parameters that will contain the values of the columns retrieved through the call to the stored procedure:

```
cmdEvent.Parameters.Append cmdEvent.CreateParameter _
     ("EventName", adVarChar, adParamOutput, 50)
cmdEvent.Parameters.Append cmdEvent.CreateParameter _
     ("StartDate", adVarChar, adParamOutput, 50)
cmdEvent.Parameters.Append cmdEvent.CreateParameter _
     ("EndDate", adVarChar, adParamOutput, 50)
cmdEvent.Parameters.Append cmdEvent.CreateParameter _
     ("Location", adVarChar, adParamOutput, 1000)
cmdEvent.Parameters.Append cmdEvent.CreateParameter _
     ("TheDescription", adVarChar, adParamOutput, 8000)
```

You then execute the Command object:

```
cmdEvent.Execute
```

If the status returned is 1, you have a valid record:

```
If cmdEvent("ReturnStatus") = 1 Then
```

In that case, you store the ID of the event retrieved:

```
CurrentID = cmdEvent("EventID")
```

and place the values of the parameters returned from the stored procedure into the text boxes on the form:

```
[txtEventName] = cmdEvent("EventName")
[txtStartDate] = cmdEvent("StartDate")
[txtEndDate] = cmdEvent("EndDate")
[txtLocation] = cmdEvent("Location")
[txtTheDescription] = cmdEvent("TheDescription")
```

You then call your procedure that will populate the combo box:

```
RefreshComboBox
```

and the list box:

```
RefreshAttendeeList
```

Then you set focus to the Event Name text box:

```
txtEventName.SetFocus
```

If the status returned through the Command object was not successful, the code flows here and you display the message to the user:

```
MsgBox cmdEvent("ReturnMessage")
```

When the user changes the selected item in the combo box, you need to display the event that they selected.

```
Private Sub cmbEventID_Change()
    Dim cmdEvent As New ADODB.Command
    Set cmdEvent.ActiveConnection = MyDB
    cmdEvent.CommandText = "EventRecord"
    cmdEvent.CommandType = adCmdStoredProc
    cmdEvent.Parameters.Append cmdEvent.CreateParameter _
        ("ReturnStatus", adInteger, adParamOutput)
    cmdEvent.Parameters.Append cmdEvent.CreateParameter _
        ("ReturnMessage", adVarChar, adParamOutput, 50)
    cmdEvent.Parameters.Append cmdEvent.CreateParameter _
        ("EventID", adInteger, adParamInputOutput, , [cmbEventID])
    cmdEvent.Parameters.Append cmdEvent.CreateParameter _
        ("EventName", adVarChar, adParamOutput, 50)
    cmdEvent.Parameters.Append cmdEvent.CreateParameter _
        ("StartDate", adVarChar, adParamOutput, 50)
    cmdEvent.Parameters.Append cmdEvent.CreateParameter _
        ("EndDate", adVarChar, adParamOutput, 50)
```

```
        cmdEvent.Parameters.Append cmdEvent.CreateParameter _
            ("Location", adVarChar, adParamOutput, 1000)
        cmdEvent.Parameters.Append cmdEvent.CreateParameter _
            ("TheDescription", adVarChar, adParamOutput, 8000)
        cmdEvent.Execute
        If cmdEvent("ReturnStatus") = 1 Then
            CurrentID = [cmbEventID]
            [txtEventName] = cmdEvent("EventName")
            [txtStartDate] = cmdEvent("StartDate")
            [txtEndDate] = cmdEvent("EndDate")
            [txtLocation] = cmdEvent("Location")
            [txtTheDescription] = cmdEvent("TheDescription")
            RefreshAttendeeList
            txtEventName.SetFocus
        Else
            MsgBox cmdEvent("ReturnMessage")
        End If
    End Sub
```

The procedure needs a Command object:

```
Dim cmdEvent As New ADODB.Command
```

which will use your Public database connection:

```
Set cmdEvent.ActiveConnection = MyDB
```

It will call EventRecord:

```
cmdEvent.CommandText = "EventRecord"
```

which is a stored procedure:

```
cmdEvent.CommandType = adCmdStoredProc
```

The stored procedure requires numerous parameters. The first two are output parameters, which return the status of the call to the procedure:

```
cmdEvent.Parameters.Append cmdEvent.CreateParameter _
    ("ReturnStatus", adInteger, adParamOutput)
cmdEvent.Parameters.Append cmdEvent.CreateParameter _
    ("ReturnMessage", adVarChar, adParamOutput, 50)
```

The third parameter is used to pass in the ID of the event whose data you want retrieved. Note that you pass into it the value selected in the combo box:

```
cmdEvent.Parameters.Append cmdEvent.CreateParameter _
      ("EventID", adInteger, adParamInputOutput, , [cmbEventID])
```

The rest of the parameters are all output parameters. After the call to the stored procedure, they will contain the values for the fields in the selected record:

```
cmdEvent.Parameters.Append cmdEvent.CreateParameter _
      ("EventName", adVarChar, adParamOutput, 50)
cmdEvent.Parameters.Append cmdEvent.CreateParameter _
      ("StartDate", adVarChar, adParamOutput, 50)
cmdEvent.Parameters.Append cmdEvent.CreateParameter _
      ("EndDate", adVarChar, adParamOutput, 50)
cmdEvent.Parameters.Append cmdEvent.CreateParameter _
      ("Location", adVarChar, adParamOutput, 1000)
cmdEvent.Parameters.Append cmdEvent.CreateParameter _
      ("TheDescription", adVarChar, adParamOutput, 8000)
```

You then call the stored procedure:

```
cmdEvent.Execute
```

and check to see whether it ran successfully:

```
If cmdEvent("ReturnStatus") = 1 Then
```

If it did, you store the ID of the event into your private variable:

```
CurrentID = [cmbEventID]
```

and use the other values returned to populate the text boxes on the form:

```
[txtEventName] = cmdEvent("EventName")
[txtStartDate] = cmdEvent("StartDate")
[txtEndDate] = cmdEvent("EndDate")
[txtLocation] = cmdEvent("Location")
[txtTheDescription] = cmdEvent("TheDescription")
```

You also need to update the list box so that it will show the attendees of the selected event:

```
RefreshAttendeeList
```

and you set focus to the Event Name text box:

```
txtEventName.SetFocus
```

If the call to the stored procedure returned an error message, you display that to the user here:

```
MsgBox cmdEvent("ReturnMessage")
```

When the user clicks the Add button, the next code block fires.

```
Private Sub cmdAdd_Click()
    Dim cmdEvent As New ADODB.Command
    Set cmdEvent.ActiveConnection = MyDB
    cmdEvent.CommandText = "EventAdd"
    cmdEvent.CommandType = adCmdStoredProc
    cmdEvent.Parameters.Append cmdEvent.CreateParameter _
        ("ReturnStatus", adInteger, adParamOutput)
    cmdEvent.Parameters.Append cmdEvent.CreateParameter _
        ("ReturnMessage", adVarChar, adParamOutput, 50)
    cmdEvent.Parameters.Append cmdEvent.CreateParameter _
        ("EventID", adInteger, adParamOutput)
    cmdEvent.Parameters.Append cmdEvent.CreateParameter _
        ("EventName", adVarChar, adParamInput, 50, _
        Replace([txtEventName], "'", "''", 1, -1, vbTextCompare))
    cmdEvent.Parameters.Append cmdEvent.CreateParameter _
        ("StartDate", adVarChar, adParamInput, 50, [txtStartDate])
    cmdEvent.Parameters.Append cmdEvent.CreateParameter _
        ("EndDate", adVarChar, adParamInput, 50, [txtEndDate])
    cmdEvent.Parameters.Append cmdEvent.CreateParameter _
        ("Location", adVarChar, adParamInput, 1000, _
        Replace([txtLocation], "'", "''", 1, -1, vbTextCompare))
    cmdEvent.Parameters.Append cmdEvent.CreateParameter _
        ("TheDescription", adVarChar, adParamInput, 8000, _
        Replace([txtTheDescription], "'", "''", 1, -1, vbTextCompare))
    cmdEvent.Execute
    If cmdEvent("ReturnStatus") = 1 Then
        CurrentID = cmdEvent("EventID")
```

```
            RefreshComboBox
            RefreshAttendeeList
            txtEventName.SetFocus
        Else
            MsgBox cmdEvent("ReturnMessage")
        End If
End Sub
```

The procedure needs a Command object:

```
Dim cmdEvent As New ADODB.Command
```

which will use your public connection:

```
Set cmdEvent.ActiveConnection = MyDB
```

The Command object will call EventAdd:

```
cmdEvent.CommandText = "EventAdd"
```

which is a stored procedure:

```
cmdEvent.CommandType = adCmdStoredProc
```

The first two parameters of the stored procedure are used to return the status of the call:

```
cmdEvent.Parameters.Append cmdEvent.CreateParameter _
      ("ReturnStatus", adInteger, adParamOutput)
cmdEvent.Parameters.Append cmdEvent.CreateParameter _
      ("ReturnMessage", adVarChar, adParamOutput, 50)
```

The next parameter is an output parameter, which returns the ID of the event just added:

```
cmdEvent.Parameters.Append cmdEvent.CreateParameter _
      ("EventID", adInteger, adParamOutput)
```

The rest of the parameters contain the values for the record being added. Note that you use the Replace function to replace any single apostrophes with two so that they will be properly added to the database:

```
cmdEvent.Parameters.Append cmdEvent.CreateParameter _
      ("EventName", adVarChar, adParamInput, 50, _
```

```
        Replace([txtEventName], "'", "''", 1, -1, vbTextCompare))
cmdEvent.Parameters.Append cmdEvent.CreateParameter _
        ("StartDate", adVarChar, adParamInput, 50, [txtStartDate])
cmdEvent.Parameters.Append cmdEvent.CreateParameter _
        ("EndDate", adVarChar, adParamInput, 50, [txtEndDate])
cmdEvent.Parameters.Append cmdEvent.CreateParameter _
        ("Location", adVarChar, adParamInput, 1000, _
        Replace([txtLocation], "'", "''", 1, -1, vbTextCompare))
cmdEvent.Parameters.Append cmdEvent.CreateParameter _
  ("TheDescription", adVarChar, adParamInput, 8000, _
        Replace([txtTheDescription], "'", "''", 1, -1, vbTextCompare))
```

You then call the stored procedure:

```
cmdEvent.Execute
```

If it returns a success status:

```
If cmdEvent("ReturnStatus") = 1 Then
```

you set the CurrentID variable so that it contains the ID of the event just added:

```
CurrentID = cmdEvent("EventID")
```

refresh the combo box and the list box:

```
RefreshComboBox
RefreshAttendeeList
```

and set focus to the first field on the form:

```
txtEventName.SetFocus
```

If the call to the stored procedure returned an error status, you display the message to the user:

```
MsgBox cmdEvent("ReturnMessage")
```

The next code block fires when the Update button is clicked.

```
Private Sub cmdUpdate_Click()
    Dim cmdEvent As New ADODB.Command
    If CurrentID = "0" Then
        cmdAdd_Click
```

```
        Exit Sub
    End If
    Set cmdEvent.ActiveConnection = MyDB
    cmdEvent.CommandText = "EventEdit"
    cmdEvent.CommandType = adCmdStoredProc
    cmdEvent.Parameters.Append cmdEvent.CreateParameter _
        ("ReturnStatus", adInteger, adParamOutput)
    cmdEvent.Parameters.Append cmdEvent.CreateParameter _
        ("ReturnMessage", adVarChar, adParamOutput, 50)
    cmdEvent.Parameters.Append cmdEvent.CreateParameter _
        ("EventID", adInteger, adParamInput, , CurrentID)
    cmdEvent.Parameters.Append cmdEvent.CreateParameter _
        ("EventName", adVarChar, adParamInput, 50, _
        Replace([txtEventName], "'", "''", 1, -1, vbTextCompare))
    cmdEvent.Parameters.Append cmdEvent.CreateParameter _
        ("StartDate", adVarChar, adParamInput, 50, [txtStartDate])
    cmdEvent.Parameters.Append cmdEvent.CreateParameter _
        ("EndDate", adVarChar, adParamInput, 50, [txtEndDate])
    cmdEvent.Parameters.Append cmdEvent.CreateParameter _
        ("Location", adVarChar, adParamInput, 1000, _
        Replace([txtLocation], "'", "''", 1, -1, vbTextCompare))
    cmdEvent.Parameters.Append cmdEvent.CreateParameter _
        ("TheDescription", adVarChar, adParamInput, 8000, _
        Replace([txtTheDescription], "'", "''", 1, -1, vbTextCompare))
    cmdEvent.Execute
    If cmdEvent("ReturnStatus") = 1 Then
        RefreshComboBox
        txtEventName.SetFocus
    Else
        MsgBox cmdEvent("ReturnMessage")
    End If
End Sub
```

The procedure needs a Command object:

```
Dim cmdEvent As New ADODB.Command
```

If the CurrentID is set to 0, the user is in Add mode, not Update mode:

```
If CurrentID = "0" Then
```

Therefore, you call the Add procedure:

```
cmdAdd_Click
```

and leave this procedure:

```
Exit Sub
```

Otherwise, you set the database connection for the Command object:

```
Set cmdEvent.ActiveConnection = MyDB
```

It will call the EventEdit stored procedure:

```
cmdEvent.CommandText = "EventEdit"
cmdEvent.CommandType = adCmdStoredProc
```

You need to pass in two output parameters to the stored procedure that will return the status of the call:

```
cmdEvent.Parameters.Append cmdEvent.CreateParameter _
      ("ReturnStatus", adInteger, adParamOutput)
cmdEvent.Parameters.Append cmdEvent.CreateParameter _
      ("ReturnMessage", adVarChar, adParamOutput, 50)
```

The next parameter passed into the stored procedure is the ID of the event to be edited:

```
cmdEvent.Parameters.Append cmdEvent.CreateParameter _
      ("EventID", adInteger, adParamInput, , CurrentID)
```

The other parameters passed in contain the values of the fields in the record being edited:

```
cmdEvent.Parameters.Append cmdEvent.CreateParameter _
      ("EventName", adVarChar, adParamInput, 50, _
      Replace([txtEventName], "'", "''", 1, -1, vbTextCompare))
cmdEvent.Parameters.Append cmdEvent.CreateParameter _
      ("StartDate", adVarChar, adParamInput, 50, [txtStartDate])
cmdEvent.Parameters.Append cmdEvent.CreateParameter _
      ("EndDate", adVarChar, adParamInput, 50, [txtEndDate])
cmdEvent.Parameters.Append cmdEvent.CreateParameter _
      ("Location", adVarChar, adParamInput, 1000, _
      Replace([txtLocation], "'", "''", 1, -1, vbTextCompare))
cmdEvent.Parameters.Append cmdEvent.CreateParameter _
      ("TheDescription", adVarChar, adParamInput, 8000, _
      Replace([txtTheDescription], "'", "''", 1, -1, vbTextCompare))
```

You then make the call to the stored procedure:

```
cmdEvent.Execute
```

If the call returns a success message:

```
If cmdEvent("ReturnStatus") = 1 Then
```

you update the combo box:

```
RefreshComboBox
```

and set the focus to the Event Name field:

```
txtEventName.SetFocus
```

Otherwise, you display the error message returned:

```
MsgBox cmdEvent("ReturnMessage")
```

When the Delete button is clicked, the next code block fires.

```
Private Sub cmdDelete_Click()
    Dim cmdEventDelete As New ADODB.Command
    Dim cmdEvent As New ADODB.Command
    If CurrentID = 0 Then
        cmdClear_Click
        Exit Sub
    End If
    Set cmdEventDelete.ActiveConnection = MyDB
    cmdEventDelete.CommandText = "EventDelete"
    cmdEventDelete.CommandType = adCmdStoredProc
    cmdEventDelete.Parameters.Append cmdEventDelete.CreateParameter _
        ("ReturnStatus", adInteger, adParamOutput)
    cmdEventDelete.Parameters.Append cmdEventDelete.CreateParameter _
        ("ReturnMessage", adVarChar, adParamOutput, 50)
    cmdEventDelete.Parameters.Append cmdEventDelete.CreateParameter _
        ("EventID", adInteger, adParamInput, , CurrentID)
    cmdEventDelete.Execute
    If cmdEventDelete("ReturnStatus") = 1 Then
        Set cmdEvent.ActiveConnection = MyDB
        cmdEvent.CommandText = "EventRecord"
        cmdEvent.CommandType = adCmdStoredProc
```

```
        cmdEvent.Parameters.Append cmdEvent.CreateParameter _
            ("ReturnStatus", adInteger, adParamOutput)
        cmdEvent.Parameters.Append cmdEvent.CreateParameter _
            ("ReturnMessage", adVarChar, adParamOutput, 50)
        cmdEvent.Parameters.Append cmdEvent.CreateParameter _
            ("EventID", adInteger, adParamInputOutput, , 0)
        cmdEvent.Parameters.Append cmdEvent.CreateParameter _
            ("EventName", adVarChar, adParamOutput, 50)
        cmdEvent.Parameters.Append cmdEvent.CreateParameter _
            ("StartDate", adVarChar, adParamOutput, 50)
        cmdEvent.Parameters.Append cmdEvent.CreateParameter _
            ("EndDate", adVarChar, adParamOutput, 50)
        cmdEvent.Parameters.Append cmdEvent.CreateParameter _
            ("Location", adVarChar, adParamOutput, 1000)
        cmdEvent.Parameters.Append cmdEvent.CreateParameter _
            ("TheDescription", adVarChar, adParamOutput, 8000)
        cmdEvent.Execute
        If cmdEvent("ReturnStatus") = 1 Then
            CurrentID = cmdEvent("EventID")
            [txtEventName] = cmdEvent("EventName")
            [txtStartDate] = cmdEvent("StartDate")
            [txtEndDate] = cmdEvent("EndDate")
            [txtLocation] = cmdEvent("Location")
            [txtTheDescription] = cmdEvent("TheDescription")
            RefreshComboBox
            RefreshAttendeeList
            txtEventName.SetFocus
        Else
            CurrentID = 0
            cmdClear_Click
        End If
    Else
        MsgBox cmdEventDelete("ReturnMessage")
    End If
End Sub
```

The procedure will need two Command objects. The first will be used to delete the current record:

```
Dim cmdEventDelete As New ADODB.Command
```

The other will be used to retrieve another record after the current record is deleted:

```
Dim cmdEvent As New ADODB.Command
```

If the ID of the current event is 0, you are in Add mode:

```
If CurrentID = 0 Then
```

In that case, you just need to clear the form:

```
cmdClear_Click
```

and leave this procedure:

```
Exit Sub
```

Otherwise, you set up the Command object for the record deletion so that it points to your Connection object:

```
Set cmdEventDelete.ActiveConnection = MyDB
```

and set it to call the procedure name EventDelete:

```
cmdEventDelete.CommandText = "EventDelete"
```

which is a stored procedure:

```
cmdEventDelete.CommandType = adCmdStoredProc
```

The stored procedure requires two output parameters for the return status of the call:

```
cmdEventDelete.Parameters.Append cmdEventDelete.CreateParameter _
      ("ReturnStatus", adInteger, adParamOutput)
cmdEventDelete.Parameters.Append cmdEventDelete.CreateParameter _
      ("ReturnMessage", adVarChar, adParamOutput, 50)
```

The other parameter passed in contains the ID of the event being deleted:

```
cmdEventDelete.Parameters.Append cmdEventDelete.CreateParameter _
      ("EventID", adInteger, adParamInput, , CurrentID)
```

You then make the call to the stored procedure:

```
cmdEventDelete.Execute
```

If it executed successfully:

```
If cmdEventDelete("ReturnStatus") = 1 Then
```

the code flows here and you need to display another record on the form. So, you set up the other Command object:

```
Set cmdEvent.ActiveConnection = MyDB
```

It will call the EventRecord stored procedure:

```
cmdEvent.CommandText = "EventRecord"
cmdEvent.CommandType = adCmdStoredProc
```

That stored procedure requires parameters for the return status:

```
cmdEvent.Parameters.Append cmdEvent.CreateParameter _
      ("ReturnStatus", adInteger, adParamOutput)
cmdEvent.Parameters.Append cmdEvent.CreateParameter _
      ("ReturnMessage", adVarChar, adParamOutput, 50)
```

and parameters for the values of the record retrieved:

```
cmdEvent.Parameters.Append cmdEvent.CreateParameter _
      ("EventID", adInteger, adParamInputOutput, , 0)
cmdEvent.Parameters.Append cmdEvent.CreateParameter _
      ("EventName", adVarChar, adParamOutput, 50)
cmdEvent.Parameters.Append cmdEvent.CreateParameter _
      ("StartDate", adVarChar, adParamOutput, 50)
cmdEvent.Parameters.Append cmdEvent.CreateParameter _
      ("EndDate", adVarChar, adParamOutput, 50)
cmdEvent.Parameters.Append cmdEvent.CreateParameter _
      ("Location", adVarChar, adParamOutput, 1000)
cmdEvent.Parameters.Append cmdEvent.CreateParameter _
      ("TheDescription", adVarChar, adParamOutput, 8000)
```

You then execute that stored procedure:

```
cmdEvent.Execute
```

If it ran successfully:

```
If cmdEvent("ReturnStatus") = 1 Then
```

you store the value of the EventID:

```
CurrentID = cmdEvent("EventID")
```

and place the other values returned into the text boxes on the form:

```
[txtEventName] = cmdEvent("EventName")
[txtStartDate] = cmdEvent("StartDate")
[txtEndDate] = cmdEvent("EndDate")
[txtLocation] = cmdEvent("Location")
[txtTheDescription] = cmdEvent("TheDescription")
```

You then repopulate the combo box and the list box:

```
RefreshComboBox
RefreshAttendeeList
```

and set the focus to the Event Name field:

```
txtEventName.SetFocus
```

If the code flows here, you weren't able to retrieve a record from the database:

```
CurrentID = 0
cmdClear_Click
```

If it flows here, you were unable to delete the record:

```
MsgBox cmdEventDelete("ReturnMessage")
```

The next code block fires when the user clicks the Clear button on the form.

```
Private Sub cmdClear_Click()
    [txtEventName] = ""
    [txtStartDate] = ""
    [txtEndDate] = ""
    [txtLocation] = ""
    [txtTheDescription] = ""
    CurrentID = 0
    RefreshAttendeeList
    txtEventName.SetFocus
End Sub
```

The procedure clears the text boxes:

```
[txtEventName] = ""
[txtStartDate] = ""
[txtEndDate] = ""
[txtLocation] = ""
[txtTheDescription] = ""
```

the CurrentID:

```
CurrentID = 0
```

and the list box:

```
RefreshAttendeeList
```

before setting focus to the Event Name field:

```
txtEventName.SetFocus
```

The next code block fires when the Add Attendees button is clicked.

```
Private Sub cmdAddAttendee_Click()
    DoCmd.OpenForm "frmAddAttendee", acNormal, _
        , , , acDialog, CurrentID
    RefreshAttendeeList
End Sub
```

The procedure calls the Add Attendee form. It calls it in a dialog box form so that the code stops with the call until the user is done with that form. And you pass into that form the ID of the event that the attendee should be added to.

```
DoCmd.OpenForm "frmAddAttendee", acNormal, _
     , , , acDialog, CurrentID
```

After the call is made, you need to refresh the list box:

```
RefreshAttendeeList
```

The last procedure on this form fires when the Delete Attendee button is clicked. It deletes the currently selected attendee from the event.

```
Private Sub cmdDeleteAttendee_Click()
    Dim cmdEA As New ADODB.Command
```

```
    If Not IsNull([lstAttendees]) Then
        Set cmdEA.ActiveConnection = MyDB
        cmdEA.CommandText = "EventAttendeeDelete"
        cmdEA.CommandType = adCmdStoredProc
        cmdEA.Parameters.Append cmdEA.CreateParameter _
            ("ReturnStatus", adInteger, adParamOutput)
        cmdEA.Parameters.Append cmdEA.CreateParameter _
            ("ReturnMessage", adVarChar, adParamOutput, 50)
        cmdEA.Parameters.Append cmdEA.CreateParameter _
            ("EventAttendeeID", adInteger, adParamInput, , [lstAttendees])
        cmdEA.Execute
        RefreshAttendeeList
    End If
End Sub
```

The procedure will need a Command object:

```
Dim cmdEA As New ADODB.Command
```

But before taking any action, you need to make sure the user has selected an attendee to delete:

```
If Not IsNull([lstAttendees]) Then
```

If they have, you set up the Command object:

```
Set cmdEA.ActiveConnection = MyDB
```

It will call the EventAttendeeDelete stored procedure:

```
cmdEA.CommandText = "EventAttendeeDelete"
cmdEA.CommandType = adCmdStoredProc
```

You pass message parameters into it:

```
cmdEA.Parameters.Append cmdEA.CreateParameter _
      ("ReturnStatus", adInteger, adParamOutput)
cmdEA.Parameters.Append cmdEA.CreateParameter _
      ("ReturnMessage", adVarChar, adParamOutput, 50)
```

and the ID of the record to delete:

```
cmdEA.Parameters.Append cmdEA.CreateParameter _
      ("EventAttendeeID", adInteger, adParamInput, , [lstAttendees])
```

You then call the stored procedure:

```
cmdEA.Execute
```

and repopulate the list box:

```
RefreshAttendeeList
```

Attendees Form

The code on the Attendees form allows the user to add, edit, delete, and view Attendee records. The code is almost identical to the same procedures on the Events form. Please refer to that section to review the code.

Add Attendees Form

The code on the Add Attendees form allows the user to add an attendee to an event. When the form first loads, the Load event fires. That event populates the combo box on the form.

```
Private Sub Form_Load()
    Dim cmdList As New ADODB.Command
    Set cmdList.ActiveConnection = MyDB
    cmdList.CommandText = "AttendeeComboBox"
    cmdList.CommandType = adCmdStoredProc
    cmdList.Parameters.Append cmdList.CreateParameter _
        ("TheList", adVarChar, adParamOutput, 8000)
    cmdList.Execute
    cmbAttendeeID.RowSource = cmdList("TheList")
End Sub
```

The procedure needs a Command object:

```
Dim cmdList As New ADODB.Command
```

The Command object will use your public database connection:

```
Set cmdList.ActiveConnection = MyDB
```

and will call the AttendeeComboBox stored procedure:

```
cmdList.CommandText = "AttendeeComboBox"
cmdList.CommandType = adCmdStoredProc
```

You pass to that stored procedure an output parameter that will contain the text for the combo box:

```
cmdList.Parameters.Append cmdList.CreateParameter _
      ("TheList", adVarChar, adParamOutput, 8000)
```

You then execute the stored procedure:

```
cmdList.Execute
```

and use its return to populate the list portion of the combo box:

```
cmbAttendeeID.RowSource = cmdList("TheList")
```

When the user clicks the OK button on the form, you need to add the Attendee that they selected to the Event.

```
Private Sub cmdOK_Click()
    Dim cmdEA As New ADODB.Command
    Set cmdEA.ActiveConnection = MyDB
    cmdEA.CommandText = "EventAttendeeAdd"
    cmdEA.CommandType = adCmdStoredProc
    cmdEA.Parameters.Append cmdEA.CreateParameter _
        ("ReturnStatus", adInteger, adParamOutput)
    cmdEA.Parameters.Append cmdEA.CreateParameter _
        ("ReturnMessage", adVarChar, adParamOutput, 50)
    cmdEA.Parameters.Append cmdEA.CreateParameter _
        ("EventID", adInteger, adParamInput, , Me.OpenArgs)
    cmdEA.Parameters.Append cmdEA.CreateParameter _
        ("AttendeeID", adInteger, adParamInput, , [cmbAttendeeID])
    cmdEA.Execute
    DoCmd.Close acForm, "frmAddAttendee"
End Sub
```

The procedure will need a stored procedure:

```
Dim cmdEA As New ADODB.Command
```

swhich will point to your public database connection:

```
Set cmdEA.ActiveConnection = MyDB
```

It will call the EventAttendeeAdd stored procedure:

```
cmdEA.CommandText = "EventAttendeeAdd"
cmdEA.CommandType = adCmdStoredProc
```

and pass to it two output parameters that will contain the status of the call:

```
cmdEA.Parameters.Append cmdEA.CreateParameter _
      ("ReturnStatus", adInteger, adParamOutput)
cmdEA.Parameters.Append cmdEA.CreateParameter _
      ("ReturnMessage", adVarChar, adParamOutput, 50)
```

You also pass to it the ID of the event that the attendee is attending. That value is passed into this form through the OpenArgs parameter:

```
cmdEA.Parameters.Append cmdEA.CreateParameter _
      ("EventID", adInteger, adParamInput, , Me.OpenArgs)
```

You also need to pass to the stored procedure the ID of the attendee being added:

```
cmdEA.Parameters.Append cmdEA.CreateParameter _
      ("AttendeeID", adInteger, adParamInput, , [cmbAttendeeID])
```

You then call the stored procedure:

```
cmdEA.Execute
```

and close this form:

```
DoCmd.Close acForm, "frmAddAttendee"
```

If the user clicks the Cancel button on the form, you simply close it:

```
Private Sub cmdCancel_Click()
   DoCmd.Close acForm, "frmAddAttendee"
End Sub
```

CHAPTER 13

Project Management

IN THIS CHAPTER:

C13SQLObjects.sql

Projects.txt

ProjectSteps.txt

C13FrontEnd.mdb

In this chapter, you will look at a simple SQL Server/Access application that allows a user to manage projects and the steps needed to complete a project. As you review the application, pay particular attention to the triggers.

Projects and Steps

The application uses SQL Server triggers to keep summary information about the project up to date. Also note the use of a user-defined function within a view. You will see how a problem within a view brings forth a solution from a user-defined function.

Application Walk-Through

When the user launches the Access front end, they are asked to supply their SQL Server user name and password. If they successfully enter that information, they will see the menu for the Project Manager application, displayed in Figure 13-1.

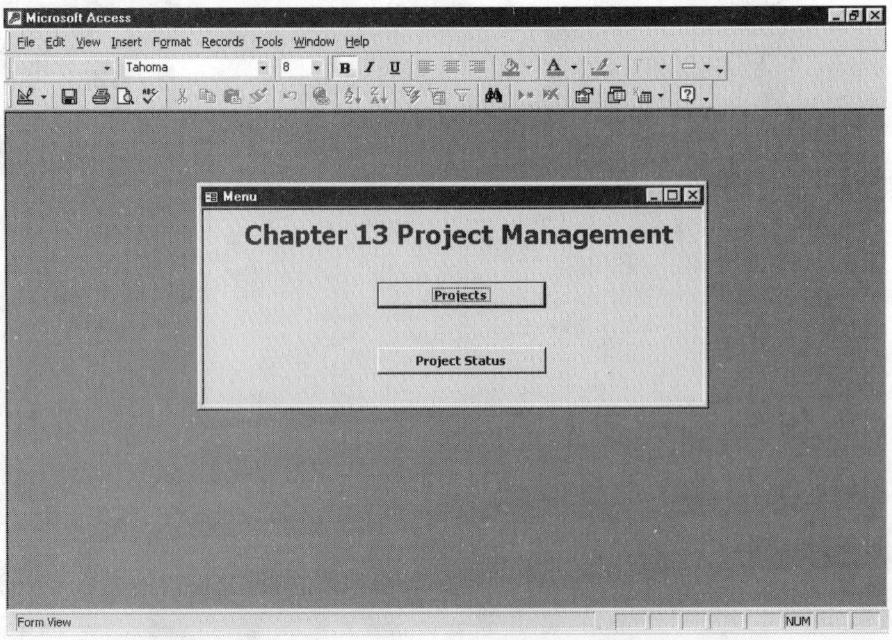

Figure 13-1 *Project Management menu*

From the menu, the user can access two different parts of the application. The main form is the Projects form, which is accessible to the user by clicking the Projects button.

The Projects form shown in Figure 13-2 allows the user to add, edit, delete, and view the different projects in the database. The user navigates to the desired project that they wish to work with by selecting it in the combo box at the bottom of the form. Note that in the title bar the project status is listed. Also note the label that displays the total number of steps and the total number of steps completed.

The triggers in the database automatically keep these tallies and status information up to date. A project has the status of pending until all the steps in the project are marked as complete.

The user marks a step as being complete by selecting the step in the list and then clicking the Mark Step as Complete button. When they do that, the status and tally labels are automatically updated.

If the user wants to add a step to the current project, they click the Add Step button, which displays the form shown in Figure 13-3.

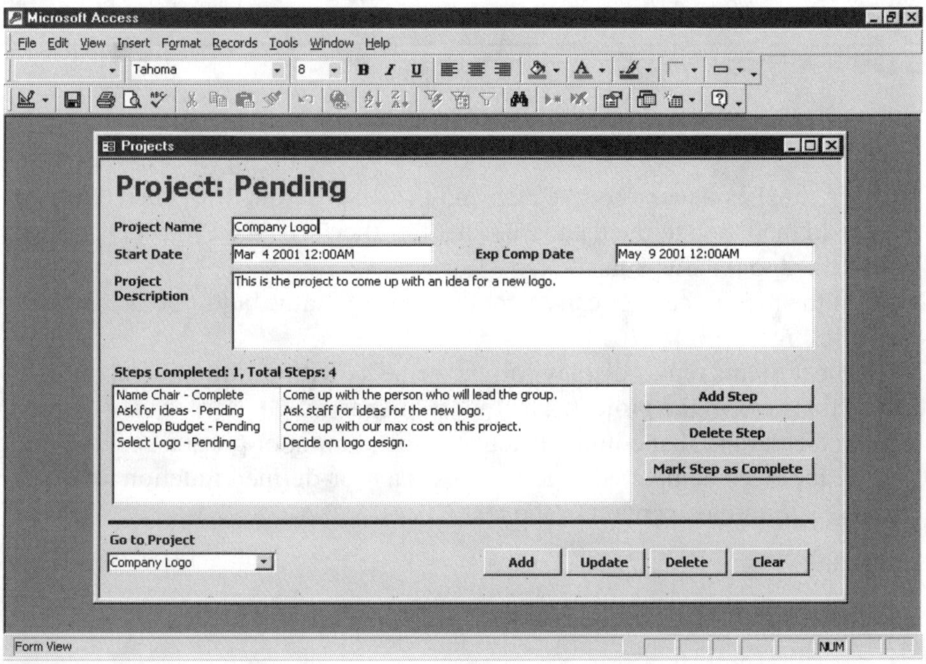

Figure 13-2 *Projects form*

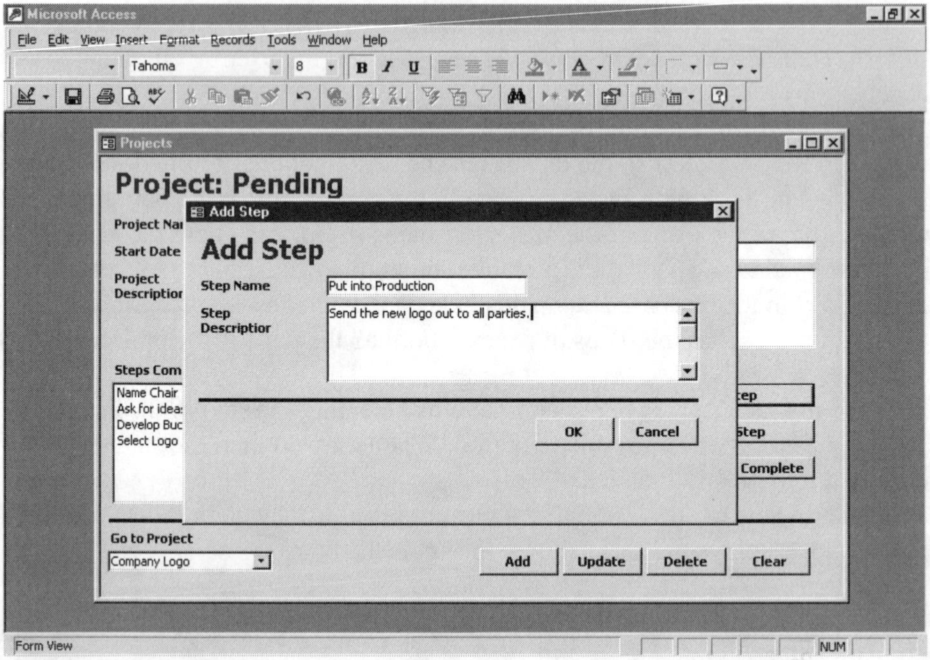

Figure 13-3 *Add Step form*

The user supplies a name for the step and the description. They then click the OK button to add their step to the database. The user then sees the Projects form with the new step added to the Steps list box.

Back on the menu, the user can select the Project Status button to see the report displayed in Figure 13-4.

The Project Status report displays all the projects with information about their status and the steps in the project. The report links to a SQL Server view. Note the Complete % column. That column calculates the amount of progress on the project in terms of the steps completed. The view uses a user-defined function to accomplish the result of returning a percent or the text NA.

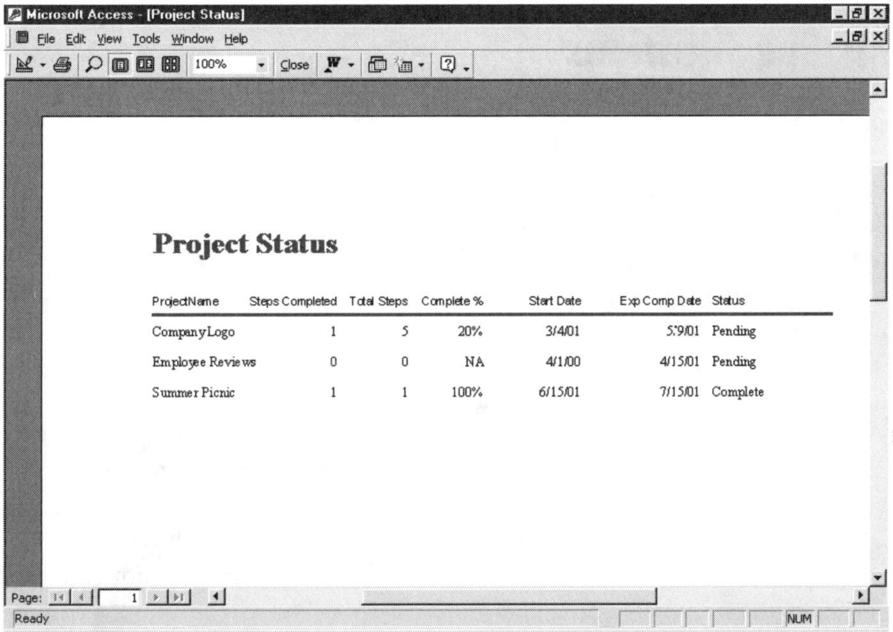

Figure 13-4 *Project Status report*

Tables and Relationships

C13SQLObjects.sql

Projects Table

The Projects table is the top-level table in this database. It stores summary and specific information about the project.

ProjectSteps Table

The ProjectSteps table stores the information about the steps within a project. The table relates to the Projects table in a one-to-many relationship. Each of the projects can have many steps, but each step belongs to a single project.

Fields Specifications

Projects Table

Projects.txt

The field specifications for the Projects table are displayed in Table 13-1.

The ProjectID field is the primary key for this table. Since it is an identity column, it is automatically populated.

The StepsCompleted field stores the number of steps for the project that have been marked as Completed. The field has a default value of 0 and is automatically kept up to date through triggers on the ProjectSteps table.

The TotalSteps field stores the total number of steps within the project. The field also has a default value of 0 and is updated through triggers on the ProjectSteps table.

A rule is enforced on the date fields through stored procedures. The ExpectedCompletionDate must be greater than the StartDate column.

The Status field has the default value of "Pending." The field is not editable by the user; and when all the steps in the project are marked as complete, a trigger in the ProjectSteps table changes the value to "Complete."

ProjectSteps Table

ProjectSteps.txt

The field specifications for the ProjectSteps table are displayed in Table 13-2.

The ProjectStepID column is the primary key in this table. The ProjectID field is a foreign key that links this table to the Projects table.

Field Name	Field Type	Notes
ProjectID	int	Primary Key, Identity Column
ProjectName	varchar	Length = 50
StepsCompleted	int	
TotalSteps	int	
StartDate	datetime	
ExpectedCompletionDate	datetime	
Status	varchar	Length = 50
Project Description	varchar	Length = 5000

Table 13-1 *Projects Table Field Specifications*

Field Name	Field Type	Notes
ProjectStepID	int	Primary Key, Identity Column
ProjectID	int	Foreign Key
StepName	varchar	Length = 50
Status	varchar	Length = 50
StepDescription	varchar	Length = 2000

Table 13-2 *ProjectSteps Table Field Specifications*

The Status field stores the status of the step. When a record is first added, the field contains the text "Pending." The text can change to the value "Complete" through a stored procedure.

Triggers

UpdateInsertSteps Trigger

The UpdateInsertSteps trigger fires whenever a record is added or updated in the ProjectSteps table. The triggers updates fields in the Projects table according to the record affected in the ProjectSteps table.

```
CREATE TRIGGER UpdateInsertSteps ON dbo.ProjectSteps
AFTER INSERT, UPDATE
AS
BEGIN
      DECLARE
      @TotalSteps integer,
      @StepsCompleted integer,
      @OverAllStatus varchar(50)
      Select @TotalSteps = Count(ProjectStepID) from ProjectSteps
            Where ProjectID = (Select ProjectID from Inserted)
      Select @StepsCompleted = Count(ProjectStepID) from ProjectSteps
            Where ProjectID = (Select ProjectID from Inserted) and
            Status = 'Complete'
      If @TotalSteps > 0 and @TotalSteps = @StepsCompleted
            BEGIN
```

```
                    Set @OverAllStatus = 'Complete'
              END
        Else
              BEGIN
                    Set @OverAllStatus = 'Pending'
              END
        Update Projects set
              TotalSteps = @TotalSteps,
              StepsCompleted = @StepsCompleted,
              Status = @OverAllStatus
              Where ProjectID = (Select ProjectID from Inserted)
END
```

The trigger fires after a record is added or updated:

```
AFTER INSERT, UPDATE
```

The trigger will need local variables to store the total number of steps in the project:

```
@TotalSteps integer,
```

The total number of steps marked as complete:

```
@StepsCompleted integer,
```

and the current status of the project:

```
@OverAllStatus varchar(50)
```

You then retrieve the total number of steps for the project designated by the ProjectID of the record being added or updated. That is the data in the temporary Inserted table:

```
Select @TotalSteps = Count(ProjectStepID) from ProjectSteps
      Where ProjectID = (Select ProjectID from Inserted)
```

Next, you retrieve the total number of steps complete for the project that has a step being added or updated as given by the ProjectID of that project and the Status field in the steps having the value "Complete":

```
Select @StepsCompleted = Count(ProjectStepID) from ProjectSteps
      Where ProjectID = (Select ProjectID from Inserted) and
      Status = 'Complete'
```

If the project has steps and all the steps have been marked as complete:

```
If @TotalSteps > 0 and @TotalSteps = @StepsCompleted
```

the project itself has the status of complete:

```
Set @OverAllStatus = 'Complete'
```

Otherwise, the project is pending:

```
Set @OverAllStatus = 'Pending'
```

You then update the project record with the values determined in the preceding code:

```
Update Projects set
      TotalSteps = @TotalSteps,
      StepsCompleted = @StepsCompleted,
      Status = @OverAllStatus
      Where ProjectID = (Select ProjectID from Inserted)
```

DeleteSteps Trigger

When a record is deleted from the ProjectSteps table, you also need a trigger to fire that updates the information in the Projects table. For example, a project may have only one step that is still pending. If that step was deleted, the status of the project would need to change to "Complete." The DeleteSteps trigger takes this action.

```
CREATE TRIGGER DeleteSteps ON dbo.ProjectSteps
AFTER DELETE
AS
BEGIN
      DECLARE
      @TotalSteps integer,
      @StepsCompleted integer,
      @OverAllStatus varchar(50)
      Select @TotalSteps = Count(ProjectStepID) from ProjectSteps
            Where ProjectID = (Select ProjectID from Deleted)
      Select @StepsCompleted = Count(ProjectStepID) from ProjectSteps
            Where ProjectID = (Select ProjectID from Deleted) and
            Status = 'Complete'
      If @TotalSteps > 0 and @TotalSteps = @StepsCompleted
            BEGIN
                  Set @OverAllStatus = 'Complete'
```

```
            END
        Else
            BEGIN
                Set @OverAllStatus = 'Pending'
            END
        Update Projects set
            TotalSteps = @TotalSteps,
            StepsCompleted = @StepsCompleted,
            Status = @OverAllStatus
            Where ProjectID = (Select ProjectID from Deleted)
END
```

The trigger fires after a record is deleted from the ProjectSteps table:

```
AFTER DELETE
```

The trigger needs local variables to store the total number of steps in the project:

```
@TotalSteps integer,
```

the total number of steps marked as complete:

```
@StepsCompleted integer,
```

and the status of the project:

```
@OverAllStatus varchar(50)
```

You then retrieve the total number of steps for the project given the ID of the project for which a step was just deleted. Note that you retrieve that ID from the temporary table, Deleted, which is available in a trigger to retrieve the values in the fields of the record being deleted:

```
Select @TotalSteps = Count(ProjectStepID) from ProjectSteps
      Where ProjectID = (Select ProjectID from Deleted)
```

You then retrieve the total number of steps marked as completed for this project:

```
Select @StepsCompleted = Count(ProjectStepID) from ProjectSteps
      Where ProjectID = (Select ProjectID from Deleted) and
      Status = 'Complete'
```

Next, you check to see if all the steps in the project are marked as complete:

```
If @TotalSteps > 0 and @TotalSteps = @StepsCompleted
```

If so, the status of the project is complete:

```
Set @OverAllStatus = 'Complete'
```

Otherwise, the project is still pending:

```
Set @OverAllStatus = 'Pending'
```

Now that all these values have been retrieved, you can use them to update the values in the project:

```
Update Projects set
      TotalSteps = @TotalSteps,
      StepsCompleted = @StepsCompleted,
      Status = @OverAllStatus
      Where ProjectID = (Select ProjectID from Deleted)
```

User-Defined Functions

ProjectIDCheck User-Defined Function

In some of the stored procedures, you need to determine whether the ID of a project entered is valid. This function determines that. If the ID is valid, it returns a nonzero number. If the ID is invalid, the function returns 0.

```
CREATE FUNCTION ProjectIDCheck (@TheID integer)
RETURNS Integer AS
BEGIN
      Declare @TheCount Integer
      Select @TheCount = Count(ProjectID) from Projects
            Where ProjectID = @TheID
      Return @TheCount
END
```

The function requires a single parameter, the ID of the project to check for:

```
CREATE FUNCTION ProjectIDCheck (@TheID integer)
```

The function returns the results as an integer:

```
RETURNS Integer AS
```

Locally, a variable that will store the number of occurrences of the ID in the Projects table is required:

```
Declare @TheCount Integer
```

You then set that value:

```
Select @TheCount = Count(ProjectID) from Projects
     Where ProjectID = @TheID
```

and return it:

```
Return @TheCount
```

PercentComplete User-Defined Function

The SQL Server back-end database contains a view called ProjectStatus that is used to produce the Project Status report in the Access front end. The view contains a field that shows the percentage of the project that is complete. The field needs to display the text "NA" if the project does not have any steps. The PercentComplete function returns the value for that column in the view.

```
CREATE FUNCTION PercentComplete (@StepsComplete integer, @TotalSteps integer)
RETURNS varchar(6) AS
BEGIN
     Declare @TempReturn varchar(6)
     If @TotalSteps = 0
          BEGIN
               Set @TempReturn =  'NA'
          END
     Else
          BEGIN
               Set @TempReturn =  Convert
               (varchar(5), @StepsComplete * 100 / @TotalSteps) + '%'
          END
     Return @TempReturn
END
```

The function requires two parameters. These are the values for the steps completed and the total number of steps:

```
CREATE FUNCTION PercentComplete (@StepsComplete integer, @TotalSteps integer)
```

The function will return a string that is six characters long:

```
RETURNS varchar(6) AS
```

Within the function, you need a variable to store the return value:

```
Declare @TempReturn varchar(6)
```

You then check to see how many steps are in the project:

```
If @TotalSteps = 0
```

If the value is 0, the text "NA" is displayed:

```
Set @TempReturn =  'NA'
```

Otherwise, you return the total number of steps complete as a percentage of the total number of steps:

```
Set @TempReturn =  Convert
      (varchar(5), @StepsComplete * 100 / @TotalSteps) + '%'
```

The value calculated within the If statement is returned from the function:

```
Return @TempReturn
```

Stored Procedures

ProjectAdd Stored Procedure

The ProjectAdd stored procedure provides the mechanism for adding records to the Projects table.

```
CREATE PROCEDURE ProjectAdd
@ReturnStatus integer OUTPUT,
@ReturnMessage varchar(50) OUTPUT,
@NewID integer OUTPUT,
@ProjectName varchar(50),
@StartDate datetime,
@ExpectedCompletionDate datetime,
@ProjectDescription varchar(5000)
AS
```

```
If @ExpectedCompletionDate < @StartDate
      BEGIN
            set @ReturnStatus = 0
            set @ReturnMessage = 'Expected completion date must ' +
                  ' be after start date!'
            set @NewID = 0
      END
Else
      BEGIN
            Insert Into Projects
                  (ProjectName, StartDate, ExpectedCompletionDate,
                        ProjectDescription)
                  values (@ProjectName, @StartDate,
                        @ExpectedCompletionDate, @ProjectDescription)
            set @ReturnStatus = 1
            set @ReturnMessage = 'Success'
            set @NewID = @@Identity
      END
GO
```

The procedure requires three output parameters. The first two are used to pass back the status of the call to this procedure:

```
@ReturnStatus integer OUTPUT,
@ReturnMessage varchar(50) OUTPUT,
```

The next parameter returns the ID of the project just added:

```
@NewID integer OUTPUT,
```

The rest of the parameters are used to pass in the values for the columns being inserted into the Projects table:

```
@ProjectName varchar(50),
@StartDate datetime,
@ExpectedCompletionDate datetime,
@ProjectDescription varchar(5000)
```

But before you insert a record into the Projects table, you need to make sure that the end date is after the start date:

```
If @ExpectedCompletionDate < @StartDate
```

If it isn't, you return an error message to the calling application:

```
set @ReturnStatus = 0
set @ReturnMessage = 'Expected completion date must ' +
      ' be after start date!'
```

and set the ID of the record being added to an invalid value:

```
set @NewID = 0
```

Otherwise, you can insert a new record in the Projects table based on the values passed into this procedure:

```
Insert Into Projects
      (ProjectName, StartDate, ExpectedCompletionDate,
      ProjectDescription)
      values (@ProjectName, @StartDate,
      @ExpectedCompletionDate, @ProjectDescription)
```

You then return a success message:

```
set @ReturnStatus = 1
set @ReturnMessage = 'Success'
```

and the ID of the record just added to the database:

```
set @NewID = @@Identity
```

ProjectEdit Stored Procedure

The ProjectEdit stored procedure provides the mechanism for editing an existing record in the Projects table.

```
CREATE PROCEDURE ProjectEdit
@ReturnStatus integer OUTPUT,
@ReturnMessage varchar(50) OUTPUT,
@ProjectID integer,
@ProjectName varchar(50),
@StartDate datetime,
@ExpectedCompletionDate datetime,
@ProjectDescription varchar(5000)
AS
If (dbo.ProjectIDCheck(@ProjectID)) = 0
      BEGIN
            set @ReturnStatus = 0
            set @ReturnMessage = 'The Project ID entered ' +
                  'was not found.'
      END
Else
      If @ExpectedCompletionDate < @StartDate
```

```
            BEGIN
                  set @ReturnStatus = 0
            set @ReturnMessage = 'Expected completion date must ' +
                  ' be after start date!'
            END
      Else
            BEGIN
                  Update Projects set
                        ProjectName = @ProjectName,
                        StartDate = @StartDate,
                        ExpectedCompletionDate = @ExpectedCompletionDate,
                        ProjectDescription = @ProjectDescription
                        Where ProjectID = @ProjectID
                  set @ReturnStatus = 1
                  set @ReturnMessage = 'Success.'
            END
GO
```

The procedure expects parameters that are used to return a status message regarding the current call:

```
@ReturnStatus integer OUTPUT,
@ReturnMessage varchar(50) OUTPUT,
```

The procedure also expects to receive the ID of the project to be edited:

```
@ProjectID integer,
```

and the new values for the editable fields:

```
@ProjectName varchar(50),
@StartDate datetime,
@ExpectedCompletionDate datetime,
@ProjectDescription varchar(5000)
```

Before editing a record, you need to perform two checks. First, you check to make sure that the ID of the record being edited exists:

```
If (dbo.ProjectIDCheck(@ProjectID)) = 0
```

If it doesn't, you return an error message to the calling application:

```
set @ReturnStatus = 0
set @ReturnMessage = 'The Project ID entered ' +
      'was not found.'
```

Next, you make sure that the end date is after the start date:

```
If @ExpectedCompletionDate < @StartDate
```

If it isn't, you return a different error message:

```
set @ReturnStatus = 0
set @ReturnMessage = 'Expected completion date must ' +
      ' be after start date!'
```

Otherwise, you can update the requested project based on the values passed into this procedure:

```
Update Projects set
      ProjectName = @ProjectName,
      StartDate = @StartDate,
      ExpectedCompletionDate = @ExpectedCompletionDate,
      ProjectDescription = @ProjectDescription
      Where ProjectID = @ProjectID
```

and return a success message:

```
set @ReturnStatus = 1
set @ReturnMessage = 'Success.'
```

ProjectDelete Stored Procedure

The ProjectDelete stored procedure allows the calling application to delete a record from the Projects table.

```
CREATE PROCEDURE ProjectDelete
@ReturnStatus integer OUTPUT,
@ReturnMessage varchar(50) OUTPUT,
@ProjectID integer
AS
If (dbo.ProjectIDCheck(@ProjectID)) = 0
      BEGIN
            set @ReturnStatus = 0
```

```
            set @ReturnMessage = 'The Project ID entered ' +
                  'was not found.'
      END
Else
      BEGIN
            Delete from Projects
                  Where ProjectID = @ProjectID
            set @ReturnStatus = 1
            set @ReturnMessage = 'Success.'
      END
GO
```

The procedure expects three parameters. The first two are output parameters and will be used to pass back a message from this procedure:

```
@ReturnStatus integer OUTPUT,
@ReturnMessage varchar(50) OUTPUT,
```

The other parameter is the ID of the project being deleted:

```
@ProjectID integer
```

Before deleting, you make sure that the record being deleted is valid:

```
If (dbo.ProjectIDCheck(@ProjectID)) = 0
```

If it isn't, you return an error message:

```
set @ReturnStatus = 0
set @ReturnMessage = 'The Project ID entered ' +
      'was not found.'
```

Otherwise, you delete the offending record:

```
Delete from Projects
      Where ProjectID = @ProjectID
```

and return a success message:

```
set @ReturnStatus = 1
set @ReturnMessage = 'Success.'
```

ProjectRecord Stored Procedure

The ProjectRecord stored procedure is used to return the contents of a specific project record or the first project record in the Projects table.

```
CREATE PROCEDURE ProjectRecord
@ReturnStatus integer OUTPUT,
@ReturnMessage varchar(50) OUTPUT,
@ProjectID integer = 0 OUTPUT,
@ProjectName varchar(50) OUTPUT,
@StepsCompleted integer = 0 OUTPUT,
@TotalSteps integer = 0 OUTPUT,
@StartDate varchar(50) OUTPUT,
@ExpectedCompletionDate varchar(50) OUTPUT,
@Status varchar(50) OUTPUT,
@ProjectDescription varchar(5000) OUTPUT
AS
If (dbo.ProjectIDCheck(@ProjectID)) = 0 and @ProjectID <> 0
      BEGIN
            set @ReturnStatus = 0
            set @ReturnMessage = 'The EventID entered ' +
                  'was not found.'
      END
Else
      If @ProjectID = 0
            BEGIN
                  Declare CurProject Cursor
                  For Select ProjectID, ProjectName, StepsCompleted,
                        TotalSteps, StartDate, ExpectedCompletionDate,
                        Status, ProjectDescription
                        From Projects
                        Where ProjectID = (Select Min(ProjectID)
                        from Projects)
                  Open CurProject
                  Fetch CurProject
                        Into @ProjectID, @ProjectName, @StepsCompleted,
                        @TotalSteps, @StartDate, @ExpectedCompletionDate,
                        @Status, @ProjectDescription
                  If @@Fetch_Status = 0
                        BEGIN
                              set @ReturnStatus = 1
                              set @ReturnMessage = 'Success'
                              Close CurProject
```

```
                        Deallocate CurProject
                END
            Else
                BEGIN
                        set @ReturnStatus = 1
                        set @ReturnMessage = 'No records found'
                        set @ProjectName = ''
                        set @StepsCompleted = 0
                        set @TotalSteps = 0
                        set @StartDate = ''
                        set @ExpectedCompletionDate = ''
                        set @Status = ''
                        set @ProjectDescription = ''
                        Close CurProject
                        Deallocate CurProject
                END
            END
    Else
        BEGIN
            Declare CurProject Cursor
            For Select ProjectName, StepsCompleted,
                TotalSteps, StartDate, ExpectedCompletionDate,
                Status, ProjectDescription
                From Projects
                Where ProjectID = @ProjectID
            Open CurProject
            Fetch CurProject
                Into @ProjectName, @StepsCompleted,
                @TotalSteps, @StartDate, @ExpectedCompletionDate,
                @Status, @ProjectDescription
            set @ReturnStatus = 1
            set @ReturnMessage = 'Success'
            Close CurProject
            Deallocate CurProject
        END
GO
```

The project requires many parameters. The first two are used to return the status of the call to the procedure:

```
@ReturnStatus integer OUTPUT,
@ReturnMessage varchar(50) OUTPUT,
```

The next is an input/output parameter that is optional. If omitted, it is set to the value 0. The parameter is used to store and return the ID of the record to be returned.

If the parameter has the value of 0, the procedure returns the first record in the Projects table:

```
@ProjectID integer = 0 OUTPUT,
```

You also need output parameters that are used to return all the values for the columns in the desired record:

```
@ProjectName varchar(50) OUTPUT,
@StepsCompleted integer = 0 OUTPUT,
@TotalSteps integer = 0 OUTPUT,
@StartDate varchar(50) OUTPUT,
@ExpectedCompletionDate varchar(50) OUTPUT,
@Status varchar(50) OUTPUT,
@ProjectDescription varchar(5000) OUTPUT
```

The first condition you check for is where the ID of the project is not 0 and is not found in the Projects table:

```
If (dbo.ProjectIDCheck(@ProjectID)) = 0 and @ProjectID <> 0
```

In that case, you have an invalid ID request and you pass back an error message:

```
set @ReturnStatus = 0
set @ReturnMessage = 'The EventID entered ' +
      'was not found.'
```

The next condition you test for is where the calling application is seeking the first record in the table:

```
If @ProjectID = 0
```

So you will need a cursor object to retrieve the record that has the lowest ID in the table as returned from the subquery:

```
Declare CurProject Cursor
      For Select ProjectID, ProjectName, StepsCompleted,
            TotalSteps, StartDate, ExpectedCompletionDate,
            Status, ProjectDescription
            From Projects
            Where ProjectID = (Select Min(ProjectID)
            from Projects)
```

That cursor is opened:

```
Open CurProject
```

and the record is retrieved into your output parameters:

```
Fetch CurProject
      Into @ProjectID, @ProjectName, @StepsCompleted,
      @TotalSteps, @StartDate, @ExpectedCompletionDate,
      @Status, @ProjectDescription
```

You then make sure you found a record:

```
If @@Fetch_Status = 0
```

If you did, you return a success message along with the output parameters set previously:

```
set @ReturnStatus = 1
set @ReturnMessage = 'Success'
```

You also need to clean up your Cursor object:

```
Close CurProject
Deallocate CurProject
```

If the code flows here, that means that there are not any records in the table. In that case, you return such a message:

```
set @ReturnStatus = 1
set @ReturnMessage = 'No records found'
```

and empty values for all the fields in the record:

```
set @ProjectName = ''
set @StepsCompleted = 0
set @TotalSteps = 0
set @StartDate = ''
set @ExpectedCompletionDate = ''
set @Status = ''
set @ProjectDescription = ''
```

You also need to close and release your Cursor object:

```
Close CurProject
Deallocate CurProject
```

The last code block in this procedure fires when the ID passed in is a valid ID of an existing Project record. In that case, you will need a Cursor object:

```
Declare CurProject Cursor
```

that is set to retrieve the values for the desired project:

```
For Select ProjectName, StepsCompleted,
      TotalSteps, StartDate, ExpectedCompletionDate,
      Status, ProjectDescription
      From Projects
      Where ProjectID = @ProjectID
```

That cursor is opened:

```
Open CurProject
```

and the values retrieved into your output parameters:

```
Fetch CurProject
      Into @ProjectName, @StepsCompleted,
      @TotalSteps, @StartDate, @ExpectedCompletionDate,
      @Status, @ProjectDescription
```

You then return a success message:

```
set @ReturnStatus = 1
set @ReturnMessage = 'Success'
```

and clean up your Cursor object:

```
Close CurProject
Deallocate CurProject
```

ProjectComboBox Stored Procedure

On the Projects form in the Access front end, the user uses a combo box to navigate to the records in the Projects table. The ProjectComboBox stored procedure returns the values for that list.

```
CREATE PROCEDURE ProjectComboBox
@TheList varchar(8000) OUTPUT
AS
Declare
@ProjectID varchar(10),
@ProjectName varchar(50)
Declare CurProjects Cursor
For Select ProjectID, ProjectName from Projects
Order By ProjectName
Select @TheList = ''
Open CurProjects
Fetch CurProjects
      Into @ProjectID, @ProjectNAme
While @@Fetch_Status = 0
      BEGIN
            Select @TheList = @TheList + @ProjectID + ';"'
                  + @ProjectName + '";'
            Fetch CurProjects
                  Into @ProjectID, @ProjectNAme
      END
Close CurProjects
Deallocate CurProjects
GO
```

The procedure has a single output parameter, the list for the combo box:

```
@TheList varchar(8000) OUTPUT
```

The procedure needs a couple of local variables. One is used to store the ID of the project:

```
@ProjectID varchar(10),
```

the other, the name of the project:

```
@ProjectName varchar(50)
```

You also need a Cursor object:

```
Declare CurProjects Cursor
```

that will be set to the values in the Projects table:

```
For Select ProjectID, ProjectName from Projects
      Order By ProjectName
```

You then initialize the return value to an empty string:

```
Select @TheList = ''
```

and open your cursor:

```
Open CurProjects
```

placing the values of the first record in the cursor into your local variables:

```
Fetch CurProjects
      Into @ProjectID, @ProjectNAme
```

Next, you enter a loop to process each of the records in the Cursor object:

```
While @@Fetch_Status = 0
```

The ID and name of the project retrieved through the Cursor object are appended to the return value:

```
Select @TheList = @TheList + @ProjectID + ';"'
      + @ProjectName + '";'
```

Before you retrieve the next record and loop:

```
Fetch CurProjects
      Into @ProjectID, @ProjectNAme
```

After the loop, you close and release the resources of your Cursor object:

```
Close CurProjects
Deallocate CurProjects
```

ProjectStepAdd Stored Procedure

The ProjectStepAdd stored procedure provides the mechanism for adding a record to the ProjectSteps table.

```
CREATE PROCEDURE ProjectStepAdd
@ReturnStatus integer OUTPUT,
```

```
@ReturnMessage varchar(50) OUTPUT,
@ProjectID int,
@StepName varchar(50),
@StepDescription varchar(2000)
AS
BEGIN
      Insert Into ProjectSteps
            (ProjectID, StepName, StepDescription)
            values (@ProjectID, @StepName, @StepDescription)
      set @ReturnStatus = 1
      set @ReturnMessage = 'Success'
END
GO
```

The procedure requires two output parameters, which are used to pass back the status of the call to this procedure:

```
@ReturnStatus integer OUTPUT,
@ReturnMessage varchar(50) OUTPUT,
```

The procedure also requires three input parameters that contain the values for the editable fields of the record to be added:

```
@ProjectID int,
@StepName varchar(50),
@StepDescription varchar(2000)
```

You then use a T-SQL Insert statement to add the new record based on the values passed in:

```
Insert Into ProjectSteps
      (ProjectID, StepName, StepDescription)
      values (@ProjectID, @StepName, @StepDescription)
```

and you return a success message:

```
set @ReturnStatus = 1
set @ReturnMessage = 'Success'
```

ProjectStepComplete Stored Procedure

On the Projects form in the Access front end, there is a button labeled Mark Step as Complete. That button changes the status of a step from Pending to Complete. The ProjectStepComplete stored procedure performs that task.

```
CREATE PROCEDURE ProjectStepComplete
@ReturnStatus integer OUTPUT,
@ReturnMessage varchar(50) OUTPUT,
@ProjectStepID integer
AS
BEGIN
      Update ProjectSteps
            set Status = 'Complete'
            Where ProjectStepID = @ProjectStepID
      set @ReturnStatus = 1
      set @ReturnMessage = 'Success.'
END
GO
```

The procedure requires three parameters. The first two are for the return of a status message:

```
@ReturnStatus integer OUTPUT,
@ReturnMessage varchar(50) OUTPUT,
```

and the third is used to pass in the ID of the step that needs to be marked as complete:

```
@ProjectStepID integer
```

You then update the status of the desired step:

```
Update ProjectSteps
      set Status = 'Complete'
      Where ProjectStepID = @ProjectStepID
```

and return a success message:

```
set @ReturnStatus = 1
set @ReturnMessage = 'Success.'
```

ProjectStepDelete Stored Procedure

The ProjectStepDelete stored procedure provides the mechanism for the calling application to delete a record from the ProjectSteps table.

```
CREATE PROCEDURE ProjectStepDelete
@ReturnStatus integer OUTPUT,
@ReturnMessage varchar(50) OUTPUT,
@ProjectStepID integer
AS
BEGIN
      Delete from ProjectSteps
            Where ProjectStepID = @ProjectStepID
      set @ReturnStatus = 1
      set @ReturnMessage = 'Success.'
END
GO
```

The procedure requires parameters that return the status of the call:

```
@ReturnStatus integer OUTPUT,
@ReturnMessage varchar(50) OUTPUT,
```

and a parameter that passes in the ID of the step to be deleted:

```
@ProjectStepID integer
```

You then delete the offending step:

```
Delete from ProjectSteps
      Where ProjectStepID = @ProjectStepID
```

and return a success message:

```
set @ReturnStatus = 1
set @ReturnMessage = 'Success.'
```

ProjectStepListBox Stored Procedure

The Projects form in the Access front end contains a list box that lists all the steps in the current project. The ProjectStepListBox stored procedure returns the text for that list box.

```
CREATE PROCEDURE ProjectStepListBox
@ProjectID int,
@TheList varchar(8000) OUTPUT
AS
Declare
@ProjectStepID varchar(10),
@StepName varchar(50),
@Status varchar(50),
@StepDescription varchar(100)
Declare CurSteps Cursor
For Select ProjectStepID, StepName, Status, StepDescription
      from ProjectSteps
      Where ProjectID = @ProjectID
Select @TheList = ''
Open CurSteps
Fetch CurSteps
      Into @ProjectStepID, @StepName,
      @Status, @StepDescription
While @@Fetch_Status = 0
      Begin
            Select @TheList = @TheList + @ProjectStepID
                  + ';"' + @StepName + ' - '
                  + @Status + '";"' + @StepDescription
                  + '";'
            Fetch CurSteps
                  Into @ProjectStepID, @StepName,
                  @Status, @StepDescription
      End
Close CurSteps
Deallocate CurSteps
GO
```

The procedure has one input parameter, the ID of the project for which you want steps retrieved:

```
@ProjectID int,
```

The procedure requires a single output parameter, which will return the value for the list:

```
@TheList varchar(8000) OUTPUT
```

Locally, the procedure needs variables that will store the fields for the records in the ProjectSteps table:

```
@ProjectStepID varchar(10),
@StepName varchar(50),
@Status varchar(50),
@StepDescription varchar(100)
```

You will also need a Cursor object:

```
Declare CurSteps Cursor
```

that is set to retrieve data from the ProjectSteps table:

```
For Select ProjectStepID, StepName, Status, StepDescription
      from ProjectSteps
      Where ProjectID = @ProjectID
```

Next, you need to initialize your return value:

```
Select @TheList = ''
```

open your cursor:

```
Open CurSteps
```

and grab the first record from the ProjectSteps table, placing the fields retrieved into the local variables:

```
Fetch CurSteps
      Into @ProjectStepID, @StepName,
      @Status, @StepDescription
```

You then enter a loop so that you can process each of the records in the Cursor object:

```
While @@Fetch_Status = 0
```

The text of the return value is then formatted so that the fields will be displayed correctly in a list box:

```
Select @TheList = @TheList + @ProjectStepID
      + ';"' + @StepName + ' - '
      + @Status + '";"' + @StepDescription
      + '";'
```

The next record is then retrieved before you loop:

```
Fetch CurSteps
      Into @ProjectStepID, @StepName,
      @Status, @StepDescription
```

After the loop you need to clean up the Cursor object:

```
Close CurSteps
Deallocate CurSteps
```

Views

ProjectStatus View

The ProjectStatus view returns summary information about each project. The data is then used by the Project Status report in the front-end Access application.

```
SELECT ProjectName, StepsCompleted, TotalSteps,
      dbo.PercentComplete(StepsCompleted, TotalSteps)
      AS CompletePercent, StartDate,
      ExpectedCompletionDate, Status
      FROM      dbo.Projects
```

NOTE

The CompletePercent column gets its value by calling the PercentComplete function discussed in the "User-Defined Functions" section.

Application Notes

C13FrontEnd.mdb

The Access front end does not contain any of its own local tables. It relies entirely on the SQL Server back end for the data. The front end does link to the ProjectStatus view, which is used for the Project Status report. For the application to work correctly, a DSN that points to the back end database must be created, and it must have the following name:

```
C13ProjectManagement
```

Modules

GeneralProcs Module

The Access front end contains a single module called GeneralProcs. In the General Declarations of that module, a database connection object is declared as Public so that it is available to any of the procedures in the application:

```
Public MyDB As New ADODB.Connection
```

When the user opens the application, an AutoExec macro fires. That macro calls a procedure named StartUp. That procedure sets up your database connection.

```
Public Function StartUp()
    On Error GoTo HandleError
    Dim SQLUserName As String
    Dim SQLPassword As String
    SQLUserName = InputBox("Please enter your user name.", "User Name")
    SQLPassword = InputBox("Please enter your password.", "Password")
    MyDB.Open "DSN=C13ProjectManagement;UID=" & SQLUserName _
        & ";Password=" & SQLPassword
    DoCmd.OpenForm "frmMenu"
    Exit Function
HandleError:
    MsgBox Err.Number & ": " & Err.Description & _
```

```
        ". Closing application.", vbCritical, "Can't Start Application"
    Application.CloseCurrentDatabase
End Function
```

The procedure will need to trap any errors that occur:

```
On Error GoTo HandleError
```

You will need variables to store the name and password of the user:

```
Dim SQLUserName As String
Dim SQLPassword As String
```

You then prompt the user for that information:

```
SQLUserName = InputBox("Please enter your user name.", "User Name")
SQLPassword = InputBox("Please enter your password.", "Password")
```

You then use the name and password that they entered to attempt a connection to the database:

```
MyDB.Open "DSN=C13ProjectManagement;UID=" & SQLUserName _
      & ";Password=" & SQLPassword
```

If the login is successful, the code flows here and you open the menu form:

```
DoCmd.OpenForm "frmMenu"
```

If not, the code flows here:

```
HandleError:
```

You then inform the user of the problem:

```
MsgBox Err.Number & ": " & Err.Description & _
      ". Closing application.", vbCritical, "Can't Start Application"
```

and close the database:

```
Application.CloseCurrentDatabase
```

Forms

Menu Form

The code on the Menu form allows the user to enter the different parts of the front-end application. When the user clicks the Projects button, the OpenForm method of the DoCmd object is used to take them to the Projects form:

```
Private Sub cmdProjects_Click()
    DoCmd.OpenForm "frmProjects"
End Sub
```

The other button on the form uses the OpenReport method to display the Project Status report when it is clicked:

```
Private Sub cmdProjectStatus_Click()
    DoCmd.OpenReport "Project Status", acViewPreview
End Sub
```

Projects Form

The code on the Projects form provides all the needed functionality to manage the projects through the back-end stored procedures. The form declares a variable with Private scope in the General Declarations section. That variable is used to store the ID of the current project and is available to any of the procedures on this form:

```
Private CurrentID As Long
```

The form contains three user-defined procedures that are called from other procedures on the form. The first displays a record on the form.

```
Public Sub DisplayProjectRecord(ID2Use As Long)
    Dim cmdProject As New ADODB.Command
    Set cmdProject.ActiveConnection = MyDB
    cmdProject.CommandText = "ProjectRecord"
    cmdProject.CommandType = adCmdStoredProc
    cmdProject.Parameters.Append cmdProject.CreateParameter _
        ("ReturnStatus", adInteger, adParamOutput)
    cmdProject.Parameters.Append cmdProject.CreateParameter _
        ("ReturnMessage", adVarChar, adParamOutput, 50)
    cmdProject.Parameters.Append cmdProject.CreateParameter _
```

```
        ("ProjectID", adInteger, adParamInputOutput, , ID2Use)
    cmdProject.Parameters.Append cmdProject.CreateParameter _
        ("ProjectName", adVarChar, adParamOutput, 50)
    cmdProject.Parameters.Append cmdProject.CreateParameter _
        ("StepsCompleted", adInteger, adParamOutput)
    cmdProject.Parameters.Append cmdProject.CreateParameter _
        ("TotalSteps", adInteger, adParamOutput)
    cmdProject.Parameters.Append cmdProject.CreateParameter _
        ("StartDate", adVarChar, adParamOutput, 50)
    cmdProject.Parameters.Append cmdProject.CreateParameter _
        ("ExpectedCompletionDate", adVarChar, adParamOutput, 50)
    cmdProject.Parameters.Append cmdProject.CreateParameter _
        ("Status", adVarChar, adParamOutput, 50)
    cmdProject.Parameters.Append cmdProject.CreateParameter _
        ("ProjectDescription", adVarChar, adParamOutput, 5000)
    cmdProject.Execute
    If cmdProject("ReturnStatus") = 1 Then
        CurrentID = cmdProject("ProjectID")
        [txtProjectName] = cmdProject("ProjectName")
        lblSteps.Caption = "Steps Completed: " _
            & cmdProject("StepsCompleted") _
            & ", Total Steps: " _
            & cmdProject("TotalSteps")
        [txtStartDate] = cmdProject("StartDate")
        [txtExpectedCompletionDate] = cmdProject("ExpectedCompletionDate")
        lblTitle.Caption = "Project: " _
            & cmdProject("Status")
        [txtProjectDescription] = cmdProject("ProjectDescription")
        txtProjectName.SetFocus
    Else
        MsgBox cmdProject("ReturnMessage")
    End If
End Sub
```

The procedure expects a single parameter, the ID of the project for which data is to be retrieved:

```
Public Sub DisplayProjectRecord(ID2Use As Long)
```

The procedure will need a Command object:

```
Dim cmdProject As New ADODB.Command
```

which is connected to the active database connection:

```
Set cmdProject.ActiveConnection = MyDB
```

The command will call ProjectRecord:

```
cmdProject.CommandText = "ProjectRecord"
```

which is a stored procedure:

```
cmdProject.CommandType = adCmdStoredProc
```

The call expects many parameters. The first two are for the return message from the stored procedure:

```
cmdProject.Parameters.Append cmdProject.CreateParameter _
      ("ReturnStatus", adInteger, adParamOutput)
cmdProject.Parameters.Append cmdProject.CreateParameter _
      ("ReturnMessage", adVarChar, adParamOutput, 50)
```

The next passes into the stored procedure the ID of the project, which is actually passed into this procedure:

```
cmdProject.Parameters.Append cmdProject.CreateParameter _
      ("ProjectID", adInteger, adParamInputOutput, , ID2Use)
```

The remaining parameters are used to retrieve the values for the fields on the form for the selected project record:

```
cmdProject.Parameters.Append cmdProject.CreateParameter _
      ("ProjectName", adVarChar, adParamOutput, 50)
cmdProject.Parameters.Append cmdProject.CreateParameter _
      ("StepsCompleted", adInteger, adParamOutput)
cmdProject.Parameters.Append cmdProject.CreateParameter _
      ("TotalSteps", adInteger, adParamOutput)
cmdProject.Parameters.Append cmdProject.CreateParameter _
      ("StartDate", adVarChar, adParamOutput, 50)
cmdProject.Parameters.Append cmdProject.CreateParameter _
      ("ExpectedCompletionDate", adVarChar, adParamOutput, 50)
cmdProject.Parameters.Append cmdProject.CreateParameter _
      ("Status", adVarChar, adParamOutput, 50)
cmdProject.Parameters.Append cmdProject.CreateParameter _
      ("ProjectDescription", adVarChar, adParamOutput, 5000)
```

You then make the call to the stored procedure:

```
cmdProject.Execute
```

and check to see whether it ran successfully:

```
If cmdProject("ReturnStatus") = 1 Then
```

If it did, you set the ID of the current project:

```
CurrentID = cmdProject("ProjectID")
```

populate the text boxes and labels on the form:

```
[txtProjectName] = cmdProject("ProjectName")
lblSteps.Caption = "Steps Completed: " _
      & cmdProject("StepsCompleted") _
      & ", Total Steps: " _
      & cmdProject("TotalSteps")
[txtStartDate] = cmdProject("StartDate")
[txtExpectedCompletionDate] = cmdProject("ExpectedCompletionDate")
lblTitle.Caption = "Project: " _
      & cmdProject("Status")
[txtProjectDescription] = cmdProject("ProjectDescription")
```

and set focus to the first field on the form:

```
txtProjectName.SetFocus
```

Otherwise, you display the error returned from the procedure:

```
MsgBox cmdProject("ReturnMessage")
```

The next procedure is used to populate the contents of the combo box on the form.

```
Public Sub RefreshComboBox()
    Dim cmdList As New ADODB.Command
    Set cmdList.ActiveConnection = MyDB
    cmdList.CommandText = "ProjectComboBox"
    cmdList.CommandType = adCmdStoredProc
    cmdList.Parameters.Append cmdList.CreateParameter _
        ("TheList", adVarChar, adParamOutput, 8000)
    cmdList.Execute
```

```
    cmbProjectID.RowSource = cmdList("TheList")
End Sub
```

The procedure will need a Command object:

```
Dim cmdList As New ADODB.Command
```

that uses your database connection:

```
Set cmdList.ActiveConnection = MyDB
```

The Command object will call the ProjectComboBox stored procedure:

```
cmdList.CommandText = "ProjectComboBox"
cmdList.CommandType = adCmdStoredProc
```

and pass to it a parameter that will contain the list for the combo box after the call:

```
cmdList.Parameters.Append cmdList.CreateParameter _
      ("TheList", adVarChar, adParamOutput, 8000)
```

You then make the call to the stored procedure:

```
cmdList.Execute
```

and use the return from the call to populate the combo box:

```
cmbProjectID.RowSource = cmdList("TheList")
```

The next procedure populates the list box on the form, which displays the steps for the current project.

```
Public Sub RefreshStepsList()
    Dim cmdList As New ADODB.Command
    Set cmdList.ActiveConnection = MyDB
    cmdList.CommandText = "ProjectStepListBox"
    cmdList.CommandType = adCmdStoredProc
    cmdList.Parameters.Append cmdList.CreateParameter _
        ("ProjectID", adInteger, adParamInput, , CurrentID)
    cmdList.Parameters.Append cmdList.CreateParameter _
        ("TheList", adVarChar, adParamOutput, 8000)
    cmdList.Execute
    lstSteps.RowSource = cmdList("TheList")
End Sub
```

The procedure needs a Command object:

```
Dim cmdList As New ADODB.Command
```

which points to the database pointed to by the Public database connection:

```
Set cmdList.ActiveConnection = MyDB
```

The command will call the ProjectStepListBox stored procedure:

```
cmdList.CommandText = "ProjectStepListBox"
cmdList.CommandType = adCmdStoredProc
```

and pass to it the ID of the project for which you want steps retrieved as determined by the ID of the current project:

```
cmdList.Parameters.Append cmdList.CreateParameter _
      ("ProjectID", adInteger, adParamInput, , CurrentID)
```

You also pass to it a parameter that will contain the text for the list after the call:

```
cmdList.Parameters.Append cmdList.CreateParameter _
      ("TheList", adVarChar, adParamOutput, 8000)
```

Next, the stored procedure is executed:

```
cmdList.Execute
```

and the return from the call is used to populate the list box:

```
lstSteps.RowSource = cmdList("TheList")
```

When the form first loads, the code in the Load event fires.

```
Private Sub Form_Load()
    DisplayProjectRecord 0
    RefreshComboBox
    RefreshStepsList
End Sub
```

The procedure calls your procedure, DisplayProjectRecord discussed previously, to display the first record in the Projects table:

```
DisplayProjectRecord 0
```

list all the projects in the combo box:

```
RefreshComboBox
```

and display the steps for the current project in the list box:

```
RefreshStepsList
```

Each time the user changes the value in the Projects combo box, the Change event fires.

```
Private Sub cmbProjectID_Change()
    DisplayProjectRecord [cmbProjectID]
    RefreshStepsList
End Sub
```

The procedure displays the contents of the selected project:

```
DisplayProjectRecord [cmbProjectID]
```

and displays its steps:

```
RefreshStepsList
```

The next event fires when the Add button is clicked:

```
Private Sub cmdAdd_Click()
    Dim cmdProject As New ADODB.Command
    Set cmdProject.ActiveConnection = MyDB
    cmdProject.CommandText = "ProjectAdd"
    cmdProject.CommandType = adCmdStoredProc
    cmdProject.Parameters.Append cmdProject.CreateParameter _
        ("ReturnStatus", adInteger, adParamOutput)
    cmdProject.Parameters.Append cmdProject.CreateParameter _
        ("ReturnMessage", adVarChar, adParamOutput, 50)
    cmdProject.Parameters.Append cmdProject.CreateParameter _
        ("ProjectID", adInteger, adParamOutput)
    cmdProject.Parameters.Append cmdProject.CreateParameter _
        ("ProjectName", adVarChar, adParamInput, 50, _
        Replace([txtProjectName], "'", "''", 1, -1, vbTextCompare))
```

```
    cmdProject.Parameters.Append cmdProject.CreateParameter _
        ("StartDate", adVarChar, adParamInput, 50, [txtStartDate])
    cmdProject.Parameters.Append cmdProject.CreateParameter _
        ("ExpectedCompletionDate", adVarChar, adParamInput, 50, _
        [txtExpectedCompletionDate])
    cmdProject.Parameters.Append cmdProject.CreateParameter _
        ("ProjectDescription", adVarChar, adParamInput, 1000, _
        Replace([txtProjectDescription], "'", "''", 1, -1, vbTextCompare))
    cmdProject.Execute
    If cmdProject("ReturnStatus") = 1 Then
        CurrentID = cmdProject("ProjectID")
        RefreshComboBox
        RefreshStepsList
        txtProjectName.SetFocus
    Else
        MsgBox cmdProject("ReturnMessage")
    End If
End Sub
```

The procedure needs a Command object:

```
Dim cmdProject As New ADODB.Command
```

that will use your Public database connection:

```
Set cmdProject.ActiveConnection = MyDB
```

The command will call the ProjectAdd stored procedure:

```
cmdProject.CommandText = "ProjectAdd"
cmdProject.CommandType = adCmdStoredProc
```

The command needs numerous parameters. The first two are output parameters that will contain the status of the call:

```
cmdProject.Parameters.Append cmdProject.CreateParameter _
      ("ReturnStatus", adInteger, adParamOutput)
cmdProject.Parameters.Append cmdProject.CreateParameter _
      ("ReturnMessage", adVarChar, adParamOutput, 50)
```

The next will contain the ID of the project just added.

```
cmdProject.Parameters.Append cmdProject.CreateParameter _
      ("ProjectID", adInteger, adParamOutput)
```

The rest of the parameters are input parameters that contain the values for the fields in the new record:

```
cmdProject.Parameters.Append cmdProject.CreateParameter _
      ("ProjectName", adVarChar, adParamInput, 50, _
      Replace([txtProjectName], "'", "''", 1, -1, vbTextCompare))
cmdProject.Parameters.Append cmdProject.CreateParameter _
      ("StartDate", adVarChar, adParamInput, 50, [txtStartDate])
cmdProject.Parameters.Append cmdProject.CreateParameter _
      ("ExpectedCompletionDate", adVarChar, adParamInput, 50, _
      [txtExpectedCompletionDate])
cmdProject.Parameters.Append cmdProject.CreateParameter _
      ("ProjectDescription", adVarChar, adParamInput, 1000, _
      Replace([txtProjectDescription], "'", "''", 1, -1, vbTextCompare))
```

You then make the call to the stored procedure:

```
cmdProject.Execute
```

If it returns successfully:

```
If cmdProject("ReturnStatus") = 1 Then
```

you use the ID of the project returned:

```
CurrentID = cmdProject("ProjectID")
```

refresh the combo box and the list box:

```
RefreshComboBox
RefreshStepsList
```

and set the focus back to the Project Name text box:

```
txtProjectName.SetFocus
```

Otherwise, you display the error message:

```
MsgBox cmdProject("ReturnMessage")
```

The next code block fires when the Update button is clicked.

```
Private Sub cmdUpdate_Click()
    Dim cmdProject As New ADODB.Command
    If CurrentID = "0" Then
        cmdAdd_Click
        Exit Sub
    End If
    Set cmdProject.ActiveConnection = MyDB
    cmdProject.CommandText = "ProjectEdit"
    cmdProject.CommandType = adCmdStoredProc
    cmdProject.Parameters.Append cmdProject.CreateParameter _
        ("ReturnStatus", adInteger, adParamOutput)
    cmdProject.Parameters.Append cmdProject.CreateParameter _
        ("ReturnMessage", adVarChar, adParamOutput, 50)
    cmdProject.Parameters.Append cmdProject.CreateParameter _
        ("ProjectID", adInteger, adParamInput, , CurrentID)
    cmdProject.Parameters.Append cmdProject.CreateParameter _
        ("ProjectName", adVarChar, adParamInput, 50, _
        Replace([txtProjectName], "'", "''", 1, -1, vbTextCompare))
    cmdProject.Parameters.Append cmdProject.CreateParameter _
        ("StartDate", adVarChar, adParamInput, 50, [txtStartDate])
    cmdProject.Parameters.Append cmdProject.CreateParameter _
        ("ExpectedCompletionDate", adVarChar, adParamInput, _
        50, [txtExpectedCompletionDate])
    cmdProject.Parameters.Append cmdProject.CreateParameter _
        ("ProjectDescription", adVarChar, adParamInput, 5000, _
        Replace([txtProjectDescription], "'", "''", 1, -1, vbTextCompare))
    cmdProject.Execute
    If cmdProject("ReturnStatus") = 1 Then
        RefreshComboBox
        txtProjectName.SetFocus
    Else
        MsgBox cmdProject("ReturnMessage")
    End If
End Sub
```

The procedure will need a Command object:

```
Dim cmdProject As New ADODB.Command
```

You first make sure that the user is not in Add mode.

```
If CurrentID = "0" Then
```

If they are, you really need to add a record instead of updating one:

```
cmdAdd_Click
Exit Sub
```

Otherwise, the Command object uses the Public database connection:

```
Set cmdProject.ActiveConnection = MyDB
```

and will call the ProjectEdit stored procedure:

```
cmdProject.CommandText = "ProjectEdit"
cmdProject.CommandType = adCmdStoredProc
```

That stored procedure requires status parameters:

```
cmdProject.Parameters.Append cmdProject.CreateParameter _
     ("ReturnStatus", adInteger, adParamOutput)
cmdProject.Parameters.Append cmdProject.CreateParameter _
     ("ReturnMessage", adVarChar, adParamOutput, 50)
```

and parameters for the values of the project being edited:

```
cmdProject.Parameters.Append cmdProject.CreateParameter _
     ("ProjectID", adInteger, adParamInput, , CurrentID)
cmdProject.Parameters.Append cmdProject.CreateParameter _
     ("ProjectName", adVarChar, adParamInput, 50, _
     Replace([txtProjectName], "'", "''", 1, -1, vbTextCompare))
cmdProject.Parameters.Append cmdProject.CreateParameter _
     ("StartDate", adVarChar, adParamInput, 50, [txtStartDate])
cmdProject.Parameters.Append cmdProject.CreateParameter _
     ("ExpectedCompletionDate", adVarChar, adParamInput, _
     50, [txtExpectedCompletionDate])
cmdProject.Parameters.Append cmdProject.CreateParameter _
     ("ProjectDescription", adVarChar, adParamInput, 5000, _
     Replace([txtProjectDescription], "'", "''", 1, -1, vbTextCompare))
```

You then call the stored procedure:

```
cmdProject.Execute
```

and check to see whether it ran successfully:

```
If cmdProject("ReturnStatus") = 1 Then
```

If it did, you need to update the combo box:

```
RefreshComboBox
```

and set focus to the Project Name text box:

```
txtProjectName.SetFocus
```

Otherwise, you display the error message returned by the stored procedure:

```
MsgBox cmdProject("ReturnMessage")
```

The next code block fires when the Delete button is clicked.

```
Private Sub cmdDelete_Click()
    Dim cmdProjectDelete As New ADODB.Command
    If CurrentID = 0 Then
        cmdClear_Click
        Exit Sub
    End If
    Set cmdProjectDelete.ActiveConnection = MyDB
    cmdProjectDelete.CommandText = "ProjectDelete"
    cmdProjectDelete.CommandType = adCmdStoredProc
    cmdProjectDelete.Parameters.Append cmdProjectDelete.CreateParameter _
        ("ReturnStatus", adInteger, adParamOutput)
    cmdProjectDelete.Parameters.Append cmdProjectDelete.CreateParameter _
        ("ReturnMessage", adVarChar, adParamOutput, 50)
    cmdProjectDelete.Parameters.Append cmdProjectDelete.CreateParameter _
        ("ProjectID", adInteger, adParamInput, , CurrentID)
    cmdProjectDelete.Execute
    If cmdProjectDelete("ReturnStatus") = 1 Then
        DisplayProjectRecord 0
        RefreshComboBox
        RefreshStepsList
    Else
        MsgBox cmdProjectDelete("ReturnMessage")
    End If
End Sub
```

The procedure needs a Command object to delete a record:

```
Dim cmdProjectDelete As New ADODB.Command
```

But before deleting, you make sure you are not in Add mode:

```
If CurrentID = 0 Then
```

If that is the case, you really just need to clear the contents of the form:

```
cmdClear_Click
```

Otherwise, you connect the Command object to the database:

```
Set cmdProjectDelete.ActiveConnection = MyDB
```

which will call the ProjectDelete stored procedure:

```
cmdProjectDelete.CommandText = "ProjectDelete"
cmdProjectDelete.CommandType = adCmdStoredProc
```

The procedure expects output parameters for the status of the call:

```
cmdProjectDelete.Parameters.Append cmdProjectDelete.CreateParameter _
      ("ReturnStatus", adInteger, adParamOutput)
cmdProjectDelete.Parameters.Append cmdProjectDelete.CreateParameter _
      ("ReturnMessage", adVarChar, adParamOutput, 50)
```

and an input parameter that contains the ID of the project being deleted:

```
cmdProjectDelete.Parameters.Append cmdProjectDelete.CreateParameter _
      ("ProjectID", adInteger, adParamInput, , CurrentID)
```

You then make the call to the stored procedure:

```
cmdProjectDelete.Execute
```

If it ran successfully:

```
If cmdProjectDelete("ReturnStatus") = 1 Then
```

you display a valid record on the form:

```
DisplayProjectRecord 0
```

and refresh the combo box:

```
RefreshComboBox
```

as well as the list box:

```
    RefreshStepsList
```

Otherwise, you display the error message returned by the stored procedure:

```
MsgBox cmdProjectDelete("ReturnMessage")
```

When the user clicks the Clear button, the code clears the form.

```
Private Sub cmdClear_Click()
    [txtProjectName] = ""
    [txtStartDate] = ""
    [txtExpectedCompletionDate] = ""
    [txtProjectDescription] = ""
    CurrentID = 0
    RefreshStepsList
    txtProjectName.SetFocus
End Sub
```

First, it clears the text boxes on the form:

```
[txtProjectName] = ""
[txtStartDate] = ""
[txtExpectedCompletionDate] = ""
[txtProjectDescription] = ""
```

You then set the ID so you are in Add mode:

```
CurrentID = 0
```

You clear the list box:

```
RefreshStepsList
```

and set focus to the first field on the form:

```
txtProjectName.SetFocus
```

The next three procedures deal with the steps related to a project. When the user clicks the Add Step button, the next code block fires.

```
Private Sub cmdAddStep_Click()
    DoCmd.OpenForm "frmAddStep", acNormal, _
        , , , acDialog, CurrentID
    RefreshStepsList
    DisplayProjectRecord CurrentID
End Sub
```

The procedure calls the Add Step form to add a step. Note that it is displayed as a dialog box and that you pass into it the value of the current ProjectID:

```
DoCmd.OpenForm "frmAddStep", acNormal, _
      , , , acDialog, CurrentID
```

Since it is displayed as a dialog box, the next line of code does not run until the user closes the Add Step form. Once they are done with that form, you need to update the list box:

```
RefreshStepsList
```

and update the current project so the status and step tallies will be displayed correctly:

```
DisplayProjectRecord CurrentID
```

When the user clicks the Delete Step button, the next code block fires.

```
Private Sub cmdDeleteStep_Click()
    Dim cmdStep As New ADODB.Command
    If Not IsNull([lstSteps]) Then
        Set cmdStep.ActiveConnection = MyDB
        cmdStep.CommandText = "ProjectStepDelete"
        cmdStep.CommandType = adCmdStoredProc
        cmdStep.Parameters.Append cmdStep.CreateParameter _
            ("ReturnStatus", adInteger, adParamOutput)
        cmdStep.Parameters.Append cmdStep.CreateParameter _
            ("ReturnMessage", adVarChar, adParamOutput, 50)
```

```
        cmdStep.Parameters.Append cmdStep.CreateParameter _
            ("ProjectStepID", adInteger, adParamInput, , [lstSteps])
        cmdStep.Execute
        RefreshStepsList
        DisplayProjectRecord CurrentID
    End If
End Sub
```

The procedure needs a Command object:

```
Dim cmdStep As New ADODB.Command
```

First though, you need to make sure that the user has selected an item in the list box that is to be deleted:

```
If Not IsNull([lstSteps]) Then
```

If so, you set up the command object so that it uses the Public database connection:

```
Set cmdStep.ActiveConnection = MyDB
```

The Command object will call the ProjectStepDelete stored procedure:

```
cmdStep.CommandText = "ProjectStepDelete"
cmdStep.CommandType = adCmdStoredProc
```

It will pass to it parameters for the status of the call:

```
cmdStep.Parameters.Append cmdStep.CreateParameter _
      ("ReturnStatus", adInteger, adParamOutput)
cmdStep.Parameters.Append cmdStep.CreateParameter _
      ("ReturnMessage", adVarChar, adParamOutput, 50)
```

and the ID of the step to be deleted:

```
cmdStep.Parameters.Append cmdStep.CreateParameter _
      ("ProjectStepID", adInteger, adParamInput, , [lstSteps])
```

You then make the call:

```
cmdStep.Execute
```

and update the list box so that it no longer shows the deleted record:

```
RefreshStepsList
```

Also, you need to update the form so that it displays the proper summary information about the steps:

```
DisplayProjectRecord CurrentID
```

The last procedure on this form fires when the Mark Step as Complete button is clicked.

```
Private Sub cmdMarkComplete_Click()
    Dim cmdMC As New ADODB.Command
    If Not IsNull([lstSteps]) Then
        Set cmdMC.ActiveConnection = MyDB
        cmdMC.CommandText = "ProjectStepComplete"
        cmdMC.CommandType = adCmdStoredProc
        cmdMC.Parameters.Append cmdMC.CreateParameter _
            ("ReturnStatus", adInteger, adParamOutput)
        cmdMC.Parameters.Append cmdMC.CreateParameter _
            ("ReturnMessage", adVarChar, adParamOutput, 50)
        cmdMC.Parameters.Append cmdMC.CreateParameter _
            ("ProjectStepID", adInteger, adParamInput, , [lstSteps])
        cmdMC.Execute
        RefreshStepsList
        DisplayProjectRecord CurrentID
    End If
End Sub
```

The procedure will need a Command object to mark the step complete:

```
Dim cmdMC As New ADODB.Command
```

but the procedure runs only if the user has selected a step to mark:

```
If Not IsNull([lstSteps]) Then
```

If that is the case, the Command object is set to use your Public connection:

```
Set cmdMC.ActiveConnection = MyDB
```

The command will call the ProjectStepComplete stored procedure:

```
cmdMC.CommandText = "ProjectStepComplete"
cmdMC.CommandType = adCmdStoredProc
```

and pass to it parameters for the status of the return from the call:

```
cmdMC.Parameters.Append cmdMC.CreateParameter _
      ("ReturnStatus", adInteger, adParamOutput)
cmdMC.Parameters.Append cmdMC.CreateParameter _
      ("ReturnMessage", adVarChar, adParamOutput, 50)
```

You also pass to it the ID of the step to be deleted:

```
cmdMC.Parameters.Append cmdMC.CreateParameter _
      ("ProjectStepID", adInteger, adParamInput, , [lstSteps])
```

You then execute the stored procedure:

```
cmdMC.Execute
```

After the call, you need to update the list box:

```
RefreshStepsList
```

as well as the summary information for the project:

```
DisplayProjectRecord CurrentID
```

Add Step Form

The Add Step form contains two procedures. The first fires when the OK button is clicked, adding the step to the database.

```
Private Sub cmdOK_Click()
    Dim cmdStep As New ADODB.Command
    Set cmdStep.ActiveConnection = MyDB
    cmdStep.CommandText = "ProjectStepAdd"
    cmdStep.CommandType = adCmdStoredProc
    cmdStep.Parameters.Append cmdStep.CreateParameter _
        ("ReturnStatus", adInteger, adParamOutput)
    cmdStep.Parameters.Append cmdStep.CreateParameter _
        ("ReturnMessage", adVarChar, adParamOutput, 50)
    cmdStep.Parameters.Append cmdStep.CreateParameter _
```

```
        ("ProjectID", adInteger, adParamInput, , Me.OpenArgs)
    cmdStep.Parameters.Append cmdStep.CreateParameter _
        ("StepName", adVarChar, adParamInput, 50, _
        [txtStepName])
    cmdStep.Parameters.Append cmdStep.CreateParameter _
        ("StepDescription", adVarChar, adParamInput, 2000, _
        [txtStepDescription])
    cmdStep.Execute
    DoCmd.Close acForm, "frmAddStep"
End Sub
```

To add the step, you will need a Command object:

```
Dim cmdStep As New ADODB.Command
```

which uses your Public database connection:

```
Set cmdStep.ActiveConnection = MyDB
```

It will call the ProjectStepAdd stored procedure:

```
cmdStep.CommandText = "ProjectStepAdd"
cmdStep.CommandType = adCmdStoredProc
```

and pass to it parameters for the status of the call:

```
cmdStep.Parameters.Append cmdStep.CreateParameter _
      ("ReturnStatus", adInteger, adParamOutput)
cmdStep.Parameters.Append cmdStep.CreateParameter _
      ("ReturnMessage", adVarChar, adParamOutput, 50)
```

You also pass in the ID of the project that the step is being added to, which was passed into this form through the OpenArgs parameter:

```
cmdStep.Parameters.Append cmdStep.CreateParameter _
      ("ProjectID", adInteger, adParamInput, , Me.OpenArgs)
```

You also need to set up parameters for the name and description of the step whose values come from the text boxes on this form:

```
cmdStep.Parameters.Append cmdStep.CreateParameter _
      ("StepName", adVarChar, adParamInput, 50, _
      [txtStepName])
```

```
cmdStep.Parameters.Append cmdStep.CreateParameter _
      ("StepDescription", adVarChar, adParamInput, 2000, _
      [txtStepDescription])
```

The stored procedure is then executed:

```
cmdStep.Execute
```

and the form is closed:

```
DoCmd.Close acForm, "frmAddStep"
```

The other procedure on this form fires when the Cancel button is clicked. The code uses the Close method of the DoCmd object to close the form:

```
Private Sub cmdCancel_Click()
    DoCmd.Close acForm, "frmAddStep"
End Sub
```

CHAPTER

14

Managing Collections

IN THIS CHAPTER:

C14SQLObjects.sql

Collections.txt

CollectionItems.txt

C14FrontEnd.mdb

In this chapter, you will look at a solution that allows the user to manage items in a collection. The application allows the user to define what types of collections they want to manage.

Working with Collections of Items

The application can be used to manage a book collection, a stamp collection, or any other basic collection. In fact, the application allows the user to manage items from many different collections. The user simply selects the active collection that they want to work with, and that is the data that they see.

Application Walk-Through

When the user first enters the application through Access, they are prompted for their SQL Server user name and password. If they enter a valid login, they will see the menu displayed in Figure 14-1.

From the Menu form, the user can access the two other forms in the Access database. When the user clicks the Collections button, they are shown the form displayed in Figure 14-2.

The application allows the user to manage items in a variety of different collections. The user uses the Collection forms to define the different types of collections that they wish to work with and the attributes for each collection. By defining the data on this form, they are defining how data is entered for the collection.

All the different collections have a name and an Item Name field. Each collection can also contain one of the four optional fields Text1, Text2, Date1, and Date2. The Collection Items form is based on the checks selected and the captions for the different fields.

So, back on the menu, the user must first select the active collection that they want to work with from the combo box at the bottom of the Menu form. If they selected Stamps as the active collection and then clicked the Work With Current Collection button, they would see the Collection Items form displayed in Figure 14-3.

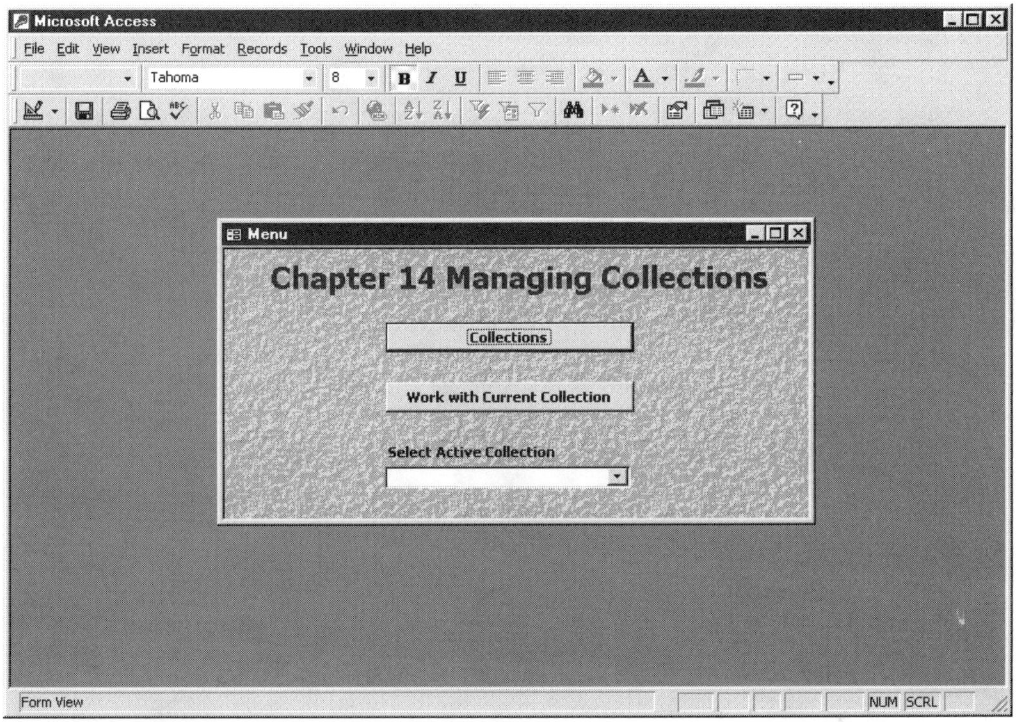

Figure 14-1 *Menu form*

Notice that the Collection Items form shows the two optional text fields and date fields. Also notice that the captions for the fields on the form match what was entered on the Collections form in Figure 14-2.

But the form can have a different appearance for a different collection. Take a look at Figure 14-4.

Notice that the Books collection has different data for the captions. And also notice that the collection does not use Text2 or Date2. So, if the user makes this their active collection, the Collection Items form looks like what you see in Figure 14-5.

Now the form uses the Books collection. And the form does not show the Text2 and Date2 fields, since they are not used with this collection.

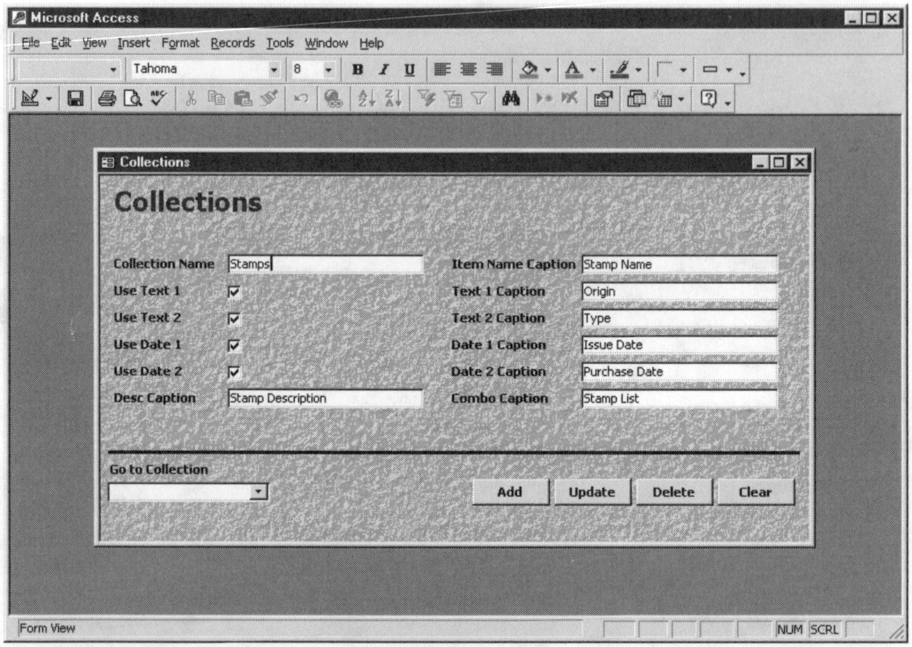

Figure 14-2 *Collections form*

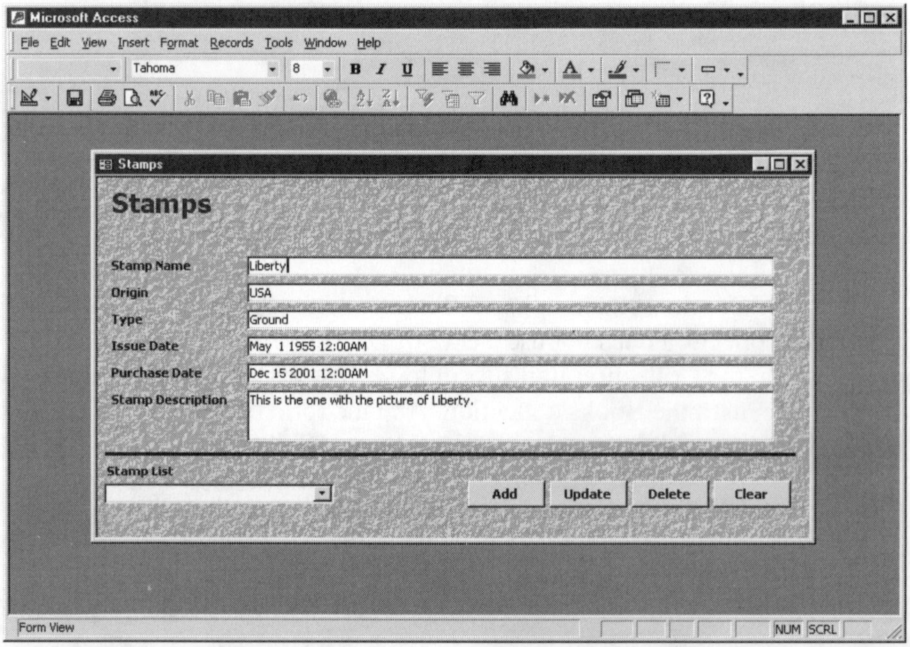

Figure 14-3 *Collection Items form based on the Stamps collection*

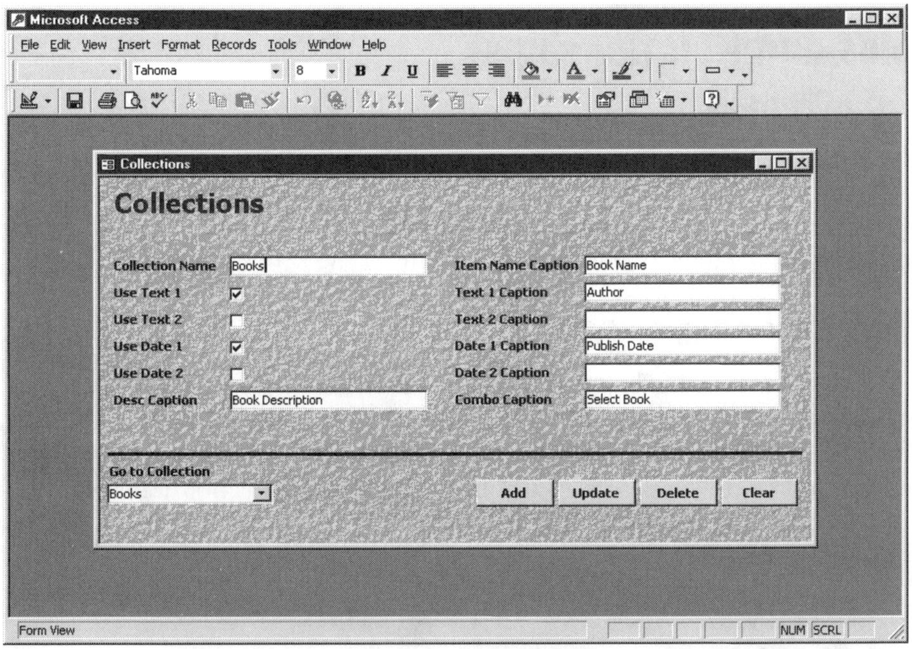

Figure 14-4 *Collections form for the Books collection*

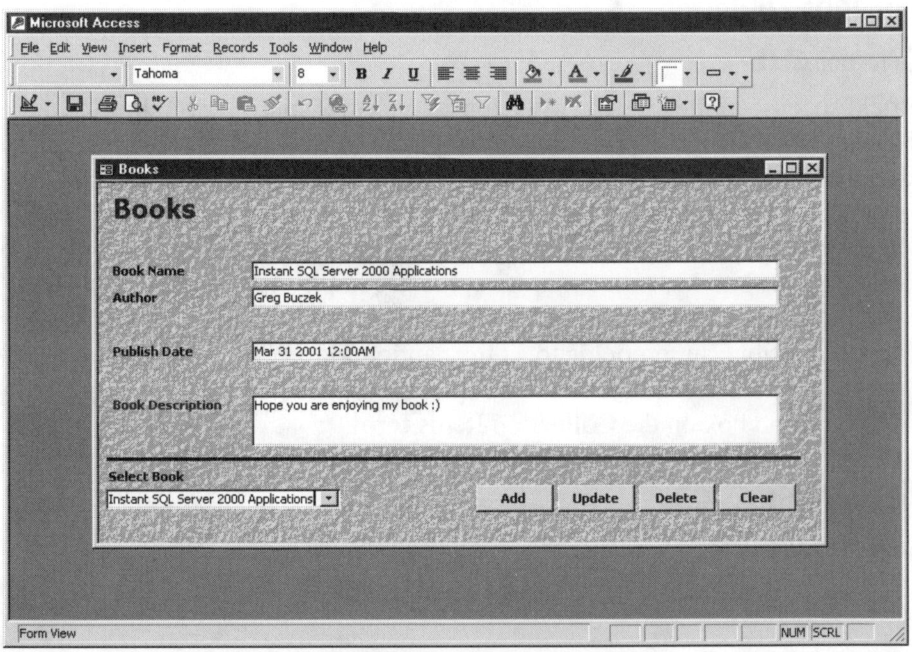

Figure 14-5 *Collection Items form for the Books collection*

Tables and Relationships

C14SQLObjects.sql

Collections Table

The Collections table stores the metadata about the collections. The data is then used to correctly display the Collections Items form for the active collection.

CollectionItems Table

The CollectionItems table stores information about all the items in all the collections. The table links to the Collections table in a one-to-many relationship. Each of the items belongs to one collection, but one collection can have many items. When the Collection Items form is displayed, only the CollectionItems records from the active collection are displayed.

Field Specifications

Collections Table

Collections.txt

The field specifications for the Collections table are displayed in Table 14-1.

The CollectionID is the primary key for the table. The CollectionName field is used as the text displayed in the title of the Collection Items form. The data in the ItemNameCaption field is used in the item name label on the Collection Items form.

The four "use" fields are Boolean fields that store whether the four optional fields are to be included in this collection. If so, the accompanying caption field stores the text for the label for that field.

The DescriptionCaption field stores the caption for the memo box on the Collection Items form, and the ComboCaption field stores the text to be placed above the combo box on the Collection Items form.

CollectionItems Table

CollectionItems.txt

The field specifications for the CollectionItems table are displayed in Table 14-2.

Field Name	Field Type	Notes
CollectionID	int	Primary Key, Identity Column
CollectionName	varchar	Length = 50
ItemNameCaption	varchar	Length = 50
UseText1	int	
Text1Caption	varchar	Length = 50
UseText2	int	
Text2Caption	varchar	Length = 50
UseDate1	int	
Date1Caption	varchar	Length = 50
UseDate2	int	
Date2Caption	varchar	Length = 50
DescriptionCaption	varchar	Length = 50
ComboCaption	varchar	Length = 50

Table 14-1 *Collections Table Field Specifications*

The CollectionItemID field is the primary key for this table. The CollectionID field is a foreign key that links this table to the Collections table. The rest of the fields store the specification information about the item in the collection.

Field Name	Field Type	Notes
CollectionItemID	int	Primary Key, Identity Column
CollectionID	int	Foreign Key
CollectionName	varchar	Length = 50
ItemName	varchar	Length = 50
Text1	varchar	Length = 1000
Text2	varchar	Length = 1000
Date1	datetime	
Date2	datetime	
ItemDescription	varchar	Length = 5000

Table 14-2 *CollectionItems Table Field Specifications*

User-Defined Functions

CollectionIDCheck Function

In a couple of stored procedures, you need to know whether a CollectionID is a valid ID. The CollectionIDCheck function provides that functionality.

```
CREATE FUNCTION CollectionIDCheck (@TheID integer)
RETURNS Integer AS
BEGIN
      Declare @TheCount Integer
      Select @TheCount = Count(CollectionID) from Collections
            Where CollectionID = @TheID
      Return @TheCount
END
```

The function requires a single parameter, the CollectionID to test:

```
CREATE FUNCTION CollectionIDCheck (@TheID integer)
```

It returns the number of times the ID was found as an integer:

```
RETURNS Integer AS
```

The function requires a local variable:

```
Declare @TheCount Integer
```

which is set to the number of occurrences of the CollectionID:

```
Select @TheCount = Count(CollectionID) from Collections
      Where CollectionID = @TheID
```

That value is returned from the function:

```
Return @TheCount
```

CollectionItemIDCheck Function

The CollectionItemIDCheck function is used to test whether a CollectionItemID is valid.

```
CREATE FUNCTION CollectionItemIDCheck (@TheID integer)
RETURNS Integer AS
BEGIN
      Declare @TheCount Integer
      Select @TheCount = Count(CollectionItemID) from CollectionItems
            Where CollectionItemID = @TheID
      Return @TheCount
END
```

The function requires as a parameter the ID to be tested:

```
CREATE FUNCTION CollectionItemIDCheck (@TheID integer)
```

It returns data as an integer:

```
RETURNS Integer AS
```

You then declare a variable:

```
Declare @TheCount Integer
```

that is set to the count of the requested ID from the CollectionItems table:

```
Select @TheCount = Count(CollectionItemID) from CollectionItems
      Where CollectionItemID = @TheID
```

That value is returned from the function:

```
Return @TheCount
```

Stored Procedures

CollectionAdd Stored Procedure

The CollectionAdd stored procedure provides the mechanism for inserting a record into the Collections table.

```
CREATE PROCEDURE CollectionAdd
@ReturnStatus integer OUTPUT,
@ReturnMessage varchar(50) OUTPUT,
@NewID integer OUTPUT,
```

```
@CollectionName varchar(50),
@ItemNameCaption varchar(50),
@UseText1 bit,
@Text1Caption varchar(50),
@UseText2 bit,
@Text2Caption varchar(50),
@UseDate1 bit,
@Date1Caption varchar(50),
@UseDate2 bit,
@Date2Caption varchar(50),
@DescriptionCaption varchar(50),
@ComboCaption varchar(50)
AS
BEGIN
      Insert Into Collections
            (CollectionName, ItemNameCaption, UseText1,
                  Text1Caption, UseText2, Text2Caption,
                  UseDate1, Date1Caption, UseDate2,
                  Date2Caption, DescriptionCaption, ComboCaption)
            values (@CollectionName, @ItemNameCaption, @UseText1,
                  @Text1Caption, @UseText2, @Text2Caption,
                  @UseDate1, @Date1Caption, @UseDate2,
                  @Date2Caption, @DescriptionCaption, @ComboCaption)
      set @ReturnStatus = 1
      set @ReturnMessage = 'Success'
      set @NewID = @@Identity
END
GO
```

The procedure requires many parameters. The first two are output parameters that return the status of the call to this procedure:

```
@ReturnStatus integer OUTPUT,
@ReturnMessage varchar(50) OUTPUT,
```

The next parameter is also an output parameter. It returns the ID of the collection just added:

```
@NewID integer OUTPUT,
```

The rest of the parameters are all input parameters and are used to pass into the procedure the values for the fields for the inserted record:

```
@CollectionName varchar(50),
@ItemNameCaption varchar(50),
@UseText1 bit,
@Text1Caption varchar(50),
@UseText2 bit,
@Text2Caption varchar(50),
@UseDate1 bit,
@Date1Caption varchar(50),
@UseDate2 bit,
@Date2Caption varchar(50),
@DescriptionCaption varchar(50),
@ComboCaption varchar(50)
```

Then, in the body of the stored procedure, you use a SQL Insert statement to add the record to the Collections table:

```
Insert Into Collections
      (CollectionName, ItemNameCaption, UseText1,
      Text1Caption, UseText2, Text2Caption,
      UseDate1, Date1Caption, UseDate2,
      Date2Caption, DescriptionCaption, ComboCaption)
      values (@CollectionName, @ItemNameCaption, @UseText1,
      @Text1Caption, @UseText2, @Text2Caption,
      @UseDate1, @Date1Caption, @UseDate2,
      @Date2Caption, @DescriptionCaption, @ComboCaption)
```

You then return a success message:

```
set @ReturnStatus = 1
set @ReturnMessage = 'Success'
```

as well as the ID of the record just added to the Collections table:

```
set @NewID = @@Identity
```

CollectionEdit Stored Procedure

The CollectionEdit stored procedure provides the mechanism for editing an existing record in the Collections table.

```
CREATE PROCEDURE CollectionEdit
@ReturnStatus integer OUTPUT,
@ReturnMessage varchar(50) OUTPUT,
```

```
@CollectionID integer,
@CollectionName varchar(50),
@ItemNameCaption varchar(50),
@UseText1 bit,
@Text1Caption varchar(50),
@UseText2 bit,
@Text2Caption varchar(50),
@UseDate1 bit,
@Date1Caption varchar(50),
@UseDate2 bit,
@Date2Caption varchar(50),
@DescriptionCaption varchar(50),
@ComboCaption varchar(50)
AS
If (dbo.CollectionIDCheck(@CollectionID)) = 0
      BEGIN
            set @ReturnStatus = 0
            set @ReturnMessage = 'The Collection ID entered ' +
                  'was not found.'
      END
Else
      BEGIN
            Update Collections set
                  CollectionName = @CollectionName,
                  ItemNameCaption = @ItemNameCaption,
                  UseText1 = @UseText1,
                  Text1Caption = @Text1Caption,
                  UseText2 = @UseText2,
                  Text2Caption = @Text2Caption,
                  UseDate1 = @UseDate1,
                  Date1Caption = @Date1Caption,
                  UseDate2 = @UseDate2,
                  Date2Caption = @Date2Caption,
                  DescriptionCaption = @DescriptionCaption,
                  ComboCaption = @ComboCaption
                  Where CollectionID = @CollectionID
            set @ReturnStatus = 1
            set @ReturnMessage = 'Success.'
      END
GO
```

The first two parameters of the procedure return the status of the call to this procedure:

```
@ReturnStatus integer OUTPUT,
@ReturnMessage varchar(50) OUTPUT,
```

The next parameter stores the ID of the Collections record being edited:

```
@CollectionID integer,
```

The rest of the parameters store the new values for the fields in the record:

```
@CollectionName varchar(50),
@ItemNameCaption varchar(50),
@UseText1 bit,
@Text1Caption varchar(50),
@UseText2 bit,
@Text2Caption varchar(50),
@UseDate1 bit,
@Date1Caption varchar(50),
@UseDate2 bit,
@Date2Caption varchar(50),
@DescriptionCaption varchar(50),
@ComboCaption varchar(50)
```

First, you need to make sure that the ID of the collection being edited is valid by calling your user-defined procedure:

```
If (dbo.CollectionIDCheck(@CollectionID)) = 0
```

If the ID was not valid, you return an error message to the calling application:

```
set @ReturnStatus = 0
set @ReturnMessage = 'The Collection ID entered ' +
      'was not found.'
```

Otherwise, you can update the desired record:

```
Update Collections set
      CollectionName = @CollectionName,
```

```
        ItemNameCaption = @ItemNameCaption,
        UseText1 = @UseText1,
        Text1Caption = @Text1Caption,
        UseText2 = @UseText2,
        Text2Caption = @Text2Caption,
        UseDate1 = @UseDate1,
        Date1Caption = @Date1Caption,
        UseDate2 = @UseDate2,
        Date2Caption = @Date2Caption,
        DescriptionCaption = @DescriptionCaption,
        ComboCaption = @ComboCaption
        Where CollectionID = @CollectionID
```

and return a success record:

```
set @ReturnStatus = 1
set @ReturnMessage = 'Success.'
```

CollectionDelete Stored Procedure

The CollectionDelete procedure is used by the calling application to delete a collection record.

```
CREATE PROCEDURE CollectionDelete
@ReturnStatus integer OUTPUT,
@ReturnMessage varchar(50) OUTPUT,
@CollectionID integer
AS
If (dbo.CollectionIDCheck(@CollectionID)) = 0
      BEGIN
            set @ReturnStatus = 0
            set @ReturnMessage = 'The Collection ID entered ' +
                  'was not found.'
      END
Else
      BEGIN
            Delete from Collections
                  Where CollectionID = @CollectionID
            set @ReturnStatus = 1
            set @ReturnMessage = 'Success.'
      END
GO
```

The procedure requires three parameters. The first two are used for the return message:

```
@ReturnStatus integer OUTPUT,
@ReturnMessage varchar(50) OUTPUT,
```

The third is used to pass in the ID of the record being deleted:

```
@CollectionID integer
```

First, you make sure that the ID of the record to be deleted is a valid ID:

```
If (dbo.CollectionIDCheck(@CollectionID)) = 0
```

If it isn't, you return an error message:

```
set @ReturnStatus = 0
set @ReturnMessage = 'The Collection ID entered ' +
      'was not found.'
```

Otherwise, you delete the desired record:

```
Delete from Collections
      Where CollectionID = @CollectionID
```

and return a success message:

```
set @ReturnStatus = 1
set @ReturnMessage = 'Success.'
```

CollectionRecord Stored Procedure

On both the Collections form and the CollectionItems form, you need to retrieve the data in a specific collection record. The CollectionRecord stored procedure performs that task.

```
CREATE PROCEDURE CollectionRecord
@ReturnStatus integer OUTPUT,
@ReturnMessage varchar(50) OUTPUT,
@CollectionID integer = 0 OUTPUT,
@CollectionName varchar(50) OUTPUT,
@ItemNameCaption varchar(50) OUTPUT,
@UseText1 bit OUTPUT,
@Text1Caption varchar(50) OUTPUT,
@UseText2 bit OUTPUT,
```

```
@Text2Caption varchar(50) OUTPUT,
@UseDate1 bit OUTPUT,
@Date1Caption varchar(50) OUTPUT,
@UseDate2 bit OUTPUT,
@Date2Caption varchar(50) OUTPUT,
@DescriptionCaption varchar(50) OUTPUT,
@ComboCaption varchar(50) OUTPUT
AS
If (dbo.CollectionIDCheck(@CollectionID)) = 0 and @CollectionID <> 0
      BEGIN
            set @ReturnStatus = 0
            set @ReturnMessage = 'The Collection ID entered ' +
                  'was not found.'
      END
Else
      If @CollectionID = 0
            BEGIN
                  Declare CurCollection Cursor
                  For Select CollectionID, CollectionName, ItemNameCaption,
                        UseText1, Text1Caption, UseText2, Text2Caption,
                        UseDate1, Date1Caption, UseDate2, Date2Caption,
                        DescriptionCaption, ComboCaption
                        From Collections
                        Where CollectionID = (Select Min(CollectionID)
                        from Collections)
                  Open CurCollection
                  Fetch CurCollection
                        Into @CollectionID, @CollectionName, @ItemNameCaption,
                        @UseText1, @Text1Caption, @UseText2, @Text2Caption,
                        @UseDate1, @Date1Caption, @UseDate2, @Date2Caption,
                        @DescriptionCaption, @ComboCaption
                  If @@Fetch_Status = 0
                        BEGIN
                              set @ReturnStatus = 1
                              set @ReturnMessage = 'Success'
                              Close CurCollection
                              Deallocate CurCollection
                        END
                  Else
                        BEGIN
                              set @ReturnStatus = 1
                              set @ReturnMessage = 'No records found'
                              set @CollectionName = ''
                              set @ItemNameCaption = ''
                              set @UseText1 = 0
                              set @Text1Caption = ''
                              set @UseText2 = 0
                              set @Text2Caption = ''
```

```
                    set @UseDate1= 0
                    set @Date1Caption = ''
                    set @UseDate2 = 0
                    set @Date2Caption = ''
                    set @DescriptionCaption = ''
                    set @ComboCaption = ''
                    Close CurCollection
                    Deallocate CurCollection
                END
            END
    Else
        BEGIN
            Declare CurCollection Cursor
            For Select CollectionID, CollectionName, ItemNameCaption,
                UseText1, Text1Caption, UseText2, Text2Caption,
                UseDate1, Date1Caption, UseDate2, Date2Caption,
                DescriptionCaption, ComboCaption
                From Collections
                Where CollectionID = @CollectionID
            Open CurCollection
            Fetch CurCollection
                Into @CollectionID, @CollectionName, @ItemNameCaption,
                @UseText1, @Text1Caption, @UseText2, @Text2Caption,
                @UseDate1, @Date1Caption, @UseDate2, @Date2Caption,
                @DescriptionCaption, @ComboCaption
            set @ReturnStatus = 1
            set @ReturnMessage = 'Success'
            Close CurCollection
            Deallocate CurCollection
        END
GO
```

The procedure's first two parameters are for the return message:

```
@ReturnStatus integer OUTPUT,
@ReturnMessage varchar(50) OUTPUT,
```

The next parameter is used to pass in the ID of the collection to be retrieved. It defaults to 0 and it also returns the value of the ID actually retrieved:

```
@CollectionID integer = 0 OUTPUT,
```

The rest of the parameters are output parameters that return the values of the fields in the collection record:

```
@CollectionName varchar(50) OUTPUT,
@ItemNameCaption varchar(50) OUTPUT,
@UseText1 bit OUTPUT,
```

```
@Text1Caption varchar(50) OUTPUT,
@UseText2 bit OUTPUT,
@Text2Caption varchar(50) OUTPUT,
@UseDate1 bit OUTPUT,
@Date1Caption varchar(50) OUTPUT,
@UseDate2 bit OUTPUT,
@Date2Caption varchar(50) OUTPUT,
@DescriptionCaption varchar(50) OUTPUT,
@ComboCaption varchar(50) OUTPUT
```

The first condition you test for is where the ID is not found in the Collections table and the ID passed in is not 0:

```
If (dbo.CollectionIDCheck(@CollectionID)) = 0 and @CollectionID <> 0
```

If that is the case, the ID requested is not in the table. Therefore, you return an error message:

```
set @ReturnStatus = 0
set @ReturnMessage = 'The Collection ID entered ' +
      'was not found.'
```

The next test condition means that the calling application wants the first record in the table:

```
If @CollectionID = 0
```

You will need a cursor:

```
Declare CurCollection Cursor
```

that returns all the fields from the first record in the Collections table:

```
For Select CollectionID, CollectionName, ItemNameCaption,
      UseText1, Text1Caption, UseText2, Text2Caption,
      UseDate1, Date1Caption, UseDate2, Date2Caption,
      DescriptionCaption, ComboCaption
      From Collections
      Where CollectionID = (Select Min(CollectionID)from Collections)
```

That cursor is then opened and the record is fetched into the return parameters:

```
Open CurCollection
Fetch CurCollection
      Into @CollectionID, @CollectionName, @ItemNameCaption,
      @UseText1, @Text1Caption, @UseText2, @Text2Caption,
```

```
    @UseDate1, @Date1Caption, @UseDate2, @Date2Caption,
    @DescriptionCaption, @ComboCaption
```

You then make sure that you actually found a record in the table by checking the @@FetchStatus variable:

```
If @@Fetch_Status = 0
```

If the value of that public variable is 0, you found a record. Therefore, you return a success message:

```
set @ReturnStatus = 1
set @ReturnMessage = 'Success'
```

and close your Cursor object:

```
Close CurCollection
Deallocate CurCollection
```

Otherwise, the table does not have any records:

```
set @ReturnStatus = 1
set @ReturnMessage = 'No records found'
```

So, you clear all the output parameters:

```
set @CollectionName = ''
set @ItemNameCaption = ''
set @UseText1 = 0
set @Text1Caption = ''
set @UseText2 = 0
set @Text2Caption = ''
set @UseDate1= 0
set @Date1Caption = ''
set @UseDate2 = 0
set @Date2Caption = ''
set @DescriptionCaption = ''
set @ComboCaption = ''
```

and close your cursor:

```
Close CurCollection
Deallocate CurCollection
```

The next condition means that the calling application is requesting the data of a specific, valid collection. You will need a Cursor object.

```
Declare CurCollection Cursor
```

that will retrieve the contents of the specified record:

```
For Select CollectionID, CollectionName, ItemNameCaption,
      UseText1, Text1Caption, UseText2, Text2Caption,
      UseDate1, Date1Caption, UseDate2, Date2Caption,
      DescriptionCaption, ComboCaption
      From Collections
      Where CollectionID = @CollectionID
```

You then open that cursor and retrieve the record into your output parameters:

```
Open CurCollection
Fetch CurCollection
      Into @CollectionID, @CollectionName, @ItemNameCaption,
      @UseText1, @Text1Caption, @UseText2, @Text2Caption,
      @UseDate1, @Date1Caption, @UseDate2, @Date2Caption,
      @DescriptionCaption, @ComboCaption
```

return a success message:

```
set @ReturnStatus = 1
set @ReturnMessage = 'Success'
```

and close your Cursor object:

```
Close CurCollection
Deallocate CurCollection
```

CollectionComboBox Stored Procedure

The Menu form and the Collections form contain a combo box that displays all the collections in the Collections table. The CollectionComboBox procedure is used to return the contents for that combo box.

```
CREATE PROCEDURE CollectionComboBox
@TheList varchar(8000) OUTPUT
AS
Declare
@CollectionID varchar(10),
@CollectionName varchar(50)
Declare CurCollections Cursor
```

```
For Select CollectionID, CollectionName from Collections
Order By CollectionName
Select @TheList = ''
Open CurCollections
Fetch CurCollections
      Into @CollectionID, @CollectionName
While @@Fetch_Status = 0
      BEGIN
            Select @TheList = @TheList + @CollectionID + ';"'
                  + @CollectionName + '";'
            Fetch CurCollections
                  Into @CollectionID, @CollectionName
      END
Close CurCollections
Deallocate CurCollections
GO
```

The procedure requires a single output parameter that returns the contents for the combo box:

```
@TheList varchar(8000) OUTPUT
```

Within the procedure, you need two variables that are used to store data from the Collections table:

```
@CollectionID varchar(10),
@CollectionName varchar(50)
```

You will also need a Cursor object that will retrieve the name and ID of each collection:

```
Declare CurCollections Cursor
For Select CollectionID, CollectionName from Collections
Order By CollectionName
```

You initialize your return variable:

```
Select @TheList = ''
```

and retrieve the first record from the Collections table into your local variables:

```
Open CurCollections
Fetch CurCollections
      Into @CollectionID, @CollectionName
```

You then enter a loop so that you can process each of the Collections records:

```
While @@Fetch_Status = 0
```

Within that loop you concatenate each of the IDs and names of the collections so that they are formatted for a combo box in Access:

```
Select @TheList = @TheList + @CollectionID + ';"'
     + @CollectionName + '";'
```

You then retrieve the next record so that it can be processed:

```
Fetch CurCollections
      Into @CollectionID, @CollectionName
```

After the loop, you close the cursor:

```
Close CurCollections
Deallocate CurCollections
```

CollectionItemAdd Stored Procedure

The CollectionItemAdd stored procedure provides the mechanism for adding a record to the CollectionItems table.

```
CREATE PROCEDURE CollectionItemAdd
@ReturnStatus integer OUTPUT,
@ReturnMessage varchar(50) OUTPUT,
@NewID integer OUTPUT,
@CollectionID integer,
@ItemName varchar(50),
@Text1 varchar(1000),
@Text2 varchar(1000),
@Date1 datetime,
@Date2 datetime,
@ItemDescription varchar(5000)
AS
BEGIN
      Insert Into CollectionItems
            (CollectionID, ItemName, Text1, Text2,
            Date1, Date2, ItemDescription)
            values (@CollectionID, @ItemName, @Text1, @Text2,
            @Date1, @Date2, @ItemDescription)
```

```
        set @ReturnStatus = 1
        set @ReturnMessage = 'Success'
        set @NewID = @@Identity
END
GO
```

The procedure requires three output parameters. The first two are for the status of the procedure call:

```
@ReturnStatus integer OUTPUT,
@ReturnMessage varchar(50) OUTPUT,
```

The other returns the ID of the record added:

```
@NewID integer OUTPUT,
```

The other variables store the data for the record to be inserted:

```
@CollectionID integer,
@ItemName varchar(50),
@Text1 varchar(1000),
@Text2 varchar(1000),
@Date1 datetime,
@Date2 datetime,
@ItemDescription varchar(5000)
```

You then use an Insert statement to add the data to the CollectionItems table:

```
Insert Into CollectionItems
      (CollectionID, ItemName, Text1, Text2,
      Date1, Date2, ItemDescription)
      values (@CollectionID, @ItemName, @Text1, @Text2,
      @Date1, @Date2, @ItemDescription)
```

You then set your return message:

```
set @ReturnStatus = 1
set @ReturnMessage = 'Success'
```

as well as the ID of the record just added:

```
set @NewID = @@Identity
```

CollectionItemEdit Stored Procedure

The CollectionItemEdit stored procedure is used to edit an existing CollectionItems record.

```
CREATE PROCEDURE CollectionItemEdit
@ReturnStatus integer OUTPUT,
@ReturnMessage varchar(50) OUTPUT,
@CollectionItemID integer,
@CollectionID integer,
@ItemName varchar(50),
@Text1 varchar(1000),
@Text2 varchar(1000),
@Date1 datetime,
@Date2 datetime,
@ItemDescription varchar(5000)
AS
If (dbo.CollectionItemIDCheck(@CollectionItemID)) = 0
      BEGIN
            set @ReturnStatus = 0
            set @ReturnMessage = 'The Collection Item entered ' +
                  'was not found.'
      END
Else
      BEGIN
            Update CollectionItems set
                  CollectionID = @CollectionID,
                  ItemName = @ItemName,
                  Text1 = @Text1,
                  Text2 = @Text2,
                  Date1 = @Date1,
                  Date2 = @Date2,
                  ItemDescription = @ItemDescription
                  Where CollectionItemID = @CollectionItemID
            set @ReturnStatus = 1
            set @ReturnMessage = 'Success.'
      END
GO
```

The first two parameters are used for the return message:

```
@ReturnStatus integer OUTPUT,
@ReturnMessage varchar(50) OUTPUT,
```

The next specifies the ID of the item to be edited:

```
@CollectionItemID integer,
```

The rest of the parameters store the new values for the fields in the record:

```
@CollectionID integer,
@ItemName varchar(50),
@Text1 varchar(1000),
@Text2 varchar(1000),
@Date1 datetime,
@Date2 datetime,
@ItemDescription varchar(5000)
```

You first check to see whether the ID of the record being edited is valid:

```
If (dbo.CollectionItemIDCheck(@CollectionItemID)) = 0
```

If it doesn't exist, you return an error message:

```
set @ReturnStatus = 0
set @ReturnMessage = 'The Collection Item entered ' +
      'was not found.'
```

Otherwise, you update the desired record:

```
Update CollectionItems set
      CollectionID = @CollectionID,
      ItemName = @ItemName,
      Text1 = @Text1,
      Text2 = @Text2,
      Date1 = @Date1,
      Date2 = @Date2,
      ItemDescription = @ItemDescription
      Where CollectionItemID = @CollectionItemID
And return a success message:
set @ReturnStatus = 1
set @ReturnMessage = 'Success.'
```

CollectionItemDelete Stored Procedure

The CollectionItemDelete stored procedure is used to delete a CollectionItems record.

```
CREATE PROCEDURE CollectionItemDelete
@ReturnStatus integer OUTPUT,
@ReturnMessage varchar(50) OUTPUT,
@CollectionItemID integer
AS
If (dbo.CollectionItemIDCheck(@CollectionItemID)) = 0
      BEGIN
            set @ReturnStatus = 0
            set @ReturnMessage = 'The Collection ItemID entered ' +
                  'was not found.'
      END
Else
      BEGIN
            Delete from CollectionItems
                  Where CollectionItemID = @CollectionItemID
            set @ReturnStatus = 1
            set @ReturnMessage = 'Success.'
      END
GO
```

The procedure requires parameters for the return message:

```
@ReturnStatus integer OUTPUT,
@ReturnMessage varchar(50) OUTPUT,
```

as well as the ID of the item to be deleted:

```
@CollectionItemID integer
```

You need to make sure that the ID of the item to be deleted exists:

```
If (dbo.CollectionItemIDCheck(@CollectionItemID)) = 0
```

If it doesn't, you return an error message:

```
set @ReturnStatus = 0
set @ReturnMessage = 'The Collection ItemID entered ' +
      'was not found.'
```

Otherwise, you delete the offending record:

```
Delete from CollectionItems
      Where CollectionItemID = @CollectionItemID
```

and return a success message:

```
set @ReturnStatus = 1
set @ReturnMessage = 'Success.'
```

CollectionItemRecord Stored Procedure

The CollectionItemRecord stored procedure returns the contents of a single collection item through output parameters.

```
CREATE PROCEDURE CollectionItemRecord
@ReturnStatus integer OUTPUT,
@ReturnMessage varchar(50) OUTPUT,
@CollectionItemID integer = 0 OUTPUT,
@CollectionID integer OUTPUT,
@ItemName varchar(50) OUTPUT,
@Text1 varchar(1000) OUTPUT,
@Text2 varchar(1000) OUTPUT,
@Date1 varchar(50) OUTPUT,
@Date2 varchar(50) OUTPUT,
@ItemDescription varchar(5000) OUTPUT
AS
If (dbo.CollectionItemIDCheck(@CollectionItemID)) = 0 and @CollectionItemID <> 0
      BEGIN
            set @ReturnStatus = 0
            set @ReturnMessage = 'The Collection Item ID entered ' +
                  'was not found.'
      END
Else
      If @CollectionItemID = 0
            BEGIN
                  Declare CurItem Cursor
                  For Select CollectionItemID, CollectionID, ItemName,
                        Text1, Text2, Date1, Date2, ItemDescription
                        From CollectionItems
                        Where CollectionItemID = (Select Min(CollectionItemID)
                        from CollectionItems where CollectionID = @CollectionID)
                  Open CurItem
                  Fetch CurItem
                        Into @CollectionItemID, @CollectionID, @ItemName,
                        @Text1, @Text2, @Date1, @Date2, @ItemDescription
                  If @@Fetch_Status = 0
                        BEGIN
                              set @ReturnStatus = 1
                              set @ReturnMessage = 'Success'
                              Close CurItem
```

```
                    Deallocate CurItem
                END
            Else
                BEGIN
                    set @ReturnStatus = 1
                    set @ReturnMessage = 'No records found'
                    set @CollectionID = 0
                    set @ItemName = ''
                    set @Text1 = ''
                    set @Text2 = ''
                    set @Date1 = ''
                    set @Date2 = ''
                    set @ItemDescription = ''
                    Close CurItem
                    Deallocate CurItem
                END
            END
    Else
        BEGIN
            Declare CurItem Cursor
            For Select CollectionID, ItemName,
                Text1, Text2, Date1, Date2, ItemDescription
                From CollectionItems
                Where CollectionItemID = @CollectionItemID
            Open CurItem
            Fetch CurItem
                Into @CollectionID, @ItemName,
                @Text1, @Text2, @Date1, @Date2, @ItemDescription
            set @ReturnStatus = 1
            set @ReturnMessage = 'Success'
            Close CurItem
            Deallocate CurItem
        END
GO
```

The procedure requires two output parameters for the status of the call:

```
@ReturnStatus integer OUTPUT,
@ReturnMessage varchar(50) OUTPUT,
```

The next parameter passes in and returns the ID of the item:

```
@CollectionItemID integer = 0 OUTPUT,
```

The rest of the parameters return the values for the fields in the record:

```
@CollectionID integer OUTPUT,
@ItemName varchar(50) OUTPUT,
```

```
@Text1 varchar(1000) OUTPUT,
@Text2 varchar(1000) OUTPUT,
@Date1 varchar(50) OUTPUT,
@Date2 varchar(50) OUTPUT,
@ItemDescription varchar(5000) OUTPUT
```

First, you check to see whether the ID requested exists:

```
If (dbo.CollectionItemIDCheck(@CollectionItemID)) = 0 and @CollectionItemID <> 0
```

If not, you return an error message:

```
set @ReturnStatus = 0
set @ReturnMessage = 'The Collection Item ID entered ' +
      'was not found.'
```

Then you check to see if the calling application wants the first item in a collection:

```
If @CollectionItemID = 0
```

In that case, you need a Cursor object:

```
Declare CurItem Cursor
```

which is set to retrieve the first item in the specified collection:

```
For Select CollectionItemID, CollectionID, ItemName,
      Text1, Text2, Date1, Date2, ItemDescription
      From CollectionItems
      Where CollectionItemID = (Select Min(CollectionItemID)
      from CollectionItems where CollectionID = @CollectionID)
```

You then open the cursor and retrieve the data into the return parameters:

```
Open CurItem
Fetch CurItem
      Into @CollectionItemID, @CollectionID, @ItemName,
      @Text1, @Text2, @Date1, @Date2, @ItemDescription
```

If a record in the specified collection was found, the fetch variable will be set to 0:

```
If @@Fetch_Status = 0
```

In that case, you return a success message:

```
set @ReturnStatus = 1
set @ReturnMessage = 'Success'
```

and release the cursor's resources:

```
Close CurItem
Deallocate CurItem
```

Otherwise, no record was found. Therefore, you return a different message:

```
set @ReturnStatus = 1
set @ReturnMessage = 'No records found'
```

and clear the output parameters:

```
set @CollectionID = 0
set @ItemName = ''
set @Text1 = ''
set @Text2 = ''
set @Date1 = ''
set @Date2 = ''
set @ItemDescription = ''
```

and release the cursor:

```
Close CurItem
Deallocate CurItem
```

The last condition of the main If block means that the calling application is requesting a valid record. You will need a Cursor object that will retrieve the desired record:

```
Declare CurItem Cursor
For Select CollectionID, ItemName,
      Text1, Text2, Date1, Date2, ItemDescription
      From CollectionItems
      Where CollectionItemID = @CollectionItemID
```

which is placed into the output parameters:

```
Open CurItem
Fetch CurItem
      Into @CollectionID, @ItemName,
      @Text1, @Text2, @Date1, @Date2, @ItemDescription
```

You then return a success message:

```
set @ReturnStatus = 1
set @ReturnMessage = 'Success'
```

and release the cursor:

```
Close CurItem
Deallocate CurItem
```

CollectionItemComboBox Stored Procedure

The CollectionItemComboBox procedure returns all the items in the specified collection so that they can be displayed in a combo box.

```
CREATE PROCEDURE CollectionItemComboBox
@CollectionID integer,
@TheList varchar(8000) OUTPUT
AS
Declare
@CollectionItemID varchar(10),
@ItemName varchar(50)
Declare CurItems Cursor
For Select CollectionItemID, ItemName from CollectionItems
      Where CollectionID = @CollectionID
      Order By ItemName
Select @TheList = ''
Open CurItems
Fetch CurItems
      Into @CollectionItemID, @ItemName
While @@Fetch_Status = 0
      BEGIN
            Select @TheList = @TheList + @CollectionItemID + ';"'
                  + @ItemName + '";'
            Fetch CurItems
                  Into @CollectionItemID, @ItemName
      END
Close CurItems
Deallocate CurItems
GO
```

Passed into the procedure is the ID of the collection for which you want the items retrieved:

```
@CollectionID integer,
@TheList varchar(8000) OUTPUT
AS
Declare
@CollectionItemID varchar(10),
```

Returned from the procedure is the list of the items formatted for a combo box:

```
@ItemName varchar(50)
```

You need a cursor object that retrieves the names and IDs of the items from the specified collection:

```
Declare CurItems Cursor
For Select CollectionItemID, ItemName from CollectionItems
      Where CollectionID = @CollectionID
      Order By ItemName
```

Next, you initialize the return variable:

```
Select @TheList = ''
```

and retrieve the first item record:

```
Open CurItems
Fetch CurItems
      Into @CollectionItemID, @ItemName
```

You then enter a loop so that you can process all the items in the collection:

```
While @@Fetch_Status = 0
```

Each item is appended to the return value:

```
Select @TheList = @TheList + @CollectionItemID + ';"'
      + @ItemName + '";'
```

before you move on to the next record:

```
Fetch CurItems
      Into @CollectionItemID, @ItemName
```

Finally, you release the cursor:

```
Close CurItems
Deallocate CurItems
```

Application Notes

C14FrontEnd.mdb

The Access front end does not contain any of its own local tables. It relies entirely on the SQL Server back end for the data. For the application to work correctly, a DSN that points to the back-end database must be created, and it must have the following name:

```
C14ManagingCollections
```

Modules

GeneralProcs Module

The Access front end contains a single module called GeneralProcs. In the General Declarations section of that module, two public variables are declared:

```
Public MyDB As New ADODB.Connection
Public CurrentCollectionID As Integer
```

The first is the Connection object that is used throughout the application to connect to the SQL Server database. The other stores the ID of the active collection, which is used by the Collection Items form to display the correct items.

When the Access front end is first opened, a macro called Autoexec fires. That macro calls the following procedure.

```
Public Function StartUp()
    On Error GoTo HandleError
    Dim SQLUserName As String
    Dim SQLPassword As String
    SQLUserName = InputBox("Please enter your user name.", "User Name")
    SQLPassword = InputBox("Please enter your password.", "Password")
    MyDB.Open "DSN=C14ManagingCollections;UID=" & SQLUserName _
        & ";Password=" & SQLPassword
    DoCmd.OpenForm "frmMenu"
    Exit Function
```

```
HandleError:
    MsgBox Err.Number & ": " & Err.Description & _
        ". Closing application.", vbCritical, "Can't Start Application"
    Application.CloseCurrentDatabase
End Function
```

The function will watch for errors:

```
On Error GoTo HandleError
```

It will need two local variables:

```
Dim SQLUserName As String
Dim SQLPassword As String
```

that are set to the user's name and password:

```
SQLUserName = InputBox("Please enter your user name.", "User Name")
SQLPassword = InputBox("Please enter your password.", "Password")
```

You then attempt to connect to the SQL Server database using the login provided:

```
MyDB.Open "DSN=C14ManagingCollections;UID=" & SQLUserName _
      & ";Password=" & SQLPassword
```

If the login was successful, the code will flow here and you open the Menu form:

```
DoCmd.OpenForm "frmMenu"
```

Otherwise, the code flows here and you display the error message:

```
MsgBox Err.Number & ": " & Err.Description & _
". Closing application.", vbCritical, "Can't Start Application"
```

before exiting the database:

```
Application.CloseCurrentDatabase
```

Forms

Menu Form

The Menu form provides access to the other forms in the database, and it also provides the user with a way of selecting the active collection. When the form first opens, the Load event fires.

```
Private Sub Form_Load()
    Dim cmdList As New ADODB.Command
    Set cmdList.ActiveConnection = MyDB
    cmdList.CommandText = "CollectionComboBox"
    cmdList.CommandType = adCmdStoredProc
    cmdList.Parameters.Append cmdList.CreateParameter _
        ("TheList", adVarChar, adParamOutput, 8000)
    cmdList.Execute
    cmbCollectionID.RowSource = cmdList("TheList")
End Sub
```

The event is used to populate the Collections combo box. So you need a command object that connects to your SQL Server database:

```
Dim cmdList As New ADODB.Command
Set cmdList.ActiveConnection = MyDB
```

It will call your CollectionComboBox stored procedure:

```
cmdList.CommandText = "CollectionComboBox"
cmdList.CommandType = adCmdStoredProc
```

You pass to that procedure a single parameter, which will contain the contents for the list:

```
cmdList.Parameters.Append cmdList.CreateParameter _
      ("TheList", adVarChar, adParamOutput, 8000)
```

You then make the call to the stored procedure:

```
cmdList.Execute
```

and use the return to populate the list:

```
cmbCollectionID.RowSource = cmdList("TheList")
```

When the user selects a collection in the combo box, the public variable is set to the ID of that collection so that it can be used on the Collection Items form:

```
Private Sub cmbCollectionID_Change()
    CurrentCollectionID = [cmbCollectionID]
End Sub
```

When the user clicks the Collections button, they are taken to the Collections form through the OpenForm method of the DoCmd object:

```
Private Sub cmdCollections_Click()
    DoCmd.OpenForm "frmCollections"
End Sub
```

The other procedure on the Menu form fires when the Work With Current Collection button is clicked.

```
Private Sub cmdItems_Click()
    If CurrentCollectionID = 0 Then
        MsgBox "Please select a collection to work with first!"
    Else
        DoCmd.OpenForm "frmCollectionItems"
    End If
End Sub
```

The procedure checks to see whether the user has yet selected an active collection:

```
If CurrentCollectionID = 0 Then
```

If they haven't, you inform them of the problem:

```
MsgBox "Please select a collection to work with first!"
```

Otherwise, you open the Collection Items form:

```
DoCmd.OpenForm "frmCollectionItems"
```

Collections Form

The Collections form provides the user with the functionality needed to manage the collections. In the General Declarations section of the form, a public variable is declared that stores the ID of the collection that the user is currently working with on the form:

```
Private CurrentID As Long
```

The form contains two procedures of its own that are called from other places on this form. The first one populates the form with the desired record.

```
Public Sub DisplayCollectionRecord(ID2Use As Long)
    Dim cmdCollection As New ADODB.Command
    Set cmdCollection.ActiveConnection = MyDB
    cmdCollection.CommandText = "CollectionRecord"
    cmdCollection.CommandType = adCmdStoredProc
    cmdCollection.Parameters.Append cmdCollection.CreateParameter _
        ("ReturnStatus", adInteger, adParamOutput)
    cmdCollection.Parameters.Append cmdCollection.CreateParameter _
        ("ReturnMessage", adVarChar, adParamOutput, 50)
    cmdCollection.Parameters.Append cmdCollection.CreateParameter _
        ("CollectionID", adInteger, adParamInputOutput, , ID2Use)
    cmdCollection.Parameters.Append cmdCollection.CreateParameter _
        ("CollectionName", adVarChar, adParamOutput, 50)
    cmdCollection.Parameters.Append cmdCollection.CreateParameter _
        ("ItemNameCaption", adVarChar, adParamOutput, 50)
    cmdCollection.Parameters.Append cmdCollection.CreateParameter _
        ("UseText1", adBoolean, adParamOutput)
    cmdCollection.Parameters.Append cmdCollection.CreateParameter _
        ("Text1Caption", adVarChar, adParamOutput, 50)
    cmdCollection.Parameters.Append cmdCollection.CreateParameter _
        ("UseText2", adBoolean, adParamOutput)
    cmdCollection.Parameters.Append cmdCollection.CreateParameter _
        ("Text2Caption", adVarChar, adParamOutput, 50)
    cmdCollection.Parameters.Append cmdCollection.CreateParameter _
        ("UseDate1", adBoolean, adParamOutput)
    cmdCollection.Parameters.Append cmdCollection.CreateParameter _
        ("Date1Caption", adVarChar, adParamOutput, 50)
    cmdCollection.Parameters.Append cmdCollection.CreateParameter _
        ("UseDate2", adBoolean, adParamOutput)
    cmdCollection.Parameters.Append cmdCollection.CreateParameter _
        ("Date2Caption", adVarChar, adParamOutput, 50)
    cmdCollection.Parameters.Append cmdCollection.CreateParameter _
        ("DescriptionCaption", adVarChar, adParamOutput, 50)
    cmdCollection.Parameters.Append cmdCollection.CreateParameter _
        ("ComboCaption", adVarChar, adParamOutput, 50)
    cmdCollection.Execute
    If cmdCollection("ReturnStatus") = 1 Then
        CurrentID = cmdCollection("CollectionID")
        [txtCollectionName] = cmdCollection("CollectionName")
        [txtItemNameCaption] = cmdCollection("ItemNameCaption")
        [chkUseText1] = cmdCollection("UseText1")
```

```
        [txtText1Caption] = cmdCollection("Text1Caption")
        [chkUseText2] = cmdCollection("UseText2")
        [txtText2Caption] = cmdCollection("Text2Caption")
        [chkUseDate1] = cmdCollection("UseDate1")
        [txtDate1Caption] = cmdCollection("Date1Caption")
        [chkUseDate2] = cmdCollection("UseDate2")
        [txtDate2Caption] = cmdCollection("Date2Caption")
        [txtDescriptionCaption] = cmdCollection("DescriptionCaption")
        [txtComboCaption] = cmdCollection("ComboCaption")
        txtCollectionName.SetFocus
    Else
        MsgBox cmdCollection("ReturnMessage")
    End If
End Sub
```

The procedure takes a single parameter, the ID of the collection record to be retrieved.

```
Public Sub DisplayCollectionRecord(ID2Use As Long)
```

The procedure will need a Command object, which will use your SQL Server database:

```
Dim cmdCollection As New ADODB.Command
Set cmdCollection.ActiveConnection = MyDB
```

The Command object will call the CollectionRecord stored procedure:

```
cmdCollection.CommandText = "CollectionRecord"
cmdCollection.CommandType = adCmdStoredProc
```

and pass to it parameters for the return message from the call:

```
cmdCollection.Parameters.Append cmdCollection.CreateParameter _
      ("ReturnStatus", adInteger, adParamOutput)
cmdCollection.Parameters.Append cmdCollection.CreateParameter _
      ("ReturnMessage", adVarChar, adParamOutput, 50)
```

as well as the ID of the record to retrieve:

```
cmdCollection.Parameters.Append cmdCollection.CreateParameter _
      ("CollectionID", adInteger, adParamInputOutput, , ID2Use)
```

The rest of the parameters passed will be set to the values in the selected record:

```
cmdCollection.Parameters.Append cmdCollection.CreateParameter _
      ("CollectionName", adVarChar, adParamOutput, 50)
cmdCollection.Parameters.Append cmdCollection.CreateParameter _
      ("ItemNameCaption", adVarChar, adParamOutput, 50)
cmdCollection.Parameters.Append cmdCollection.CreateParameter _
      ("UseText1", adBoolean, adParamOutput)
cmdCollection.Parameters.Append cmdCollection.CreateParameter _
      ("Text1Caption", adVarChar, adParamOutput, 50)
cmdCollection.Parameters.Append cmdCollection.CreateParameter _
      ("UseText2", adBoolean, adParamOutput)
cmdCollection.Parameters.Append cmdCollection.CreateParameter _
      ("Text2Caption", adVarChar, adParamOutput, 50)
cmdCollection.Parameters.Append cmdCollection.CreateParameter _
      ("UseDate1", adBoolean, adParamOutput)
cmdCollection.Parameters.Append cmdCollection.CreateParameter _
      ("Date1Caption", adVarChar, adParamOutput, 50)
cmdCollection.Parameters.Append cmdCollection.CreateParameter _
      ("UseDate2", adBoolean, adParamOutput)
cmdCollection.Parameters.Append cmdCollection.CreateParameter _
      ("Date2Caption", adVarChar, adParamOutput, 50)
cmdCollection.Parameters.Append cmdCollection.CreateParameter _
      ("DescriptionCaption", adVarChar, adParamOutput, 50)
cmdCollection.Parameters.Append cmdCollection.CreateParameter _
      ("ComboCaption", adVarChar, adParamOutput, 50)
```

You then make the call to the stored procedure:

```
cmdCollection.Execute
```

and check to see whether it returned successfully:

```
If cmdCollection("ReturnStatus") = 1 Then
```

If it did, you populate the form based on the values retrieved:

```
CurrentID = cmdCollection("CollectionID")
[txtCollectionName] = cmdCollection("CollectionName")
[txtItemNameCaption] = cmdCollection("ItemNameCaption")
[chkUseText1] = cmdCollection("UseText1")
[txtText1Caption] = cmdCollection("Text1Caption")
[chkUseText2] = cmdCollection("UseText2")
```

```
[txtText2Caption] = cmdCollection("Text2Caption")
[chkUseDate1] = cmdCollection("UseDate1")
[txtDate1Caption] = cmdCollection("Date1Caption")
[chkUseDate2] = cmdCollection("UseDate2")
[txtDate2Caption] = cmdCollection("Date2Caption")
[txtDescriptionCaption] = cmdCollection("DescriptionCaption")
[txtComboCaption] = cmdCollection("ComboCaption")
```

You then set the focus to the first field on the form:

```
txtCollectionName.SetFocus
```

Otherwise, you display the error returned from the procedure to the user:

```
MsgBox cmdCollection("ReturnMessage")
```

The other procedure that this form declares is used to populate the combo box on the form.

```
Public Sub RefreshComboBox()
    Dim cmdList As New ADODB.Command
    Set cmdList.ActiveConnection = MyDB
    cmdList.CommandText = "CollectionComboBox"
    cmdList.CommandType = adCmdStoredProc
    cmdList.Parameters.Append cmdList.CreateParameter _
        ("TheList", adVarChar, adParamOutput, 8000)
    cmdList.Execute
    cmbCollectionID.RowSource = cmdList("TheList")
End Sub
```

The procedure requires a Command object, which points to your Connection object:

```
Dim cmdList As New ADODB.Command
Set cmdList.ActiveConnection = MyDB
```

The Command object will call the CollectionComboBox stored procedure:

```
cmdList.CommandText = "CollectionComboBox"
cmdList.CommandType = adCmdStoredProc
```

You pass to it a parameter that will contain the contents of the list after the call:

```
cmdList.Parameters.Append cmdList.CreateParameter _
      ("TheList", adVarChar, adParamOutput, 8000)
```

You then make the call:

```
cmdList.Execute
```

and use the return parameter to populate the combo box:

```
cmbCollectionID.RowSource = cmdList("TheList")
```

When the form is loaded, the Load event fires.

```
Private Sub Form_Load()
    DisplayCollectionRecord 0
    RefreshComboBox
End Sub
```

The event calls your procedure to display the first record in the Collections table:

```
DisplayCollectionRecord 0
```

and then loads the combo box:

```
RefreshComboBox
```

When the user changes the contents of the combo box, the code in the Change event fires. That code updates the form so that it displays the contents of the collection selected:

```
Private Sub cmbCollectionID_Change()
    DisplayCollectionRecord [cmbCollectionID]
End Sub
```

The next code block fires when the Add button is clicked.

```
Private Sub cmdAdd_Click()
    Dim cmdCollection As New ADODB.Command
    Set cmdCollection.ActiveConnection = MyDB
    cmdCollection.CommandText = "CollectionAdd"
    cmdCollection.CommandType = adCmdStoredProc
    cmdCollection.Parameters.Append cmdCollection.CreateParameter _
```

```
        ("ReturnStatus", adInteger, adParamOutput)
    cmdCollection.Parameters.Append cmdCollection.CreateParameter _
        ("ReturnMessage", adVarChar, adParamOutput, 50)
    cmdCollection.Parameters.Append cmdCollection.CreateParameter _
        ("CollectionID", adInteger, adParamOutput)
    cmdCollection.Parameters.Append cmdCollection.CreateParameter _
        ("CollectionName", adVarChar, adParamInput, 50, _
        Replace([txtCollectionName], "'", "''", 1, -1, vbTextCompare))
    cmdCollection.Parameters.Append cmdCollection.CreateParameter _
        ("ItemNameCaption", adVarChar, adParamInput, 50, _
        Replace([txtItemNameCaption], "'", "''", 1, -1, vbTextCompare))
    cmdCollection.Parameters.Append cmdCollection.CreateParameter _
        ("UseText1", adBoolean, adParamInput, , _
        [chkUseText1])
    cmdCollection.Parameters.Append cmdCollection.CreateParameter _
        ("Text1Caption", adVarChar, adParamInput, 50, _
        Replace([txtText1Caption], "'", "''", 1, -1, vbTextCompare))
    cmdCollection.Parameters.Append cmdCollection.CreateParameter _
        ("UseText2", adBoolean, adParamInput, , _
        [chkUseText2])
    cmdCollection.Parameters.Append cmdCollection.CreateParameter _
        ("Text2Caption", adVarChar, adParamInput, 50, _
        Replace([txtText2Caption], "'", "''", 1, -1, vbTextCompare))
    cmdCollection.Parameters.Append cmdCollection.CreateParameter _
        ("UseDate1", adBoolean, adParamInput, , _
        [chkUseDate1])
    cmdCollection.Parameters.Append cmdCollection.CreateParameter _
        ("Date1Caption", adVarChar, adParamInput, 50, _
        Replace([txtDate1Caption], "'", "''", 1, -1, vbTextCompare))
    cmdCollection.Parameters.Append cmdCollection.CreateParameter _
        ("UseDate2", adBoolean, adParamInput, , _
        [chkUseDate2])
    cmdCollection.Parameters.Append cmdCollection.CreateParameter _
        ("Date2Caption", adVarChar, adParamInput, 50, _
        Replace([txtDate2Caption], "'", "''", 1, -1, vbTextCompare))
    cmdCollection.Parameters.Append cmdCollection.CreateParameter _
        ("DescriptionCaption", adVarChar, adParamInput, 50, _
        Replace([txtDescriptionCaption], "'", "''", 1, -1, vbTextCompare))
    cmdCollection.Parameters.Append cmdCollection.CreateParameter _
        ("ComboCaption", adVarChar, adParamInput, 50, _
        Replace([txtComboCaption], "'", "''", 1, -1, vbTextCompare))
    cmdCollection.Execute
    If cmdCollection("ReturnStatus") = 1 Then
```

```
        CurrentID = cmdCollection("CollectionID")
        RefreshComboBox
        txtCollectionName.SetFocus
    Else
        MsgBox cmdCollection("ReturnMessage")
    End If
End Sub
```

The procedure will need a Command object:

```
Dim cmdCollection As New ADODB.Command
```

That Command object will use the database pointed to by your Connection object:

```
Set cmdCollection.ActiveConnection = MyDB
```

It will call your CollectionAdd stored procedure:

```
cmdCollection.CommandText = "CollectionAdd"
cmdCollection.CommandType = adCmdStoredProc
```

and pass to it parameters for the return message:

```
cmdCollection.Parameters.Append cmdCollection.CreateParameter _
      ("ReturnStatus", adInteger, adParamOutput)
cmdCollection.Parameters.Append cmdCollection.CreateParameter _
      ("ReturnMessage", adVarChar, adParamOutput, 50)
```

as well as an output parameter that will contain the ID of the collection just added:

```
cmdCollection.Parameters.Append cmdCollection.CreateParameter _
      ("CollectionID", adInteger, adParamOutput)
```

The rest of the parameters are input parameters that pass the data for the new record into the stored procedure from the text boxes on the form. You use the Replace function to check for any ' characters so that they will be properly placed into the database:

```
cmdCollection.Parameters.Append cmdCollection.CreateParameter _
      ("CollectionName", adVarChar, adParamInput, 50, _
      Replace([txtCollectionName], "'", "''", 1, -1, vbTextCompare))
cmdCollection.Parameters.Append cmdCollection.CreateParameter _
      ("ItemNameCaption", adVarChar, adParamInput, 50, _
```

```
        Replace([txtItemNameCaption], "'", "''", 1, -1, vbTextCompare))
cmdCollection.Parameters.Append cmdCollection.CreateParameter _
        ("UseText1", adBoolean, adParamInput, , _
        [chkUseText1])
cmdCollection.Parameters.Append cmdCollection.CreateParameter _
        ("Text1Caption", adVarChar, adParamInput, 50, _
        Replace([txtText1Caption], "'", "''", 1, -1, vbTextCompare))
cmdCollection.Parameters.Append cmdCollection.CreateParameter _
        ("UseText2", adBoolean, adParamInput, , _
        [chkUseText2])
cmdCollection.Parameters.Append cmdCollection.CreateParameter _
        ("Text2Caption", adVarChar, adParamInput, 50, _
        Replace([txtText2Caption], "'", "''", 1, -1, vbTextCompare))
cmdCollection.Parameters.Append cmdCollection.CreateParameter _
        ("UseDate1", adBoolean, adParamInput, , _
        [chkUseDate1])
cmdCollection.Parameters.Append cmdCollection.CreateParameter _
        ("Date1Caption", adVarChar, adParamInput, 50, _
        Replace([txtDate1Caption], "'", "''", 1, -1, vbTextCompare))
cmdCollection.Parameters.Append cmdCollection.CreateParameter _
        ("UseDate2", adBoolean, adParamInput, , _
        [chkUseDate2])
cmdCollection.Parameters.Append cmdCollection.CreateParameter _
        ("Date2Caption", adVarChar, adParamInput, 50, _
        Replace([txtDate2Caption], "'", "''", 1, -1, vbTextCompare))
cmdCollection.Parameters.Append cmdCollection.CreateParameter _
        ("DescriptionCaption", adVarChar, adParamInput, 50, _
        Replace([txtDescriptionCaption], "'", "''", 1, -1, vbTextCompare))
cmdCollection.Parameters.Append cmdCollection.CreateParameter _
        ("ComboCaption", adVarChar, adParamInput, 50, _
        Replace([txtComboCaption], "'", "''", 1, -1, vbTextCompare))
```

You then make the call to the procedure:

```
cmdCollection.Execute
```

If it ran successfully:

```
If cmdCollection("ReturnStatus") = 1 Then
```

you set the ID of the record you are currently working with:

```
CurrentID = cmdCollection("CollectionID")
```

refresh the combo box:

```
RefreshComboBox
```

and set focus to the Collection Name text box:

```
txtCollectionName.SetFocus
```

Otherwise, you display the error message to the user:

```
MsgBox cmdCollection("ReturnMessage")
```

The next code block fires when the Update button is clicked.

```
Private Sub cmdUpdate_Click()
    Dim cmdCollection As New ADODB.Command
    If CurrentID = "0" Then
        cmdAdd_Click
        Exit Sub
    End If
    Set cmdCollection.ActiveConnection = MyDB
    cmdCollection.CommandText = "CollectionEdit"
    cmdCollection.CommandType = adCmdStoredProc
    cmdCollection.Parameters.Append cmdCollection.CreateParameter _
        ("ReturnStatus", adInteger, adParamOutput)
    cmdCollection.Parameters.Append cmdCollection.CreateParameter _
        ("ReturnMessage", adVarChar, adParamOutput, 50)
    cmdCollection.Parameters.Append cmdCollection.CreateParameter _
        ("CollectionID", adInteger, adParamInput, , CurrentID)
    cmdCollection.Parameters.Append cmdCollection.CreateParameter _
        ("CollectionName", adVarChar, adParamInput, 50, _
        Replace([txtCollectionName], "'", "''", 1, -1, vbTextCompare))
    cmdCollection.Parameters.Append cmdCollection.CreateParameter _
        ("ItemNameCaption", adVarChar, adParamInput, 50, _
        Replace([txtItemNameCaption], "'", "''", 1, -1, vbTextCompare))
    cmdCollection.Parameters.Append cmdCollection.CreateParameter _
        ("UseText1", adBoolean, adParamInput, , _
        [chkUseText1])
    cmdCollection.Parameters.Append cmdCollection.CreateParameter _
        ("Text1Caption", adVarChar, adParamInput, 50, _
```

```
        Replace([txtText1Caption], "'", "''", 1, -1, vbTextCompare))
    cmdCollection.Parameters.Append cmdCollection.CreateParameter _
        ("UseText2", adBoolean, adParamInput, , _
        [chkUseText2])
    cmdCollection.Parameters.Append cmdCollection.CreateParameter _
        ("Text2Caption", adVarChar, adParamInput, 50, _
        Replace([txtText2Caption], "'", "''", 1, -1, vbTextCompare))
    cmdCollection.Parameters.Append cmdCollection.CreateParameter _
        ("UseDate1", adBoolean, adParamInput, , _
        [chkUseDate1])
    cmdCollection.Parameters.Append cmdCollection.CreateParameter _
        ("Date1Caption", adVarChar, adParamInput, 50, _
        Replace([txtDate1Caption], "'", "''", 1, -1, vbTextCompare))
    cmdCollection.Parameters.Append cmdCollection.CreateParameter _
        ("UseDate2", adBoolean, adParamInput, , _
        [chkUseDate2])
    cmdCollection.Parameters.Append cmdCollection.CreateParameter _
        ("Date2Caption", adVarChar, adParamInput, 50, _
        Replace([txtDate2Caption], "'", "''", 1, -1, vbTextCompare))
    cmdCollection.Parameters.Append cmdCollection.CreateParameter _
        ("DescriptionCaption", adVarChar, adParamInput, 50, _
        Replace([txtDescriptionCaption], "'", "''", 1, -1, vbTextCompare))
    cmdCollection.Parameters.Append cmdCollection.CreateParameter _
        ("ComboCaption", adVarChar, adParamInput, 50, _
        Replace([txtComboCaption], "'", "''", 1, -1, vbTextCompare))
    cmdCollection.Execute
    If cmdCollection("ReturnStatus") = 1 Then
        RefreshComboBox
        txtCollectionName.SetFocus
    Else
        MsgBox cmdCollection("ReturnMessage")
    End If
End Sub
```

The procedure will need a Command object:

```
Dim cmdCollection As New ADODB.Command
```

But, first, you make sure you are not in Add mode:

```
If CurrentID = "0" Then
```

If you are, you need to call the Add procedure instead of the Update:

```
cmdAdd_Click
```

Otherwise, you can connect your Command object:

```
Set cmdCollection.ActiveConnection = MyDB
```

and set it to call your CollectionEdit stored procedure:

```
cmdCollection.CommandText = "CollectionEdit"
cmdCollection.CommandType = adCmdStoredProc
```

You pass to it parameters for the return message:

```
cmdCollection.Parameters.Append cmdCollection.CreateParameter _
      ("ReturnStatus", adInteger, adParamOutput)
cmdCollection.Parameters.Append cmdCollection.CreateParameter _
      ("ReturnMessage", adVarChar, adParamOutput, 50)
```

the ID of the record being updated:

```
cmdCollection.Parameters.Append cmdCollection.CreateParameter _
      ("CollectionID", adInteger, adParamInput, , CurrentID)
```

and values for all the fields in the record:

```
cmdCollection.Parameters.Append cmdCollection.CreateParameter _
      ("CollectionName", adVarChar, adParamInput, 50, _
      Replace([txtCollectionName], "'", "''", 1, -1, vbTextCompare))
cmdCollection.Parameters.Append cmdCollection.CreateParameter _
      ("ItemNameCaption", adVarChar, adParamInput, 50, _
      Replace([txtItemNameCaption], "'", "''", 1, -1, vbTextCompare))
cmdCollection.Parameters.Append cmdCollection.CreateParameter _
      ("UseText1", adBoolean, adParamInput, , _
      [chkUseText1])
cmdCollection.Parameters.Append cmdCollection.CreateParameter _
      ("Text1Caption", adVarChar, adParamInput, 50, _
      Replace([txtText1Caption], "'", "''", 1, -1, vbTextCompare))
cmdCollection.Parameters.Append cmdCollection.CreateParameter _
      ("UseText2", adBoolean, adParamInput, , _
      [chkUseText2])
cmdCollection.Parameters.Append cmdCollection.CreateParameter _
```

```
        ("Text2Caption", adVarChar, adParamInput, 50, _
        Replace([txtText2Caption], "'", "''", 1, -1, vbTextCompare))
cmdCollection.Parameters.Append cmdCollection.CreateParameter _
        ("UseDate1", adBoolean, adParamInput, , _
        [chkUseDate1])
cmdCollection.Parameters.Append cmdCollection.CreateParameter _
        ("Date1Caption", adVarChar, adParamInput, 50, _
        Replace([txtDate1Caption], "'", "''", 1, -1, vbTextCompare))
cmdCollection.Parameters.Append cmdCollection.CreateParameter _
        ("UseDate2", adBoolean, adParamInput, , _
        [chkUseDate2])
cmdCollection.Parameters.Append cmdCollection.CreateParameter _
        ("Date2Caption", adVarChar, adParamInput, 50, _
        Replace([txtDate2Caption], "'", "''", 1, -1, vbTextCompare))
cmdCollection.Parameters.Append cmdCollection.CreateParameter _
        ("DescriptionCaption", adVarChar, adParamInput, 50, _
        Replace([txtDescriptionCaption], "'", "''", 1, -1, vbTextCompare))
cmdCollection.Parameters.Append cmdCollection.CreateParameter _
        ("ComboCaption", adVarChar, adParamInput, 50, _
        Replace([txtComboCaption], "'", "''", 1, -1, vbTextCompare))
```

You then call the procedure:

```
cmdCollection.Execute
```

and check the return value:

```
If cmdCollection("ReturnStatus") = 1 Then
```

If it ran successfully, you need to update the combo box:

```
RefreshComboBox
```

and set focus to the first field on the form:

```
txtCollectionName.SetFocus
```

Otherwise, you display the error message returned from the stored procedure:

```
MsgBox cmdCollection("ReturnMessage")
```

The next procedure fires when the Delete button is clicked.

```
Private Sub cmdDelete_Click()
    Dim cmdCollectionDelete As New ADODB.Command
    If CurrentID = 0 Then
        cmdClear_Click
        Exit Sub
    End If
    Set cmdCollectionDelete.ActiveConnection = MyDB
    cmdCollectionDelete.CommandText = "CollectionDelete"
    cmdCollectionDelete.CommandType = adCmdStoredProc
    cmdCollectionDelete.Parameters.Append cmdCollectionDelete.CreateParameter _
        ("ReturnStatus", adInteger, adParamOutput)
    cmdCollectionDelete.Parameters.Append cmdCollectionDelete.CreateParameter _
        ("ReturnMessage", adVarChar, adParamOutput, 50)
    cmdCollectionDelete.Parameters.Append cmdCollectionDelete.CreateParameter _
        ("CollectionID", adInteger, adParamInput, , CurrentID)
    cmdCollectionDelete.Execute
    If cmdCollectionDelete("ReturnStatus") = 1 Then
        DisplayCollectionRecord 0
        RefreshComboBox
    Else
        MsgBox cmdCollectionDelete("ReturnMessage")
    End If
End Sub
```

The procedure will need a Command object:

```
Dim cmdCollectionDelete As New ADODB.Command
```

But, first, you make sure you are not in Add mode:

```
If CurrentID = 0 Then
```

If you are, you just need to clear the form by calling that procedure:

```
cmdClear_Click
```

Otherwise, you can connect to your SQL Server database:

```
Set cmdCollectionDelete.ActiveConnection = MyDB
```

and set the Command object to call the CollectionDelete stored procedure:

```
cmdCollectionDelete.CommandText = "CollectionDelete"
cmdCollectionDelete.CommandType = adCmdStoredProc
```

You pass to that procedure parameters for the return value:

```
cmdCollectionDelete.Parameters.Append cmdCollectionDelete.CreateParameter _
      ("ReturnStatus", adInteger, adParamOutput)
cmdCollectionDelete.Parameters.Append cmdCollectionDelete.CreateParameter _
      ("ReturnMessage", adVarChar, adParamOutput, 50)
```

and a parameter that contains the ID of the record you want to delete:

```
cmdCollectionDelete.Parameters.Append cmdCollectionDelete.CreateParameter _
      ("CollectionID", adInteger, adParamInput, , CurrentID)
```

You then call the procedure:

```
cmdCollectionDelete.Execute
```

and check the return value:

```
If cmdCollectionDelete("ReturnStatus") = 1 Then
```

If the return value was successful, you display a different record on the form:

```
DisplayCollectionRecord 0
```

and refresh the combo box:

```
RefreshComboBox
```

Otherwise, you display the error message to the user:

```
MsgBox cmdCollectionDelete("ReturnMessage")
```

The other procedure on the form clears the form when the Clear button is clicked.

```
Private Sub cmdClear_Click()
    [txtCollectionName] = ""
    [txtItemNameCaption] = ""
    [chkUseText1] = 0
    [txtText1Caption] = ""
```

```
    [chkUseText2] = 0
    [txtText2Caption] = ""
    [chkUseDate1] = 0
    [txtDate1Caption] = ""
    [chkUseDate2] = 0
    [txtDate2Caption] = ""
    [txtDescriptionCaption] = ""
    [txtComboCaption] = ""
    CurrentID = 0
    txtCollectionName.SetFocus
End Sub
```

The procedure clears all the text boxes and check boxes:

```
[txtCollectionName] = ""
[txtItemNameCaption] = ""
[chkUseText1] = 0
[txtText1Caption] = ""
[chkUseText2] = 0
[txtText2Caption] = ""
[chkUseDate1] = 0
[txtDate1Caption] = ""
[chkUseDate2] = 0
[txtDate2Caption] = ""
[txtDescriptionCaption] = ""
[txtComboCaption] = ""
```

sets the current ID to 0, putting you in Add mode:

```
CurrentID = 0
```

and returns the focus to the Collection Name text box:

```
txtCollectionName.SetFocus
```

Collection Items Form

The code on the Collection Items form is nearly identical to that on the Collections form except for when the form first loads. The code in the Load event needs to set up the form so that the captions read properly for the active collection and so that the correct optional fields are displayed.

```
Private Sub Form_Load()
    Dim cmdCollection As New ADODB.Command
    Set cmdCollection.ActiveConnection = MyDB
    cmdCollection.CommandText = "CollectionRecord"
    cmdCollection.CommandType = adCmdStoredProc
    cmdCollection.Parameters.Append cmdCollection.CreateParameter _
        ("ReturnStatus", adInteger, adParamOutput)
    cmdCollection.Parameters.Append cmdCollection.CreateParameter _
        ("ReturnMessage", adVarChar, adParamOutput, 50)
    cmdCollection.Parameters.Append cmdCollection.CreateParameter _
        ("CollectionID", adInteger, adParamInputOutput, , CurrentCollectionID)
    cmdCollection.Parameters.Append cmdCollection.CreateParameter _
        ("CollectionName", adVarChar, adParamOutput, 50)
    cmdCollection.Parameters.Append cmdCollection.CreateParameter _
        ("ItemNameCaption", adVarChar, adParamOutput, 50)
    cmdCollection.Parameters.Append cmdCollection.CreateParameter _
        ("UseText1", adBoolean, adParamOutput)
    cmdCollection.Parameters.Append cmdCollection.CreateParameter _
        ("Text1Caption", adVarChar, adParamOutput, 50)
    cmdCollection.Parameters.Append cmdCollection.CreateParameter _
        ("UseText2", adBoolean, adParamOutput)
    cmdCollection.Parameters.Append cmdCollection.CreateParameter _
        ("Text2Caption", adVarChar, adParamOutput, 50)
    cmdCollection.Parameters.Append cmdCollection.CreateParameter _
        ("UseDate1", adBoolean, adParamOutput)
    cmdCollection.Parameters.Append cmdCollection.CreateParameter _
        ("Date1Caption", adVarChar, adParamOutput, 50)
    cmdCollection.Parameters.Append cmdCollection.CreateParameter _
        ("UseDate2", adBoolean, adParamOutput)
    cmdCollection.Parameters.Append cmdCollection.CreateParameter _
        ("Date2Caption", adVarChar, adParamOutput, 50)
    cmdCollection.Parameters.Append cmdCollection.CreateParameter _
        ("DescriptionCaption", adVarChar, adParamOutput, 50)
    cmdCollection.Parameters.Append cmdCollection.CreateParameter _
        ("ComboCaption", adVarChar, adParamOutput, 50)
    cmdCollection.Execute
    If cmdCollection("ReturnStatus") = 1 Then
        Me.Caption = cmdCollection("CollectionName")
```

```
        lblTitle.Caption = cmdCollection("CollectionName")
        lblItemNameCaption.Caption = cmdCollection("ItemNameCaption")
        If cmdCollection("UseText1") = True Then
            lblText1Caption.Visible = True
            txtText1.Visible = True
            lblText1Caption.Caption = cmdCollection("Text1Caption")
        End If
        If cmdCollection("UseText2") = True Then
            lblText2Caption.Visible = True
            txtText2.Visible = True
            lblText2Caption.Caption = cmdCollection("Text2Caption")
        End If
        If cmdCollection("UseDate1") = True Then
            lblDate1Caption.Visible = True
            txtDate1.Visible = True
            lblDate1Caption.Caption = cmdCollection("Date1Caption")
        End If
        If cmdCollection("UseDate2") = True Then
            lblDate2Caption.Visible = True
            txtDate2.Visible = True
            lblDate2Caption.Caption = cmdCollection("Date2Caption")
        End If
        lblDescriptionCaption.Caption = cmdCollection("DescriptionCaption")
        lblComboCaption.Caption = cmdCollection("ComboCaption")
        txtItemName.SetFocus
    Else
        MsgBox cmdCollection("ReturnMessage")
    End If
    DisplayCollectionItemRecord 0
    RefreshComboBox
End Sub
```

The procedure needs a Command object that points to your SQL Server database:

```
Dim cmdCollection As New ADODB.Command
Set cmdCollection.ActiveConnection = MyDB
```

The Command object will call the CollectionRecord stored procedure:

```
cmdCollection.CommandText = "CollectionRecord"
cmdCollection.CommandType = adCmdStoredProc
```

You pass in parameters for the return message:

```
cmdCollection.Parameters.Append cmdCollection.CreateParameter _
     ("ReturnStatus", adInteger, adParamOutput)
cmdCollection.Parameters.Append cmdCollection.CreateParameter _
     ("ReturnMessage", adVarChar, adParamOutput, 50)
```

as well as the ID of the current active collection that the user is working with:

```
cmdCollection.Parameters.Append cmdCollection.CreateParameter _
     ("CollectionID", adInteger, adParamInputOutput, , CurrentCollectionID)
```

The rest of the parameters will contain the information about the collection:

```
cmdCollection.Parameters.Append cmdCollection.CreateParameter _
     ("CollectionName", adVarChar, adParamOutput, 50)
cmdCollection.Parameters.Append cmdCollection.CreateParameter _
     ("ItemNameCaption", adVarChar, adParamOutput, 50)
cmdCollection.Parameters.Append cmdCollection.CreateParameter _
     ("UseText1", adBoolean, adParamOutput)
cmdCollection.Parameters.Append cmdCollection.CreateParameter _
     ("Text1Caption", adVarChar, adParamOutput, 50)
cmdCollection.Parameters.Append cmdCollection.CreateParameter _
     ("UseText2", adBoolean, adParamOutput)
cmdCollection.Parameters.Append cmdCollection.CreateParameter _
     ("Text2Caption", adVarChar, adParamOutput, 50)
cmdCollection.Parameters.Append cmdCollection.CreateParameter _
     ("UseDate1", adBoolean, adParamOutput)
cmdCollection.Parameters.Append cmdCollection.CreateParameter _
     ("Date1Caption", adVarChar, adParamOutput, 50)
cmdCollection.Parameters.Append cmdCollection.CreateParameter _
     ("UseDate2", adBoolean, adParamOutput)
cmdCollection.Parameters.Append cmdCollection.CreateParameter _
     ("Date2Caption", adVarChar, adParamOutput, 50)
cmdCollection.Parameters.Append cmdCollection.CreateParameter _
     ("DescriptionCaption", adVarChar, adParamOutput, 50)
cmdCollection.Parameters.Append cmdCollection.CreateParameter _
     ("ComboCaption", adVarChar, adParamOutput, 50)
```

You then call the procedure:

```
cmdCollection.Execute
```

and check to see whether it ran successfully:

```
If cmdCollection("ReturnStatus") = 1 Then
```

If it did, you set the title of the form and the title label on the form to the name of the active collection:

```
Me.Caption = cmdCollection("CollectionName")
lblTitle.Caption = cmdCollection("CollectionName")
```

You also set the caption for the Item Name label:

```
lblItemNameCaption.Caption = cmdCollection("ItemNameCaption")
```

Next, you check to see whether the active collection uses the optional Text1 field:

```
If cmdCollection("UseText1") = True Then
```

If it does, you display that field and its label on the form:

```
lblText1Caption.Visible = True
txtText1.Visible = True
```

and set the caption for that label:

```
lblText1Caption.Caption = cmdCollection("Text1Caption")
```

You do the same for the other optional text field:

```
If cmdCollection("UseText2") = True Then
      lblText2Caption.Visible = True
      txtText2.Visible = True
      lblText2Caption.Caption = cmdCollection("Text2Caption")
End If
```

as well as the two date fields:

```
If cmdCollection("UseDate1") = True Then
      lblDate1Caption.Visible = True
      txtDate1.Visible = True
      lblDate1Caption.Caption = cmdCollection("Date1Caption")
End If
If cmdCollection("UseDate2") = True Then
      lblDate2Caption.Visible = True
        txtDate2.Visible = True
      lblDate2Caption.Caption = cmdCollection("Date2Caption")
End If
```

You also need to set the captions for the description field, as well as the caption for the combo box on the form:

```
lblDescriptionCaption.Caption = cmdCollection("DescriptionCaption")
lblComboCaption.Caption = cmdCollection("ComboCaption")
```

Finally, you set focus to the first field on the form:

```
txtItemName.SetFocus
```

If the procedure did not run successfully, you inform the user of the problem:

```
Else
      MsgBox cmdCollection("ReturnMessage")
End If
```

You also need to display the first item in the active collection:

```
DisplayCollectionItemRecord 0
```

and refresh the combo box:

```
RefreshComboBox
```

PART IV

ASP / SQL Server Applications

CHAPTER

15

ASP As a Front End to SQL Server

In this section of the book, you will look at using Active Server Pages and Active Server Page applications as the interface for SQL Server databases. The solutions will show you how to write code in ASP that manipulates and browses through data in several SQL Server databases.

Using ASP with SQL Server

But first, in this chapter, we will discuss the advantages and disadvantages of choosing ASP as the front end for your solutions. Then we will look at how you use ADO within ASP to access your database objects. After that, we will look at how the concept of an application works within ASP.

Advantages and Disadvantages of Using ASP

Active Server Pages and Active Server Page applications provide a wonderful option for you to get your data and your applications out to the rest of the world. First, it is fast to develop in. You can use one of the many commercial tools to design a Web page or a Web site that has all the elements in place. Then you can insert your ASP code in blocks or inline with your HTML to quickly create a dynamic Web site.

Creating Active Server Pages and Active Server Page applications makes your applications immediately available to a vast audience. Once you create your tool, all your users need is a standard browser and the address to your site and they can access your tool. You don't have to worry about whether your installation will work on one computer or another because if the visitor has already installed a browser, there is no installation necessary.

Plus your code is cross-platform. Since the result of running your code can produce just straight, simple HTML, any computer that has a browser, regardless of the operating system, should be able to view your site.

Another benefit of using ASP is the ease with which you can update your code. Since the code runs on the server, you don't need to worry about which version of a tool the visitor is using. They are running the most recent version that you have posted. And when it is time for a new version, you simply post it in the location of the old version and the visitors have been upgraded to your new system.

And, since the code runs on the server, you can expand the capabilities of your tool by adding components to it that the visitor does not need to have. For example, in all the solutions presented in this section of the book—in fact, in all the solution chapters—you use ADO to access the data. With Visual Basic and Access, that means that the user needs to have the ADO library installed and registered on the client machine. But with ASP, it doesn't matter whether the visitor has ADO, since all the ADO code runs on the server.

And you don't have to write your applications for the whole world with ASP. You could develop a solution using ASP that runs on your local networked server that only allows employees at your company to use the tool.

So, what about the negatives? Well, the biggest negative comes from one of the biggest positives of using ASP. As just mentioned, all the code runs on the server, removing the worry about what components the visitor has installed. But that means that the server must have the computing power to handle those components and the client requests.

With an ASP application, you don't have a distributed solution, you have a client/server solution. In fact, the client often acts as a dumb terminal. It merely displays the text and graphics doled out by the server and sends requests to the server.

Another negative about using ASP to develop your tools is a negative that also arises when using Access to develop your front-end applications. It is the perception of the consumer market. If you want to sell your solution, you must realize that the consumer has the perception that tools and applications online should be free. They expect not to have to pay to use your Loan Calculator, Chat Board, or Online Personal Information Manager. If you are looking to sell such a tool, Visual Basic would be perceived by the consumer as a tangible application that they are more likely to pay for. What online companies do instead is offer such tools free as part of their service, hoping to make their money from the service that they offer or through some other mechanism such as banner ads.

Using ADO in ASP

Active Server Page code has just a single data type called a *variant.* This data type can act as any of the standard data types, but you can't initially assign it to a type. When you coded a data type in Visual Basic or Access, you could do something like this:

```
Dim I as Integer
Dim TheMessage as String
```

The first variable is implicitly declared as an Integer, and the second, as a String. But in ASP, you would code this:

```
Dim I
Dim TheMessage
```

Both variables have been declared as variants. Each could be an integer or a string or even a complex object. That means that they could even be an ADO object. Therefore, in Visual Basic and in Access, you had this code:

```
Dim MyConn as New ADODB.Connection
```

What you are saying with this line of code is that you want to create a variable called MyConn. And the variable needs to be an instance of the Connection object of the ADODB library. All the methods and properties of that object are now available to it. So the next line of code could set one of the properties of the object:

```
MyConn.ConnectionString = "driver={SQL Server};" _
      & "server=MyServer;uid=SomeUser" _
      & ";pwd=SomePassword;database=SomeDB"
```

But, since ASP only has one data type, the variant, you would have this declaration:

```
Dim MyConn
```

The compiler knows nothing about the variable at this point. It could be a String, a Long, or a Connection object. The compiler will remain clueless until you assign a value or an object to that variant variable:

```
Set MyConn = Server.Createobject ("ADODB.Connection")
```

First, note the use of the Set statement. This tells the compiler that you are assigning an object type to the MyConn variable. You then use the method CreateObject of the intrinsic Server object to create an instance of the Connection object, which is an object of the ADO library. The library type that you want to instantiate is passed to the CreateObject method through the parameter.

After this line of code, you can now assign values to the properties of the Connection object, like the connection string:

```
MyConn.ConnectionString = "driver={SQL Server};" _
      & "server=MyServer;uid=SomeUser" _
      & ";pwd=SomePassword;database=SomeDB"
```

and then call one of the methods of the Connection object to open the connection to the database:

```
MyConn.Open
```

This same procedure of using the CreateObject method to instantiate an object type can be used to instantiate many different libraries. Here, the same procedure is used to create an e-mail object that is used to send out an e-mail message through ASP code:

```
Dim objMail
Set objMail = CreateObject("CDONTS.NewMail")
objMail.Send "from@na.com", "to@na.com", _
      "Subject Text", "The text of the message."
Set objMail = Nothing
```

Application Issues

If Active Server Pages stood on their own without the interaction of a series of pages acting together as an application, they would not be very useful. That is where Active Server Page applications come into play. Active Server Page applications allow you to store information about the visitor's state and pass their information on from page to page.

For example, if you have a secure site, you need to pass on the identity of the visitor from page to page. Without Active Server Page applications, you would need to ask the visitor to log in at each page they entered. In this section, you will look at how to create and use the features of Active Server Page applications that are essential to using ASP as the front end to your SQL Server databases.

The first thing you need to do is establish that a series of Active Server Pages is an Active Server Page application. An *Active Server Page application* is a series of Active Server Pages that are found in the same location either within the same file folder, or within subfolders of the parent directory of the application.

From your server computer, launch your Internet Services Manager and browse to the folder that contains the files that you want to make into an Active Server Page application. Such a folder is displayed in Figure 15-1.

The files that you want to establish as being part of an application are in the folder called Chat. Right-click the folder and select Properties. You should then see a dialog box such as the one displayed in Figure 15-2.

Notice the section labeled Application Settings. This is where you tell the Internet Services Manager that this folder is an Active Server Page application. Click the Create button.

The Application Name property should now be enabled, and you can enter a name for the application like the one displayed in Figure 15-3.

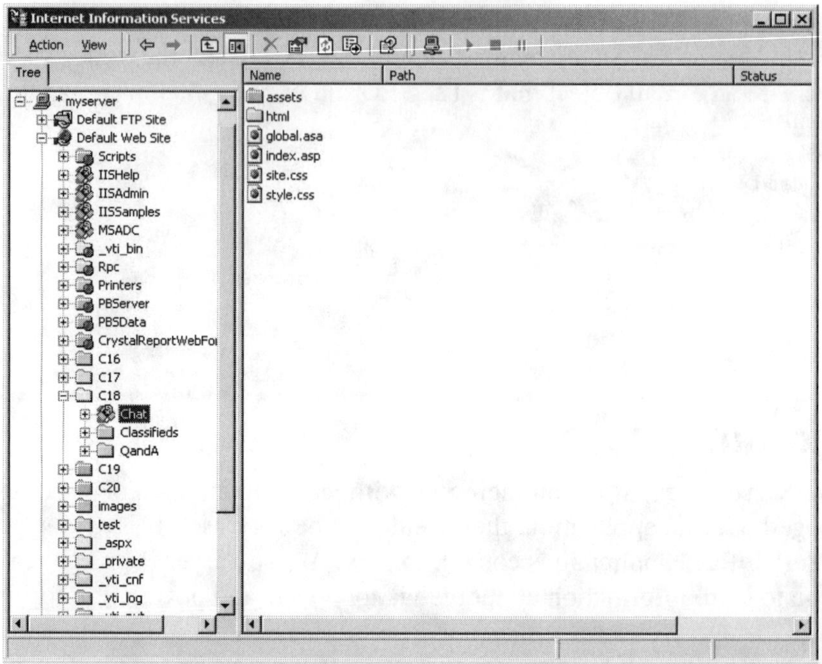

Figure 15-1 *Internet Services Manager*

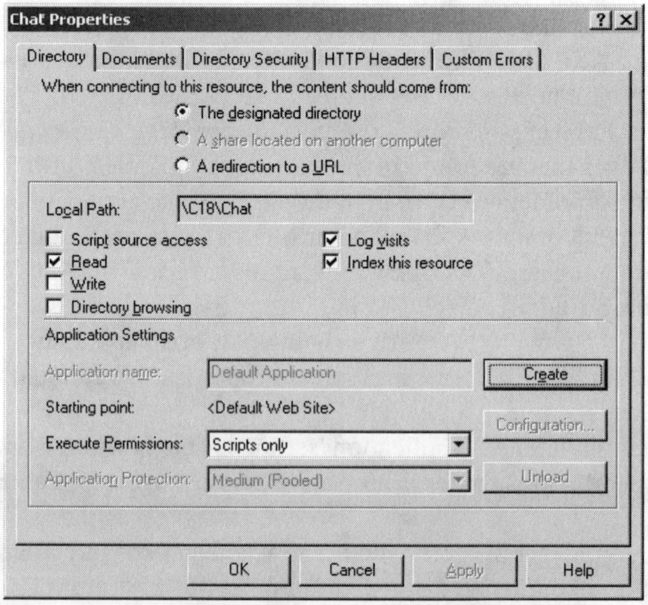

Figure 15-2 *Folder Properties without the folder as an application*

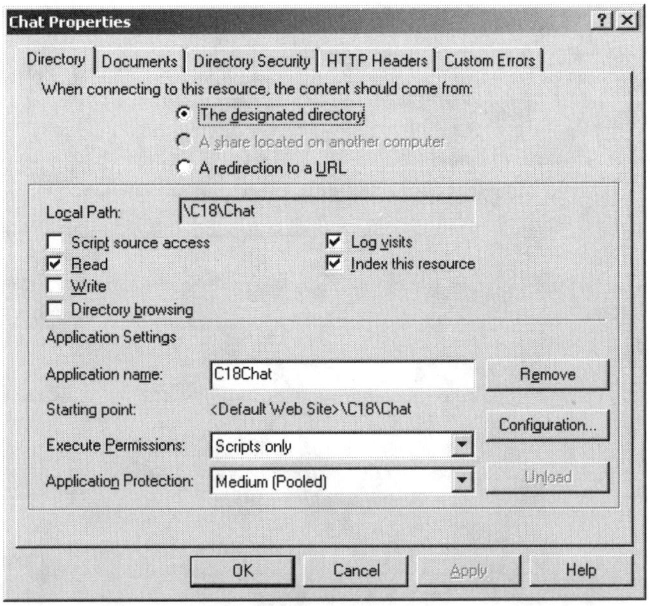

Figure 15-3 *Folder Properties with the folder as an application*

Notice the drop-down menu labeled Execute Permissions; make sure that it is set to Scripts Only. This setting allows the Active Server Pages in this folder to be run. The property can also be set to None, which means that no code in this folder can be executed through a browser. The third setting for this property is Scripts and Executables. This allows code to run in your ASP pages, as well as in standard executable files.

Now take a look at the Application Protection drop-down. This property is used to determine the isolation mode in which your code runs. Setting the property determines whether problems with this application can affect other Active Server Page applications and the performance of the server.

The first option is Low. If the property is set to this value, the application takes up fewer resources but the Active Server Page application can potentially take down IIS if the application fails.

The second setting is the default setting of Medium. With this value, the application runs pooled with other ASP applications; so if your application fails, it could bring down other applications but shouldn't bring down IIS with it.

The third setting of High uses the most resources. It isolates this Active Server Page application into its own process space.

Next, click the Configuration button to see the dialog box displayed in Figure 15-4.

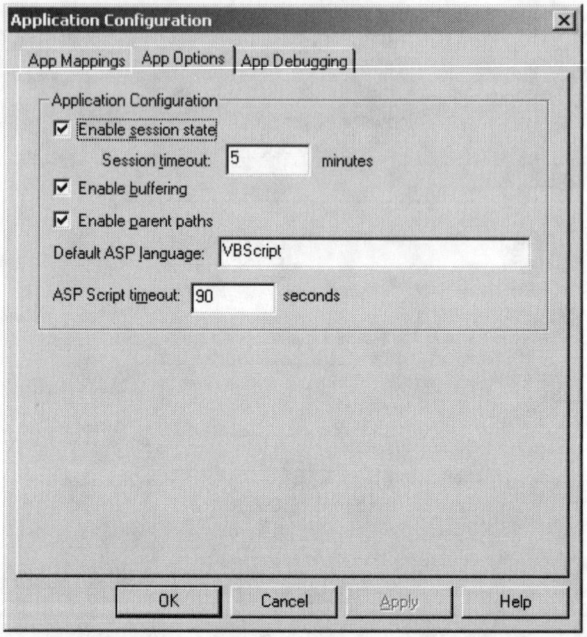

Figure 15-4 *App Options tab of the Application Configuration dialog box*

The second tab in the Application Configuration dialog box is App Options. Here, you set properties relating to the state of your Active Server Page application.

The first property is whether to Enable Session State. If this property is selected, the pages within your ASP application can share information through the use of Session variables and Application variables.

A *session* in ASP lingo refers to requests made by an individual visitor as they travel from page to page in your site. A session does not have knowledge or awareness of the state of other sessions, only its own. Session variables allow you to pass data on from page to page, and save it between page calls until the visitor's session ends.

For example, say you have a Web site where you are allowing a student to answer a series of questions on a test. You probably would want to store the ID of the student, the ID of the test, and the ID of the current question. You would then want that information passed from page to page to maintain the visitor's state as they take the test. You would have code like this:

```
Session("StudentID") = 10
Session("TestID") = 42
Session("QuestionID") = 145
```

Since the variables are Session variables, any of the pages in the Active Server Page application can retrieve or set their value. So, as you go from page to page in the test, you know what question to display, and on the results page of the test you can display the visitor's score.

Application variables are a little different. Just like Session variables, they can be retrieved or set in any page of the Active Server Pages application. But their scope goes beyond a single session. They are available to any session within the Active Server Page application.

In the preceding example, you stored the ID of the student in a Session variable. Another session could not access the value in this session. It would have its own instance of the variable. This is how you want it. You don't want one session to know the ID of another student.

But sometimes you do need to pass information on between sessions. You do this through Application variables. Let's take the school example a bit further. Say that you had many online schools on your server. You managed them all, but each with its own content. You could store all the test and course information in the same database and then access that data through separate ASP applications, each with its own school ID. Each session would have to know the ID of the school that the session belonged to in order to display the correct content. You could create an Application variable to store the ID of the school:

```
Application("SchoolID") = 2
```

Now, each session would know what school data to use.

So, checking the Enable Session State property on the App Options tab enables the use of these variables.

The next property on this page is the Session Timeout property. A session ends when you call the Abandon method of the Session object:

```
Session.Abandon
```

or when the time between requests made by the visitors exceeds the number of minutes in the Session Timeout property.

If Enable Buffering is checked, all the code on your page runs before the results of the code are sent to the visitor's browser. If Enable Parent Paths is checked, you can use relative positioning of a page in your code instead of specifying the full path to each page call.

The Default ASP Language is used to tell the compiler what language to use if you don't indicate a language name in your code. The last property on this page is the ASP Script Timeout property. This property represents the number of seconds you want to allow your code to run before it returns an error indicating that the code on the page did not complete. This is helpful when your code is fresh and may contain endless loops. Instead of running on until the whole application crashes, the script will just stop running if not complete by the number of seconds indicated in this property.

Now, select the App Debugging tab to see the dialog box displayed in Figure 15-5.

On this tab, you set debugging properties for your ASP application. If the first box, Enable ASP Server-Side Script Debugging, is checked, when an error occurs on a page in this application, the Script Debugger will open on the server at the point of the error. The second box, Enable ASP Client-Side Script Debugging, does nothing at this point. Microsoft is reserving it for some possible future use.

The bottom section of the dialog box allows you to determine what the visitor sees when an error does occur. If the first option is selected, the visitor will see the standard error message with the error number description and the erring line of code when an error occurs. If the second option is selected, the visitor sees a text message that you enter into the provided text box.

Now close the dialog box and select the Documents tab from the Folder Properties dialog box as displayed in Figure 15-6.

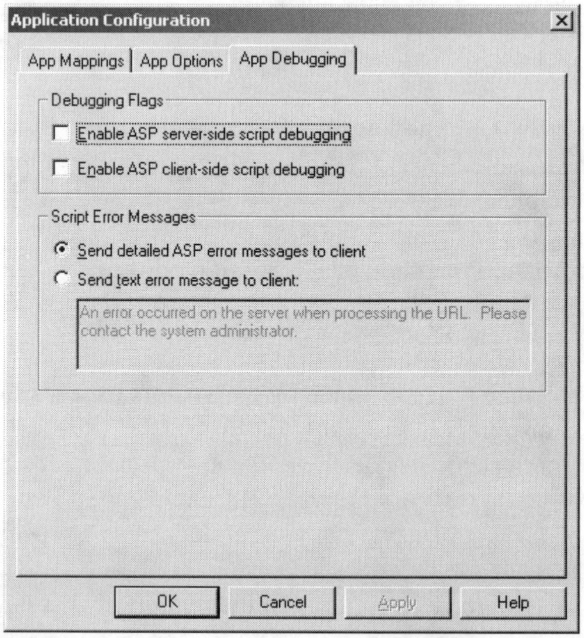

Figure 15-5 *App Debugging tab of the Application Configuration dialog box*

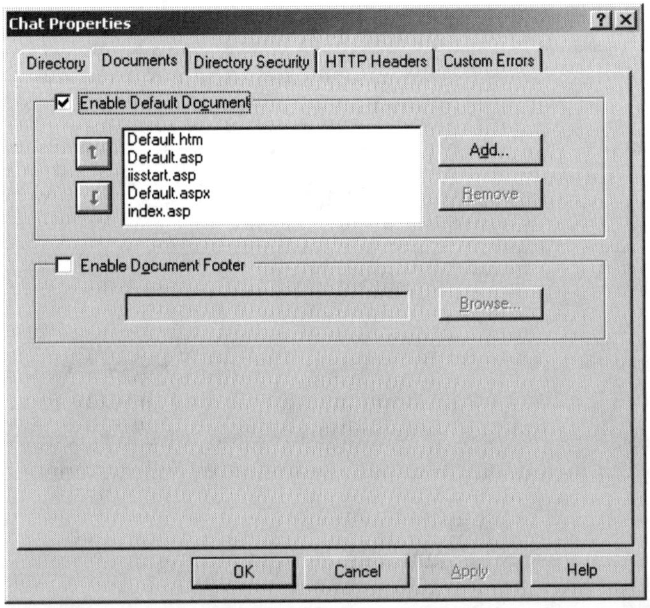

Figure 15-6 *Documents tab of the Folder Properties dialog box*

This dialog box allows you to determine which page to view when the visitor does not enter a specific page name when they browse to a Web site through its domain name:

```
http://www.whatever.com
```

or through a folder name at a site:

```
http://www.whatever.com/somefolder
```

In both of the examples, the visitor didn't request a specific page. So IIS looks at the list of possible default pages on the Documents tab and displays the first match it finds. I prefer using the default name of Index.asp, which is not part of the list. So, to use that filename, you need to click the Add button and add that name to the Default Document list.

The entry point directory of the Active Server Page application can contain a special file called global.asa. The global.asa file is simply a text file with the name global.asa that is placed in the root directory of your Web application. In this text file, you can define four events that are summarized in Table 15-1.

Event	Purpose
Application_OnStart	Runs when the first ASP is viewed with your application by any user
Application_OnEnd	Runs when your application is shut down
Session_OnStart	Runs when a visitor enters or returns to your application
Session_OnEnd	Runs when the user leaves your Web site

Table 15-1 *Active Server Page Application Events*

The purpose of these events is to allow you to run code or create variables that will persist across the life of your application or during the stay of a visitor. Thus, you can create login variables, constant information for use across your site, or dedicated connections to a data source. The code that follows contains a sample global.asa file.

```
<SCRIPT LANGUAGE=VBScript RUNAT=Server>
Sub Application_OnStart
set Application("Gconn") = Gconn
Application("Gconn").open "DSN", "sa", "password"
      Application("Discount") = .1
End Sub
Sub Application_OnEnd
      'Insert script to be executed when the application ends
End Sub

Sub Session_OnStart
      Session("LoginEmpID") = " "
End Sub

Sub Session_OnEnd
      'Insert script to be executed when a session ends
End Sub
</SCRIPT>
```

The first thing you will notice with this listing is that you are using this code:

```
<SCRIPT LANGUAGE=VBScript RUNAT=Server>
</SCRIPT>
```

to denote the beginning and end of the code, and the language of the code. Each of the events starts with the word "Sub," followed by the name of the event:

```
Sub Application_OnEnd
```

and ends with:

```
End Sub
```

In that event, you create an Application variable:

```
Application("Discount") = .1
```

You have defined a variable for which the value is available anywhere within your ASP application. This is very powerful because instead of defining a discount on 10 different pages, you define it in one place and access the value in all of your pages. When it comes time to change the discount, you only have to change the information in one place. Similarly you can define Session variables for which the scope, as discussed earlier in this chapter, is only for a specific user's focus throughout your ASP application. This allows you to keep track of an order as a visitor selects more items throughout your e-commerce site, or to keep track of security as a user goes from page to page.

In this example, you could manage sessions with the TimeOut property and the Abandon method of the Session object. The TimeOut property could be set in the Session_OnStart event:

```
Session.TimeOut = 30
```

A visitor's session will be considered over when they go through a period of 30 minutes without requesting a page. Or you could end a session with the Abandon method:

```
Session.Abandon
```

Once the session is abandoned or times out, the code in the Session_OnEnd event will run.

CHAPTER

16

Online Store

IN THIS CHAPTER:

C16SQLObjects.sql

Products.txt

Categories.txt

ProductsInCategories.txt

Visitors.txt

VisitorItems.txt

Index.asp

Products.asp

Shopping_Cart.asp

Check_Out.asp

Receipt.asp

In this chapter, you will look at a Web site that allows the visitor to access the products that your company offers. The visitor will be able to browse through products grouped by the categories that they are in. Those products can then be placed in a shopping cart and the customer can check out when their order is complete.

Allowing Customers to Shop Online

As you review this chapter, note the use of HTML elements within the stored procedures to generate script from there. Also note that the visitor accesses the database through a Web account that strictly limits their access to the database. And triggers are used on the tables in the back-end database to keep track of tally information as products are added and removed from the visitor's shopping cart.

The Online Store is implemented as a store that sells fish. But, if you removed the data from the database and changed the text on the site, it could be used to sell a variety of products.

Web Site Walk-Through

When the visitor first enters the site, they see the welcome page displayed in Figure 16-1.

The page provides introductory text. Here you would want to include information about your company and contact information. If the visitor clicks the Start Shopping link, they are taken to the Products page displayed in Figure 16-2.

Note the elements of the Products page. At the top, the visitor sees the category that they are currently in. They can select a different category and click the OK Change Category button to change to a different category. The next section on the page displays a product from the current category. Note that each category must have at least one product in it. But a product can be in many categories.

The visitor sees the extended information about the product and a picture of the product. If the user clicks the picture, they see a larger image of the product.

Note the list at the bottom of the page. That list displays all the products in the current category. The visitor can select a different product and click the OK Change Product button to see the information on that product. Figure 16-3 shows the Products page displaying the Cat Fish product.

When the visitor is ready to add an item to their shopping cart, they enter a quantity and click the Add to Shopping Cart button. When they do that, they are taken to the Shopping Cart page shown in Figure 16-4.

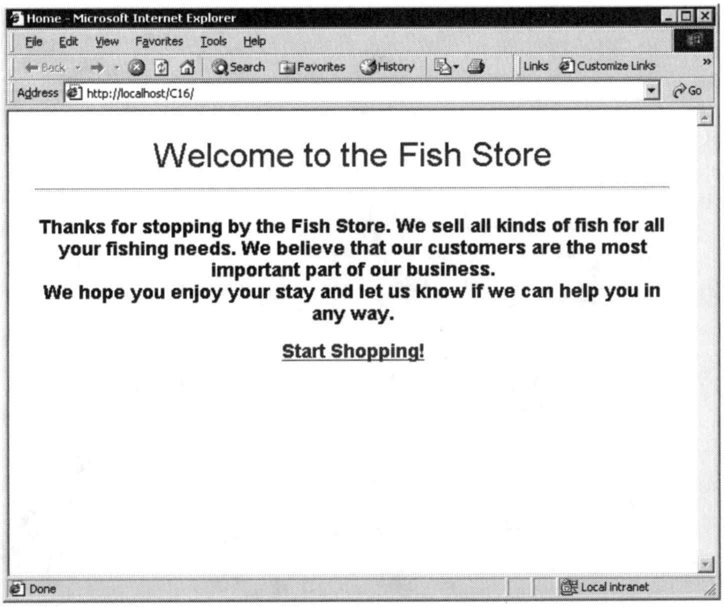

Figure 16-1 *Welcome page*

Figure 16-2 *Products page*

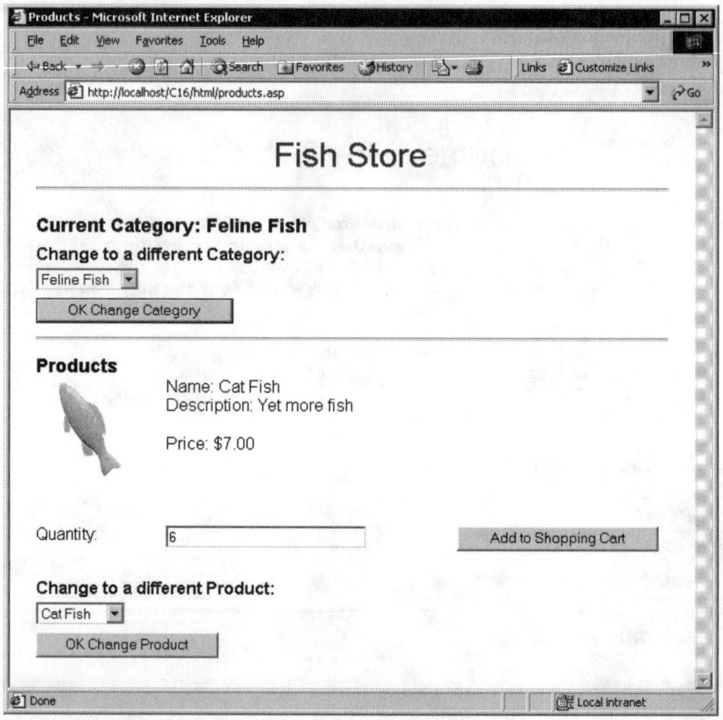

Figure 16-3 *Product page showing Cat Fish product*

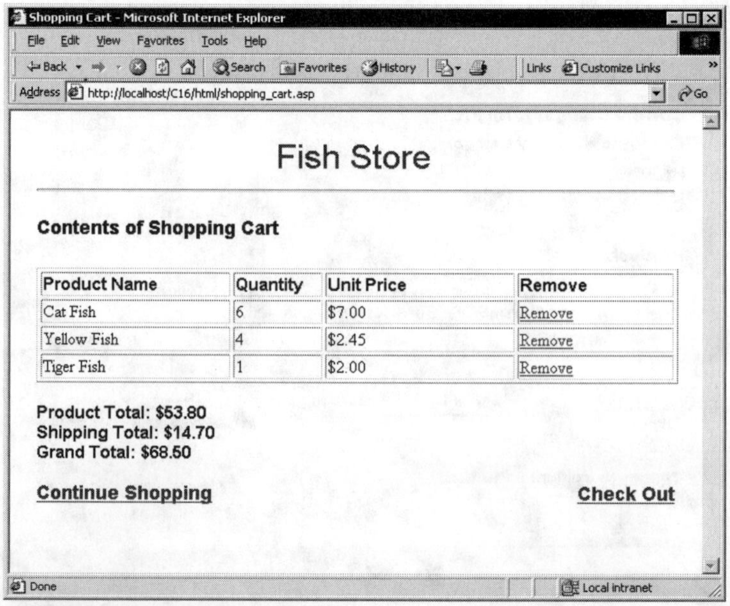

Figure 16-4 *Shopping Cart page*

The top of the page shows the contents of the visitor's shopping cart in the form of an HTML table. The visitor sees the products they ordered, the quantity, and the price for each item. The visitor can remove an item from their shopping cart by clicking the Remove link in the fourth column of the HTML table. So, if the visitor were to click the Remove link in the Tiger Fish row, that item would be removed, as shown in Figure 16-5.

Beneath the HTML table, the user sees the total for their order. As you will see when you look at the database, the totals are maintained through triggers. Therefore, whenever items are added to or removed from the shopping cart, these tallies are kept up to date.

From this page, the user can elect to continue shopping through the catalog or to Check Out. If they click the Check Out link, they are taken to the Check Out page displayed in Figure 16-6.

Note that the Check Out page also shows the visitor the amount of their order. The visitor would then enter their personal information on the Check Out page and click the Check Out button. When they do that, they are taken to the Receipt page displayed in Figure 16-7.

The Receipt page provides the visitor with a copy of the order for their records. The first section of the receipt displays the personal information on the order. Then the section under that shows the visitor the products that were included with the order.

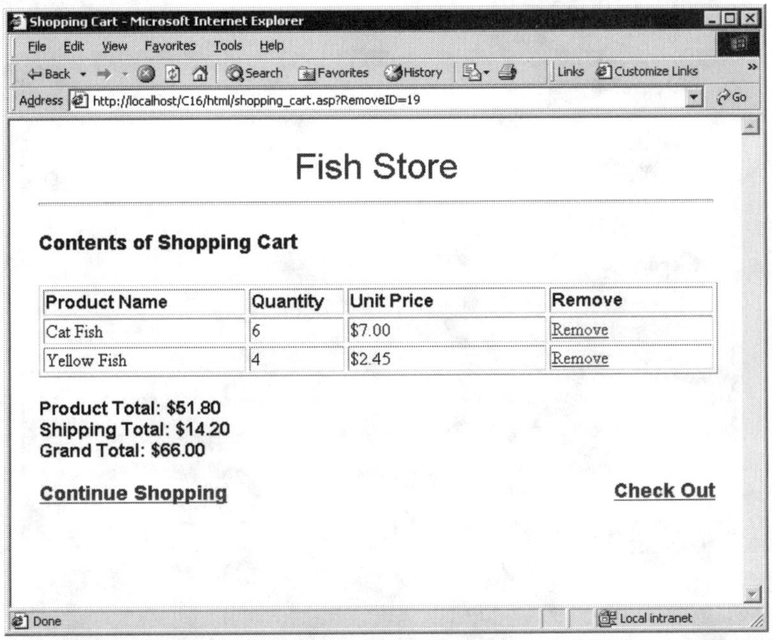

Figure 16-5 *Shopping cart with item removed*

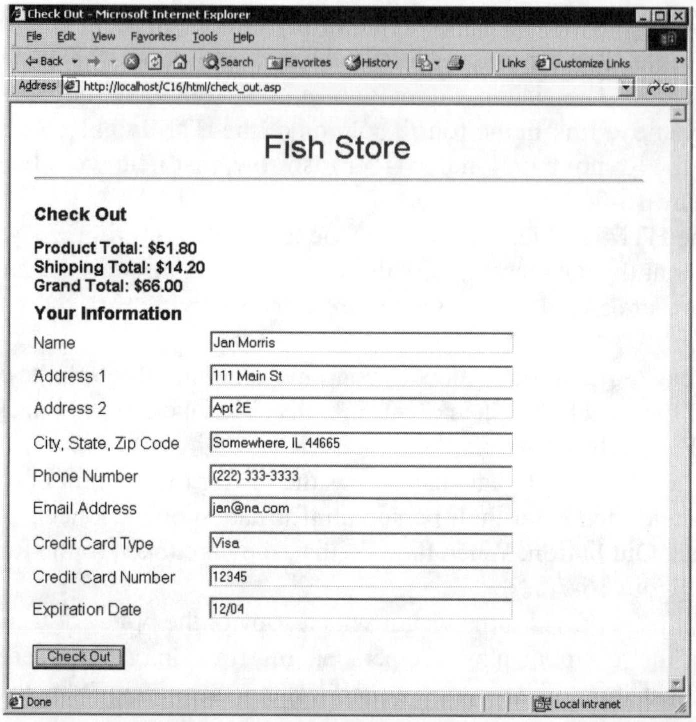

Figure 16-6 *Check Out page*

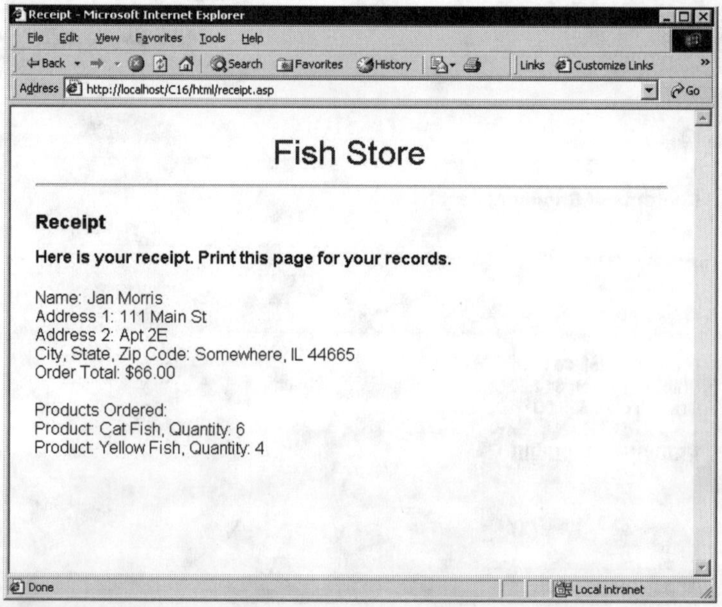

Figure 16-7 *Receipt page*

Tables and Relationships

C16SQLObjects.sql

Products Table

The Products table stores information about the products in the catalog. That information is displayed on the Products page and is used when placing items in the shopping cart.

Categories Table

When the visitor enters the Products page, they select a category in which they want to view products. The names of the different products are stored in the Categories table.

ProductsInCategories Table

Each product can be in many categories, and each category can have many products. Therefore, the Products table and the Categories table are in a many-to-many relationship. The ProductsInCategories table satisfies that relationship by acting as the connecting table. Each product can have many records in the ProductsInCategories table, and each category can also have many records in the table.

Visitors Table

The Visitors table stores the table-level information about the people who visit the Online Store. Whenever a visitor comes to the home page, a record for them is created in this table.

VisitorItems Table

The VisitorItems table stores the contents of the visitor's shopping cart. Each item they place in their shopping cart produces a record in this table. The VisitorItems table is in a one-to-many relationship with the Visitors table. Each visitor can have many items in their shopping cart, but each item goes with a specific visitor.

Field Specifications

Products Table

Products.txt

The field specifications for the Products table are displayed in Table 16-1.

Field Name	Field Type	Notes
ProductID	int	Primary Key, Identity Column
ProductName	varchar	Length = 60
ProductDescription	varchar	Length = 1000
ProductPrice	money	
ProductShipping	money	
SmallImageName	varchar	Length = 50
BigImageName	varchar	Length = 50

Table 16-1 *Products Table Field Specifications*

The ProductID field is the primary key in this table. Since it is an identity column, it is automatically populated when a new record is added to this table.

The ProductPrice field stores the amount that a single unit of this product costs. The ProductShipping field stores the amount charged for each unit for shipping.

The SmallImageName field stores the filename of the graphic used as the thumbnail image on the Products page. The BigImageName field stores the name of the file that contains the large image of the product that is viewed when the thumbnail image is clicked on the Products page. Both files must be located in a folder of the main root of the Web site called Pics for the images to be displayed properly.

Categories Table

Categories.txt

The field specifications for the Categories table are displayed in Table 16-2.

The CategoryID field is the primary key in this table. The other field stores the name of the category. These names are then used in the Category list on the Products page.

ProductsInCategories Table

ProductsInCategories.txt

The field specifications for the ProductsInCategories table are displayed in Table 16-3.

The ProductInCategoryID field is the primary key in this table. The ProductID field is a foreign key that links this table to the Products table. The CategoryID field is also a foreign key. It links this table to the Categories table.

Field Name	Field Type	Notes
CategoryID	int	Primary Key, Identity Column
CategoryName	varchar	Length = 60

Table 16-2 *Categories Table Field Specifications*

Field Name	Field Type	Notes
ProductInCategoryID	int	Primary Key, Identity Column
ProductID	int	Foreign Key
CategoryID	int	Foreign Key

Table 16-3 *ProductsInCategories Table Field Specifications*

Visitors Table

Visitors.txt

The field specifications for the Visitors table are displayed in Table 16-4.

The VisitorID field uniquely identifies each record. The Status field stores the status of the order. When a record is first added, it is set to Open. When the visitor checks out, the field is set to Order Placed.

The money fields store the total dollar amount for the products purchased, the shipping charge, and the grand total. The fields are automatically populated according to triggers in the VisitorItems table.

VisitorItems Table

VisitorItems.txt

The field specifications for the VisitorItems table are displayed in Table 16-5.

Field Name	Field Type	Notes
VisitorID	int	Primary Key, Identity Column
VisitorName	varchar	Length = 100
Address1	varchar	Length = 100
Address2	varchar	Length = 100
CSZ	varchar	Length = 100
PhoneNumber	varchar	Length = 100
EmailAddress	varchar	Length = 100
CCType	varchar	Length = 100
CCNumber	varchar	Length = 100
CCExpirationDate	varchar	Length = 100
Status	varchar	Length = 50
ProductTotal	money	
ShippingTotal	money	
GrandTotal	money	

Table 16-4 *Visitors Table Field Specifications*

Field Name	Field Type	Notes
VisitorItemID	int	Primary Key, Identity Column
VisitorID	int	Foreign Key
ProductName	varchar	Length = 60
Quantity	int	
UnitPrice	money	
UnitShipping	money	

Table 16-5 *VisitorItems Table Field Specifications*

The primary key for this table is the VisitorItemID field. The VisitorID field is a foreign key that links this table back to the Visitors table.

Triggers

InsertItem Trigger

When a record is added to the VisitorItems table, the tally fields in the Visitors table for that visitor need to be updated. The InsertItem trigger provides that functionality.

```
CREATE TRIGGER InsertItem ON dbo.VisitorItems
AFTER INSERT
AS
BEGIN
      DECLARE
      @ProductTotal money,
      @ShippingTotal money
      Select @ProductTotal = Sum(Quantity * UnitPrice)
            from VisitorItems
            Where VisitorID = (Select VisitorID from Inserted)
      Select @ShippingTotal = Sum(Quantity * UnitShipping)
            from VisitorItems
            Where VisitorID = (Select VisitorID from Inserted)
      Update Visitors set
            ProductTotal = @ProductTotal,
            ShippingTotal = @ShippingTotal,
            GrandTotal = @ProductTotal + @ShippingTotal
            Where VisitorID = (Select VisitorID from Inserted)
END
```

The trigger runs on the VisitorItems table:

```
CREATE TRIGGER InsertItem ON dbo.VisitorItems
```

It fires after a record is inserted into that table:

```
AFTER INSERT
```

The trigger will need a variable to store the product total:

```
DECLARE
@ProductTotal money,
```

and the shipping total:

```
@ShippingTotal money
```

You then retrieve the sum of the products ordered multiplied by the number of each product ordered and place that result into a variable. Note the Where clause limits the records summed to only those for the visitor who just added something into the shopping cart:

```
Select @ProductTotal = Sum(Quantity * UnitPrice)
      from VisitorItems
      Where VisitorID = (Select VisitorID from Inserted)
```

You then do the same for the shipping total:

```
Select @ShippingTotal = Sum(Quantity * UnitShipping)
      from VisitorItems
      Where VisitorID = (Select VisitorID from Inserted)
```

An Update query is then used to update the tally fields for the visitor who just inserted an item into their shopping cart based on the totals you just retrieved:

```
Update Visitors set
      ProductTotal = @ProductTotal,
      ShippingTotal = @ShippingTotal,
      GrandTotal = @ProductTotal + @ShippingTotal
      Where VisitorID = (Select VisitorID from Inserted)
```

DeleteItem Trigger

The visitor can also remove items from their shopping cart. When they do that, you need to update their tallies in the Visitors table. The DeleteItem trigger takes this action.

```
CREATE TRIGGER DeleteItem ON dbo.VisitorItems
AFTER DELETE
AS
BEGIN
      DECLARE
      @ProductTotal money,
      @ShippingTotal money
      Select @ProductTotal = Sum(Quantity * UnitPrice)
            from VisitorItems
            Where VisitorID = (Select VisitorID from Deleted)
      Select @ShippingTotal = Sum(Quantity * UnitShipping)
            from VisitorItems
            Where VisitorID = (Select VisitorID from Deleted)
      Update Visitors set
            ProductTotal = @ProductTotal,
            ShippingTotal = @ShippingTotal,
            GrandTotal = @ProductTotal + @ShippingTotal
            Where VisitorID = (Select VisitorID from Deleted)
END
```

The trigger fires when a record is deleted from the VisitorItems table:

```
CREATE TRIGGER DeleteItem ON dbo.VisitorItems
AFTER DELETE
```

One variable is needed to retrieve the new sum of the products ordered:

```
@ProductTotal money,
```

and one is used to retrieve the total amount of shipping on the order:

```
@ShippingTotal money
```

You then total the amount for the products from the VisitorItems table for the visitor who just deleted a record:

```
Select @ProductTotal = Sum(Quantity * UnitPrice)
      from VisitorItems
      Where VisitorID = (Select VisitorID from Deleted)
```

You also need to retrieve the amount for the shipping:

```
Select @ShippingTotal = Sum(Quantity * UnitShipping)
      from VisitorItems
      Where VisitorID = (Select VisitorID from Deleted)
```

Those values are then used to update the three total fields in the Visitors table for the current visitor:

```
Update Visitors set
      ProductTotal = @ProductTotal,
      ShippingTotal = @ShippingTotal,
      GrandTotal = @ProductTotal + @ShippingTotal
      Where VisitorID = (Select VisitorID from Deleted)
```

Stored Procedures

VisitorNew Stored Procedure

When a visitor first enters your site, you need to create a visitor record for them so that they can add items to the shopping cart. The VisitorNew stored procedure accomplishes this task.

```
CREATE PROCEDURE VisitorNew AS
BEGIN
      Insert Into Visitors
            (Status) values ('Open')
      Select @@Identity as VisitorID
END
GO
```

The procedure simply adds a new record to the Visitors table and sets the status of the visitor to open:

```
Insert Into Visitors
      (Status) values ('Open')
```

The ID of the visitor record just added is returned from the procedure:

```
Select @@Identity as VisitorID
```

CategoryList Stored Procedure

The Products page contains a list of all the categories of products. The CategoryList stored procedure returns the Option tags for the HTML Select control that displays that list.

```
CREATE PROCEDURE CategoryList
AS
Declare
@AllOfIt varchar(8000),
@CategoryID varchar(10),
@CategoryName varchar(60)
Declare CurCategories Cursor
For Select CategoryID, CategoryName from Categories
      order by CategoryName
Open CurCategories
Fetch CurCategories
      Into @CategoryID, @CategoryName
Select @AllOfIt = ''
While @@Fetch_Status = 0
      BEGIN
            Select @AllOfIt = @AllOfIt + '<OPTION VALUE="' +
                  @CategoryID + '">' + @CategoryName
                  + '</OPTION>'
            Fetch CurCategories
                  Into @CategoryID, @CategoryName
      END
Close CurCategories
Deallocate CurCategories
Select @AllOfIt as TheList
GO
```

You will need a variable to store the options for the Select control:

```
@AllOfIt varchar(8000),
```

You also need variables that will store the ID of each category retrieved:

```
@CategoryID varchar(10),
```

and the name of that category:

```
@CategoryName varchar(60)
```

A Cursor object is then declared:

```
Declare CurCategories Cursor
```

that will be used to retrieve the names and IDs of all the categories from the database:

```
For Select CategoryID, CategoryName from Categories
      order by CategoryName
```

You then open the Cursor:

```
Open CurCategories
```

and retrieve the first record into your local variables:

```
Fetch CurCategories
      Into @CategoryID, @CategoryName
```

You need to initialize your return list of Option tags:

```
Select @AllOfIt = ''
```

and enter a loop so that you can process each of the category records:

```
While @@Fetch_Status = 0
```

Each category needs to be displayed on the Web page as an Option tag for a Select control. So you open that tag:

```
Select @AllOfIt = @AllOfIt + '<OPTION VALUE="' +
```

and place the ID of the category into the Value parameter. This is the data that is sent when the HTML form is submitted. After that, the name of the category is entered into the tag, which is what the visitor sees:

```
@CategoryID + '">' + @CategoryName
```

You then close the tag:

```
+ '</OPTION>'
```

retrieve the next record:

```
Fetch CurCategories
      Into @CategoryID, @CategoryName
```

and loop to process it:

```
End
```

After the loop, you need to close your Cursor object:

```
Close CurCategories
```

and release its resources:

```
Deallocate CurCategories
```

You then return the Option tags to the calling application:

```
Select @AllOfIt as TheList
```

ProductItem Stored Procedure

The Products page displays one of the products in the product catalog. Either the item selected by the visitor is displayed or the first item in the current category is displayed. The ProductItem stored procedure returns the data for a single product formatted for the Products page.

```
CREATE PROCEDURE ProductItem
@ProductID  int = 0,
@CategoryID int = 0
AS
Declare
@ProductInfo varchar(2000),
@ProductName varchar(60),
@ProductDescription varchar(1000),
@ProductPrice varchar(20),
@SmallImageName varchar(50),
@BigImageName varchar(50)
if @ProductID = 0
      BEGIN
            Select @ProductID = Min(Products.ProductID)
                  From Products
                  Left Join ProductsInCategories On
                  Products.ProductID = ProductsInCategories.ProductID
                  Where CategoryID = @CategoryID
      END
Select @ProductName = ProductName,
```

```
      @ProductDescription = ProductDescription,
      @ProductPrice = convert(varchar(20), ProductPrice),
      @SmallImageName = SmallImageName,
      @BigImageName = BigImageName from Products
      Where ProductID = @ProductID
Set @ProductInfo = 'Name: ' + @ProductName
      + '<BR>Description: ' + @ProductDescription
      + '</P> <P>Price: $' + @ProductPrice + '</P>'
Select @ProductInfo as ProductInfo,
      @ProductID as ProductID,
      @SmallImageName as SmallImageName,
      @BigImageName as BigImageName
GO
```

The first parameter is optional and is used to pass in the ID of the product to retrieve. If it is omitted, it is set to the special value of 0. Note that you use 0 to indicate that the first record should be returned. This is used to display some record when the Products page is first opened or when a different category is selected:

```
@ProductID  int = 0,
```

The other parameter passed in is also optional and set to 0 by default. If the ProductID is omitted or set to 0, then this parameter is used to indicate which category the first product should be retrieved from:

```
@CategoryID int = 0
```

Within the procedure you will need some variables. The first will store the general information about the product:

```
@ProductInfo varchar(2000),
```

The next will be used to retrieve the name of the product:

```
@ProductName varchar(60),
```

its description:

```
@ProductDescription varchar(1000),
```

and price:

```
@ProductPrice varchar(20),
```

You also need to retrieve the path to the thumbnail image of the product:

```
@SmallImageName varchar(50),
```

and the full-size image of the product:

```
@BigImageName varchar(50)
```

Now you can check to see whether you need to look up a product ID or whether one was submitted:

```
if @ProductID = 0
```

If the parameter is set to 0, you need to retrieve the lowest product ID in the category for which the ID was passed into this procedure:

```
Select @ProductID = Min(Products.ProductID)
      From Products
      Left Join ProductsInCategories On
      Products.ProductID = ProductsInCategories.ProductID
      Where CategoryID = @CategoryID
```

After the If block, you have a product ID, the value of which is used to retrieve the data into your local variables:

```
Select @ProductName = ProductName,
      @ProductDescription = ProductDescription,
      @ProductPrice = convert(varchar(20), ProductPrice),
      @SmallImageName = SmallImageName,
      @BigImageName = BigImageName from Products
      Where ProductID = @ProductID
```

You need to return the information on the product in summary form so that it can be displayed on the Products page. Therefore, you concatenate the field values with text and HTML elements:

```
Set @ProductInfo = 'Name: ' + @ProductName
      + '<BR>Description: ' + @ProductDescription
      + '</P> <P>Price: $' + @ProductPrice + '</P>'
```

You then return that information, as well as the ID and image paths, for the product to the calling application:

```
Select @ProductInfo as ProductInfo,
      @ProductID as ProductID,
      @SmallImageName as SmallImageName,
      @BigImageName as BigImageName
```

ProductList Stored Procedure

The ProductList stored procedure returns Option tags for an HTML Select control. These options contain the names and IDs of the products in a particular category or in the first category.

```
CREATE PROCEDURE ProductList
@CategoryID  int = 0
AS
Declare
@CategoryName varchar(60),
@AllOfIt varchar(8000),
@ProductID varchar(10),
@ProductName varchar(60)
if @CategoryID = 0
      BEGIN
            Select @CategoryID = Min(CategoryID)
                  From Categories
      END
Select @CategoryName = CategoryName from Categories
      Where CategoryID = @CategoryID
Declare CurProducts Cursor
For Select Products.ProductID, ProductName from Products
      Left Join ProductsInCategories On
      Products.ProductID = ProductsInCategories.ProductID
      Where CategoryID = @CategoryID
      order by ProductName
Open CurProducts
Fetch CurProducts
      Into @ProductID, @ProductName
Select @AllOfIt = ''
```

```
While @@Fetch_Status = 0
     BEGIN
          Select @AllOfIt = @AllOfIt + '<OPTION VALUE="' +
               @ProductID + '">' + @ProductName
               + '</OPTION>'
          Fetch CurProducts
               Into @ProductID, @ProductName
     END
Close CurProducts
Deallocate CurProducts
Select @CategoryID as CategoryID,
     @CategoryName as CategoryName,
     @AllOfIt as TheList
GO
```

The procedure has a single parameter: the ID of the Category from which you want to return products. The parameter is optional:

```
@CategoryID  int = 0
```

Locally, you will need to retrieve the name of the category so that it can be returned:

```
@CategoryName varchar(60),
```

This variable will store the Option tags as they are being built:

```
@AllOfIt varchar(8000),
```

and the other two will store the ID and name of the product as you retrieve them one at a time from the database:

```
@ProductID varchar(10),
@ProductName varchar(60)
```

You then check to see whether you need to retrieve the lowest CategoryID:

```
if @CategoryID = 0
```

If so, you use the Min aggregate function to retrieve the lowest CategoryID:

```
Select @CategoryID = Min(CategoryID)
     From Categories
```

You can now retrieve the name of the current category and store it in your local variable:

```
Select @CategoryName = CategoryName from Categories
      Where CategoryID = @CategoryID
```

Next, you declare a Cursor object:

```
Declare CurProducts Cursor
```

It will be used to retrieve the names and IDs for all the products that are in the current category. Note that you need to link to the ProductsInCategories table to retrieve just those products in a specific category:

```
For Select Products.ProductID, ProductName from Products
      Left Join ProductsInCategories On
      Products.ProductID = ProductsInCategories.ProductID
      Where CategoryID = @CategoryID
      order by ProductName
```

You then open the cursor:

```
Open CurProducts
```

and retrieve the ID and name of the first product into your local variables:

```
Fetch CurProducts
      Into @ProductID, @ProductName
```

You then initialize the variable that will store the Option tags:

```
Select @AllOfIt = ''
```

Next, a loop is started that will continue until you run out of records:

```
While @@Fetch_Status = 0
```

Within that loop, each product is added as an Option tag to your return value. Note that the tag is built so that the visitor would see the name of the product, but that actually the ID of the product would be passed when the form was submitted:

```
Select @AllOfIt = @AllOfIt + '<OPTION VALUE="' +
      @ProductID + '">' + @ProductName
      + '</OPTION>'
```

You then retrieve the next product record:

```
Fetch CurProducts
      Into @ProductID, @ProductName
And Loop to process it:
End
```

After the loop, you need to release the resources of the Cursor object:

```
Close CurProducts
Deallocate CurProducts
```

You then return the ID and name of the current category, as well as the Option tags for the Products HTML Select control:

```
Select @CategoryID as CategoryID,
      @CategoryName as CategoryName,
      @AllOfIt as TheList
```

VisitorItemAdd Stored Procedure

When the visitor adds a product to their shopping cart, the VisitorItemAdd stored procedure is used to add the item to the VisitorItems table.

```
CREATE PROCEDURE VisitorItemAdd
@VisitorID integer,
@ProductID int,
@Quantity int
AS
DECLARE
@ProductName varchar(60),
@ProductPrice money,
@ProductShipping money
Select @ProductName = ProductName,
      @ProductPrice = ProductPrice,
      @ProductShipping = ProductShipping
      From Products
      Where ProductID = @ProductID
Insert Into VisitorItems
      (VisitorID, ProductName, Quantity,
      UnitPrice, UnitShipping) Values
      (@VisitorID, @ProductName, @Quantity,
            @ProductPrice, @ProductShipping)
GO
```

Passed into this procedure is the ID of the visitor who is adding an item:

```
@VisitorID integer,
```

the ID of the product being added:

```
@ProductID int,
```

and the quantity of products being added:

```
@Quantity int
```

You need variables to store the name of the product:

```
@ProductName varchar(60),
```

the product cost:

```
@ProductPrice money,
```

and the shipping cost for the product:

```
@ProductShipping money
```

You then retrieve those values from the Products table according to the ProductID passed into this procedure:

```
Select @ProductName = ProductName,
      @ProductPrice = ProductPrice,
      @ProductShipping = ProductShipping
      From Products
      Where ProductID = @ProductID
```

A SQL Insert statement is then used to add the item to the VisitorItems table according to the values passed in and retrieved in the preceding Select statement:

```
Insert Into VisitorItems
      (VisitorID, ProductName, Quantity,
      UnitPrice, UnitShipping) Values
      (@VisitorID, @ProductName, @Quantity,
      @ProductPrice, @ProductShipping)
```

VisitorItemDelete Stored Procedure

The VisitorItemDelete stored procedure is used by the calling application to remove a record from the VisitorItems table. This procedure is called when the visitor clicks the Remove link on the Shopping Cart page.

```
CREATE PROCEDURE VisitorItemDelete
@VisitorItemID integer
AS
BEGIN
      Delete From VisitorItems
            Where VisitorItemID = @VisitorItemID
END
GO
```

Passed into the procedure is the ID of the record to be deleted:

```
@VisitorItemID integer
```

The record with that ID is then removed from the VisitorItems table:

```
Delete From VisitorItems
      Where VisitorItemID = @VisitorItemID
```

ShoppingCart Stored Procedure

The ShoppingCart stored procedure returns all the items that the visitor has in their shopping cart formatted as rows for an HTML table. The procedure also returns summary text about the total amounts on the order, which is also displayed on the Shopping Cart page.

```
CREATE PROCEDURE ShoppingCart
@VisitorID integer
AS
DECLARE
@AllofIt varchar(5000),
@VisitorItemID integer,
@ProductName varchar(60),
@Quantity integer,
@UnitPrice money,
@ProductTotal money,
@ShippingTotal money,
@GrandTotal money,
@TotalText varchar(1000)
Declare CurItems Cursor
```

```
For Select VisitorItemID, ProductName, Quantity,
      UnitPrice from VisitorItems
      Where VisitorID = @VisitorID
Open CurItems
Fetch CurItems
      Into @VisitorItemID, @ProductName, @Quantity,
      @UnitPrice
Select @AllOfIt = ''
While @@Fetch_Status = 0
      Begin
            Select @AllOfIt = @AllOfIt + '<TR>'
                  + '<TD>' + @ProductName + '</TD>'
                  + '<TD>' + convert(varchar(10), @Quantity) + '</TD>'
                  + '<TD>$' + convert(varchar(20), @UnitPrice) + '</TD>'
                  + '<TD><A HREF="./shopping_cart.asp?RemoveID='
                  + convert(varchar(10), @VisitorItemID) + '"><FONT COLOR="#000099">'
                  + 'Remove</FONT></TD>'
                  + '</TR>'
            Fetch CurItems
                  Into @VisitorItemID, @ProductName, @Quantity,
                  @UnitPrice
      End
Close CurItems
Deallocate CurItems
Select @ProductTotal = ProductTotal,
      @ShippingTotal = ShippingTotal,
      @GrandTotal = GrandTotal
      From Visitors
      Where VisitorID = @VisitorID
Select @TotalText = 'Product Total: $' + convert(varchar(50), @ProductTotal)
            + '<BR>Shipping Total: $' + convert(varchar(50), @ShippingTotal)
            + '<BR>Grand Total: $' + convert(varchar(50), @GrandTotal)
Select @AllOfIt as TheList, @TotalText as TotalText
GO
```

Passed into the procedure is the ID of the visitor whose shopping cart is to be returned:

```
@VisitorID integer
```

Within the procedure, you will need many variables. One will store the contents of the HTML rows for the shopping cart:

```
@AllofIt varchar(5000),
```

The next four will be used to retrieve the values for the visitor's records in the VisitorItems table:

```
@VisitorItemID integer,
@ProductName varchar(60),
@Quantity integer,
@UnitPrice money,
```

The three money variables will be used to retrieve the current totals on the order:

```
@ProductTotal money,
@ShippingTotal money,
@GrandTotal money,
```

which will be formatted and returned through this variable:

```
@TotalText varchar(1000)
```

You will need a Cursor object:

```
Declare CurItems Cursor
```

It will contain all the records in the VisitorItems table for the current visitor. These are the items that the visitor has placed into their shopping cart:

```
For Select VisitorItemID, ProductName, Quantity,
      UnitPrice from VisitorItems
      Where VisitorID = @VisitorID
```

That cursor is opened:

```
Open CurItems
```

and the values for the first record retrieved are placed into your local variables:

```
Fetch CurItems
      Into @VisitorItemID, @ProductName, @Quantity,
      @UnitPrice
```

You then clear your variable that will contain the text for the shopping cart:

```
Select @AllOfIt = ''
```

and cnter a loop so that each item in the shopping cart can be processed:

```
While @@Fetch_Status = 0
```

Each record is concatenated into your local variable. Each record is formatted so that it is returned as an HTML row for an HTML table:

```
Select @AllOfIt = @AllOfIt + '<TR>'
```

The first cell in the row contains the name of the product:

```
+ '<TD>' + @ProductName + '</TD>'
```

followed by the quantity ordered:

```
+ '<TD>' + convert(varchar(10), @Quantity) + '</TD>'
```

and the cost for each item:

```
+ '<TD>$' + convert(varchar(20), @UnitPrice) + '</TD>'
```

The next cell in the row contains the Remove link. This allows the visitor to remove the item from the shopping cart. Note that the link is formatted so that it links to the Shopping Cart page, passing to it the ID of the current shopping cart item:

```
+ '<TD><A HREF="./shopping_cart.asp?RemoveID='
+ convert(varchar(10), @VisitorItemID) + '"><FONT COLOR="#000099">'
+ 'Remove</FONT></TD>'
```

You then close the current row tag:

```
+ '</TR>'
```

retrieve the next record, and loop so that it can be processed:

```
Fetch CurItems
      Into @VisitorItemID, @ProductName, @Quantity,
      @UnitPrice
End
```

After the loop, you need to release the Cursor object:

```
Close CurItems
Deallocate CurItems
```

In addition to the contents of the shopping cart, the procedure needs to return text for the order total that is displayed on the Shopping Cart page. So the current totals for the visitor are retrieved from their record:

```
Select @ProductTotal = ProductTotal,
      @ShippingTotal = ShippingTotal,
      @GrandTotal = GrandTotal
      From Visitors
      Where VisitorID = @VisitorID
```

You then format the total retrieved so that it will be displayed properly as HTML on the Shopping Cart page:

```
Select @TotalText = 'Product Total: $' + convert(varchar(50), @ProductTotal)
      + '<BR>Shipping Total: $' + convert(varchar(50), @ShippingTotal)
      + '<BR>Grand Total: $' + convert(varchar(50), @GrandTotal)
```

Finally, you return the contents of the shopping cart and the summary text to the calling application:

```
Select @AllOfIt as TheList, @TotalText as TotalText
```

TotalStuff Stored Procedure

When the visitor enters the Check Out page, they see their order total. The TotalStuff stored procedure returns that text to the Active Server Page.

```
CREATE PROCEDURE TotalStuff
@VisitorID integer
AS
DECLARE
@ProductTotal money,
@ShippingTotal money,
@GrandTotal money,
@TotalText varchar(1000)
Select @ProductTotal = ProductTotal,
      @ShippingTotal = ShippingTotal,
      @GrandTotal = GrandTotal
      From Visitors
      Where VisitorID = @VisitorID
Select @TotalText = 'Product Total: $' + convert(varchar(50), @ProductTotal)
            + '<BR>Shipping Total: $' + convert(varchar(50), @ShippingTotal)
            + '<BR>Grand Total: $' + convert(varchar(50), @GrandTotal)
Select @TotalText as TotalText
GO
```

Passed into the procedure is the ID of the visitor whose totals need to be returned:

```
@VisitorID integer
```

Within the procedure, you will need variables to store the totals:

```
@ProductTotal money,
@ShippingTotal money,
@GrandTotal money,
```

as well as the totals formatted into text for the Check Out page:

```
@TotalText varchar(1000)
```

You then retrieve the totals for the VisitorID passed into the procedure:

```
Select @ProductTotal = ProductTotal,
      @ShippingTotal = ShippingTotal,
      @GrandTotal = GrandTotal
      From Visitors
      Where VisitorID = @VisitorID
```

You then concatenate the total variables with text and HTML tags:

```
Select @TotalText = 'Product Total: $' + convert(varchar(50), @ProductTotal)
            + '<BR>Shipping Total: $' + convert(varchar(50), @ShippingTotal)
            + '<BR>Grand Total: $' + convert(varchar(50), @GrandTotal)
```

That text is then returned to the calling application:

```
Select @TotalText as TotalText
```

VisitorCheckOut Stored Procedure

The VisitorCheckOut stored procedure modifies the visitor's record with their personal information and marks the order as having been placed. The procedure is called from the Check Out page.

```
CREATE PROCEDURE VisitorCheckOut
@VisitorID integer,
@VisitorName varchar(100),
@Address1 varchar(100),
@Address2 varchar(100),
@CSZ varchar(100),
@PhoneNumber varchar(100),
@EmailAddress varchar(100),
@CCType varchar(100),
@CCNumber varchar(100),
```

```
@CCExpirationDate varchar(100)
AS
BEGIN
      Update Visitors set
            VisitorName = @VisitorName,
            Address1 = @Address1,
            Address2 = @Address2,
            CSZ = @CSZ,
            PhoneNumber = @PhoneNumber,
            EmailAddress = @EmailAddress,
            CCType = @CCType,
            CCNumber = @CCNumber,
            CCExpirationDate = @CCExpirationDate,
            Status = 'Order Placed'
            Where VisitorID = @VisitorID
END
GO
```

Passed into the procedure is the ID of the visitor who is checking out:

```
@VisitorID integer,
```

Also passed in is the personal information that the visitor entered when they checked out through the Check Out page:

```
@VisitorName varchar(100),
@Address1 varchar(100),
@Address2 varchar(100),
@CSZ varchar(100),
@PhoneNumber varchar(100),
@EmailAddress varchar(100),
@CCType varchar(100),
@CCNumber varchar(100),
@CCExpirationDate varchar(100)
```

You then update the visitor's record according to the parameters passed into this procedure:

```
Update Visitors set
      VisitorName = @VisitorName,
      Address1 = @Address1,
      Address2 = @Address2,
      CSZ = @CSZ,
      PhoneNumber = @PhoneNumber,
      EmailAddress = @EmailAddress,
      CCType = @CCType,
      CCNumber = @CCNumber,
      CCExpirationDate = @CCExpirationDate,
```

The record is also marked as Order Placed:

```
Status = 'Order Placed'
Where VisitorID = @VisitorID
```

StoreReceipt Stored Procedure

The StoreReceipt stored procedure returns the contents of the visitor's order formatted for the Receipt page.

```
CREATE PROCEDURE StoreReceipt
@VisitorID integer
AS
DECLARE
@VisitorName varchar(100),
@Address1 varchar(100),
@Address2 varchar(100),
@CSZ varchar(100),
@GrandTotal money,
@ProductName varchar(60),
@Quantity integer,
@ReceiptText varchar(2000)
Declare CurItems Cursor
For Select ProductName, Quantity from VisitorItems
      Where VisitorID = @VisitorID
Select @VisitorName = VisitorName,
      @Address1 = Address1,
      @Address2 = Address2,
      @CSZ = CSZ,
      @GrandTotal = GrandTotal
      From Visitors
      Where VisitorID = @VisitorID
Select @ReceiptText = 'Name: ' + @VisitorName
      + '<BR>Address 1: ' + @Address1
      + '<BR>Address 2: ' + @Address2
      + '<BR>City, State, Zip Code: ' + @CSZ
      + '<BR>Order Total: $' + Convert(varchar(20), @GrandTotal)
      + '<BR><BR>Products Ordered:<BR>'
Open CurItems
Fetch CurItems
      Into @ProductName, @Quantity
While @@Fetch_Status = 0
      Begin
            Select @ReceiptText = @ReceiptText +
```

```
                    'Product: ' + @ProductName
                    + ', Quantity: ' + Convert(varchar(10), @Quantity)
                    + '<BR>'
               Fetch CurItems
                    Into @ProductName, @Quantity
     End
Close CurItems
Deallocate CurItems
Select @ReceiptText as ReceiptText
GO
```

The procedure expects one parameter, the ID of the visitor whose receipt is to be returned:

```
@VisitorID integer
```

You will need variables to retrieve personal information for the receipt from the Visitors table:

```
@VisitorName varchar(100),
@Address1 varchar(100),
@Address2 varchar(100),
@CSZ varchar(100),
@GrandTotal money,
```

You also need variables that will be used to retrieve the names and quantities of the products that the visitor ordered:

```
@ProductName varchar(60),
@Quantity integer,
```

One last variable will contain the text of the receipt as you build it in this procedure:

```
@ReceiptText varchar(2000)
```

You also need a Cursor object:

```
Declare CurItems Cursor
```

that will be used to return the names and quantities of the products ordered by the visitor:

```
For Select ProductName, Quantity from VisitorItems
     Where VisitorID = @VisitorID
```

Next, you retrieve the visitor's personal information into your local variables:

```
Select @VisitorName = VisitorName,
      @Address1 = Address1,
      @Address2 = Address2,
      @CSZ = CSZ,
      @GrandTotal = GrandTotal
      From Visitors
      Where VisitorID = @VisitorID
```

You place this data concatenated with text and HTML tags into your return variable:

```
Select @ReceiptText = 'Name: ' + @VisitorName
      + '<BR>Address 1: ' + @Address1
      + '<BR>Address 2: ' + @Address2
      + '<BR>City, State, Zip Code: ' + @CSZ
      + '<BR>Order Total: $' + Convert(varchar(20), @GrandTotal)
      + '<BR><BR>Products Ordered:<BR>'
```

Now you need to add the products ordered to the receipt. So you open the Cursor object:

```
Open CurItems
```

retrieve the first item ordered:

```
Fetch CurItems
      Into @ProductName, @Quantity
```

and enter a loop so that each item ordered can be processed:

```
While @@Fetch_Status = 0
```

Within the loop, you concatenate each item to your return variable:

```
Select @ReceiptText = @ReceiptText +
      'Product: ' + @ProductName
      + ', Quantity: ' + Convert(varchar(10), @Quantity)
      + '<BR>'
```

before moving on to the next record:

```
Fetch CurItems
      Into @ProductName, @Quantity
```

After the loop, you release the Cursor object from memory:

```
Close CurItems
Deallocate CurItems
```

The text of the Receipt is then returned to the calling application:

```
Select @ReceiptText as ReceiptText
```

Users

WebUser16 User

In addition to the default Administrator account, the database has the user WebUser16 associated with it. The only access that user has to the database is through the ten stored procedures. No other permissions are granted to this user.

Active Server Pages

Index Active Server Page

Index.asp

The code on the Index Active Server Page initializes the visitor into the Online Store. The only code on the page appears in the code block at the top.

```
<%
Option Explicit
Dim DBConn
Dim RSNew
If IsEmpty(Session("VisitorID")) Then
      set DBConn = Server.Createobject ("ADODB.Connection")
      DBConn.ConnectionString = "driver={SQL Server};" _
            & "server=MyServer;uid=WebUser16" _
            & ";pwd=WebUser16;" & "database=C16OnlineStore"
      DBConn.Open
      Set RSNew = DBConn.Execute("Exec VisitorNew")
      Session("VisitorID") = RSNew("VisitorID")
End If
%>
```

You start by telling the compiler that variables will be declared:

```
Option Explicit
```

You then declare a variable for your Database Connection object:

```
Dim DBConn
```

and one for a Recordset object:

```
Dim RSNew
```

The Session variable here is used to keep track of the visitor as they traverse the Web site. So you check to see whether they are just entering the site:

```
If IsEmpty(Session("VisitorID")) Then
```

If so, you will need to connect to the database:

```
set DBConn = Server.Createobject ("ADODB.Connection")
DBConn.ConnectionString = "driver={SQL Server};" _
      & "server=MyServer;uid=WebUser16" _
      & ";pwd=WebUser16;" & "database=C16OnlineStore"
DBConn.Open
```

and retrieve an ID for this new visitor:

```
Set RSNew = DBConn.Execute("Exec VisitorNew")
```

and place that ID into the Session variable:

```
Session("VisitorID") = RSNew("VisitorID")
```

Products Active Server Page

Products.asp

The Products page is responsible for displaying products and categories, and adding items to the shopping cart. The page has four states. One state is when the visitor first enters the page, the second state is when the visitor changes to a new category, the third state occurs when the visitor selects a product to view, and the fourth state occurs when the visitor adds an item to the shopping cart. The action taken based on these states is controlled through If statements in the main code block at the top of the Active Server Page.

```
<%
Option Explicit
```

```
Dim DBConn
Dim RSCategoryList
Dim RSProducts
Dim RSCurrentProduct
set DBConn = Server.Createobject ("ADODB.Connection")
DBConn.ConnectionString = "driver={SQL Server};" _
      & "server=MyServer;uid=WebUser16" _
      & ";pwd=WebUser16;" & "database=C16OnlineStore"
DBConn.Open
If Not IsEmpty(Request.Form("AddToShoppingCart")) Then
      DBConn.Execute "Exec VisitorItemAdd " _
            & Session("VisitorID") _
            & ", " & Request.Form("LastProductID") _
            & ", " & Request.Form("Quantity")
      Response.Redirect "./shopping_cart.asp"
End If
Set RSCategoryList = DBConn.Execute("Exec CategoryList")
If IsEmpty(Request.Form("OKChangeCategory")) and _
      IsEmpty(Request.Form("OKChangeProduct")) Then
      Set RSProducts = DBConn.Execute _
            ("Exec ProductList")
      Set RSCurrentProduct = DBConn.Execute _
            ("Exec ProductItem 0, " _
            & RSProducts("CategoryID"))
ElseIf Not IsEmpty(Request.Form("OKChangeCategory")) Then
      Set RSProducts = DBConn.Execute _
            ("Exec ProductList " _
            & Request.Form("CategoryID"))
      Set RSCurrentProduct = DBConn.Execute _
            ("Exec ProductItem 0, " _
            & RSProducts("CategoryID"))
ElseIf Not IsEmpty(Request.Form("OKChangeProduct")) Then
      Set RSProducts = DBConn.Execute _
            ("Exec ProductList " _
            & Request.Form("LastCategoryID"))
      Set RSCurrentProduct = DBConn.Execute _
                  ("Exec ProductItem " _
                  & Request.Form("ProductID"))
End If
%>
```

You start by telling the compiler that variables will be declared:

```
Option Explicit
```

You declare a variable that will be used to connect to your database:

```
Dim DBConn
```

and three Recordset objects may be needed:

```
Dim RSCategoryList
Dim RSProducts
Dim RSCurrentProduct
```

You then instantiate your Connection object:

```
set DBConn = Server.Createobject ("ADODB.Connection")
```

set the connect string for your Online Store database:

```
DBConn.ConnectionString = "driver={SQL Server};" _
      & "server=MyServer;uid=WebUser16" _
      & ";pwd=WebUser16;" & "database=C16OnlineStore"
```

and open the connection:

```
DBConn.Open
```

Next, you check to see whether the visitor is adding an item to their shopping cart by looking for the Add to Shopping Cart button:

```
If Not IsEmpty(Request.Form("AddToShoppingCart")) Then
```

If the button is found, you call your stored procedure to add the item to the shopping cart:

```
DBConn.Execute "Exec VisitorItemAdd " _
      & Session("VisitorID") _
      & ", " & Request.Form("LastProductID") _
      & ", " & Request.Form("Quantity")
```

and send the visitor to the Shopping Cart page:

```
Response.Redirect "./shopping_cart.asp"
```

Otherwise, you retrieve the list for the shopping cart:

```
Set RSCategoryList = DBConn.Execute("Exec CategoryList")
```

and check to see whether this is the entrance into the Products page:

```
If IsEmpty(Request.Form("OKChangeCategory")) and _
    IsEmpty(Request.Form("OKChangeProduct")) Then
```

In that case, the Products list will be for the first category:

```
Set RSProducts = DBConn.Execute _
    ("Exec ProductList")
```

and you will display the first item in that category:

```
Set RSCurrentProduct = DBConn.Execute _
    ("Exec ProductItem 0, " _
    & RSProducts("CategoryID"))
```

The next condition means that the visitor is changing categories:

```
ElseIf Not IsEmpty(Request.Form("OKChangeCategory")) Then
```

In that case, you retrieve all the products for the category selected:

```
Set RSProducts = DBConn.Execute _
    ("Exec ProductList " _
    & Request.Form("CategoryID"))
```

and retrieve information for the first product in that category:

```
Set RSCurrentProduct = DBConn.Execute _
    ("Exec ProductItem 0, " _
    & RSProducts("CategoryID"))
```

If the code flows here, the visitor has selected a product that they wish to view:

```
ElseIf Not IsEmpty(Request.Form("OKChangeProduct")) Then
```

In that case, the product list will be based on the category that you were in before the page was submitted:

```
Set RSProducts = DBConn.Execute _
    ("Exec ProductList " _
    & Request.Form("LastCategoryID"))
```

and the product retrieved is the one that the visitor has selected from the Select control:

```
Set RSCurrentProduct = DBConn.Execute _
            ("Exec ProductItem " _
            & Request.Form("ProductID"))
```

The Form tag on the page submits the contents of the Form back to this Products page:

```
<FORM ACTION="./products.asp" METHOD=POST>
```

Two hidden elements are placed on the form. One contains the ID of the current product so that you can use it when adding an item to the shopping cart:

```
<INPUT TYPE=HIDDEN NAME="LastProductID" VALUE="
<% Response.Write RSCurrentProduct("ProductID") %>">
```

The other stores the ID of the current category so that it is available when the form on the page is submitted:

```
<INPUT TYPE=HIDDEN NAME="LastCategoryID" VALUE="
<% Response.Write RSProducts("CategoryID") %>">
```

Inline on the page, you display the contents of the Category Select control:

```
<SELECT ID="FormsComboBox1" NAME="CategoryID">
      <% Response.Write RSCategoryList("TheList") %>
</SELECT>
```

as well as the contents of the Products Select control:

```
<SELECT ID="FormsComboBox2" NAME="ProductID">
      <% Response.Write RSProducts("TheList") %>
</SELECT>
```

Also on the page you need to display the information for the current product:

```
<% Response.Write RSCurrentProduct("ProductInfo") %>
```

and the thumbnail for the current product:

```
<A HREF="../pics/<% Response.Write RSCurrentProduct("BigImageName") %>">
<IMG ID="Picture1" HEIGHT=100 WIDTH=100
SRC="../pics/<% Response.Write RSCurrentProduct("SmallImageName") %>"
 BORDER=0></A>
```

Shopping Cart Active Server Page

Shopping_Cart.asp

The code on the Shopping Cart page uses your stored procedures to display the contents of the shopping cart and to remove items from it. The main code block is at the top of the form.

```
<%
Option Explicit
Dim DBConn
Dim RSShoppingCart
set DBConn = Server.Createobject ("ADODB.Connection")
DBConn.ConnectionString = "driver={SQL Server};" _
      & "server=MyServer;uid=WebUser16" _
      & ";pwd=WebUser16;" & "database=C16OnlineStore"
DBConn.Open
If Not IsEmpty(Request.QueryString("RemoveID")) Then
      DBConn.Execute "Exec VisitorItemDelete " _
            & Request.QueryString("RemoveID")
End If
Set RSShoppingCart = DBConn.Execute("Exec ShoppingCart " _
      & Session("VisitorID"))
%>
```

You start by telling the compiler that variables will be declared:

```
Option Explicit
```

You then declare a variable for your Connection object:

```
Dim DBConn
```

and for a Recordset object:

```
Dim RSShoppingCart
```

You then connect to your SQL Server database:

```
set DBConn = Server.Createobject ("ADODB.Connection")
DBConn.ConnectionString = "driver={SQL Server};" _
      & "server=MyServer;uid=WebUser16" _
      & ";pwd=WebUser16;" & "database=C16OnlineStore"
DBConn.Open
```

Next, you check to see whether the visitor is trying to remove an item from the shopping cart:

```
If Not IsEmpty(Request.QueryString("RemoveID")) Then
```

If so, you call your stored procedure to delete the desired record:

```
DBConn.Execute "Exec VisitorItemDelete " _
      & Request.QueryString("RemoveID")
```

After that, you retrieve the contents of the shopping cart:

```
Set RSShoppingCart = DBConn.Execute("Exec ShoppingCart " _
      & Session("VisitorID"))
```

Then, within the HTML, you display the contents of the shopping cart:

```
<% Response.Write RSShoppingCart("TheList") %>
```

as well as the summary billing information:

```
<% Response.Write RSShoppingCart("TotalText") %>
```

Check Out Active Server Page

Check_Out.asp

The code on the Check Out page calls stored procedures to mark the visitor's record as checked out and to display the price summary information on the page. The main code block is at the top of the page.

```
<%
Option Explicit
Dim DBConn
Dim RSTotalStuff
set DBConn = Server.Createobject ("ADODB.Connection")
DBConn.ConnectionString = "driver={SQL Server};" _
      & "server=MyServer;uid=WebUser16" _
      & ";pwd=WebUser16;" & "database=C16OnlineStore"
DBConn.Open
If Not IsEmpty(Request.Form("CheckOut")) Then
      DBConn.Execute "Exec VisitorCheckOut " _
            & Session("VisitorID") & ", " _
            & "'" & Request.Form("VisitorName") & "', " _
            & "'" & Request.Form("Address1") & "', " _
```

```
            & "'" & Request.Form("Address2") & "', " _
            & "'" & Request.Form("CSZ") & "', " _
            & "'" & Request.Form("PhoneNumber") & "', " _
            & "'" & Request.Form("EmailAddress") & "', " _
            & "'" & Request.Form("CCType") & "', " _
            & "'" & Request.Form("CCNumber") & "', " _
            & "'" & Request.Form("CCExpirationDate") & "'"
      Response.Redirect "./receipt.asp"
End If
Set RSTotalStuff = DBConn.Execute("Exec TotalStuff " _
      & Session("VisitorID"))
%>
```

You start by telling the compiler that you will declare your variables:

```
Option Explicit
```

You then declare variables for a Connection object:

```
Dim DBConn
```

and for a Recordset object:

```
Dim RSTotalStuff
```

Next, a connection to your database is opened:

```
set DBConn = Server.Createobject ("ADODB.Connection")
DBConn.ConnectionString = "driver={SQL Server};" _
      & "server=MyServer;uid=WebUser16" _
      & ";pwd=WebUser16;" & "database=C16OnlineStore"
DBConn.Open
```

and you check to see whether the form on the page has been submitted:

```
If Not IsEmpty(Request.Form("CheckOut")) Then
```

If so, the visitor is checking out. You pass their personal information on to the VisitorCheckOut stored procedure:

```
DBConn.Execute "Exec VisitorCheckOut " _
      & Session("VisitorID") & ", " _
      & "'" & Request.Form("VisitorName") & "', " _
```

```
      & "'" & Request.Form("Address1") & "', " _
      & "'" & Request.Form("Address2") & "', " _
      & "'" & Request.Form("CSZ") & "', " _
      & "'" & Request.Form("PhoneNumber") & "', " _
      & "'" & Request.Form("EmailAddress") & "', " _
      & "'" & Request.Form("CCType") & "', " _
      & "'" & Request.Form("CCNumber") & "', " _
      & "'" & Request.Form("CCExpirationDate") & "'"
```

and send them to the Receipt page:

```
Response.Redirect "./receipt.asp"
```

Otherwise, you need to retrieve the summary order information on the Check Out page:

```
Set RSTotalStuff = DBConn.Execute("Exec TotalStuff " _
      & Session("VisitorID"))
```

That information is then placed on the page:

```
<% Response.Write RSTotalStuff("TotalText") %>
```

Receipt Active Server Page

Receipt.asp

The code on the Receipt Active Server Page calls your stored procedure to retrieve the visitor's receipt before ending their session.

```
<%
Option Explicit
Dim DBConn
Dim RSStoreReceipt
set DBConn = Server.Createobject ("ADODB.Connection")
DBConn.ConnectionString = "driver={SQL Server};" _
      & "server=MyServer;uid=WebUser16" _
      & ";pwd=WebUser16;" & "database=C16OnlineStore"
DBConn.Open
Set RSStoreReceipt = DBConn.Execute("Exec StoreReceipt " _
      & Session("VisitorID"))
Session.Abandon
%>
```

You will need Connection and Recordset objects:

```
Dim DBConn
Dim RSStoreReceipt
```

You then connect to your database:

```
set DBConn = Server.Createobject ("ADODB.Connection")
DBConn.ConnectionString = "driver={SQL Server};" _
      & "server=MyServer;uid=WebUser16" _
      & ";pwd=WebUser16;" & "database=C16OnlineStore"
DBConn.Open
```

and retrieve the customer's receipt:

```
Set RSStoreReceipt = DBConn.Execute("Exec StoreReceipt " _
      & Session("VisitorID"))
```

You then close the visitor's session:

```
Session.Abandon
```

Then within the HTML, you place the text of their receipt:

```
<% Response.Write RSStoreReceipt("ReceiptText") %>
```

CHAPTER

17

Online School

IN THIS CHAPTER:

C17SQLObjects.sql

Students.txt

Courses.txt

StudentCourses.txt

Topics.txt

Contents.txt

Questions.txt

Answers.txt

HelpTopics.txt

Index.asp

Courses.asp

Topic_List.asp

Content.asp

Quiz.asp

Result.asp

Help.asp

In this chapter, we will look at a solution that uses an Active Server Page application front end and a SQL Server back end. The solution provides a way for a student to select from a list of courses that they are enrolled in. They then select a topic within that course, view its contents, and take a quiz on that topic.

Web Site Walk-Through

When the visitor first enters any page of the site except for the Help page, they are taken to the Log In page shown in Figure 17-1.

From this page, the student enters their name and password to gain access to most of the application. If they try to go directly to one of the other pages on the site,

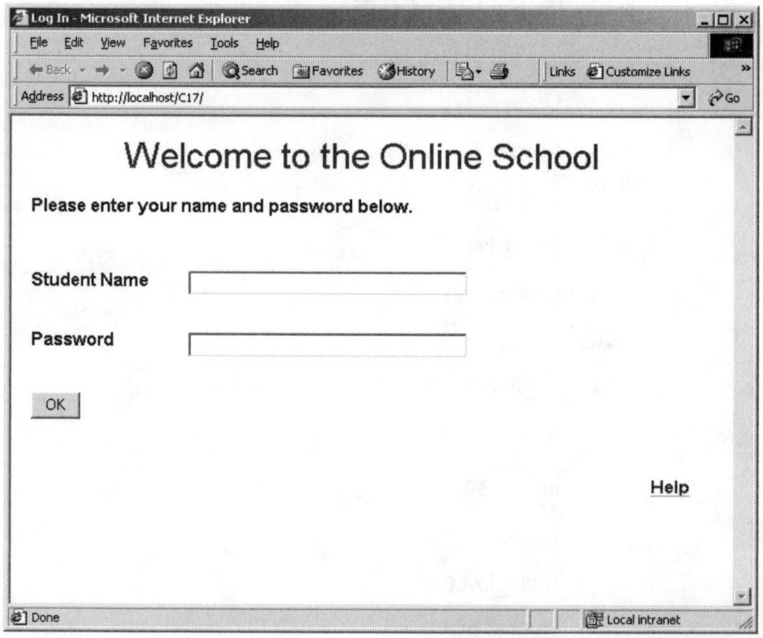

Figure 17-1 *Log In page*

except the Help page, they are sent to this page instead to log in. If the student enters an invalid login, they see a different message and can try to log in again.

Note the link to the Help page at the bottom of the Log In page. That page is displayed in Figure 17-2.

The Help page is accessible from all the other pages in the site. The page uses the database, stored procedures, and ASP code to display a list of questions and an answer to the selected question. The student would find their question in the list and then click OK to see the answer to that question.

Back on the Log In page, if the student enters a valid user name and password, they are taken to the Courses page displayed in Figure 17-3.

The Courses page displays a list of all the courses that the student is signed up for. Another student may see a very different list.

The student uses this page to select the course that they want to work with. Once they click OK, they are taken to the Topic List page displayed in Figure 17-4.

Each course is divided into topics. *Topics* are logical units of information within the overall framework of a course. The Topic List page lists all the topics for the course that the student selected on the previous page. So here the student selected the Cooking Basics course and is selecting the Eggs topic.

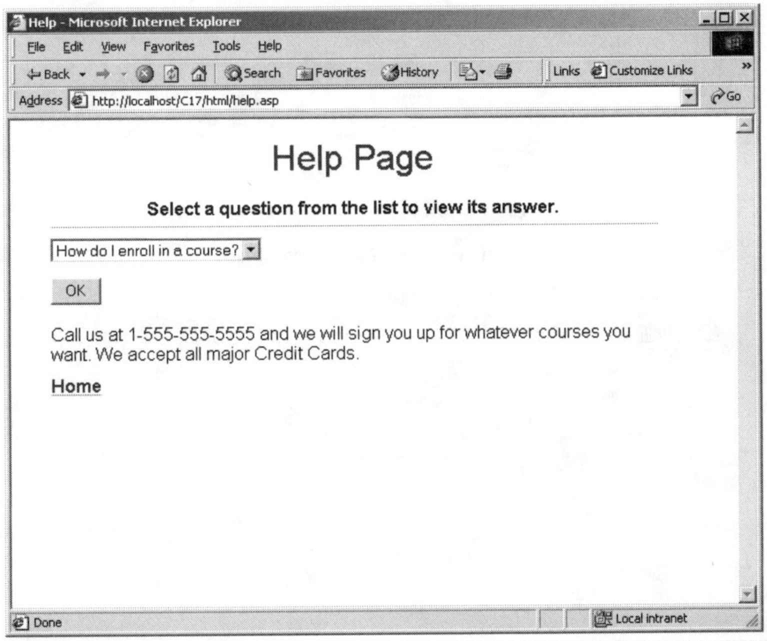

Figure 17-2 *Help page*

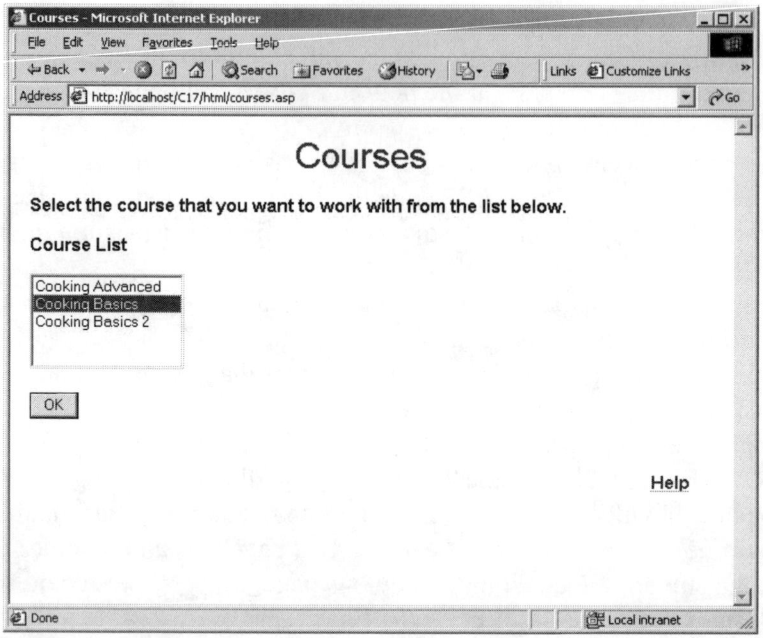

Figure 17-3 *Courses page*

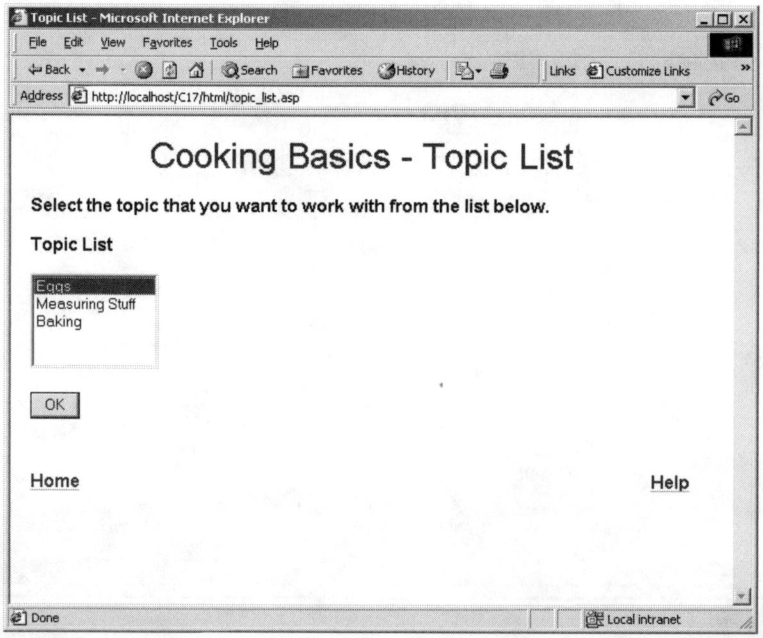

Figure 17-4 *Topic List page*

When the student clicks OK on the Topics List page, they are taken to the page shown in Figure 17-5.

The Content page lists information about the topic that the student has selected. Each topic must have at least one set of content, but it could have many more sets. The Content page displays a specific piece of information on the topic that the student selected.

When the student is done with this Content page, they click the Next link to see the next Content page displayed in Figure 17-6.

The content within a topic is displayed one unit at a time in the order indicated in the database. The student continues to go from page to page until all the content has been reviewed. They then see the Quiz page displayed in Figure 17-7.

Each topic must have at least one quiz question, but each topic can have many questions. Each question can contain one or more answers. So for a True/False question, you could display just those answers, but for another question you may want seven different answers to choose from. The Quiz page displays all the questions and all the answers to each question for the current topic.

When the student is done with the quiz, they click OK to see the Result page displayed in Figure 17-8.

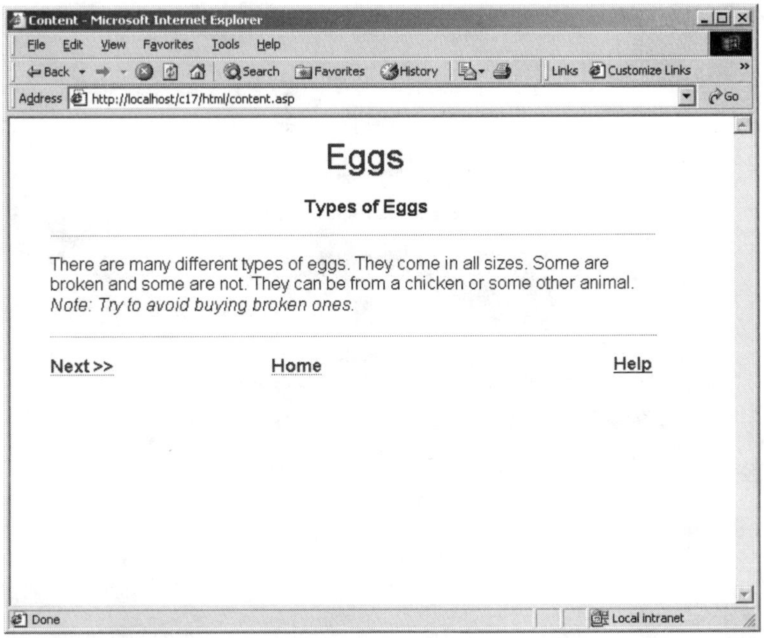

Figure 17-5 *Content page showing first content*

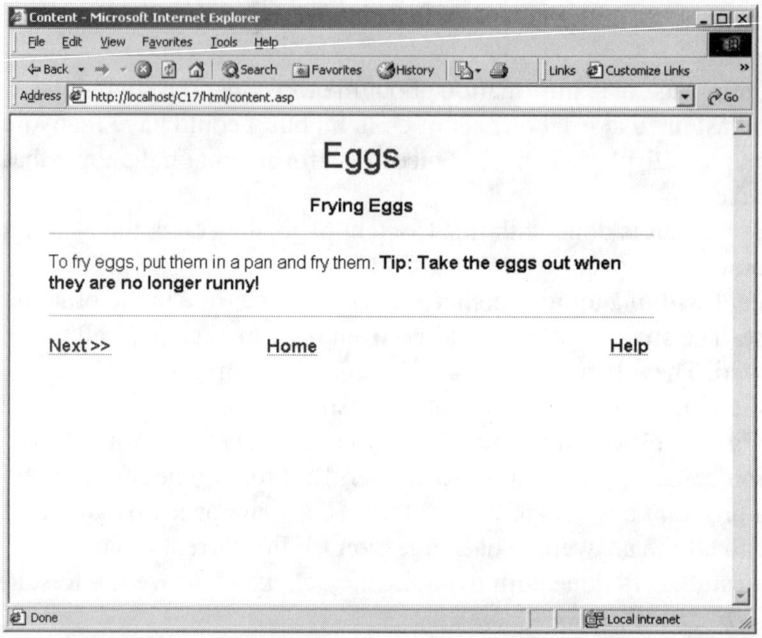

Figure 17-6 *Content page showing second page of text*

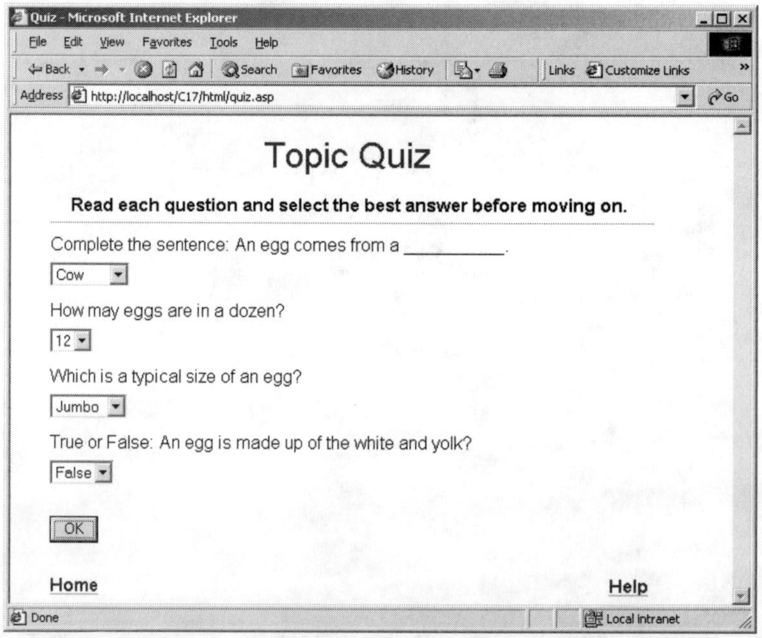

Figure 17-7 *Quiz page*

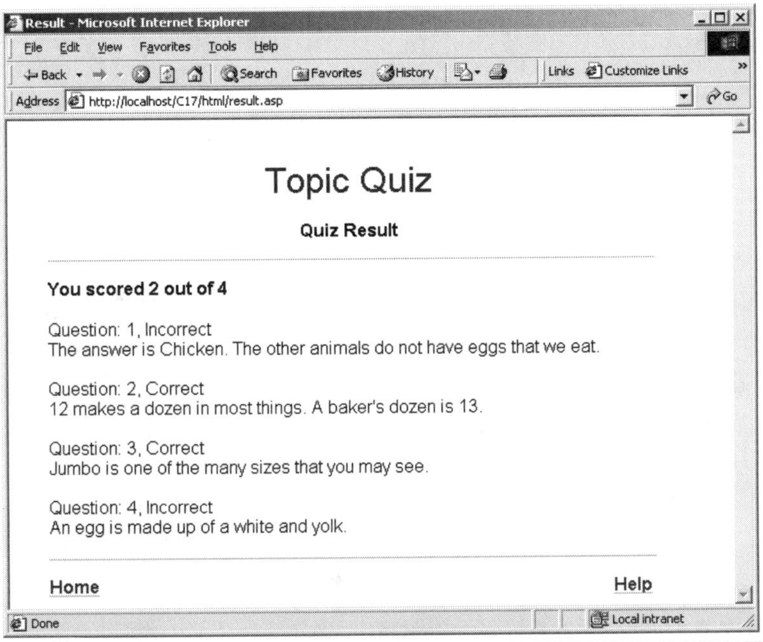

Figure 17-8 *Result page*

The Result page shows the student their total score on the quiz. It also displays the result of each question, as well as an explanation of the question.

The student can then click the Home button to be taken back to the Courses page to move on to another topic.

Tables and Relationships

C17SQLObjects.sql

Students Table

The Students table is a top-level table that stores information about the students who are enrolled in courses. The table is used to log students into the Active Server Page application.

Courses Table

The Courses table is another top-level table. It stores information about the Courses and is related to many of the other tables in the database.

StudentCourses Table

Each student can be enrolled in many courses. Each course can have many students enrolled in it. Therefore, a many-to-many relationship exists between the Students table and the Courses table. The StudentCourses table satisfies that relationship by acting as the connecting table, since it is in a one-to-many relationship with the Students table and the Courses table.

Topics Table

Each course is divided into topics. The Topics table stores that information. The table is in a one-to-many relationship with the Courses table.

Contents Table

Each topic is divided into content pages. The text and titles for those pages are stored in the Contents table. The table is in a one-to-many relationship with the Topics table.

Questions Table

Each topic can have many questions that appear at the end of the topic. The Questions table stores those questions. That table is in a one-to-many relationship with the Topics table.

Answers Table

The Answers table stores the possible answers for each question. The table is in a one-to-many relationship with the Questions table. Each question can have many possible answers, but each answer goes with a specific question.

HelpTopics Table

The HelpTopics table is a stand-alone table that stores help questions and answers. That information is then used on the Help page.

Field Specifications

Students.txt

Students Table

The field specifications for the Students table are displayed in Table 17-1.

Field Name	Field Type	Notes
StudentID	int	Primary Key, Identity Column
StudentName	varchar	Length = 100
StudentPassword	varchar	Length = 100
Address1	varchar	Length = 100
Address2	varchar	Length = 100
CSZ	varchar	Length = 100
PhoneNumber	varchar	Length = 100
EmailAddress	varchar	Length = 100

Table 17-1 *Students Table Field Specifications*

The StudentID field is the primary key in this table. The StudentName and StudentPassword fields are used to log the student into the application. The rest of the fields store information about the student.

Courses Table

Courses.txt

The field specifications for the Courses table are displayed in Table 17-2.

The CourseID field is a primary key and is automatically populated when a new record is added to the table. The rest of the fields store information about the course. The DateCreated field has this default value:

```
GetDate()
```

Therefore, it is set to the current system date and time when a record is added and the field is omitted.

Field Name	Field Type	Notes
CourseID	int	Primary Key, Identity Column
CourseName	varchar	Length = 50
CourseDescription	varchar	Length = 1000
DateCreated	datetime	

Table 17-2 *Courses Table Field Specifications*

Field Name	Field Type	Notes
StudentCourseID	int	Primary Key, Identity Column
StudentID	int	Foreign Key
CourseID	int	Foreign Key

Table 17-3 *StudentCourses Table Field Specifications*

StudentCourses Table

StudentCourses.txt

The field specifications for the StudentCourses table are displayed in Table 17-3.

The StudentCourseID field is the primary key for this table. The StudentID field is a foreign key that links this table to the Students table. The CourseID field is also a foreign key that links this table to the Courses table.

Topics Table

Topics.txt

The field specifications for the Topics table are displayed in Table 17-4.

The TopicID is the primary key in this table. The CourseID field is a foreign key that links this table to the Courses table. The SequenceNumber field is used to indicate the order of the topics within a specific course.

Contents Table

Contents.txt

The field specifications for the Contents table are displayed in Table 17-5.

Field Name	Field Type	Notes
TopicID	int	Primary Key, Identity Column
CourseID	int	Foreign Key
SequenceNumber	int	
TopicName	varchar	Length = 50
TopicDescription	varchar	Length = 50

Table 17-4 *Topics Table Field Specifications*

Field Name	Field Type	Notes
ContentID	int	Primary Key, Identity Column
TopicID	int	Foreign Key
SequenceNumber	int	
ContentTitle	varchar	Length = 50
ContentText	varchar	Length = 500

Table 17-5 *Contents Table Field Specifications*

The ContentID field is the primary key in this table. The TopicID field links this table to the Topics table. The SequenceNumber field is used to indicate the order of the content records within a topic. The other fields store information about the content.

Questions Table

Questions.txt

The field specifications for the Questions table are displayed in Table 17-6.

The QuestionID field is the primary key for this table. The TopicID field is a foreign key that links this table to the Topics table. The SequenceNumber field is used to indicate the order of the questions on the Quiz page.

The QuestionText field stores the text of the question. The CorrectAnswer is the exact match for the correct answer to the question. A record with the same text must also appear in the Answers table to give the student the opportunity to answer a

Field Name	Field Type	Notes
QuestionID	int	Primary Key, Identity Column
TopicID	int	Foreign Key
SequenceNumber	int	
QuestionText	varchar	Length = 255
CorrectAnswer	varchar	Length = 50
ResponseText	varchar	Length = 255

Table 17-6 *Questions Table Field Specifications*

Field Name	Field Type	Notes
AnswerID	int	Primary Key, Identity Column
QuestionID	int	Foreign Key
AnswerText	varchar	Length = 50

Table 17-7 *Answers Table Field Specifications*

question correctly. The ResponseText field stores the text that is displayed on the Result page that explains the question.

Answers Table

Answers.txt

The field specifications for the Answers table are displayed in Table 17-7.

The AnswerID field is the primary key. The QuestionID field links the record to a question record in the Questions table. The AnswerText field stores the text of the answer as it appears in the Select control on the Quiz page.

HelpTopics Table

HelpTopics.txt

The field specifications for the HelpTopics table are displayed in Table 17-8.

The HelpTopicID field is the primary key in this table. The other fields store the text of the question and the answer that appear on the Help page.

Field Name	Field Type	Notes
HelpTopicID	int	Primary Key, Identity Column
QuestionText	varchar	Length = 100
AnswerText	varchar	Length = 2000

Table 17-8 *HelpTopics Table Field Specifications*

Stored Procedures

StudentLogin Stored Procedure

The StudentLogin stored procedure is used by the calling application to validate an entry into the Active Server Page application.

```
CREATE PROCEDURE StudentLogin
@StudentName varchar(100),
@Password varchar(100)
AS
Declare
@TheCount as Integer
Select @TheCount = Count(StudentID)
      From Students
      Where StudentName = @StudentName
      And StudentPassword = @Password
If @TheCount = 0
      BEGIN
            Select 0 as StudentID
      END
Else
      BEGIN
            Select StudentID from Students
                  Where StudentName = @StudentName
                  And StudentPassword = @Password
      END
GO
```

The procedure requires two parameters to be passed into it. The first is the student's name:

```
@StudentName varchar(100),
```

The other is the password of the student:

```
@Password varchar(100)
```

Within the procedure a variable is declared that will be used to check and see if a record with the passed-in student name and password is in the database:

```
@TheCount as Integer
```

You then set that variable to the number of occurrences of the student's name and password:

```
Select @TheCount = Count(StudentID)
      From Students
      Where StudentName = @StudentName
      And StudentPassword = @Password
```

If the name and password were not found, the count variable is set to 0.

```
If @TheCount = 0
```

In that case, you return a 0 to the calling application:

```
Select 0 as StudentID
```

Otherwise, you return the ID of the student matching the name and password passed in:

```
Select StudentID from Students
      Where StudentName = @StudentName
      And StudentPassword = @Password
```

CourseList Stored Procedure

The CourseList stored procedure is called from the Courses Active Server Page and returns all the courses that a student is enrolled in as options for a Select control.

```
CREATE PROCEDURE CourseList
@StudentID integer
AS
Declare
@AllOfIt varchar(8000),
@CourseID varchar(10),
@CourseName varchar(50)
Declare CurCourses Cursor
For Select Courses.CourseID, Courses.CourseName
      from Courses
```

```
        Inner Join StudentCourses On
        Courses.CourseID = StudentCourses.CourseID
        Where StudentCourses.StudentID = @StudentID
        Order By CourseName
Open CurCourses
Fetch CurCourses
        Into @CourseID, @CourseName
Select @AllOfIt = ''
While @@Fetch_Status = 0
        BEGIN

                Select @AllOfIt = @AllOfIt + '<OPTION VALUE="' +
                        @CourseID + '">' + @CourseName
                        + '</OPTION>'
                Fetch CurCourses
                        Into @CourseID, @CourseName
        END
Close CurCourses
Deallocate CurCourses
Select @AllOfIt as TheList
GO
```

The procedure expects one parameter, the ID of the student whose course list is to be returned:

```
@StudentID integer
```

Within the procedure, you need a variable that will store the option list as it is being concatenated:

```
@AllOfIt varchar(8000),
```

Also, variables will be needed to store the ID:

```
@CourseID varchar(10),
```

and names of the courses:

```
@CourseName varchar(50)
```

You need a Cursor object to retrieve the courses from the Courses table:

```
Declare CurCourses Cursor
```

You set that to return the names and IDs for the courses that the current student is enrolled in. Note that you have to join the Courses table with the StudentCourses table so that you can retrieve just the courses that this student is enrolled in:

```
For Select Courses.CourseID, Courses.CourseName
      from Courses
      Inner Join StudentCourses On
      Courses.CourseID = StudentCourses.CourseID
      Where StudentCourses.StudentID = @StudentID
      Order By CourseName
```

You then open that cursor:

```
Open CurCourses
```

retrieve the first record into your local variables:

```
Fetch CurCourses
      Into @CourseID, @CourseName
```

and initialize your return variable:

```
Select @AllOfIt = ''
```

You then enter a loop that allows you to iterate through all the course records:

```
While @@Fetch_Status = 0
```

Each record needs to be returned as an Option for a Select control. The tag is set up so that the student sees the name of the course, but the ID of the course is submitted with the form that the Option tags appears on:

```
Select @AllOfIt = @AllOfIt + '<OPTION VALUE="' +
      @CourseID + '">' + @CourseName
      + '</OPTION>'
```

You then retrieve the next record and loop to process it:

```
Fetch CurCourses
      Into @CourseID, @CourseName
```

After the loop, you release the resources used by the cursor:

```
Close CurCourses
Deallocate CurCourses
```

and return the Option tags:

```
Select @AllOfIt as TheList
```

TopicList Stored Procedure

The TopicList stored procedure returns a list of all the topics within a course as Options for an HTML Select element. Also returned is the name of the course.

```
CREATE PROCEDURE TopicList
@CourseID integer
AS
Declare
@AllOfIt varchar(8000),
@TopicID varchar(10),
@TopicName varchar(50),
@CourseName varchar(50)
Select @CourseName = CourseName
      From Courses
      Where CourseID = @CourseID
Declare CurTopics Cursor
For Select TopicID, TopicName
      from Topics
      Where CourseID = @CourseID
      Order By SequenceNumber
Open CurTopics
Fetch CurTopics
      Into @TopicID, @TopicName
Select @AllOfIt = ''
While @@Fetch_Status = 0
      BEGIN

            Select @AllOfIt = @AllOfIt + '<OPTION VALUE="' +
                  @TopicID + '">' + @TopicName
                  + '</OPTION>'
```

```
            Fetch CurTopics
                  Into @TopicID, @TopicName
      END
Close CurTopics
Deallocate CurTopics
Select @AllOfIt as TheList, @CourseName as CourseName
GO
```

The procedure expects one parameter, the ID of the course from which the topics are to be retrieved:

```
@CourseID integer
```

Within the procedure you will need a variable to store the topic list that is returned:

```
@AllOfIt varchar(8000),
```

as well as the ID and name of each topic as they are retrieved from the Topics table:

```
@TopicID varchar(10),
@TopicName varchar(50),
```

This variable will be used to return the name of the course corresponding to the ID passed in:

```
@CourseName varchar(50)
```

You then retrieve that course name and place it in your local variable:

```
Select @CourseName = CourseName
      From Courses
      Where CourseID = @CourseID
```

Within the procedure you need a Cursor object to retrieve all the topics:

```
Declare CurTopics Cursor
```

You then set the cursor up so that it just retrieves the topics matching the course ID passed in:

```
For Select TopicID, TopicName
      from Topics
      Where CourseID = @CourseID
      Order By SequenceNumber
```

The cursor is then opened:

```
Open CurTopics
```

the first record is retrieved:

```
Fetch CurTopics
      Into @TopicID, @TopicName
```

and your variable that will store the Option list is initialized:

```
Select @AllOfIt = ''
```

You then enter a loop so that each record can be processed:

```
While @@Fetch_Status = 0
```

Each record is concatenated to your local variable as an Option for an HTML Select control:

```
Select @AllOfIt = @AllOfIt + '<OPTION VALUE="' +
      @TopicID + '">' + @TopicName
      + '</OPTION>'
```

You then retrieve the next record and loop:

```
Fetch CurTopics
      Into @TopicID, @TopicName
End
```

You then release your Cursor object:

```
Close CurTopics
Deallocate CurTopics
```

and return both the Option list and the name of the course to the calling application:

```
Select @AllOfIt as TheList, @CourseName as CourseName
```

GetContent Stored Procedure

The GetContent stored procedure returns the next content record for a particular topic according to a sequence number. If the end-of-content record has been reached, the procedure returns 0.

```
CREATE PROCEDURE GetContent
@TopicID integer,
@LastSequence integer
AS
Declare
@TheCount Integer,
@TopicName varchar(50),
@ContentID integer,
@ContentTitle varchar(50),
@ContentText varchar(5000)
Select @TheCount = Count(ContentID)
      from Contents
      Where TopicID = @TopicID
      And SequenceNumber = @LastSequence
If @TheCount = 0
      BEGIN
            Select 0 as ContentID
      END
Else
      BEGIN
            Select @TopicName = TopicName
                  From Topics
                  Where TopicID = @TopicID
            Select @ContentID = ContentID,
                  @ContentTitle = ContentTitle,
                  @ContentText = ContentText
                  from Contents
                  Where TopicID = @TopicID
                  And SequenceNumber = @LastSequence
            Select @TopicName as TopicName,
                  @ContentID as ContentID,
                  @ContentTitle as ContentTitle,
                  @ContentText as ContentText
      END
GO
```

Passed into the procedure is the ID of the topic for which content is to be returned:

```
@TopicID integer,
```

as well as the sequence number for the content item:

```
@LastSequence integer
```

Within the procedure, you need a variable to check for the existence of the desired content record:

```
@TheCount Integer,
```

You need to return the name of the current topic:

```
@TopicName varchar(50),
```

You need variables to retrieve the ID:

```
@ContentID integer,
```

the title:

```
@ContentTitle varchar(50),
```

and the text of the content:

```
@ContentText varchar(5000)
```

You then check to see if a record with the specified sequence number for the specified topic exists:

```
Select @TheCount = Count(ContentID)
      from Contents
      Where TopicID = @TopicID
      And SequenceNumber = @LastSequence
```

If it doesn't:

```
If @TheCount = 0
```

the code flows here and you return a 0, which tells the content page that you are done with content and need to move on to the Quiz page:

```
Select 0 as ContentID
```

Otherwise, you need to retrieve the name of the current topic:

```
Select @TopicName = TopicName
      From Topics
      Where TopicID = @TopicID
```

You also need to retrieve the information for the current content record:

```
Select @ContentID = ContentID,
      @ContentTitle = ContentTitle,
      @ContentText = ContentText
      from Contents
      Where TopicID = @TopicID
      And SequenceNumber = @LastSequence
```

Those variables are then returned to the calling application:

```
Select @TopicName as TopicName,
      @ContentID as ContentID,
      @ContentTitle as ContentTitle,
      @ContentText as ContentText
```

QuizPage Stored Procedure

The QuizPage stored procedure returns all the questions and answers for the quiz corresponding to the passed-in topic to the calling application in the form of an HTML table that displays the information correctly on the Quiz page.

The code uses two loops, one inside the other. The outer loop loops through the questions, and the inner loop loops through all the answers for each question. A Cursor object is used for each loop.

```
CREATE PROCEDURE QuizPage
@TopicID integer
AS
Declare
@AllOfIt varchar(8000),
@QuestionID integer,
@QuestionText varchar(255),
@AnswerText varchar(50)
Declare CurQuestions Cursor
For Select QuestionID, QuestionText
      from Questions
      Where TopicID = @TopicID
      Order By SequenceNumber
Open CurQuestions
Fetch CurQuestions
      Into @QuestionID, @QuestionText
Select @AllOfIt = ''
```

```
While @@Fetch_Status = 0
      BEGIN
            Select @AllOfIt = @AllOfIt
                  + '<TR VALIGN=TOP ALIGN=LEFT>'
                  + '<TD COLSPAN=7 HEIGHT=10></TD>'
                  + '</TR>'
                  + '<TR VALIGN=TOP ALIGN=LEFT>'
                  + '<TD COLSPAN=2></TD>'
                  + '<TD COLSPAN=3 WIDTH=540 CLASS="TextObject">'
                  + '<P>' + @QuestionText + '</P>'
                  + '</TD>'
                  + '<TD COLSPAN=2></TD>'
                  + '</TR>'
                  + '<TR VALIGN=TOP ALIGN=LEFT>'
                  + '<TD COLSPAN=7 HEIGHT=8></TD>'
                  + '</TR>'
                  + '<TR VALIGN=TOP ALIGN=LEFT>'
                  + '<TD COLSPAN=2 HEIGHT=24></TD>'
                  + '<TD COLSPAN=2 WIDTH=283>'
                  + '<SELECT ID="FormsComboBox1" NAME="A'
                  + convert(varchar(10), @QuestionID) + '">'
            Declare CurAnswers Cursor
            For Select AnswerText
                  from Answers
                  Where QuestionID = @QuestionID
            Open CurAnswers
            Fetch CurAnswers
                  Into @AnswerText
            While @@Fetch_Status = 0
                  Begin
                  Select @AllOfIt = @AllOfIt
                                                + '<OPTION VALUE="'
                        + @AnswerText + '">'
                        + @AnswerText + '</OPTION>'
                  Fetch CurAnswers
                        Into @AnswerText
                  END
            Close CurAnswers
            Deallocate CurAnswers
            Select @AllOfIt = @AllOfIt
                  + '</SELECT>'
                  + '</TD>'
                  + '<TD COLSPAN=3></TD>'
```

```
                    + '</TR>'
              Fetch CurQuestions
                    Into @QuestionID, @QuestionText
      END
Close CurQuestions
Deallocate CurQuestions
Select @AllOfIt as ThePage
GO
```

Passed into the procedure is the ID of the topic that the quiz is based on:

```
@TopicID integer
```

This variable will be used to return the contents of the quiz page returned from this procedure:

```
@AllOfIt varchar(8000),
```

You will need to retrieve the IDs of the questions:

```
@QuestionID integer,
```

the text of the questions:

```
@QuestionText varchar(255),
```

and the answers to the questions:

```
@AnswerText varchar(50)
```

The first Cursor object declared will retrieve data from the Questions table:

```
Declare CurQuestions Cursor
```

It is set to retrieve just the questions based on the TopicID passed in sorted by the SequenceNumber field:

```
For Select QuestionID, QuestionText
      from Questions
      Where TopicID = @TopicID
      Order By SequenceNumber
```

You then open that cursor:

```
Open CurQuestions
```

and retrieve the ID and text of the first question from the Questions table for the specified topic into your local variables:

```
Fetch CurQuestions
      Into @QuestionID, @QuestionText
```

You need to initialize your return variable:

```
Select @AllOfIt = ''
```

and start the outer loop that processes the question records:

```
While @@Fetch_Status = 0
```

Each question needs to appear formatted so that it appears correctly on the quiz page. The page uses table definitions to place items on the page in a precise location. That formatting starts with a spacer row:

```
Select @AllOfIt = @AllOfIt
      + '<TR VALIGN=TOP ALIGN=LEFT>'
      + '<TD COLSPAN=7 HEIGHT=10></TD>'
      + '</TR>'
```

Then in the next row, you place the text of the question:

```
+ '<TR VALIGN=TOP ALIGN=LEFT>'
+ '<TD COLSPAN=2></TD>'
+ '<TD COLSPAN=3 WIDTH=540 CLASS="TextObject">'
+ '<P>' + @QuestionText + '</P>'
+ '</TD>'
+ '<TD COLSPAN=2></TD>'
+ '</TR>'
```

After that, you have more space:

```
+ '<TR VALIGN=TOP ALIGN=LEFT>'
+ '<TD COLSPAN=7 HEIGHT=8></TD>'
+ '</TR>'
```

Then the Select control appears, containing the possible answers to the question. Note how the Select control is named. It starts with the letter A followed by the ID of the question. So if the question has the ID 10, the name of the Select control is A10. This convention is used when the answers to the questions are scored:

```
+ '<TR VALIGN=TOP ALIGN=LEFT>'
+ '<TD COLSPAN=2 HEIGHT=24></TD>'
+ '<TD COLSPAN=2 WIDTH=283>'
+ '<SELECT ID="FormsComboBox1" NAME="A'
+ convert(varchar(10), @QuestionID) + '">'
```

Now you are at the point in the HTML where the Options tags for the Select control need to appear. So you need another Cursor object:

```
Declare CurAnswers Cursor
```

which is used to retrieve all the answers to the current question in the outer loop:

```
For Select AnswerText
      from Answers
      Where QuestionID = @QuestionID
```

You then open the cursor:

```
Open CurAnswers
```

and retrieve the first answer into your local variable:

```
Fetch CurAnswers
      Into @AnswerText
```

Now you enter the inner loop, which processes all the answers to the current question:

```
While @@Fetch_Status = 0
```

Each answer is concatenated to the return text as an Option tag of the Select control:

```
Select @AllOfIt = @AllOfIt
      + '<OPTION VALUE="'
      + @AnswerText + '">'
      + @AnswerText + '</OPTION>'
```

You can then retrieve the next answer:

```
Fetch CurAnswers
      Into @AnswerText
```

and iterate in the inner loop:

```
END
```

At this point in the code, you are outside of the inner loop. You need to release the Answer cursor's resources:

```
Close CurAnswers
Deallocate CurAnswers
```

and put the closing tag onto the Select control:

```
Select @AllOfIt = @AllOfIt
      + '</SELECT>'
      + '</TD>'
      + '<TD COLSPAN=3></TD>'
      + '</TR>'
```

You can now retrieve the question:

```
Fetch CurQuestions
      Into @QuestionID, @QuestionText
```

and loop back to the top of the outer loop:

```
End
```

At this point in the code, you are outside of both loops. You simply need to release the Cursor object:

```
Close CurQuestions
Deallocate CurQuestions
```

and return the text of the Quiz page:

```
Select @AllOfIt as ThePage
```

CheckAnswer Stored Procedure

The CheckAnswer stored procedure checks to see if the answer provided is the correct answer to one of the questions. It returns values based on that answer, as well as the explanation text for the given question. This information is then used on the Result page.

```
CREATE PROCEDURE CheckAnswer
@QuestionID integer,
@PassedAnswer varchar(50)
AS
DECLARE
@CorrectAnswer varchar(50),
@ResponseText varchar(255),
@AnswerValue integer,
@AnswerPrompt varchar(9)
Select @CorrectAnswer = CorrectAnswer,
      @ResponseText = ResponseText
      From Questions
      Where QuestionID = @QuestionID
If @PassedAnswer = @CorrectAnswer
      BEGIN
            Select @AnswerValue = 1
            Select @AnswerPrompt = 'Correct'
      END
Else
      BEGIN
            Select @AnswerValue = 0
            Select @AnswerPrompt = 'Incorrect'
      END
Select @AnswerValue as AnswerValue,
      @AnswerPrompt as AnswerPrompt,
      @ResponseText as ResponseText
GO
```

Two parameters are passed into the stored procedure. The first is the ID of the question for which an answer is being checked:

```
@QuestionID integer,
```

The other is the text of the user-supplied answer that is to be checked against the correct answer:

```
@PassedAnswer varchar(50)
```

You will need to retrieve the correct answer:

```
@CorrectAnswer varchar(50),
```

and the explanation text for the question:

```
@ResponseText varchar(255),
```

You will also return a value based on whether the answer was correct or incorrect:

```
@AnswerValue integer,
```

and the word Correct or Incorrect according to the result:

```
@AnswerPrompt varchar(9)
```

First you need to retrieve the correct answer to the question and the explanation text:

```
Select @CorrectAnswer = CorrectAnswer,
      @ResponseText = ResponseText
      From Questions
      Where QuestionID = @QuestionID
```

Then you can check to see if the answer supplied was correct:

```
If @PassedAnswer = @CorrectAnswer
```

If it was, the value of the answer is set to 1:

```
Select @AnswerValue = 1
```

and the text prompt is set to Correct:

```
Select @AnswerPrompt = 'Correct'
```

Otherwise, the value is set to 0:

```
Select @AnswerValue = 0
```

and a prompt of incorrect will be used:

```
Select @AnswerPrompt = 'Incorrect'
```

You then return that value, prompt, and explanation text to the calling application:

```
Select @AnswerValue as AnswerValue,
      @AnswerPrompt as AnswerPrompt,
      @ResponseText as ResponseText
```

HelpTopicListAndAnswer Stored Procedure

The HelpTopicListAndAnswer stored procedure returns a list of the Help questions in the form of Option tags for a Select control for the Help page. It also returns the text of an answer as determined by either the question passed in or the first question in the HelpTopics table.

```
CREATE PROCEDURE HelpTopicListAndAnswer
@PassedHelpTopicID integer
AS
Declare
@AllOfIt varchar(8000),
@HelpTopicID varchar(10),
@QuestionText varchar(60),
@AnswerText varchar(2000)
If @PassedHelpTopicID = 0
      BEGIN
            Select @PassedHelpTopicID = Min(HelpTopicID) from HelpTopics
      END
Select @AnswerText = AnswerText from HelpTopics
      Where HelpTopicID = @PassedHelpTopicID
Declare CurHelpTopics Cursor
For Select HelpTopicID, QuestionText from HelpTopics
      order by QuestionText
Open CurHelpTopics
Fetch CurHelpTopics
      Into @HelpTopicID, @QuestionText
Select @AllOfIt = ''
While @@Fetch_Status = 0
      BEGIN
            If @PassedHelpTopicID = @HelpTopicID
                  BEGIN
                        Select @AllOfIt = @AllOfIt + '<OPTION VALUE="' +
                              @HelpTopicID + '" SELECTED>' + @QuestionText
                              + '</OPTION>'
```

```
                END
        Else
                BEGIN
                        Select @AllOfIt = @AllOfIt + '<OPTION VALUE="' +
                                @HelpTopicID + '">' + @QuestionText
                                + '</OPTION>'
                END
        Fetch CurHelpTopics
                Into @HelpTopicID, @QuestionText
    END
Close CurHelpTopics
Deallocate CurHelpTopics
Select @AllOfIt as TheList, @AnswerText as AnswerText
GO
```

Passed into the procedure is the ID of the question being asked:

```
@PassedHelpTopicID integer
```

Locally, you will need variables to store the return text:

```
@AllOfIt varchar(8000),
```

the ID of each help topic:

```
@HelpTopicID varchar(10),
```

the text of each question:

```
@QuestionText varchar(60),
```

and the answer to the current question:

```
@AnswerText varchar(2000)
```

The ID passed in can be set to 0. That means that the calling application wants to use a default question and answer because none have been selected:

```
If @PassedHelpTopicID = 0
```

If that is the case, the code flows here and you retrieve the first help topic ID:

```
Select @PassedHelpTopicID = Min(HelpTopicID) from HelpTopics
```

Now you can retrieve the answer to either the first question or the question of the ID passed in:

```
Select @AnswerText = AnswerText from HelpTopics
      Where HelpTopicID = @PassedHelpTopicID
```

You then declare a Cursor object:

```
Declare CurHelpTopics Cursor
```

that will be used to retrieve the list of all the questions for the Select control:

```
For Select HelpTopicID, QuestionText from HelpTopics
      order by QuestionText
```

That cursor is opened:

```
Open CurHelpTopics
```

the first record is retrieved:

```
Fetch CurHelpTopics
      Into @HelpTopicID, @QuestionText
```

and you initialize the variable that will return the Option tags:

```
Select @AllOfIt = ''
```

You then enter a loop so that you can process each question:

```
While @@Fetch_Status = 0
```

You want the current question passed in to appear in the Select control as the selected question. That way, the student will see the text of the question they asked, together with the answer. So you check to see if the ID of the current help topic is the same as the ID of the one passed into the procedure:

```
If @PassedHelpTopicID = @HelpTopicID
```

If it is, you set the Option tag up with the parameter "Selected" so that it will appear as the selected item in the Select control:

```
Select @AllOfIt = @AllOfIt + '<OPTION VALUE="' +
      @HelpTopicID + '" SELECTED>' + @QuestionText
      + '</OPTION>'
```

Otherwise, the help topic question is not displayed as the selected one:

```
Select @AllOfIt = @AllOfIt + '<OPTION VALUE="' +
            @HelpTopicID + '">' + @QuestionText
            + '</OPTION>'
```

You then move on to process the next help topic:

```
Fetch CurHelpTopics
      Into @HelpTopicID, @QuestionText
```

and loop:

```
End
```

After the loop, you release the resources of the Cursor object:

```
Close CurHelpTopics
Deallocate CurHelpTopics
```

and return the options for the Select control as well as the answer to the selected question:

```
Select @AllOfIt as TheList, @AnswerText as AnswerText
```

Users

WebUser User

In addition to the default Administrator account, the database has the user WebUser associated with it. The only access that user has to the database is through the stored procedures. No other permissions are granted to this user.

Active Server Pages

Index Active Server Page

Index.asp

The code on the Index or Log In Active Server Page validates the student's attempt to enter the Active Server Page application. The main code block is at the top of the page.

```
<%
Option Explicit
Dim DBConn
Dim RSLogin
Dim TheMessage
If IsEmpty(Request.Form("OK")) Then
      TheMessage = "Please enter " _
            & "your name and password below."
Else
      set DBConn = Server.Createobject ("ADODB.Connection")
      DBConn.ConnectionString = "driver={SQL Server};" _
            & "server=MyServer;uid=WebUser" _
            & ";pwd=WebUser;database=C17OnlineSchool"
      DBConn.Open
      Set RSLogin = DBConn.Execute _
            ("Exec StudentLogin '" _
            & Request.Form("StudentName") & "', '" _
            & Request.Form("Password") & "'")
      If RSLogin("StudentID") = 0 then
            TheMessage = "Incorrect log in attempt. " _
                  & "Please try again."
      Else
            Session("StudentID") = RSLogin("StudentID")
            Response.Redirect "./html/courses.asp"
      End If
End If
%>
```

You start by telling the compiler that you will declare your variables:

```
Option Explicit
```

For the code on this page, you will need an ADO Connection object:

```
Dim DBConn
```

a Recordset object:

```
Dim RSLogin
```

and a string to hold the message displayed on the page:

```
Dim TheMessage
```

First, you check to see if the student has just entered this page by seeing if the OK button is absent in the Form collection:

```
If IsEmpty(Request.Form("OK")) Then
```

If that is the case, you set up your string variable to display an initial message:

```
TheMessage = "Please enter " _
      & "your name and password below."
```

Otherwise, you need to connect to the database:

```
set DBConn = Server.Createobject ("ADODB.Connection")
DBConn.ConnectionString = "driver={SQL Server};" _
      & "server=MyServer;uid=WebUser" _
      & ";pwd=WebUser;database=C17OnlineSchool"
DBConn.Open
```

and check to see if the login information entered by the student is valid:

```
Set RSLogin = DBConn.Execute _
      ("Exec StudentLogin '" _
      & Request.Form("StudentName") & "', '" _
      & Request.Form("Password") & "'")
```

If your stored procedure returns 0:

```
If RSLogin("StudentID") = 0 then
```

that means the login was not found. So you will tell the student this:

```
TheMessage = "Incorrect log in attempt. " _
      & "Please try again."
```

Otherwise, you store the ID of the student returned through your stored procedure in a Session variable:

```
Session("StudentID") = RSLogin("StudentID")
```

and send the student to the Courses page:

```
Response.Redirect "./html/courses.asp"
```

In the body of the page, within the HTML, you display the message string:

```
<% Response.Write TheMessage %>
```

Courses Active Server Page

Courses.asp

The code on the Courses page calls your stored procedure to display all the courses that the student is signed up for. The main code block is at the top of the page.

```
<%
Option Explicit
Dim DBConn
Dim RSCOurses
If IsEmpty(Session("StudentID")) Then
      Response.Redirect "../index.asp"
End If
if IsEmpty(Request.Form("CourseID")) Then
      set DBConn = Server.Createobject ("ADODB.Connection")
      DBConn.ConnectionString = "driver={SQL Server};" _
            & "server=MyServer;uid=WebUser" _
            & ";pwd=WebUser;database=C17OnlineSchool"
      DBConn.Open
      Set RSCOurses = DBConn.Execute _
            ("Exec CourseList " _
            & Session("StudentID"))
Else
      Session("CourseID") = Request.Form("CourseID")
      Response.Redirect "./topic_list.asp"
End If
%>
```

You start by telling the compiler that variables will be declared:

```
Option Explicit
```

You will need a Connection object:

```
Dim DBConn
```

and a Recordset object:

```
Dim RSCOurses
```

First, you need to make sure that the student has logged into the application by looking for the StudentID Session variable:

```
If IsEmpty(Session("StudentID")) Then
```

If they haven't, you send them to the Log In page:

```
Response.Redirect "../index.asp"
```

Otherwise, you check to see if the student has just entered the page by making sure that the CourseID Form collection item is empty:

```
if IsEmpty(Request.Form("CourseID")) Then
```

If that is the case, you need to connect to your SQL Server database:

```
set DBConn = Server.Createobject ("ADODB.Connection")
DBConn.ConnectionString = "driver={SQL Server};" _
      & "server=MyServer;uid=WebUser" _
      & ";pwd=WebUser;database=C17OnlineSchool"
DBConn.Open
```

and retrieve, through your stored procedure, the list of courses that the student is enrolled in:

```
Set RSCOurses = DBConn.Execute _
      ("Exec CourseList " _
      & Session("StudentID"))
```

Otherwise, you store the course selected by the student into a Session variable:

```
Session("CourseID") = Request.Form("CourseID")
```

and send the student to the Topic List page:

```
Response.Redirect "./topic_list.asp"
```

Within the HTML, the return from the stored procedure is used to populate the Option tags for the Select control:

```
<SELECT ID="FormsComboBox1" NAME="CourseID" SIZE=5>
      <% Response.Write RSCOurses("TheList") %>
</SELECT>
```

Topic List Active Server Page

Topic_List.asp

The code on the Topic List page displays all the topics for the course selected by the student. Once a Topic is selected, the code transfers the student to the Content page. The main code block is at the top of the page.

```
<%
Option Explicit
Dim DBConn
Dim RSTopics
If IsEmpty(Session("StudentID")) Then
      Response.Redirect "../index.asp"
End If
If IsEmpty(Session("CourseID")) Then
      Response.Redirect "./courses.asp"
End If
if IsEmpty(Request.Form("TopicID")) Then
      set DBConn = Server.Createobject ("ADODB.Connection")
      DBConn.ConnectionString = "driver={SQL Server};" _
            & "server=MyServer;uid=WebUser" _
            & ";pwd=WebUser;database=C17OnlineSchool"
      DBConn.Open
      Set RSTopics = DBConn.Execute _
            ("Exec TopicList " _
            & Session("CourseID"))
Else
      Session("TopicID") = Request.Form("TopicID")
      Session("ContentSequence") = 0
      Response.Redirect "./content.asp"
End If
%>
```

You start with the compiler directive indicating that your variables will be declared:

```
Option Explicit
```

Then you declare a Connection object:

```
Dim DBConn
```

and a Recordset object:

```
Dim RSTopics
```

The page should not be entered if the student has not yet logged in:

```
If IsEmpty(Session("StudentID")) Then
```

If they haven't, they are sent to the login page:

```
Response.Redirect "../index.asp"
```

The page should also not be entered without the student first selecting a course. So you check for the CourseID session variable:

```
If IsEmpty(Session("CourseID")) Then
```

If it is not found, the student is sent to the Courses page:

```
Response.Redirect "./courses.asp"
```

Otherwise, the Student can be on this page. You then check to see if the page has just been entered or whether the form on the page has been submitted:

```
if IsEmpty(Request.Form("TopicID")) Then
```

If the page has just been entered, you need to connect to the database:

```
set DBConn = Server.Createobject ("ADODB.Connection")
DBConn.ConnectionString = "driver={SQL Server};" _
      & "server=MyServer;uid=WebUser" _
      & ";pwd=WebUser;database=C17OnlineSchool"
DBConn.Open
```

and retrieve the topics for the current course:

```
Set RSTopics = DBConn.Execute _
      ("Exec TopicList " _
      & Session("CourseID"))
```

Otherwise, you store the topic selected by the student into a session variable

```
Session("TopicID") = Request.Form("TopicID")
```

and reset the content sequence pointer within the topic to the beginning of the topic. This variable will be used on the Content page to maintain a progression of content records:

```
Session("ContentSequence") = 0
```

You then send the student to the Content page:

```
Response.Redirect "./content.asp"
```

Within the HTML, you need to display the name of the current course:

```
<% Response.Write RSTopics("CourseName") %> - Topic List
```

and the list of the topics in the course:

```
<SELECT ID="FormsComboBox1" NAME="TopicID" SIZE=5>
      <% Response.Write RSTopics("TheList") %>
</SELECT>
```

Content Active Server Page

Content.asp

The code on the Contents page calls your stored procedure to return the content for the current topic. It also moves the student onto the Quiz page when the student has finished with all the Content pages for the current topic.

```
<%
Option Explicit
Dim DBConn
Dim RSContent
If IsEmpty(Session("StudentID")) Then
      Response.Redirect "../index.asp"
```

```
End If
If IsEmpty(Session("CourseID")) Then
      Response.Redirect "./courses.asp"
End If
If IsEmpty(Session("TopicID")) Then
      Response.Redirect "./topic_list.asp"
End If
Session("ContentSequence") = Session("ContentSequence") + 1
set DBConn = Server.Createobject ("ADODB.Connection")
DBConn.ConnectionString = "driver={SQL Server};" _
      & "server=MyServer;uid=WebUser" _
      & ";pwd=WebUser;database=C17OnlineSchool"
DBConn.Open
Set RSContent = DBConn.Execute _
      ("Exec GetContent " _
      & Session("TopicID") _
      & ", "       & Session("ContentSequence"))
If RSContent("ContentID") = 0 Then
      Response.Redirect "./quiz.asp"
End If
%>
```

You will declare your variables:

```
Option Explicit
```

which will include a Connection object:

```
Dim DBConn
```

and a Recordset object:

```
Dim RSContent
```

However, you need to make sure that the page was entered correctly. The page should not be viewed if the student has not logged in:

```
If IsEmpty(Session("StudentID")) Then
```

If that is the case, you send the student to the Log In page:

```
Response.Redirect "../index.asp"
```

The page should not be entered if the student has not yet selected a course to work with:

```
If IsEmpty(Session("CourseID")) Then
```

If that is the case, you send the student to the Courses page:

```
Response.Redirect "./courses.asp"
```

You also need to make sure that a topic has been selected:

```
If IsEmpty(Session("TopicID")) Then
```

If it hasn't, you need to send the student to the Topic List page:

```
Response.Redirect "./topic_list.asp"
```

Otherwise, you move the student onto the next content sequence number:

```
Session("ContentSequence") = Session("ContentSequence") + 1
```

connect to the database:

```
set DBConn = Server.Createobject ("ADODB.Connection")
DBConn.ConnectionString = "driver={SQL Server};" _
      & "server=MyServer;uid=WebUser" _
      & ";pwd=WebUser;database=C17OnlineSchool"
DBConn.Open
```

and retrieve the content record:

```
Set RSContent = DBConn.Execute _
      ("Exec GetContent " _
      & Session("TopicID") _
      & ", "       & Session("ContentSequence"))
```

If the student has finished viewing all the content for the current topic, the stored procedure will return 0:

```
If RSContent("ContentID") = 0 Then
```

In that case, you send the student to the Quiz page:

```
Response.Redirect "./quiz.asp"
```

Otherwise, within the HTML you display the name of the Topic:

```
<% Response.Write RSContent("TopicName") %>
```

the name of the content record:

```
<% Response.Write RSContent("ContentTitle") %>
```

and the text of the content record:

```
<% Response.Write RSContent("ContentText") %>
```

Quiz Active Server Page

Quiz.asp

The code on the Quiz page calls your stored procedure to display the contents of the quiz for the current topic. The main code block is at the top of the page.

```
<%
Option Explicit
Dim DBConn
Dim RSQuizPage
If IsEmpty(Session("StudentID")) Then
      Response.Redirect "../index.asp"
End If
If IsEmpty(Session("CourseID")) Then
      Response.Redirect "./courses.asp"
End If
If IsEmpty(Session("TopicID")) Then
      Response.Redirect "./topic_list.asp"
End If
set DBConn = Server.Createobject ("ADODB.Connection")
DBConn.ConnectionString = "driver={SQL Server};" _
      & "server=MyServer;uid=WebUser" _
      & ";pwd=WebUser;database=C17OnlineSchool"
DBConn.Open
Set RSQuizPage = DBConn.Execute _
      ("Exec QuizPage " _
      & Session("TopicID"))
%>
```

You start with your compiler directive:

```
Option Explicit
```

and declare a Connection object:

```
Dim DBConn
```

and a Recordset object:

```
Dim RSQuizPage
```

If the student hasn't logged into the site, you send them to the login page:

```
If IsEmpty(Session("StudentID")) Then
     Response.Redirect "../index.asp"
End If
```

If they got to this page without selecting a course, you send them to the Courses page:

```
If IsEmpty(Session("CourseID")) Then
     Response.Redirect "./courses.asp"
End If
```

You also need to make sure that they didn't skip to this page without first selecting a topic. If they have, you send the student to the Topic List page:

```
If IsEmpty(Session("TopicID")) Then
     Response.Redirect "./topic_list.asp"
End If
```

If all those Session variables are found, the student can be on this page. You connect to the database:

```
set DBConn = Server.Createobject ("ADODB.Connection")
DBConn.ConnectionString = "driver={SQL Server};" _
     & "server=MyServer;uid=WebUser" _
     & ";pwd=WebUser;database=C17OnlineSchool"
DBConn.Open
```

and retrieve the HTML text of the quiz:

```
Set RSQuizPage = DBConn.Execute _
     ("Exec QuizPage " _
     & Session("TopicID"))
```

Then on the page, you display the Quiz with all its questions and answers as returned from your stored procedure:

```
<% Response.Write RSQuizPage("ThePage") %>
```

Result Active Server Page

Result.asp

When the student finishes a quiz, they click the OK button on that page to submit the contents of the form on that page to the Result page. The code on the Result page checks each of the student's answers through your stored procedure and displays the quiz results to the student.

The code does this by iterating through the Form collection submitted to it from the Quiz page. The Quiz page displays each answer's Select control with a name that contains the ID of that question. So in the code here, you iterate through each of the Select controls, checking them against the correct answers.

The main code block is at the top of the page.

```
<%
Option Explicit
Dim DBConn
Dim RSAnswer
Dim TheControl
Dim TotalQuestions
Dim TotalAnswersCorrect
Dim PageText
If IsEmpty(Session("StudentID")) Then
      Response.Redirect "../index.asp"
End If
If IsEmpty(Session("CourseID")) Then
      Response.Redirect "./courses.asp"
End If
If IsEmpty(Session("TopicID")) Then
      Response.Redirect "./topic_list.asp"
End If
set DBConn = Server.Createobject ("ADODB.Connection")
DBConn.ConnectionString = "driver={SQL Server};" _
      & "server=MyServer;uid=WebUser" _
      & ";pwd=WebUser;database=C17OnlineSchool"
DBConn.Open
TotalQuestions = 0
TotalAnswersCorrect = 0
```

```
For Each TheControl in Request.Form
      If left(TheControl, 1) = "A" Then
            TotalQuestions = TotalQuestions + 1
            Set RSAnswer = DBConn.Execute _
                  ("Exec CheckAnswer " _
                  & Mid(TheControl, 2) _
                  & ", '" & Request.Form(TheControl) _
                  & "'")
            TotalAnswersCorrect = TotalAnswersCorrect _
                  + RSAnswer("AnswerValue")
            PageText = PageText & "<BR><BR>" _
                  & "Question: " & TotalQuestions _
                  & ", " & RSAnswer("AnswerPrompt") _
                  & "<BR>" & RSAnswer("ResponseText")
      End If
Next
PageText = "<B>You scored " & TotalAnswersCorrect _
      & " out of " & TotalQuestions & "</B>" _
      & PageText
%>
```

You start with Option Explicit:

```
Option Explicit
```

In code, you will need a Connection object:

```
Dim DBConn
```

and a Recordset object:

```
Dim RSAnswer
```

You will also need a Form control object as you iterate through all the Select controls submitted:

```
Dim TheControl
```

This variable will store the total number of questions scored:

```
Dim TotalQuestions
```

and the number that were correct:

```
Dim TotalAnswersCorrect
```

One other variable will store the text for the Result page as you build it:

```
Dim PageText
```

First, you make sure the page was entered correctly. If the student hasn't logged in, you send them to the Log In page:

```
If IsEmpty(Session("StudentID")) Then
      Response.Redirect "../index.asp"
End If
```

If the student hasn't selected a course, they are sent to the Courses page:

```
If IsEmpty(Session("CourseID")) Then
      Response.Redirect "./courses.asp"
End If
```

And if they haven't selected a topic, they are sent to the Topic List page:

```
If IsEmpty(Session("TopicID")) Then
      Response.Redirect "./topic_list.asp"
End If
```

Otherwise, you can connect to your SQL Server database:

```
set DBConn = Server.Createobject ("ADODB.Connection")
DBConn.ConnectionString = "driver={SQL Server};" _
      & "server=MyServer;uid=WebUser" _
      & ";pwd=WebUser;database=C17OnlineSchool"
DBConn.Open
```

you initialize your counter variables to 0:

```
TotalQuestions = 0
TotalAnswersCorrect = 0
```

and enter a loop so that you can process each of the controls that were submitted to this page through the Quiz page:

```
For Each TheControl in Request.Form
```

The form on the Quiz page contains, in addition to the Select controls that store the answers selected by the student, a Submit button. You don't want to process that button or any other elements on that form except for the Select controls. You do that by making sure that the control's name starts with "A", which is how you created the Select controls for the Quiz page through your stored procedure:

```
If left(TheControl, 1) = "A" Then
```

If it does start with "A", it is a valid question and you need to increment your total questions counter:

```
TotalQuestions = TotalQuestions + 1
```

Then you need to check the student's answer to the question:

```
Set RSAnswer = DBConn.Execute _
      ("Exec CheckAnswer " _
      & Mid(TheControl, 2) _
      & ", '" & Request.Form(TheControl) _
      & "'")
```

Remember that the CheckAnswer stored procedure returns a value for the answer: a 1 for correct and a 0 for incorrect. That number is used to increment your total correct tally:

```
TotalAnswersCorrect = TotalAnswersCorrect _
      + RSAnswer("AnswerValue")
```

You then place the number of the question, whether it was correct or incorrect, and the explanation text into your variable that will be displayed on this page:

```
PageText = PageText & "<BR><BR>" _
      & "Question: " & TotalQuestions _
      & ", " & RSAnswer("AnswerPrompt") _
      & "<BR>" & RSAnswer("ResponseText")
```

You then move on to process the next control on the page:

```
Next
```

After the loop, you place the summary information about the quiz result into your page text variable:

```
PageText = "<B>You scored " & TotalAnswersCorrect _
      & " out of " & TotalQuestions & "</B>" _
      & PageText
```

That variable is then displayed to the student within the body of the HTML page:

```
<% Response.Write PageText %>
```

Help Active Server Page

Help.asp

The code on the Help page calls your stored procedure to display a list of questions to the student and the answer to the question that was selected by the user.

```
<%
Option Explicit
Dim DBConn
Dim RSHelpPage
set DBConn = Server.Createobject ("ADODB.Connection")
DBConn.ConnectionString = "driver={SQL Server};" _
      & "server=MyServer;uid=WebUser" _
      & ";pwd=WebUser;database=C17OnlineSchool"
DBConn.Open
If IsEmpty(Request.Form("QuestionID")) Then
      Set RSHelpPage = DBConn.Execute _
            ("Exec HelpTopicListAndAnswer 3")
Else
      Set RSHelpPage = DBConn.Execute _
            ("Exec HelpTopicListAndAnswer " _
            & Request.Form("QuestionID"))
End If
%>
```

You start with Option Explicit:

```
Option Explicit
```

You will need a Connection object:

```
Dim DBConn
```

and a Recordset object:

```
Dim RSHelpPage
```

You then connect to the database:

```
set DBConn = Server.Createobject ("ADODB.Connection")
DBConn.ConnectionString = "driver={SQL Server};" _
```

```
        & "server=MyServer;uid=WebUser" _
        & ";pwd=WebUser;database=C17OnlineSchool"
DBConn.Open
```

and check to see if the student has selected a question that they want the answer for:

```
If IsEmpty(Request.Form("QuestionID")) Then
```

If that is the case, you call your stored procedure, passing to it the ID of the question selected by the student:

```
Set RSHelpPage = DBConn.Execute _
        ("Exec HelpTopicListAndAnswer 3")
```

Otherwise, you will retrieve and display the answer to the first question:

```
Set RSHelpPage = DBConn.Execute _
        ("Exec HelpTopicListAndAnswer " _
        & Request.Form("QuestionID"))
```

Either way, within the body of the HTML page, you display the question list in the Select control:

```
<SELECT ID="FormsComboBox1" NAME="QuestionID">
        <% Response.Write RSHelpPage("TheList") %>
</SELECT>
```

and the answer for the question selected in that list:

```
<% Response.Write RSHelpPage("AnswerText") %>
```

CHAPTER 18

Web Site Enhancements

IN THIS CHAPTER:

C18ChatSQLObjects.sql

Chats.txt

Global.asp

Index.asp

Chat.asp

Body_Chat.asp

Footer_ChatPage.asp

C18ClassifiedsSQLObjects.sql

ClassifiedCategories.txt

Classifieds.txt

Classifieds.asp

Add_Ad.asp

Remove_Ad.asp

C18QandASQLObjects.sql

QandAs.txt

Answer.asp

In this chapter, we will look at tools that expand the capabilities of your Web site. The tools all use a SQL Server back end with ASP on the front end.

Tools That Add a Dimension to Your Web Site

First we will look at the Chat tool. The Chat tool allows visitors to your site to engage in written live communication with each other.

Then we will look at the Classifieds tool. The Classifieds tool allows the visitor to browse through items posted for sale. They can also add items and remove them.

After that, we will look at the Question and Answer tool. This tool allows you to take the visitor through a series of questions. Each answer they give leads them down a different path until eventually they reach an answer to their question.

Chat Tool

The Chat tool allows visitors to have a live text-based conversation with each other. Once the visitor logs into the site, they can then send a message out to all connected visitors or to a specific visitor.

Web Site Walk-Through

When the visitor first enters the Chat site, they see the page displayed in Figure 18-1.

From this page, the visitor enters the screen name that they want to use during the chat. But the name must not be in use by another chatter. If it is, they see the message displayed in Figure 18-2.

Once the user enters a valid login name, they are taken to the Chat page displayed in Figure 18-3.

The top part of the page displays the thread of the chat conversation. When the visitor first enters this page, they see a message from the server that they have entered the site, as well as one previous message. The visitor can then send a message out to everyone else connected. They do this by selecting Everyone from the To list, entering the message and clicking the Send button.

Their message is then sent out to everyone connected to the chat. The message appears in the thread part of the page, as shown in Figure 18-4.

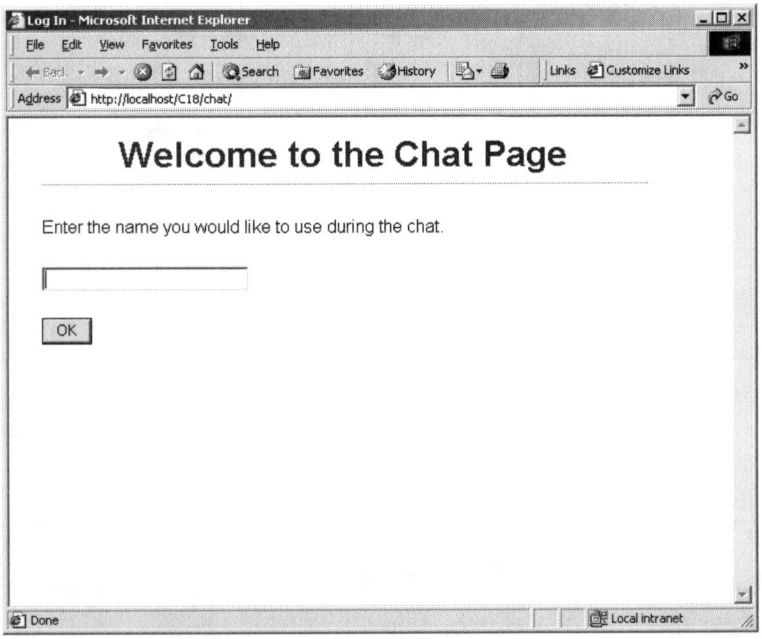

Figure 18-1 *Initial view of the Chat Login page*

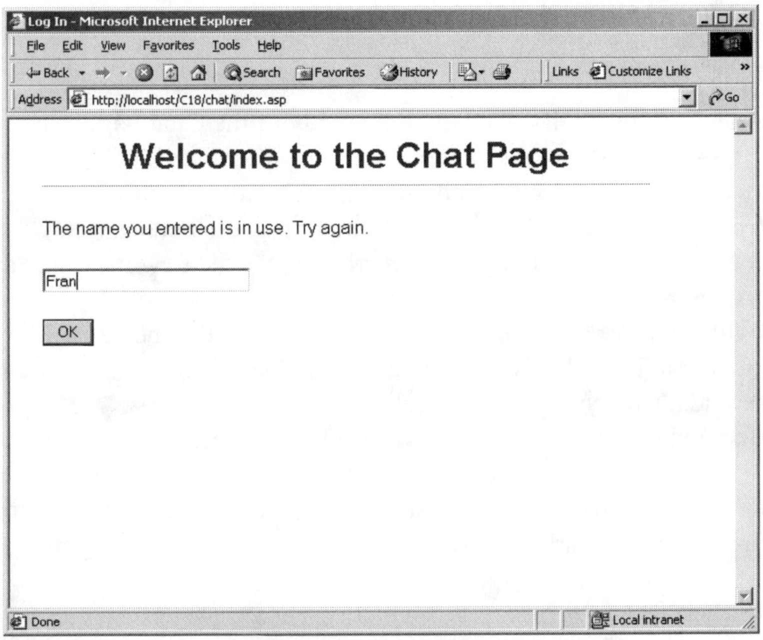

Figure 18-2 *Log In page after failed login attempt*

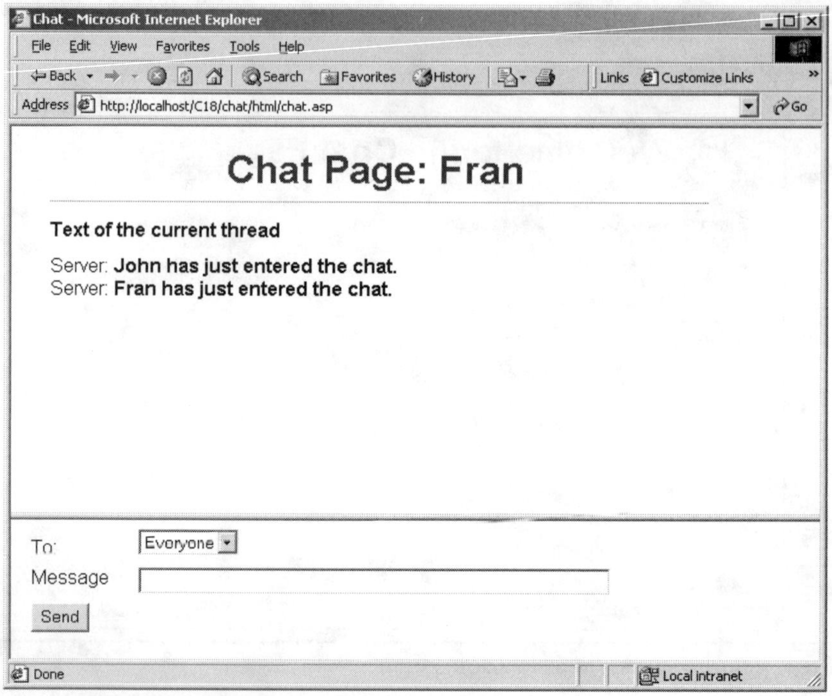

Figure 18-3 *Initial entry into the Chat page*

The message automatically appears in the body of the Chat page, since that frame updates itself every 10 seconds.

The visitor can also choose to send out a message to a specific person in the chat. This is known as a whisper. They do this by selecting the person who is to receive the whisper from the To list. Only that person will see the new message, as is displayed in Figure 18-5.

Note the different types of fonts used in the thread of the message. Messages from the server appear in bold. Messages that are available for everyone to view are in regular text, and a whisper appears in italics.

The To list updates every time the visitor submits a message with all the visitors active in the chat. As you will see when we look at the code, when the session expires the user is removed from the list and a server message is posted to the thread regarding their departure. Such a message is displayed in Figure 18-6.

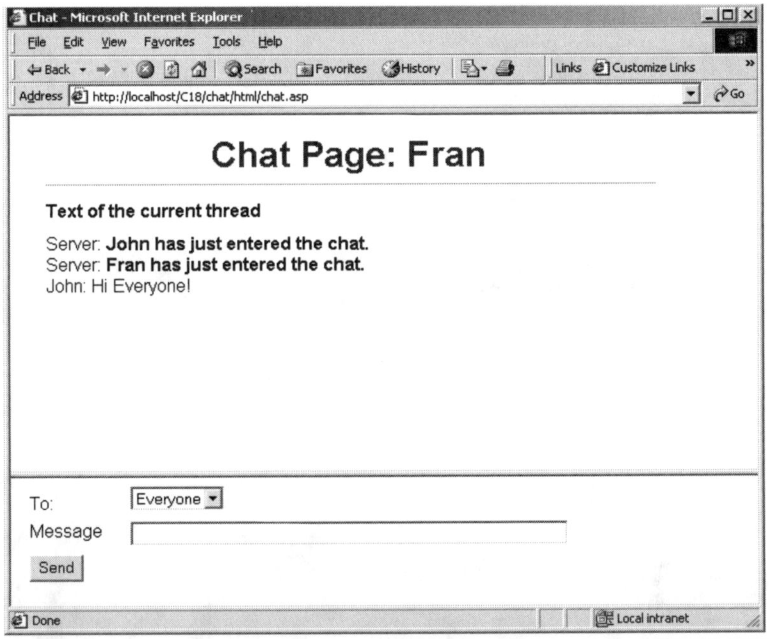

Figure 18-4 *Chat page with new message sent out to all visitors*

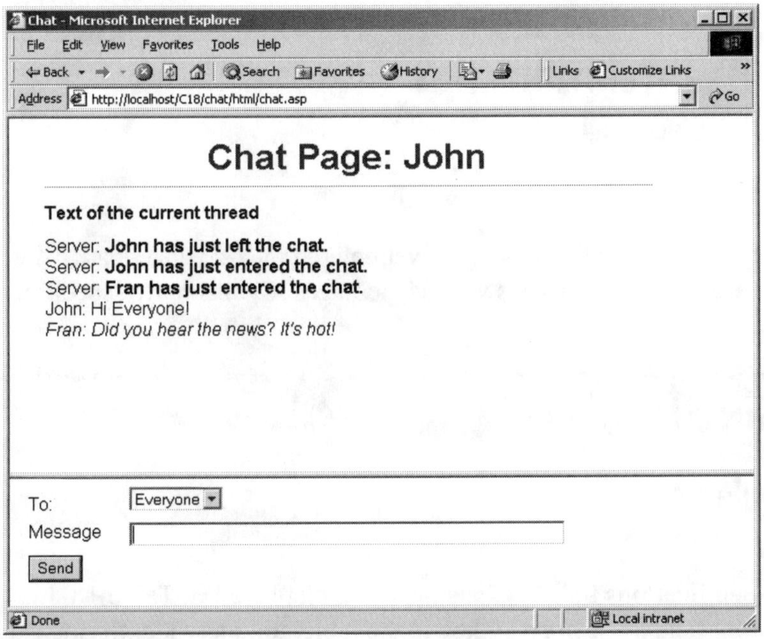

Figure 18-5 *Chat page with a whisper message added*

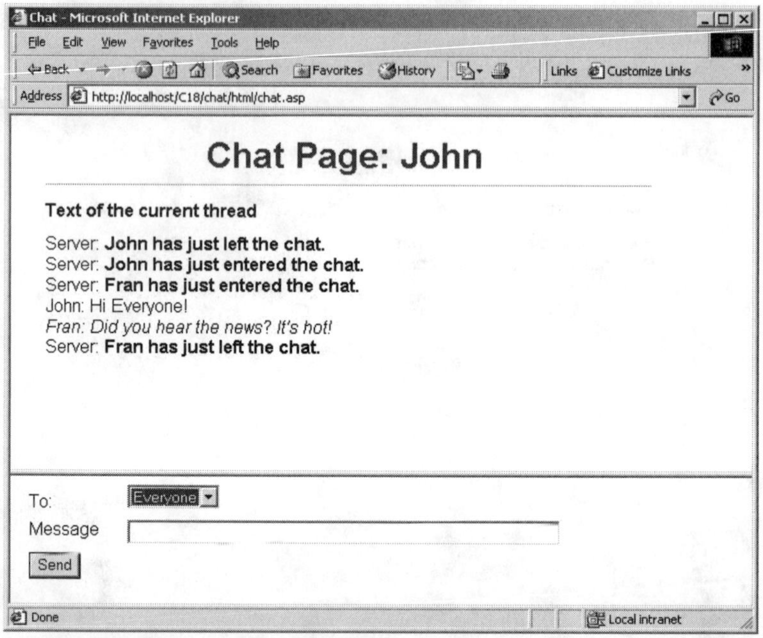

Figure 18-6 *Chat page displaying server departure message*

Tables and Relationships

C18ChatSQLObjects.sql

Chats Table

The Chats table stores all the messages ever entered into the chat board. This thread trail includes messages to everyone, as well as messages whispered to a specific visitor.

Field Specifications

Chats Table

Chats.txt

The field specifications for the Chats table are displayed in Table 18-1.

The ChatID field is the primary key in the table, uniquely identifying each record. The WhenEntered field stores the date and time that the record was added to the table.

Field Name	Field Type	Notes
ChatID	int	Primary Key, Identity Column
WhenEntered	datetime	
EnteredBy	varchar	Length = 50
EnteredTo	varchar	Length = 50
TheMessage	varchar	Length = 255

Table 18-1 *Chats Table Field Specifications*

The field has the following code in the Default Value property:

```
GetDate()
```

So the field will contain the current system date and time if it is omitted from the field list in a SQL Insert statement.

The EnteredBy field stores the name of the visitor who entered the message. The EnteredTo field stores who the message was sent to, or it can contain the text "Everyone" to signify that the message is for all the visitors. The TheMessage field stores the text of the message.

Stored Procedures

ChatStartingID Stored Procedure

When the visitor first enters the Chat tool, that moment marks the point that they see all the chat messages from. The ChatStartingID is called to return the ID of the record that was entered just before the visitor logged in to the site.

```
CREATE PROCEDURE ChatStartingID
AS
BEGIN
      Select Max(ChatID) - 1 as TheID
            From Chats
END
GO
```

The procedure takes no parameters. It simply retrieves the ID of the last entered record and subtracts one from it so that the visitor will begin their session in the spot previous to the message posted at the time that they have entered the chat:

```
Select Max(ChatID) - 1 as TheID
      From Chats
```

ChatGetMessages Stored Procedure

Whenever the body of the Chat page is updated, it needs to display all the messages to everyone, as well as whispered messages to the current visitor since they have logged into the tool. The ChatGetMessages stored procedure returns that information.

```
CREATE PROCEDURE ChatGetMessages
@StartingPoint integer,
@ChatName varchar(50)
AS
Declare
@AllOfIt varchar(8000),
@EnteredBy varchar(50),
@EnteredTo varchar(50),
@TheMessage varchar(255)
Declare CurChats Cursor
For Select Enteredby, EnteredTo, TheMessage
      from Chats
      Where (EnteredTo = 'EveryOne'
      Or EnteredTo = @ChatName)
      And ChatID >= @StartingPoint
      order by WhenEntered
Open CurChats
Fetch CurChats
      Into @EnteredBy, @EnteredTo,
      @TheMessage
Select @AllOfIt = ''
While @@Fetch_Status = 0
      BEGIN
            If @EnteredTo = 'EveryOne'
                  BEGIN
                        Select @AllOfIt = @AllOfIt + @EnteredBy
                              + ': ' + @TheMessage
                              + '<BR>'
                  END
            Else
                  BEGIN
                        Select @AllOfIt = @AllOfIt + '<I>' + @EnteredBy
                              + ': ' + @TheMessage + '</I>'
```

```
                              + '<BR>'
                        END
                  Fetch CurChats
                        Into @EnteredBy, @EnteredTo,
                        @TheMessage
            END
Close CurChats
Deallocate CurChats
Select @AllOfIt as TheMessage
GO
```

The procedure takes two parameters. The first is the point that the visitor entered the Chat page:

```
@StartingPoint integer,
```

and the other is the name of the chatter:

```
@ChatName varchar(50)
```

Within the procedure, you need a variable to store the return text as it is being concatenated:

```
@AllOfIt varchar(8000),
```

You also need variables to store the fields from the Chats table as you are retrieving them:

```
@EnteredBy varchar(50),
@EnteredTo varchar(50),
@TheMessage varchar(255)
```

You will also need a Cursor object:

```
Declare CurChats Cursor
```

which is used to retrieve all the chat records to this visitor or to all visitors since they logged in:

```
For Select Enteredby, EnteredTo, TheMessage
      from Chats
      Where (EnteredTo = 'EveryOne'
      Or EnteredTo = @ChatName)
```

```
      And ChatID >= @StartingPoint
      order by WhenEntered
```

You then open the Cursor object:

```
Open CurChats
```

and retrieve the first record into your local variables:

```
Fetch CurChats
      Into @EnteredBy, @EnteredTo,
      @TheMessage
```

Next, you need to initialize your return variable:

```
Select @AllOfIt = ''
```

and enter a loop that will iterate through all the records in the Cursor object:

```
While @@Fetch_Status = 0
```

Within the loop, you check to see if the message retrieved was to everyone:

```
If @EnteredTo = 'EveryOne'
```

If that is the case, you format the thread message so that it will appear on its own line in the HTML as standard text:

```
Select @AllOfIt = @AllOfIt + @EnteredBy
            + ': ' + @TheMessage
            + '<BR>'
```

Otherwise, the specific message must be for this specific visitor. So the text will need to be in italics:

```
Select @AllOfIt = @AllOfIt + '<I>' + @EnteredBy
      + ': ' + @TheMessage + '</I>'
      + '<BR>'
```

You then retrieve the next record and loop so that it, too, can be processed:

```
Fetch CurChats
      Into @EnteredBy, @EnteredTo,
      @TheMessage
```

After the loop, you release the resources used by the Cursor object:

```
Close CurChats
Deallocate CurChats
```

and return the entire thread of the chat:

```
Select @AllOfIt as TheMessage
```

ChatAdd Stored Procedure

The ChatAdd stored procedure, called from the footer of the Chat page, is used to add a new chat message to the database. The procedure is also called from code to add a chat message whenever a visitor enters the application or leaves the application.

```
CREATE PROCEDURE ChatAdd
@EnteredBy varchar(50),
@EnteredTo varchar(50),
@TheMessage varchar(255)
AS
BEGIN
      Insert Into Chats
            (EnteredBy, EnteredTo, TheMessage) values
            (@EnteredBy, @EnteredTo, @TheMessage)
END
GO
```

The procedure requires that the name of the visitor entering the message be passed in:

```
@EnteredBy varchar(50),
```

as well as the ID of the person the message is to:

```
@EnteredTo varchar(50),
```

and the text of the message:

```
@TheMessage varchar(255)
```

Those values are then used in the value list portion of a SQL Insert statement:

```
Insert Into Chats
      (EnteredBy, EnteredTo, TheMessage) values
      (@EnteredBy, @EnteredTo, @TheMessage)
```

Users

WebUser User

In addition to the default Administrator account, the database has the user WebUser associated with it. The only access that user has to the database is through the stored procedures. No other permissions are granted to this user.

Global.asa File

Global.asp

The Chat tool is implemented as an Active Server Page application that uses the Global.asa file. Therefore, you need to set up the site as an Active Server Page application from within the Internet Services Manager, as is shown in Chapter 15.

The following coded events can be found in the Global.asa file.

```
Sub Application_OnStart
      Application("ChatNames") = "Everyone~"
End Sub
Sub Session_OnEnd
      Dim DBConn
      set DBConn = Server.Createobject ("ADODB.Connection")
      DBConn.ConnectionString = "driver={SQL Server};" _
            & "server=MyServer;uid=WebUser" _
            & ";pwd=WebUser;database=C18WSE"
      DBConn.Open
      DBCOnn.Execute "Exec ChatAdd 'Server', 'Everyone', " _
            & "'<B>" &  Session("ChatName") & " has just " _
            & "left the chat.</B>'"
      Application("ChatNames") = _
```

```
            Replace(Application("ChatNames"), _
            Session("ChatName") & "~", "")
End Sub
```

The first event coded for is the Application OnStart event. This event fires when the application is first launched or the Global.asa file is changed and saved:

```
Sub Application_OnStart
```

Within that event, you initialize an application variable that will contain the names of all the chatters. The list also needs to include the special chat name Everyone, which is used to broadcast a message out to all the chatters. Note the "~" at the end of the name. As you will see in the footer code, that character is used to indicate the end of a chatter name when building the To Select control on that page:

```
Application("ChatNames") = "Everyone~"
```

The other event that is coded for in this file is the Session OnEnd event. That event fires when the visitor's session ends, that is, when they leave the application:

```
Sub Session_OnEnd
```

Within that event, you will need an ADO Connection object:

```
Dim DBConn
```

which is instantiated:

```
set DBConn = Server.Createobject ("ADODB.Connection")
```

and the connection to the database is made:

```
DBConn.ConnectionString = "driver={SQL Server};" _
      & "server=MyServer;uid=WebUser" _
      & ";pwd=WebUser;database=C18WSE"
DBConn.Open
```

You then add a chat message from the server that the visitor whose session is ending has left the chat:

```
DBCOnn.Execute "Exec ChatAdd 'Server', 'Everyone', " _
      & "'<B>" &  Session("ChatName") & " has just " _
      & "left the chat.</B>'"
```

You also need to remove the visitor's name from the chat names list:

```
Application("ChatNames") = _
     Replace(Application("ChatNames"), _
     Session("ChatName") & "~", "")
```

Active Server Pages

Index or Log In Active Server Page

Index.asp

The code on the Index or Log In page validates the user's attempt to enter the chat. The main code block can be found at the top of that page.

```
<%
Option Explicit
Dim TheMessage
Dim DBConn
Dim RSStartingPoint
If IsEmpty(Request.Form("ChatName")) Then
     TheMessage = "Enter the name you would " _
          & "like to use during the chat."
Else
     if InStr(UCase(Application("ChatNames")), _
          UCase(Request.Form("ChatName")) & "~") Then
          TheMessage = "The name you entered is in use. " _
               & "Try again."
     Else
          Session("ChatName") = Request.Form("ChatName")
          Application("ChatNames") = Application("ChatNames") _
               & Request.Form("ChatName") & "~"
          set DBConn = Server.Createobject ("ADODB.Connection")
          DBConn.ConnectionString = "driver={SQL Server};" _
               & "server=MyServer;uid=WebUser" _
               & ";pwd=WebUser;database=C18WSE"
          DBConn.Open
          DBCOnn.Execute "Exec ChatAdd 'Server', 'Everyone', " _
               & "'<B>" &  Session("ChatName") & " has just " _
               & "entered the chat.</B>'"
          Set RSStartingPoint = DBConn.Execute("Exec ChatStartingID")
```

```
            Session("StartingPoint") = RSStartingPoint("TheID")
            Response.Redirect "./html/chat.asp"
        End If
End If
%>
```

You start by indicating that you will declare all your variables:

```
Option Explicit
```

This variable will store the prompt message on the page:

```
Dim TheMessage
```

You will also need a Connection object:

```
Dim DBConn
```

as well as a Recordset object to store the entry point in the chat thread for the visitor:

```
Dim RSStartingPoint
```

You then check to see if the form on the page has been submitted:

```
If IsEmpty(Request.Form("ChatName")) Then
```

If it hasn't, this is the first viewing of the page and the visitor needs to see the initial instructions:

```
TheMessage = "Enter the name you would " _
      & "like to use during the chat."
```

Otherwise, the visitor is attempting to log into the chat. You need to make sure that the name they have entered is not in use by another user:

```
if InStr(UCase(Application("ChatNames")), _
      UCase(Request.Form("ChatName")) & "~") Then
```

If it is, you inform the user of the problem:

```
TheMessage = "The name you entered is in use. " _
      & "Try again."
```

Otherwise, you store the name that the visitor entered into a session variable:

```
Session("ChatName") = Request.Form("ChatName")
```

You also add that name to the visitor name list that will be displayed in the Select control on the Chat Footer page:

```
Application("ChatNames") = Application("ChatNames") _
      & Request.Form("ChatName") & "~"
```

You also need to connect to the database:

```
set DBConn = Server.Createobject ("ADODB.Connection")
DBConn.ConnectionString = "driver={SQL Server};" _
      & "server=MyServer;uid=WebUser" _
      & ";pwd=WebUser;database=C18WSE"
DBConn.Open
```

and insert a message from the server that the visitor has entered the Chat tool:

```
DBCOnn.Execute "Exec ChatAdd 'Server', 'Everyone', " _
      & "'<B>" &  Session("ChatName") & " has just " _
      & "entered the chat.</B>'"
```

You also need to retrieve the point in the Chats table where their chatting begins:

```
Set RSStartingPoint = DBConn.Execute("Exec ChatStartingID")
```

and store that value in a Session variable:

```
Session("StartingPoint") = RSStartingPoint("TheID")
```

Finally, you send the visitor to the Chat page:

```
Response.Redirect "./html/chat.asp"
```

Within the body of the page, you display the instructions to the visitor:

```
<% Response.Write TheMessage %>
```

Chat Active Server Page

Chat.asp

The Chat page is a frames-based page that is made up of the body and the footer, which are described in the next sections. But the Chat page itself, which defines the frames, also contains some ASP code. The code makes sure that the visitor has logged in before coming to this page.

```
<%
Option Explicit
If IsEmpty(Session("ChatName")) Then
      Response.Redirect "../index.asp"
End If
%>
```

You check to see if the chat name session variable is empty:

```
If IsEmpty(Session("ChatName")) Then
```

If it is, the visitor is sent back to the Log In page:

```
Response.Redirect "../index.asp"
```

Chat Body Active Server Page

Body_Chat.asp

The code on the Chat Body page displays the current chat thread to the visitor. The page automatically updates because of this Meta tag found in the head of the page:

```
<META HTTP-EQUIV="REFRESH" CONTENT="15;URL=body_chat.asp">
```

The tag tells the browser to refresh the page every 15 seconds with the contents of the page indicated in the URL parameter.

At the top of the page, you will find the main code block.

```
<%
Option Explicit
Dim DBConn
Dim RSChats
set DBConn = Server.Createobject ("ADODB.Connection")
```

```
DBConn.ConnectionString = "driver={SQL Server};" _
     & "server=MyServer;uid=WebUser" _
     & ";pwd=WebUser;database=C18WSE"
DBConn.Open
Set RSChats = DBCOnn.Execute("Exec ChatGetMessages " _
     & Session("StartingPoint") & ", " _
     & "'" & Session("ChatName") & "'")
%>
```

You start by telling the compiler that you will be declaring all your variables:

```
Option Explicit
```

You will need a Connection object:

```
Dim DBConn
```

and a Recordset object:

```
Dim RSChats
```

You then instantiate the Connection object:

```
set DBConn = Server.Createobject ("ADODB.Connection")
```

point it to your SQL Server database using the WebUser account:

```
DBConn.ConnectionString = "driver={SQL Server};" _
     & "server=MyServer;uid=WebUser" _
     & ";pwd=WebUser;database=C18WSE"
```

and open that connection:

```
DBConn.Open
```

You then call your stored procedure to retrieve all the messages in the chat thread for everyone or the current visitor since they logged in:

```
Set RSChats = DBCOnn.Execute("Exec ChatGetMessages " _
     & Session("StartingPoint") & ", " _
     & "'" & Session("ChatName") & "'")
```

Within the body of the page, you display the name of the current chatter:

```
Chat Page: <% Response.Write Session("ChatName") %>
```

and the text of the current thread:

```
<% Response.Write RSChats("TheMessage") %>
```

Chat Footer Active Server Page

Footer_ChatPage.asp

The code on the Chat Footer page submits the message entered by the visitor to the database and displays a list of all the logged-in chatters. The main code block is at the top of the page.

```
<%
Option Explicit
Dim ToOptions
Dim CurrentName
Dim AllOfIt
Dim DBConn
AllOfIt = Application("ChatNames")
Do Until AllOfIt = ""
      CurrentName = Left(AllOfIt, Instr(AllOfIt, "~") - 1)
      ToOptions = ToOptions _
            & "<OPTION VALUE=""" & CurrentName _
            & """>" & CurrentName & "</OPTION>"
      AllOfIt = Mid(AllOfIt, Instr(AllOfIt, "~") + 1)
Loop
If Not IsEmpty(Request.Form("Message")) Then
      set DBConn = Server.Createobject ("ADODB.Connection")
      DBConn.ConnectionString = "driver={SQL Server};" _
            & "server=MyServer;uid=WebUser" _
            & ";pwd=WebUser;database=C18WSE"
      DBConn.Open
      DBCOnn.Execute "Exec ChatAdd '" & Session("ChatName") _
            & "', '" & Request.Form("To") & "', " _
            & "'" & Replace(Request.Form("Message"), "'", "''") & "'"
End If
%>
```

You start by telling the compiler that you will declare your variables:

```
Option Explicit
```

One variable will contain the Options for the Select control:

```
Dim ToOptions
```

Another will contain the name of the current visitor as you add them to the Select control:

```
Dim CurrentName
```

The third will contain a list of all the visitors that you will parse names out of into the CurrentName variable:

```
Dim AllOfIt
```

You will also need a Connection object:

```
Dim DBConn
```

You place the list of all the chatter names into a local variable:

```
AllOfIt = Application("ChatNames")
```

and enter a loop so that you can parse and process each of the chatter names:

```
Do Until AllOfIt = ""
```

Within that loop, you chop out the name of each chatter:

```
CurrentName = Left(AllOfIt, Instr(AllOfIt, "~") - 1)
```

and set it up so that it will be an option in your Select control:

```
ToOptions = ToOptions _
      & "<OPTION VALUE=""" & CurrentName _
      & """>" & CurrentName & "</OPTION>"
```

You then remove the name you just added from the list of all the chatters:

```
AllOfIt = Mid(AllOfIt, Instr(AllOfIt, "~") + 1)
```

and Loop so that you can process the next chatter name:

```
Loop
```

After the loop, you check to see if the visitor has entered a new message:

```
If Not IsEmpty(Request.Form("Message")) Then
```

If so, you need to connect to the database:

```
set DBConn = Server.Createobject ("ADODB.Connection")
DBConn.ConnectionString = "driver={SQL Server};" _
      & "server=MyServer;uid=WebUser" _
      & ";pwd=WebUser;database=C18WSE"
DBConn.Open
```

and call your procedure to insert the message into the Chats table:

```
DBCOnn.Execute "Exec ChatAdd '" & Session("ChatName") _
      & "', '" & Request.Form("To") & "', " _
      & "'" & Replace(Request.Form("Message"), "'", "''") & "'"
```

Within the body of the HTML of the footer page, you write the Option tags for the Select control:

```
<SELECT ID="FormsComboBox1" NAME="To">
      <% Response.Write ToOptions %>
</SELECT>
```

Classifieds Tool

The Classifieds tool adds pages to your Web site that allow visitors to browse through items that they or others have posted for sale. The tool also allows visitors to add and remove ads that they have posted.

Web Site Walk-Through

The entry page into the tool is displayed in Figure 18-7.

On the entry page, the visitor is presented with a list of all the categories that a product can be in. Listed with the name of the category is the number of items that have been posted in that category.

When the visitor selects one of the categories, they see the items listed in that category, as shown in Figure 18-8.

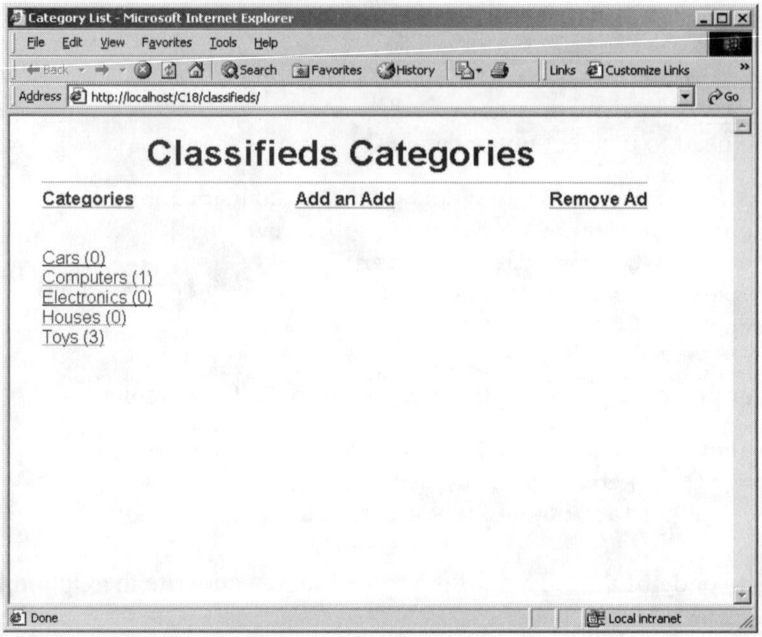

Figure 18-7 *Classifieds Entry page listing categories*

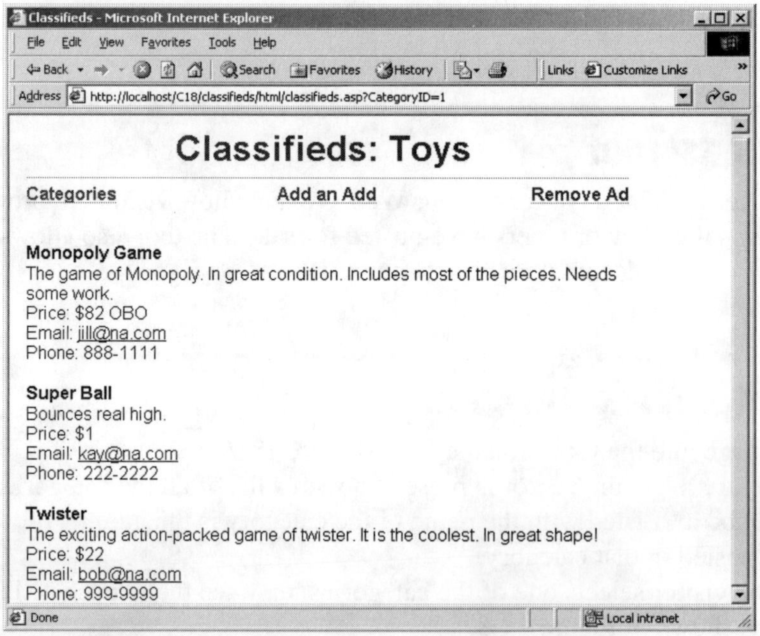

Figure 18-8 *Classifieds page displaying items in the Toys category*

At the top of the page, the visitor sees the name of the category that they are browsing. Then the main part of the page shows all the information about all the items in that category.

Toward the top of this page, as well as the top of all the other pages, the visitor can click links to take them to other pages in the tool. When they select the Add an Ad link, they are taken to the page displayed in Figure 18-9.

From this page, the visitor can enter in the information for the item that they wish to sell. When they click the OK button, their item is added to the Classifieds table and they see the message displayed in Figure 18-10.

If the visitor wants to remove their Ad at some point, they will need to take down this information. To be able to delete an ad, they need their password and the ID of the classified that they just entered.

When the visitor does wish to do that, they select the Remove Ad link and are taken to the page displayed in Figure 18-11.

The visitor simply enters the ID of their classified and their password before clicking the OK button. Their item is then removed from the Classifieds table.

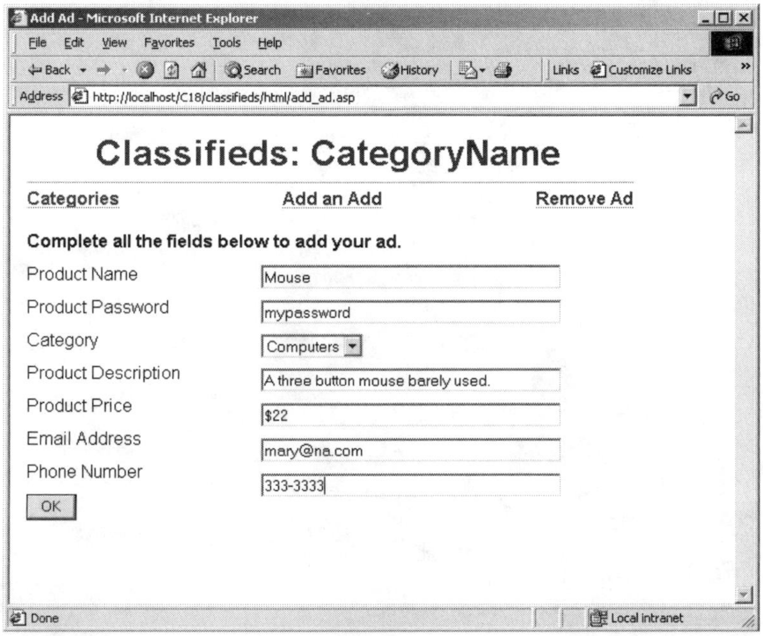

Figure 18-9 *Add Ad page with new ad entered*

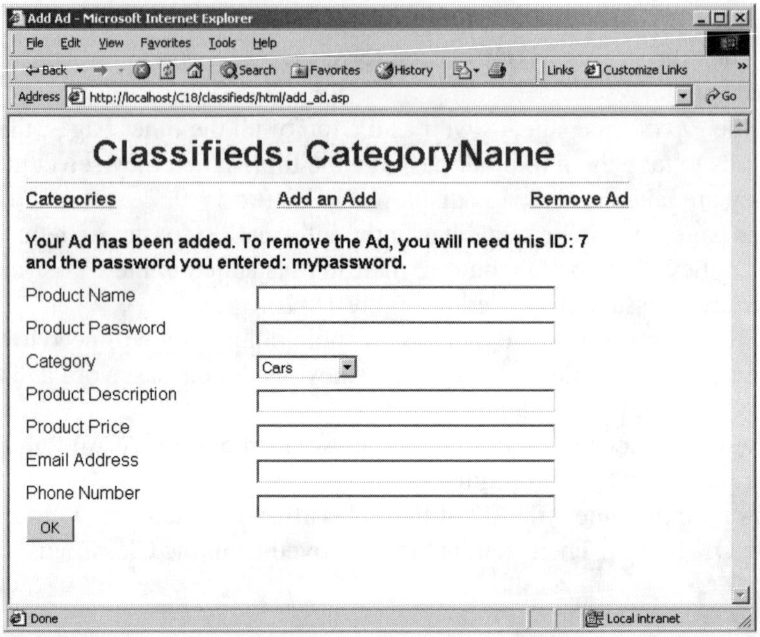

Figure 18-10 *Add Ad page with message after Ad has been added*

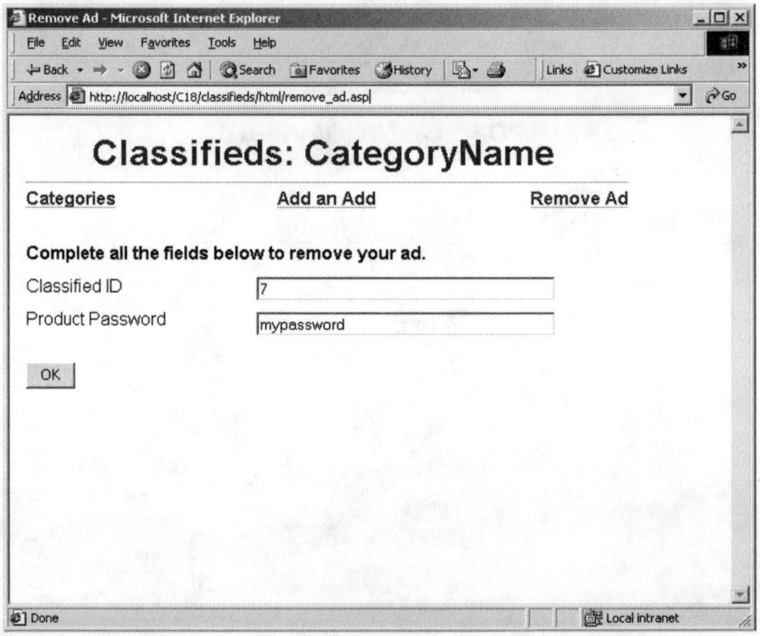

Figure 18-11 *Remove Ad page*

Tables and Relationships

C18ClassifiedsSQLObjects.sql

ClassifiedCategories Table

The ClassifiedCategories table stores the names and amounts of each category that a classified ad can be in.

Classifieds Table

The Classifieds table stores all the information about the classified ads contained in the application. The table is in a one-to-many relationship with the ClassifiedCategories table. Each ad goes in a specific category, but each category can have many ads.

Field Specifications

ClassifiedCategories.txt

ClassifiedCategories Table

The field specifications for the ClassifiedCategories table are displayed in Table 18-2.

The CategoryID field is a primary key. Since it is an identity column, it is automatically populated when a new record is added. The CategoryName field stores the name of the category, and the TotalItems field stores the total number of entries for this category in the Classifieds table. This field defaults to 0 when a new record is added, and it is automatically updated through triggers on the Classifieds table.

Classifieds Table

Classifieds.txt

The field specifications for the Classifieds table are displayed in Table 18-3.

Field Name	Field Type	Notes
CategoryID	int	Primary Key, Identity Column
CategoryName	varchar	Length = 50
TotalItems	int	

Table 18-2 *ClassifiedCategories Table Field Specifications*

Field Name	Field Type	Notes
ClassifiedID	int	Primary Key, Identity Column
CategoryID	varchar	
ProductName	int	Length = 50
ProductPassword	varchar	Length = 50
ProductDescription	varchar	Length = 255
ProductPrice	varchar	Length = 50
EmailAddress	varchar	Length = 50
PhoneNumber	varchar	Length = 50

Table 18-3 *Classifieds Table Field Specifications*

The ClassifiedID field is the primary key in this table. The CategoryID field is a foreign key that links this table to the ClassifiedCategories table. The rest of the fields store data about the classified ad.

Triggers

InsertClassifieds Trigger

Whenever a record is added to the Classifieds table, the category that that item is in needs to be updated so that it contains the correct total number of items in it. The InsertClassifieds trigger takes that action.

```
CREATE TRIGGER InsertClassifieds ON dbo.Classifieds
AFTER INSERT
AS
BEGIN
      DECLARE
      @TotalItems integer
      Select @TotalItems = Count(ClassifiedID) from Classifieds
            Where CategoryID = (Select CategoryID from Inserted)
      Update ClassifiedCategories set
            TotalItems = @TotalItems
            Where CategoryID = (Select CategoryID from Inserted)
END
```

The trigger fires on the Classifieds table:

```
CREATE TRIGGER InsertClassifieds ON dbo.Classifieds
```

after a record is added:

```
AFTER INSERT
```

Within the trigger, you need a variable to store the total number of items in the category that the classified ad was placed in:

```
@TotalItems integer
```

You then retrieve the total number of items that are in the current category and place that value into the local variable:

```
Select @TotalItems = Count(ClassifiedID) from Classifieds
      Where CategoryID = (Select CategoryID from Inserted)
```

and update the category record so that it contains this new total:

```
Update ClassifiedCategories set
      TotalItems = @TotalItems
      Where CategoryID = (Select CategoryID from Inserted)
```

DeleteClassifieds Trigger

Similarly, when a record is deleted from the Classifieds table, you need to update the tally for that category in the ClassifiedCategories table. The DeleteClassifieds trigger takes that action.

```
CREATE TRIGGER DeleteClassifieds ON dbo.Classifieds
AFTER DELETE
AS
BEGIN
      DECLARE
      @TotalItems integer
      Select @TotalItems = Count(ClassifiedID) from Classifieds
            Where CategoryID = (Select CategoryID from Deleted)
      Update ClassifiedCategories set
            TotalItems = @TotalItems
            Where CategoryID = (Select CategoryID from Deleted)
END
```

The trigger runs on the Classifieds table:

```
CREATE TRIGGER DeleteClassifieds ON dbo.Classifieds
```

after a record is deleted:

```
AFTER DELETE
```

Within the trigger, you need a variable to store the total number of items in the category:

```
@TotalItems integer
```

You then retrieve that total according to the ID of the category that the deleted classified ad was in:

```
Select @TotalItems = Count(ClassifiedID) from Classifieds
      Where CategoryID = (Select CategoryID from Deleted)
```

The value retrieved is then used in a SQL Update statement:

```
Update ClassifiedCategories set
      TotalItems = @TotalItems
      Where CategoryID = (Select CategoryID from Deleted)
```

Stored Procedures

ClassifiedsCategoryList Stored Procedure

When the visitor first enters the tool, they see a list of all the categories. The ClassifiedsCategoryList stored procedure returns that list.

```
CREATE PROCEDURE ClassifiedsCategoryList
AS
Declare
@AllOfIt varchar(8000),
@CategoryID varchar(10),
@CategoryName varchar(50),
@TotalItems varchar(100)
Declare CurCategories Cursor
For Select * from ClassifiedCategories
```

```
      order by CategoryName
Open CurCategories
Fetch CurCategories
      Into @CategoryID, @CategoryName,
      @TotalItems
Select @AllOfIt = ''
While @@Fetch_Status = 0
      BEGIN
            Select @AllOfIt = @AllOfIt
                  + '<A HREF="./html/classifieds.asp?'
                  + 'CategoryID=' + @CategoryID
                  + '"><SPAN STYLE="color: rgb(0,0,153);">'
                  + @CategoryName + ' ('
                  + @TotalItems + ')</SPAN></A><BR>'
            Fetch CurCategories
                  Into @CategoryID, @CategoryName,
                  @TotalItems
      END
Close CurCategories
Deallocate CurCategories
Select @AllOfIt as TheHTML
GO
```

The procedure does not have any parameters. But it does need a variable to store the text of the return as it is being formatted:

```
@AllOfIt varchar(8000),
```

as well as variables to store the ID of the category:

```
@CategoryID varchar(10),
```

the name of the category:

```
@CategoryName varchar(50),
```

and the total number of items in the category:

```
@TotalItems varchar(100)
```

You will also need a Cursor object:

```
Declare CurCategories Cursor
```

that will retrieve all the category records:

```
For Select * from ClassifiedCategories
      order by CategoryName
```

You then open the Cursor object:

```
Open CurCategories
```

and retrieve the first record into your local variables:

```
Fetch CurCategories
      Into @CategoryID, @CategoryName,
      @TotalItems
```

You then initialize your return variable:

```
Select @AllOfIt = ''
```

and enter a loop so that each of the records can be processed:

```
While @@Fetch_Status = 0
```

Within the loop, each of the categories needs to be returned as formatted HTML that displays the name of the category and the number of items in the category, which links to your Classifieds page:

```
Select @AllOfIt = @AllOfIt
      + '<A HREF="./html/classifieds.asp?'
      + 'CategoryID=' + @CategoryID
      + '"><SPAN STYLE="color: rgb(0,0,153);">'
      + @CategoryName + ' ('
      + @TotalItems + ')</SPAN></A><BR>'
```

You then retrieve the next record:

```
Fetch CurCategories
      Into @CategoryID, @CategoryName,
      @TotalItems
```

and loop to process it:

```
End
```

After the loop, you release the Cursor object:

```
Close CurCategories
Deallocate CurCategories
```

and return the HTML that you built:

```
Select @AllOfIt as TheHTML
```

ClassifiedList Stored Procedure

The ClassifiedList stored procedure returns all the classifieds items in a category formatted as HTML, which are displayed on the Classifieds page.

```
CREATE PROCEDURE ClassifiedList
@CategoryID integer
AS
Declare
@AllOfIt varchar(8000),
@CategoryName varchar(50),
@ProductName varchar(50),
@ProductDescription varchar(255),
@ProductPrice varchar(50),
@EmailAddress varchar(50),
@PhoneNumber varchar(50)
Select @CategoryName = CategoryName
      From ClassifiedCategories
      Where CategoryID = @CategoryID
Declare CurClassifieds Cursor
For Select ProductName, ProductDescription,
      ProductPrice, EmailAddress, PhoneNumber
      From Classifieds
      Where CategoryID = @CategoryID
      order by ProductName
Open CurClassifieds
Fetch CurClassifieds
      Into @ProductName, @ProductDescription,
      @ProductPrice, @EmailAddress, @PhoneNumber
Select @AllOfIt = ''
While @@Fetch_Status = 0
      BEGIN
            Select @AllOfIt = @AllOfIt
                  + '<P><B>' + @ProductName
```

```
                    + '</B><BR>' + @ProductDescription
                    + '<BR>Price: ' + @ProductPrice
                    + '<BR>Email: <A HREF="mailto:'
                    + @EmailAddress + '">' + @EmailAddress
                    + '</A><BR>Phone: ' + @PhoneNumber
                    + '</P>'
            Fetch CurClassifieds
                    Into @ProductName, @ProductDescription,
                    @ProductPrice, @EmailAddress, @PhoneNumber
      END
Close CurClassifieds
Deallocate CurClassifieds
Select @AllOfIt as TheHTML, @CategoryName as CategoryName
GO
```

Passed into the procedure is the ID of the category from which the ads are to be retrieved:

```
@CategoryID integer
```

Within the procedure, you need a variable to store the HTML text as you are building it:

```
@AllOfIt varchar(8000),
```

You also need a variable to store the name of the category:

```
@CategoryName varchar(50),
```

and variables to store fields from the Classifieds table as they are retrieved through a Cursor object:

```
@ProductName varchar(50),
@ProductDescription varchar(255),
@ProductPrice varchar(50),
@EmailAddress varchar(50),
@PhoneNumber varchar(50)
```

You then retrieve the name of the category corresponding to the ID passed in. That name will be returned at the end of the procedure:

```
Select @CategoryName = CategoryName
      From ClassifiedCategories
      Where CategoryID = @CategoryID
```

You then declare your Cursor object:

```
Declare CurClassifieds Cursor
```

and set it to retrieve the records from the Classifieds table according to the ID of the category passed in:

```
For Select ProductName, ProductDescription,
      ProductPrice, EmailAddress, PhoneNumber
      From Classifieds
      Where CategoryID = @CategoryID
      order by ProductName
```

That cursor is opened:

```
Open CurClassifieds
```

and the first record is retrieved into your local variables:

```
Fetch CurClassifieds
      Into @ProductName, @ProductDescription,
      @ProductPrice, @EmailAddress, @PhoneNumber
```

You then initialize the variable that will store the HTML return text:

```
Select @AllOfIt = ''
```

and enter a loop to process each of the records:

```
While @@Fetch_Status = 0
```

Within the loop, each classified ad in the category passed in is formatted as HTML so that it will be displayed as desired on the Classifieds page:

```
Select @AllOfIt = @AllOfIt
      + '<P><B>' + @ProductName
      + '</B><BR>' + @ProductDescription
      + '<BR>Price: ' + @ProductPrice
      + '<BR>Email: <A HREF="mailto:'
      + @EmailAddress + '">' + @EmailAddress
      + '</A><BR>Phone: ' + @PhoneNumber
      + '</P>'
```

You then retrieve the next record and loop so that it can be processed:

```
Fetch CurClassifieds
      Into @ProductName, @ProductDescription,
      @ProductPrice, @EmailAddress, @PhoneNumber
```

The resources used by the cursor are then released:

```
Close CurClassifieds
Deallocate CurClassifieds
```

and you return the HTML-formatted classified ads and the name of the current category:

```
Select @AllOfIt as TheHTML, @CategoryName as CategoryName
```

ClassifiedsCategoryOptions Stored Procedure

The ClassifiedsCategoryOptions stored procedure returns a list of categories in the form of HTML Option tags for an HTML Select control. The procedure is used on the Add Ad page to display a list of all the categories.

```
CREATE PROCEDURE ClassifiedsCategoryOptions
AS
Declare
@AllOfIt varchar(8000),
@CategoryID varchar(10),
@CategoryName varchar(50)
Declare CurCategories Cursor
For Select CategoryID, CategoryName
      from ClassifiedCategories
      order by CategoryName
Open CurCategories
Fetch CurCategories
      Into @CategoryID, @CategoryName
Select @AllOfIt = ''
While @@Fetch_Status = 0
      BEGIN
            Select @AllOfIt = @AllOfIt
                  + '<OPTION VALUE="'
                  + @CategoryID + '">'
                  + @CategoryName + '</OPTION>'
            Fetch CurCategories
                  Into @CategoryID, @CategoryName
```

```
      END
Close CurCategories
Deallocate CurCategories
Select @AllOfIt as TheList
GO
```

Within the procedure, you need a variable to store the text of the return as it is being built:

```
@AllOfIt varchar(8000),
```

You also need variables that will contain the ID and the name of the category as they are retrieved from the ClassifiedCategories table:

```
@CategoryID varchar(10),
@CategoryName varchar(50)
```

Also a Cursor object is needed:

```
Declare CurCategories Cursor
```

which will retrieve all the category records:

```
For Select CategoryID, CategoryName
      from ClassifiedCategories
      order by CategoryName
```

You then open the cursor:

```
Open CurCategories
```

and retrieve the first record through the cursor into your local variables:

```
Fetch CurCategories
      Into @CategoryID, @CategoryName
```

Next, you initialize the return variable:

```
Select @AllOfIt = ''
```

and enter a loop so that each record retrieved can be processed:

```
While @@Fetch_Status = 0
```

Each record is formatted as an HTML Option tag with the name of the category visible but the ID of the category passed when the form is submitted:

```
Select @AllOfIt = @AllOfIt
      + '<OPTION VALUE="'
      + @CategoryID + '">'
      + @CategoryName + '</OPTION>'
```

You then retrieve the next record:

```
Fetch CurCategories
      Into @CategoryID, @CategoryName
```

and loop so that it can be processed:

```
End
```

After the loop, you release the cursor:

```
Close CurCategories
Deallocate CurCategories
```

and return the HTML Option tag text:

```
Select @AllOfIt as TheList
```

ClassifiedsAddAd Stored Procedure

The ClassifiedsAddAd stored procedure provides the mechanism for adding a new record to the Classifieds table. The procedure is called from the Add Ad page.

```
CREATE PROCEDURE ClassifiedsAddAd
@ProductName varchar(50),
@ProductPassword varchar(50),
@CategoryID integer,
@ProductDescription varchar(255),
@ProductPrice varchar(50),
@EmailAddress varchar(50),
@PhoneNumber varchar(50)
AS
BEGIN
      Insert Into Classifieds
            (ProductName, ProductPassword,
```

```
            CategoryID, ProductDescription,
            ProductPrice, EmailAddress,
            PhoneNumber) values
            (@ProductName, @ProductPassword,
            @CategoryID, @ProductDescription,
            @ProductPrice, @EmailAddress,
            @PhoneNumber)
      Select @@Identity as TheID
End
GO
```

Passed into the procedure are the values for the fields for the record being added:

```
@ProductName varchar(50),
@ProductPassword varchar(50),
@CategoryID integer,
@ProductDescription varchar(255),
@ProductPrice varchar(50),
@EmailAddress varchar(50),
@PhoneNumber varchar(50)
```

Those parameters are then used in the value list portion of a SQL Insert statement:

```
Insert Into Classifieds
      (ProductName, ProductPassword,
      CategoryID, ProductDescription,
      ProductPrice, EmailAddress,
      PhoneNumber) values
      (@ProductName, @ProductPassword,
      @CategoryID, @ProductDescription,
      @ProductPrice, @EmailAddress,
      @PhoneNumber)
```

You then return the ID of the record just added:

```
Select @@Identity as TheID
```

ClassifiedDelete Stored Procedure

The ClassifiedDelete stored procedure is used to delete a classified record. The procedure is called from the Remove Ad page.

```
CREATE PROCEDURE ClassifiedDelete
@ClassifiedID integer,
@ProductPassword varchar(50)
AS
BEGIN
      Delete From Classifieds
            Where ClassifiedID = @ClassifiedID
            And ProductPassword = @ProductPassword
END
GO
```

Passed into the procedure are the ID of the classified ad to be deleted:

```
@ClassifiedID integer,
```

and the password for that item:

```
@ProductPassword varchar(50)
```

The record that matches that ID and password is then deleted from the Classifieds table:

```
Delete From Classifieds
      Where ClassifiedID = @ClassifiedID
      And ProductPassword = @ProductPassword
```

Users

WebUser User

In addition to the default Administrator account, the database has the user WebUser associated with it. The only access that user has to the database is through the stored procedures. No other permissions are granted to this user.

Active Server Pages

Category List Active Server Page

Index.asp

The code on the Category List page calls your stored procedure to display the list of all the categories. The main code block is at the top of the page.

```
<%
Option Explicit
Dim DBConn
Dim RSCategories
set DBConn = Server.Createobject ("ADODB.Connection")
DBConn.ConnectionString = "driver={SQL Server};" _
      & "server=MyServer;uid=WebUser" _
      & ";pwd=WebUser;database=C18WSE"
DBConn.Open
Set RSCategories = DBConn.Execute("Exec ClassifiedsCategoryList")
%>
```

You start by telling the compiler that all the variables will be declared:

```
Option Explicit
```

Next, you declare a variable for an ADO Connection object:

```
Dim DBConn
```

and one for a Recordset object:

```
Dim RSCategories
```

You then open a connection to your SQL Server database:

```
set DBConn = Server.Createobject ("ADODB.Connection")
DBConn.ConnectionString = "driver={SQL Server};" _
      & "server=MyServer;uid=WebUser" _
      & ";pwd=WebUser;database=C18WSE"
DBConn.Open
```

and retrieve the category list:

```
Set RSCategories = DBConn.Execute("Exec ClassifiedsCategoryList")
```

Then in the body of the page, you write out that category list:

```
<P><% Response.Write RSCategories("TheHTML") %></P>
```

Classifieds Active Server Page

Classifieds.asp

The code on the Classifieds page displays the list of all the items in the selected category by calling one of your stored procedures. The main code block is at the top of the page.

```
<%
Option Explicit
Dim DBConn
Dim RSClassifieds
If IsEmpty(Request.QueryString("CategoryID")) Then
      Response.Redirect "../index.asp"
End If
set DBConn = Server.Createobject ("ADODB.Connection")
DBConn.ConnectionString = "driver={SQL Server};" _
      & "server=MyServer;uid=WebUser" _
      & ";pwd=WebUser;database=C18WSE"
DBConn.Open
Set RSClassifieds = DBConn.Execute("Exec ClassifiedList " _
      & Request.QueryString("CategoryID"))
%>
```

You start by telling the compiler that you will declare all your variables:

```
Option Explicit
```

You then declare a variable to store a Connection object:

```
Dim DBConn
```

and a Recordset object:

```
Dim RSClassifieds
```

The page should not be viewed without the ID of a category being passed in through the QueryString collection. You check for that item here:

```
If IsEmpty(Request.QueryString("CategoryID")) Then
```

If it is not found, you send the visitor back to the Categories page:

```
Response.Redirect "../index.asp"
```

Otherwise, you can connect to the database:

```
set DBConn = Server.Createobject ("ADODB.Connection")
DBConn.ConnectionString = "driver={SQL Server};" _
      & "server=MyServer;uid=WebUser" _
      & ";pwd=WebUser;database=C18WSE"
DBConn.Open
```

and retrieve all the classifieds in the selected category:

```
Set RSClassifieds = DBConn.Execute("Exec ClassifiedList " _
      & Request.QueryString("CategoryID"))
```

Then in the body of the page, you write the name of the category:

```
Classifieds: <% Response.Write RSClassifieds("CategoryName") %>
```

and the list of classifieds:

```
<% Response.Write RSClassifieds("TheHTML") %>
```

Add Ad Active Server Page

Add_Ad.asp

The code on the Add Ad page calls your stored procedure to add the ad entered by the visitor into the database. The code is also used to populate the Options of the Select control.

```
<%
Option Explicit
Dim DBConn
Dim RSCategories
Dim RSNewID
Dim TheMessage
set DBConn = Server.Createobject ("ADODB.Connection")
DBConn.ConnectionString = "driver={SQL Server};" _
      & "server=MyServer;uid=WebUser" _
      & ";pwd=WebUser;database=C18WSE"
DBConn.Open
Set RSCategories = DBConn.Execute("Exec ClassifiedsCategoryOptions")
If IsEmpty(Request.Form("OK")) Then
      TheMessage = "Complete all the fields below to add your ad."
Else
      Set RSNewID = DBConn.Execute("Exec ClassifiedsAddAd " _
            & "'" & Request.Form("ProductName") & "', " _
            & "'" & Request.Form("ProductPassword") & "', " _
            & "" & Request.Form("CategoryID") & ", " _
            & "'" & Request.Form("ProductDescription") & "', " _
            & "'" & Request.Form("ProductPrice") & "', " _
            & "'" & Request.Form("EmailAddress") & "', " _
            & "'" & Request.Form("PhoneNumber") & "'")
      TheMessage = "Your Ad has been added. To remove the Ad, you will " _
```

```
                & "need this ID: " & RSNewID("TheID") _
                & " and the password you entered: " _
                & Request.Form("ProductPassword") & "."
End If
%>
```

You start with the compiler directive:

```
Option Explicit
```

and declare variables that will store the database connection:

```
Dim DBConn
```

a recordset for the categories list:

```
Dim RSCategories
```

and the ID of the classified added:

```
Dim RSNewID
```

You also need a variable to store the text of the message displayed on the page to the visitor:

```
Dim TheMessage
```

You start by connecting to the database:

```
set DBConn = Server.Createobject ("ADODB.Connection")
DBConn.ConnectionString = "driver={SQL Server};" _
     & "server=MyServer;uid=WebUser" _
     & ";pwd=WebUser;database=C18WSE"
DBConn.Open
```

Then you use the connection to retrieve the category list for the Select control:

```
Set RSCategories = DBConn.Execute("Exec ClassifiedsCategoryOptions")
```

You then check to see if the form on the page has been submitted:

```
If IsEmpty(Request.Form("OK")) Then
```

If it hasn't, you will need to display your default message:

```
TheMessage = "Complete all the fields below to add your ad."
```

Otherwise, you call your stored procedure to add the ad entered by the visitor to the database:

```
Set RSNewID = DBConn.Execute("Exec ClassifiedsAddAd " _
            & "'" & Request.Form("ProductName") & "', " _
            & "'" & Request.Form("ProductPassword") & "', " _
            & "" & Request.Form("CategoryID") & ", " _
            & "'" & Request.Form("ProductDescription") & "', " _
            & "'" & Request.Form("ProductPrice") & "', " _
            & "'" & Request.Form("EmailAddress") & "', " _
            & "'" & Request.Form("PhoneNumber") & "'")
```

The visitor sees a different message after an ad has been added, which tells them how they can remove their ad:

```
TheMessage = "Your Ad has been added. To remove the Ad, you will " _
      & "need this ID: " & RSNewID("TheID") _
      & " and the password you entered: " _
      & Request.Form("ProductPassword") & "."
```

Then in the body of the page, you write the message variable:

```
<P><B><% Response.Write TheMessage %></B></P>
```

as well as the Option tags for the Select control:

```
<SELECT ID="FormsComboBox1" NAME="CategoryID">
      <% Response.Write RSCategories("TheList") %>
</SELECT>
```

Remove Ad Active Server Page

Remove_Ad.asp

The code on the Remove Ad page calls your stored procedure to remove an ad from the database when the form on the page is submitted. All the code is at the top of the page.

```
<%
Option Explicit
Dim DBConn
set DBConn = Server.Createobject ("ADODB.Connection")
DBConn.ConnectionString = "driver={SQL Server};" _
      & "server=MyServer;uid=WebUser" _
```

```
        & ";pwd=WebUser;database=C18WSE"
DBConn.Open
If Not IsEmpty(Request.Form("OK")) Then
        DBCOnn.Execute "Exec ClassifiedDelete " _
                & Request.Form("ClassifiedID") & ", " _
                & "'" & Request.Form("ProductPassword") _
                & "'"
End If
%>
```

You start with your compiler directive:

```
Option Explicit
```

declare a variable for your database connection:

```
Dim DBConn
```

and connect to the database:

```
set DBConn = Server.Createobject ("ADODB.Connection")
DBConn.ConnectionString = "driver={SQL Server};" _
        & "server=MyServer;uid=WebUser"_
        & ";pwd=WebUser;database=C18WSE"
DBConn.Open
```

You then check to see if the form on the page has been submitted:

```
If Not IsEmpty(Request.Form("OK")) Then
```

If so, you call your stored procedure to delete the record entered by the visitor:

```
DBCOnn.Execute "Exec ClassifiedDelete " _
        & Request.Form("ClassifiedID") & ", " _
        & "'" & Request.Form("ProductPassword") _
        & "'"
```

Question and Answer Tool

The Question and Answer tool allows you to ask the visitor questions. Each time they answer the question, they can be presented with another question. This process can go on for as many questions as you like. Then eventually the response they make to a question takes them to the answer for their problem.

A tool like this could be used to support the products and services you offer. Using information given by the visitor, you could supply them with a possible resolution.

Web Site Walk-Through

When the visitor first enters the site, they are presented with the top-level question displayed in Figure 18-12.

The visitor then reads the question and selects the most appropriate response to that question. That response could lead to another question as is displayed in Figure 18-13.

The visitor continues to answer questions that can lead to other questions as they proceed through. Eventually they select a response that does not lead to another question. Instead it leads to an answer. The answer is displayed on the Answer page, which you can see in Figure 18-14.

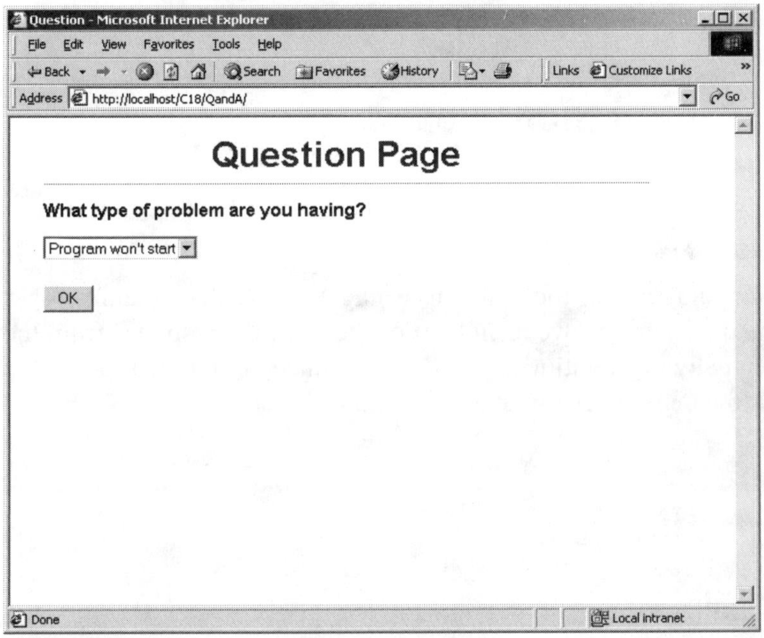

Figure 18-12 *Top-level question on the Questions page*

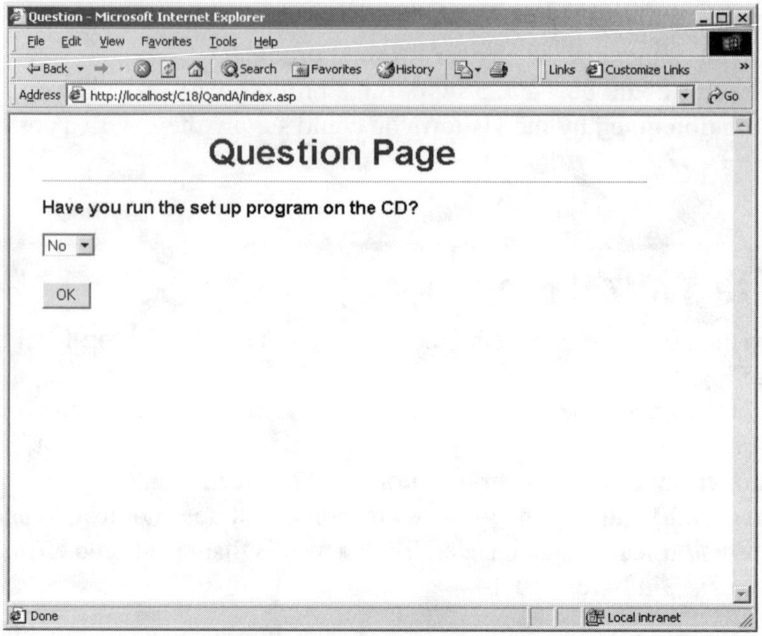

Figure 18-13 *Second-level question on the Questions page*

Tables and Relationships

C18QandASQLObjects.sql

QandAs Table

The Question and Answer tool contains a single table called QandAs. That table contains the questions, answers, and options text for the response from the visitor. The table is really in a relationship with itself, since all but the top-level question relate back to another question that elicited the choice.

Field Specifications

QandAs Table

QandAs.txt

The field specifications for the QandAs table are displayed in Table 18-4.

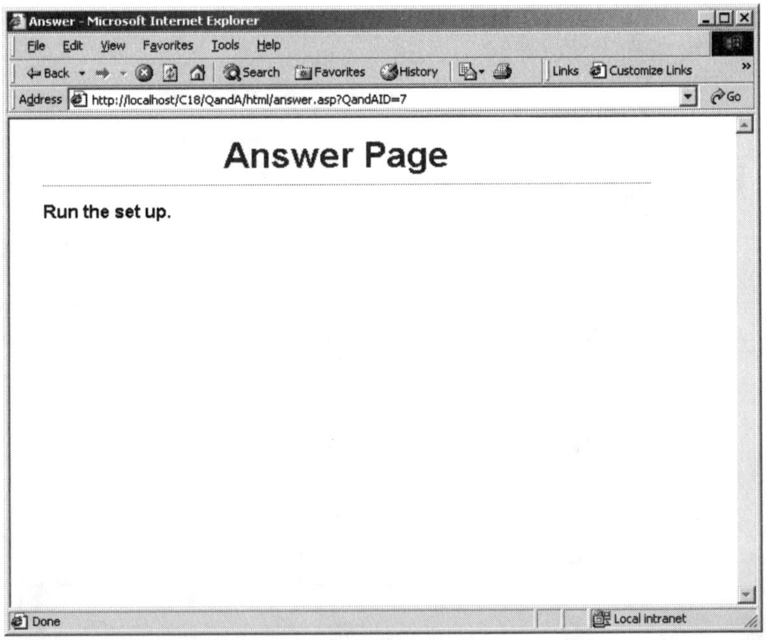

Figure 18-14 *Answer page*

The QandAID field is the primary key in this table. The ParentID field is a foreign key that links this table to itself. Stored in this field is the ID of the QandAs record that this record is a response for.

The QandAText field stores the text of the question if this record is a question or the text of an answer if this record is an answer. The OptionText field stores the text that is displayed for this item in the Select control on the Questions page.

FieldName	FieldType	Notes
QandAID	int	Primary Key, Identity Column
ParentID	int	Foreign Key
QandAText	varchar	Length = 2000
OptionText	varchar	Length = 100
OptionType	varchar	Length = 1

Table 18-4 *QandAs Table Field Specifications*

The OptionType field can contain either "A" or "Q". "A" means that the record is an answer, and "Q" means that the record is a question.

Stored Procedures

QuestionStuff Stored Procedure

The QuestionStuff stored procedure returns the text of the question and the possible responses to that question for the Select control according to the ID passed into it.

```
CREATE PROCEDURE QuestionStuff
@QandAIDIn integer
AS
Declare
@AllOfIt varchar(8000),
@QandAText varchar(2000),
@QandAID varchar(10),
@OptionText varchar(100),
@OptionType varchar(1)
If @QandAIDIn = 0
      BEGIN
            Select @QandAIDIn = QandAID
                  From QandAs
                  Where ParentID = 0
      END
Select @QandAText = QandAText
      From QandAs
      Where QandAID = @QandAIDIn
Declare CurQandA Cursor
For Select QandAID, OptionText, OptionType
      From QandAs
      Where ParentID = @QandAIDIn
Open CurQandA
Fetch CurQandA
      Into @QandAID, @OptionText, @OptionType
Select @AllOfIt = ''
While @@Fetch_Status = 0
      BEGIN
            Select @AllOfIt = @AllOfIt
                  + '<OPTION VALUE="'
                  + @OptionType + @QandAID
```

```
                    + '">' + @OptionText
                    + '</OPTION>'
              Fetch CurQandA
                    Into @QandAID, @OptionText, @OptionType
      END
Close CurQandA
Deallocate CurQandA
Select @AllOfIt as TheOptions, @QandAText as QandAText
GO
```

Passed into the procedure is the ID of the question for which the calling application wants to retrieve the text and responses:

```
@QandAIDIn integer
```

Within the procedure, you need a variable to store the text of the options as you are building them:

```
@AllOfIt varchar(8000),
```

Another variable will be used to return the text of the question:

```
@QandAText varchar(2000),
```

You also need variables to store the fields from the QandAs table as you retrieve them:

```
@QandAID varchar(10),
@OptionText varchar(100),
@OptionType varchar(1)
```

If the calling application passes in a value of 0 through the parameter, that means that they want the top-level question. The procedure is called in this way when from the Questions page when it is initially viewed. You check for that here:

```
If @QandAIDIn = 0
```

If that is the case, you retrieve the ID of the question for which the parent ID is set to 0, which is a special value indicating that the record is the top-level record:

```
Select @QandAIDIn = QandAID
      From QandAs
      Where ParentID = 0
```

After that, you can retrieve and store in your local variable the text of the question:

```
Select @QandAText = QandAText
     From QandAs
     Where QandAID = @QandAIDIn
```

Next, you declare a Cursor object:

```
Declare CurQandA Cursor
```

and set it to retrieve all the records that are possible responses to the current question:

```
For Select QandAID, OptionText, OptionType
     From QandAs
     Where ParentID = @QandAIDIn
```

That cursor is opened:

```
Open CurQandA
```

the first record is retrieved:

```
Fetch CurQandA
     Into @QandAID, @OptionText, @OptionType
```

you initialize your return variable:

```
Select @AllOfIt = ''
```

and enter a loop so that each record can be processed:

```
While @@Fetch_Status = 0
```

Each response is formatted as an HTML Option tag for an HTML Select control. Note that the visitor sees the text of the response, but the type and ID of the response are passed:

```
Select @AllOfIt = @AllOfIt
     + '<OPTION VALUE="'
     + @OptionType + @QandAID
```

```
        + '">' + @OptionText
        + '</OPTION>'
```

You then retrieve the next record:

```
Fetch CurQandA
      Into @QandAID, @OptionText, @OptionType
```

and loop so that it can be processed:

```
End
```

After the loop, the cursor is released:

```
Close CurQandA
Deallocate CurQandA
```

and you return the Option tags as well as the text of the question:

```
Select @AllOfIt as TheOptions, @QandAText as QandAText
```

AnswerStuff Stored Procedure

The AnswerStuff stored procedure is called from the Answer page and is used to return the text of an answer.

```
CREATE PROCEDURE AnswerStuff
@QandAID integer
AS
BEGIN
      Select QandAText from QandAs
            where QandAID = @QandAID
END
GO
```

Passed into the procedure is the ID of the record for which you want the answer retrieved:

```
@QandAID integer
```

That ID is then used in a SQL Select statement that returns the text of the answer.

```
Select QandAText from QandAs
      where QandAID = @QandAID
```

Users

WebUser User

In addition to the default Administrator account, the database has the user WebUser associated with it. The only access that user has to the database is through the stored procedures. No other permissions are granted to this user.

Active Server Pages

Question Active Server Page

Index.asp

The code on the Question page displays the text of the question and the possible responses to the visitor in the Select control by calling your stored procedure. The code also redirects the visitor to the answer page when they reach an answer record. The main code block is at the top of the page.

```
<%
Option Explicit
Dim DBConn
Dim RSQStuff
Dim ID2Use
If IsEmpty(Request.Form("QandAID")) Then
      ID2Use = 0
ElseIf Left(Request.Form("QandAID"), 1) = "Q" Then
      ID2Use = Mid(Request.Form("QandAID"), 2)
Else
      Response.Redirect "./html/answer.asp?QandAID=" _
           & Mid(Request.Form("QandAID"), 2)
End If
set DBConn = Server.Createobject ("ADODB.Connection")
DBConn.ConnectionString = "driver={SQL Server};" _
      & "server=MyServer;uid=WebUser" _
      & ";pwd=WebUser;database=C18WSE"
DBConn.Open
```

```
Set RSQstuff = DBConn.Execute("Exec QuestionStuff " _
      & ID2Use)
%>
```

You start by telling the compiler that you will be declaring your variables:

```
Option Explicit
```

You then declare a variable for your database connection:

```
Dim DBConn
```

one for a Recordset object:

```
Dim RSQStuff
```

and one to store the ID of the question that is to be retrieved:

```
Dim ID2Use
```

Next, you need to determine the state of the form. You check to see if the form has not been submitted, meaning that this is the first viewing of the page:

```
If IsEmpty(Request.Form("QandAID")) Then
```

If that is the case, you need to display the top-level question, which means that the ID to use variable needs to be set to 0:

```
ID2Use = 0
```

Next, you check to see if the response selected by the visitor leads to another question by seeing if the item starts with "Q":

```
ElseIf Left(Request.Form("QandAID"), 1) = "Q" Then
```

If it does, you will use that ID for your next question:

```
ID2Use = Mid(Request.Form("QandAID"), 2)
```

Otherwise, the visitor is at the point of an answer and is sent to the Answer page:

```
Response.Redirect "./html/answer.asp?QandAID=" _
      & Mid(Request.Form("QandAID"), 2)
```

If the code flows here, the visitor needs to see a question. So you connect to the database:

```
set DBConn = Server.Createobject ("ADODB.Connection")
DBConn.ConnectionString = "driver={SQL Server};" _
      & "server=MyServer;uid=WebUser" _
      & ";pwd=WebUser;database=C18WSE"
DBConn.Open
```

and retrieve the question and responses from your stored procedure:

```
Set RSQstuff = DBConn.Execute("Exec QuestionStuff " _
      & ID2Use)
```

Then in the body of the page, you display the text of the question:

```
<P><B><% Response.Write RSQstuff("QandAText") %></B></P>
```

as well as the Options for the Select control:

```
<SELECT ID="FormsComboBox1" NAME="QandAID">
      <% Response.Write RSQstuff("TheOptions") %>
</SELECT>
```

Answer Active Server Page

Answer.asp

The code on the Answer page displays the text of an answer to the visitor according to the ID passed into the page. The main code block is at the top of the page.

```
<%
Option Explicit
Dim DBConn
Dim RSAStuff
If IsEmpty(Request.QueryString("QandAID")) Then
      Response.Redirect "../index.asp"
End If
set DBConn = Server.Createobject ("ADODB.Connection")
DBConn.ConnectionString = "driver={SQL Server};" _
      & "server=MyServer;uid=WebUser" _
      & ";pwd=WebUser;database=C18WSE"
DBConn.Open
Set RSAstuff = DBConn.Execute("Exec AnswerStuff " _
```

```
      & Request.QueryString("QandAID"))
%>
```

You start with your compiler directive:

```
Option Explicit
```

declare variables for a Connection object:

```
Dim DBConn
```

and a Recordset object:

```
Dim RSAStuff
```

The page should not be entered without a QandAID being passed into it. You check for one here:

```
If IsEmpty(Request.QueryString("QandAID")) Then
```

If it isn't present, the visitor is sent back to the question page:

```
Response.Redirect "../index.asp"
```

Otherwise, you can connect to the database:

```
set DBConn = Server.Createobject ("ADODB.Connection")
DBConn.ConnectionString = "driver={SQL Server};" _
      & "server=MyServer;uid=WebUser" _
      & ";pwd=WebUser;database=C18WSE"
DBConn.Open
```

and retrieve the text of the answer:

```
Set RSAstuff = DBConn.Execute("Exec AnswerStuff " _
      & Request.QueryString("QandAID"))
```

That text is then displayed to the visitor on the body of the page:

```
<P><B><% Response.Write RSAstuff("QandAText") %></B></P>
```

CHAPTER 19

Company Site Tools

IN THIS CHAPTER:

C19ContactsSQLObjects.sql

Departments.txt

Contacts.txt

Index.asp

Contact_Matches.asp

Contact.asp

C19SurveySQLObjects.sql

SurveyResponses.txt

Results.asp

C19OrderStatusQLObjects.sql

Orders.txt

OrderDetails.txt

Order_Status.asp

In this chapter, we will look at Active Server Page applications that could be used to enhance a company's internal intranet or external Internet site. First, we will look at the Contacts tool. The Contacts tool allows the visitor to search or browse through contact listings from a company.

Then we will review the Survey tool. That tool allows you to record responses made by visitors to questions and then to review the results of survey questions.

Finally, we will review the Order Status tool. This tool allows your visitors to view the status of their order, as well as the products in their order.

Contacts Tool

The Contacts tool provides a way for visitors to your site to search through your Contacts list. They can view all the contacts in a specific department, or they can search the contact records. The visitor then selects a specific contact to view their complete information.

Web Site Walk-Through

When the visitor first enters this tool, they see the page displayed in Figure 19-1.

From the home page, the visitor selects how they want to browse through the Contacts records. Their first option is to select a department and view all the contacts in that department. When they do that, they see the Contacts Matches page displayed in Figure 19-2.

At the top of the page, the visitor sees the name of the department that they are viewing the records for. Under that, they see a table of all the contacts in that department with their summary contact information.

Back on the Contacts page, the visitor can choose to search the Contacts record. They enter a search word or part of a word. The code then looks for any matches on that term in a variety of fields and displays the matches, such as those shown in Figure 19-3.

In this example, the visitor entered the search term "Smith." Displayed on this page are all the records that have the term "Smith" in one of the search fields.

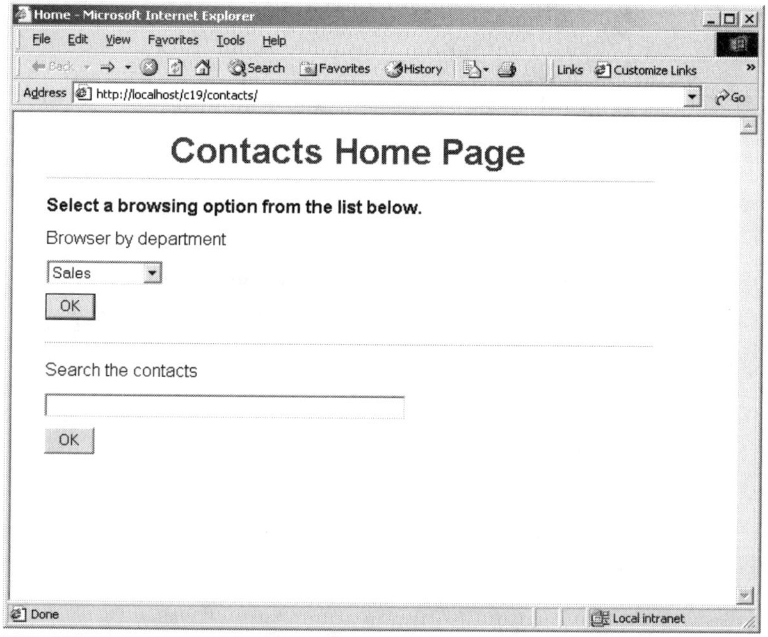

Figure 19-1 *Contacts tool home page*

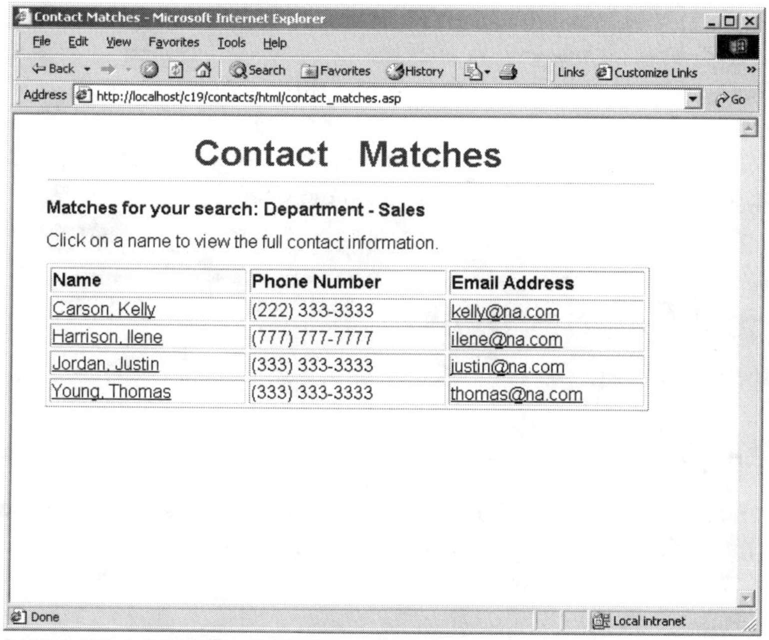

Figure 19-2 *Contacts Matches page for a department*

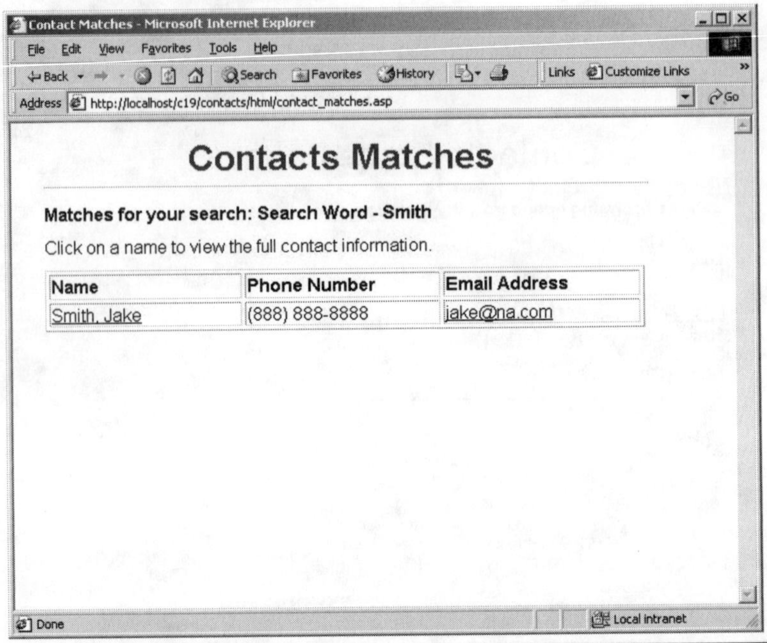

Figure 19-3 *Contacts Matches page displaying the results of a search*

Regardless of whether the visitor searches or browses a department's contacts, they can click the name of the visitor to see the full contact information, which is displayed in Figure 19-4.

The top of the Contact page shows the contact's name. Then, in the body of the page, the visitor sees all the information about the contact.

Tables and Relationships

C19ContactsSQLObjects.sql

Departments Table

The Departments table stores the IDs and names of the departments. Those values are used in the Select control on the Contacts home page.

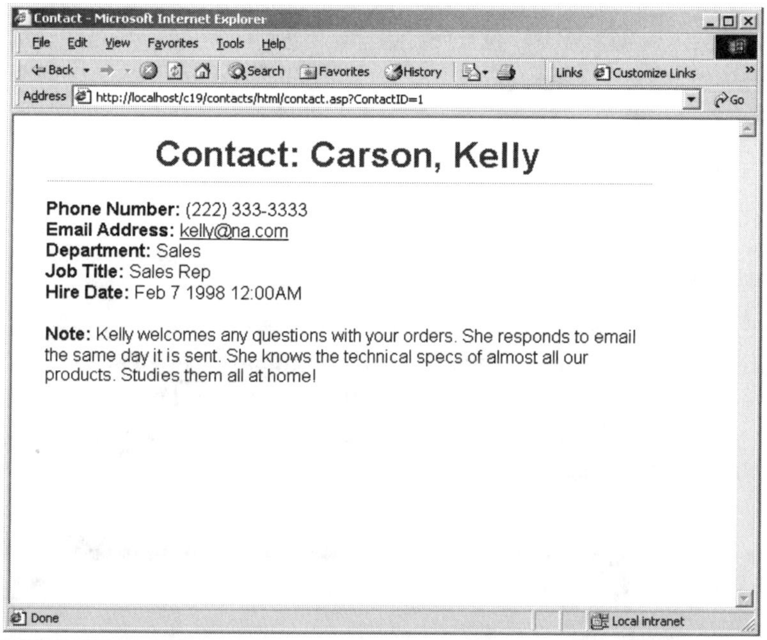

Figure 19-4 *Contact page*

Contacts Table

The Contacts table stores all the data about the contacts used by this application. The table is in a one-to-many relationship with the Departments table. Each contact record goes with a specific department but each department can have many contacts.

Field Specifications

Departments Table

Departments.txt

The field specifications for the Departments table are displayed in Table 19-1.

The DepartmentID field is the primary key in this table. It is an identity column, so values are automatically entered into this field when a new record is added. The DepartmentName field stores the name of the department.

Field Name	Field Type	Notes
DepartmentID	int	Primary Key, Identity Column
DepartmentName	varchar	Length = 50

Table 19-1 *Departments Table Field Specifications*

Contacts Table

Contacts.txt

The field specifications for the Contacts table are displayed in Table 19-2.

The ContactID field is the primary key in this table. The DepartmentID field is a foreign key that links this table to the Departments table. The rest of the fields store information about the contact.

Stored Procedures

DepartmentList Stored Procedure

On the home page of the Contacts tool, the visitor is presented with a list of departments in the form of an HTML Select control. The DepartmentList stored procedure return the options for that Select control.

Field Name	Field Type	Notes
ContactID	int	Primary Key, Identity Column
DepartmentID	int	Foreign Key
LastName	varchar	Length = 50
FirstName	varchar	Length = 50
PhoneNumber	varchar	Length = 50
EmailAddress	varchar	Length = 50
JobTitle	varchar	Length = 50
HireDate	datetime	
TheNote	varchar	Length = 3000

Table 19-2 *Contacts Table Field Specifications*

```
CREATE PROCEDURE DepartmentList
AS
Declare
@AllOfIt varchar(8000),
@DepartmentID varchar(10),
@DepartmentName varchar(50)
Declare CurDepartments Cursor
For Select DepartmentID, DepartmentName
      from Departments
      order by DepartmentName
Open CurDepartments
Fetch CurDepartments
      Into @DepartmentID, @DepartmentName
Select @AllOfIt = ''
While @@Fetch_Status = 0
      BEGIN
            Select @AllOfIt = @AllOfIt
                  + '<OPTION VALUE="'
                  + @DepartmentID + '">'
                  + @DepartmentName + '</OPTION>'
            Fetch CurDepartments
                  Into @DepartmentID, @DepartmentName
      END
Close CurDepartments
Deallocate CurDepartments
Select @AllOfIt as TheOptions
GO
```

The procedure does not require any parameters. You will need local variables to store the option list as you build it:

```
@AllOfIt varchar(8000),
```

Also, variables are needed to store the ID and name of the department as you retrieve them from the database:

```
@DepartmentID varchar(10),
@DepartmentName varchar(50)
```

Those variables will be retrieved through a Cursor object, which is declared next:

```
Declare CurDepartments Cursor
```

The Cursor will retrieve all the records from the Departments table:

```
For Select DepartmentID, DepartmentName
     from Departments
     order by DepartmentName
```

That cursor is opened:

```
Open CurDepartments
```

and the first record is retrieved into your local variables:

```
Fetch CurDepartments
      Into @DepartmentID, @DepartmentName
```

You need to initialize your variable because it will be concatenated to:

```
Select @AllOfIt = ''
```

and enter a loop so that you can process each record in the Departments table:

```
While @@Fetch_Status = 0
```

Within the loop, each record is concatenated to your return value as an HTML Option tag:

```
Select @AllOfIt = @AllOfIt
      + '<OPTION VALUE="'
      + @DepartmentID + '">'
      + @DepartmentName + '</OPTION>'
```

The next record is retrieved:

```
Fetch CurDepartments
      Into @DepartmentID, @DepartmentName
```

and this End statement marks where you loop to process that next record:

```
End
```

After the loop, the Cursor is released:

```
Close CurDepartments
Deallocate CurDepartments
```

and you return the Option tags to the calling application:

```
Select @AllOfIt as TheOptions
```

DepartmentMatches Stored Procedure

The DepartmentMatches stored procedure is called from the Contacts Matches page when the visitor selects a department to browse. It returns the name of the department, as well as rows for an HTML table containing all the contacts in the department specified.

```
CREATE PROCEDURE DepartmentMatches
@DepartmentID integer
AS
Declare
@AllOfIt varchar(8000),
@DepartmentName varchar(50),
@ContactID varchar(10),
@LastName varchar(50),
@FirstName varchar(50),
@PhoneNumber varchar(50),
@EmailAddress varchar(50)
Select @DepartmentName = DepartmentName
      From Departments
      Where DepartmentID = @DepartmentID
Declare CurContacts Cursor
For Select ContactID, LastName, FirstName,
      PhoneNumber, EmailAddress
      from Contacts
      Where DepartmentID = @DepartmentID
      order by LastName, FirstName
Open CurContacts
Fetch CurContacts
      Into @ContactID, @LastName, @FirstName,
      @PhoneNumber, @EmailAddress
Select @AllOfIt = ''
While @@Fetch_Status = 0
      BEGIN
            Select @AllOfIt = @AllOfIt
                  + '<TR>'
                  + '<TD WIDTH=171>'
                  + '<P><A HREF="./contact.asp?ContactID='
                  + @ContactID + '">' + @LastName
```

```
                    + ', ' + @FirstName + '</A></P>'
                    + '</TD>'
                    + '<TD WIDTH=171>'
                    + '<P>' + @PhoneNumber + '</P>'
                    + '</TD>'
                    + '<TD WIDTH=172>'
                    + '<P><A HREF="mailto:'
                    + @EmailAddress + '">' + @EmailAddress
                    + '</A></P></TD>'
                    + '</TR>'
              Fetch CurContacts
                    Into @ContactID, @LastName, @FirstName,
                    @PhoneNumber, @EmailAddress
        END
Close CurContacts
Deallocate CurContacts
Select @AllOfIt as TheTable, @DepartmentName as DepartmentName
GO
```

Passed into the procedure is the ID of the department from which contacts are to be returned:

```
@DepartmentID integer
```

Within the procedure, you need a variable that will contain the rows of your HTML table:

```
@AllOfIt varchar(8000),
```

and one for the name of the department so that it can be returned:

```
@DepartmentName varchar(50),
```

The other variables will store the values from the fields in the Contacts table as you retrieve records:

```
@ContactID varchar(10),
@LastName varchar(50),
@FirstName varchar(50),
@PhoneNumber varchar(50),
@EmailAddress varchar(50)
```

Next, you retrieve the name of the department corresponding to the ID passed in:

```
Select @DepartmentName = DepartmentName
      From Departments
      Where DepartmentID = @DepartmentID
```

You then declare a Cursor object:

```
Declare CurContacts Cursor
```

and set it to retrieve all the basic contact information from the Contacts table for the specified department:

```
For Select ContactID, LastName, FirstName,
      PhoneNumber, EmailAddress
      from Contacts
      Where DepartmentID = @DepartmentID
      order by LastName, FirstName
```

The Cursor is opened:

```
Open CurContacts
```

and the first record is retrieved into your local variable:

```
Fetch CurContacts
      Into @ContactID, @LastName, @FirstName,
      @PhoneNumber, @EmailAddress
```

You need to initialize the variable that will store the HTML table rows:

```
Select @AllOfIt = ''
```

and enter a loop to process each of the contact records:

```
While @@Fetch_Status = 0
```

Within the loop, each contact is concatenated to your return value as a row for an HTML table:

```
Select @AllOfIt = @AllOfIt
      + '<TR>'
```

Then, within that row, the name of the contact goes in the first cell, with the text linking to your Contact page.

```
+ '<TD WIDTH=171>'
+ '<P><A HREF="./contact.asp?ContactID='
+ @ContactID + '">' + @LastName
+ ', ' + @FirstName + '</A></P>'
+ '</TD>'
```

In the next cell, you place the contact's phone number:

```
+ '<TD WIDTH=171>'
+ '<P>' + @PhoneNumber + '</P>'
+ '</TD>'
```

And, in the third cell, you place the e-mail address, which is also a link to the e-mail address:

```
+ '<TD WIDTH=172>'
+ '<P><A HREF="mailto:'
+ @EmailAddress + '">' + @EmailAddress
+ '</A></P></TD>'
+ '</TR>'
```

After concatenating the row to your return value, you retrieve the next record and loop:

```
Fetch CurContacts
      Into @ContactID, @LastName, @FirstName,
      @PhoneNumber, @EmailAddress
```

After the loop, the cursor is released:

```
Close CurContacts
Deallocate CurContacts
```

and you return the contents of the HTML table, as well as the name of the department:

```
Select @AllOfIt as TheTable, @DepartmentName as DepartmentName
```

SearchMatches Stored Procedure

The SearchMatches stored procedure returns contact records that match the search text passed in. The records are returned as rows for an HTML table and are displayed on the Contacts Matches page.

```
CREATE PROCEDURE SearchMatches
@SearchWord varchar(50)
AS
Declare
@AllOfIt varchar(8000),
@ContactID varchar(10),
@LastName varchar(50),
@FirstName varchar(50),
@PhoneNumber varchar(50),
@EmailAddress varchar(50)
Set @SearchWord = '%' + @SearchWord + '%'
Declare CurContacts Cursor
For Select ContactID, LastName, FirstName,
      PhoneNumber, EmailAddress
      from Contacts
      Where LastName Like @SearchWord
      Or FirstName Like @SearchWord
      Or JobTitle Like @SearchWord
      Or TheNote Like @SearchWord
      order by LastName, FirstName
Open CurContacts
Fetch CurContacts
      Into @ContactID, @LastName, @FirstName,
      @PhoneNumber, @EmailAddress
Select @AllOfIt = ''
While @@Fetch_Status = 0
      BEGIN
            Select @AllOfIt = @AllOfIt
                  + '<TR>'
                  + '<TD WIDTH=171>'
                  + '<P><A HREF="./contact.asp?ContactID='
                  + @ContactID + '">' + @LastName
                  + ', ' + @FirstName + '</A></P>'
                  + '</TD>'
                  + '<TD WIDTH=171>'
                  + '<P>' + @PhoneNumber + '</P>'
                  + '</TD>'
                  + '<TD WIDTH=172>'
                  + '<P><A HREF="mailto:'
                  + @EmailAddress + '">' + @EmailAddress
                  + '</A></P></TD>'
                  + '</TR>'
            Fetch CurContacts
```

```
                    Into @ContactID, @LastName, @FirstName,
                    @PhoneNumber, @EmailAddress
      END
Close CurContacts
Deallocate CurContacts
Select @AllOfIt as TheTable
GO
```

The search text is passed into the procedure as a parameter:

```
@SearchWord varchar(50)
```

You will need a variable to store the HTML rows:

```
@AllOfIt varchar(8000),
```

and variables for the contact records as they are being retrieved:

```
@ContactID varchar(10),
@LastName varchar(50),
@FirstName varchar(50),
@PhoneNumber varchar(50),
@EmailAddress varchar(50)
```

The search text will be part of a wildcard search in your SQL statement. So you need to surround the text with the wildcard character:

```
Set @SearchWord = '%' + @SearchWord + '%'
```

Next, you declare your cursor object:

```
Declare CurContacts Cursor
```

and use it to return records from the Contacts table that has the search text in the contact's name, title, or note:

```
For Select ContactID, LastName, FirstName,
      PhoneNumber, EmailAddress
      from Contacts
      Where LastName Like @SearchWord
      Or FirstName Like @SearchWord
      Or JobTitle Like @SearchWord
```

```
Or TheNote Like @SearchWord
order by LastName, FirstName
```

You then open the cursor:

```
Open CurContacts
```

and retrieve the first record:

```
Fetch CurContacts
      Into @ContactID, @LastName, @FirstName,
      @PhoneNumber, @EmailAddress
```

You also need to initialize your return variable:

```
Select @AllOfIt = ''
```

You then start a loop to process each record:

```
While @@Fetch_Status = 0
```

Each record is concatenated to your return value as a row for an HTML table:

```
Select @AllOfIt = @AllOfIt
      + '<TR>'
      + '<TD WIDTH=171>'
      + '<P><A HREF="./contact.asp?ContactID='
      + @ContactID + '">' + @LastName
      + ', ' + @FirstName + '</A></P>'
      + '</TD>'
      + '<TD WIDTH=171>'
      + '<P>' + @PhoneNumber + '</P>'
      + '</TD>'
      + '<TD WIDTH=172>'
      + '<P><A HREF="mailto:'
      + @EmailAddress + '">' + @EmailAddress
      + '</A></P></TD>'
      + '</TR>'
```

The next record is retrieved into the local variables:

```
Fetch CurContacts
      Into @ContactID, @LastName, @FirstName,
      @PhoneNumber, @EmailAddress
```

After each record is processed, you can close the cursor:

```
Close CurContacts
Deallocate CurContacts
```

and return the HTML rows:

```
Select @AllOfIt as TheTable
```

ContactRecord Stored Procedure

The ContactRecord stored procedure returns the contents of a specific contact record. The record is returned as formatted HTML so that it can appear correctly on the Contact page.

```
CREATE PROCEDURE ContactRecord
@ContactID integer
AS
Declare
@LastName varchar(50),
@FirstName varchar(50),
@PhoneNumber varchar(50),
@EmailAddress varchar(50),
@DepartmentName varchar(50),
@JobTitle varchar(50),
@HireDate varchar(50),
@TheNote varchar(3000)
Select @LastName = LastName,
      @FirstName = FirstName,
      @PhoneNumber = PhoneNumber,
      @EmailAddress = EmailAddress,
      @DepartmentName = DepartmentName,
      @JobTitle = JobTitle,
      @HireDate = HireDate,
      @TheNote = TheNote
      From Contacts
      Left Join Departments On
      Contacts.DepartmentID = Departments.DepartmentID
      Where ContactID = @ContactID
Select @LastName + ', ' + @FirstName as TheName,
      '<P><B>Phone Number: </B>' + @PhoneNumber
```

```
      + '<BR><B>Email Address: </B><A HREF="mailto:'
      + @EmailAddress + '">' + @EmailAddress + '</A><BR>'
      + '<B>Department: </B>' + @DepartmentName + '<BR>'
      + '<B>Job Title: </B>' + @JobTitle + '<BR>'
      + '<B>Hire Date: </B>' + @HireDate + '</P>'
      + '<P><B>Note: </B>' + @TheNote + '</P>'
      as TheContact
GO
```

Passed into the procedure is the ID of the contact for which the record is to be returned:

```
@ContactID integer
```

You then declare variables that will be used to store the data from the Contacts table for the record specified:

```
@LastName varchar(50),
@FirstName varchar(50),
@PhoneNumber varchar(50),
@EmailAddress varchar(50),
@DepartmentName varchar(50),
@JobTitle varchar(50),
@HireDate varchar(50),
@TheNote varchar(3000)
```

Those variables are then set to their corresponding fields according to the ID passed into the procedure:

```
Select @LastName = LastName,
      @FirstName = FirstName,
      @PhoneNumber = PhoneNumber,
      @EmailAddress = EmailAddress,
      @DepartmentName = DepartmentName,
      @JobTitle = JobTitle,
      @HireDate = HireDate,
      @TheNote = TheNote
      From Contacts
      Left Join Departments On
      Contacts.DepartmentID = Departments.DepartmentID
      Where ContactID = @ContactID
```

You then return first the contact's name and then the rest of the contact information with appropriate HTML formatting:

```
Select @LastName + ', ' + @FirstName as TheName,
      '<P><B>Phone Number: </B>' + @PhoneNumber
      + '<BR><B>Email Address: </B><A HREF="mailto:'
      + @EmailAddress + '">' + @EmailAddress + '</A><BR>'
      + '<B>Department: </B>' + @DepartmentName + '<BR>'
      + '<B>Job Title: </B>' + @JobTitle + '<BR>'
      + '<B>Hire Date: </B>' + @HireDate + '</P>'
      + '<P><B>Note: </B>' + @TheNote + '</P>'
      as TheContact
```

Users

WebUser User

In addition to the default Administrator account, the database has the user WebUser associated with it. The only access that user has to the database is through the four stored procedures. No other permissions are granted to this user.

Active Server Pages

Contacts Home Active Server Page

Index.asp

The code on the Contacts page calls a stored procedure to populate the department list. The main code block is at the top of the page.

```
<%
Option Explicit
Dim DBConn
Dim RSDepartments
set DBConn = Server.Createobject ("ADODB.Connection")
DBConn.ConnectionString = "driver={SQL Server};" _
      & "server=MyServer;uid=WebUser" _
      & ";pwd=WebUser;database=C19Contacts"
DBConn.Open
```

```
Set RSDepartments = DBConn.Execute("Exec DepartmentList")
%>
```

You start by telling the compiler that variables will be declared:

```
Option Explicit
```

You then declare a variable for a database connection:

```
Dim DBConn
```

and for a Recordset object:

```
Dim RSDepartments
```

You then set up your Connect string, using the WebUser account:

```
set DBConn = Server.Createobject ("ADODB.Connection")
DBConn.ConnectionString = "driver={SQL Server};" _
      & "server=MyServer;uid=WebUser" _
      & ";pwd=WebUser;database=C19Contacts"
```

and open that connection:

```
DBConn.Open
```

You then call your stored procedure to retrieve the department list as HTML Option tags:

```
Set RSDepartments = DBConn.Execute("Exec DepartmentList")
```

Within the body of the HTML, you write those Option tags:

```
<SELECT ID="FormsComboBox1" NAME="DepartmentID">
      <% Response.Write RSDepartments("TheOptions") %>
</SELECT>
```

Contacts Matches Active Server Page

Contact_Matches.asp

The code on the Contacts Matches page displays the contacts resulting from a search or within a department. The main code block is at the top of the page.

```
<%
Option Explicit
Dim DBConn
Dim RSContacts
Dim TheMessage
If Not IsEmpty(Request.Form("OKDepartment")) Then
      set DBConn = Server.Createobject ("ADODB.Connection")
      DBConn.ConnectionString = "driver={SQL Server};" _
            & "server=MyServer;uid=WebUser" _
            & ";pwd=WebUser;database=C19Contacts"
      DBConn.Open
      Set RSContacts = DBConn.Execute("Exec DepartmentMatches " _
            & Request.Form("DepartmentID"))
      TheMessage = "Department - " _
            & RSContacts("DepartmentName")
ElseIf Not IsEmpty(Request.Form("OKSearch")) Then
      set DBConn = Server.Createobject ("ADODB.Connection")
      DBConn.ConnectionString = "driver={SQL Server};" _
            & "server=MyServer;uid=WebUser"_
            & ";pwd=WebUser;database=C19Contacts"
      DBConn.Open
      Set RSContacts = DBConn.Execute("Exec SearchMatches '"_
            & Request.Form("SearchWord") & "'")
      TheMessage = "Search Word - " _
            & Request.Form("SearchWord")
Else
      Response.Redirect "../index.asp"
End If
%>
```

To ease debugging, you start by telling the compiler to throw an error if you use a variable that is not declared:

```
Option Explicit
```

You then declare a variable for a database connection:

```
Dim DBConn
```

and a Recordset object:

```
Dim RSContacts
```

as well as a variable to store some title text:

```
Dim TheMessage
```

Next, you check to see whether the visitor entered this page by selecting a department that they want to browse:

```
If Not IsEmpty(Request.Form("OKDepartment")) Then
```

If so, you need to connect to the database:

```
set DBConn = Server.Createobject ("ADODB.Connection")
DBConn.ConnectionString = "driver={SQL Server};" _
      & "server=MyServer;uid=WebUser" _
      & ";pwd=WebUser;database=C19Contacts"
DBConn.Open
```

call the stored procedure that returns contact records based on a department:

```
Set RSContacts = DBConn.Execute("Exec DepartmentMatches " _
      & Request.Form("DepartmentID"))
```

and set your message variable to contain the name of the department:

```
TheMessage = "Department - " _
      & RSContacts("DepartmentName")
```

Next, you check to see whether the visitor entered this page by using a search word:

```
ElseIf Not IsEmpty(Request.Form("OKSearch")) Then
```

If so, you need to connect to the database:

```
set DBConn = Server.Createobject ("ADODB.Connection")
DBConn.ConnectionString = "driver={SQL Server};" _
      & "server=MyServer;uid=WebUser" _
      & ";pwd=WebUser;database=C19Contacts"
DBConn.Open
```

and retrieve all the contact records that match that search term:

```
Set RSContacts = DBConn.Execute("Exec SearchMatches '" _
      & Request.Form("SearchWord") & "'")
```

You then set up your message variable so that the visitor will see the search text they entered:

```
TheMessage = "Search Word - " _
    & Request.Form("SearchWord")
```

If the code flows here, the visitor entered this page without going through the home page. So you send them there:

```
Response.Redirect "../index.asp"
```

Within the body of the page, you write your message variable:

```
<P><B>Matches for your search: <% Response.Write TheMessage %></B></P>
```

You also write the rows for the HTML table that were returned from your stored procedure:

```
<% Response.Write RSContacts("TheTable") %>
```

Contact Active Server Page

Contact.asp

The code on the Contact page calls your stored procedure to retrieve full information on the contact requested. The main code block is at the top of the page:

```
<%
Option Explicit
Dim DBConn
Dim RSContact
If IsEmpty(Request.QueryString("ContactID")) Then
      Response.Redirect "../index.asp"
End If
set DBConn = Server.Createobject ("ADODB.Connection")
DBConn.ConnectionString = "driver={SQL Server};" _
      & "server=MyServer;uid=WebUser" _
      & ";pwd=WebUser;database=C19Contacts"
```

```
DBConn.Open
Set RSContact = DBConn.Execute("Exec ContactRecord " _
      & Request.QueryString("ContactID"))
%>
```

You start by telling the compiler that you will declare your variables:

```
Option Explicit
```

Then you declare a Connection object:

```
Dim DBConn
```

and a Recordset object:

```
Dim RSContact
```

The page should only be entered if the visitor selected a Contact from the Contacts Matches page. You check for that here:

```
If IsEmpty(Request.QueryString("ContactID")) Then
```

If they didn't, you send them back to the home page:

```
Response.Redirect "../index.asp"
```

Otherwise, you can connect to the database:

```
set DBConn = Server.Createobject ("ADODB.Connection")
DBConn.ConnectionString = "driver={SQL Server};" _
      & "server=MyServer;uid=WebUser" _
      & ";pwd=WebUser;database=C19Contacts"
DBConn.Open
```

You then retrieve the contact record through your stored procedure:

```
Set RSContact = DBConn.Execute("Exec ContactRecord " _
      & Request.QueryString("ContactID"))
```

Within the body of the HTML, you write the name of the contact:

```
Contact: <% Response.Write RSContact("TheName") %>
```

You also write the content of the Contact record:

```
<% Response.Write RSContact("TheContact") %>
```

Survey Tool

The Survey tool provides a way for you to track responses made by visitors to questions. The tool also provides a page for reviewing the answers given by respondents.

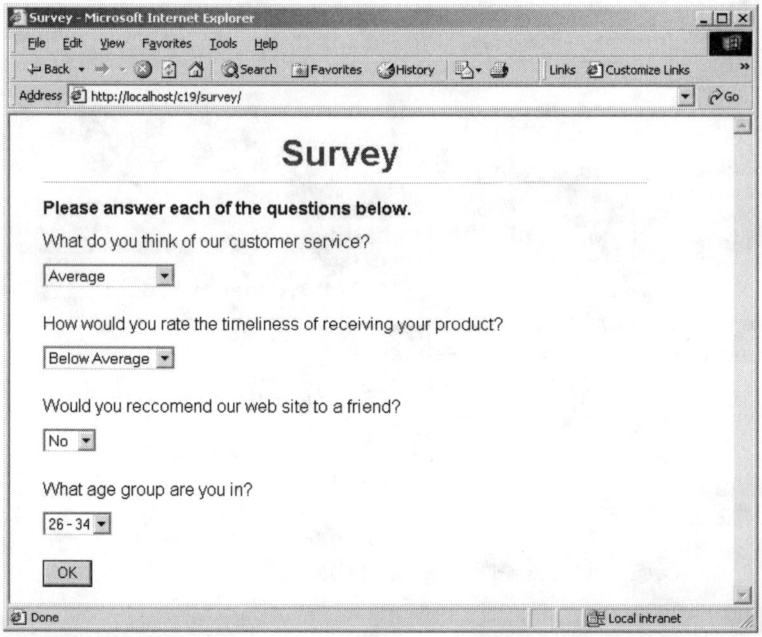

Figure 19-5 *Survey page*

Web Site Walk-Through

Once the visitor first enters the tool, they see the Survey displayed in Figure 19-5.

The visitor would complete each question. They are then taken to the Results page displayed in Figure 19-6.

The Results page allows the visitor to select any of the questions from the survey. Then, in the bottom of the form, they see the percentages of respondents that offered the different responses. The visitor also sees the total number of responses to this question.

Note that since this page displays the results of a survey, you may not want to redirect the visitor here. Instead, you may want this page to be used just by those in your company.

Back on the Survey page, each of the Select controls has a name that is used to categorize the response. So the list displayed on the Results page comes from the names of those Select controls on the Survey page.

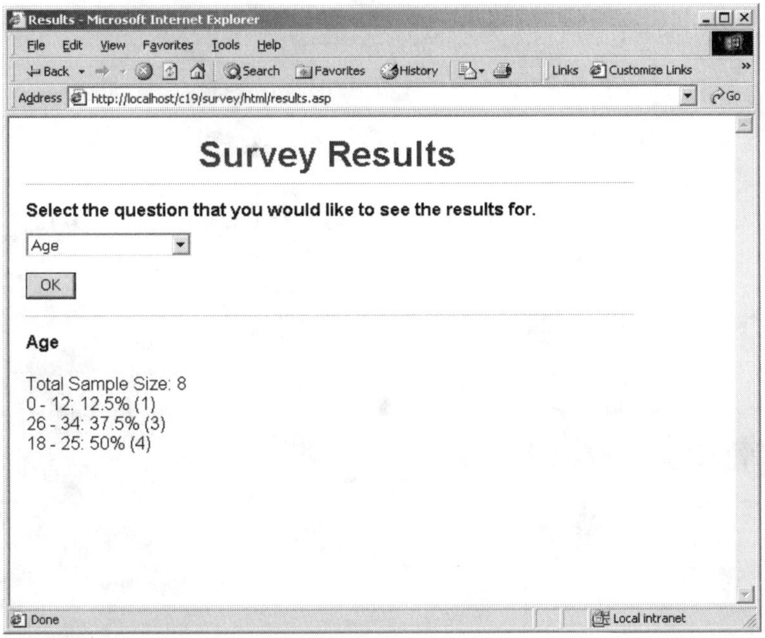

Figure 19-6 *Survey Results page*

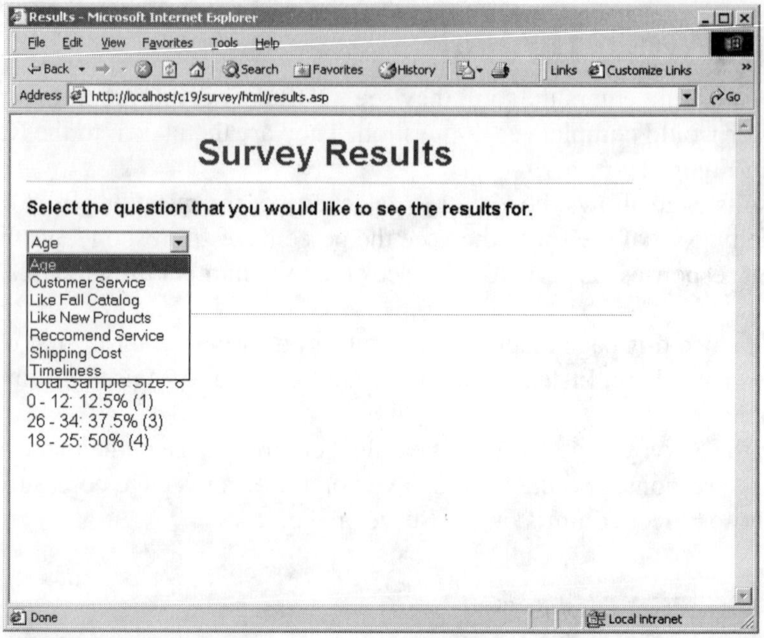

Figure 19-7 *Results page displaying all the questions*

That means that the tool displays results not just from this survey but from any survey that has used the format of this tool. Take a look at Figure 19-7.

The question list shows questions other than the ones that you have on the Survey page. So you could use this tool to pool the results of many survey pages and then display the results of all the surveys on the Results page.

Tables and Relationships

C19SurveySQLObjects.sql

SurveyResponses Table

SurveyResponses.txt

The Survey tool's date is stored in one table, the SurveyResponses table. That table stores all the responses to all the questions across all the surveys.

Field Name	Field Type	Notes
SurveyResponseID	int	Primary Key, Identity Column
SurveyQuestion	varchar	Length = 50
SurveyResponse	varchar	Length = 50

Table 19-3 *SurveyResponses Table Field Specifications*

Field Specifications

SurveyResponses Table

The field specifications for the SurveyResponses table are displayed in Table 19-3.

The SurveyResponseID field is the primary key in the table. The SurveyQuestion field stores the short text of the question, which comes from the name of the Select control on the Survey page. The SurveyResponse field stores the response selected by the visitor to the particular question.

Stored Procedures

AddResponse Stored Procedure

The AddResponse stored procedure provides the mechanism for adding a response by the visitor to the SurveyResponses table. The procedure is called from the Survey page.

```
CREATE PROCEDURE AddResponse
@SurveyQuestion varchar(50),
@SurveyResponse varchar(50)
AS
BEGIN
      Insert Into SurveyResponses
            (SurveyQuestion, SurveyResponse)
            Values
            (@SurveyQuestion, @SurveyResponse)
END
GO
```

The procedure requires two parameters to be passed in. The first is the text of the question:

```
@SurveyQuestion varchar(50),
```

The second is the response selected by the visitor:

```
@SurveyResponse varchar(50)
```

Those values are used in the value list of a SQL Insert statement:

```
Insert Into SurveyResponses
      (SurveyQuestion, SurveyResponse)
      Values
      (@SurveyQuestion, @SurveyResponse)
```

SurveyQuestionList Stored Procedure

The SurveyQuestionList stored procedure returns options for an HTML Select control based on all the questions in the SurveyResponses table.

```
CREATE PROCEDURE SurveyQuestionList
AS
Declare
@AllOfIt varchar(8000),
@SurveyQuestion varchar(50)
Declare CurQuestions Cursor
For Select Distinct SurveyQuestion
      from SurveyResponses
      order by SurveyQuestion
Open CurQuestions
Fetch CurQuestions
      Into @SurveyQuestion
Select @AllOfIt = ''
While @@Fetch_Status = 0
      BEGIN
            Select @AllOfIt = @AllOfIt
                  + '<OPTION VALUE="'
                  + @SurveyQuestion + '">'
                  + @SurveyQuestion + '</OPTION>'
            Fetch CurQuestions
                  Into @SurveyQuestion
      END
```

```
Close CurQuestions
Deallocate CurQuestions
Select @AllOfIt as TheOptions
GO
```

The procedure does not require any parameters. But you need to declare a variable that will store the option tags as you are building them:

```
@AllOfIt varchar(8000),
```

Another variable is declared that will store the text of the question as you retrieve it from the database:

```
@SurveyQuestion varchar(50)
```

You also need a Cursor object:

```
Declare CurQuestions Cursor
```

that will retrieve all the text of all the unique questions. Since each question is asked more than once, to more than one visitor, you use the Distinct keyword to retrieve a unique list of questions:

```
For Select Distinct SurveyQuestion
      from SurveyResponses
      order by SurveyQuestion
```

You then open the cursor:

```
Open CurQuestions
```

and retrieve the first question into your local variable:

```
Fetch CurQuestions
      Into @SurveyQuestion
```

The return variable needs to be initialized:

```
Select @AllOfIt = ''
```

You then enter a loop so that you can process each question:

```
While @@Fetch_Status = 0
```

The text of each question is concatenated to your return value as an option tag:

```
Select @AllOfIt = @AllOfIt
      + '<OPTION VALUE="'
      + @SurveyQuestion + '">'
      + @SurveyQuestion + '</OPTION>'
```

You then retrieve the next record so that it can be processed:

```
Fetch CurQuestions
      Into @SurveyQuestion
```

After the loop, you close the cursor:

```
Close CurQuestions
Deallocate CurQuestions
```

and return the Option tags:

```
Select @AllOfIt as TheOptions
```

SurveyResult Stored Procedure

On the Results page the SurveyResult stored procedure is called to return the summary results for the question selected.

```
CREATE PROCEDURE SurveyResult
@SurveyQuestion varchar(50)
AS
Declare
@AllOfIt varchar(8000),
@TotalResponses integer,
@SurveyResponse varchar(50),
@TheCount integer,
@ThePercent float
Declare CurResponses Cursor
For Select SurveyResponse,
      Count(SurveyResponseID) as TheCount
      From SurveyResponses
      Where SurveyQuestion = @SurveyQuestion
      Group By SurveyResponse
      Order By TheCount
Open CurResponses
```

```
Fetch CurResponses
      Into @SurveyResponse, @TheCount
Select @TotalResponses = Count(SurveyResponseID)
      From SurveyResponses
      Where SurveyQuestion = @SurveyQuestion
Select @AllOfIt = '<P>Total Sample Size: '
      + Convert(varchar(10), @TotalResponses)
While @@Fetch_Status = 0
      BEGIN
            Select @ThePercent = (Convert(float,@TheCount) /
                  Convert(float,@TotalResponses)) * 100
            Select @AllOfIt = @AllOfIt
                  + '<BR>' + @SurveyResponse
                  + ': '
                  + Convert(varchar(10), @ThePercent)
                  + '% (' + Convert(varchar(10), @TheCount)
                  + ')'
            Fetch CurResponses
                  Into @SurveyResponse, @TheCount
      END
Close CurResponses
Deallocate CurResponses
Select @AllOfIt = @AllOfIt + '</P>'
Select @AllOfIt as TheStuff
GO
```

Passed into the procedure is the text of the question whose summary information needs to be returned:

```
@SurveyQuestion varchar(50)
```

Locally, you need a variable to store the return text as it is being built:

```
@AllOfIt varchar(8000),
```

Variables are also needed to retrieve the total number of responses to the question passed in:

```
@TotalResponses integer,
```

the text of the response:

```
@SurveyResponse varchar(50),
```

the number of times a response was selected:

```
@TheCount integer,
```

and the percentage of that response to all the responses for the question:

```
@ThePercent float
```

You also need a Cursor object:

```
Declare CurResponses Cursor
```

that will return the total number of each response according to the question passed in:

```
For Select SurveyResponse,
      Count(SurveyResponseID) as TheCount
      From SurveyResponses
      Where SurveyQuestion = @SurveyQuestion
      Group By SurveyResponse
      Order By TheCount
```

The cursor is opened:

```
Open CurResponses
```

and the first response with its count is retrieved:

```
Fetch CurResponses
      Into @SurveyResponse, @TheCount
```

Next, you retrieve the total number of responses to the question:

```
Select @TotalResponses = Count(SurveyResponseID)
      From SurveyResponses
      Where SurveyQuestion = @SurveyQuestion
```

and place that, with HTML formatting, into your return variable:

```
Select @AllOfIt = '<P>Total Sample Size: '
      + Convert(varchar(10), @TotalResponses)
```

You then enter a loop so that you can process each of the responses to the questions:

```
While @@Fetch_Status = 0
```

First, within the loop, you calculate the percentage for the current responses in terms of the total number of responses:

```
Select @ThePercent = (Convert(float,@TheCount) /
      Convert(float,@TotalResponses)) * 100
```

Then, you format the response text with HTML into your return variable:

```
Select @AllOfIt = @AllOfIt
      + '<BR>' + @SurveyResponse
      + ': '
```

as well as the response percent:

```
+ Convert(varchar(10), @ThePercent)
```

and the raw number of responses:

```
+ '% (' + Convert(varchar(10), @TheCount)
+ ')'
```

You then retrieve the next record so that it, too, can be processed:

```
Fetch CurResponses
      Into @SurveyResponse, @TheCount
```

After the loop, the cursor is released from memory:

```
Close CurResponses
Deallocate CurResponses
```

You add a closing HTML tag to your return variable:

```
Select @AllOfIt = @AllOfIt + '</P>'
```

and return it to the calling application:

```
Select @AllOfIt as TheStuff
```

Users

WebUser User

In addition to the default Administrator account, the database has the user WebUser associated with it. The only access that user has to the database is through the four stored procedures. No other permissions are granted to this user.

Active Server Pages

Survey Active Server Page

Index.asp

The code on the Survey page calls your stored procedure to add responses made by the visitor to the database. All the code is at the top of the page.

```
<%
Option Explicit
Dim DBConn
Dim TheControl
If Not IsEmpty(Request.Form("OK")) Then
      set DBConn = Server.Createobject ("ADODB.Connection")
      DBConn.ConnectionString = "driver={SQL Server};" _
            & "server=MyServer;uid=WebUser" _
            & ";pwd=WebUser;database=C19Survey"
      DBConn.Open
      For Each TheControl in Request.Form
            If TheControl <> "OK" Then
                  DBConn.Execute _
                  ("Exec AddResponse '" _
                  & TheControl _
                  & "', '" & Request.Form(TheControl) _
                  & "'")
            End If
      Next
```

```
        Response.Redirect "./html/results.asp"
End If
%>
```

You start by telling the compiler that the variables will be declared:

```
Option Explicit
```

You then declare an ADO Connection object:

```
Dim DBConn
```

You also declare a variable that will store controls from the form as you iterate through the collection:

```
Dim TheControl
```

Next, you check to see whether the form on the page has been submitted:

```
If Not IsEmpty(Request.Form("OK")) Then
```

If it has, you need to connect to the database:

```
set DBConn = Server.Createobject ("ADODB.Connection")
DBConn.ConnectionString = "driver={SQL Server};" _
        & "server=MyServer;uid=WebUser" _
        & ";pwd=WebUser;database=C19Survey"
DBConn.Open
```

You then enter a loop so that you can process all the controls on the form:

```
For Each TheControl in Request.Form
```

The form consists of the Select controls plus the Submit button. Each of the Select controls represents one of the questions on the survey; therefore, they need to be processed. But the OK button should not be. So you check here to see if the current control that you have iterated to through the collection of controls is the OK button:

```
                If TheControl <> "OK" Then
```

If it isn't, you call your stored procedure to add a response to a question. You pass to it the text of the question, which comes from the name of the Select control. You also pass it the response selected by the visitor, shown next.

```
DBConn.Execute _
      ("Exec AddResponse '" _
      & TheControl _
      & "', '" & Request.Form(TheControl) _
      & "'")
```

After the loop, you send the visitor to the Results page.

```
Response.Redirect "./html/results.asp"
```

Results Active Server Page

Results.asp

The code on the Results page calls your stored procedures to populate the Select control with the questions and to show the results of the selected question. The main code block is at the top of the page.

```
<%
Option Explicit
Dim DBConn
Dim RSQuestions
Dim CurrentQuestion
Dim RSSurveyResult
Dim TheStats
set DBConn = Server.Createobject ("ADODB.Connection")
DBConn.ConnectionString = "driver={SQL Server};" _
      & "server=MyServer;uid=WebUser" _
      & ";pwd=WebUser;database=C19Survey"
DBConn.Open
Set RSQuestions = DBCOnn.Execute("Exec SurveyQuestionList")
If Not IsEmpty(Request.Form("SurveyQuestion")) Then
      CurrentQuestion = Request.Form("SurveyQuestion")
      Set RSSurveyResult = DBConn.Execute("Exec SurveyResult '" _
            & CurrentQuestion & "'")
      TheStats = RSSurveyResult("TheStuff")
End If
%>
```

You start by telling the compiler that variables will be declared:

```
Option Explicit
```

You then declare a variable that will be used as a Connection object:

```
Dim DBConn
```

and a Recordset object:

```
Dim RSQuestions
```

This variable will store the text of the question selected by the visitor:

```
Dim CurrentQuestion
```

Another Recordset object will be used to retrieve the results of the question selected:

```
Dim RSSurveyResult
```

and this variable will store the HTML for those results:

```
Dim TheStats
```

You then connect to the database:

```
set DBConn = Server.Createobject ("ADODB.Connection")
DBConn.ConnectionString = "driver={SQL Server};" _
      & "server=MyServer;uid=WebUser" _
      & ";pwd=WebUser;database=C19Survey"
DBConn.Open
```

and retrieve the text of the questions as options for the Select control:

```
Set RSQuestions = DBCOnn.Execute("Exec SurveyQuestionList")
```

Next, you check to see whether the form on the page has been submitted:

```
If Not IsEmpty(Request.Form("SurveyQuestion")) Then
```

If it has, you store the text of the question selected by the visitor:

```
CurrentQuestion = Request.Form("SurveyQuestion")
```

and retrieve the summary results of the question through your stored procedure:

```
Set RSSurveyResult = DBConn.Execute("Exec SurveyResult '" _
      & CurrentQuestion & "'")
```

That summary information is stored in a variable:

```
TheStats = RSSurveyResult("TheStuff")
```

Then, in the body of the page, you populate the options of the Select control:

```
<SELECT ID="FormsComboBox1" NAME="SurveyQuestion">
      <% Response.Write RSQuestions("TheOptions") %>
</SELECT>
```

You also write out to the browser the question selected by the visitor:

```
<P><B><% Response.Write CurrentQuestion %></B></P>
```

and the summary information about that question:

```
<% Response.Write TheStats %>
```

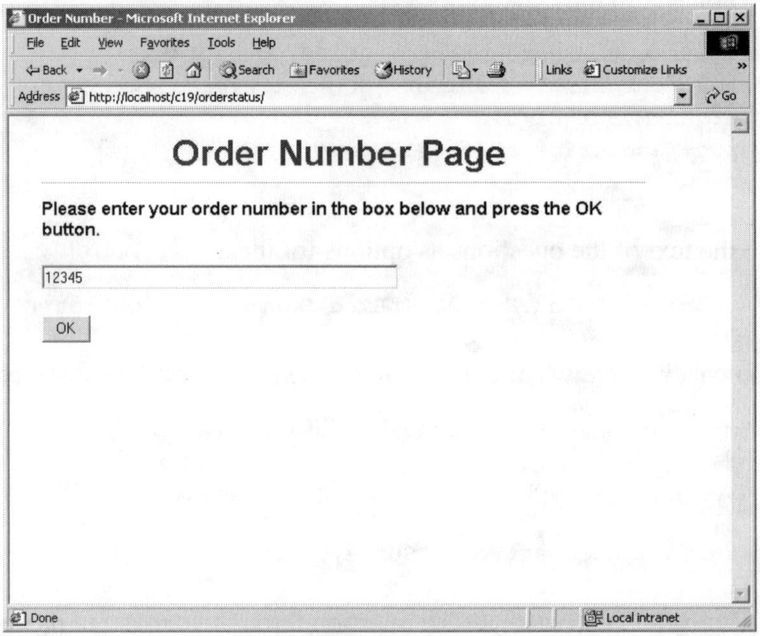

Figure 19-8 *Order Number page on initial view*

Order Status Tool

The Order Status tool allows the visitor to view the status of their order. They can also see the status of each item in their order.

Web Site Walk-Through

When the visitor first enters this tool, they see the Order Number page displayed in Figure 19-8.

The visitor uses this page by entering their order number. If they enter an invalid order number, they see the message displayed in Figure 19-9.

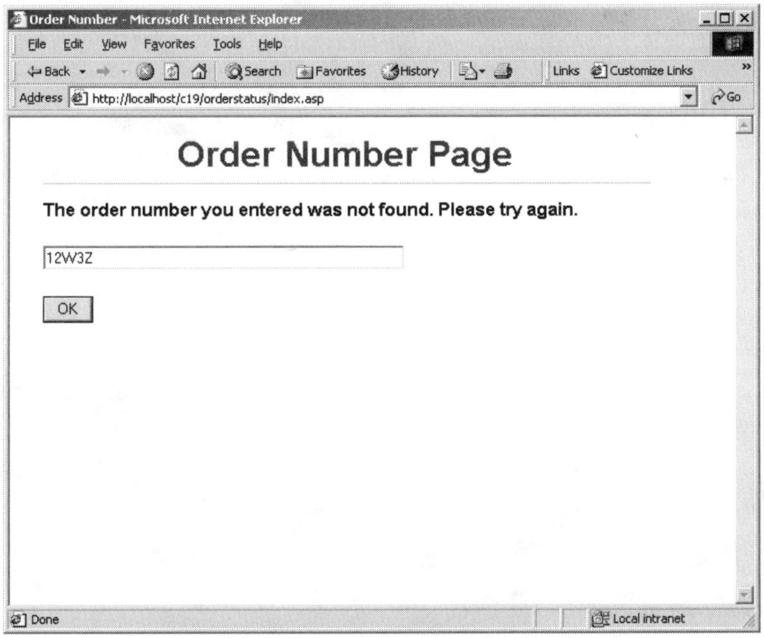

Figure 19-9 *Order Number page after an invalid number was entered*

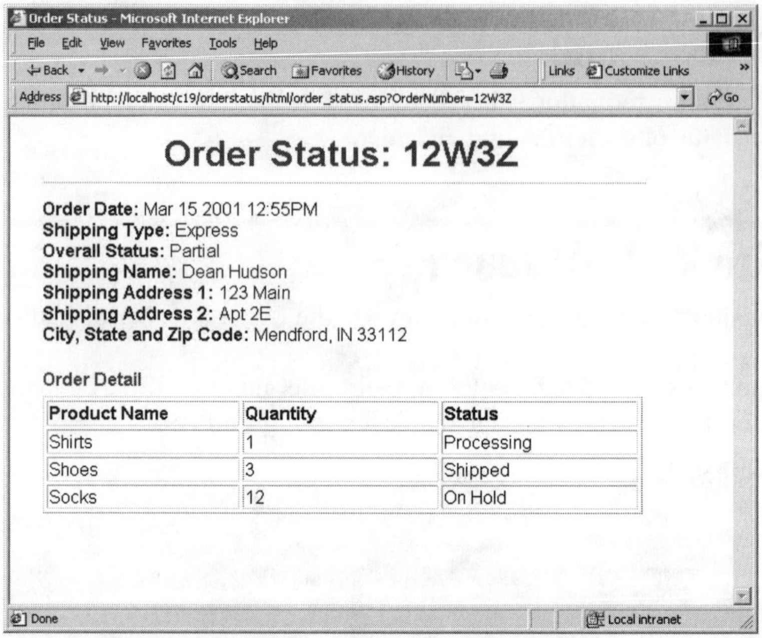

Figure 19-10 *Order Status page*

The message informs the visitor of the problem and lets them try again. Once they enter a valid order number, they are taken to the Order Status page, which is displayed in Figure 19-10.

In the title text of the page, the visitor sees the order number that they entered. Then, at the top of the body of the page, they see the top-level information about the order. Under that in the HTML table, the visitor sees each item in their order and its status.

Tables and Relationships

C19OrderStatusQLObjects.sql

Orders Table

Orders.txt

The Orders table is the top-level table in the database. It stores information about the order itself.

Field Name	Field Type	Notes
OrderID	int	Primary Key, Identity Column
OrderNumber	varchar	Length = 50
OrderDate	datetime	
ShippingType	varchar	Length = 50
OverallStatus	varchar	Length = 50
ShippingName	varchar	Length = 50
ShippingAddress1	varchar	Length = 100
ShippingAddress2	varchar	Length = 100
CSZ	varchar	Length = 100

Table 19-4 *Orders Table Field Specifications*

OrderDetails Table

OrderDetails.txt

The OrderDetails table stores the items that the visitor has in their order. The table is in a one-to-many relationship with the Orders table. Each order can have many items, but each item goes with a specific order.

Field Specifications

Orders Table

The field specifications for the Orders table are displayed in Table 19-4.

Field Name	Field Type	Notes
OrderDetailID	int	Primary Key, Identity Column
OrderID	int	Foreign Key
ProductName	varchar	Length = 50
QuantityOrdered	int	
Status	varchar	Length = 50

Table 19-5 *OrderDetails Table Field Specifications*

The OrderID field is the primary key in this table. The OrderNumber field would be the number given to the customer to identify this order. The other fields store information about the order.

OrderDetails Table

The field specifications for the OrderDetails table are displayed in Table 19-5.

The OrderDetailID field is the primary key in this table. The OrderID is a foreign key that links this table to the Orders table in a one-to-many relationship.

Stored Procedures

ValidateOrderNumber Stored Procedure

The ValidateOrderNumber stored procedure is called from the Order Number page and is used to determine whether the order number entered is valid.

```
CREATE PROCEDURE ValidateOrderNumber
@OrderNumber varchar(50)
AS
BEGIN
      Select Count(OrderID) as TheCount
            From Orders
            Where OrderNumber = @OrderNumber
END
GO
```

The procedure requires one parameter, the order number to test:

```
@OrderNumber varchar(50)
```

You then return the number of records that match that order number:

```
Select Count(OrderID) as TheCount
      From Orders
      Where OrderNumber = @OrderNumber
```

OrderInformation Stored Procedure

The OrderInformation stored procedure is called from the Order Status page. It returns the top-level information about the order, as well as the product information in the order formatted with HTML tags.

```
CREATE PROCEDURE OrderInformation
@OrderNumber varchar(50)
AS
Declare
@OrderID integer,
@OrderDate varchar(20),
@ShippingType varchar(50),
@OverallStatus varchar(50),
@ShippingName varchar(50),
@ShippingAddress1 varchar(100),
@ShippingAddress2 varchar(100),
@CSZ varchar(100),
@TopStuff varchar(1000),
@ProductName varchar(50),
@QuantityOrdered varchar(10),
@Status varchar(50),
@BottomStuff varchar(3000)
Select @OrderID = OrderID,
      @OrderDate = OrderDate,
      @ShippingType = ShippingType,
      @OverallStatus = OverallStatus,
      @ShippingName = ShippingName,
      @ShippingAddress1 = ShippingAddress1,
      @ShippingAddress2 = ShippingAddress2,
      @CSZ = CSZ
      From Orders
      Where OrderNumber = @OrderNumber
Select @TopStuff = '<P><B>Order Date: </B>'
      + @OrderDate
      + '<BR><B>Shipping Type: </B>'  + @ShippingType
      + '<BR><B>Overall Status: </B>' + @OverallStatus
      + '<BR><B>Shipping Name: </B>' + @ShippingName
      + '<BR><B>Shipping Address 1: </B>' + @ShippingAddress1
      + '<BR><B>Shipping Address 2: </B>' + @ShippingAddress2
      + '<BR><B>City, State and Zip Code: </B>'
      + @CSZ + '</P>'
```

```
Declare CurDetails Cursor
For Select ProductName, QuantityOrdered, Status
      From OrderDetails
      Where OrderID = @OrderID
      order by ProductName
Open CurDetails
Fetch CurDetails
      Into @ProductName, @QuantityOrdered,
      @Status
Select @BottomStuff = ''
While @@Fetch_Status = 0
      Begin
            Select @BottomStuff = @BottomStuff
                  + '<TR>'
                  + '<TD WIDTH=171>'
                  + '<P>' + @ProductName + '</P>'
                  + '</TD>'
                  + '<TD WIDTH=171>'
                  + '<P>' + @QuantityOrdered + '</P>'
                  + '</TD>'
                  + '<TD WIDTH=172>'
                  + '<P>' + @Status + '</P>'
                  + '</TD>'
                  + '</TR>'
            Fetch CurDetails
                  Into @ProductName, @QuantityOrdered,
                  @Status
      END
Close CurDetails
Deallocate CurDetails
Select @TopStuff as TopStuff, @BottomStuff as BottomStuff
GO
```

The procedure requires one parameter, the order number that is to be used:

```
@OrderNumber varchar(50)
```

From the Orders table you will need to retrieve all the information about the order. So, you declare variables to store that information:

```
@OrderID integer,
@OrderDate varchar(20),
@ShippingType varchar(50),
```

```
@OverallStatus varchar(50),
@ShippingName varchar(50),
@ShippingAddress1 varchar(100),
@ShippingAddress2 varchar(100),
@CSZ varchar(100),
```

This variable will store the return HTML tags with the order information:

```
@TopStuff varchar(1000),
```

You also need variables that will store the product information in the order:

```
@ProductName varchar(50),
@QuantityOrdered varchar(10),
@Status varchar(50),
```

and a variable to store the product information as it is formatted with HTML tags:

```
@BottomStuff varchar(3000)
```

You then retrieve the top-level order information corresponding to the order number passed into this procedure:

```
Select @OrderID = OrderID,
      @OrderDate = OrderDate,
      @ShippingType = ShippingType,
      @OverallStatus = OverallStatus,
      @ShippingName = ShippingName,
      @ShippingAddress1 = ShippingAddress1,
      @ShippingAddress2 = ShippingAddress2,
      @CSZ = CSZ
      From Orders
      Where OrderNumber = @OrderNumber
```

Those values retrieved are then combined with HTML tags and are stored in a variable that will be returned from this procedure:

```
Select @TopStuff = '<P><B>Order Date: </B>'
      + @OrderDate
      + '<BR><B>Shipping Type: </B>'  + @ShippingType
      + '<BR><B>Overall Status: </B>' + @OverallStatus
      + '<BR><B>Shipping Name: </B>' + @ShippingName
      + '<BR><B>Shipping Address 1: </B>' + @ShippingAddress1
```

```
        + '<BR><B>Shipping Address 2: </B>' + @ShippingAddress2
        + '<BR><B>City, State and Zip Code: </B>'
        + @CSZ + '</P>'
```

Next, you need to declare a Cursor object:

```
Declare CurDetails Cursor
```

that will retrieve the details of this order as defined by the ID of the order:

```
For Select ProductName, QuantityOrdered, Status
      From OrderDetails
      Where OrderID = @OrderID
      order by ProductName
```

That cursor is opened:

```
Open CurDetails
```

and the first record is retrieved:

```
Fetch CurDetails
      Into @ProductName, @QuantityOrdered,
      @Status
```

You then initialize the variable that will contain the order details:

```
Select @BottomStuff = ''
```

and enter a loop to process each of the order items:

```
While @@Fetch_Status = 0
```

Each item in the order needs to be returned as a row in an HTML table so that it will be displayed as on the Order Status page, shown earlier in Figure 19-10:

```
    Select @BottomStuff = @BottomStuff
          + '<TR>'
          + '<TD WIDTH=171>'
          + '<P>' + @ProductName + '</P>'
          + '</TD>'
          + '<TD WIDTH=171>'
          + '<P>' + @QuantityOrdered + '</P>'
          + '</TD>'
          + '<TD WIDTH=172>'
          + '<P>' + @Status + '</P>'
          + '</TD>'
          + '</TR>'
```

You then retrieve the next record and loop so that it can be processed:

```
Fetch CurDetails
      Into @ProductName, @QuantityOrdered,
      @Status
```

After the loop, you release the cursor from memory:

```
Close CurDetails
Deallocate CurDetails
```

and return the top-level order information, as well as the order detail information:

```
Select @TopStuff as TopStuff, @BottomStuff as BottomStuff
```

Users

WebUser User

In addition to the default Administrator account, the database has the user WebUser associated with it. The only access that user has to the database is through the four stored procedures. No other permissions are granted to this user.

Active Server Pages

Order Number Active Server Page

Index.asp

The code on the Order Number page validates the order number that was entered by the visitor by calling your stored procedure. The main code block is at the top of the page.

```
<%
Option Explicit
Dim DBConn
Dim RSValidate
Dim TheMessage
If Not IsEmpty(Request.Form("OrderNumber")) Then
      set DBConn = Server.Createobject ("ADODB.Connection")
      DBConn.ConnectionString = "driver={SQL Server};" _
            & "server=MyServer;uid=WebUser" _
            & ";pwd=WebUser;database=C19OrderStatus"
      DBConn.Open
      Set RSValidate = DBConn.Execute("Exec ValidateOrderNumber '" _
            & Request.Form("OrderNumber") & "'")
      If RSValidate("TheCount") > 0 Then
            Response.Redirect "./html/order_status.asp?OrderNumber=" _
                  & Request.Form("OrderNumber")
      Else
            TheMessage = "The order number you entered was not found. " _
                  & "Please try again."
      End If
Else
      TheMessage = "Please enter your order number in the box " _
            & "below and press the OK button."
End If
%>
```

You start by telling the compiler that variables will be declared:

```
Option Explicit
```

Next, you declare a variable for a Connection object:

```
Dim DBConn
```

a Recordset object:

```
Dim RSValidate
```

and one that will store the prompt on the page:

```
Dim TheMessage
```

Now you need to check to see if the form on the page has been submitted:

```
If Not IsEmpty(Request.Form("OrderNumber")) Then
```

If it has, you open a connection to the database:

```
set DBConn = Server.Createobject ("ADODB.Connection")
DBConn.ConnectionString = "driver={SQL Server};" _
      & "server=MyServer;uid=WebUser" _
      & ";pwd=WebUser;database=C19OrderStatus"
DBConn.Open
```

and call a procedure to check to see whether the order number is valid:

```
Set RSValidate = DBConn.Execute("Exec ValidateOrderNumber '" _
      & Request.Form("OrderNumber") & "'")
```

If it is, your procedure will return a positive number:

```
If RSValidate("TheCount") > 0 Then
```

In that case, you send them to the Order Status page:

```
Response.Redirect "./html/order_status.asp?OrderNumber=" _
      & Request.Form("OrderNumber")
```

Otherwise, you tell the visitor that the order number they entered was not found:

```
TheMessage = "The order number you entered was not found. " _
      & "Please try again."
```

If the code flows here, it means that the visitor is entering the page for the first time:

```
Else
```

So you will use your initial prompt.

```
TheMessage = "Please enter your order number in the box " _
      & "below and click the OK button."
```

Then, within the HTML, you write the message out to the visitor:

```
<P><B><% Response.Write TheMessage %></B></P>
```

Order Status Active Server Page

Order_Status.asp

The code on the Order Status page calls your stored procedure to display the contents on the page. The main code block is at the top of the page.

```
<%
Option Explicit
Dim DBConn
Dim RSOrderInformation
If IsEmpty(Request.QueryString("OrderNumber")) Then
      Response.Redirect "../index.asp"
End If
set DBConn = Server.Createobject ("ADODB.Connection")
DBConn.ConnectionString = "driver={SQL Server};" _
      & "server=MyServer;uid=WebUser" _
      & ";pwd=WebUser;database=C19OrderStatus"
DBConn.Open
Set RSOrderInformation = DBConn.Execute("Exec OrderInformation '" _
      & Request.QueryString("OrderNumber") & "'")
%>
```

You start by telling the compiler that variables will be declared:

```
Option Explicit
```

You then declare one variable for your database connection object:

```
Dim DBConn
```

and one for a Recordset object:

```
Dim RSOrderInformation
```

Next, you make sure that the visitor entered this page with an order number:

```
If IsEmpty(Request.QueryString("OrderNumber")) Then
```

If they didn't, they are sent back to the Order Number page:

```
Response.Redirect "../index.asp"
```

Otherwise, you can connect to the database:

```
set DBConn = Server.Createobject ("ADODB.Connection")
DBConn.ConnectionString = "driver={SQL Server};" _
      & "server=MyServer;uid=WebUser" _
      & ";pwd=WebUser;database=C19OrderStatus"
DBConn.Open
```

and retrieve the contents of the page by calling your stored procedure:

```
Set RSOrderInformation = DBConn.Execute("Exec OrderInformation '" _
      & Request.QueryString("OrderNumber") & "'")
```

Within the body of the page, you write out the order number:

```
Order Status: <% Response.Write Request.QueryString("OrderNumber") %>
```

the top-level order information:

```
<% Response.Write RSOrderInformation("TopStuff") %>
```

and the rows for the HTML table:

```
<% Response.Write RSOrderInformation("BottomStuff") %>
```

CHAPTER

20

E-Books and E-Help Files

IN THIS CHAPTER:

- C20EBookSQLObjects.sql
- Books.txt
- Chapters.txt
- Sections.txt
- GlossaryTerms.txt
- Index.asp
- Chapters.asp
- Section.asp
- Book_Page.asp
- Glossary.asp
- Search_Results.asp
- C20EHelpSQLObjects.sql
- Topics.txt
- Keywords.txt
- Left_Index.asp
- Body_Index.asp

In this chapter, we will look at a pair of tools that provide a way for your visitor to access lengthy content that your business may offer. First, we will look at the E-Book tool. The E-Book tool allows visitors to browse, search, and read the contents of books through their browser. Then we will review the E-Help tool. The E-Help tool provides a way for you to convey documentation or help information about your products or services to your customers.

E-Book Tool

The E-Books tool allows visitors to search and browse through the contents of online books. The content of the books can be hyperlinked to contain pictures or other files, and the terms used in the content of a page can be linked to a glossary.

Web Site Walk-Through

When the visitor first enters the E-Book tool, they are presented with the page displayed in Figure 20-1.

The entry page in the tool allows the visitor to select the book that they want to work with. Your site could contain a single book, or you could offer hundreds of books and booklets.

Once the visitor selects a book title and clicks the OK button, they are taken to the Chapters page, displayed in Figure 20-2.

Listed on the Chapters page are all the chapters in the book that the visitor selected. The visitor selects the chapter that they want to read by clicking it and is presented with the page displayed in Figure 20-3.

The Section page displays all the sections in the chapter selected. A book is divided into chapters, and a chapter is divided into sections. The visitor selects the section that they want to read by clicking it. They are then taken to the page displayed in Figure 20-4.

The Book Content page is where the visitor reads the contents of a section of a chapter of a book. At the top of the page, the visitor sees the book title, the chapter title, and even the section title.

Since the text of the book is displayed as HTML, it can contain links. Take a look at Figure 20-5.

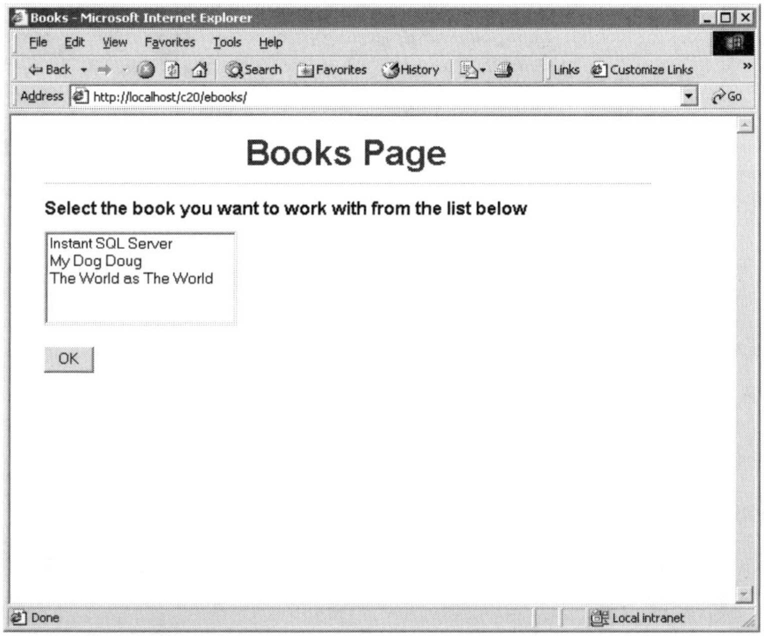

Figure 20-1 *Books page*

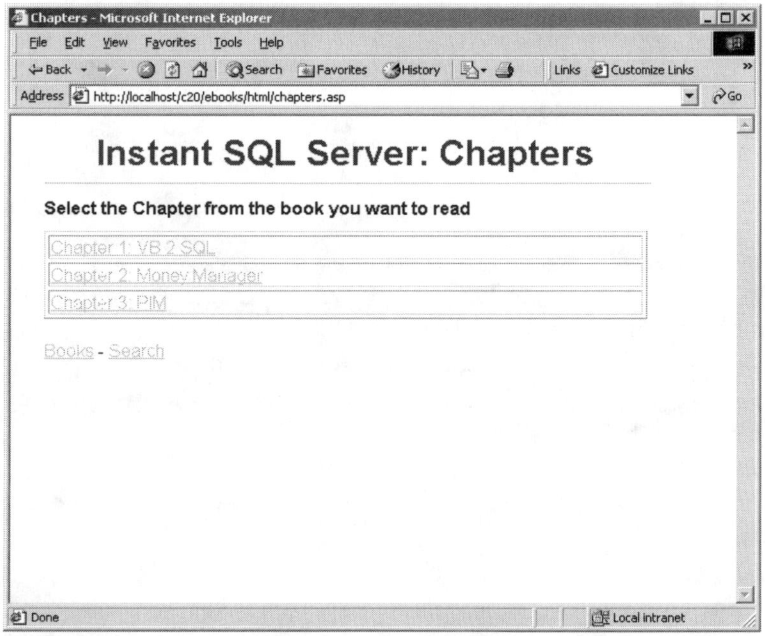

Figure 20-2 *Chapters page*

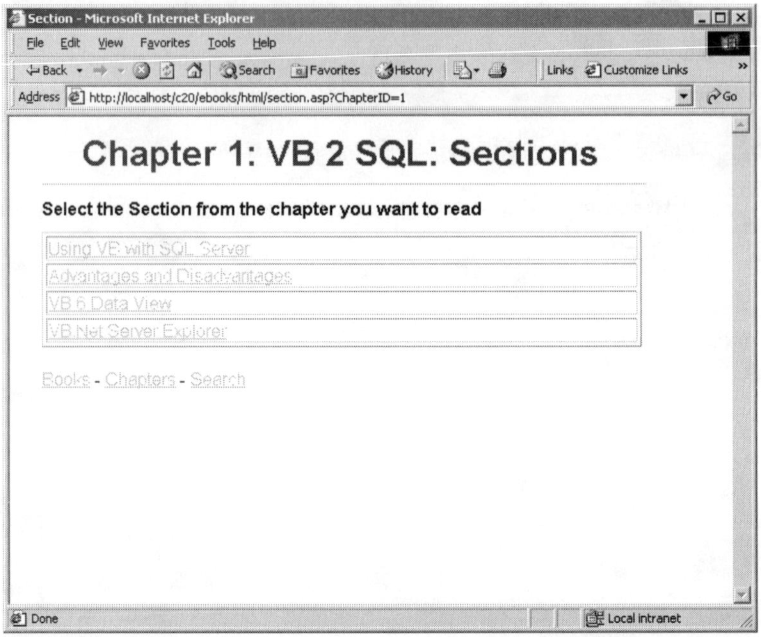

Figure 20-3 *Sections page*

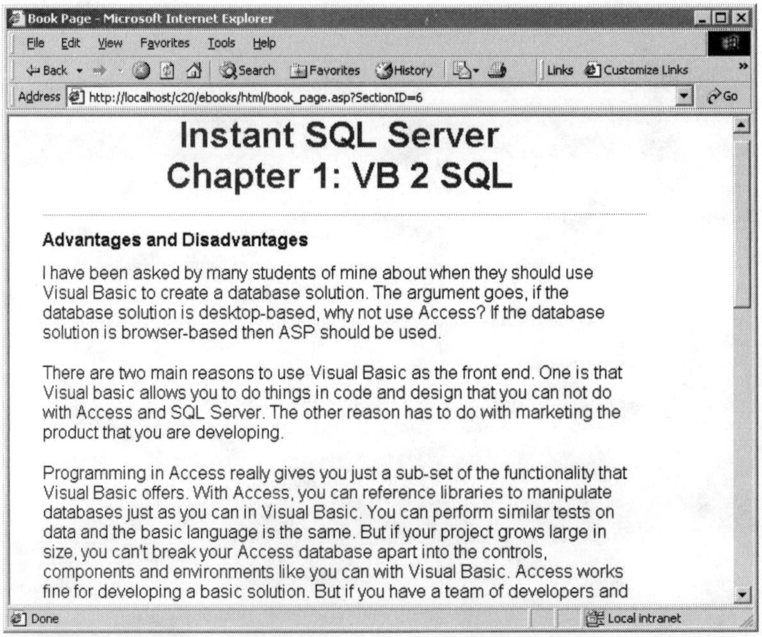

Figure 20-4 *Book Content page*

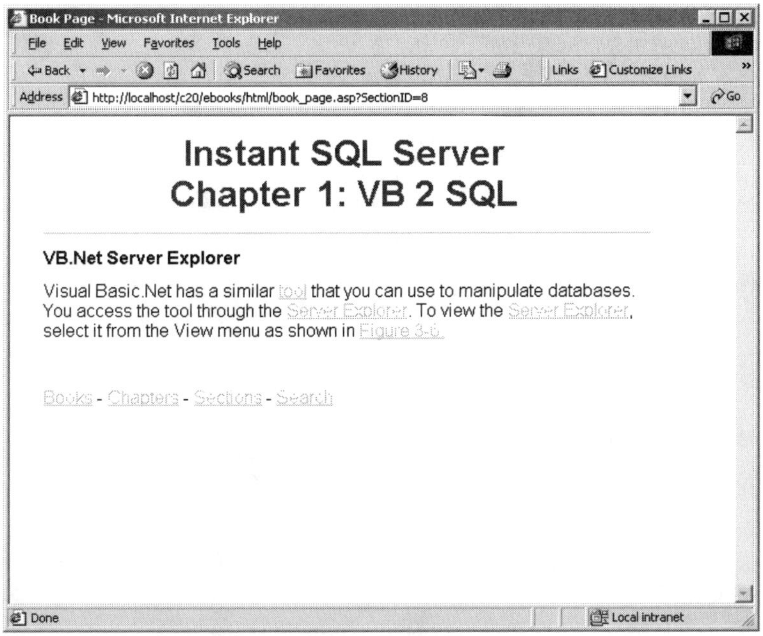

Figure 20-5 *Book Content page with links*

This time, the content on the page contains links. Two types are shown here. First the visitor could click one of the terms, such as Server Explorer. When they do that, they are taken to the Glossary page, displayed in Figure 20-6.

The Glossary page displays the definition of a term. The terms can be used across chapters or even books. Therefore, you only need to enter a definition of a term once.

The other type of link on the Book Content page is a file link. If the visitor were to click the "Figure 3-6" link, they would see a page like that displayed in Figure 20-7.

But even though I have used a picture here, you are not limited to that format. You could link the visitor to sound, video, animation, or some other file type.

At the bottom of the Chapters, Sections, and Book Content pages, the visitor can browse to the Search page, which is displayed in Figure 20-8.

The Search page allows the visitor to search the contents of the current book. The visitor enters their search term on this page and clicks the OK button to be taken to the Search Results page shown in Figure 20-9.

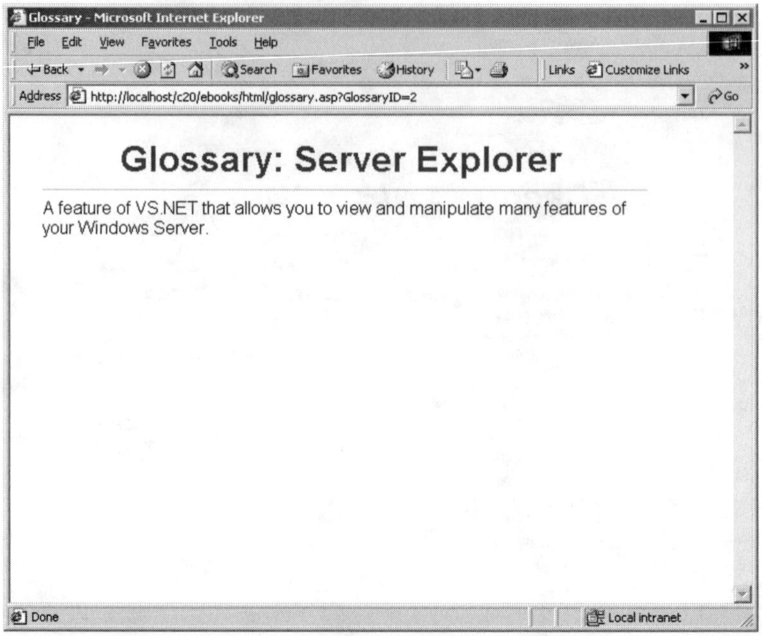

Figure 20-6 *Glossary page*

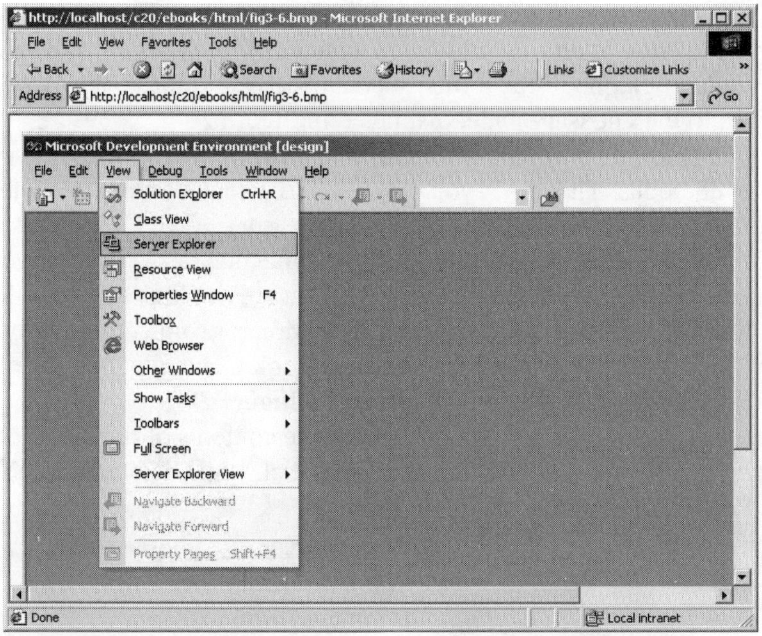

Figure 20-7 *Book content linking to a file*

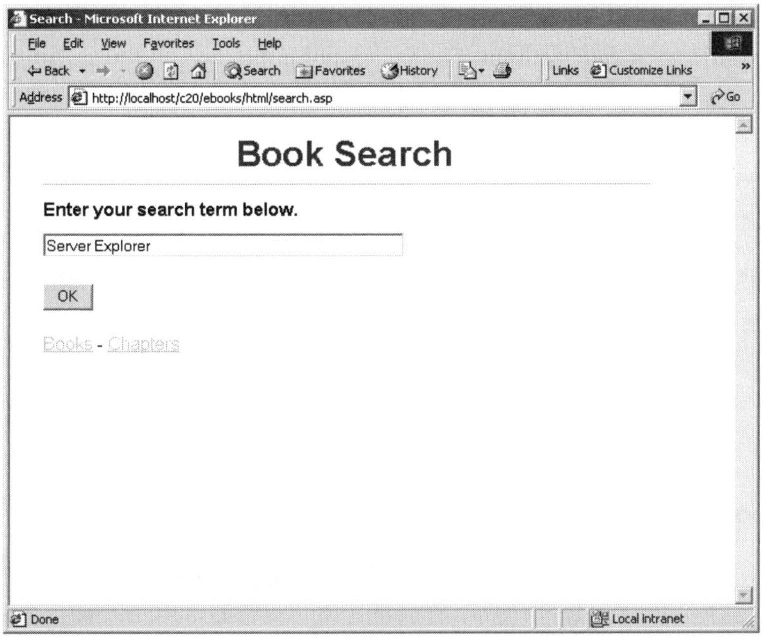

Figure 20-8 *Search page*

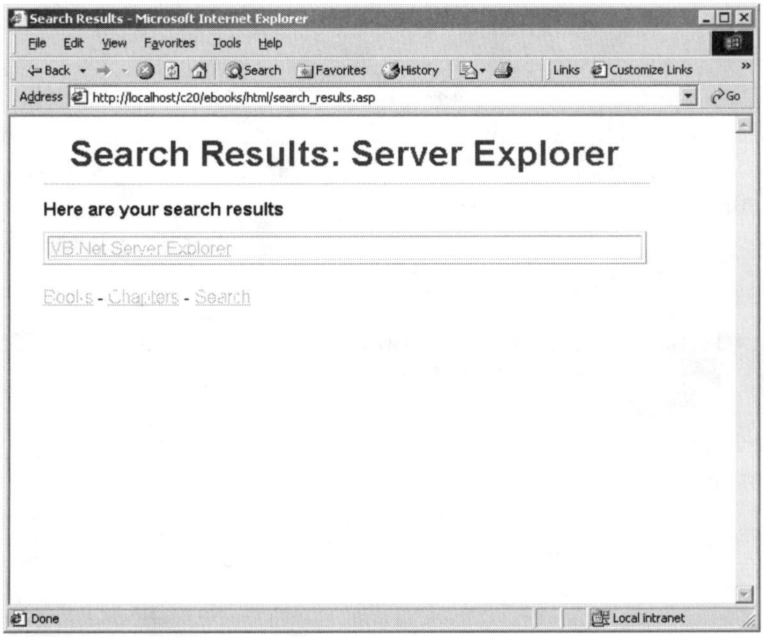

Figure 20-9 *Search Results page*

Listed on the Search Results page are all the sections that contain the search word in their title or in their content. The visitor could then select the section to view its content.

Tables and Relationships

C20EBookSQLObjects.sql

Books Table

The top table in this database is the Books table. It stores information on the books themselves.

Chapters Table

Under the Books table is the Chapters table. The Chapters table stores information about the chapters in a book. The table is in a one-to-many relationship with the Books table. Each book can contain many chapters, but each chapter goes with a specific book.

Sections Table

Beneath the Chapters table is the Sections table. The Sections table stores information about the section, including the content for that section. The table is in a one-to-many relationship with the Chapters table. Each chapter can have many sections, but each section belongs to a specific chapter.

GlossaryTerms Table

The GlossaryTerms table stores information about data that can be linked to through the Glossary page. The table is a stand-alone table.

Field Name	Field Type	Notes
BookID	int	Primary Key, Identity Column
BookName	varchar	Length = 50

Table 20-1 *Books Table Field Specifications*

Field Specifications

Books Table

Books.txt

The field specifications for the Books table are displayed in Table 20-1.

The BookID field is the primary key in this table. The BookName field stores the name of the book.

Chapters Table

Chapters.txt

The field specifications for the Chapters table are displayed in Table 20-2.

The ChapterID field is the primary key in this table. The BookID field is a foreign key that links this table to the Books table. The SequenceNumber field is used in sorting the chapters for the book. This is the order that the chapters are listed as appearing in the book.

Field Name	Field Type	Notes
ChapterID	int	Primary Key, Identity Column
BookID	int	Foreign Key
SequenceNumber	int	
ChapterName	varchar	Length = 50

Table 20-2 *Chapters Table Field Specifications*

Field Name	Field Type	Notes
SectionID	int	Primary Key, Identity Column
ChapterID	int	Foreign Key
SequenceNumber	int	
SequenceName	varchar	Length = 50

Table 20-3 *Sections Table Field Specifications*

Sections Table

Sections.txt

The field specifications for the Sections table are displayed in Table 20-3.

The SectionID field is the primary key in this table. The ChapterID field links the table to the Chapters table. As in the Chapters table, the SequenceNumber field is used for sorting the records. The BookPage field stores the text content for this section as it appears on the Book Content page.

GlossaryTerms Table

GlossaryTerms.txt

The field specifications for the GlossaryTerms table are displayed in Table 20-4.

The GlossaryID field is the primary key in this stand-alone table. The GlossaryTerm field stores the name of the term. And the definition of the term is stored in the TermDefinition field.

Field Name	Field Type	Notes
GlossaryID	int	Primary Key, Identity Column
GlossaryTerm	varchar	Length = 100
TermDefinition	varchar	Length = 3000

Table 20-4 *GlossaryTerms Table Field Specifications*

Stored Procedures

BookList Stored Procedure

The BookList stored procedure returns a list of Option HTML tags for each of the books in the Books table. The stored procedure is called from the Books page.

```
CREATE PROCEDURE BookList
AS
Declare
@AllOfIt varchar(8000),
@BookID varchar(10),
@BookName varchar(50)
Declare CurBooks Cursor
For Select BookID, BookName
      from Books
      order by BookName
Open CurBooks
Fetch CurBooks
      Into @BookID, @BookName
Select @AllOfIt = ''
While @@Fetch_Status = 0
      BEGIN
            Select @AllOfIt = @AllOfIt
                  + '<OPTION VALUE="'
                  + @BookID + '">'
                  + @BookName + '</OPTION>'
            Fetch CurBooks
                  Into @BookID, @BookName
      END
Close CurBooks
Deallocate CurBooks
Select @AllOfIt as TheOptions
GO
```

The procedure does not require any parameters. A local variable that will store the return value is declared:

```
@AllOfIt varchar(8000),
```

The next two variables are used to retrieve data from the Books table:

```
@BookID varchar(10),
@BookName varchar(50)
```

You also need a Cursor object:

```
Declare CurBooks Cursor
```

that is set to retrieve all the records from the Books table:

```
For Select BookID, BookName
      from Books
      order by BookName
```

The cursor is opened:

```
Open CurBooks
```

You retrieve the first record through your Cursor object:

```
Fetch CurBooks
      Into @BookID, @BookName
```

initialize your return variable:

```
Select @AllOfIt = ''
```

and enter a loop so that you can process each of the records:

```
While @@Fetch_Status = 0
```

Each record needs to be formatted as an HTML Option tag with the ID of the book submitted with the form and the name of the book visible to the visitor:

```
Select @AllOfIt = @AllOfIt
      + '<OPTION VALUE="'
      + @BookID + '">'
      + @BookName + '</OPTION>'
```

You then retrieve the next record:

```
Fetch CurBooks
      Into @BookID, @BookName
```

After looping through each record, you can close the cursor:

```
Close CurBooks
Deallocate CurBooks
```

and return the HTML Option tags:

```
Select @AllOfIt as TheOptions
```

ChapterList Stored Procedure

The ChapterList stored procedure returns a list of chapters for the specified book in the form of HTML Table Row tags.

```
CREATE PROCEDURE ChapterList
@BookID integer
AS
Declare
@AllOfIt varchar(8000),
@BookName varchar(50),
@ChapterID varchar(10),
@ChapterName varchar(50)
Select @BookName = BookName
      From Books
      Where BookID = @BookID
Declare CurChapters Cursor
For Select ChapterID, ChapterName
      from Chapters
      Where BookID = @BookID
      order by SequenceNumber
Open CurChapters
Fetch CurChapters
      Into @ChapterID, @ChapterName
Select @AllOfIt = ''
While @@Fetch_Status = 0
      BEGIN
            Select @AllOfIt = @AllOfIt
                  + '<TR><TD WIDTH=528>'
                  + '<P><A HREF="./section.asp?ChapterID='
                  + @ChapterID + '">' + @ChapterName
                  + '</A></P></TD></TR>'
            Fetch CurChapters
                  Into @ChapterID, @ChapterName
```

```
        END
Close CurChapters
Deallocate CurChapters
Select @AllOfIt as TheTable, @BookName as BookName
GO
```

Passed into the procedure is the ID of the book, which needs the chapter list returned:

```
@BookID integer
```

Within the procedure, you declare a variable for the return list:

```
@AllOfIt varchar(8000),
```

the returned name of the book:

```
@BookName varchar(50),
```

and variables that are used to retrieve data from the Chapters table:

```
@ChapterID varchar(10),
@ChapterName varchar(50)
```

You then retrieve the name of the book corresponding to the ID passed in:

```
Select @BookName = BookName
      From Books
      Where BookID = @BookID
```

Next, you need to declare a Cursor object:

```
Declare CurChapters Cursor
```

that will retrieve all the chapters in the book specified. Note that the records are sorted by the sequence number field:

```
For Select ChapterID, ChapterName
      from Chapters
      Where BookID = @BookID
      order by SequenceNumber
```

You then open the cursor:

```
Open CurChapters
```

and retrieve the first record:

```
Fetch CurChapters
      Into @ChapterID, @ChapterName
```

You need to initialize the variable that will return the HTML text:

```
Select @AllOfIt = ''
```

and enter a loop so that you can process each of the chapter records:

```
While @@Fetch_Status = 0
```

Within the loop, you format each chapter as an HTML Row tag. Note that the name of the chapter appears in the row but the text is linked to the Sections page. Passed to the Sections page is the ID of the chapter:

```
Select @AllOfIt = @AllOfIt
      + '<TR><TD WIDTH=528>'
      + '<P><A HREF="./section.asp?ChapterID='
      + @ChapterID + '">' + @ChapterName
      + '</A></P></TD></TR>'
```

You then retrieve the next record:

```
Fetch CurChapters
      Into @ChapterID, @ChapterName
```

After the loop, you release the cursor:

```
Close CurChapters
Deallocate CurChapters
```

and return the table rows and the name of the book:

```
Select @AllOfIt as TheTable, @BookName as BookName
```

SectionList Stored Procedure

The SectionList stored procedure returns a list of all the sections in a chapter that are displayed on the Sections page.

```
CREATE PROCEDURE SectionList
@ChapterID integer
AS
Declare
@AllOfIt varchar(8000),
@ChapterName varchar(50),
@SectionID varchar(10),
@SectionName varchar(50)
Select @ChapterName = ChapterName
      From Chapters
      Where ChapterID = @ChapterID
Declare CurSections Cursor
For Select SectionID, SectionName
      from Sections
      Where ChapterID = @ChapterID
      order by SequenceNumber
Open CurSections
Fetch CurSections
      Into @SectionID, @SectionName
Select @AllOfIt = ''
While @@Fetch_Status = 0
      BEGIN
            Select @AllOfIt = @AllOfIt
                  + '<TR><TD WIDTH=528>'
                  + '<P><A HREF="./book_page.asp?SectionID='
                  + @SectionID + '">' + @SectionName
                  + '</A></P></TD></TR>'
            Fetch CurSections
                  Into @SectionID, @SectionName
      END
Close CurSections
Deallocate CurSections
Select @AllOfIt as TheTable, @ChapterName as ChapterName
GO
```

The ID of the chapter that the sections are to be returned for is passed into the procedure:

```
@ChapterID integer
```

Within the procedure, you need a local variable to store the section list:

```
@AllOfIt varchar(8000),
```

the name of the chapter:

```
@ChapterName varchar(50),
```

and data from the Sections table:

```
@SectionID varchar(10),
@SectionName varchar(50)
```

You then retrieve the name of the chapter corresponding to the ID passed in:

```
Select @ChapterName = ChapterName
      From Chapters
      Where ChapterID = @ChapterID
```

Also needed in this procedure is a Cursor object:

```
Declare CurSections Cursor
```

that will retrieve all the sections for the chapter specified:

```
For Select SectionID, SectionName
      from Sections
      Where ChapterID = @ChapterID
      order by SequenceNumber
```

The cursor is then opened:

```
Open CurSections
```

and the first record is retrieved:

```
Fetch CurSections
      Into @SectionID, @SectionName
```

You need to initialize your return variable, since it is being concatenated to:

```
Select @AllOfIt = ''
```

and enter a loop so that each section can be processed:

```
While @@Fetch_Status = 0
```

Each section is returned as a row for an HTML table. The visitor sees the name of the section. When they click that name, they are linked to the Book Contents page:

```
Select @AllOfIt = @AllOfIt
      + '<TR><TD WIDTH=528>'
      + '<P><A HREF="./book_page.asp?SectionID='
      + @SectionID + '">' + @SectionName
      + '</A></P></TD></TR>'
```

You then retrieve the next record so that it can be processed and continue looping through all the records:

```
Fetch CurSections
      Into @SectionID, @SectionName
```

After the loop, the cursor is released:

```
Close CurSections
Deallocate CurSections
```

The rows and name of the chapter are returned to the calling application:

```
Select @AllOfIt as TheTable, @ChapterName as ChapterName
```

PageText Stored Procedure

The GetPageText stored procedure is called from the Book Contents page. It returns the text for the page, as well as the different title text.

```
CREATE PROCEDURE GetPageText
@SectionID integer
AS
Declare
@BookPage varchar(8000),
@SectionName varchar(50),
@ChapterID integer,
@ChapterName varchar(50),
@BookID integer,
@BookName varchar(50)
BEGIN
      Select @BookPage = BookPage,
            @SectionName = SectionName,
            @ChapterID = ChapterID
```

```
            from Sections
            Where SectionID = @SectionID
      Select @ChapterName = ChapterName,
            @BookID = BookID
            From Chapters
            Where ChapterID = @ChapterID
      Select @BookName = BookName
            From Books
            Where BookID = @BookID
      Select @BookPage as BookPage,
            @SectionName as SectionName,
            @ChapterName as ChapterName,
            @BookName as BookName
END
GO
```

The procedure expects one parameter, the ID of the section that the content is to be retrieved for:

```
@SectionID integer
```

Locally, you declare a variable to store that text:

```
@BookPage varchar(8000),
```

as well as the name of the section:

```
@SectionName varchar(50),
```

the ID of the chapter that the section is in:

```
@ChapterID integer,
```

the name of the chapter that the section is in:

```
@ChapterName varchar(50),
```

the ID of the book that the chapter is in:

```
@BookID integer,
```

and also the name of that book.

```
@BookName varchar(50)
```

First, you need to retrieve the section information according to the ID of the section passed in:

```
Select @BookPage = BookPage,
      @SectionName = SectionName,
      @ChapterID = ChapterID
      from Sections
      Where SectionID = @SectionID
```

You can then retrieve the chapter name:

```
Select @ChapterName = ChapterName,
      @BookID = BookID
      From Chapters
      Where ChapterID = @ChapterID
```

and finally the name of the book:

```
Select @BookName = BookName
      From Books
      Where BookID = @BookID
```

The text of the section, as well as the different title information for the section, is returned from the procedure:

```
Select @BookPage as BookPage,
      @SectionName as SectionName,
      @ChapterName as ChapterName,
      @BookName as BookName
```

GetGlossaryTerm Stored Procedure

The GetGlossaryTerm stored procedure returns the text of a glossary term. The procedure is called from the Glossary page.

```
CREATE PROCEDURE GetGlossaryTerm
@GlossaryID integer
AS
BEGIN
      Select GlossaryTerm, TermDefinition
            From GlossaryTerms
```

```
            Where GlossaryID = @GlossaryID
END
GO
```

Passed into the procedure is the ID of the glossary term:

```
@GlossaryID integer
```

That ID is then used to return the definition to the calling application:

```
Select GlossaryTerm, TermDefinition
      From GlossaryTerms
      Where GlossaryID = @GlossaryID
```

SearchSectionList Stored Procedure

The SearchSectionList stored procedure returns all the sections that match the search text passed in. The procedure is called from the Search Results page.

```
CREATE PROCEDURE SearchSectionList
@SearchTerm varchar(102)
AS
Declare
@AllOfIt varchar(8000),
@SectionID varchar(10),
@SectionName varchar(50)
Select @SearchTerm = '%' + @SearchTerm + '%'
Declare CurSections Cursor
For Select SectionID, SectionName
      from Sections
      Where SectionName Like @SearchTerm
      Or BookPage Like @SearchTerm
      order by SequenceNumber
Open CurSections
Fetch CurSections
      Into @SectionID, @SectionName
Select @AllOfIt = ''
While @@Fetch_Status = 0
      BEGIN
            Select @AllOfIt = @AllOfIt
                  + '<TR><TD WIDTH=528>'
                  + '<P><A HREF="./book_page.asp?SectionID='
                  + @SectionID + '">' + @SectionName
```

```
                    + '</A></P></TD></TR>'
              Fetch CurSections
                    Into @SectionID, @SectionName
        END
Close CurSections
Deallocate CurSections
Select @AllOfIt as TheTable
GO
```

Passed into the procedure is the search text:

```
@SearchTerm varchar(102)
```

Within the procedure, you declare a variable that will contain the matching sections as HTML Row tags:

```
@AllOfIt varchar(8000),
```

You also declare variables that are used to retrieve data from the Sections table:

```
@SectionID varchar(10),
@SectionName varchar(50)
```

For a section record to match the search text, it can contain the search text anywhere in the name or text of the section. Therefore, you need to surround the search text with wildcard characters:

```
Select @SearchTerm = '%' + @SearchTerm + '%'
```

Next you declare a cursor object:

```
Declare CurSections Cursor
```

that retrieves the sections that have the search text in the name of the section or in the content of the section:

```
For Select SectionID, SectionName
      from Sections
      Where SectionName Like @SearchTerm
      Or BookPage Like @SearchTerm
      order by SequenceNumber
```

You then open the cursor:

```
Open CurSections
```

and retrieve the first record:

```
Fetch CurSections
      Into @SectionID, @SectionName
```

You need to initialize your return variable:

```
Select @AllOfIt = ''
```

and enter a loop so that you can process each matching section:

```
While @@Fetch_Status = 0
```

Within the loop, each matching record is returned as an HTML Row tag:

```
Select @AllOfIt = @AllOfIt
      + '<TR><TD WIDTH=528>'
      + '<P><A HREF="./book_page.asp?SectionID='
      + @SectionID + '">' + @SectionName
      + '</A></P></TD></TR>'
```

You then retrieve the next record:

```
Fetch CurSections
      Into @SectionID, @SectionName
```

After the loop, the cursor is released:

```
Close CurSections
Deallocate CurSections
```

and you return the matching records as rows from an HTML Table:

```
Select @AllOfIt as TheTable
```

Users

WebUser User

In addition to the default Administrator account, the database has the user WebUser associated with it. The only access that user has to the database is through the four stored procedures. No other permissions are granted to this user.

Active Server Pages

Index.asp

Books Active Server Page

The code on the Books page displays the list of books to the visitor by calling your stored procedure.

```
<%
Option Explicit
Dim DBConn
Dim RSOptions
If Not IsEmpty(Request.Form("BookID")) Then
      Session("BookID") = Request.Form("BookID")
      Response.Redirect "./html/chapters.asp"
End If
set DBConn = Server.Createobject ("ADODB.Connection")
DBConn.ConnectionString = "driver={SQL Server};" _
      & "server=MyServer;uid=WebUser" _
      & ";pwd=WebUser;database=C20EBooks"
DBConn.Open
Set RSOptions = DBConn.Execute("Exec BookList")
%>
```

You start by telling the compiler that variables will be declared:

```
Option Explicit
```

You will need an ADO Connection object:

```
Dim DBConn
```

and a Recordset object:

```
Dim RSOptions
```

Next, you check to see whether the visitor has submitted the form on the page:

```
If Not IsEmpty(Request.Form("BookID")) Then
```

If so, you store the ID of the book selected by the visitor into a Session variable:

```
Session("BookID") = Request.Form("BookID")
```

You then send the visitor to the Chapters page:

```
Response.Redirect "./html/chapters.asp"
```

If the form has not been submitted, the code will flow here and you need to connect to the database:

```
set DBConn = Server.Createobject ("ADODB.Connection")
DBConn.ConnectionString = "driver={SQL Server};" _
      & "server=MyServer;uid=WebUser" _
      & ";pwd=WebUser;database=C20EBooks"
DBConn.Open
```

and retrieve the list of books:

```
Set RSOptions = DBConn.Execute("Exec BookList")
```

which are written in the body of the page:

```
<SELECT ID="FormsComboBox1" NAME="BookID" SIZE=5>
      <% Response.Write RSOptions("TheOptions") %>
</SELECT>
```

Chapters Active Server Page

Chapters.asp

The code on the Chapters page displays a list of chapters to the visitor. The main code block is at the top of the page.

```
<%
Option Explicit
```

```
Dim DBConn
Dim RSChapters
If IsEmpty(Session("BookID")) Then
      Response.Redirect "../index.asp"
End If
set DBConn = Server.Createobject ("ADODB.Connection")
DBConn.ConnectionString = "driver={SQL Server};" _
      & "server=MyServer;uid=WebUser" _
      & ";pwd=WebUser;database=C20EBooks"
DBConn.Open
Set RSChapters = DBConn.Execute("Exec ChapterList " _
      & Session("BookID"))
%>
```

You start by telling the compiler that variables will be declared:

```
Option Explicit
```

You will need a Connection object:

```
Dim DBConn
```

and a Recordset object:

```
Dim RSChapters
```

But the page should not be entered without first selecting a book. You check for one here:

```
If IsEmpty(Session("BookID")) Then
```

And if the visitor has not selected a book, you send them back to the Books page:

```
Response.Redirect "../index.asp"
```

Otherwise, you can connect to the database:

```
set DBConn = Server.Createobject ("ADODB.Connection")
DBConn.ConnectionString = "driver={SQL Server};" _
      & "server=MyServer;uid=WebUser" _
      & ";pwd=WebUser;database=C20EBooks"
DBConn.Open
```

and retrieve the chapter list through your stored procedure:

```
Set RSChapters = DBConn.Execute("Exec ChapterList " _
      & Session("BookID"))
```

Within the body of the page, you write out the name of the book:

```
<% Response.Write RSChapters("BookName") %>: Chapters
```

and the chapter list:

```
<% Response.Write RSChapters("TheTable") %>
```

Sections Active Server Page

Section.asp

The code on the Sections page displays a list of sections to the visitor corresponding to the chapter that they have selected. The main code block is at the top of the page.

```
<%
Option Explicit
Dim DBConn
Dim RSSections
If Not IsEmpty(Request.QueryString("ChapterID")) Then
      Session("ChapterID") = Request.QueryString("ChapterID")
End If
If IsEmpty(Session("ChapterID")) Then
      Response.Redirect "./chapters.asp"
End If
set DBConn = Server.Createobject ("ADODB.Connection")
DBConn.ConnectionString = "driver={SQL Server};" _
      & "server=MyServer;uid=WebUser" _
      & ";pwd=WebUser;database=C20EBooks"
DBConn.Open
Set RSSections = DBConn.Execute("Exec SectionList " _
      & Session("ChapterID"))
%>
```

You start with your compiler directive:

```
Option Explicit
```

and declare a Connection object and a Recordset object:

```
Dim DBConn
Dim RSSections
```

Next, you check to see whether the ID of the current chapter was passed into the page:

```
If Not IsEmpty(Request.QueryString("ChapterID")) Then
```

If so, you store it in a Session variable:

```
Session("ChapterID") = Request.QueryString("ChapterID")
```

Next, you make sure that you have the ID of a chapter stored:

```
If IsEmpty(Session("ChapterID")) Then
```

If not, the visitor is sent back to the Chapters page:

```
Response.Redirect "./chapters.asp"
```

Otherwise, you can connect to the database:

```
set DBConn = Server.Createobject ("ADODB.Connection")
DBConn.ConnectionString = "driver={SQL Server};" _
      & "server=MyServer;uid=WebUser" _
      & ";pwd=WebUser;database=C20EBooks"
DBConn.Open
```

and call your stored procedure to retrieve the list of sections in this chapter:

```
Set RSSections = DBConn.Execute("Exec SectionList " _
      & Session("ChapterID"))
```

Within the body of the page, the name of the chapter is displayed to the visitor:

```
<% Response.Write RSSections("ChapterName") %>: Sections
```

and the section list is written:

```
<% Response.Write RSSections("TheTable") %>
```

Book Content Active Server Page

Book_Page.asp

The code on the Book Content page calls your stored procedure to display the text of the section selected by the visitor. The main code block is at the top of the page.

```
<%
Option Explicit
Dim DBConn
Dim RSPage
If IsEmpty(Request.QueryString("SectionID")) Then
      Response.Redirect "./section.asp"
End If
set DBConn = Server.Createobject ("ADODB.Connection")
DBConn.ConnectionString = "driver={SQL Server};" _
      & "server=MyServer;uid=WebUser" _
      & ";pwd=WebUser;database=C20EBooks"
DBConn.Open
Set RSPage = DBConn.Execute("Exec GetPageText " _
      & Request.QueryString("SectionID"))
%>
```

You start with the compiler directive:

```
Option Explicit
```

and then declare Connection and Recordset objects:

```
Dim DBConn
Dim RSPage
```

The page should not be entered without the ID of a section passed in:

```
If IsEmpty(Request.QueryString("SectionID")) Then
```

If it was, the visitor is sent back to the Sections page:

```
Response.Redirect "./section.asp"
```

Otherwise, you can connect to the database:

```
set DBConn = Server.Createobject ("ADODB.Connection")
DBConn.ConnectionString = "driver={SQL Server};" _
      & "server=MyServer;uid=WebUser" _
      & ";pwd=WebUser;database=C20EBooks"
DBConn.Open
```

and retrieve the text for the page:

```
Set RSPage = DBConn.Execute("Exec GetPageText " _
      & Request.QueryString("SectionID"))
```

Within the body of the page, you write out the name of the book and the name of the chapter:

```
<% Response.Write RSPage("BookName") %><BR><% Response.Write RSPage("ChapterName") %>
```

You also write out the name of the section:

```
<P><B><% Response.Write RSPage("SectionName") %></B></P>
```

and the text of the section:

```
<% Response.Write RSPage("BookPage") %>
```

Glossary Active Server Page

Glossary.asp

The code on the Glossary page displays the text of a glossary term by calling your stored procedure. The main code block is at the top of the page.

```
<%
Option Explicit
Dim DBConn
Dim RSTerm
If IsEmpty(Request.QueryString("GlossaryID")) Then
      Response.Redirect "./section.asp"
End If
set DBConn = Server.Createobject ("ADODB.Connection")
DBConn.ConnectionString = "driver={SQL Server};" _
      & "server=MyServer;uid=WebUser" _
      & ";pwd=WebUser;database=C20EBooks"
DBConn.Open
Set RSTerm = DBConn.Execute("Exec GetGlossaryTerm " _
      & Request.QueryString("GLossaryID"))
%>
```

You start by telling the compiler that variables will be declared:

```
Option Explicit
```

Next, you declare Connection and Recordset objects:

```
Dim DBConn
Dim RSTerm
```

and make sure that the ID of a glossary term was passed into the page:

```
If IsEmpty(Request.QueryString("GlossaryID")) Then
```

If it wasn't, you send the visitor back to the Section page:

```
Response.Redirect "./section.asp"
```

Otherwise, you can connect to the database:

```
set DBConn = Server.Createobject ("ADODB.Connection")
DBConn.ConnectionString = "driver={SQL Server};" _
      & "server=MyServer;uid=WebUser" _
      & ";pwd=WebUser;database=C20EBooks"
DBConn.Open
```

and retrieve the definition of the glossary term:

```
Set RSTerm = DBConn.Execute("Exec GetGlossaryTerm " _
      & Request.QueryString("GLossaryID"))
```

Within the body of the page, the glossary term:

```
Glossary: <% Response.Write RSTerm("GlossaryTerm") %>
```

and definition are written:

```
<P><% Response.Write RSTerm("TermDefinition") %></P>
```

Search Results Active Server Page

Search_Results.asp

The code on the Search Results page displays a table of all the sections that match the visitor's search given the search text that they entered.

```
<%
Option Explicit
Dim DBConn
Dim RSSections
If IsEmpty(Request.Form("SearchTerm")) Then
      Response.Redirect "./search.asp"
```

```
End If
set DBConn = Server.Createobject ("ADODB.Connection")
DBConn.ConnectionString = "driver={SQL Server};" _
      & "server=MyServer;uid=WebUser" _
      & ";pwd=WebUser;database=C20EBooks"
DBConn.Open
Set RSSections = DBConn.Execute("Exec SearchSectionList '" _
      & Request.Form("SearchTerm") & "'")
%>
```

You inform the compiler that a variable declaration will be required:

```
Option Explicit
```

and you declare a Connection object and a Recordset object:

```
Dim DBConn
Dim RSSections
```

The page should not be entered without search text passed into it:

```
If IsEmpty(Request.Form("SearchTerm")) Then
```

If it wasn't, the visitor is sent back to the Search page:

```
Response.Redirect "./search.asp"
```

Otherwise, you connect to the database:

```
set DBConn = Server.Createobject ("ADODB.Connection")
DBConn.ConnectionString = "driver={SQL Server};" _
      & "server=MyServer;uid=WebUser" _
      & ";pwd=WebUser;database=C20EBooks"
DBConn.Open
```

and retrieve the matching sections:

```
Set RSSections = DBConn.Execute("Exec SearchSectionList '" _
      & Request.Form("SearchTerm") & "'")
```

Then in the body of the page, you write out the matching sections that were returned from your stored procedure:

```
<% Response.Write RSSections("TheTable") %>
```

E-Help Tool

The E-Help tool provides a way for you to share help information that may relate to products and services that you offer with your visitors. The tool allows the visitor to browse through help topics and keywords.

Web Site Walk-Through

When the visitor first enters the tool, they see the page displayed in Figure 20-10.

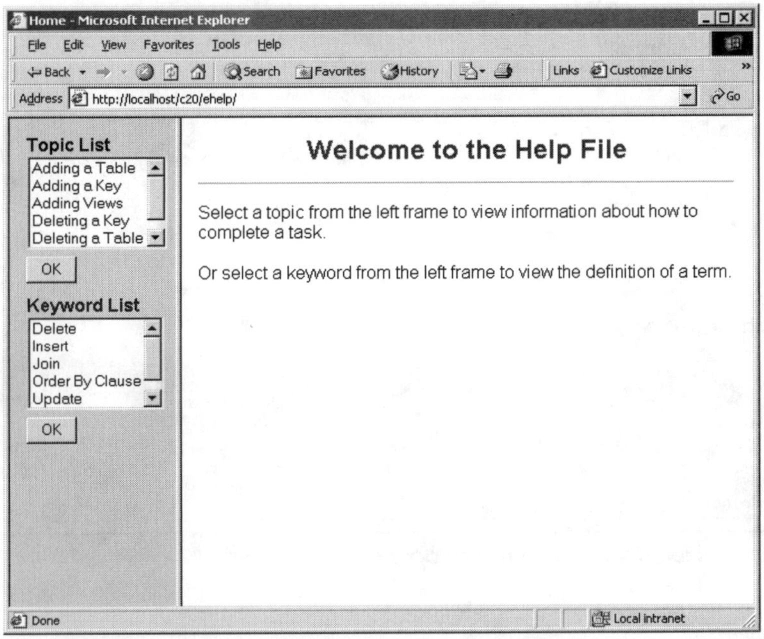

Figure 20-10 *Initial view of the E-Help tool*

In the body of the page, the visitor sees a welcome message that describes how the tool works. The page is divided into a left frame and a body frame. The main frame displays content, and the left frame lists topics and keywords.

At the top of the left frame is a list of all the topics in the help file. When the visitor selects a topic and clicks the OK button, they see the contents of that topic, as displayed in Figure 20-11.

The topics are meant to take the visitor through completing a task, which is different from a keyword item. A keyword item is shown in Figure 20-12.

Keyword entries are meant to convey a definition of a feature or term. Regardless of the type that the entry is, since the entry is displayed as HTML, you could insert tags that linked the visitor to other locations or that displayed support files that go with the entry.

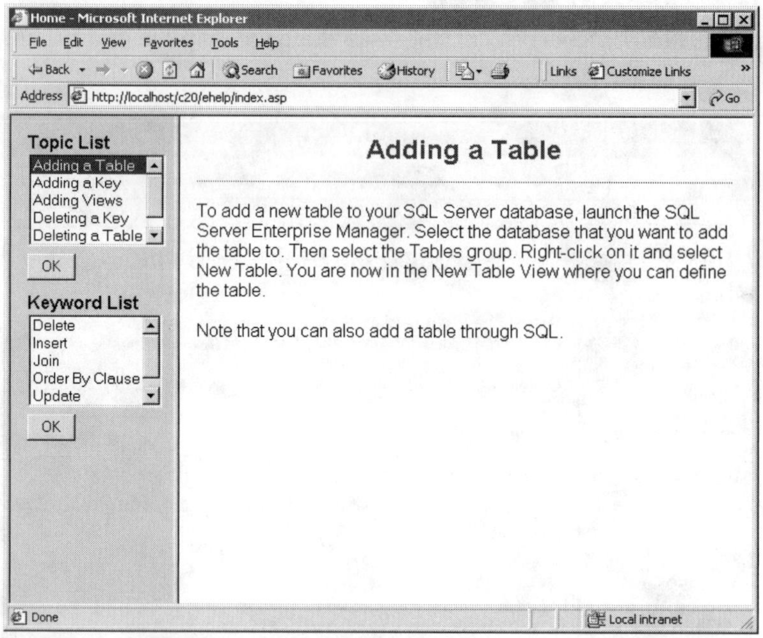

Figure 20-11 *E-Help tool displaying a topic entry*

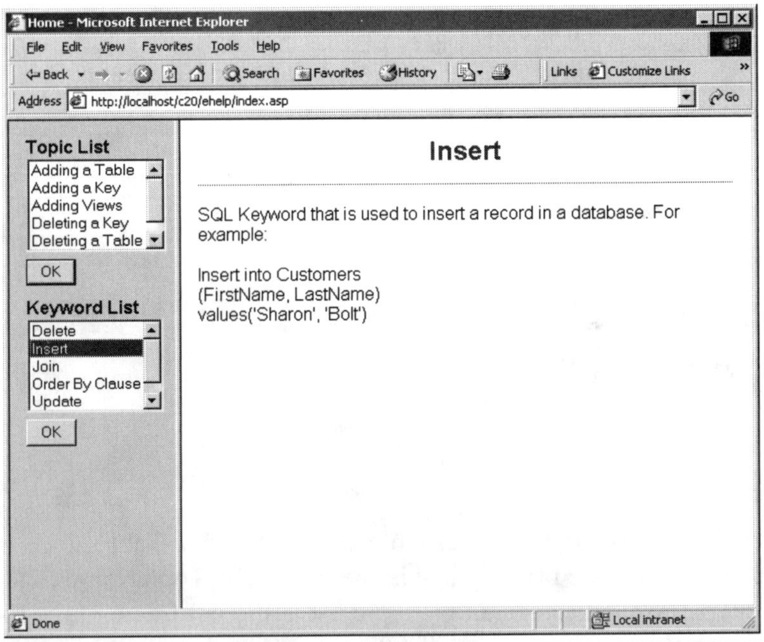

Figure 20-12 *E-Help tool displaying a keyword item*

Tables and Relationships

C20EHelpSQLObjects.sql

Topics Table

The Topics table is a stand-alone top-level table. It stores information on the topics that are displayed in the left frame and the body frame of the E-Help tool.

Keywords Table

The other table in the database is the Keywords table. This table stores the information about keywords that is displayed in the bottom list of the left frame.

Field Name	Field Type	Notes
TopicID	int	Primary Key, Identity Column
TopicName	varchar	Length = 50
TopicText	varchar	Length = 2000

Table 20-5 *Topics Table Field Specifications*

Field Specifications

Topics Table

Topics.txt

The field specifications for the Topics table are displayed in Table 20-5.

The TopicID field is the primary key in the table. The TopicName field stores the name of the topic, which appears in the topic list in the left frame of the E-Help tool. The TopicText field stores the content of the topic.

Keywords Table

Keywords.txt

The field specifications for the Keywords table are displayed in Table 20-6.

The primary key in this table is the KeywordID field. The other fields store the data about the keyword.

Field Name	Field Type	Notes
KeywordID	int	Primary Key, Identity Column
KeywordName	varchar	Length = 50
KeywordText	varchar	Length = 2000

Table 20-6 *Keywords Table Field Specifications*

Stored Procedures

TopicList Stored Procedure

The TopicList stored procedure is called from the left frame and returns a list of all the topic items formatted as Option tags.

```
CREATE PROCEDURE TopicList
AS
Declare
@AllOfIt varchar(8000),
@TopicID varchar(10),
@TopicName varchar(50)
Declare CurTopics Cursor
For Select TopicID, TopicName
      from Topics
      order by TopicName
Open CurTopics
Fetch CurTopics
      Into @TopicID, @TopicName
Select @AllOfIt = ''
While @@Fetch_Status = 0
      BEGIN
            Select @AllOfIt = @AllOfIt
                  + '<OPTION VALUE="'
                  + @TopicID + '">'
                  + @TopicName + '</OPTION>'
            Fetch CurTopics
                  Into @TopicID, @TopicName
      END
Close CurTopics
Deallocate CurTopics
Select @AllOfIt as TheOptions
GO
```

You need a variable that will be used to store the return value as you concatenate records to it:

```
@AllOfIt varchar(8000),
```

You also need variables that will store the contents of the topic record as it is retrieved for the database:

```
@TopicID varchar(10),
@TopicName varchar(50)
```

A cursor is declared:

```
Declare CurTopics Cursor
```

which is set to retrieve all the topics from the Topics table:

```
For Select TopicID, TopicName
      from Topics
      order by TopicName
```

You then open the cursor:

```
Open CurTopics
```

and place the contents of the first record into your local variables:

```
Fetch CurTopics
      Into @TopicID, @TopicName
```

You need to initialize your return variable:

```
Select @AllOfIt = ''
```

and enter a loop that will allow you to process each record:

```
While @@Fetch_Status = 0
```

Within the loop, each record is concatenated to your return variable as an HTML Option tag:

```
Select @AllOfIt = @AllOfIt
      + '<OPTION VALUE="'
      + @TopicID + '">'
      + @TopicName + '</OPTION>'
```

You then retrieve the next record from the Topics table into your local variables and loop so that each record in turn can be processed:

```
Fetch CurTopics
      Into @TopicID, @TopicName
```

After the loop, you release the cursor:

```
Close CurTopics
Deallocate CurTopics
```

and return the option list:

```
Select @AllOfIt as TheOptions
```

KeywordList Stored Procedure

The KeywordList stored procedure returns the options for the other list control on the left frame.

```
CREATE PROCEDURE KeywordList
AS
Declare
@AllOfIt varchar(8000),
@KeywordID varchar(10),
@KeywordName varchar(50)
Declare CurKeywords Cursor
For Select KeywordID, KeywordName
      from Keywords
      order by KeywordName
Open CurKeywords
Fetch CurKeywords
      Into @KeywordID, @KeywordName
Select @AllOfIt = ''
While @@Fetch_Status = 0
      BEGIN
            Select @AllOfIt = @AllOfIt
                  + '<OPTION VALUE="'
                  + @KeywordID + '">'
                  + @KeywordName + '</OPTION>'
            Fetch CurKeywords
```

```
                        Into @KeywordID, @KeywordName
      END
Close CurKeywords
Deallocate CurKeywords
Select @AllOfIt as TheOptions
GO
```

You will need a variable to store the return value as you concatenate Option tags to it:

```
@AllOfIt varchar(8000),
```

Also, local variables are needed to retrieve data from the Keywords table:

```
@KeywordID varchar(10),
@KeywordName varchar(50)
```

as is a cursor object:

```
Declare CurKeywords Cursor
```

which is set to retrieve all the records from the Keywords table sorted by the name of the keyword:

```
For Select KeywordID, KeywordName
      from Keywords
      order by KeywordName
```

You then open the cursor:

```
Open CurKeywords
```

and retrieve the first record:

```
Fetch CurKeywords
      Into @KeywordID, @KeywordName
```

Also, you need to initialize your return variable:

```
Select @AllOfIt = ''
```

and enter a loop so that each record can be processed:

```
While @@Fetch_Status = 0
```

Each record is formatted as an HTML Option tag:

```
Select @AllOfIt = @AllOfIt
      + '<OPTION VALUE="'
      + @KeywordID + '">'
      + @KeywordName + '</OPTION>'
```

before you retrieve the next record and loop:

```
Fetch CurKeywords
      Into @KeywordID, @KeywordName
```

After the loop, the cursor object is closed:

```
Close CurKeywords
Deallocate CurKeywords
```

and the option list is returned:

```
Select @AllOfIt as TheOptions
```

GetTopic Stored Procedure

The body page needs to display the contents of a topic when the visitor selects an item from the Topics list. The GetTopic stored procedure returns a topic's contents.

```
CREATE PROCEDURE GetTopic
@TopicID integer
AS
BEGIN
      Select TopicName, TopicText
            From Topics
            Where TopicID = @TopicID
END
GO
```

Passed into the procedure is the ID of the topic that the calling application wants to retrieve the data for:

```
@TopicID integer
```

You then use that ID to return the contents of the topic:

```
Select TopicName, TopicText
      From Topics
      Where TopicID = @TopicID
```

GetKeyword Stored Procedure

The GetKeyword stored procedure returns the contents of a keyword record for the body page.

```
CREATE PROCEDURE GetKeyword
@KeywordID integer
AS
BEGIN
      Select KeywordName, KeywordText
            From Keywords
            Where KeywordID = @KeywordID
END
GO
```

Passed into the procedure is the ID of the keyword:

```
@KeywordID integer
```

That ID is used in the Where clause of a SQL statement so that the keyword data can be retrieved:

```
Select KeywordName, KeywordText
      From Keywords
      Where KeywordID = @KeywordID
```

Active Server Pages

Index Active Server Page

Index.asp

The E-Help tool is made up of a single framed page. The page that defines the frames is the Index page. That page has code in it that passes the section of the visitor from the left frame to the body frame. The main code block is at the top of the page.

```
<%
Option Explicit
Dim TheMainLink
If Not IsEmpty(Request.Form("OKTopic")) Then
      TheMainLink = "./body_index.asp?Type=Topic" _
```

```
            & "&TheID=" & Request.Form("TopicID")
ElseIf Not IsEmpty(Request.Form("OKKeyword")) Then
      TheMainLink = "./body_index.asp?Type=Keyword" _
            & "&TheID=" & Request.Form("KeywordID")
Else
      TheMainLink = "./body_index.asp?Type=New"
End If
%>
```

You start by telling the compiler that you will declare your variables:

```
Option Explicit
```

You then declare a variable that will store the link information passed onto the body page:

```
Dim TheMainLink
```

Next, you check to see whether the visitor has selected a Topic that they want to view by checking to see whether the OK button is present in the Form fields collection:

```
If Not IsEmpty(Request.Form("OKTopic")) Then
```

If it is present, you pass on information to the body page so that it knows what is to be displayed is a topic:

```
TheMainLink = "./body_index.asp?Type=Topic" _
      & "&TheID=" & Request.Form("TopicID")
```

Next, you check to see whether the visitor wants to see a keyword:

```
ElseIf Not IsEmpty(Request.Form("OKKeyword")) Then
```

In that case, you pass on to the body page the fact that the type of call is a keyword and you pass the ID of the keyword on:

```
TheMainLink = "./body_index.asp?Type=Keyword" _
      & "&TheID=" & Request.Form("KeywordID")
```

If the code flows here, it means that the visitor has not clicked either button:

```
Else
```

In that case, you tell the body page that this is a new visitor:

```
TheMainLink = "./body_index.asp?Type=New"
```

Then within the Frame tag, you write this link for the body frame:

```
<FRAME NAME="body" SRC="<% Response.Write TheMainLink %>"
SCROLLING=AUTO MARGINWIDTH=0 MARGINHEIGHT=0>
```

Left Active Server Page

Left_Index.asp

The code on the left page calls your stored procedures to display the topic and keyword lists. The main code block is at the top of the page.

```
<%
Option Explicit
Dim DBConn
Dim RSKeywordOptions
Dim RSTopicOptions
set DBConn = Server.Createobject ("ADODB.Connection")
DBConn.ConnectionString = "driver={SQL Server};" _
    & "server=MyServer;uid=WebUser" _
    & ";pwd=WebUser;database=C20EHelp"
DBConn.Open
Set RSKeywordOptions = DBConn.Execute("Exec KeywordList")
Set RSTopicOptions = DBConn.Execute("Exec TopicList")
%>
```

You start with a compiler directive:

```
Option Explicit
```

and then declare a Connection object and two Recordset objects:

```
Dim DBConn
Dim RSKeywordOptions
Dim RSTopicOptions
```

You then connect to the database:

```
set DBConn = Server.Createobject ("ADODB.Connection")
DBConn.ConnectionString = "driver={SQL Server};" _
```

```
        & "server=MyServer;uid=WebUser" _
        & ";pwd=WebUser;database=C20EHelp"
DBConn.Open
```

and retrieve the keyword list:

```
Set RSKeywordOptions = DBConn.Execute("Exec KeywordList")
```

as well as the topics list:

```
Set RSTopicOptions = DBConn.Execute("Exec TopicList")
```

In the body of the page, those lists are written:

```
<SELECT ID="FormsComboBox1" NAME="TopicID" SIZE=5>
      <% Response.Write RSTopicOptions("TheOptions") %>
</SELECT>
<SELECT ID="FormsComboBox2" NAME="KeywordID" SIZE=5>
      <% Response.Write RSKeywordOptions("TheOptions") %>
</SELECT>
```

Body Active Server Page

Body_Index.asp

The code on the body page displays the content on the page corresponding to the keyword or topic selected by the visitor. The main code block is at the top of the page.

```
<%
Option Explicit
Dim DBConn
Dim RSContent
Dim TheTitle
Dim TheContent
If Request.QueryString("Type") = "Keyword" Then
      set DBConn = Server.Createobject ("ADODB.Connection")
      DBConn.ConnectionString = "driver={SQL Server};" _
            & "server=MyServer;uid=WebUser" _
            & ";pwd=WebUser;database=C20EHelp"
      DBConn.Open
      Set RSContent = DBConn.Execute("Exec GetKeyword " _
            & Request.QueryString("TheID"))
```

```
        TheTitle = RSContent("KeywordName")
        TheContent = RSContent("KeywordText")
ElseIf Request.QueryString("Type") = "Topic" Then
        set DBConn = Server.Createobject ("ADODB.Connection")
        DBConn.ConnectionString = "driver={SQL Server};" _
              & "server=MyServer;uid=WebUser" _
              & ";pwd=WebUser;database=C20EHelp"
        DBConn.Open
        Set RSContent = DBConn.Execute("Exec GetTopic " _
              & Request.QueryString("TheID"))
        TheTitle = RSContent("TopicName")
        TheContent = RSContent("TopicText")
Else
        TheTitle = "Welcome to the Help File"
        TheContent = "Select a topic from the left frame to " _
              & "view information about how to complete a " _
              & "task.</P><P>Or select a keyword from the " _
              & "left frame to view the definition of a term."
End If
%>
```

You start by telling the compiler that you will declare your variables:

```
Option Explicit
```

Then you declare a Connection object:

```
Dim DBConn
```

a Recordset object:

```
Dim RSContent
```

and variables to store the text of the page:

```
Dim TheTitle
Dim TheContent
```

The first condition you test for is whether the visitor has selected a keyword that they want to view:

```
If Request.QueryString("Type") = "Keyword" Then
```

If that is the case, you need to connect to the database:

```
set DBConn = Server.Createobject ("ADODB.Connection")
DBConn.ConnectionString = "driver={SQL Server};" _
      & "server=MyServer;uid=WebUser" _
      & ";pwd=WebUser;database=C20EHelp"
DBConn.Open
```

and retrieve the content of the keyword:

```
Set RSContent = DBConn.Execute("Exec GetKeyword " _
      & Request.QueryString("TheID"))
```

You then place the name of the keyword and its text into your local variables:

```
TheTitle = RSContent("KeywordName")
TheContent = RSContent("KeywordText")
```

The next condition you test for is whether the visitor has selected a topic that they want to view:

```
ElseIf Request.QueryString("Type") = "Topic" Then
```

If that is the case, you connect to the database:

```
set DBConn = Server.Createobject ("ADODB.Connection")
DBConn.ConnectionString = "driver={SQL Server};" _
      & "server=MyServer;uid=WebUser" _
      & ";pwd=WebUser;database=C20EHelp"
DBConn.Open
```

and retrieve the topic requested by the visitor through your stored procedure:

```
Set RSContent = DBConn.Execute("Exec GetTopic " _
      & Request.QueryString("TheID"))
```

The content retrieved through the procedure is placed into your local variables:

```
TheTitle = RSContent("TopicName")
TheContent = RSContent("TopicText")
```

If the code flows here, it means that the visitor is in the initial view of the page:

```
Else
```

So you place the welcome text and instructions into your local variables:

```
TheTitle = "Welcome to the Help File"
TheContent = "Select a topic from the left frame to " _
     & "view information about how to complete a " _
     & "task.</P><P>Or select a keyword from the " _
     & "left frame to view the definition of a term."
```

Then, in the body of the page, you write the title text:

```
<% Response.Write TheTitle %>
```

and the content of the page:

```
<P><% Response.Write TheContent %></P>
```

PART V

Appendixes

APPENDIX

A

Visual Basic and Visual Basic.NET Quick Reference

In this appendix, many of the procedures available in Visual Basic and Visual Basic.NET are defined. Each procedure is listed with the description of the procedures, any parameters, any return value, and a sample use of the procedures. If the syntax for Visual Basic.NET is different, that syntax is also presented.

Abs

Returns the absolute value of a number. In VB.NET, use Math.Abs.

Syntax:

```
X = Abs(Num)
```

VB.NET:

```
X = Math.Abs(Num)
```

Num is a numeric value for which the absolute value needs to be determined. Returned from the function is the absolute value of Num.

Example:

```
MsgBox Abs(5)
MsgBox Abs(-5)
```

VB.NET:

```
MsgBox(Math.Abs(5))
MsgBox(Math.Abs(-5))
```

Entered in a message box would be:

```
5
5
```

Asc

Returns the numeric ASCII value of a character.

Syntax:

```
X = Asc(TheLetter)
```

TheLetter is the character for which you want to determine the ASCII value. Returned from the method would be the numeric ASCII value.

Example:

```
MsgBox Asc("B")
MsgBox Asc("?")
```

VB.NET:

```
MsgBox Asc("B")
MsgBox Asc("?")
```

Entered in a message box would be:

```
66
63
```

Conversion Functions (CBool, CByte, CCur, CDate, CDbl, CInt, CLng, Csng, CStr)

Converts a variable of one type to a variable of another type.

Syntax:

```
X = CStr(ValueToConvert)
```

The syntax is the same for all the conversion functions. Passed to the function is the value you wish to convert. Returned from the function is the converted number.

Example:

```
X = CInt("44")
```

X would contain an integer with the value 44.

Chr

Converts an ASCII value to its character representation.

Syntax:

```
X = Chr(TheValue)
```

TheValue is the ASCII number you wish to return a character from. The value converted is returned from the function.

Example:

```
Response.Write Chr(72) & "<P>"
Response.Write Chr(74) & "<P>"
```

Entered to the browser would be:

```
H
J
```

Date (VB.NET: Today) Returns the current system date.

Syntax:

```
X = Date
```

VB.NET:

```
X = Today()
```

X would contain the current system date.

Example:

```
MsgBox Date
MsgBox (Today())
```

Entered in a message would be the current system date.

DateAdd Adds a value to a date or time.

Syntax:

```
X = DateAdd(Part2Add, Number2Add, Date)
```

The first parameter in Visual Basic is a string representing what you want to add to a date, like days or hours. For this parameter, *yyyy* represents years, *q* represents quarters, *m* represents months, *y* represents day of year, *d* represents days, *w* represents weekdays, *ww* represents week of year, *h* represents hours, *n* represents minutes, and *s* represents seconds.

In VB.NET, the first parameter is a numeric constant. For this parameter

> Microsoft.VisualBasic.DateInterval.Year represents years,
> Microsoft.VisualBasic.DateInterval.Quarter represents quarters,
> Microsoft.VisualBasic.DateInterval.Month represents months,
> Microsoft.VisualBasic.DateInterval.DayOfYear represents day of year,

Microsoft.VisualBasic.DateInterval.Day represents days,
Microsoft.VisualBasic.DateInterval.Week represents weeks,
Microsoft.VisualBasic.DateInterval.Hour represents hours,
Microsoft.VisualBasic.DateInterval.Minute represents minutes, and
Microsoft.VisualBasic.DateInterval.Second represents seconds.

Num2Add is the quantity that you want to add. Use a negative number to perform date subtraction. Date is the date that you want to add to.

Example:

```
MsgBox DateAdd("h", 4, "5:15")
MsgBox DateAdd("yyyy", -3, "5/5/1940")
```

VB.NET:

```
MsgBox(DateAdd(Microsoft.VisualBasic.DateInterval.Hour , 4, "5:15"))
MsgBox(DateAdd(Microsoft.VisualBasic.DateInterval.Year , -3, "5/5/1940"))
```

Entered in a message box would be:

```
9:15:00 AM
5/5/37
```

DateDiff

Subtracts two dates and returns the difference.

Syntax:

```
X= DateDiff(Part2Diff, Date1, Date2)
```

In Visual Basic, the first parameter is a string representing what you want to use to subtract, like days or hours. For this parameter, *yyyy* represents years, *q* represents quarters, *m* represents months, *y* represents day of year, *d* represents days, *w* represents weekdays, *ww* represents week of year, *h* represents hours, *n* represents minutes, and *s* represents seconds.

In VB.NET, the first parameter is a numeric constant. For this parameter

Microsoft.VisualBasic.DateInterval.Year represents years,
Microsoft.VisualBasic.DateInterval.Quarter represents quarters,
Microsoft.VisualBasic.DateInterval.Month represents months,
Microsoft.VisualBasic.DateInterval.DayOfYear represents day of year,
Microsoft.VisualBasic.DateInterval.Day represents days,

Microsoft.VisualBasic.DateInterval.Week represents weeks,
Microsoft.VisualBasic.DateInterval.Hour represents hours,
Microsoft.VisualBasic.DateInterval.Minute represents minutes, and
Microsoft.VisualBasic.DateInterval.Second represents seconds.

The second parameter is the date that you want to subtract from the third parameter.

Example:

```
MsgBox DateDiff("yyyy", "4/1/1952", "3/1/2005")
MsgBox DateDiff("n", "1:15", "1:25")
```

VB.NET:

```
MsgBox(DateDiff(Microsoft.VisualBasic.DateInterval.Year _
    , "4/1/1952", "3/1/2005"))
MsgBox(DateDiff(Microsoft.VisualBasic.DateInterval.Minute, _
    "1:15", "1:25"))
```

Entered to the browser would be:

```
53
10
```

DatePart Returns a portion of a date or time.

Syntax:

```
X = DatePart(Part2Return, Date)
```

In VB, the first parameter is a string representing what part you want to return, such as day or hour. For this parameter, *yyyy* represents years, *q* represents quarters, *m* represents months, *y* represents day of year, *d* represents days, *w* represents weekdays, *ww* represents week of year, *h* represents hours, *n* represents minutes, and *s* represents seconds.

In VB.NET, the first parameter is a numeric constant. For this parameter

Microsoft.VisualBasic.DateInterval.Year represents years,
Microsoft.VisualBasic.DateInterval.Quarter represents quarters,
Microsoft.VisualBasic.DateInterval.Month represents months,
Microsoft.VisualBasic.DateInterval.DayOfYear represents day of year,

Microsoft.VisualBasic.DateInterval.Day represents days,
Microsoft.VisualBasic.DateInterval.Week represents weeks,
Microsoft.VisualBasic.DateInterval.Hour represents hours,
Microsoft.VisualBasic.DateInterval.Minute represents minutes, and
Microsoft.VisualBasic.DateInterval.Second represents seconds.

The second parameter is the date that you want to parse from. Returned is the portion of the date requested.

Example:

```
MsgBox DatePart("yyyy", "4/1/1952")
MsgBox DatePart("n", "1:15")
```

VB.NET:

```
MsgBox(DatePart(Microsoft.VisualBasic.DateInterval.Year _
    , "4/1/1952"))
MsgBox(DatePart(Microsoft.VisualBasic.DateInterval.Minute _
    , "1:15"))
```

Entered to the browser would be:

```
1952
15
```

DateSerial Returns a date from the parts year, month, and day.

Syntax:

```
X = DateSerial(year, month, day)
```

Returned from the function is the concatenation of the date parts.

Example:

```
Response.Write DateSerial("1955", "4", "22") & "<P>
Response.Write DateSerial("2022", "8", "11") & "<P>"
```

Entered to the browser would be:

```
4/22/55
8/11/22
```

Day Returns the day portion of a date. In VB.NET, use the DatePart function.

Syntax:

```
X = Day(Date)
```

Returned from the function would be the day of the Date.

Example:

```
Response.Write Day("5/1/1971 5:15:32") & "<P>
Response.Write Day("9/21/2002 12:32:54") & "<P>"
```

Entered to the browser would be:

```
1
21
```

Do...Loop Repeats a chunk of code until a condition is met.

Syntax:

```
Do Condition
    'Code Block
Loop
```

The code would run until the condition was met.

Example:

```
X = 0
Do Until X = 5
    MsgBox "Not Yet"
    X = X + 1
Loop
```

VB.NET:

```
X = 0
Do Until X = 5
    MsgBox("Not Yet")
    X = X + 1
Loop
```

"Not Yet" would be written over and over again in a message box until X was 5.

Fix Returns the integer portion of a number.

Syntax:

```
X = Fix(TheNumber)
```

X would be set to the integer portion of TheNumber.

Example:

```
Response.Write Fix(2.999) & "<P>"
Response.Write Fix(0.1) & "<P>"
```

Entered to the browser would be:

```
2
0
```

For...Each Allows you to iterate through a collection of objects.

Syntax:

```
For Each MyItem in TheCollection
    'take action on the collection
Next
```

The code would perform the code block through each of the items in TheCollection.

Example:

```
For Each TheField in RS.Fields
    Response.Write TheField.Name
Next
```

Entered to the browser would be the name of each field in a Recordset object.

For...Next Iterates from one number to another, performing a block of code with each cycle.

Syntax:

```
For TheNumber = Start to End
    'code block
Next
```

The block would iterate until TheNumber was equal to End.

Example:

```
For I = 1 to 5
   Response.Write I
Next
```

Entered to the browser would be the numbers 1 through 5.

FormatCurrency

Formats a number as currency.

Syntax:

```
X = FormatCurrency(Number2Format)
```

X is set to Number2Format converted to currency.

Example:

```
MsgBox FormatCurrency(2.999)
MsgBox FormatCurrency(0.1)
```

VB.NET:

```
MsgBox(FormatCurrency(2.999))
MsgBox(FormatCurrency(0.1))
```

Entered in a message box would be:

```
$3.00
$0.10
```

FormatDateTime

Formats a string in a date format.

Syntax:

```
X = FormatDateTime(TheDate)
```

X would be set to the formatted date version of TheDate.

Example:

```
Response.Write FormatDateTime("12/6/1989", 0) & "<P>"
Response.Write FormatDateTime("12/6/1989", 1) & "<P>"
Response.Write FormatDateTime("12/6/1989", 2) & "<P>"
```

Entered to the browser would be:

```
12/6/89
Wednesday, December 06, 1989
12/6/89
```

FormatNumber

Formats a number.

Syntax:

```
X = FormatNumber(TheNumber)
```

X will be set to the formatted version of TheNumber.

Example:

```
Response.Write FormatNumber(1234567) & "<P>"
Response.Write FormatNumber(.1) & "<P>"
```

Entered to the browser would be:

```
1,234,567.00
0.10
```

FormatPercent

Formats a number as a percentage.

Syntax:

```
X = FormatPercent(TheNumber)
```

X would be set to the value of TheNumber written as a percentage.

Example:

```
Response.Write FormatPercent(12.1) & "<P>"
Response.Write FormatPercent(.1877) & "<P>"
```

Entered to the browser would be:

```
1,210.00%
18.77%
```

Hex Returns a string representing the hexadecimal value of a number.

Syntax:

```
X = Hex(TheNumber)
```

X is set to a string containing the hexadecimal value of TheNumber.

Example:

```
MsgBox Hex(255)
MsgBox Hex(16)
```

VB.NET:

```
MsgBox(Hex(255))
MsgBox(Hex(16))
```

Entered in a message box would be:

```
FF
10
```

Hour Returns the hour portion of a time. In VB.NET, use the DatePart function.

Syntax:

```
X = Hour(TheTime)
```

X would be set to the hour of TheTime.

Example:

```
Response.Write Hour("5/1/1971 5:15:32") & "<P>"
Response.Write Hour("9/21/2002 12:32:54") & "<P>"
```

Entered to the browser would be:

```
5
12
```

If Provides for code to run given a condition.

Syntax:

```
If Condition1 Then
    'Code block
ElseIf Condition2 Then
    'Code block
Else
    'Code block
End If
```

If Condition1 evaluates to True, then the first code block would run. If not, the code would test Condition2. If it evaluated to True, then the second code block would run. Otherwise, the code in the third code block would run. The ElseIf and Else portions of an If statement are not required.

Example:

```
If Month(Date) = 9 then
    Response.Write "September"
Else
    Response.Write "Not September"
End If
```

Entered to the browser would be September if the current month is September. Otherwise, Not September would be written.

InputBox Displays a small window with a prompt and a text box for entering information. Not available in ASP.

Syntax:

```
X = InputBox(ThePrompt, TheTitle, TheDefault)
```

ThePrompt is the text that is displayed in a label in the input box. TheTitle is the text displayed in the title bar of the input box. TheDefault is an optional default value displayed in the text box on the input box. X is set to the value entered into the text box. If Cancel is clicked, X is set to an empty string.

Example:

```
X = InputBox("Please enter your name:", "LogIn", _
     "Admin")
```

InStr Searches for a string within a string.

Syntax:

```
X = Instr(String2Search, SearchString)
```

X is set to the first occurrence of the SearchString within the String2Search. If the SearchString is not found, the function returns 0.

Example:

```
Response.Write Instr("Hello", "e") & "<P>"
Response.Write Instr("Hello", "R") & "<P>"
```

Entered to the browser would be:

```
2
0
```

InStrRev Same as Instr except that the search begins at the end of the string.

Syntax:

```
X = Instr(String2Search, SearchString)
```

X would be set to the last occurrence of the SearchString within the String2Search.

Example:

```
MsgBox(InstrRev("Hello World", "l"))
MsgBox(InstrRev("Hello", "R"))
```

VB.NET:

```
MsgBox(InstrRev("Hello World", "l"))
MsgBox(InstrRev("Hello", "R"))
```

Entered in a message box would be:

```
10
5
```

Int
Returns the integer portion of a number.

Syntax:

```
X = Int(TheNumber)
```

X would be set to the integer portion of TheNumber.

Example:

```
Response.Write Int(2.999) & "<P>"
Response.Write Int(0.1) & "<P>"
```

Entered to the browser would be:

```
2
0
```

IsDate
Tests a value to see if it is a date.

Syntax:

```
X = IsDate(TheDate)
```

X will be set to True or False depending upon whether TheDate is a date.

Example:

```
Response.Write IsDate("12/44/55") & "<P>"
Response.Write IsDate("12/14/55") & "<P>"
```

Entered to the browser would be:

```
False
True
```

IsEmpty
Tests to see if a variable is empty. In VB.NET, use IsNothing.

Syntax:

```
X = IsEmpty(TheVariable)
```

VB.NET:

```
X = IsNothing(TheVariable)
```

X will be set to True or False depending upon whether TheVariable is empty.

Example:

```
If Not IsEmpty(Request.Form("Submit")) Then
    'form submitted
Else
    'Form not submitted
End If
```

In this code example, if a form field called Submit was present, then the first code block would run. Otherwise, the second code block would run.

IsNumeric Tests to see if a value is a number.

Syntax:

```
X = IsNumeric(TheValue)
```

X would be set to True or False depending upon whether TheValue was a number.

Example:

```
MsgBox IsNumeric("Hello")
MsgBox IsNumeric("33")
```

VB.NET:

```
MsgBox(IsNumeric("Hello"))
MsgBox(IsNumeric("33"))
```

Entered in a message box would be:

```
False
True
```

LCase Converts text to lowercase.

Syntax:

```
X = LCase(TheValue)
```

X would be set to the lowercase text of the variable TheValue.

Example:

```
Response.Write LCase("HELLO") & "<P>"
Response.Write LCase("123") & "<P>"
```

Entered to the browser would be:

```
hello
123
```

Left
Chops characters off the left side of a string.

Syntax:

```
X = Left(String2Chop, NumCharacters)
```

String2Chop is the string that you want to chop characters from. NumCharacters is the number of characters you want to chop. Returned to X would be the chopped string.

Example:

```
MsgBox Left("Hello", 2)
```

VB.NET:

```
MsgBox(Left("Hello", 2))
```

Entered in a message box would be:

```
He
```

Len
Returns the length, in characters, of a string.

Syntax:

```
X = Len(TheString)
```

X would be set to the number of characters in TheString.

Example:

```
MsgBox Len("Hello")
MsgBox Len("Hello World")
```

VB.NET:

```
MsgBox(Len("Hello"))
MsgBox(Len("Hello World"))
```

Entered to the browser would be:

```
5
11
```

LTrim Returns a string without any leading spaces.

Syntax:

```
X = Ltrim(TheString)
```

X would be set to TheString without any leading spaces.

Example:

```
X = Ltrim("   Hello   ")
```

X would be set to the string “Hello”.

Mid Returns characters from the middle of the string.

Syntax:

```
X = Mid(TheString, StartPosition, NumCharacters)
```

TheString is the string to pull characters from. StartPosition is the spot to start retrieving characters from. NumCharacters is the number of characters to chop out of the middle. If the third parameter is left off, the function returns all characters after the start position.

Example:

```
MsgBox Mid("Hello", 2, 3)
MsgBox Mid("Hello", 2)
```

VB.NET:

```
MsgBox(Mid("Hello", 2, 3))
MsgBox(Mid("Hello", 2))
```

Entered in a message box would be:

```
ell
ello
```

Minute Returns the minute from a time. In VB.NET, use DatePart.

Syntax:

```
X = Minute(TheTime)
```

X would be set to the minutes within the TheTime variable.

Example:

```
Response.Write Hour("5/1/1971 5:15:32") & "<P>"
Response.Write Hour("9/21/2002 12:32:54") & "<P>"
```

Entered to the browser would be:

```
15
32
```

Month Returns the month portion of a date as a number. In VB.NET, use DatePart.

Syntax:

```
X = Month(TheDate)
```

X would be set to the month of TheDate.

Example:

```
MsgBox Month("5/1/1971 5:15:32")
MsgBox Month("9/21/2002 12:32:54")
```

Entered in a message box would be:

```
5
9
```

MonthName Returns the month name for a number from 1 to 12.

Syntax:

```
X = MonthName(TheNumber)
```

X will be set to the text name of the month corresponding to the number in TheNumber.

Example:

```
MsgBox Month(3)
```

VB.NET:

```
MsgBox(Month(3))
```

Entered in a message box would be

```
March
```

Now Returns the current system date and time.

Syntax:

```
X = Now
```

X would be set to the current system date and time.

Example:

```
Response.Write Now
```

Entered to the browser would be the current system date and time.

Oct Returns the octal value of a number.

Syntax:

```
X = Oct(TheNumber)
```

X would contain a string representing the octal value of TheNumber.

Example:

```
Response.Write Oct(9) & "<P>"
Response.Write Oct(12) & "<P>"
```

Entered to the browser would be:

```
11
14
```

Randomize Initializes the random number generator.

Syntax:

```
Randomize
```

The random number generator would be initialized.

Example:

```
Randomize
```

Replace Replaces one character in a string with another.

Syntax:

```
X = Replace(String2Fix, Character2Replace, What2ReplaceWith)
```

X would contain a converted String2Fix that would have Character2Replace substituted with What2ReplaceWith.

Example:

```
Response.Write Replace("Mississippi", "i", "o") & "<P>"
```

Entered to the browser would be:

```
Mossossoppo
```

Right Chops characters off the right side of a string.

Syntax:

```
X = Right(String2Chop, NumCharacters)
```

X would contain the right-most characters of String2Chop, in terms of the number in NumCharacters.

Example:

```
MsgBox Right("Hello", 2)
```

VB.NET:

```
MsgBox Right("Hello", 2)
```

Entered in a message box would be:

```
lo
```

Rnd Returns a random number.

Syntax:

```
X = Rnd
```

X would contain a random number.

Example:

```
Response.Write Int(Rnd * 6) + 1
```

Entered to the browser would be a number between 1 and 6.

Round Rounds a number to the number of decimal places specified. In VB.NET, use Decimal.Round.

Syntax:

```
X = Round(TheNumber, NumPlaces)
```

VB.NET:

```
X = Decimal.Round(TheNumber, NumPlaces)
```

X would contain the rounded TheNumber rounded to NumPlaces.

Example:

```
MsgBox Round(4.555, 2)
```

VB.NET:

```
MsgBox Decimal.Round(4.555, 2)
```

Entered in a message box would be:

```
4.56
```

RTrim Returns a string with any trailing spaces removed.

Syntax:

```
X = Rtrim(TheString)
```

X is set to TheString without any trailing spaces.

Example:

```
X = Rtrim("   Hello   ")
```

X would be set to the string "Hello".

Second Returns the seconds from a time. In VB.NET, use the DatePart function.

Syntax:

```
X = Second(TheTime)
```

Returns the number of seconds chopped from a time.

Example:

```
Response.Write Second("5/1/1971 5:15:32") & "<P>"
Response.Write Second("9/21/2002 12:32:54") & "<P>"
```

Entered to the browser would be:

```
32
54
```

Select...Case The Select...Case structure allows you to have code run depending on a condition.

Syntax:

```
Select Case X
    Case 1
        'first code block
    Case 2
        'second code block
    Case Else
End Select
```

The code will run a code block determined by the value of X. If X is 1, the first code block will run. If X is 2, the second code block will run. Otherwise, the Else code block will run.

Example:

```
X = 1
Select Case X
    Case 1
        Response.Write "This one."
    Case 2
        Response.Write "Not this one."
    Case Else
        Response.Write "Not this one."
End Select
```

Entered to the browser would be "This one."

Space Returns a number of spaces as a string.

Syntax:

```
X = Space(TheNumber)
```

X would contain a string of TheNumber spaces.

Example:

```
X = Space(5)
```

X would be set to the value "   ".

Sqr Returns the square root of a number. Tshis function is called Math.Sqrt in VB.NET.

Syntax:

```
X = Sqr(TheNumber)
```

VB.NET:

```
X = Math.Sqrt(TheNumber)
```

X would be set to the square root of the number.

Example:

```
MsgBox Sqr(9)
```

VB.NET:

```
MsgBox(Math.Sqrt(9))
```

Entered in a message box would be:

```
3
```

StrComp Compares two strings and returns a value based on that comparison.

Syntax:

```
X = StrComp(String1,String2)
```

If the two strings are equal, X will contain 0. If string 1 is greater, X will contain 1. Otherwise, X will contain –1.

Example:

```
Response.Write StrComp("Hello", "Hello") & "<P>"
Response.Write StrComp("Hello", "World") & "<P>"
Response.Write StrComp("World", "Hello") & "<P>"
```

Entered to the browser would be:

```
0
-1
1
```

String Returns a character repeated depending on the parameters passed. This function is not available in VB.NET.

Syntax:

```
X = String(TheNumber, TheCharacter)
```

X will contain the character TheCharacter repeated TheNumber times.

Example:

```
Response.Write String(4,"R")
```

Entered to the browser would be:

```
RRRR
```

StrReverse Reverses the characters in a string.

Syntax:

```
X = StrReverse(TheString)
```

X will contain TheString backward.

Example:

```
MsgBox StrReverse("Hello")
```

VB.NET:

```
MsgBox StrReverse("Hello")
```

Entered in a message box would be:

```
olleH
```

Time Returns the current system time. In VB.NET, use TimeOfDay.

Syntax:

```
X = Time
```

VB.NET:

```
X = TimeOfDay()
```

X would contain the current system time.

Example:

```
MsgBox Time
```

VB.NET:

```
MsgBox(TimeOfDay())
```

Entered in a message box would be the current system time.

TimeSerial

Returns a time concatenated from an hour, minute, and second.

Syntax:

```
X = TimeSerial(Hour, Minute, Second)
```

X would contain the time specified by the values of Hour, Minute, and Second.

Example:

```
X = TimeSerial("5", "17", "32")
```

X would contain the time 5:17:32.

Trim

Removes the spaces from both ends of a string.

Syntax:

```
X = Trim(TheString)
```

X would contain the string TheString with all the spaces removed.

Example:

```
X = Trim("   Hello   ")
```

X would be set to the string "Hello".

Ucase Converts a string to its uppercase value.

Syntax:

```
X = UCase(TheString)
```

X would contain the string TheString with the characters all in uppercase.

Example:

```
MsgBox UCase("hello")
```

VB.NET:

```
MsgBox(UCase("hello"))
```

Entered in a message box would be:

```
HELLO
```

Weekday Returns the numeric weekday of a date from 1 to 7. In VB.NET, use the DatePart function.

Syntax:

```
X = WeekDay(TheDate)
```

X will contain a number 1 to 7 depending on the weekday of TheDate.

Example:

```
Response.Write Weekday("5/1/1971 5:15:32") & "<P>"
Response.Write Weekday("9/21/2002 12:32:54") & "<P>"
```

Entered to the browser would be:

```
7
7
```

WeekdayName Returns the name of a weekday matching its number.

Syntax:

```
X = WeekdayName(TheNumber)
```

X will contain the name of the day matching the number, where Sunday is 1 and Saturday is 7.

Example:

```
MsgBox WeekdayName(1)
MsgBox WeekdayName(7)
```

VB.NET

```
MsgBox(WeekdayName(1))
MsgBox(WeekdayName(7))
```

Entered in a message box would be:

```
Sunday
Saturday
```

Year Returns the year portion of a date. In VB.NET, use the DatePart function.

Syntax:

```
X = Year(TheDate)
```

X will be set to the year portion of TheDate.

Example:

```
Response.Write Year("5/1/1971 5:15:32") & "<P>"
Response.Write Year("9/21/2002 12:32:54") & "<P>"
```

Entered to the browser would be:

```
1971
2001
```

APPENDIX

B

T-SQL Language Reference

In this appendix the basics of SQL Server's structured query language, called T-SQL, will be reviewed. The review will look at Select, Insert, Update, and Delete statements, as well as clauses within those statements.

T-SQL Basics

This appendix will also demonstrate the use of the T-SQL statements against a sample database. The database is made up of two tables—tblEmps and tblDepartments. The first table contains data about employees, and the other table contains data about departments at some company. The two tables are related in a one-to-many relationship. Each employee works in a single department but each department can have many employees.

Select Statements

The most basic SQL statement retrieves all the records and all the fields from a table:

```
Select * from tblEmps
```

When you use a Select statement, you are saying that you want to select fields and records to be returned from the database. In a basic SQL statement like this, the word Select is followed by the name of the fields that you want to return. Then the statement has the keyword From, which is followed by the name of the table from which you want to retrieve records.

The result of that query is displayed in the following table:

	FirstName	LastName	DepartmentID	Salary	BirthDate
1	Michelle	Morgan	1	$35,000	5/1/62
2	Jack	Gordon	1	$35,000	6/15/48
3	Jamie	Lesser	2	$22,000	8/21/55
4	Amanda	Smith	5	$88,000	5/2/59

The * in this Query means that you want all the fields from the table indicated in the From clause.

But you often don't need all the fields. You should only retrieve the fields that you are going to use because it is much more efficient. Think about the number of bytes that would be required if you returned one of the fields versus all of the fields.

So in T-SQL, if you just wanted the employees' names, the SQL statement would be this:

```
Select LastName, FirstName from tblEmps
```

The result of that query is shown in the following table:

FirstName	LastName
Michelle	Morgan
Jack	Gordon
Jamie	Lesser
Amanda	Smith

When you want to return specific fields, you just list them separated by commas. You can also combine and extract from fields to produce fields that are outputted but not part of the table. For example, you may want to display the full name of the employee as a single field. You would do that in T-SQL like this:

```
Select LastName + ', ' + FirstName as FullName from tblEmps
```

In T-SQL you use the + to indicate concatenation. The result of that query is displayed in the following table:

FullName
Morgan, Michelle
Gordon, Jack
Lesser, Jamie
Smith, Amanda

The new field outputted is called FullName. Again, note that this does not become part of the table. It is merely a temporary field in this output. Whenever you create a field like this, you use the AS keyword to indicate what the temporary field should be called. Also notice that the concatenation is in three parts. The first part is the last name of the employee. That is followed by a comma and a space. Concatenated to that is the first name of the employee.

You can also extract parts of a field. The next table reviews some of the common functions used in T-SQL statements.

T-SQL	Purpose
DatePart(yy, date)	Returns the year for the date passed to the function.
DatePart(mm, date)	Returns the month for the date passed to the function.
DatePart(dd, date)	Returns the day of the month for the date passed to the function.
DatePart(hh, time)	Returns the hour for the time passed to the function.
DatePart(mi, time)	Returns the minute for the time passed to the function.
DatePart(ss, time)	Returns the second for the time passed to the function.
GetDate	Returns the current system date and time.

Say you want to retrieve just the month in which the person was born and their first name. From T-SQL you would write this query:

```
Select FirstName, DatePart(mm, Birthdate) as MonthBorn from tblEmps
```

The result of that query is shown in the following table:

FirstName	MonthBorn
Michelle	5
Jack	6
Jamie	8
Amanda	5

This time, a temporary field called MonthBorn was outputted from the database with the employee's first name. The T-SQL function, DatePart, was used to extract the month from the BirthDate field. The first parameter of the function is the part of the date you want. The second part is the date to extract from.

Sometimes you only want to retrieve the unique values for a field. For example, if you wanted to display a list of all the salaries, but didn't want to see duplicates, you would use this T-SQL statement:

```
Select Distinct Salary from tblEmps
```

The result of this query is shown in the following table:

Salary
$35,000
$22,000
$88,000

Notice in this result that the salary amount $35,000 is shown only once even though it occurs in two records.

It is also simple to retrieve summary information about your data. For example, if you wanted to know the salary of the highest paid person you would code:

```
Select Max(Salary) as TopSalary from tblEmps
```

The output of this query in T-SQL would be $88,000. So the Max function retrieves the highest values for the field. You can also retrieve the lowest salary:

```
Select Min(Salary) as LowSalary from tblEmps
```

You can even add up all the salaries and get a total amount:

```
Select Sum(Salary) as TotalSalary from tblEmps
```

Another summary function is the Count function that counts the number of records, as in the following:

```
Select Count(EmpID) as TotalRecords from tblEmps
```

That statement would return the value 4 since there are four records in the table.

Where Clause

So far you have limited your output to all the records. But you often want just some of the records. You limit the records outputted with the Where clause. For example, if you wanted to view only those people who made more than $30,000, you would use this statement:

```
Select * from tblEmps where Salry > 30000
```

That query would result in the output shown in the following table:

EmplID	FirstName	LastName	DepartmentID	Salary	BirthDate
1	Michelle	Morgan	1	$35,000	5/1/62
2	Jack	Gordon	1	$35,000	6/15/48
4	Amanda	Smith	5	$88,000	5/2/59

In T-SQL, you can use =, <, >, >=, <>, or <= in the Where clause to limit output from the table. If you are looking for a numeric field in the Where clause, as you did with the search on the salary field, you just put the number in the query. If you have a text field you are searching, you surround the text you are searching for with single quotes:

```
Select * from tblEmps where FirstName = 'Jack'
```

The results of that query are displayed in the following table:

EmplID	FirstName	LastName	DepartmentID	Salary	BirthDate
2	Jack	Gordon	1	$35,000	6/15/48

If you wanted to use a date in the Where clause you would surround the date in single quotes for T-SQL:

```
Select * from tblEmps where BirthDate > '1/1/56'
```

The result of this query is displayed in the following table:

EmplID	FirstName	LastName	DepartmentID	Salary	BirthDate
1	Michelle	Morgan	1	$35,000	5/1/62
4	Amanda	Smith	5	$88,000	5/2/59

Another way you can limit the output is with a wild card. You use a wild card to represent any character combinations. For example, in T-SQL, if you wanted to display all the employees whose first name started with a *J*, you would have a query like this:

```
Select * from tblEMps where FirstName Like 'J%'
```

The results of that query are displayed in the following table:

EmplID	FirstName	LastName	DepartmentID	Salary	BirthDate
2	Jack	Gordon	1	$35,000	6/15/48
3	Jamie	Lesser	2	$22,000	8/21/55

The Where clause selects all employees whose first name starts with the letter *J*. The % character is the wild card character.

You can also combine more than one criteria with an "and" or an "or." If you wanted to see all those employees in Department 5 that have a salary of more than $34,000, you would type:

```
Select * from tblEmps where DepartmentID = 5 and Salary > 34000
```

The result of that query is displayed in the following table:

EmplID	FirstName	LastName	DepartmentID	Salary	BirthDate
4	Amanda	Smith	5	$88,000	5/2/59

This means that both criteria must match. If an "or" was used instead, the result of the query would be everyone in Department 5 and also include anyone who makes more than $34,000. This result is shown in the following table:

EmplID	FirstName	LastName	DepartmentID	Salary	BirthDate
1	Michelle	Morgan	1	$35,000	5/1/62
2	Jack	Gordon	1	$35,000	6/15/48
4	Amanda	Smith	5	$88,000	5/2/59

Order By Clause

The Order By clause allows you to sort the outputted records. The Order By clause comes after the Where clause and looks like this:

```
Select * from tblEMps order by Salary
```

The outputted records would now be sorted by employee salary, as shown in the following table:

EmplID	FirstName	LastName	DepartmentID	Salary	BirthDate
4	Amanda	Smith	5	$88,000	5/2/59
1	Michelle	Morgan	1	$35,000	5/1/62
2	Jack	Gordon	1	$35,000	6/15/48
3	Jamie	Lesser	2	$22,000	8/21/55

You could also sort the records in the reverse order by using the DESC qualifier, which means descending:

```
Select * from tblEMps order by Salary
```

The outputted records would now be sorted from lowest to highest salary, as shown in the next table.

EmplID	FirstName	LastName	DepartmentID	Salary	BirthDate
3	Jamie	Lesser	2	$22,000	8/21/55
2	Jack	Gordon	1	$35,000	6/15/48
1	Michelle	Morgan	1	$35,000	5/1/62
4	Amanda	Smith	5	$88,000	5/2/59

You can also sort by more than one field in the Order By clause. If you wanted to sort the records by the LastName field and the FirstName field, you would code this:

```
Select * from tblEMps order by LastName, FirstName
```

Joins

Sometimes you need to retrieve data that is across more than one table. For example, you may want to output the employee's name with the name of the department they work in. To do this, you need to use the Join keyword.

```
Select tblEmps.FirstName, tblEmps.LastName, tblDepartments.DepartmentName from tblEmps
Inner Join tblDepartments on tblEmps.DepartmentID = tblDepartments.DepartmentID
```

This query combines both tables and displays just the name and department for each employee, as shown in the following table:

FirstName	LastName	DepartmentName
Michelle	Morgan	Administrative
Jack	Gordon	Administrative
Jamie	Lesser	IS

The words "Inner Join" are followed with the name of the table to join with. That is followed with the names of the fields that link the two tables together.

Notice that the employee Amanda Smith isn't in this output. This is because the department for that employee is number 5 and there is no Department 5 in tblDepartments. This is what an Inner Join does. It will only output matches in both tables. If you want to see all the employees, even if they don't have a matching department, you need to change Inner Join to Left Join. If you wanted to see all the departments, even if they didn't have an employee, then you would change Inner Join to Right Join.

Add, Edit, and Delete

Beyond viewing records in your database in T-SQL, you will need to Add, Edit, and Delete records.

To add records, you use an Insert statement as in this example:

```
Insert into tblEMps (FirstName, LastName, DepartmentID, Salary, BirthDate) values
('John', 'Doe', 2, 45000, '3/22/66')
```

Now the tblEmps table would have the records shown in the following table:

EmplID	FirstName	LastName	DepartmentID	Salary	BirthDate
1	Michelle	Morgan	1	$35,000	5/1/62
2	Jack	Gordon	1	$35,000	6/15/48
3	Jamie	Lesser	2	$22,000	8/21/55
4	Amanda	Smith	5	$88,000	5/2/59
5	John	Doe	2	$45,000	3/22/66

The Insert statement starts with the term "Insert." That is followed with the Into keyword and the name of the table you are adding a record into. Then, surrounded by parentheses, are the names of all the fields that you are adding data to for this new record. That is followed by the keyword values. Then another set of parentheses surrounds the data being inserted into the table.

You use an Update statement to edit an existing record. The Update statement takes the following form:

```
Update tblEmps set Salary = 35000, DepartmentID = 3 where EmployeeID = 1
```

That action would result in the data looking like that displayed in the following table:

EmplID	FirstName	LastName	DepartmentID	Salary	BirthDate
1	Michelle	Morgan	1	$35,000	5/1/62
2	Jack	Gordon	1	$35,000	6/15/48
3	Jamie	Lesser	2	$22,000	8/21/55
4	Amanda	Smith	5	$88,000	5/2/59
5	John	Doe	2	$45,000	3/22/66

The Update statement begins with the Update keyword followed by the name of the table to update. Then the set keyword is used, followed by field/value pairs that are each separated by commas. At the end of the statement is usually a Where clause indicating which record or records to update.

To delete a record or records, you use an SQL Delete statement. That statement takes the following form:

```
Delete from tblEmps where EmployeeID = 2
```

This action would result in your table looking like that displayed in the following table:

EmplID	FirstName	LastName	DepartmentID	Salary	BirthDate
1	Michelle	Morgan	1	$35,000	5/1/62
3	Jamie	Lesser	2	$22,000	8/21/55
4	Amanda	Smith	5	$88,000	5/2/59
5	John	Doe	2	$45,000	3/22/66

The statement starts with Delete From, followed by the name of the table where the record needed to be deleted is located. That is usually followed by a Where clause, limiting the records to be deleted.

APPENDIX

C

Using the CD

The CD that accompanies this book contains all the solutions detailed in Chapters 4 through 20, excluding Chapters 9 and 15. Each chapter has its own folder on the CD. If you want to use the files from Chapter 16, go to the Chapter 16 folder on the CD.

Within that folder you will find the front-end files, either in VB, VB.NET, Access, or ASP, depending on the chapter. Also within the folder you will find the files needed to rebuild the objects within the back-end database as well as placing into the tables the sample data used with the presentations of the book. The procedure necessary to import those objects and data are reviewed here.

Before importing the data, you need to re-create the database structure. So, after you have created the database that you want to place the solution in, highlight that database within the SQL Server Enterprise Manager. Then select SQL Query Analyzer from the Tools menu. You should then see the query analyzer window, like the one displayed in the following illustration.

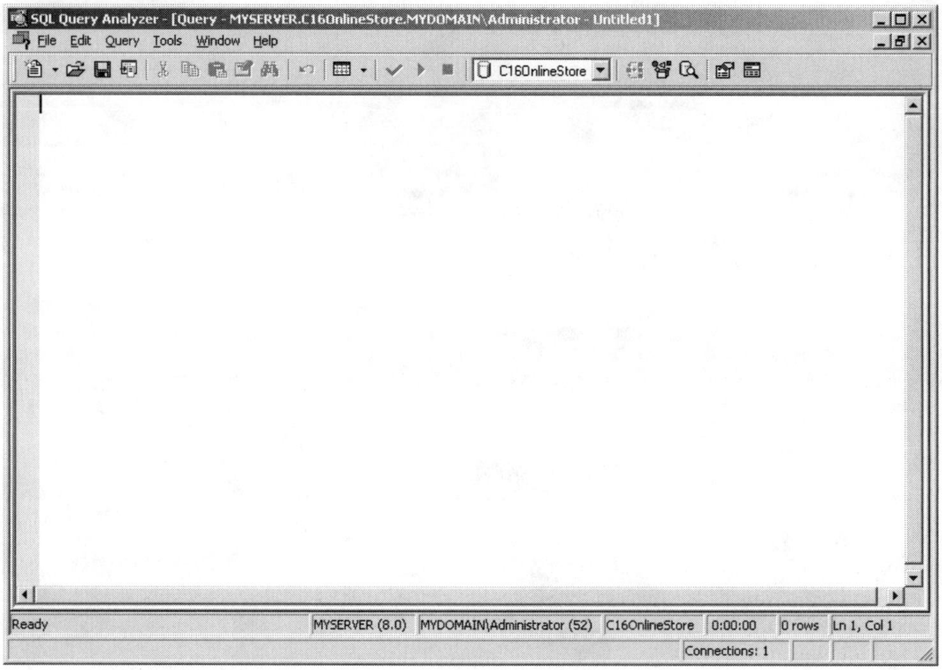

This tool is used to run SQL scripts. You could use it to write and display the results of a SQL statement, or you can use it to load a script that creates the structure of a database. That is what you need to do.

Select the Open from the File menu and browse to the script you want to load. The file on the CD that contains the script to create the database object is located in the chapter folder and has a name like this:

```
C16SQLObjects.sql
```

Once you find the file, click OK and it will be opened in the SQL Query Analyzer, as shown in the following illustration.

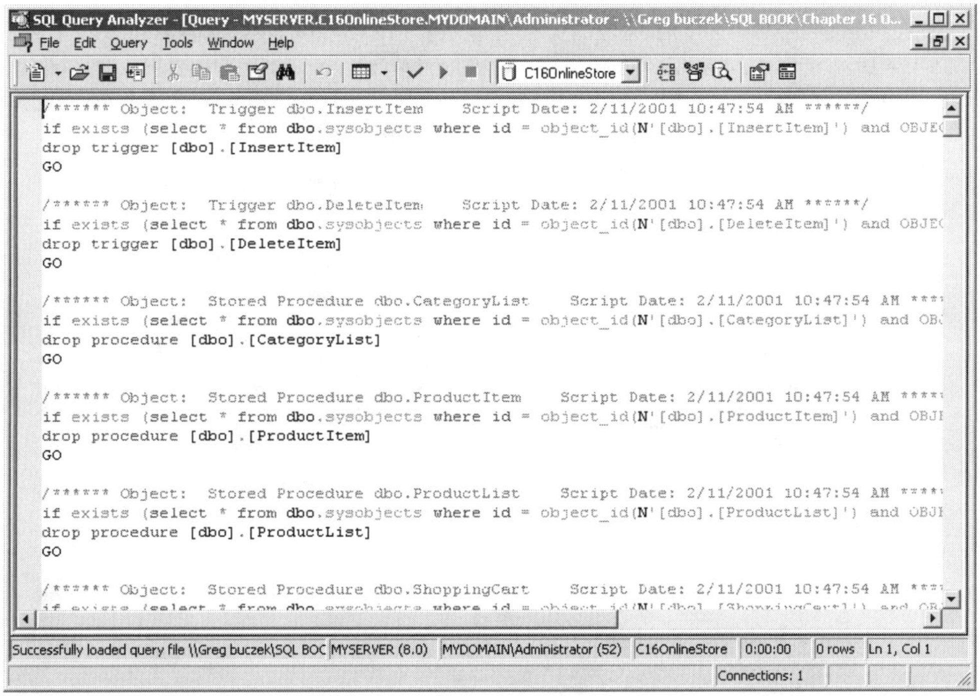

Note something very important about the scripts: they include Drop tags. This means that if you have an object in the database that you are running the script on that has the same name as the object in the script, it will be replaced with the scripted object. In other words, don't run this script on an existing database unless you are starting one of the solutions from scratch.

Next, click the green arrow button on the toolbar or select Execute from the Query menu. The script should run and the structure of the database should now exist in your database.

Optionally, you can now import test data that I created with the solution into the newly created tables. On the CD within the chapter folder you will find files that have a name like this:

```
Products.txt
```

This file contains the data for the Products table. Each table created in the database should have a matching text file within the same location on the CD that contains the data for that table.

To import data into the table, browse the table within the database that you want to import into and right-click on it. Then select All Tasks followed by Import Data. You should then be in the first step of the Data Transformation Service. Click Next to see the figure displayed in the following illustration.

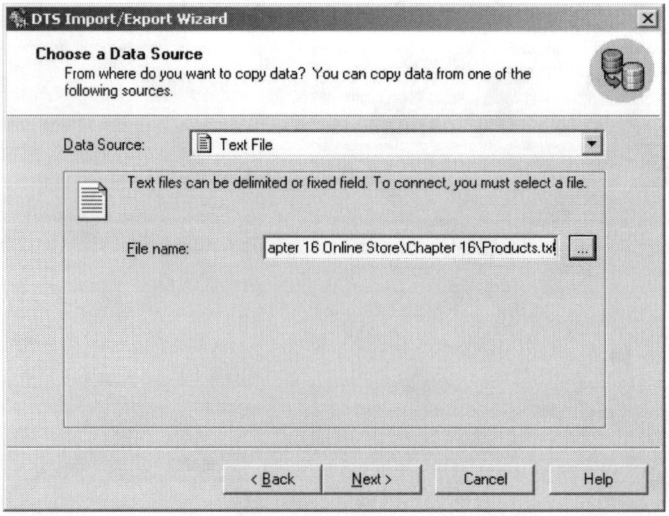

From this page of the DTS wizard, you need to change the data source that you are importing from to a text file. Then browse to the text file that contains the data. Click Next to see the next step displayed in the following illustration.

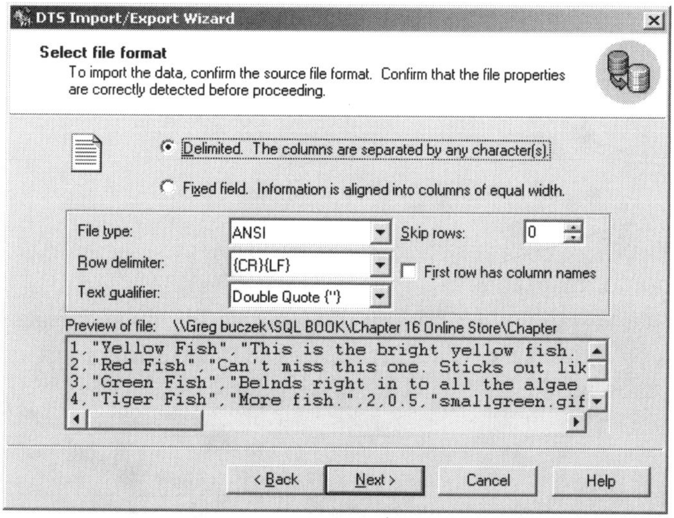

You shouldn't need to make any changes on this page. The Delimited item should be selected and the other properties should be as are displayed. Click Next to see something like what is displayed in the following illustration.

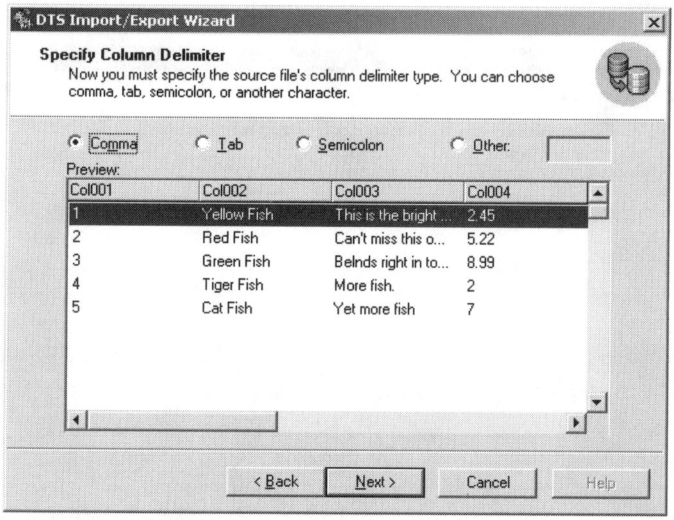

On this step of the wizard, make sure that Comma is selected as the delimiter type. The data should appear correctly in columnar format in the preview list as it does in this figure. Click Next to see the next step displayed in the following illustration.

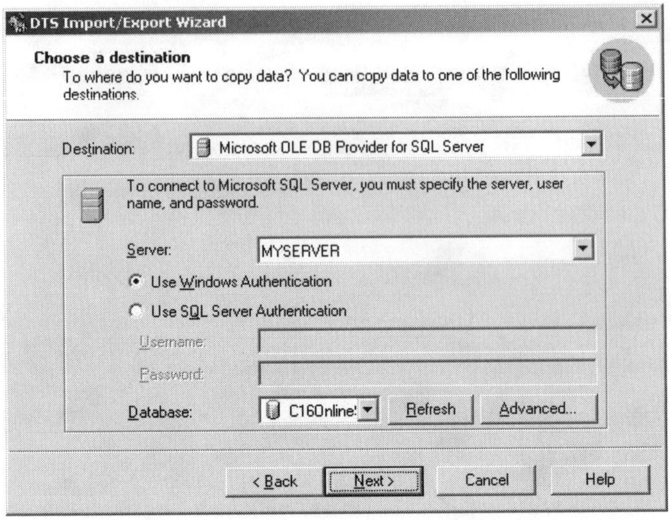

If you entered the DTS by right-clicking on the correct target table, you shouldn't need to change anything here. For the destination, you should see the SQL Server database that you are importing into. Again, click Next to see what is displayed in the following illustration.

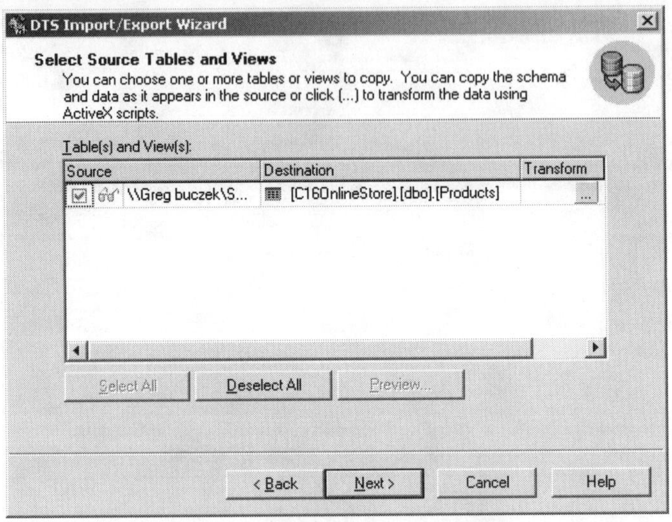

As with the last step, if you selected the correct table to import into, this page of the wizard should already be correct. But what you should see in the destination is the name of the table that you are importing into. Click Next once again to see the page displayed in the following illustration.

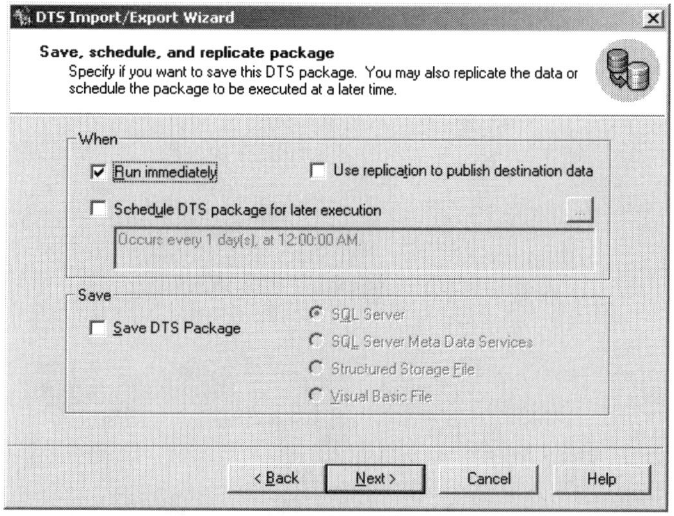

Select Run Immediately from the When section and click Next to take yourself to the final page. On the last page of the wizard, click Finish. The data should now have been imported into your SQL Server table.

Index

A

D

E

F

G

M

N

O

P

Q

R

S

T

U

Z

INTERNATIONAL CONTACT INFORMATION

AUSTRALIA
McGraw-Hill Book Company Australia Pty. Ltd.
TEL +61-2-9417-9899
FAX +61-2-9417-5687
http://www.mcgraw-hill.com.au
books-it_sydney@mcgraw-hill.com

CANADA
McGraw-Hill Ryerson Ltd.
TEL +905-430-5000
FAX +905-430-5020
http://www.mcgrawhill.ca

GREECE, MIDDLE EAST, NORTHERN AFRICA
McGraw-Hill Hellas
TEL +30-1-656-0990-3-4
FAX +30-1-654-5525

MEXICO (Also serving Latin America)
McGraw-Hill Interamericana Editores S.A. de C.V.
TEL +525-117-1583
FAX +525-117-1589
http://www.mcgraw-hill.com.mx
fernando_castellanos@mcgraw-hill.com

SINGAPORE (Serving Asia)
McGraw-Hill Book Company
TEL +65-863-1580
FAX +65-862-3354
http://www.mcgraw-hill.com.sg
mghasia@mcgraw-hill.com

SOUTH AFRICA
McGraw-Hill South Africa
TEL +27-11-622-7512
FAX +27-11-622-9045
robyn_swanepoel@mcgraw-hill.com

UNITED KINGDOM & EUROPE (Excluding Southern Europe)
McGraw-Hill Education Europe
TEL +44-1-628-502500
FAX +44-1-628-770224
http://www.mcgraw-hill.co.uk
computing_neurope@mcgraw-hill.com

ALL OTHER INQUIRIES Contact:
Osborne/McGraw-Hill
TEL +1-510-549-6600
FAX +1-510-883-7600
http://www.osborne.com
omg_international@mcgraw-hill.com

WARNING: BEFORE OPENING THE DISC PACKAGE, CAREFULLY READ THE TERMS AND CONDITIONS OF THE FOLLOWING COPYRIGHT STATEMENT AND LIMITED CD-ROM WARRANTY.

Copyright Statement

This software is protected by both United States copyright law and international copyright treaty provision. Except as noted in the contents of the CD-ROM, you must treat this software just like a book. However, you may copy it into a computer to be used and you may make archival copies of the software for the sole purpose of backing up the software and protecting your investment from loss. By saying, "just like a book," The McGraw-Hill Companies, Inc. ("Osborne/McGraw-Hill") means, for example, that this software may be used by any number of people and may be freely moved from one computer location to another, so long as there is no possibility of its being used at one location or on one computer while it is being used at another. Just as a book cannot be read by two different people in two different places at the same time, neither can the software be used by two different people in two different places at the same time.

Limited Warranty

Osborne/McGraw-Hill warrants the physical compact disc enclosed herein to be free of defects in materials and workmanship for a period of sixty days from the purchase date. If you live in the U.S. and the CD included in your book has defects in materials or workmanship, please call McGraw-Hill at 1-800-217-0059, 9 A.M. to 5 P.M., Monday through Friday, Eastern Standard Time, and McGraw-Hill will replace the defective disc. If you live outside the U.S., please contact your local McGraw-Hill office. You can find contact information for most offices on the International Contact Information page immediately following the index of this book, or send an e-mail to omg_international@mcgraw-hill.com.

The entire and exclusive liability and remedy for breach of this Limited Warranty shall be limited to replacement of the defective disc, and shall not include or extend to any claim for or right to cover any other damages, including but not limited to, loss of profit, data, or use of the software, or special incidental, or consequential damages or other similar claims, even if Osborne/McGraw-Hill has been specifically advised of the possibility of such damages. In no event will Osborne/McGraw-Hill's liability for any damages to you or any other person ever exceed the lower of the suggested list price or actual price paid for the license to use the software, regardless of any form of the claim.

OSBORNE/McGRAW-HILL SPECIFICALLY DISCLAIMS ALL OTHER WARRANTIES, EXPRESS OR IMPLIED, INCLUDING BUT NOT LIMITED TO, ANY IMPLIED WARRANTY OF MERCHANTABILITY OR FITNESS FOR A PARTICULAR PURPOSE. Specifically, Osborne/McGraw-Hill makes no representation or warranty that the software is fit for any particular purpose, and any implied warranty of merchantability is limited to the sixty-day duration of the Limited Warranty covering the physical disc only (and not the software), and is otherwise expressly and specifically disclaimed.

This limited warranty gives you specific legal rights; you may have others which may vary from state to state. Some states do not allow the exclusion of incidental or consequential damages, or the limitation on how long an implied warranty lasts, so some of the above may not apply to you.

This agreement constitutes the entire agreement between the parties relating to use of the Product. The terms of any purchase order shall have no effect on the terms of this Agreement. Failure of Osborne/McGraw-Hill to insist at any time on strict compliance with this Agreement shall not constitute a waiver of any rights under this Agreement. This Agreement shall be construed and governed in accordance with the laws of New York. If any provision of this Agreement is held to be contrary to law, that provision will be enforced to the maximum extent permissible, and the remaining provisions will remain in force and effect.

NO TECHNICAL SUPPORT IS PROVIDED WITH THIS CD-ROM.